Programming
Collaborative
Web Applications
Microsoft®
Exchange 2000
Server

Mindy Martin

PUBLISHED BY
Microsoft Press
A Division of Microsoft Corporation
One Microsoft Way
Redmond, Washington 98052-6399

Library of Congress Cataloging-in-Publication Data
Martin, Mindy C.
    Programming Collaborative Web Applications with Microsoft Exchange 2000 Server/
Mindy Martin.
       p. cm.
  Includes index.
  ISBN 0-7356-0772-9
    1. Internet programming. 2. Web sites--Design. 3. Microsft Exchange Server
(Computer file). I. Title.

  QA76.625.M329 2000
  005.7'13769--dc21   00-034855

Printed and bound in the United States of America.

1 2 3 4 5 6 7 8 9   WCWC   5 4 3 2 1 0

Distributed in Canada by Penguin Books Canada Limited.

A CIP catalogue record for this book is available from the British Library.

Microsoft Press books are available through booksellers and distributors worldwide. For further information about international editions, contact your local Microsoft Corporation office or contact Microsoft Press International directly at fax (425) 936-7329. Visit our Web site at mspress.microsoft.com. Send comments to *mspinput@microsoft.com*.

Active Directory, ActiveX, FrontPage, Hotmail, IntelliSense, JScript, Microsoft, Microsoft Press, MS-DOS, MSDN, Outlook, PowerPoint, Visual Basic, Visual C++, Visual InterDev, Visual Studio, Win32, Windows, and Windows NT are either registered trademarks or trademarks of Microsoft Corporation in the United States and/or other countries. Other product and company names mentioned herein may be the trademarks of their respective owners.

Unless otherwise noted, the example companies, organizations, products, people, and events depicted herein are fictitious. No association with any real company, organization, product, person, or event is intended or should be inferred.

Acquisitions Editor: Eric Stroo
Project Editor: Victoria Thulman

To Peter Waxman, who made it possible for me to write this book and still maintain some of my sanity. Thank you, Peter, for your love and understanding and for giving me the occasional and much needed kick in the butt.

Koogamasha!

Table of Contents

ACKNOWLEDGEMENTS XXVII

INTRODUCTION XXIX

Who Should Read This Book xxix

How This Book Is Organized xxx

Section I—Welcome to Exchange 2000 Server xxx

Section II—Data Access xxxi

Section III—Extending Your Application xxxiii

Section IV—Building for the Web xxxiv

Section V—Preparing for the Enterprise xxxiv

Appendixes xxxv

System Requirements xxxvi

About the Companion CD xxxvi

What's On the CD xxxvi

Installing the Chapter Sample Code Files xxxvii

Setting Up the Sample Application xxxviii

Setting Up Zoo Management Folder Structure xxxviii

Setting Up ZooWeb xxxix

About the Helper Tools xl

About ZipOut 2000 xli

Conventions Used in This Book xlii

SECTION I: WELCOME TO EXCHANGE 2000 SERVER 1

CHAPTER 1: DEVELOPING WITH THE EXCHANGE PLATFORM 3

A Tour of Exchange 2000 4

    Exchange System Manager 4

    Active Directory 5

    The Web Storage System 7

    Protocol Support 8

    Web Storage System Schema 9

Using Data Access Tools 9

    Understanding the Data Access Paradigm 10

    Using ADO 11

    Using CDO for Exchange 14

    Using ADSI 16

    Using XML 19

Displaying Your Data 22

    Using Outlook 2000 23

    Using Outlook Web Access 24

    Reusing Outlook Web Access 26

    Using Web Storage System Forms 28

Enhancing Your Application 29

    Using Web Storage System Events 30

    Using Workflow Logic 31

Wrapping It Up 33

    Adding Security Features 33

    Deploying a Web Storage System Application 34

Summary 35

CHAPTER 2: EXCHANGE AND THE WEB STORAGE SYSTEM 37

Using Exchange for Data Storage 38

    Benefits of the Web Storage System 38

    Exchange vs. SQL Server 40

Understanding the Architecture of Exchange Data Storage 41

Exchange–Then and Now 42

Web Storage System vs. Exchange Databases 44

Why Use Multiple Public Web Storage Systems? 45

Understanding Names Used in Exchange 48

Creating a New Web Storage System 49

Creating a Public Folder Tree 50

Creating and Mounting a Public Web Storage System 51

Creating a Virtual Directory 54

Using URLs with Exchange 56

URL Basics 57

Accessing Public Stores 58

Accessing Mailboxes 59

Accessing Individual Items 61

Using Additional Data Access Options 62

Windows Explorer 62

Open and Save Dialog Boxes 64

Custom Clients 65

Doing More with the Web Storage System 65

Querying a Web Storage System 65

Replicating Web Storage System Folder Trees 66

Summary 66

SECTION II: DATA ACCESS..**67**

CHAPTER 3: WEB STORAGE SYSTEM SCHEMA **69**

Overview of the Web Storage System Schema 70

Understanding the Web Storage System Schema 70

Understanding Property and Namespace Names 72

Web Storage System Namespaces 73

Introducing Content Classes 75

   Understanding Content Classes 75

   Folder Content Classes 76

   Item Content Classes 79

   Searching for a Specific Content Class 82

   Learning About Content Classes by Using the Content Class Browser 84

Schema Access Scenarios 86

   URLs and HTTP 87

   Web Applications Using ASP Technology 88

   Microsoft Outlook 2000 89

Using a Custom Application Schema 89

   Benefits of Employing a Custom Schema 90

   How a Custom Schema Works 91

   Defining the Application Schema 93

      Creating the Application Schema Folder 93

      Configuring Application Folders 96

   Defining Properties 99

      Data Types 102

   Defining Content Classes 103

Creating a Custom Schema 106

   Defining the Zoo Management Schema 106

      Creating the Schema Folder Structure 109

      Defining the Custom Properties 110

      Defining the Animal Content Class 111

   Creating an Instance of the Animal Content Class 112

Returning Application Schema Information 113

Summary 116

CHAPTER 4: ACTIVEX DATA OBJECTS AND EXCHANGE **117**

Overview of ActiveX Data Objects 2.5 and Exchange 118

ADO 2.5 Object Model 118

Exchange OLE DB Provider 121

Understanding the Relationship Between Records and Recordsets 122

Understanding Security in ADO 123

Connecting to a Web Storage System 124

Building URLs for ExOLEDB 124

Accessing Public Web Storage System Folders 125

Accessing Mailboxes 126

Accessing Items 127

Using a Connection Object 127

Opening and Closing a Connection 128

Using Relative URLs 129

Using Transactions 131

Handling Errors 133

Using the Record Object 135

Using the Open Method 136

Understanding the Mode Parameter 137

Understanding the CreateOptions Parameter 138

Opening a Resource 139

Enumerating Properties 140

Reading Single-Valued Properties 141

Reading Multi-Valued Properties 142

Saving a Record 142

Creating a Resource 143

Creating a Folder 144

Creating an Item 145

Appending a Custom Property to a Resource 146

Understanding ADO Data Types 148

Using the Recordset Object 150

    Opening a Recordset 150

        Using the GetChildren Method 151

        Using the Open Method of a Recordset Object 151

    Moving Through a Recordset 152

    Using ADO to Get the Contents of a Folder 153

Querying a Web Storage System by Using SQL SELECT Statements 155

    Using the AddQuotes Function 155

    Building a Simple SELECT Statement 156

        SELECT: Choose the Properties to Return 156

        FROM: Indicating Where to Look for Records 157

        WHERE: Filtering the Results 158

        ORDER BY: Sorting the Results 159

    Opening a Recordset with the Query Results 161

    Saving a Recordset as XML 163

Doing More Using ADO 165

    Copying a Resource 165

    Moving a Resource 166

    Deleting a Resource 167

    Streaming Contents 169

        Opening and Reading the Default Stream for an Item 169

        Saving a Stream to a File 169

Using ADO with Microsoft Internet Publishing Provider 171

Summary 173

CHAPTER 5: INTRODUCTION TO CDO FOR EXCHANGE 175

Overview of CDO 176

    CDO Object Models 177

    Understanding the CDO for Exchange 2000 Server Object Model 178

    Understanding the CDO for Exchange Management Objects Object
    Model 179

    Understanding the CDO Workflow for Exchange Object Model 180

Getting Started with CDO 181

   Creating Objects from Classes 181

   Using Interfaces 182

   Accessing Schema Properties 184

   Using URLs 185

Understanding and Using the IDataSource Interface 186

   IDataSource Interface Properties and Methods 186

   How the IDataSource Interface Works 187

   Opening a Resource by Using CDO 188

   Detecting and Saving Changes 190

   Creating a New Resource by Using CDO 192

      Saving to a URL 192

      Saving to a Container 194

   Opening CDO Objects from Other Objects 196

   Checking for the Existence of a Folder or Item 199

Working with Folders 200

   CDO Folder Object Properties 201

   Creating a Folder by Using CDO 202

   Enabling a Folder for E-mail 203

   Counting the Contents of a Folder 205

Working with Contact Information 207

   Contact Properties 208

   Creating a Contact in the Web Storage System 220

   Retrieving vCard Information 221

Summary 223

CHAPTER 6: CDO MESSAGING **225**

Overview of CDO Messaging 226

   CDO Messaging Classes and Interfaces 227

   Dissecting a MIME Message 228

Composing and Sending Messages 231

   Sending a Simple Message 231

   Addressing a Message 233

      Specifying Who Is Sending the Message 234

      Specifying Who Is Receiving the Message 234

      Configuring for Replies 235

   Adding the Body Text 235

      Using Plain-Text Formatting 236

      Using HTML Formatting 236

      Using MHTML Formatting 238

   Adding Attachments 240

   Useful Schema Properties for Messaging 242

   Sending to a Folder 245

   Posting to a Newsgroup 246

Composing More Complex Messages 248

   Using a Persistent Configuration Object 248

   Resolving an Address in Your Domain 250

      Checking for User Existence 251

      Handling Ambiguous Names 254

Processing Messages 255

   Finding a Message 255

   Opening a Message 255

   Detecting and Saving Attachments 257

   Reading a Message as BodyPart Objects 259

      Using Shortcut Properties 259

      Identifying the Media Type of a BodyPart Object 260

      Streaming BodyPart Objects 262

   Replying to a Message 264

   Forwarding a Message 266

   Saving a Message to a File 268

Summary 270

CHAPTER 7: CDO CALENDARING 271

Overview of CDO Calendaring 272

  CDO Calendaring Classes and Interfaces 272

  Understanding How Exchange Stores and Formats Dates and Times 274

  Indicating a Time Zone 276

Using the Appointment Object 277

  Creating a Simple Appointment 277

  Appointment Properties 279

  Using a Persistent Configuration Object 281

Scheduling Meetings 282

  Scheduling a New Meeting 282

    Setting the Meeting Organizer 285

    Adding Attendees 285

    Sending a Meeting Request 287

  Checking Free/Busy Status 287

    Checking the User Existence 288

    Using the GetFreeBusy Method 288

  Publishing a Meeting 291

    Keeping Track of Attendees of a Published Event 293

Scheduling Recurring Appointments and Meetings 294

  Configuring the Master Appointment 294

  Defining a Recurrence Pattern 297

  Using Exceptions 301

  Getting the Recurrence Master 305

Working with Existing Appointments and Meeting Requests 309

  Converting Dates and Times 309

  Querying a Calendar 311

    Identifying Appointment Types 315

    Telling the Difference Between a Meeting and a Simple Appointment...317

    Using Calendar Browser 317

Sending Updates 319

Canceling and Deleting Appointments and Meetings 319

Canceling an Appointment 320

Canceling a Meeting 322

Processing a Meeting Request 323

Setting Reminders 325

Summary 326

CHAPTER 8: INTERACTING WITH ACTIVE DIRECTORY 327

Connecting to Active Directory 328

LDAP 328

ADSI 329

CDO for Exchange 332

Choosing Between CDO and ADSI 333

Building the LDAP Binding String 334

ADSI for the Exchange Developer 336

Common Supported Interfaces 336

Opening an Object 338

Accessing the Domain 338

Opening a Container or Organizational Unit 339

Opening Group and User Objects 339

Opening with Logon Credentials 340

Understanding the Property Cache 342

Getting Property Values 343

Using the Get Method 343

Using the GetEx Method 344

Using the GetList Method 344

Setting Property Values 345

Using the Put Method 345

Using the PutEx Method 346

Using the SetInfo Method 347

Creating Objects 348

Deleting Objects 349

Understanding Active Directory Contacts, Users, and Mailboxes 350

Person, Contact, and User Objects 350

Understanding Mail-Enabled vs. Mailbox-Enabled 351

Creating Contact and User Objects 352

Creating an Active Directory Contact Object 353

Creating a User Account 354

Active Directory Properties for Address Book Information 357

Mail-Enabling an Object 360

Working with Mailboxes 362

Mailbox-Specific Properties in Active Directory 362

Creating a Mailbox 366

Customizing Mailbox Settings 370

Moving a Mailbox 372

Deleting a Mailbox 374

Managing User and Contact Objects 374

Using CDO to Open User and Contact Objects 375

Using ADSI to Open User and Contact Objects 376

Moving User and Contact Objects 376

Deleting User and Contact Objects 378

Enumerating User and Contact Objects 379

Working with Groups 381

Using Group Type and Group Scope 381

Understanding Group Type 381

Understanding Group Scope 382

Creating a Group Object 383

Creating a Mail-Enabled Distribution Group 383

Indicating the Group Type 385

Setting the sAMAccountName 386

Handling Group Membership 386

Adding Members 386

Checking User Membership 387

Removing Members 388

Enumerating Members of a Group 388

Managing Group Objects 390

Opening a Group Object 390

Moving Group Objects 391

Deleting a Group Object 392

Enumerating Only Group Objects in a Container 393

Querying Active Directory 394

Querying by Using ADO 395

Building the Core SELECT Statement 396

Adding Filter Criteria 398

Searching for Object Types 399

Setting Command Options 400

Using the SearchScope Property 401

Using the Time Limit and TimeOut Properties 402

Using the Page Size Property 402

Using the Cache Results Property 403

Using the Chase Referrals Property 403

Using ADSI to Return Information About Your Domain 404

Identifying Your Active Directory Server 404

Identifying Your Domain 406

Identifying the Current User 408

Returning Exchange Mailboxes 409

Returning Exchange Servers 411

Returning an Exchange Server from an E-mail Address 413

Summary 415

SECTION III: EXTENDING YOUR APPLICATION 417

CHAPTER 9: USING WEB STORAGE SYSTEM EVENTS 419

Overview of Events in Exchange 2000 420

  Why Incorporate Events? 420

  Understanding Event Types 421

    Synchronous Events 422

    Asynchronous Events 423

    System Events 423

  Understanding the Event Paradigm 424

  Security and Event Sinks 426

Building an Event Sink 426

  Creating the Dynamic-Link Library 427

    Setting the References 427

    Building the Event Procedures 428

    Using CDO to Send Notifications 430

    Using the EventSinkTemplate Project 431

  Reacting to Synchronous Events 432

    Using the OnSyncDelete Event Procedure 434

    Using the OnSyncSave Event Procedure 435

    Checking for the Phase of a Transaction 438

    Distinguishing Between a New Item and a Changed Item 439

    Modifying the Event Item in a Synchronous Event Sink 440

    Aborting a Synchronous Event 441

  Reacting to Asynchronous Events 442

    Using the OnDelete Event Procedure 443

    Using the OnSave Event Procedure 444

    Accessing the Event Item in an Asynchronous Event Sink 446

Reacting to System Events 446

Using the OnMDBStartUp Event Procedure 447

Using the OnMDBShutDown Event Procedure 447

Using the OnTimer Event Procedure 447

Installing the Event Sink as a COM+ Application 448

Making the .dll File 448

Registering the .dll file 448

Creating the COM+ Components 449

Creating a New COM+ Application for Event Sink Components..... 449

Adding Components to a COM+ Application................................. 453

Changing an Event Sink 456

Creating an Event Registration Item 457

Creating an Event Registration Item by Using ADO 458

Setting the Required Event Properties 461

Identifying the Source Events.. 461

Identifying the Event Sink 462

Setting Optional Event Properties 462

Defining the Range of an Event Registration Item.......................... 463

Restricting Event Items.. 465

Prioritizing Multiple Event Registrations 466

Registering for an OnTimer Event.. 467

Creating an Event Registration by Using the RegEvent Script 467

Managing Event Registration Items 469

Returning Event Registration Information 469

Disabling an Event Registration 471

Deleting an Event Registration 472

Using Custom Properties with Events 473

Defining Custom Properties in the Event Registration Item 474

Reading the Custom Fields in the Event Sink 475

Investigating Event Errors with the Application Log 476

Summary 477

CHAPTER 10: DESIGNING WORKFLOW APPLICATIONS 479

Overview of Workflow 480

   Workflow Background 480

   Understanding the Workflow Process 480

   Understanding Actions 482

   Setting Security in Workflow 483

      Running Script in Restricted Mode 483

      Running Script in Privileged Mode 484

   Building Workflow Applications 485

Before You Begin 486

   Defining the Workflow System Account 487

   Registering Workflow Authors 489

Using Workflow Designer for Exchange 491

   Introducing Workflow Designer 491

   Using Workflow Designer: A Simple Example 493

      Connecting to a Workflow Folder with Workflow Designer 493

      Creating a New Process 494

      Adding States 495

      Adding Actions 496

      Adding Script 498

         Creating Condition Script Statements.....................................499

         Creating Action Script 499

         Creating Compensating Actions 500

         Using External Script Files 500

      Using Multiple Actions on a Single State 501

      Adding Final Touches to Your Workflow Process 501

   Importing and Exporting Processes 502

Scripting the Workflow Item 504

   WorkflowSession Properties and Methods 504

   Adding an Audit Entry 506

   Identifying the Sender 507

   Sending a Notification Message 508

   Reading the State Information 510

   Deleting the Workflow Item 510

Debugging Workflow Script 511

   Checking Script Syntax 511

   Using Event Viewer 512

   Using Script Debugger 512

Summary 512

CHAPTER 11: DEVELOPING WITH OUTLOOK 2000 513

Introducing the MAPI Folder Tree 514

Developing for the Outlook Environment 515

   Creating Folders in the MAPI Folder Tree 515

   Creating Items in the MAPI Folder Tree 517

Developing in the Outlook Environment 522

   Adding Collaboration Features 522

   Accessing Web Storage System Schema Properties in Outlook Forms 523

      Using Field Chooser to Access Schema Properties 523

      Using the Outlook Object Model to Access Schema Properties 526

   Querying Other Web Storage Systems from Outlook Forms 526

Summary 528

SECTION IV: BUILDING FOR THE WEB 529

CHAPTER 12: BUILDING WEB APPLICATIONS FOR EXCHANGE 531

Overview of Web Applications 532

Approaches to Web Development 532

Thinking in Terms of Data, Not Forms 533

Understanding How Web Storage System Forms Work 533

Using Forms Registry and Forms Registrations 536

    Configuring a Forms Registry 537

        Configuring a Forms Registry Folder 537

        Taking Advantage of Custom Content Classes 538

        Using the Folder Composition Tool 539

    Using Form Registrations 540

        Creating a Form Registration 541

        Accessing the Form Registration Parameters from a Web Page 544

        Using the Forms Registry Explorer 545

Setting Up a Web Development Environment 547

    Setting Execute Permissions and Access Rights 548

        Setting Execute Permissions 548

        Using Anonymous Access 549

    Using a Web Development Tool 551

        Using FrontPage 2000 to Create a Web Development Environment ... 551

        Using ADO and CDO Constants in Web Pages 552

Creating and Registering Web Storage System Forms 554

    Choosing a Folder for Web Page Storage 554

    Creating a Simple Home Page 555

    Creating a Frameset Home Page 557

        Understanding the Frameset Page 558

        Understanding the Contents Page 559

        Understanding the Main Page 562

    Getting Folder Contents 563

    Displaying an Item 568

    Creating an Item 573

    Saving an Item 574

    Deleting an Item 579

    Reusing Outlook Web Access 581

Summary 584

CHAPTER 13: XML AND EXCHANGE 585

Overview of XML and Exchange 586

    Why Develop Using XML? 586

    Building Applications by Using XML 587

    Understanding HTTP and WebDAV 588

Understanding the Basics of XML 589

    Building an XML Document 590

    Creating XML Elements 592

    Integrating XML Namespaces 594

    Generating XML with an ASP Page 595

    Using XML Data Islands 601

Making HTTP Requests from a Client 603

    XMLHTTP Methods and Properties 603

    Making a Simple HTTP Request 605

    Using the Open Method 606

    Setting Header Fields 608

    Sending the HTTP Request and Getting the Results 609

    Checking the State of an Asynchronous Connection 611

Using XMLHTTP 613

    Returning a Resource with All Properties 613

        Returning All the Properties for a Resource 613

        Returning an Item with Specific Properties 614

        Returning Folder Contents 615

    Creating a Folder 617

    Creating an Item 618

    Copying a Resource 619

    Moving a Resource 620

    Deleting a Resource 621

Rendering XML with XSL 622

   How It Works 623

   Using XSL-Specific Elements 623

   Building an XSL Template as a Stand-Alone File 624

   Identifying XML Elements with XSL Patterns 626

   Building a Table 628

   Using an XML Data Island for an XSL Template 631

Response Codes 635

Summary 639

SECTION V: PREPARING FOR THE ENTERPRISE 641

CHAPTER 14: SETTING SECURITY AND PERMISSIONS 643

Understanding Exchange 2000 Server Security 644

   How Exchange 2000 Server Security Works 644

   Planning Security in Applications 645

Managing Client Permissions on Web Storage System Folders 646

   Assigning Client Permissions by Using the User Interface 646

      Assigning Permissions to MAPI Public Folders 647

      Assigning Permissions to Non-MAPI Folders 650

   Understanding Permissions Inheritance 653

   Overlapping Permissions 657

Using the Security Descriptor Property 658

   Understanding the Security Descriptor Property 658

   Interpreting a DACL 663

      Using Access Masks 664

      Reading and Building an SID 666

   Reading the Details of a Security Descriptor 668

   Building a Security Descriptor 670

Enforcing Security on Code with COM+ Components 672

   Why Use COM+ Role-Based Security? 672

Configuring COM+ Role-Based Security 673

Enabling Security for the COM+ Application 674

Defining COM+ Roles 675

Adding Users to COM+ Roles 677

Assigning COM+ Roles to Components 678

Disabling Anonymous Access to Effectively Use COM+ Roles 679

Summary 681

CHAPTER 15: TESTING AND DEPLOYING YOUR APPLICATIONS.................... 683

Setting Up Exchange in a Single Server Domain 684

Installing Windows 2000 Server 684

Configuring Your Domain Controller 686

Installing Exchange 2000 Server 688

Creating a New Administrator Account 690

Setting Up the Development Environment 691

Installing Office 2000 and FrontPage Server Extensions 691

Installing Development Environments and Tools 692

Creating an Exchange Development MMC Console 692

Adding additional users 696

Deploying Application-Specific Tools 696

Using Windows Script Files to Automate Installations 698

Summary 700

APPENDIX A: WEB STORAGE SYSTEM SCHEMA PROPERTIES 701

DAV 701

CDO Configuration 706

CDO NNTP Envelope 713

CDO SMTP Envelope 714

CDO Workflow 715

Exchange 718

Event Registrations 727

Exchange Security 729

Full Text Querying 732

Calendar 734

Contacts 742

HTTP Mail 754

Mail Header 759

Data Types 765

Exchange Data 765

Form Registrations 768

Microsoft Office 770

XML Data 777

APPENDIX B: DESIGNING FORMS WITH OUTLOOK 2000.......................... 779

Introduction to Outlook Forms Designer 780

Using Outlook Form Events 782

    Creating an Event Procedure 783

    Canceling an Event 785

    Using Control Events 787

    Order of Event Firing 787

        Opening 787

        Saving and Closing 788

        Sending 789

        Replying 789

        Forwarding 789

Using Script to Access Parts of an Outlook Form 790

    Returning the Current Item 791

    Getting the Inspector 791

    Controlling Pages 791

        Activating a Page 792

        Hiding and Showing Pages 792

        Accessing Controls on a Page 793

    Delving into Custom Fields 794

Controlling Controls 795
Controlling Text Boxes 795
Controlling List Controls 795
Populating a List Control Array 796
Returning a Value from a List Control 798
Detecting When Data Changes 798
Moving Focus to a Control and Selecting Text 799
Controlling the Body of Items 800
Using Word as the Editor 801
Using HTML as the Editor 803
Using Custom Command Bars 804
Creating the Command Bar with the Open Event 804
Making Command Bars Temporary 805
Distributing Outlook Forms 806
Protecting Your Form Design 807
Saving the Current Instance of a Form 807
Creating a Form Template 808
Publishing to a Forms Library 808
Understanding How Published Forms Work 809
Publishing with the Form Definition 811
Using a Custom Form as the Default Form in a Folder 812
Managing and Maintaining Outlook Forms 812
Distributing a New Version of a Form 812
Updating the MessageClass Property 813

GLOSSARY 815

INDEX 829

Acknowledgements

I have spent many months writing the content for this book, but lots of people helped produce the book you now hold in your hands. First and foremost, I would like to thank Eric Lockard, for giving me the opportunity to write this book to help developers everywhere learn just how great Exchange is for development. Thank you, Eric, for this wonderful experience and the chance to work with the best team at Microsoft! I would also like to raise a big glass of Barolo to Charles Eliot, for coming up with the idea for this book and for getting the project started. Thanks, Charles, for believing in me. Thanks also to Janine Harrison for adopting the project and me when Charles moved on to bigger and better things. Janine, your support and continued guidance were greatly appreciated. I've learned much from you about managing projects.

Next, I would to thank the folks who actually had a hand in making this book. First, I would like to thank the people who were the backbone of this project, my editors: Kristine Haugseth and Lori Kane. Kristine, you stuck with me from the start, and I am forever grateful for your wisdom. We survived! Thank you for your quiet guidance, incredible editing, and forgiving ear. Lori, a writer couldn't ask for a better developmental editor. You took my words and made them understandable. Without you, this book never would have gone to press in time.

I'd also like to thank Theano Petersen, Beth Harmon, and Gwen Bloomsburg for their wonderful job creating the book template, formatting the book, and copyediting. You guys were great for adjusting to my crazy, last minute changes. Thanks to Lee and Tony Ross for indexing. Thanks also to David Vican and Kristie Smith for the art, and to Mike Birch for help with production. I would also like to thank the wonderful folks at Microsoft Press—John Pierce, Victoria Thulman, and Sally Stickney—for their advice and for handling the final hand off to the printers.

I couldn't have written this book (correctly!) without the technical guidance of the men and women of the Microsoft Exchange team. These folks tolerated a seemingly endless barrage of e-mail questions and meeting requests all while producing a great product in Microsoft Exchange 2000.

For the overall developer view, thank you to Mike Patten. I can't count the times that I barged into your office demanding to know why developers needed to know this or that. Thanks for acting like I was never interrupting anything even though I'm sure that I was.

A big thanks to Andrew Sinclair for his help with ADO, CDO, and Web Storage System events. Thanks, Andrew, for answering every one of the hundreds of e-mail you received from me asking about the tiniest details, and thanks for the (um...) *detailed* technical editing. In that same technical area, thank you to Naveen Kachroo for his unfailing help with everything CDO and Web Storage System schema. Thanks, Naveen, for going above and beyond the call of duty and editing four of my chapters. You did a fantastic job!

A special thanks to Peter Waxman for his help with the Active Directory, ADSI, and overall Exchange architecture. Thanks for your guidance in designing this book and for answering each of the many, many questions I had on "why." You were always able to explain (time and time again!) why things have to work the way they do in Exchange.

For their help on Web content, a big thanks to Alex Hopmann and Robert Brown. Thanks, Alex, for all of your help with XML. You've made an XML believer out of me! And Robert, thank you for the many hours spent explaining and building applications using the forms registry. Thanks also for letting me use your wonderful idea for the Form Registry Explorer.

I would also like to thank Sanjay Anand for his help with everything security and Jim Reitz for his help on workflow. Thanks also to Karim Batthish, Brent Ingraham, and Jamie Cool for their help on Web content.

In addition, a number of other folks helped make this project work. A very special thanks to Ken Getz for performing a technical edit of this book. You've always been a mentor to me, and you are the one who put me on this wonderful yellow brick road that I'm on. You are my teacher, my advisor, and a dear friend. Thanks to Linda Hirsh and Pam Raphael for handling the logistics of this project. And finally, a very heart felt thanks to my family: my mother Mary Lou Martin, my grandma Charlotte Winters, my aunt Theodore Chronowski, my brother and sister-in-law Mark and Kristi Martin. Thank you all for being so understanding and so supportive of my decision to come to Seattle and write this book. Thanks also to my dear friends, Lynn McCarthy, Amy Luehmann, and Denise Smith for forgiving me when I dropped off of the face of the Earth for a few months there. I'm back!

Introduction

Programming Collaborative Web Applications with Exchange 2000 Server is a guide to developing almost any solution with Microsoft Exchange 2000 Server. As technology advances and becomes more flexible in its capabilities, application developers face pressure to build bigger and better solutions in less time. Months of research went into this book in an attempt to save you time when you develop your own Exchange 2000 solutions. I hope this book gets you up and running with Exchange 2000 Server as quickly as possible and that it helps you to build the Exchange solution that best suits your application needs.

WHO SHOULD READ THIS BOOK

Programming Collaborative Web Applications with Exchange 2000 Server is for anyone who is interested in developing applications for Exchange. Whether you are a new Exchange developer ready to discover the possibilities in an Exchange application, or a seasoned Exchange developer in need of advanced tips, this book has something for you. It discusses the basics of the Exchange development paradigm as well as more advanced features, such as setting security programmatically. Because the developer features of Exchange 2000 are so different from those of its predecessors, any developer can benefit in some way from the material in each of the chapters.

Even if you've never developed for Exchange, you shouldn't have any trouble with the content of this book. The only requirement when it comes to Exchange-specific technology is to have a basic understanding of what Exchange is and what it does. You should also understand the basic principles of Exchange, including collaboration tasks such as sending e-mail and scheduling meetings. If you have used a messaging client such as Microsoft Outlook 2000, you have the right collaboration background.

However, I have had to make some assumptions about readers' programming knowledge to cover all the necessary material in the pages allotted to me. To use this book, you must have a firm grasp on the basics of the Microsoft Visual Basic programming language, such as how to use properties, methods, and variables. If you are unfamiliar with Visual Basic or Microsoft Visual Basic Scripting Edition (VBScript), you might find the material in this book too advanced to derive much benefit. If this is the case, brush up on your programming skills before you read this book.

I chose to use Visual Basic for the majority of sample code primarily due to the large number of Visual Basic and VBScript developers out there. Visual Basic is used over VBScript in most samples to provide clarity in code. You can also change Visual Basic code to VBScript without losing the automatic formatting added by Visual Basic. In addition, you use Visual Basic to create the DLLs used with Microsoft Web Storage System events, workflow, ASP applications, and COM+ components.

I also had to make some assumptions about readers' knowledge of Web development when writing the chapters that focus on Web development. These chapters don't require years of Web development experience, but they do require a basic understanding of HTML and ASP technology. If you don't have this background, you can still benefit from these chapters, but you might need to reference additional material for more detailed explanations of these technologies.

HOW THIS BOOK IS ORGANIZED

This book contains 15 chapters organized into five sections. Two appendixes, a glossary, and an index follow the chapters.

SECTION I—WELCOME TO EXCHANGE 2000 SERVER

This section is essential for even the experienced Exchange developer. It describes what Exchange 2000 Server offers the developer, including the advancements in development features from earlier versions of Exchange. Chapters include:

- **Chapter 1: Developing with the Exchange Platform**. This chapter introduces the new development platform offered by Exchange 2000 Server and Web Storage Systems. The chapter explores the tools that you can use to build anything from the simplest Exchange application involving Microsoft Outlook Web Access to more complex applications that use the Web Storage System forms registry and events. The chapter also introduces all the protocols and APIs that you can use to develop custom solutions for Exchange.

- **Chapter 2: Exchange and the Web Storage System**. This chapter gives a more detailed description of the relationship between Exchange and the Web Storage System and discusses how a Web Storage System turns simple data storage into smart storage. It explains the benefits the Web Storage System offers developers and why you would want to store data there. The chapter also discusses how data is organized in a Web Storage System and how you can get to that data from just about any client—without any code. In addition, it covers how to create multiple Web Storage Systems and configure a virtual directory by using Exchange System Manager.

SECTION II—DATA ACCESS

If you design any type of custom application with Exchange, you will want to know about the different ways to interact with the information stored in a Web Storage System as well as in the Active Directory directory service of Microsoft Windows 2000. Chapters include:

- **Chapter 3: Web Storage System Schema**. This chapter explains how data is defined with the Web Storage System schema and how to customize it to fit your application needs. The chapter begins with an introduction to schema, namespaces, and properties. You then learn how schema properties are associated with resources in a Web Storage System by using content classes. A resource is just about anything you store in Exchange, such as a mail message, a contact, or a Web file. The chapter shows how to create a custom application schema to extend your application with custom content classes and properties.

- **Chapter 4: ActiveX Data Objects and Exchange**. This chapter explores how to use ActiveX Data Objects 2.5 (ADO), which is the programmatic interface to OLE DB, to access and explore Web Storage Systems. The chapter explains how to use the Record and Recordset objects to navigate the depths of a store, how to use the Connection object for maximum application efficiency, and how to query a Web Storage System for exactly the information that you need. This chapter has lots of code samples that show the core data access tasks: opening folders and items, creating and deleting items, moving and copying items, and reading and setting properties.

- **Chapter 5: Introduction to CDO for Exchange**. This chapter introduces the premier collaboration development API: Collaboration Data Objects (CDO) for Exchange. CDO is not meant to compete with ADO but to enhance it. This chapter introduces the various DLLs that make up CDO and their associated classes and interfaces. The chapter teaches the core fundamentals for building a collaboration solution—from sending e-mail to scheduling meetings to scripting workflow. You learn how to access data in a Web Storage System for reading and writing and how to access and manipulate property values available both as CDO properties and as schema properties. In addition, this chapter describes how to use CDO objects to create and manage contacts in public folders and in Active Directory as well as how to use CDO to manage folders.

- **Chapter 6: CDO Messaging**. If you want to build a messaging solution by using CDO, this is the chapter you want. You can use this chapter to come up to speed on Multipurpose Internet Mail Extensions (MIME) messages and how CDO navigates them as a collection of BodyPart objects. The chapter teaches how to compose and send messages as well as how to process incoming messages. The chapter also discusses streaming attachments to and from a message and using the Configuration object with bulk mailings.

- **Chapter 7: CDO Calendaring**. This chapter describes how to use CDO to create calendaring solutions for Exchange 2000 Server. It covers how an Exchange server stores dates and times to manage data from multiple time zones and emphasizes that you must keep this in mind as you read and write to the store. The chapter teaches how to use CDO for everything from creating a simple appointment to scheduling a meeting, including how to schedule recurring appointments and meetings and make changes to existing patterns. Finally, the chapter explains how to successfully query a calendar from any time zone.

- **Chapter 8: Interacting with Active Directory**. This chapter moves away from the Web Storage System and focuses on Active Directory. It explains how to use Active Directory Service Interfaces (ADSI), the programmatic interface to Lightweight Directory Access Protocol (LDAP), to interact with Active Directory. It also explains how to dynamically connect to any Active Directory server to create new objects, read and set properties, and delete existing objects. It explains how to use ADSI along with CDO for Exchange 2000 to create and manage Active Directory contacts, users, and Exchange mailboxes, how to use ADSI to create and manage security groups to grant permissions on resources in your network, and how to create distribution groups—called distribution lists in earlier versions of Exchange—for e-mailing groups of people as one addressee. Finally, it discusses how to get system information from the Active Directory and how to query Active Directory for specific information, such as users that have Exchange mailboxes.

Section III—Extending Your Application

This section discusses techniques that you can use to make a good Exchange application great, but the techniques are neither essential nor applicable to every application design. Chapters include:

- **Chapter 9: Using Web Storage System Events**. This chapter introduces the new Web Storage System events that allow an application to react in a custom and intelligent way to the actions of its users. It describes the synchronous, asynchronous, and system events available in a Web Storage System for trapping various activities, such as the addition of a new item, changes to an item, or the deletion of an item. You can also create event code that executes at a specific time. Finally, the chapter describes how to build the event sinks that actually contain the event code and how to register the event sink with Exchange so it triggers the code when a certain event occurs.

- **Chapter 10: Designing Workflow Applications**. This chapter explains how to create workflow applications, which are necessary for multiple people to collaborate successfully on a project. By building workflow applications, you can control and direct the processing of documents across a team. This chapter covers how to use Workflow Designer for Exchange to build robust workflow applications.

- **Chapter 11: Developing with Outlook 2000**. This chapter describes the issues you need to be aware of when you develop a solution for Outlook 2000 clients with Exchange 2000. It explains how to create resources in a Web Storage System for both Web clients and Outlook clients and how to read custom schema properties from a custom Outlook form.

SECTION IV—BUILDING FOR THE WEB

Exchange 2000 Server is optimized for the Web, so Web applications can make the most of the development features in Exchange. This section describes the types of applications that you can build for the Web and the tools you can use to build them. Chapters include:

- **Chapter 12: Building Web Applications for Exchange**. This chapter introduces Exchange features that are specific to Web development, including the new forms registry. You can use forms registry to associate Web pages with types of Web Storage System resources. This means that you can use your own custom Web interface to display the information in a Web Storage System.

- **Chapter 13: XML and Exchange**. This chapter takes another approach to Web development and introduces you to the relatively new and quickly expanding world of Extensible Markup Language (XML). You can learn how to create Web pages that use XML and its associated components. The chapter includes an introduction to HTTP and explains how the Web Distributed Authoring and Versioning (WebDAV) extensions change into a read/write medium. You also learn how to use Extensible Stylesheet Language (XSL) to display the results several different ways.

SECTION V—PREPARING FOR THE ENTERPRISE

After you have built the application and perhaps extended it with some of the more advanced features, you are ready to prepare your Web Storage System solution for the enterprise. Chapters include:

- **Chapter 14: Setting Security and Permissions**. This chapter explains how to integrate security into your applications to keep data safe and code secure. It describes how to use the built-in security features of Exchange and Windows to control how users interact with folders in your application. You also learn how to programmatically control the same security settings and even extend them to the item level. Finally, it covers how to use COM+ roles to allow or restrict user access to your middle-tier components.

- **Chapter 15: Testing and Deploying Your Applications**. This chapter includes topics related to testing and deployment, such as how to set up your own test environment for building Web Storage System applications so you have a firm understanding of what goes into configuring an Exchange server. Rather than using the Exchange server in service, developers can use their own secure environment without concern about affecting the main messaging server. The chapter also describes some key issues to watch out for when you deploy a custom application in the enterprise.

APPENDIXES

In addition to the chapters, this book includes two appendixes:

- **Appendix A: Web Storage System Schema Properties**. This appendix includes several tables that contain descriptions of the Web Storage System schema properties. You can use this guide as a quick reference to schema properties during development or for more information about a schema property that is used in the sample code.

- **Appendix B: Designing Forms with Outlook 2000**. This appendix contains information about scripting custom Outlook forms. If you build a client-side application by using Outlook 2000, you can use this appendix as an introduction to some of the more common scripting tasks.

SYSTEM REQUIREMENTS

To view the contents of the companion CD, you do not need to have Exchange 2000 Server installed.

However, to use the tools on the CD and to complete the steps in this book, you must have Exchange 2000 Server installed. The system requirements for Exchange 2000 Server include:

- A Pentium 133 or higher

- Microsoft Windows 2000 Server

- 256 megabytes (MB) of RAM recommended (128 MB minimum)

- 200 MB of disk space available on the system drive

- 500 MB of disk space available on the install drive

- A CD ROM drive

- A video graphics adapter (VGA) or a higher resolution monitor

You can use the ZipOut 2000 tool on any client computer running Microsoft Outlook 2000. You can use the Exchange SDK on any computer.

ABOUT THE COMPANION CD

The companion CD contains sample code from each of the chapters as well as the Exchange 2000 SDK Help files. It also contains some shareware and tools to make developing with Exchange a little easier.

Please respect the copyright notices on all the code and tools. This material cannot be republished or reused in its entirety in any way. If you like the shareware, sign up for a licensed copy from the vendor.

WHAT'S ON THE CD

The companion CD to the book is organized into five folders, which, in turn, can contain subfolders:

- **Chapter Code**. This folder contains a folder for each chapter that has sample code. Each chapter folder generally contains at least one Visual Basic project and multiple .bas and .cls files. All the listings from the chapters are available in these projects. For some of the chapters that focus entirely on Web development, such as Chapter 13, "XML and Exchange," the folder contains only Microsoft FrontPage Web files.

- **Exchange SDK**. This folder contains the setup file for the official online Help file for developing with Exchange. This book makes a good companion to these Help files.

- **Sample Application**. This folder contains two folders for setting up both components of the sample application. This simple Exchange application is designed to familiarize you with the different facets of Exchange development. The code samples in the chapters use the folders created for this application.

- **Some Helper Tools**. This folder contains several folders, and each contains a tool. I created these tools to help develop applications with Exchange 2000 and found them invaluable. I continue to use them to build and test my Exchange applications. You can use these tools to learn the nuances of Exchange development and to help build various components.

- **ZipOut**. This folder contains the ZipOut.exe shareware. ZipOut 2000 is an add-in for Outlook 2000 that automatically compresses attachments to outgoing messages and items stored in your mailbox or personal folders. You can evaluate ZipOut 2000 for a 30-day trial period.

INSTALLING THE CHAPTER SAMPLE CODE FILES

The companion CD includes a folder called Chapter Code that contains child folders for each of the chapters that contain sample code. These folders have a name of Ch_*XX* where *XX* is the chapter number. In these folders, you will find a Visual Basic project with the name of Ch_XX.vbp as well as a number of supporting files. You can manually copy the files for each chapter to your computer or you can use the BookCode.exe program to extract all the chapter code files to your computer. BookCode.exe is a self-extracting ZIP file that installs all the files where you want them. The code files on the CD are read-only. If you choose to copy the files manually, you must turn off read-only access to the files in Windows Explorer.

SETTING UP THE SAMPLE APPLICATION

The code listings in this book rely on a sample application called Zoo Management. Zoo Management is an Exchange application consisting of several public folders. The custom Web version of this application is known as ZooWeb. Throughout this book, you will see references to both Zoo Management and ZooWeb. When the book references Zoo Management, it is referring to the folder structure of the application. When the book references ZooWeb, it is referring to the Web functionality incorporated into the application.

The Sample Application folder contains two folders:

- **Zoo Management Setup**. This folder contains the setup file for the folder hierarchy of the application. The setup program also creates some necessary sample items.

- **ZooWeb Setup**. This folder contains the Web pages for the Web interface of the Zoo Management application. The folder also contains the setup program to configure the Web files for use.

SETTING UP ZOO MANAGEMENT FOLDER STRUCTURE

To set up the Web Storage System that is used with the sample code in this book, you must configure a new Web Storage System and then run the ZooMgtSetup.exe program. This Web Storage System consists of one application: Zoo Management. The following tasks are discussed in detail in Chapter 2, "Exchange and the Web Storage System."

In Exchange System Manager, follow these steps:

1. Create a new public folder tree named Applications.

2. Create a new public store named Applications Store, and associate it with the new Applications folder tree.

3. Mount the store on the tree.

4. Click the Applications folder tree to enable folder access through the tree.

5. Create a new public folder in the Applications folder tree named Zoo Management (include the space).

6. Create a virtual directory named ZooWeb that maps to the Zoo Management public folder.

To finish configuring the Zoo Management sample application, you must run the ZooMgtSetup.exe program in the Zoo Management Setup folder. This program creates and configures the application folders in Zoo Management and also creates some sample items. In addition, the setup program configures the schema used by the application so that you can successfully use the ZooWeb portion of the sample application. For more information about application schemas, see Chapter 3, "Web Storage System Schema."

The Applications folder tree should look like this after you configure the folder tree and run the setup program:

Applications (Web Storage System folder tree)

--Zoo Management

   ---Animals

   ---Acquisitions

   ---Announcements

   ---Events

   ---Facilities

   ---Images (hidden folder)

   ---Research

   ---Schema (hidden folder)

   ---Staff

   ---Surgery

   ---Vets

SETTING UP ZOOWEB

To use the custom Web interface to Zoo Management known as ZooWeb, you must complete two additional tasks: copy the Web pages to the Zoo Management schema folder and run the WebApplicationSetup.exe program.

You can use Windows Explorer to copy the ZooWeb Web files. Copy the Web files from the ZooWeb Files folder on the CD to the Zoo Management application folders on drive M, where the Exchange folders are exposed in Windows Explorer:

- Copy global.asa to the Zoo Management folder.

- Copy frog.gif to the Images folder.

- Copy all the other .asp and .css files to the Schema folder.

Finally, you must configure the Web files by running the WebApplicationSetup.exe program in the ZooWeb Setup folder. This program adds some information to the Schema folder that allows the Web pages to appear instead of the default Outlook Web Access display when you open the folders and items in the application. For more information about configuring a Web application for Exchange, see Chapter 12, "Building Web Applications for Exchange."

ABOUT THE HELPER TOOLS

Besides the chapter code, the companion CD includes several compiled tools in the Some Helper Tools folder. Each tool is in a folder of the same name:

- **Content Class Browser**. Use this tool to browse the folders in a Web Storage System and view the properties on both folders and items. This is an excellent tool for learning about schema properties and content classes. For more information about using Content Class Browser, see Chapter 3, "Web Storage System Schema."

- **Calendar Browser**. Use this tool to retrieve appointment items in a folder and read the properties for each appointment. This is a great tool for learning about how Exchange handles storing dates for appointments. For more information about using Calendar Browser, see Chapter 7, "CDO Calendaring."

- **Event Registration**. Use this tool to read event registrations that exist in a Web Storage System folder and to create new event registrations. For more information about using the Event Registration tool, see Chapter 9, "Using Web Storage System Events."

- **Folder Composition**. Use this tool to view and modify the schema path for a Web Storage System application and to change the content class associated with a resource. For more information about using the Folder Composition tool, see Chapter 12, "Building Web Applications for Exchange."

- **Forms Registry Explorer**. This Web tool is built with ASP pages; use it to create and manage form registrations in a forms registry. You can use this tool to help you build a Web interface to any Exchange application. For more information about using Forms Registry Explorer. see Chapter 12, "Building Web Applications for Exchange."

Each of these folders contains an .exe file for immediate use on your server as well as the source code so that you can modify the tool for your own purposes. You can manually copy the files to your computer, or you can use the HelperTools.exe program to extract all the tool files to your computer. HelperTools.exe is a self-extracting ZIP file that installs all the tool files where you want them. The code files on the CD are read-only. If you choose to copy the files manually, you must turn off read-only access to the files in Windows Explorer.

These tools are designed to help you build applications with Exchange and to help you learn the basics behind Exchange application development. The tools are not supported, so use your best judgment when using them in your organization. In addition, please respect that the tools are not available for redistribution.

ABOUT ZIPOUT 2000

ZipOut 2000 is an Outlook 2000 add-in that automatically compresses attachments to outgoing messages and items stored in your mailbox or personal folders. ZipOut can send attachments to recipients in a .zip or self-extracting file. If you do not have a Zip utility, ZipOut provides an integral Zip file viewer. Attachment compression is done automatically; no user intervention is required.

A new addition to ZipOut 2000 is the ability to manage attachments in your mailbox or personal folders. You can compress attachments on all items in a folder and subfolders, remove HTML stationery, or simply delete attachments from a selection of messages. You can schedule automatic attachment compression in your mailbox based on a single or recurring Outlook task, and you can display the compression results in an Office 2000 Web component.

You can evaluate ZipOut 2000 for a 30-day trial period. Once the 30-day evaluation expires, you must purchase a license for ZipOut or uninstall the software. For the most recent version of the shareware, visit http://www.microeye.com/zipout/.

CONVENTIONS USED IN THIS BOOK

The following table explains some of the conventions used in this book.

Element	Example of convention	Description
Arrow keys on the keyboard	DOWN ARROW	Arrow keys appear in plain text and are uppercase. Individual direction keys are referred to by the direction of the arrow on the key to (LEFT, RIGHT, UP, DOWN). The phrase "arrow keys" is used when describing these keys collectively.
caution note	**CAUTION**	Caution notes appear in bold, are indented, and begin with a full capital followed by small capitals. A **CAUTION** advises users that failure to take or avoid a specified action could result in loss of data.

code	`Sub HellowButton_Click()`
	`Readout.Text = _`
	`"Hello, world!"`
	`End Sub`
		This font is used for code. Short code examples appear indented in this font. Complete pieces of code are labeled as Listings and are also included on the companion CD.

extensions	.exe .txt	In text, extensions appear in plain text, lowercase, and are preceded by a dot.
file names	Call.vbs	In text, file names appear in plain text and typically have the initial letter capitalized.

Continued on next page

Element	Example of convention	Description
flag values	EVT_SYNC_BEGIN EVT_SYNC_COMMITTED EVT_SYNC_ABORTED	In text, flag values appear in plain text and are uppercase.
functions (calls)	AlreadyExists CreateObject GetFrequencyPattern GetISODate	In text, functions appear in plain text, mixed case, and the initial letter is capitalized.
interfaces	IADs IBodyParts ICalendarParts IDataSource IWorkflowSession	In text, interfaces appear in plain text, mixed case, and they usually begin with an uppercase I.
keys on the keyboard	ENTER	Keyboard keys appear in plain text and are uppercase.
libraries	ExOLEDB Active DS Type Library (Activeds.lib) Active DS Type library (Activeds.dll) LDAP client library (WLDAP32.dll)	Libraries appear in plain text and match the capitalization of the library's actual name.
N/A	N/A	In tables, N/A means *not available at this time*.

Continued on next page

Element	Example of convention	Description
namespaces	http://schemas.microsoft.com/exchange/ urn:schemas:calendar: urn:schemas:contacts: DAV:	There are many types of namespaces, and they can appear several ways. They all appear in plain text. They may appear with colons, and most are lowercase. Several, like DAV: and MAIL:, are always uppercase. All namespaces are case sensitive.
new terms	*Data islands* are chunks of XML data embedded in well-formatted HTML documents.	In text, italic letters can indicate defined terms, usually the first time that they occur. Italic formatting is also used to show variables, parameters, and occasionally emphasis.
notes	**NOTE**	Notes appear in bold, are indented, and begin with a full capital followed by small capitals. A **NOTE** contains neutral or positive information that emphasizes or supplements important points of the main text. Sometimes a **NOTE** supplies information that may apply only in special cases—for example, memory limitations, equipment configurations, or details that apply to specific versions of a program.
object properties	ItemCount ActiveConnection Criteria EventRecord	In text, object properties appear in plain text and are mixed case.

Continued on next page

Element	Example of convention	Description
parameters	*adModeReadWrite* *bstrMDBGuid* *lFlags*	In text, parameters are mixed case and usually appear in italic.
path names	M:\Vb\Samples\Call.vbs	In text, path names appear in plain text, mixed case, and the drive name (for example, M) is capitalized.
schema properties	http:// schemas.microsoft.com/ cdo/configuration/ urn:schemas:calendar: timezoneid	Schema properties usually appear with the namespace name followed by the property name. Occasionally, schema property names are used without the namespace name and are noted in the body text in which they appear. They are all case sensitive.
text you are instructed to type	Type **setup**	Words that users are instructed to type appear in bold.
tips	**TIP**	Tips appear in bold, are indented, and begin with a full capital followed by small capitals. A **TIP** is designed to help users apply the techniques and procedures described in the text to their specific needs. A **TIP** suggests alternative methods that might not be obvious and is an attempt to help users understand the benefits and capabilities of the product. A **TIP** is not essential to a basic understanding of the text.

Continued on next page

Element	Example of convention	Description
user interface elements	**File** menu **Project** dialog box click **Exchange Workflow Designer**	User interface elements appear in bold. They are capitalized to match the text as it appears on-screen.
variables	*Filename*	In text, italic words can indicate placeholders for information that users supply.

Welcome to Exchange 2000 Server

Chapter:

1   Developing with the Exchange Platform   **3**

2   Exchange and the Web Storage System   **37**

Developing with the Exchange Platform

Microsoft Exchange 2000 Server has everything a database, a Web server, and a collaboration server should offer—all rolled into one product. With the new Microsoft Web Storage System technology, not only can you store just about any type of data, but you also have additional developer benefits: complete URL addressability to access your data from anywhere at any time; a fully flexible data design that adjusts to your data as your application evolves; many data access technologies to choose from, including ActiveX Data Objects (ADO), Collaboration Data Objects (CDO) for Exchange, and Extensible Markup Language (XML); and smart data storage with Web Storage System forms, events, and workflow logic. Once you learn about Exchange 2000 Server, you might not want to use anything else to develop your database, Web, and collaboration solutions.

This chapter explains the new features and possibilities of Exchange 2000 Server. Sections include:

- **A Tour of Exchange 2000**

- **Using Data Access Tools**

- **Displaying Your Data**

- **Enhancing Your Application**

- **Wrapping It Up**

A Tour of Exchange 2000

Before you construct an application with Exchange 2000 Server, you should become familiar with the Exchange environment. This section describes the administrative tools you use to define and manage an application's framework. It also explains the details of where data is stored, how to access data, and how to define data by using a schema.

Exchange System Manager

Your first step toward developing solutions with Exchange 2000 is to learn Exchange System Manager (see Figure 1.1). Exchange System Manager is the new Exchange administrator, and it has been greatly enhanced over its predecessor. With Microsoft Exchange Server 5.5, a developer had little reason to access the administrator console except to create event agents. You could do most things, such as folder creation and administration, from Microsoft Outlook 2000. But with Exchange System Manager, all that has changed.

When you develop with Exchange, use Exchange System Manager to:

- Create new Web Storage Systems and folder trees.

- Create both MAPI and non-MAPI folders and set properties on them.

- Set access rights on folders to specify who can and who cannot access a folder.

- Create virtual directories for Web Storage System folders that can be used for Web applications.

- Manage the settings for a Web application.

- Enable a folder to receive e-mail.

Exchange System Manager is a snap-in of Microsoft Management Console (MMC), which is a framework that contains such management tools. You can add any tools of Microsoft Windows to a single console as a snap-in. For example, you could create a console in MMC that uses the Exchange System Manager snap-in as well as the Events Viewer snap-in.

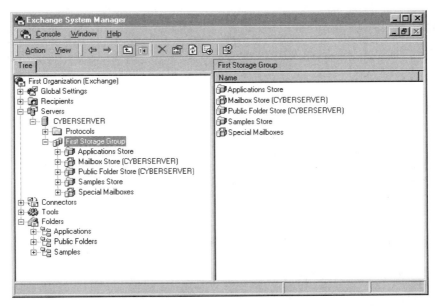

Figure 1.1
Exchange System Manager

ACTIVE DIRECTORY

The next thing you should know about Exchange 2000 Server is how it takes advantage of the Active Directory directory service of Microsoft Windows 2000 (see Figure 1.2). In Windows 2000, Active Directory manages all the user and group information in a Windows domain. Exchange 2000 turns over the user and mailbox management responsibilities to Windows 2000 and Active Directory. Because Active Directory already manages the domain accounts, it makes sense that Active Directory should also manage the mailboxes that belong to those same users. This means you get better manageability and stronger security.

In addition, Active Directory now manages the distribution groups (previously referred to as distribution lists) for Exchange. Active Directory also manages the information specific to an individual Exchange server. When you develop solutions with Exchange, use Active Directory to:

- Create users with mailboxes, or create mailboxes for existing user accounts.

- Manage information about all Exchange mailboxes in an organization, and retrieve information, such as manager information and direct reports, about those users.

- Create security groups for applying access rights to groups of individuals.

- Create distribution groups for sending e-mail to groups of recipients with one e-mail address.

- Retrieve system information, including the name of the Exchange server and the domain on which your code is running.

- Return information about the user who is currently logged on.

- Check a user's free/busy status.

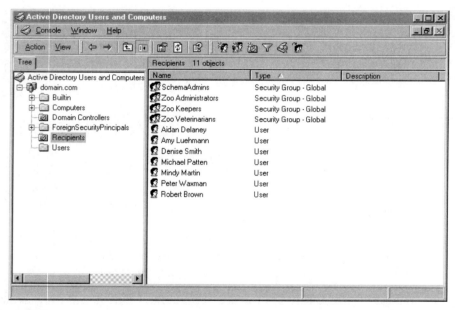

Figure 1.2
Exchange 2000 Server takes advantage of the capabilities of Active Directory.

THE WEB STORAGE SYSTEM

At the core of the Exchange development paradigm is the Web Storage System. Exchange 2000 is the first Microsoft product to employ the Web Storage System technology. The Web Storage System is not so much a new way to store data in Exchange as a new way to interact with and manage data.

As in previous versions of Exchange, Exchange 2000 is still organized into public stores and mailbox stores. But now each one of those stores is an individual Web Storage System. Each Web Storage System is organized, much like a traditional file system, as a hierarchy of folders. Each folder can contain any number of items—everything from standard Exchange items, such as appointments and contacts, to more complex files, such as Active Server Pages (ASP) files and Microsoft Office documents, as well as other folders.

However, there's much more to a Web Storage System. Each Web Storage System combines the functionality of an intranet Web server, a database server, and a collaboration server. When developing solutions with Exchange, use a Web Storage System to:

- Create multiple Web Storage Systems that can be dedicated to one application or department, in addition to the public folders store.

- Draw on the Web Storage System schema, an enormous compilation of predefined properties that Exchange uses to define resources, to create your own custom application schema with custom classes and properties.

- Build a powerful intranet Web application simply by creating a Web Storage System folder and an associated virtual directory.

- Use any number of data access APIs and protocols, including ActiveX Data Objects (ADO) 2.5, CDO for Exchange, HTTP, and XML, to build advanced custom solutions for accessing Web Storage System data.

- Include extended features, such as Web Storage System events and workflow logic, to provide intelligence to the Web Storage System data processing tasks.

For more information about using the Web Storage System, see Chapter 2, "Exchange and the Web Storage System."

PROTOCOL SUPPORT

Exchange supports a wide range of protocols for accessing the resources stored in a Web Storage System. This is why you have so much flexibility to build a client application that makes the most sense for you. Exchange supports the following protocols:

- **Hypertext Transfer Protocol (HTTP)**. HTTP is an Internet standard protocol that lets Web browsers like Microsoft Internet Explorer access Web Storage Systems.

- **Web Distributed Authoring and Versioning (WebDAV)**. WebDAV is an extension to HTTP that you can use to build applications that are writeable instead of the typical read-only Web result.

- **Simple Mail Transfer Protocol (SMTP)**. SMTP is an industry standard for Internet e-mail delivery. This is the native protocol that Exchange uses to transfer messages.

- **Network News Transfer Protocol (NNTP)**. NNTP is an Internet standard protocol used across TCP/IP networks to access newsgroups through an NNTP-compatible client such as Microsoft Outlook Express. You can use NNTP to build online discussions and set up newsgroup applications.

- **Internet Mail Access Protocol (IMAP) version 4**. IMAP4 is an Internet messaging protocol that enables a client to access e-mail on a server rather than download it to the user's computer. IMAP is designed for an environment where a user might log on to the server from different workstations.

- **Post Office Protocol (POP) version 3**. POP3 is an Internet protocol that allows a client to download e-mail from an Inbox on a server to the client computer where messages are managed. This protocol works well for computers that are unable to maintain a continuous connection to a server.

In addition to these protocols, you should also know about Lightweight Directory Access Protocol (LDAP) supported by Active Directory. LDAP is an Internet communications protocol used to communicate with a directory service. You can use an LDAP provider to access Exchange information stored in Active Directory.

WEB STORAGE SYSTEM SCHEMA

The Web Storage System schema is the data definition of a single Web Storage System. It is used to define all the resources, such as folders, items, and Web files, found in the store. The schema is an enormous compilation of predefined properties that determine the qualities, such as the display name, of a resource. You can use these properties to index, sort, and query, in the same way that you use columns in a table. However, unlike the schema associated with a standard database like Microsoft SQL Server, the Web Storage System schema is not designed to maintain rigid relational database integrity. Instead, the Web Storage System schema lets you extend existing class definitions or define your own class definitions on a per-item basis. This is why folders in the Web Storage System can store so many different types of data.

Although this huge selection of properties might be enough for you, you can easily extend it with any number of custom properties to meet even the most demanding needs of a collaboration application. You can create your own content classes, complete with custom properties. You can even define an entire application schema that you can easily reuse with other applications. For more information about using Web Storage System schema and defining a custom application schema, see Chapter 3, "Web Storage System Schema."

USING DATA ACCESS TOOLS

Probably the most significant enhancement in Exchange 2000 Server is the wide variety of data access options. Most importantly, Exchange now has an OLE DB provider, ExOLEDB. Installed with Exchange, ExOLEDB is a new, high-performance server-side provider that interacts with folders, items, and files in a Web Storage System. Both ADO 2.5 (the premier Microsoft data access API) and CDO for Exchange (the premier Microsoft collaboration API) use ExOLEDB to interact with Exchange on the server. You can also use HTTP and XML to access your data from custom Web pages and use Active Directory Services Interface (ADSI) to access the information stored in Active Directory. This section describes the Exchange data access paradigm and then explains how to use ADO, CDO, ADSI, and HTTP and XML to access Exchange data.

UNDERSTANDING THE DATA ACCESS PARADIGM

As discussed earlier in the chapter, Exchange stores information in both Web Storage Systems and Active Directory. Exchange uses the Web Storage System to store resources such as folders, items, and files, and it uses the Active Directory to store and manage data about Exchange mailboxes. This dual information source means that your applications often needs to access data from both a Web Storage System and Active Directory. Figure 1.3 shows how the development paradigm looks. To access the data in Web Storage System, you can use ADO, CDO, and even HTTP and XML. To access data in Active Directory, you can use both ADSI and CDO.

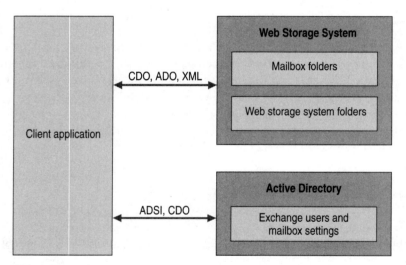

Figure 1.3
When you build an application with Exchange 2000, you use data stored in both a Web Storage System and in Active Directory.

USING ADO

When it comes to navigating among the folders and files of a Web Storage System by using code, you can't beat ADO 2.5. ADO 2.5 is the scriptable interface to OLE DB, and it is optimized to interact with any data store that has an OLE DB provider. For years, earlier versions of ADO have been used to access data stores such as Microsoft Access and SQL Server. Now you can use ADO 2.5 with the ExOLEDB provider to access a Web Storage System as easily as any other database. You can write ADO code to create new resources, delete unwanted resources, copy and move resources, and even query a Web Storage System.

Because you use URLs to identify the resource you want to access, you can navigate directly to a particular item or folder in a Web Storage System rather than navigate through the folder hierarchy until you locate the resource you want—as you must do without URLs. You use the URL to open a new ADO 2.5 Record object or a Recordset object to access a folder, an item, or a collection of both. For example, you can use a Record object to manipulate individual resources, such as copying an item from one folder to another or creating a new folder; or you can populate a Recordset object with the contents of a folder, a collection of subfolders, or a filtered set of items.

One of the biggest advantages of using ADO with Exchange is the ability to query a Web Storage System for a particular property value on any type of resource, anywhere in the store. For example, you can create a custom property that identifies the purpose of that resource and append that property to every resource in a Web Storage System application, including posts, contact, appointments, Web pages, and office documents. By using this custom property, you can query that Web Storage System application for any resource that has a particular value for that custom property. The query returns not only all the typical Exchange resources, such as the posts and appointments that meet the criteria, but also the Web pages and Office documents that meet the criteria. You can also use a modification of the FROM clause to build a query that returns resources not only from the folder being queried but also from child folders. This type of query is known as a *deep traversal*.

NOTE The code listings in this chapter are available in the Microsoft Visual Basic project CH_01.vbp on the companion CD. If you want to run the samples as they are written, you must have the Zoo Management sample installed on your Exchange 2000 server. For information about installing the application, see the introduction to the book. In addition, the code samples repeatedly call a function named GetStorageName. This function returns the name of the domain in which the code is running. For more information about the GetStorageName function, see Chapter 8, "Interacting with Active Directory."

Listing 1.1 shows how to use ADO 2.5 and the ExOLEDB provider to conduct a deep traversal of a Web Storage System for any resources, messages, contacts, custom items, Office documents, and Web pages with a specific custom property value.

Listing 1.1   Query a Web Storage System for all resources with a specific custom property value.

```
Sub SearchForCustomProperty()
    ' Look through all of the folders
    ' in a Web Storage System
    ' for resources with a specific
    ' custom property value.

    Dim cnn As ADODB.Connection
    Dim rst As ADODB.Recordset
    Dim urlQueryFld As String
    Dim strSQL As String

    ' Build the URL string
    urlQueryFld = "file://./backofficestorage/domain.com/" _
        & "Applications/Zoo Management/"

    ' Open a connection to the Applications WSS
    Set cnn = New ADODB.Connection
    With cnn
```

```
        .Provider = "exoledb.datasource"
        .Open urlQueryFld
    End With

    ' Build the SQL statement
    strSQL = _
        "SELECT " & AddQuotes("DAV:displayname") & _
        ", " & AddQuotes("DAV:href")
    strSQL = strSQL & _
        " FROM SCOPE('deep traversal of " & _
        AddQuotes(urlQueryFld) & "')"
    strSQL = strSQL & _
        " WHERE " & _
        AddQuotes("zoomgt:species") & "= 'Divine Roostrus'"
    strSQL = strSQL & _
        " ORDER BY " & AddQuotes("DAV:displayname") & " DESC"

    Set rst = New Recordset
    With rst
        .Open strSQL, cnn
    End With

    ' Return the names of the resources and their URLs
    Do Until rst.EOF
        Debug.Print _
        rst.Fields("DAV:displayname"), rst.Fields("DAV:href")
        rst.MoveNext
    Loop

    rst.Close
    cnn.Close
    Set cnn = Nothing
    Set rst = Nothing
End Sub
```

For more information about using ADO to traverse Web Storage System folders and create items, see Chapter 4, "ActiveX Data Objects and Exchange."

USING CDO FOR EXCHANGE

CDO for Exchange is the premier collaboration API for Exchange 2000. You use CDO to add collaboration capabilities to applications on the server. CDO is not a single DLL but is comprised of three different DLLs: CDO for Exchange 2000, for building standard collaboration features such as sending e-mail, scheduling, and contact management; CDO Workflow Objects for Exchange, for building workflow and routing applications; and CDO for Exchange Management, for creating and managing mailboxes and e-mail recipients.

Listing 1.2 shows how to use CDO for Exchange to schedule a meeting.

Listing 1.2 Schedule a meeting using CDO.

```
Sub ScheduleMeeting()
    ' Schedules a meeting with
    ' required and optional attendees.

    Dim cnfg As CDO.Configuration
    Dim appt As CDO.Appointment
    Dim urlCal As String

    ' URL to the calendar
    urlCal = "file://./backofficestorage/domain.com/" _
        & "mbx/mindy/calendar/"

    ' Set the configuration information
    Set cnfg = New CDO.Configuration
    With cnfg
        ' Set the meeting organizer
        .Fields(cdoSendEmailAddress) = "mindy@domain.com"
        ' Set the time zone
        .Fields(cdoTimeZoneIDURN) = cdoPacific
        .Fields.Update
    End With
```

```
' Create an appointment
Set appt = New CDO.Appointment
With appt
  ' Associate the configuration with this meeting instance
  .Configuration = cnfg

  'Set the basic properties
  .StartTime = "1:00 PM 10/09/2000"
  .EndTime = "2:00 PM 10/09/2000"
  .Subject = "Super Rooster security"
  .Location = "Super Rooster Exhibit Hall"
  .TextBody = "We need to discuss the security measures."
End With

' Add the required attendees
appt.Attendees.Add _
  "peter@domain.com, aidan@domain.com"

' Add the optional attendees
With appt.Attendees.Add
  .Address = "robert@domain.com"
  .Role = cdoOptionalParticipant
End With

' Send out the meeting requests to
' everyone who is added to the Attendees
' collection in the previous lines of code.
appt.CreateRequest.Message.Send

' Save the meeting to the organizer's calendar
appt.DataSource.SaveToContainer urlCal

' Clean up
Set cnfg = Nothing
Set appt = Nothing
End Sub
```

CDO for Exchange has very little in common with its predecessor, CDO 1.21. CDO 1.21 is used for MAPI access to Exchange, but CDO for Exchange is optimized for direct access to the Web Storage System via ExOLEDB. You can do almost everything you could do in previous releases of CDO and more.

CDO for Exchange complements ADO, rather than competing with it. Use ADO for record navigation in the Web Storage System, and use CDO for standard collaboration tasks, such as messaging and calendaring.

For more information about using CDO, see Chapter 5, "Introduction to CDO for Exchange," Chapter 6, "CDO Messaging," and Chapter 7, "CDO Calendaring."

USING ADSI

Managing the users of your Web Storage System application is as important as managing the data—sometimes even more so. As mentioned earlier, Exchange 2000 gives mailbox management responsibilities to Active Directory. This way, network users and their mailboxes are more tightly integrated.

This reassignment of management responsibilities does not change how you access directory information programmatically. As with Exchange 5.5, you access directory objects by using Active Directory Services Interface (ADSI) 2.5. ADSI is a set of Component Object Model (COM) interfaces that can use LDAP to manipulate resources stored in Active Directory. You can use ADSI to create users and groups, manage shared resources like printers and faxes, and even locate resources in the organization. You can also use CDO for Exchange (CDO) and CDO for Exchange Management (CDOExM) to manage some objects in Active Directory. For example, you can use CDO to interact with user objects in Active Directory and use CDOExM to easily set mailbox properties and return a user's free/busy status. When you incorporate ADO into the model, you can also query Active Directory for information specific to Exchange, such as the names of all Exchange servers in your organization or the names of all users with Exchange mailboxes.

Listing 1.3 shows how to return all the users in your domain that have an Exchange mailbox.

Listing 1.3   Use ADSI and ADO to query Active Directory.

```
Sub GetUserswithMailboxes()
    ' Query for all users that have
    ' a mailbox in a domain.

    Dim rootDSE As IADs
    Dim strSearchRoot As String
    Dim strADServer As String
    Dim strSQL As String
    Dim cnn As ADODB.Connection
    Dim rst As ADODB.Recordset
    Dim cmd As ADODB.Command

    ' Use the Root DS Entry to dynamically build
    ' the LDAP URL string.
    Set rootDSE = GetObject("LDAP://RootDSE")
    strADServer = rootDSE.Get("dnshostname")
    strSearchRoot = "LDAP://" & strADServer

    ' Open the connection
    Set cnn = New ADODB.Connection
    With cnn
        .Provider = "adsDSOobject"
        .Open strSearchRoot
    End With

    ' Build the SQL SELECT statement
    strSQL = _
        "SELECT adspath, cn " & _
        "FROM '" & strSearchRoot & "' " & _
        "WHERE objectcategory='person' AND MsExchMailboxGuid='*'"
```

```
' Pass the querying options to a command object
Set cmd = New ADODB.Command
With cmd
   Set .ActiveConnection = cnn
   .CommandText = strSQL
   .Properties("searchscope") = ADS_SCOPE_SUBTREE
   .Properties("cache results") = False
   .Properties("Chase Referrals") = ADS_CHASE_REFERRALS_ALWAYS
End With

' Return the results in a recordset
Set rst = cmd.Execute

' Enumerate the Exchange mailboxes
Do Until rst.EOF
   Debug.Print rst.Fields("cn"), rst.Fields("adspath")
   rst.MoveNext
Loop

' Close the ADO objects and clean up
rst.Close
cnn.Close
Set rootDSE = Nothing
Set rst = Nothing
Set cmd = Nothing
Set cnn = Nothing
End Sub
```

For more information about using ADSI and CDOEXM, see Chapter 8, "Interacting with Active Directory."

USING XML

The Web Storage System also supports building applications for Exchange by using HTTP and XML. XML is a logical choice for Web development because Exchange already stores all property definitions in a Web Storage System schema as XML. You use XML in conjunction with the XML Document Object Model (XML DOM) and Extensible Stylesheet Language (XSL) to process and display the Web Storage System data in a browser.

One way to incorporate XML into your solutions is to use XML in ASP pages. Another way to use XML in your Web solutions is to create HTML pages that use client-side script and the XML DOM to create client-side data requests. In both scenarios, your returned data is labeled with XML elements. You can then apply an XSL template, which can arrange and rearrange data on the client side without having to send another request to the server. This is one of the benefits of employing XML in your solutions: you can send the data to the client once and then allow the client to rearrange the data in multiple views without requerying the server for a new page.

Listing 1.4 shows how to use XML to submit an HTTP request from the client. The results are then rendered and displayed with XSL and HTML.

Listing 1.4   Use XML to access Web Storage System data.

```
<HTML>
<HEAD>
<TITLE>XML Sample</TITLE>
</HEAD>

<xml id="xsltemplate">
<xsl:template   xmlns:xsl="uri:xsl" xmlns:d="DAV:" xmlns:z="zoomgt:"
xmlns:c="urn:schemas:contacts:">
<xsl:for-each select="d:multistatus/d:response" order-by="c:title">
<table width="330">
<tr>
<td bgcolor="silver" colspan="2">
<b><xsl:value-of select="d:propstat/d:prop/c:fileas"/></b>
</td>
</tr>
```

```
<tr>
<td>Job title: </td>
<td><xsl:value-of select="d:propstat/d:prop/c:title"/></td>
</tr>
<tr>
<td>Email: </td>
<td><xsl:value-of select="d:propstat/d:prop/c:email1"/></td>
</tr>
<tr>
<td>Work phone: </td>
<td><xsl:value-of select="d:propstat/d:prop/c:telephoneNumber"/></td>
</tr>
</table>
<p/>
</xsl:for-each>
</xsl:template>
</xml>

<SCRIPT language="vbscript" FOR="window" EVENT="onload">
   Dim xmlo
   Dim strURL, strPropReq

   strURL = "http://cyberserver/zooweb/staff/"

   ' Build the string indicating which
   ' properties to return
   strPropReq = "<?xml version='1.0'?>"
   strPropReq = strPropReq & _
   "<d:propfind xmlns:d='DAV:' xmlns:c='urn:schemas:contacts:'>"
```

```
    strPropReq = strPropReq & "<d:prop>"
    strPropReq = strPropReq & "<d:href/>"
    strPropReq = strPropReq & "<c:fileas/>"
    strPropReq = strPropReq & "<c:telephoneNumber/>"
    strPropReq = strPropReq & "<c:email1/>"
    strPropReq = strPropReq & "<c:title/>"
    strPropReq = strPropReq & "</d:prop>"
    strPropReq = strPropReq & "</d:propfind>"


With CreateObject("microsoft.xmlhttp")
        ' Make sure to change the logon information here
        ' to your own user name and password.
        .open "PROPFIND", strURL, _
          False, "domain\user1", "password1"
        .setRequestHeader "Content-type:", "text/xml"
        .setRequestHeader "Depth", "1,noroot"
        .send (strPropReq)

        ' Return the results as XML
        Set xmlDoc = .responseXML

    ' Apply the XSL template
        ListMembersHere.innerHTML = _
          xmlDoc.transformNode(xsltemplate.documentElement)
        End With
</script>

<BODY>
<H1>Zoo Staff</H1>
<hr>
<div id="ListMembersHere"/>
</BODY>
</HTML>
```

Figure 1.4 shows what the Web page in Listing 1.4 looks like.

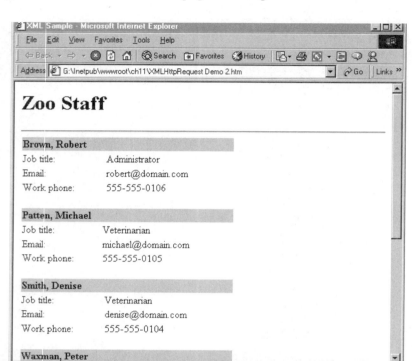

Figure 1.4
Use XML to build solutions that you can easily sort, filter, and reorganize on the client side.

For more information about using XML, see Chapter 13, "XML and Exchange."

DISPLAYING YOUR DATA

With so many options for data access, it shouldn't be surprising that you also have a number of options for displaying Exchange data. This section discusses how to access and display data by using Outlook 2000, Microsoft Outlook Web Access, and Web Storage System forms. It also discusses how to reuse Outlook Web Access.

USING OUTLOOK 2000

You can continue to use Outlook 2000 as a client interface to Exchange 2000. Outlook 2000 is a powerful personal information management tool that has increased potential when used in conjunction with a collaboration server like Exchange. Outlook 2000 delivers the same high-quality experience when used with Exchange 2000 as it does with earlier versions of Exchange. You can use Outlook for your day-to-day collaboration activities, such as sending and receiving e-mail, maintaining a calendar, and managing tasks. You can also build custom Outlook forms by using the Outlook object model and previous versions of CDO. In addition, you can access custom schema properties from an Outlook form and take advantage of the richness of the Web Storage System schema.

Figure 1.5 shows a custom Outlook form displaying an item in a Web Storage System folder that was built by using custom content classes and custom properties.

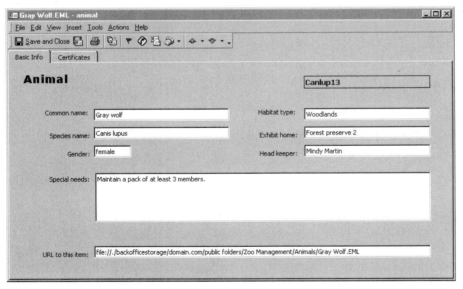

Figure 1.5
You can easily build Outlook 2000 forms that access even custom Web Storage System data.

For more information about using Outlook 2000 with Exchange 2000, see Chapter 11, "Developing with Outlook 2000."

USING OUTLOOK WEB ACCESS

Outlook Web Access is a set of Web components installed with Exchange 2000 Server. After you install Exchange, Outlook Web Access is ready for use. The version of Outlook Web Access in Exchange 2000 is significantly better than the earlier version. By using Outlook Web Access, you get the combined benefits of a rich user interface that closely mimics that of Outlook 2000 and a client that requires less network overhead. Outlook Web Access offers many advantages over its predecessor, including enhanced calendaring capabilities, such as weekly and monthly views of public calendars and personal calendars; support for embedded items, such as other messages and contact entries; and support for incorporating audio and video clips in messages.

One of the coolest new features in Exchange 2000 is URL addressibility. If you have an Exchange 2000 mailbox in your Windows 2000 domain, you can use Outlook Web Access to access it simply by entering the URL of your mailbox in a Web browser such as Internet Explorer. When you use URLs in the Web browser environment, Outlook Web Access returns the information by default. For example, you can enter a URL like this in Internet Explorer:

```
http://cyberserver/exchange/mindy/inbox
```

Outlook Web Access returns the contents of the Inbox for that alias (see Figure 1.6).

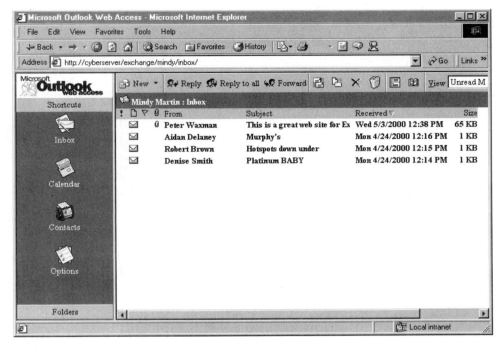

Figure 1.6
Use Outlook Web Access to view an Inbox.

Everything in Exchange is accessible with a URL: folders, messages, contact, appointments, form definitions, and Office documents such as Microsoft Word documents and Microsoft PowerPoint presentations. If you store something in a Web Storage System, you can access it by using a URL—as long as you have permission to view the information. Exchange integrates tightly with Windows 2000 and takes advantage of the security features of Windows 2000. Before you can view any Exchange information, Active Directory must authorize your logon credentials.

REUSING OUTLOOK WEB ACCESS

Outlook Web Access and URL accessibility are a nice way to access and render the content of your Inbox, but they are more significant than that. Think of Outlook Web Access in terms of reuse and data discovery. If you can use a URL in the browser text box, you can use that same URL on a Web page as a hyperlink. This means that you can easily build your own custom Web interfaces to Exchange to display needed information in the way you want it arranged. When you use a URL as a hyperlink in a Web page, Outlook Web Access automatically attempts to display the results in the browser. One way to reuse Outlook Web Access components is to use a frameset to display different folders in different frames, or use a contents frame to provide hyperlinks to different folders that are, in turn, displayed in the main frame page.

Figure 1.7 shows a custom Web page created in Microsoft FrontPage that uses a frameset with a contents page and a main page. The contents page uses hyperlinks, like the one shown in the previous section, to allow easy access to an Inbox, a calendar, and a public folder. When you click a hyperlink, Outlook Web Access displays the appropriate folder contents in the main page.

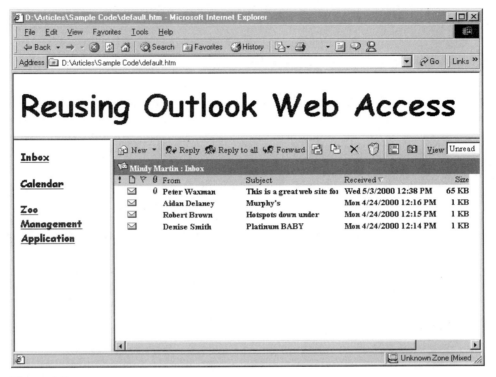

Figure 1.7
Reuse Outlook Web Access components to create custom views of Web Storage System folders.

You can also use parameters with the URL for more control over how Outlook Web Access displays the results. For example, the Inbox shown in Figure 1.7 does not display the normal Outlook Web Access navigation bar. This display is accomplished by passing a parameter that specifies Outlook Web Access should return only the contents of the folder to the Inbox URL, like this:

```
http://cyberserver/exchange/mindy/inbox?cmd=contents
```

For more information about the different parameters you can use to control Outlook Web Access, see Chapter 12, "Building Web Applications for Exchange."

USING WEB STORAGE SYSTEM FORMS

If you want more functionality from a custom client application than you can get reusing Outlook Web Access components, you can build more advanced Web applications for Exchange. You use the same skills that you use when building Web applications for other data sources such as SQL Server. You can create simple HTML pages that display static information about a folder, or you can build ASP pages that use server-side code to return the latest data whenever you access the Web page. In both of these scenarios, you can use the new Web Storage System forms technology to associate Web pages with content classes and use your own custom displays of your data instead of allowing Outlook Web Access to display the data. By associating Web pages with content classes, you take a data-driven approach to Web development that allows you to build Web solutions that react to data requests instead of to a form request. A data-driven approach means that your clients can be more focused on data than on your application.

Figure 1.8 shows a custom Web interface that is used to display the contents of a Web Storage System folder. Whenever a user enters the URL of the folder, a frameset page is returned. On the left in the contents page are hyperlinks to various subfolders. When a user clicks one of those hyperlinks, another custom Web page is returned. In this particular figure, you see the results of clicking the Animals hyperlink, which displays the contents of that folder in the right pane.

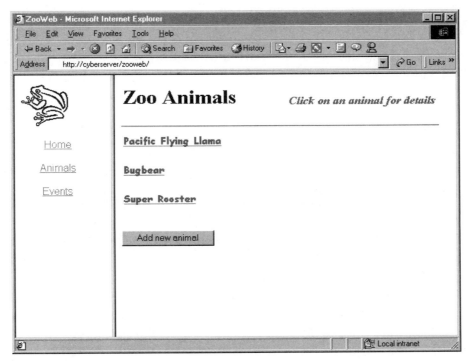

Figure 1.8
You can use custom Web pages to display the contents of a folder.

For more information about using Web Storage System forms, see Chapter 12, "Building Web Applications for Exchange."

ENHANCING YOUR APPLICATION

Sometimes a rich data storage model, extensible schema, and rich data access options are not enough. With Exchange 2000 Server, your options don't stop there. This section explains how to extend your Web Storage System even further with server-side enhancements, including Web Storage System events and workflow logic.

USING WEB STORAGE SYSTEM EVENTS

In an Exchange application, you often want code to run when a new item is added to a folder, when an existing item is changed, or when an item or folder is deleted. To execute code in these scenarios, you can use Web Storage System events. Exchange 2000 uses the new Web Storage System event model to provide a way for collaboration applications to trigger code when certain actions occur.

Events are not completely new to Exchange. When Exchange 5.5 was released, Exchange provided event agents that you could use to react to events *after* they had occurred. For example, you could write code in a Delete event agent to respond when an item in a folder is deleted. However, because the Delete event agent runs only after the item is fully removed, the code only reacts to the delete— it doesn't interact with the delete. For example, you can't write code in an Event agent that cancels an event from completing.

With the new Web Storage System event model, you can still react to events after they occur, but you can also react to an event *before* it finishes executing. For example, you can now write code in a delete event that cancels the delete and keeps the item in the folder. And because the events fire on the server, the events fire whether the client is Outlook Web Access, Outlook 2000, or a custom Web application.

Web Storage System events belong to three category types: synchronous events, asynchronous events, and system events. Synchronous events and asynchronous events react in some way to a data request. A data request can be a new resource request, a change request, a delete request, or a copy or move request. The three event types are defined as follows:

- *Synchronous* events fire before a data request is committed to the Web Storage System, which means you can modify an item before it is saved or deleted, or you can cancel the action completely.

- *Asynchronous* events are triggered after a data request is committed to the Web Storage System and are best used for simple notification.

- *System* events do not deal with data requests. Instead a system event fires at a particular system occurrence, such as when a Web Storage System shuts down.

Table 1.1 lists the Web Storage System events.

Table 1.1   Web Storage System events

Type	Event	When the event fires
Synchronous	OnSyncSave	Just before a resource is saved to a folder.
	OnSyncDelete	Just before a resource is deleted from a folder.
Asynchronous	OnSave	After a resource is saved to a folder.
	OnDelete	After a resource is deleted from a folder.
System	OnMDBStartup	After an Exchange database starts.
	OnMDBShutdown	After an Exchange database shuts down.
	OnTimer	At specific time intervals for a specific duration.

The code for events is written in event sinks, which can be built by using Microsoft Visual Basic, Microsoft Visual C++, and simple script. You can register these event sinks on parent folders and child folders at the same time, instead of creating and registering the event code on each folder individually as you do with Exchange 5.5 event agents. You can even configure Web Storage System events to fire only under specific circumstances.

For more information about incorporating events into your applications, see Chapter 9, "Using Web Storage System Events."

USING WORKFLOW LOGIC

Traditionally, a folder is nothing more than a simple container. It can hold almost anything—items such as messages and contacts, structured documents, and even other folders—but it simply stores information and does nothing more. By incorporating workflow logic into a folder, however, you can turn a simple container into smart storage. By using workflow logic, you can alert a person to do something to an item that has been submitted or changed, track what has been done to an item and what must yet be addressed, and even change the properties of an item as it progresses through its lifetime.

You can incorporate workflow into your applications in essentially two ways: by using Workflow Designer for Exchange or by defining the workflow from scratch using CDO Workflow for Exchange. For the majority of developers, Workflow Designer has the functionality and flexibility to fulfill most workflow application needs. Workflow Designer is a tool that you can use to easily and quickly build workflow logic into folders. In Workflow Designer, you use only the CDO Workflow objects and interfaces when writing script to react to actions. Figure 1.9 shows a workflow process in Workflow Designer.

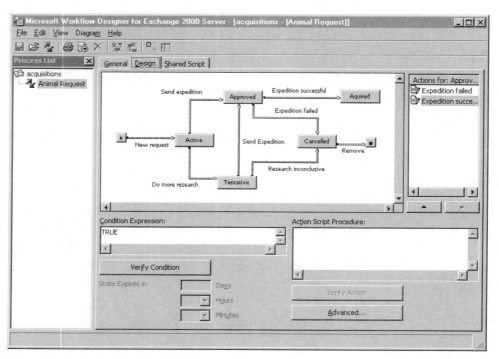

Figure 1.9
Workflow Designer for Exchange makes it easy to integrate workflow logic into a Web Storage System folder.

For more information about using Workflow Designer to build workflow solutions, see Chapter 10, "Designing Workflow Applications."

WRAPPING IT UP

After the primary development is complete, you are ready to integrate security into the application to allow or deny access rights. You are ready to test the application, and if all goes well, you can then deploy the application throughout the organization. This section describes Exchange security, one approach to testing an application, and issues to consider when deploying an application.

ADDING SECURITY FEATURES

An application is not as useful without proper security integration. Data should be easy to share among people and teams in an organization and across offices. However, you generally don't want every user in your organization to have identical access rights to the same information sources. To provide strong security benefits to Exchange users and developers alike, Exchange 2000 integrates with the security infrastructures of Windows 2000.

The Exchange 2000 Server security model is very different from that of Exchange Server 5.5. With Exchange Server 5.5, you granted rights to users of your application primarily by setting permissions on folders. With Exchange 2000 Server, you can still grant rights on folders, but now you can also:

- Grant rights to Active Directory user objects and security groups rather than address book entries.

- Explicitly deny rights to a user or security group.

- Grant rights on specific items and even on individual properties.

- Programmatically control the security information stored with each resource in a Web Storage System.

For more information about the access model used by Exchange 2000 and how to add security to your applications, see Chapter 14, "Setting Security and Permissions."

DEPLOYING A WEB STORAGE SYSTEM APPLICATION

After you successfully build an application by using Exchange 2000 Server, all you have left to do is thoroughly test it and deploy it throughout your organization. To successfully deploy an Exchange application, you should understand what an Exchange installation requires. Every developer who creates a solution for Exchange should understand how an Exchange environment is built. This is especially true if you don't have any experience administering Exchange. By building your own Exchange testing environment, you become familiar with the various components of Exchange. This familiarity can help you identify problems that might arise during deployment.

To deploy an Exchange application, keep three things in mind:

- **Exchange Server components**. Exchange specific components are the minority of objects that must be configured, but they are the most important components. Without these, your application cannot run. You must create the folder hierarchy with Exchange as well configure your application schema if you use one. If you use Web Storage System forms, you must add these to the new created folders and create the forms registration to go with them. If you use event sinks, you must create the event registrations in the appropriate folders. In addition, you must configure the proper security settings on each of the folders.

- **Active Directory components**. If you use event sinks and workflow, you also need to configure Active Directory with the proper user objects to execute event sinks and workflow. You also need to create any security groups that you use to add security to Exchange folders.

- **Middle-tier components**. If you use event sinks, you need to register the sinks on the Exchange server and then create the COM+ components for the event sinks. If you use COM+ components with Web applications, you must also register these in Component Services. In addition, if your application uses workflow, you must add users to the proper workflow roles.

For many of the Exchange and Active Directory components, you can use script files and Windows Scripting Host, which are included with Windows 2000, to automate some of the deployment work. For example, you can create a script file that builds the folder framework, creates the event registration items, and even creates the user object in Active Directory that will be used to execute the event script code.

For more information about deploying applications in your organization, see Chapter 15, "Testing and Deploying Your Applications."

SUMMARY

Exchange 2000 Server brings developers everything a database, a Web server, and a collaboration server should offer—all rolled into one product. No matter what type of developer you are, you can use your skills to build powerful collaboration solutions for your intranet and for the Web. If you are familiar with database development and ADO, use those skills to interact with the Web Storage System folders, create new items, edit existing items, and create rich querying tools. If you are experienced with developing custom forms by using Outlook 2000, use your existing skills to develop solutions with Exchange 2000. If you are familiar with ASP or XML, use those skills with Web Storage System forms to create robust Web interfaces that are automatically displayed when a client accesses a specific type of data. Every developer can integrate enhancements such as synchronous events and workflow logic.

Chapter 2, "Exchange and the Web Storage System," explains how the Web Storage System transforms Exchange from a simple data storage tool into a smart data storage tool.

2

Exchange and the Web Storage System

Microsoft Exchange 2000 Server is the first product to use the Microsoft Web Storage System. An exciting new way to manage data, the Web Storage System turns simple data storage into smart data storage that can react to the actions of your users. Not only can you use Exchange to store just about any electronic information, but you can also use just about any client to access that information. This flexibility means that you can build the applications that make the most sense for your company. In addition, the Web Storage System brings with it an event model to react to the actions of your users and an enhanced security system you can use to allow and restrict interaction all the way down to the item level. With so many benefits to the Web Storage System, Exchange may be the answer to your data storage needs.

This chapter teaches how the Web Storage System transforms Exchange from a simple data storage tool into smart data storage. Sections include:

- **Using Exchange for Data Storage**
- **Understanding the Architecture of Exchange Data Storage**
- **Using URLs with Exchange**
- **Using Additional Data Access Options**
- **Doing More with the Web Storage System**

USING EXCHANGE FOR DATA STORAGE

Continuing with the Exchange tradition of broad data storage, the Web Storage System in Exchange 2000 Server was designed to give you the ability to store just about any type of object. Exchange 2000 is perfect for knowledge management applications that must store a wide range of resources together, including classic collaboration resources such as messages and contacts, Microsoft Office documents such as Microsoft Word documents and Microsoft Excel spreadsheets, and a variety of Web pages. However, there are plenty of other reasons why you should store your application data in Exchange 2000. This section discusses why you would want to store data in Exchange and how Exchange compares with a relational database like SQL Server.

BENEFITS OF THE WEB STORAGE SYSTEM

The Web Storage System brings with it more than a snazzy new name. To accommodate the hefty requirements of collaboration application development, the Web Storage System offers features that make development easy, fast, reliable, and scalable. Some of the significant features that the Web Storage System adds to Exchange 2000 Server include:

- **Multiple databases per server**. In earlier versions of Exchange, administrators could configure only one public database and one private database for each installation of Exchange. Using Exchange 2000 Server, you can configure multiple databases on each server. This means that you can associate entire databases with specific applications. For example, you could create one public database for the sales team and another for the marketing team. In addition, administrators can arrange mailboxes on multiple private databases to improve manageability.

- **Native data storage**. In earlier versions of Exchange, messages were stored in Rich Text Format (RTF). Although Messaging Application Programming Interface (MAPI) messages did not need to be converted, Multipurpose Internet Mail Extensions (MIME) messages arriving through Simple Mail Transfer Protocol (SMTP) did. In Exchange 2000, messages are stored in the same format in which they are submitted. If a MIME message is submitted through SMTP, the message is stored in MIME format. If a MAPI message is submitted through remote procedure call (RPC), the message is stored in RTF. Exchange 2000 uses MIME as the preferred data format. In addition, Exchange 2000 also supports the direct data storage of Internet formats for calendaring contact management.

- **New database file type for streaming data**. Multimedia content types—for example, voice mail and video clips—enrich the messaging and collaboration experience for many users, but they also place new demands on a system. Earlier versions of Exchange treated a multimedia item the same way they treated a large attachment to a message. This caused problems for devices trying to access data as a sequential stream of information: either the entire item had to be loaded into memory before it could be played back, or data streaming was slow and inconsistent, leading to gaps in the playback and other glitches. Exchange 2000 provides support for large data items—from the database through high-level programming interfaces—so that multimedia data can be accessed quickly through file-streaming interfaces.

- **Enhanced security**. The security model in Exchange 2000 has been extended. In addition to the standard roles used to control user interaction with Exchange folders and items, you can now create your own custom application roles. By tightly integrating Microsoft Windows 2000 security tokens, Exchange also extends security options to include item-level security. You can specify which items a user can read, edit, or delete; this means that a user's view of the folder contents is determined per item.

- **Support for multiple clients and protocols**. The tools you use every day can now be used to access data within Exchange. Exchange data stores support Installable File System (IFS) as well as Web Distributed Authoring and Versioning (WebDAV). Exchange data is accessible using many tools—from Microsoft Internet Explorer to Microsoft Visual InterDev to any Microsoft Office 2000 **Open** dialog box. And, as always, data can still be accessed from the premier MAPI client, Microsoft Outlook.

- **OLE DB and ADO 2.5 data access**. You can take advantage of your data-access skills from other development environments, such as Microsoft Visual Basic, with Exchange 2000. Using OLE DB and Microsoft ActiveX Data Objects (ADO) 2.5, you can write code that queries Exchange data stores just as you would query databases like SQL Server or Microsoft Access. When you use OLE DB and ADO in conjunction with Collaboration Data Objects (CDO) for Exchange, you can also add, edit, and delete individual items in Exchange.

EXCHANGE VS. SQL SERVER

So why would you choose to put data in Exchange instead of SQL Server? It seems that there is no end to the discussion of why to use one and not the other. The fact is that SQL Server and Exchange are two different technologies, suited for two distinct application scenarios. SQL Server and Exchange are both excellent platforms for developing collaboration solutions that use communications, information sharing, and task coordination to solve a problem. The area in which the two differ most, however, is in data storage:

- SQL Server is a relational database system, designed to manage huge quantities of *highly structured* data. It requires that a database administrator configure the tables in the database, as well as their indexes and relationships, before developers can begin creating forms to display and enter the data. The administrator must make many assumptions about the data being stored when designing the database. SQL Server is excellent for complex, line-of-business applications.

- Exchange is built around a *semistructured* storage model, in which a folder can hold any kind of data, and there is no requirement to define the structure of the data beforehand. This loose data structure is why Exchange folders are also able to accommodate any type of object. When you add a text document to a folder, the necessary properties to define the document are defined along with it, just as when you add a post to that same folder. The number of properties often varies from resource to resource in the same folder. This makes Exchange appropriate for developing more ad hoc collaboration solutions. Exchange does offer the ability to describe schemas for items stored in the Web Storage System, but this does not require rigid table structures.

Figure 2.1 shows how these technologies differ.

Figure 2.1
If data is more structured, SQL Server is the better choice for data storage, but when data is less structured, Exchange is the better choice.

These are, however, the extreme ends of a continuum, and the truth is that many business solutions need to exploit the strengths of both platforms. You cannot apply a simple template to your situation and know which database to employ. You must investigate the individual requirements of your application, including who needs to use it, how it needs to be exposed, and what data needs to be stored.

UNDERSTANDING THE ARCHITECTURE OF EXCHANGE DATA STORAGE

Before you decide whether Exchange 2000 meets your needs, you need to understand the architecture behind it. This section explains how Exchange 2000 builds on previous versions, the difference between the Web Storage System and the Exchange databases, why you may want to use multiple Web Storage Systems, and the purpose of the names used in Exchange. Then it shows you how to create a new Web Storage System.

EXCHANGE –THEN AND NOW

Exchange 2000 has adopted the Web Storage System as its data storage technology. However, this does not replace the data storage system already established in Exchange. As with previous releases, Exchange 2000 is still organized into information stores, which can be either public stores or private mailbox stores. *Public stores* can be accessible to everyone within your organization or restricted to a subset of people such as a department or team. Either way, public stores are designed to share data among users, and each Exchange server can have multiple public stores. *Mailbox stores*, on the other hand, store data that is private to a person and contain the mailbox folders generated when a new mailbox is created for a person. These public and mailbox stores, in turn, control the interaction with the underlying Exchange database files that actually store the data. Each store is a Web Storage System. Figure 2.2 shows how multiple Web Storage Systems map to individual stores.

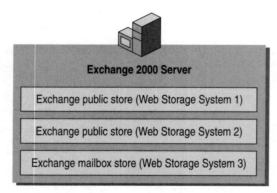

Figure 2.2
Each Exchange 2000 store is a Web Storage System.

Stores are organized into storage groups. Storage groups are created with Exchange System Manager and are used to organize multiple Web Storage Systems into more manageable units in Exchange. As a developer, the only time you really need to be aware of these storage groups is when you create or modify Exchange mailboxes in the Active Directory directory service of Windows 2000 and when you navigate to the stores in Exchange System Manager. For straight data access with a Web browser or other programmatic interfaces such as ADO and CDO, you do not need to know the storage unit. Instead, it is more important that you understand the concept of folder trees.

A Web Storage System is organized into a hierarchy of folders, very similar in structure to the standard file system. A single folder can contain child folders, which in turn can contain other child folders. This organization of folders is referred to as a *folder tree*. Typically, a folder tree represents data in a single information store. If you use code to access a Web Storage System, you use the folder tree name—not the actual information store name—to identify the exact Web Storage System you want to access. Therefore, if an information store named *Toy Store* has a folder tree name of *Toys*, you use the folder tree name *Toys* in the code. In this book, the folder tree name is the friendly name of the Web Storage System.

Each folder in the folder tree can contain any type of collaboration item or file as well as additional child folders. Anything placed in the Web Storage System is known as a resource. A *resource* can be an e-mail message, an appointment, another folder, a Web page, or any structured document. Figure 2.3 shows how a folder tree is organized into folders and items.

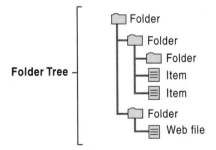

Figure 2.3
The Web Storage System is organized into a hierarchical arrangement of folders. Folders can contain child folders, items, or files. All these objects are called resources.

Web Storage System vs. Exchange Databases

The Web Storage System and the Exchange databases split the responsibility of data access and data storage between them. As a developer, you work primarily with the Web Storage System and not the databases. The Web Storage System implements basic messaging objects like mailboxes, folders, and access control lists. The Web Storage System supports the interfaces and protocols used for data access, such as OLE DB and MAPI. It is also responsible for returning Hypertext Markup Language (HTML) and Extensible Markup Language (XML) content on request from browsers.

The databases, on the other hand, are responsible for data storage and data maintenance. An Exchange database is comprised of two separate database files: an .edb file (an Exchange database file for RTF data) and an .stm file (a streaming file for handling Web content such as ASP and HTML). These files work together to store and manage Web Storage System data. As a developer, you never interact directly with a database file. All interaction occurs with the Web Storage System, which, in turn, interacts with the database files. However, you should understand what the Exchange database does. Some of the features handled by the database include:

- **Transactions**. The database uses write-ahead transaction logs to ensure data security through redundancy and to give transactional security. Committed transactions, such as saving a contact item in a folder, are guaranteed to have been written to disk. Temporary glitches, such as power losses, do not cause data loss.

- **Backups**. The database is integrated with the Windows 2000 backup system. With a well-planned and well-executed disaster-recovery strategy, you can overcome even catastrophic disk failures without loss of data.

- **Indexing**. The database manages indexes for common key fields, like message subject lines, for fast searches and look-ups.

- **Optimized storage**. The database provides efficient, optimized storage. If a message is sent to several recipients on the same server, only one copy of the message is stored. Recipients are pointed to the single copy. This is called *single instancing*.

- **Data streaming**. The database has special features for handling large items, such as multimedia attachments (bitmaps, voice mail messages, video clips, and so on) and data streaming.

WHY USE MULTIPLE PUBLIC WEB STORAGE SYSTEMS?

With Exchange 2000 you can create multiple public Web Storage Systems to replace the single public folder tree of Exchange Server 5.5. In Exchange Server 5.5, the only usable public folder tree is named *Public Folders*. Mail clients, like Outlook, see this tree under a node called *All Public Folders*. When you develop an application for Exchange Server 5.5 that will be used by your entire organization (or even a subset of individuals), you must place the application in this single public folder tree. Because you do not have a choice of another location, this single folder tree may end up housing a variety of application types as well as applications for every department within your organization. As you can imagine, the public folder tree can quickly grow out of control in a large organization. Folders become difficult to locate, as does the specific information you're seeking. This severely limits the usefulness of Exchange Server 5.5 public folders.

Figure 2.4 shows a typical approach to public folder organization in Exchange Server 5.5. The single All Public Folders tree exposes each and every subfolder even if it is used by only part of the organization. Although you can limit the visibility of folders for selected users, most users often need access to most of the folders. Hiding folders doesn't solve the problem of misuse of storage space. Exchange 2000 solves this problem.

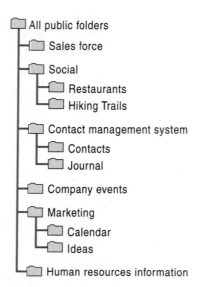

Figure 2.4
In Exchange Server 5.5, all folders are arranged in a single public folder tree regardless of how they are used and who uses them.

In Exchange 2000 Server, these mass storage and data retrieval issues are alleviated by subdividing the All Public Folders namespace into smaller, more manageable chunks or *public folder trees*. Each tree is associated with its own public folder store. Using this approach, an individual public folder tree can be associated with a particular department to create department-specific solutions. For example, you can configure Exchange to dedicate one public folder database to the Sales department, another to Marketing, and yet another to Executives, all in addition to the standard All Public Folders tree, which is visible to everybody. Figure 2.5 shows how the hierarchy shown in Figure 2.4 can be rearranged into more manageable and usable trees.

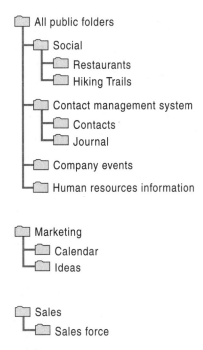

Figure 2.5
Using Exchange 2000, you can define multiple public folder trees by arranging public folders into more manageable and usable chunks.

Some additional benefits to splicing the single Exchange 5.5 public tree include:

- **Smaller replicas**. You can replicate subsets to remote sites. In earlier versions of Exchange, the entire hierarchy had to be replicated throughout the organization even if your site was only interested in one or two public folders.

- **Better backup performance and disaster recovery**. Smaller replica sets mean less data to back up and restore. In addition, each public folder database can be taken offline individually, while the others remain up and running.

When it comes to client access to these multiple public folder databases, you are somewhat limited if you use a MAPI-based e-mail client. When Exchange 2000 is first installed, a single public folder tree named *Public Folders* is configured for MAPI clients such as Microsoft Outlook. This is the only public folder tree accessible by MAPI clients.

If you create additional public folder trees, they will not be accessible to Outlook users. However, they are fully accessible through Outlook Web Access, the Web client included with Exchange 2000. These trees are configured and optimized for Internet access through Web browsers via HTTP, Internet Message Access Protocol (IMAP), Network News Transfer Protocol (NNTP), or WebDAV. The stores can also be accessed by applications developed using ADO 2.5 and CDO.

UNDERSTANDING NAMES USED IN EXCHANGE

As you'll see in the next section, Exchange provides quite a bit of freedom in naming folder trees, the information store, and the virtual directory when you create a new Web Storage System. In addition, your Exchange server might have multiple storage groups. In Exchange, each of these names is used for a different task. The following list explains the purpose of these names from a developer's perspective:

- **Storage group**. This name is used primarily for creating new mailboxes for users and for configuring mailbox settings stored in Active Directory. You do not need it to access the actual contents of a mailbox or a public Web Storage System.

- **Folder tree**. This is the friendly name of the Web Storage System and the name that you use to access the contents of a Web Storage System using ADO or CDO code. This name is needed in URLs used with the Exchange OLE DB (EXOLEDB) provider in server-side code.

- **Store**. Like the storage group name, the store name is used primarily when interacting with mailbox settings. You need this name to create new mailboxes, delete existing mailboxes, and change the properties of mailboxes.

- **Virtual directory**. This name is used to access the contents of any Web Storage System using a Web browser. The virtual directory name is used to open a mailbox as well as to browse the folders of a public store. This name is also used in URLs using the Microsoft Internet Publishing Provider (MSDAIPP), which includes both hyperlinks in Web pages and ADO client-side code. Multiple virtual directories can access different parts of the same folder tree.

The folder tree name and virtual directory name can be the same. For example, you can use the name *Applications* for both a folder tree name and the virtual directory name for the Applications Web Storage System (which you'll create in the next section). This means you access the Web Storage System with the same name from server-side code as well as from Web browsers and client-side code.

> **NOTE** Having the same name for the folder tree and the virtual directory is beneficial only if you always access the contents of the folder tree from the top folder. If you plan to use each of the child folders as independent applications, you should have a unique virtual directory name for each one and bypass creating a virtual directory for the folder tree.

CREATING A NEW WEB STORAGE SYSTEM

You configure a new public Web Storage System by using a three-step process:

1. Create a new public folder tree.

2. Create and mount a public Web Storage System onto the tree.

3. Create a virtual directory for it.

This section shows you how to set up a Web Storage System called Applications and configure a virtual directory called ZooWeb, which is used in the code samples throughout this book.

CREATING A PUBLIC FOLDER TREE

Before you can create a new store, you must first create and name the folder tree. To create a new public folder tree, follow these steps:

1. Open Exchange System Manager (see Figure 2.6) and expand the organization until you see Folders.

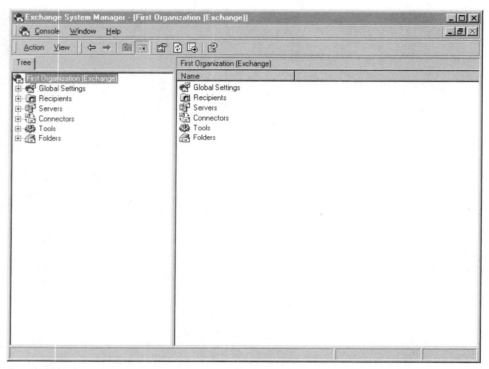

Figure 2.6
Use Exchange System Manager to create multiple public Web Storage Systems.

2. Right-click **Folders**, click **New**, and then click **Public Folder Tree**. A **Properties** dialog box (see Figure 2.7) appears. In the **Name** text box, type **Applications** as the folder tree name. Click **OK**.

Figure 2.7
Enter a name for the new public folder tree.

CREATING AND MOUNTING A PUBLIC WEB STORAGE SYSTEM

Once you have created the Applications folder tree, you can then create and mount a store onto it. To create a new Web Storage System and mount it onto a folder tree, follow these steps:

1. In Exchange System Manager, expand the Server group, and navigate to the appropriate storage group. Figure 2.8 shows what this might look like.

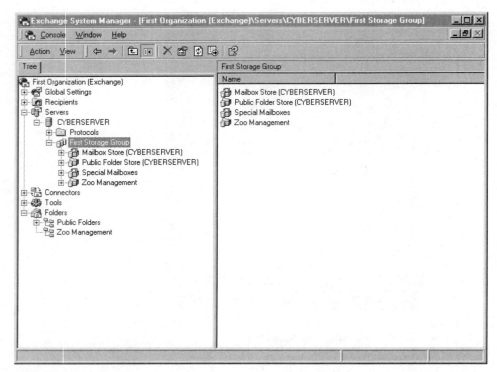

Figure 2.8
After a public folder tree has been created, you must create a new public store in one of the storage groups and mount it onto the tree.

2. Right-click the storage group name, click **New**, and then click **Public Store**. On the **Properties** dialog box that appears (see Figure 2.9), in the **Name** box, type **Applications Store** as the name for the new store.

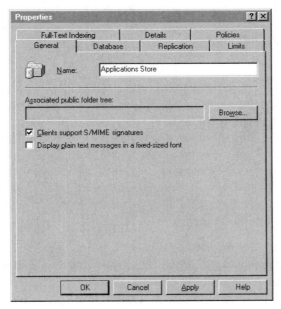

Figure 2.9
You must name the new store and then associate it with a public folder tree.

3. Click **Browse**, click the **Applications** tree you just created, and then click **OK**.

4. After Exchange creates the new store, you are prompted to mount it onto the tree. Click **Yes** to mount the store. If the mounting is successful, a dialog box appears. You now have a new Applications Web Storage System.

CREATING A VIRTUAL DIRECTORY

The last step in creating a new Web Storage System is to create a virtual directory for it. So that people in your organization can access the Applications Web Storage System by using a Web browser, you must create a virtual directory for the tree under the appropriate protocol. For example, to make the folder tree accessible with HTTP, you need to create an HTTP virtual directory.

When you create a virtual directory to a folder, all the child folders are also visible to the client, unless you specifically hide the folders. For example, if you create a virtual directory to the Applications folder tree, any application folder that you add is available using the virtual directory to the Applications folder tree. Rather than using the Applications virtual directory to access all the application folders, you can instead create a virtual directory that maps directly to each individual application folder. If you install two applications on the Applications folder tree, Zoo Management and Accounting, you can create a virtual directory for each application instead of just one to the parent folder tree.

Most of the samples and listings throughout this book use the Zoo Management application folder. Rather than using a virtual directory to the Applications folder tree to access this application, you should create a virtual directory that maps directly to the Zoo Management application. Before you can create the virtual directory, however, you must first create the folder that the virtual directory accesses. You can use Exchange System Manager to create the Zoo Management parent folder.

To create the Zoo Management folder on the Applications folder tree and then create an HTTP virtual directory for it, follow these steps:

1. In Exchange System Manager, expand Folders and right-click **Applications**. Select **New** and then click **Public Folder**. When the **Properties** dialog box appears, type **Zoo Management** as the name and click **OK** to create the folder.

2. To create the virtual directory for the new folder, expand the Server group, and navigate to the Protocols group. Expand the HTTP protocol and Exchange Virtual Server to show all of the registered virtual directories. Figure 2.10 shows what this might look like.

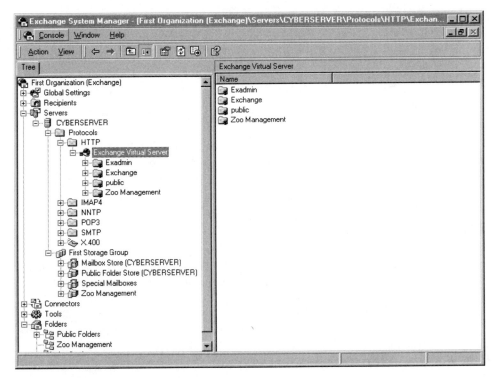

Figure 2.10
To make the new public Web Storage System accessible via HTTP, create a virtual directory for it under Exchange Virtual Server.

3. Right-click **Exchange Virtual Server**, click **New**, and then click **Virtual Directory**. When the **Properties** dialog box appears, type **ZooWeb** as the name for the virtual directory. Select the **Public Folder** option in the Exchange path group, and browse to the Zoo Management folder you just created on the Application folder tree. Click **OK** to finish creating the virtual directory.

CAUTION Use Exchange System Manager to create new virtual directories; do not use Internet Services Manager in Microsoft Internet Information Services (IIS) 5.0. Exchange configures the virtual directory differently from how IIS does it. If you attempt to create new virtual directories with IIS, you will not be able to use the Web Storage System effectively for all Web features.

USING URLS WITH EXCHANGE

The big news with Exchange 2000 is that data can be accessed through URLs— everything in Exchange is now accessible through a URL. Public folders, private stores, messages, and attachments are all accessible if you build the correct URL to them. You can use a URL to navigate to a resource in a Web Storage System just as you would use a URL to navigate to a Web site and return a Web page. The URL indicates to Exchange the thing you want to return, such as the contents of a folder or an individual item. This section discusses URL basics and shows how to use URLs to access pubic stores, mailboxes, and individual items.

NOTE You will also use URLs in your code for almost all tasks, such as navigating through folders, creating new items, editing items, and deleting items. These tasks depend on correctly formed URLs, which are formed differently from those discussed in this section. Chapter 4, "ActiveX Data Objects and Exchange," provides more details about URLs that are used in code.

URL BASICS

When you use a URL to access the Web Storage System, the server renders the item in the most appropriate format for the currently requested resource. For example, if the URL points to a folder, a list of items in the folder is returned. However, if the URL points to a message object, a note form is displayed. As an application developer, you can customize how resources are rendered when they are requested from a Web browser. As with all URLs, you can enter a URL into the address box of a Web browser or you can insert a URL as a link in a Web page. When a URL is used in this type of scenario, Outlook Web Access returns the requested information. Outlook Web Access provides many of the same features you are accustomed to in Outlook. In Outlook Web Access, you can navigate to other folders by using the Shortcuts list, display the Folder list in the navigation pane, open an item by double-clicking it in the explorer pane, and even move items between folders.

When you construct a URL, you are basically constructing an HTTP request to the server, in this case, the Web Storage System of Exchange. Therefore, you begin the URL with the HTTP indicator. Next, you indicate the name of the server that contains the Web Storage System to which you are connecting. For example, if you are attempting to access the Web Storage System on the Exchange server *CyberServer*, the URL would look something like this:

```
http://cyberserver/
```

No explicit logon information is being sent. The client automatically sends information about the current user along with the HTTP request. The server, in turn, verifies this information against Active Directory. If Active Directory verifies that the client has permission to access the requested information, the appropriate security token is generated and the data is returned in the HTTP response. If the user is not authenticated, an HTTP error code is returned instead. For more information about security tokens, see Chapter 14, "Setting Security and Permissions."

NOTE The server name, virtual directory name, and folder names used in the URL are not case sensitive.

ACCESSING PUBLIC STORES

To access the folders in a public Web Storage System, you must append the name of the virtual directory for the folder tree along with the folder path to the folder you are accessing. A forward slash separates each new level in a folder hierarchy. If you are accessing a folder in the Public Folders tree, you will use the virtual directory name *Public*. For instance, the following URL accesses a folder named ADO Samples in the default MAPI folder store on the server *CyberServer*:

```
http://cyberserver/public/ADO Samples/
```

If you are using additional Web Storage Systems, you replace the public virtual directory name with the virtual directory name of the other Web Storage System folder. For example, to access the Zoo Management folder on the Applications Web Storage System you created in the previous section, you would use a URL like this:

```
http://cyberserver/zooweb/
```

By default, Exchange uses Outlook Web Access to display the contents of the folder (see Figure 2.11). Exchange returns the requested information in an XML-based format. If the Web browser is able to render XML, the resulting Web page is displayed by using Extensible Stylesheet Language (XSL) formatting. If the Web browser is not capable of rendering XML, the results are displayed with standard HTML tags. Although Outlook Web Access is the default way to display Exchange information, you can use a custom Web page for each folder instead. This custom Web page can become a Web interface to Exchange data, providing access to additional folders of interest through other URLs, optional views, and any other information you want to include.

NOTE Internet Explorer 5 or later can render XML.

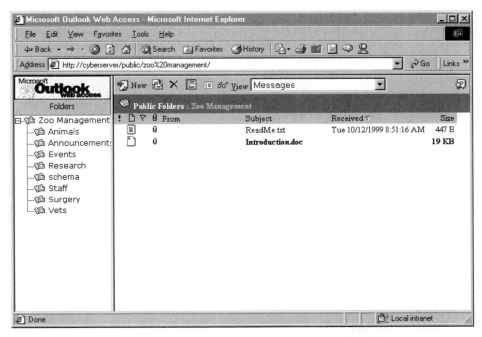

Figure 2.11
Outlook Web Access displays a public folder using a standard folder view page.

ACCESSING MAILBOXES

To return a folder in the mailbox of a user, append the keyword *Exchange* to the URL, followed by a forward slash and the user alias. By default, the Inbox for that user is returned. For instance, the following URL returns the Inbox for Mindy:

```
http://cyberserver/exchange/mindy/
```

> **TIP** If you need to access only the Inbox for the current user, you can use the shortcut URL http://cyberserver/exchange/.

To navigate to another folder in the mailbox, append the name of the subfolder (such as Inbox, Calendar, Contacts, or Sent Items) that you want to access. For instance, this URL returns Mindy's Contacts folder:

```
http://cyberserver/exchange/mindy/contacts
```

In addition, before you worry about security issues, remember that Exchange authenticates the caller before returning the requested information. If you are trying to access a mailbox other than the one for the current user, Exchange verifies that you have access to this mailbox by checking the access control list. If access is approved, the store contents are displayed in Outlook Web Access (see Figure 2.12). If access is denied, an HTTP error code is returned.

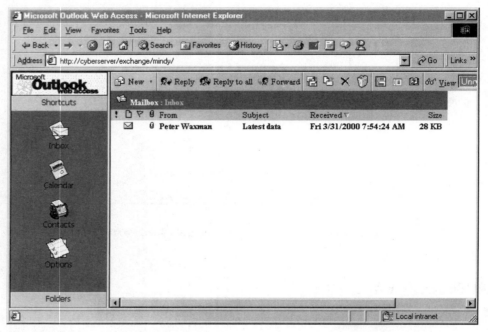

Figure 2.12
Outlook Web Access displays an Inbox after verifying access.

To access a subfolder, provide the name of each folder within the hierarchy until you reach the location you want. The following URL accesses a subfolder named Travel Info in the Inbox:

```
http://cyberserver/exchange/mindy/inbox/travel info/
```

With Exchange 2000 you can use multiple databases to organize mailboxes. This is more for the Exchange administrator's benefit than for the developer. For the developer and the end user, this storage advantage is transparent. Each mailbox can exist in only one database. Therefore, you continue to access the mailbox in the same way regardless of where the mailbox actually resides.

ACCESSING INDIVIDUAL ITEMS

If you want to open an individual item, build the URL to the appropriate Web Storage System and then append two things: the subject of the item being opened and an Exchange Message Link (EML) extension. EML is the data format returned by Exchange. For example, this URL accesses an item in an Inbox with a subject of MSDN Templates:

```
http://cyberserver/exchange/mindy/inbox/msdn templates.eml
```

The subject name and EML extension make up the schema property DAV:displayname for items. Folders do not have this extension. For more information on schema properties, see Chapter 3, "Web Storage System Schema."

Figure 2.13 shows how Outlook Web Access renders a single item in Internet Explorer 5.

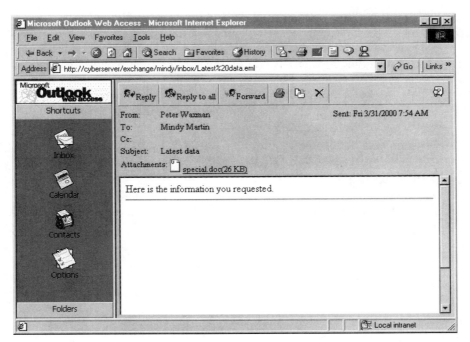

Figure 2.13
Using a URL, you can access even individual items in Exchange.

If multiple messages with the same subject exist, the first item found with the specified subject is returned. All other items with the same subject are given a suffix with a counter value to indicate a unique subject name. For instance, if you have three messages with the subject of RE:Vacation Plans, the items are referenced as:

```
http://cyberserver/exchange/mindy/inbox/RE:Vacation Plans.eml
http://cyberserver/exchange/mindy/inbox/RE:Vacation Plans-1.eml
http://cyberserver/exchange/mindy/inbox/RE:Vacation Plans-2.eml
```

> **NOTE**   If an item is moved from one folder to another folder, the item URL is automatically updated with the new folder information.

USING ADDITIONAL DATA ACCESS OPTIONS

In addition to Outlook Web Access, you can also use a number of other clients with Exchange. The client restrictions in Exchange Server 5.5 are no longer an issue. You can use a variety of clients to access existing resources and create new resources, including those tools you use every day, such as Windows Explorer and Microsoft Office. This means that you can use the client that makes the most sense for your application needs. This section describes how you can use Windows Explorer or Microsoft Office or create your own custom client application to access or create resources in Exchange.

WINDOWS EXPLORER

You can use Windows Explorer to navigate in the Web Storage Systems of Exchange 2000 Server. Using Microsoft Win32 APIs, Exchange Installable File System (IFS) exposes the Web Storage Systems available from drive M of the server. When Exchange is first installed, it attempts to mount the stores onto drive M.

If M is already in use, Exchange continues through the alphabet until it finds an available letter. Each Web Storage System is displayed as an individual file system folder underneath that drive, and the resources within the stores can then be opened like any other file. In addition, you can even share this folder in the same way as other file system folders. Figure 2.14 shows how Windows Explorer might look if you were to browse in a Web Storage System folder.

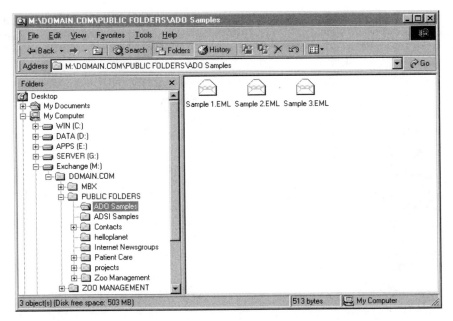

Figure 2.14
Using the Exchange integrated file system, you can navigate the Web Storage Systems of an Exchange 2000 Server just as you would navigate a file server.

However, just because you can now access Exchange data through Windows Explorer does not mean that it is treated exactly like other file system data. Exchange is still the owner of the data, so it still controls management of the data. For instance, you cannot perform standard operations, such as dragging and dropping files and performing backups, while maintaining the integrity of the data. This has to do with how the data is exposed by IFS. The API calls used by IFS to render the Exchange data do not support a mechanism for accessing custom properties, only the stream of the item. Therefore, dragging and dropping and conducting standard file system backups do not maintain custom properties. To maintain those values, you must use Exchange tools for tasks such as these.

OPEN AND SAVE DIALOG BOXES

Simplicity is a good thing, and here's the proof. Every day, users and developers alike use a standard **Open** dialog box to open file after file in the Office suite of products. They open text files, Web pages, spreadsheets, and data lists in just about any format, edit them, and save the changes. However, Exchange Server 5.5 does not support the **Open** dialog box; therefore, Exchange data was not accessible in this manner. With the release of Exchange 2000, you can use its WebDAV support to access files in a Web Storage System as easily as you would open a Microsoft Word document or an HTML page. Figure 2.15 shows the standard **Open** dialog box displaying the contents of the public folder Zoo Management.

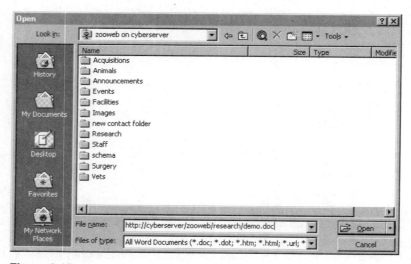

Figure 2.15
The standard Open dialog box, used throughout Microsoft Office 2000, can be used to open items in a public folder.

The benefits of this standardization become clear when you combine use of the **Open** dialog box with use of the **Save** dialog box. Consider the team maintaining an intranet site through Exchange 2000. Many people are responsible for updating data and maintaining accuracy in various documents. By storing those documents in Exchange, team members can open the files for editing in their native environment, such as Microsoft FrontPage or Word, make the changes, and then easily save the document back to the public folder. The next time the file is accessed by an intranet consumer, the most recent changes will be visible. You can also use the new item–based security features of Exchange 2000 to restrict users without permissions from editing documents and damaging data integrity.

CUSTOM CLIENTS

You can also build your own custom clients to access and display data stored in Exchange 2000 Server. Exchange supports many development environments and tools for creating custom applications. For instance, you can use Visual InterDev and FrontPage to build Web clients that can process data requests in two different ways. You can build Web clients that use Active Server Pages (ASP) technology teamed with ADO and CDO to access Exchange data. Another option is to create Web clients that use XML, XSL, and WebDAV to send a data request to Exchange. Exchange processes the request and returns the results to the client. In addition, you can continue to customize Outlook 2000 forms to access Exchange data.

For more information about these environments and tools, as well as information on the types of applications you can create, see Chapter 1, "Developing with the Exchange Platform."

DOING MORE WITH THE WEB STORAGE SYSTEM

If you've read this far, you might think that smart data storage, an enhanced security system, and the ability to use many different clients to access or create resources make Exchange worth taking a look at. But the benefits of Exchange 2000 don't stop there. This section explains the additional capabilities and flexibility that come with the Web Storage System, including querying a Web Storage System and replicating Web Storage System folder trees.

QUERYING A WEB STORAGE SYSTEM

Given the immense number of resources that can be stored in the Web Storage System of Exchange, it can be a bit difficult to locate the exact information that you need. To make the search and discovery faster and easier than a manual perusal of the stores, the Web Storage System supports querying with the standard Structured Query Language (SQL) syntax. SQL querying is conducted using the SQL SELECT statement and can be used with both OLE DB and WebDAV/XML. To query using OLE DB, you use ActiveX Data Objects (ADO) 2.5. To query using WebDAV, you use XML. For more information about querying with ADO, see Chapter 4, "ActiveX Data Objects and Exchange." For more information about querying with XML, see Chapter 13, "XML and Exchange."

REPLICATING WEB STORAGE SYSTEM FOLDER TREES

Web Storage System folder trees can be replicated from one Exchange server to another. The data itself is maintained on a central server, while the folder tree copies, also known as replicas, exist on each individual server. The Exchange servers themselves are designed to make sure that the data is up to date on each server.

Replication benefits developer and user alike. From the developer perspective, replication means that you can easily and quickly deploy an application among multiple locations. When a folder is replicated, any forms or application files stored there are replicated as well. This also minimizes time spent updating applications with newer versions of files. You need only update the master copy. Replication updates all of the replicas with the new files.

From a user perspective, replication increases a worker's performance. If an application resides only on the main corporate server, all users need to connect to that server to use the application even though the user might reside at a satellite office thousands of miles away. With replicas, the user accesses an application from the closest physical server. The user no longer needs to wait for a connection with the master server on the other side of the world.

SUMMARY

The Web Storage System is a great new way to manage data access. By implementing Web Storage System technology, Exchange 2000 Server has become a leader in smart data storage. You can use Exchange 2000 to create unique Web Storage Systems for each of your applications to optimize data storage and maintenance. You can continue to put just about anything into an Exchange store, and data is no longer converted into a single format. Instead, data is left in its native format, which maximizes access efficiency. In addition, data is accessible from almost anywhere. Everything in Exchange is now accessible through a relative URL, so you can access the information you need quickly and easily from your favorite client whether that is a Web page, the **Open** dialog box in Office 2000, or Windows Explorer. Exchange 2000 is not the answer to every data storage challenge, but it is the best solution for your collaboration applications.

Section II, "Data Access," explains how to write code to interact with Exchange data stored in a Web Storage System and in Active Directory.

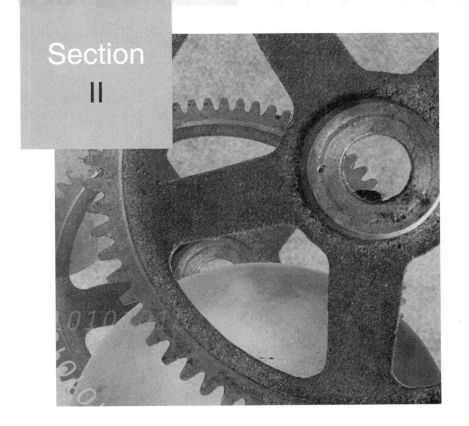

Data Access

Chapter:

3   Web Storage System Schema   **69**

4   ActiveX Data Objects and Exchange   **117**

5   Introduction to CDO for Exchange   **175**

6   CDO Messaging   **225**

7   CDO Calendaring   **271**

8   Interacting with Active Directory   **327**

3

Web Storage
System Schema

Microsoft Exchange 2000 Server is not your typical database. In fact, it is anything but a typical database. The Microsoft Web Storage System defines a hierarchy of folders for storing anything and everything, from standard Exchange items such as appointments and contacts to more complex files such as Active Server Pages (ASP) files and Microsoft Office documents. This broad storage capacity is possible thanks to the Web Storage System's semi-structured model of data storage and is fully accessible by using the Web Storage System schema. Flexible and fully extensible, the schema defines a wide range of properties that you can reuse in your own applications for nearly every collaboration scenario. And, if those properties aren't enough, you can extend the schema with your own custom properties. Properties can be assigned to specific items, shared among application folders, indexed, enumerated, and even inherited. Exchange 2000 can fit the needs of the most demanding applications.

This chapter explains the underlying data definition of the Web Storage System and shows how to extend it to meet your application needs. Sections include:

- **Overview of the Web Storage System Schema**

- **Introducing Content Classes**

- **Schema Access Scenarios**

- **Using a Custom Application Schema**

- **Creating a Custom Schema**

- **Returning Application Schema Information**

Overview of the Web Storage System Schema

A Web Storage System is built around a flexible, semi-structured core. Unlike Microsoft SQL Server, which uses a rigid, structured framework that must be defined before it can be used by a client application, a Web Storage System is available to a client application the moment you create it and mount it on a folder tree. The new folder tree automatically exposes a predefined set of properties known as the *Web Storage System schema*. This section introduces the Web Storage System schema, describes how properties and namespaces are named, and then lists the Web Storage System namespaces.

Understanding the Web Storage System Schema

The Web Storage System schema is the data definition of a single Web Storage System and is used to define all the resources, such as folders, items, and Web files, found in the store. The schema consists of a large number of predefined schema properties that determine the qualities, such as the creation date or the display name, for a resource in a Web Storage System. You can use these properties much as you would columns in a relational database table to efficiently organize, index, sort, view, and search the result sets of simple or sophisticated Structured Query Language (SQL) queries. These properties are, in turn, arranged into namespaces. Namespaces group properties based on similar purpose. For example, properties normally associated with contacts, such as home phone and last name, are organized into one namespace, while properties for appointments, such as start time and duration, are organized into another.

Namespaces also help avoid potential conflicts in property names. For example, you might have two properties named *date* that are used for two different types of information. The first date property might be used for storing information about when a resource was created, and the second date property might be used for storing information about a person's birth date. To avoid storing the wrong information in the wrong property, use a namespace name before the property name. By referring to properties in this manner, there is no conflict between similar property names in different namespaces.

A resource is not restricted to using only properties from a single namespace. Resources more often use properties from a combination of namespaces, and each resource can use a different set of properties. For example, two posts in the same folder can have two different sets of properties. This flexibility is why folders are able to store different types of data in the Web Storage System. A single folder can contain messages, contacts, Web files, and even another folder. Figure 3.1 shows the relationship among properties, namespaces, and resources in a Web Storage System.

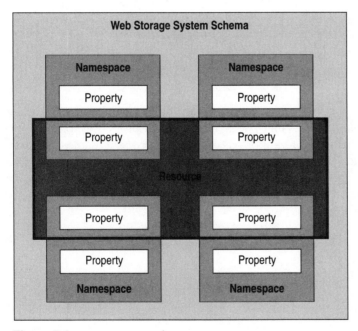

Figure 3.1
The Web Storage System schema contains a set of properties that are, in turn, organized into namespaces. A single resource in a Web Storage System can access any of these properties, regardless of the namespace in which they are located.

A Web Storage System schema is fully extensible, so if you don't find a property that fits the needs of your application, you can always define your own. The ability of the Web Storage System schema to easily accommodate new properties is what makes Exchange such a great development tool. You can extend the property base at any time to accommodate an application's growth and advancement. For example, you can create a library for storing related Microsoft Word documents and Microsoft PowerPoint presentations simply by creating a new folder in the application to hold these items. You never need to adjust the underlying schema and anticipate the types of properties that are necessary. The Web Storage System schema adapts as you add new material. You don't need to worry about creating the wrong set of properties and wasting space for properties that are never used.

UNDERSTANDING PROPERTY AND NAMESPACE NAMES

As mentioned in the previous section, schema properties are organized into virtual entities called *namespaces*. Namespaces group related properties together for easy property discovery and, more importantly, keep the property names unique. Exchange enlists the mechanism defined by the *Namespaces in XML* W3C (World Wide Web Consortium) recommendation as a mandatory convention for naming resource properties. This means that properties are not referred to with only the property name, like this:

- displayname

- href

- contentclass

- delivlength

- email1

- dtstart

Each property is instead identified by a fully qualified name that consists of a namespace and the actual property name. So the correct way to reference these schema properties is like this:

- DAV:displayname

- DAV:href

- DAV:contentclass

- http://schemas.microsoft.com/exchange/delivlength

- urn:schemas:contacts:email1

- urn:schemas:calendar:dtstart

CAUTION Schema property names, including the namespace portion, are case sensitive. If you do not use the proper case for the schema property name in your code, no error is generated, but you will not get the results that you expect.

The prefix to the namespace indicates whether the namespace is specific to a particular product or in agreement with Internet standards. For example, namespaces that begin with the string *http://schemas.microsoft.c*om are defined for use specifically with Microsoft products. Namespaces that begin with the string *urn:schemas* are defined by one of various Internet standards; these are registered namespaces and are generic enough to be applied against multiple products. For example, the namespace *http://schemas.microsoft.com/exchange* is for Microsoft Exchange Server and consists of fields optimized for that product. Developers use properties in this namespace when building applications against Exchange 2000. The namespace *urn:schemas:calendar*, on the other hand, contains properties defined for Internet-based calendaring and can be used by multiple tools and operating systems. Developers can use properties from this namespace to build generic calendaring solutions for use by any type of client.

WEB STORAGE SYSTEM NAMESPACES

Table 3.1 lists some of the predefined namespaces in the Web Storage System schema. For a complete list of namespaces and their properties, see Appendix A, "Web Storage System Schema Properties."

Table 3.1 Some of the predefined namespaces in the Web Storage System schema

Namespace	Description
DAV:	Properties for Web Distributed Authoring and Versioning (WebDAV) and is one of the most widely used namespaces.
http://schemas.microsoft.com/cdo/configuration/	Properties for setting configuration information for various Collaboration Data Objects (CDO) objects.
http://schemas.microsoft.com/cdo/workflow/	Properties for creating workflow applications.
http://schemas.microsoft.com/exchange/	Information specific to Exchange.
http://schemas.microsoft.com/exchange/events/	Properties for defining event sinks.
http://schemas.microsoft.com/exchange/security/	Properties for securing individual resources.
http://schemas.microsoft.com/mapi/	Properties defined by MAPI.
urn:schemas:calendar:	Properties used with items, such as appointments and calendar messages associated with calendars.
urn:schemas:contacts:	Properties used with items, such as person, group, and organization objects.
urn:schemas:httpmail:	Properties used to create and process the body of a message. For fields in the header of a message, use the mailheader namespace.
urn:schemas:mailheader:	Properties used to create the standard header for e-mail messages.
urn:schemas-microsoft-com:exch-data:	Properties used to control the Microsoft Web Storage System schema.

Continued on next page

Table 3.1 continued   Some of the predefined namespaces in the Web Storage System schema

Namespace	Description
urn:schemas-microsoft-com:office:forms	Information about custom form classes.
urn:schemas-microsoft-com:office:office	Properties describing features of Office documents.
urn:schemas-microsoft-com:xml-data	Properties for defining Extensible Markup Language (XML) data constructs.

INTRODUCING CONTENT CLASSES

Schema properties are associated with resources based on a content class. This section describes what content classes are and how they are stored and used, describes the folder and item content classes, and shows how to search for a specific content class and learn about content classes by using the Content Class Browser.

UNDERSTANDING CONTENT CLASSES

Every resource in Exchange has a content class. The content class identifies the intent or purpose of a resource and associates a set of default properties. For example, an e-mail message has a content class of message and, therefore, has properties commonly used for messaging. An appointment in a calendar has a content class of appointment and, therefore, has properties commonly used for calendaring.

The content class of a resource is stored in the DAV:contentclass schema property on that resource. Exchange assigns the DAV:contentclass value implicitly, or you can assign them explicitly with code. Exchange assigns the DAV:contentclass value implicitly when you use a client application, such as Microsoft Outlook 2000 or Outlook Web Access, to create the new resource. Or you can explicitly assign the content class value when you create an item with code. You can set the content class to one of the predefined content class values already registered in Exchange, or you can set it to a custom content class.

The content class, however, does not limit the properties that you can associate with a resource. The content class is more like a template of properties for that resource type that you can extend when necessary. Because content classes also support single inheritance from other content classes, you can easily extend the content class with any of the properties defined in the Web Storage System schema or with a custom property. For example, an e-mail message does not normally have the schema property *urn:schemas:contacts:givenname* associated with it by the message content class, but you can set the urn:schemas:contacts:givenname schema property for the message, and the information will be saved with the item. You can also associate custom properties with the content class in the same way. In addition, other programs, such as Office, can contribute properties to a resource if it makes sense to do so.

NOTE The DAV:contentclass schema property is similar in concept to the message class (IPM.*whatever*) used by Outlook 2000 and CDO 1.2. The DAV:contentclass does not replace the message class, nor does it do everything that the message class does. For example, the content class indicates only which set of schema properties are associated with a resource, but the message class provides information on schema properties, state, content, and the associated form. The message class is still necessary for MAPI-based clients to process folders and items correctly. For more information about using MAPI and Outlook 2000, see Chapter 11, "Developing with Outlook 2000."

FOLDER CONTENT CLASSES

When a new folder is created, it is, by default, a simple generic folder without any special properties. This allows the new folder to easily accommodate any type of item added to it. However, if a folder is used to manage a particular item, such as appointments, you should configure the folder specifically for that type of item. By indicating a content class for the folder, you can expand on this base set of schema properties. You can still put any type of information in the folder, but the folder also contains additional properties specific to the item type. For example, a calendar folder has properties specific to appointment items.

When you use a client application, such as Outlook 2000 or Outlook Web Access, to create a folder, you can choose the type of items the folder is optimized for when you create it. This action, in turn, sets the DAV:contentclass property. When you use code to create a new folder, you must explicitly set the DAV:contentclass property to one of the values in Table 3.2. If you fail to set the property, the folder is created as a generic folder with a DAV:contentclass property value of urn:content-classes:folder.

Table 3.2   Predefined folder content classes and the items each content class is expected to contain

DAV:contentclass value	Type of item that the folder is configured for
urn:content-classes:folder	No specific type
urn:content-classes:mailfolder	E-mail items
urn:content-classes:contactfolder	Contact (person) information
urn:content-classes: calendarfolder	Appointments, meetings, and requests
urn:content-classes:taskfolder	Tasks
urn:content-classes:journalfolder	Journal entries
urn:content-classes:notefolder	Notes

NOTE   For a list of the schema properties that are assigned by default to each of these folder types, see the section "Reference" in the Exchange SDK.

Listing 3.1 shows how to create a folder for contact information. The procedure sets the DAV:contentclass to urn:content-classes:contactfolder to create a folder that is optimized to store contact information. The procedure then returns all the properties that are assigned to the new folder by the content class.

Listing 3.1 Create a folder for storing contact information by setting the DAV:contentclass property of the folder.

```
Sub CreateContactFolder()
    ' Create a new contact folder
    ' in the Applications WSS
    ' named Developers.

    Dim fd As ADODB.Field
    Dim urlDeveloperFldr As String

    ' Build the URL to the resource to be created.
    ' GetStorageName is a custom function that returns
    ' the DNS name for the domain where the code is running.
    ' For more information on the function, see Chapter 8.
    ' The trailing slash is to indicate this is a folder.
    urlDeveloperFldr = _
        GetStorageName & "Applications/Developers/"

    With New ADODB.Record
        ' Create a new contact folder
        .Open urlDeveloperFldr _

            , _
            , adModeReadWrite _
            , adCreateCollection + adCreateOverwrite
        .Fields("DAV:contentclass") = _
            "urn:content-classes:contactfolder"
        .Fields.Update



    ' Enumerate through the properties
    For Each fd In .Fields
        If Not IsArray(fd.Value) Then
            ' If the property is single-valued,
            ' return the name and the current value
            Debug.Print fd.Name, fd.Value
```

```
        Else
            ' If the property is multi-valued,
            ' Identify it as such. For info on
            ' enumerating multi-valued properties, see
            ' Chapter 4 for ADO and Chapter 13 for XML
            Debug.Print fd.Name, "[MULTI-VALUED]"
        End If
    Next
    .Close
End With

    ' Clean up
    Set fd = Nothing
End Sub
```

> **NOTE** The code listings in this chapter are available in the Microsoft Visual Basic project CH_03.vbp on the companion CD. If you want to run the samples as they are written, you must have the Zoo Management sample installed on your Exchange 2000 server. For information on installing the application, see the introduction to the book. In addition, the code samples repeatedly call a function named GetStorageName. This function returns the name of the domain in which the code is running. For more information on the GetStorageName function, see Chapter 8, "Interacting with Active Directory."

ITEM CONTENT CLASSES

When you create a new item with a client tool, such as Outlook 2000 or Outlook Web Access, you specify the type of item to create by selecting it from a menu or by clicking the appropriate toolbar button. When you save the item, Exchange sets the DAV:contentclass property appropriately. When you use code to create the item, you must explicitly set the DAV:contentclass property to one of the values in Table 3.3. If you fail to set the property, the folder is created as a generic folder with a DAV:contentclass property value of urn:content-classes:message.

Table 3.3 Typical Web Storage System resources and their associated content classes

Content class	Description
urn:content-classes:appointment	Appointment or meeting.
urn:content-classes:calendarmessage	Meeting request.
urn:content-classes:contentclassdef	Predefined or custom content class definition.
urn:content-classes:document	Any structured document, including forms that use Web Storage System Forms Registry and text files. Also includes Office documents such as Word files.
urn:content-classes:dsn	Delivery status notification.
urn:content-classes:item	Generic item.
urn:content-classes:message	E-mail messages and posts in public folders.
urn:content-classes:mdn	Message delivery notification.
urn:content-classes:person	Contact entry in a folder or Active Directory.
urn:content-classes:propertydef	Predefined or custom schema property definition.
urn:content-classes:recallmessage	Recall message.
urn:content-classes:recallreport	Information on a recall.
urn:content-classes:object	Object in the store.

Listing 3.2 shows how to create a contact item in a folder by using Microsoft ActiveX Data Objects (ADO) code. The procedure sets the DAV:contentclass to urn:content-classes:person to create an item with properties specific to a contact. The procedure then returns all the properties that are assigned to the new item by the content class.

Listing 3.2   Create a contact item by setting the DAV:contentclass property.

```
Sub CreateContactItem()
    ' Create a new contact in the Developers
    ' contact folder created in the
    ' CreateContactFolder procedure.

    Dim fd As ADODB.Field
    Dim urlDeveloper As String

    ' Build the URL to the resource to be created.
    ' GetStorageName is a custom function that returns the DNS name
    ' for the domain on which the code is running.
    ' For more information on the function, see Chapter 8.
    ' The EML extension is to indicate this is an item, not a folder.
    urlDeveloper = _
        GetStorageName & "Applications/Developers/Michael Patten.EML"

    With New ADODB.Record
        ' Create a new contact folder
        .Open urlDeveloper _
            , _
            , adModeReadWrite _
            , adCreateNonCollection + adCreateOverwrite
        .Fields("DAV:contentclass") = _
            "urn:content-classes:person"
        .Fields("urn:schemas:contacts:givenname") = "Michael"
        .Fields("urn:schemas:contacts:sn") = "Patten"
        .Fields.Update
```

```
' Enumerate through the properties
For Each fd In .Fields
        If Not IsArray(fd.Value) Then
        ' If the property is single-valued,
        ' return the name and the current value
        Debug.Print fd.Name, fd.Value
    Else
        ' If the property is multi-valued,
        ' Identify it as such. For info on
        ' enumerating multi-valued properties, see
        ' Chapter 4 for ADO and Chapter 13 for XML
        Debug.Print fd.Name, "[MULTI-VALUED]"
    End If
Next

    .Close
End With

' Clean up
Set fd = Nothing
End Sub
```

NOTE For a list of the default properties that are assigned to an item for each content class, see the section "Reference" in the Exchange SDK.

SEARCHING FOR A SPECIFIC CONTENT CLASS

A Web Storage System can hold a wide variety of resources, such as folders for e-mail items, calendars, contact items, and Web documents. Although this is definitely a benefit when it comes to storing information, it can be a drawback when it comes to finding information. To solve this problem, use querying to locate resources with a specific content class. Listing 3.3 shows how to use ADO to search a Web Storage System for a particular content class. You pass the procedure one argument, which is the DAV:contentclass value that you want to search for. The procedure then searches the entire Web Storage System and returns the DAV:displayname and DAV:href value for each resource with that content class.

Listing 3.3 Loop through a collection looking for folders that contain only contact items.

```
Sub SearchForContentClass(ByVal CC As String)
    ' Look through all of the folders in the Applications WSS
    ' for resources with a specific content class

    Dim cnn As ADODB.Connection
    Dim rst As ADODB.Recordset
    Dim urlApplications As String
    Dim strSQL As String

    'Build the URL string
    urlApplications = GetStorageName() & "Applications/"

    ' Open a connection to the Applications WSS
    Set cnn = New ADODB.Connection
    With cnn
        .Provider = "exoledb.datasource"
        .Open urlApplications
    End With

    ' Build the SQL statement
    strSQL = _
        "SELECT " & AddQuotes("DAV:displayname") & _
        ", " & AddQuotes("DAV:href")
    strSQL = strSQL & _
        " FROM scope('deep traversal of " & _
        AddQuotes(urlApplications) & "')"
    strSQL = strSQL & _
        " WHERE " & _
        AddQuotes("DAV:contentclass") & "= '" & CC & "'"
    strSQL = strSQL & _
        " ORDER BY " & AddQuotes("DAV:displayname") & " DESC"

    'Create a Recordset object
    Set rst = New ADODB.Recordset
    With rst
        'Open Recordset based on the SQL string
        .Open strSQL, cnn
    End With
```

```
'Print the folder names to the debug window
Do Until rst.EOF
   Debug.Print _
   rst.Fields("DAV:displayname"), rst.Fields("DAV:href")
   rst.MoveNext
Loop

' Close the Recordset and Connection
rst.Close
cnn.Close

' Clean up
Set cnn = Nothing
Set rst = Nothing
End Sub
```

LEARNING ABOUT CONTENT CLASSES BY USING THE CONTENT CLASS BROWSER

The CH_03 Visual Basic project on the companion CD includes a form called "Content Class Browser." Content Class Browser is a handy tool for learning about content classes and their associated schema properties. You can use it to view the contents of a folder, verify the properties associated with a content class, verify the properties added to a custom content class, and check the values of certain properties. It can be invaluable during application testing as well. Figure 3.2 shows the Content Class Browser.

To use Content Class Browser, simply run the CH_03 Visual Basic project by pressing the F5 key while the project is open. After the form is displayed, in **Enter a URL to a folder**, type the URL for the folder you want to open. You can use a shortcut button to help build the URL. For example, click **Zoo Mgt Application** to build the URL for the Zoo Management application on the Applications Web Storage System. When you click **Search**, the code attempts to connect to the Exchange server on the local domain and retrieve the contents of the folder specified in the URL. By default, the search returns subfolders as well as items. If you prefer not to include subfolders in the result set, clear the **Include subfolders** check box.

Folder contents lists the contents of the folder specified in the URL. If you click an item in the list, **Content Class** displays the content class for that resource. In addition, the **Properties** list contains the properties associated with that resource. To see the value for a specific property, click it. The **Property value** box then displays the current value.

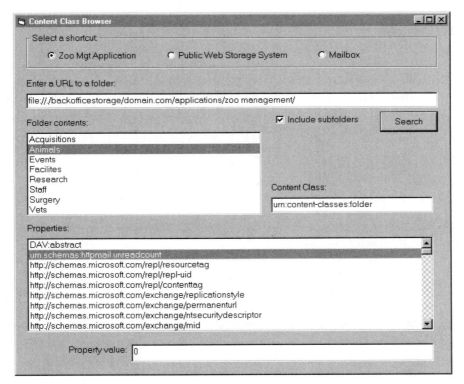

Figure 3.2
Content Class Browser is a great tool for learning the properties associated with a particular content class.

NOTE The Content Class Browser is not used to set property values or create new items. However, you can modify the tool for these tasks. The Content Class Browser is also available in the Some Helper Tools folder on the companion CD.

SCHEMA ACCESS SCENARIOS

The Web Storage System schema offers many predefined properties for your collaboration applications, and, if those aren't enough, you can always create your own custom properties and content classes. This flexibility and extensibility of the Exchange schema means you can build a broader range of applications to interact with Exchange 2000. You can:

- Enter a URL in a Web browser to use Outlook Web Access for all-around store access or generate custom requests by using WebDAV.

- Create Web applications that use ASP technology along with ADO and CDO.

- Use the client tools, such as Outlook 2000, you've always used with Exchange 5.5.

By using new ways to access the properties of the Web Storage System schema, you can build more efficient and secure collaboration solutions with Exchange 2000, if you understand how the data itself is sent and received. This section presents some of the more common data-access scenarios (URLs and HTTP, Web applications that use ASP technology, and Outlook 2000) and describes what happens to the data between the client and the Exchange server.

URLS AND HTTP

A simple scenario is using Outlook Web Access to access the Web Storage System and its schema fields. When a user enters a URL for an Inbox or public folder in a Web browser such as Microsoft Internet Explorer 5, the URL and the user's credentials are passed to the Exchange server through HTTP. Along with WebDAV extensions, HTTP allows clients to access and edit Web Storage System information over the Internet or an intranet. The actual data elements are sent through HTTP using XML as the wire-transmission format for item properties.

When Exchange receives the information, the credentials are verified and the XML is automatically parsed for the requested data. Exchange then constructs an XML response containing the appropriate schema properties and their values, and this response is then sent back through WebDAV to the browser that requested it. If the browser can parse XML (as Internet Explorer 5 can), a style sheet can be applied to the XML and the data is then displayed to the user. If the browser cannot parse XML, the page is displayed in standard HTML. Figure 3.3 shows this process. The client computer does not need any files or programs other than a Web browser to access the Web Storage System schema.

> **NOTE**   The client-side OLE DB provider for Microsoft Internet Publishing Provider (MSDAIPP) is HTTP-compliant.

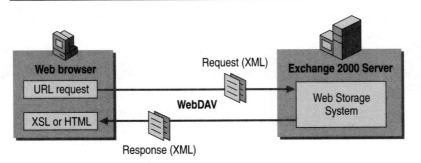

Figure 3.3
When a URL is entered in a Web browser, the information is sent as XML along with the HTTP to Exchange. It is then processed and sent back to the browser to be rendered in Extensible Stylesheet Language (XSL), if supported, or HTML.

WEB APPLICATIONS USING ASP TECHNOLOGY

Server-side processing of ADO and CDO happens most often in server-specific applications or in Web applications that use ASP technology. When a user points a Web browser to an .asp file that accesses the Web Storage System, the request is passed through plain HTTP to the Web server. There, it is intercepted by Microsoft Internet Information Services (IIS) and passed to the ASP processor. If the .asp file uses ADO or CDO, the requests for data are then sent to the Exchange OLE DB (ExOLEDB) provider. ExOLEDB provides access to local (same host) Web Storage Systems and is installed with Exchange 2000. ExOLEDB translates the data request for the Exchange server and returns the requested data to the calling .asp file, which then renders the results as HTML. The finished page is then sent back to the browser through HTTP and displayed to the user as a static HTML page. Figure 3.4 shows this process. The client has no need of ADO or CDO library files; you can install these files, and others, on the server when you install Exchange 2000.

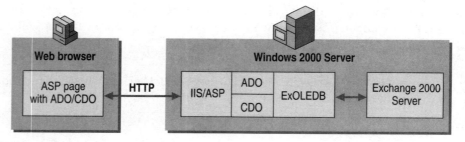

Figure 3.4
When a Web page that uses ASP technology is requested, the request is sent to the server through IIS and ASP. Any ADO or CDO calls are then translated by ExOLEDB, the OLE DB provider for Exchange 2000. The resulting data is parsed into static HTML and sent back to the browser.

MICROSOFT OUTLOOK 2000

Nothing much has changed in the way Outlook 2000 and earlier versions of Outlook access properties in the Web Storage System. Because Outlook 2000 is a MAPI client, it must still go through the MAPI on both the client and the server. Requests from the client to view private mailbox or public stores are sent as remote procedure calls (RPCs) to Exchange 2000 Server. The Web Storage System is optimized for the Web and Multipurpose Internet Mail Extensions (MIME) content, so the properties and their values are not MAPI-compliant. For a MAPI client such as Outlook 2000 to render them, properties must be mapped to their equivalent MAPI counterparts before being sent. After it is mapped to the appropriate MAPI properties, a folder or item is sent back through the MAPI layers to Outlook as an RPC. Figure 3.5 shows this process.

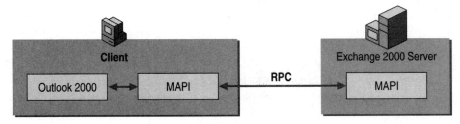

Figure 3.5
Outlook sends requests to the Exchange server by using RPCs through the MAPI interface.

USING A CUSTOM APPLICATION SCHEMA

When you build a Web Storage System application, you might find it beneficial to build your own custom application schema. You can use a custom application schema to define your own properties and content classes for an application. This section explains the benefits of using a custom application schema, explains how you define a custom schema, and shows how to define the application schema, properties, and content classes.

NOTE If you plan to use Web Storage System forms in your application, you must have a custom application schema defined. For more information about how a custom schema is used with Web Storage System forms, see Chapter 12, "Building Web Applications for Exchange."

BENEFITS OF EMPLOYING A CUSTOM SCHEMA

You do not need to use a custom schema with every application that you create. Some applications have no need of a schema. For example, if all you need is one custom property, you can append that property every time you create a new item. However, if you need to use multiple custom properties and have a variety of item types, you will find it beneficial to use a custom application schema. Some of the benefits are:

- **Querying for class type**. Although you could define custom properties for an animal entry in the Animals folder without defining the custom content class, you can use a custom content class to group similar items for faster searches. Then you can search on a content class for all items of a specific type. If instead you append the properties to each item, very different item types could potentially use the same properties. For example, you could use an AnimalId property for both exhibit and animal information. If you are querying for all animals, you might think to execute a query that looks for all items that have an AnimalId property value, but this query would also return exhibit information that has set the AnimalId property as well. However, if you have separate content classes for exhibits and animals, you can execute a query that looks for items with an animal class.

- **Consistency in property definition**. If you define a property on each item, you can inadvertently define the same property in multiple ways. For example, you might define an ID property on one item as a string data type, but you or another developer could define that same property on another item as an integer data type. By using a single definition, you don't need to worry about conflicting data types for the same property. It also reduces the chances of creating properties with the same purpose but different names.

- **Team development**. If your team has multiple developers on it, you know that it's tough to keep up-to-date with what each developer is doing. By using a single repository for properties and content classes, all developers can look in one place for a specific definition before designing a new one. For example, if a developer needs to define a new content class, they could build on what other team members have done and use inheritance to avoid building the class from scratch. Using a single application schema also eliminates the possibility that different developers might define the same property for the same purpose in two different locations.

- **Application management**. When it comes to application maintenance, a single custom namespace is easier to maintain than multiple forms and folders with unique data sets. When you must make changes to a property or content class, you can edit the definition rather than each instance that uses the property. This benefit is particularly obvious when you think about existing items. If you have a number of items that use a custom property that was added each time an item was created, you need to access each item to make the necessary changes in the code. If, however, you are using a custom content class, you just change the class definition. The changes are then made to each item that uses the content class. If you need to add a new property, you can simply add it to the existing schema and include the necessary control on the forms.

HOW A CUSTOM SCHEMA WORKS

The Web Storage System schema—also known as the global schema—is a hidden folder off the non-IPM subtree of the Web Storage System. The global schema contains all the predefined properties and content classes that you normally use in collaboration applications. You can access the global schema like any other folder by using a URL. For example, the following URL accesses the global schema for the Applications Web Storage System in domain.com:

```
File://./backofficestorage/domain.com/
    Applications/non_ipm_subtree/schema/
```

When a folder is created in a Web Storage System, by default it references the Web Storage System schema for content class and property definitions. Figure 3.6 shows a Web Storage System with a global schema. Any folders in that folder tree by default reference the global schema for properties and content classes.

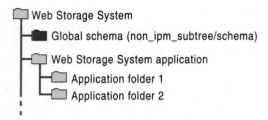

Figure 3.6
By default, a Web Storage System has only one schema defined, and all folders reference this global schema for property and content class definitions.

When you define a custom schema, you alter how application folders interact with the global schema. Instead of having the folders reference the global schema, you want those application folders to reference a schema specific to the application. To use a custom schema for an application, you must set up your own schema folder for all the custom property definitions and custom content class definitions used by your application. Figure 3.7 shows how the application looks after a custom application schema is created. You can point each of those application folders to the custom schema folder. To continue to use the standard properties and content classes in the global schema, point the application schema folder to the global schema.

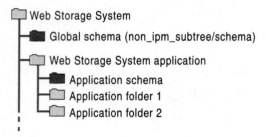

Figure 3.7
When a custom schema is employed, the application folders reference the custom schema folder for the custom properties and content classes. The application schema, in turn, references the global schema for the typical Exchange properties and content classes.

DEFINING THE APPLICATION SCHEMA

Before you can create or use any custom content classes or custom properties, you must define the application schema. You define a Web Storage System application schema by creating and configuring the schema folder that stores the custom content classes and properties and by configuring each application folder to reference that custom schema.

CREATING THE APPLICATION SCHEMA FOLDER

The application schema folder holds all the content class definitions and property definitions for your custom schema. This is the schema that all the application folders reference. You create a folder for the application schema in the same way that you create any other folder. If you are using ADO, you create a new ADO record and indicate that you are creating a folder, not an item. Then you set the urn:schemas-microsoft-com:exch-data:baseschema schema property for the folder to point to the non_ipm_subtree/Schema for the Web Storage System on which the application is installed. The urn:schemas-microsoft-com:exch-data:baseschema property is a multi-valued string property that identifies where the folder looks for schema definitions. To set the urn:schemas-microsoft-com:exch-data:baseschema property, you must use an array. The following code sample sets the urn:schemas-microsoft-com:exch-data:baseschema property to the non_IPM_subtree/schema for the Applications Web Storage System:

```
BaseSchemaURL = "file://./backofficestorage/domain.com/" & _
    "Applications/non_ipm_subtree/schema/"

rec.Fields("urn:schemas-microsoft-com:exch-data:baseschema") _
    = Array(BaseSchemaURL)
```

Because the application folders find class and property definitions in your application schema folder, the application schema folder needs to reference the global schema for the Web Storage System. This allows the resources in your application to use the Web Storage System schema properties in addition to the custom properties. Finally, you need to set the DAV:ishidden property to True to hide the folder from appearing in user interfaces such as Outlook Web Access.

Listing 3.4 shows how to use ADO to define an application schema folder. The procedure takes three arguments: the URL for the Web Storage System where the application is installed, the URL for the application schema folder to be built, and a Boolean value that indicates whether an existing schema folder at the same URL should be overwritten. The procedure either creates a new application schema folder or opens an existing one, depending on the value of the OverwriteExisting parameter. Then it points the base schema of the application schema folder to the global schema of the Web Storage System. Finally, the procedure hides the folder from user interfaces.

Listing 3.4 Create an application schema folder.

```
Sub DefineSchemaFolder( _
    ByVal WSSurl As String, _
    ByVal AppSchemaURL As String, _
    Optional OverwriteExisting As Boolean = False)

    ' This procedure creates a schema folder within
    ' the specified application folder and points
    ' its BaseSchema at the Web Storage System
    ' schema.

    Dim BaseSchemaURL As String
    Dim rec As ADODB.Record

    On Error GoTo err_DefineSchema

    ' Build the URL to the Web Storage System non IPM schema folder
    BaseSchemaURL = WSSurl & "non_ipm_subtree/schema/"

    Set rec = New ADODB.Record
    With rec
```

```
        ' Overwrite the existing application schema folder
        If OverwriteExisting = True Then
           .Open AppSchemaURL _

              , _
              , adModeReadWrite _
              , adCreateCollection + adCreateOverwrite

        ' Attempt to open the schema folder instead
        Else
           .Open AppSchemaURL _

              , _
              , adModeReadWrite _
              , adCreateCollection + adOpenIfExists
        End If

        ' Reference the global schema
        .Fields("urn:schemas-microsoft-com:exch-data:baseschema") _
           = Array(BaseSchemaURL)

        ' Hide the folder
        .Fields("DAV:ishidden") = True

        ' Save the changes and close the object
        .Fields.Update
        .Close
     End With

     ' Clean up
     Set rec = Nothing

     Exit Sub

err_DefineSchema:
     MsgBox "Unable to define the schema folder."
     Exit Sub
End Sub
```

Configuring Application Folders

After you create the application schema folder, you need to configure the application folders in the Web Storage System application so that they reference the custom application schema. By default, folders reference the global schema for the Web Storage System on which they are installed. For the folders to use the custom classes and properties, you need to configure the application folders to look to the application schema instead. Do this by setting the urn:schemas-microsoft-com:exch-data:schema-collection-ref property. Unlike the urn:schemas-microsoft-com:exch-data:baseschema property, the urn:schemas-microsoft-com:exch-data:schema-collection-ref property is a single-valued property that indicates the first place to look for schema information, which should be the application schema. The following code sample configures a folder to reference the application schema for schema definitions:

```
Const SCR As String = _
"urn:schemas-microsoft-com:exch-data:schema-collection-ref"

AppSchemaURL = "file://./backofficestorage/domain.com/" & _
  "Applications/Zoo Management/schema/"

rec.Fields _
( SCR) _
  = AppSchemaURL
```

You do not need to set the urn:schemas-microsoft-com:exch-data:baseschema property for these application folders because the schema folder is already configured to look to the global schema.

You can set this property on the application folders several different ways. Listing 3.5 uses an SQL query to return all the subfolders in a Web Storage System application and then loops through the results, setting the urn:schemas-microsoft-com:exch-data:schema-collection-ref property for each one to the URL of the application schema folder.

Listing 3.5 Configure the application folders to point to the application schema folder.

```
Function ConfigureFolders(ByVal WSSAppURL As String)
    ' Point all of the application folders
    ' to the application schema.

    Dim cnn As ADODB.Connection
    Dim rst As ADODB.Recordset
    Dim rec As ADODB.Record
    Dim strSQL As String

    Const SCR As String = _
    "urn:schemas-microsoft-com:exch-data:schema-collection-ref"

    ' Build the SQL statement
    strSQL = _
        "SELECT " & _
        AddQuotes("DAV:displayname") & ", " & _
        AddQuotes("DAV:href") & "," & _
        AddQuotes(SCR)
    strSQL = strSQL & _
        " FROM scope('Shallow traversal of " & _
        AddQuotes(WSSAppURL) & "')"
    strSQL = strSQL & _
        " WHERE " & AddQuotes("DAV:isfolder") & "= True"

    ' Open the connection
    Set cnn = New ADODB.Connection
    With cnn
        .Provider = "exoledb.datasource"
        .Open WSSAppURL
    End With

    Set rec = New ADODB.Record
```

```
' Set the SCR on the application folder
With rec
    .Open WSSAppURL, cnn, adModeReadWrite
    .Fields(SCR) = WSSAppURL & "schema/"
    .Fields.Update
    .Close
End With

' Open Recordset based on the SQL string
Set rst = New Recordset
rst.Open strSQL, cnn

' Now set the SCR on each application folder
Do Until rst.EOF
    With rec
        .Open "./" & rst.Fields("DAV:displayname") _
            , cnn, adModeReadWrite
        .Fields(SCR) = WSSAppURL & "schema/"
        .Fields.Update
        .Close
    End With
    ' Move to the next folder
    rst.MoveNext
Loop

' Close the ADO objects
rst.Close
cnn.Close

' Clean up
Set rec = Nothing
Set rst = Nothing
Set cnn = Nothing
End Function
```

DEFINING PROPERTIES

You create a custom property by defining it in the application schema folder. To define a custom property, create a new item in the application schema folder and set the item's DAV:contentclass property to urn:content-classes:propertydef. Then name the property and indicate the data type. The name you used with the URL to create the new item is only the name of the item in the folder, not the actual property name. To name the property, set the urn:schemas-microsoft-com:xml-data#name property to a qualified name. You can use anything you like as the name; however, you should include a namespace to be consistent with the Web Storage System schema. This helps reduce the possibility that your properties will conflict with existing properties and allows you to group custom properties by purpose. In addition, you might want to keep the property name in all lowercase characters to be more consistent with the properties in the Web Storage System schema. If you adopt this standard, you can always enter your property names as lowercase and be sure that you have the right case. For example, the following code sample names a property for the Zoo Management application:

```
rec.Fields("urn:schemas-microsoft-com:xml-data#name") _
    = "zoomgt:species"
```

You should also be consistent with the case of the property names. Next, set the data type for the new property definition with the urn:schemas-microsoft-com:datatypes#type property. For example, to create a property of a string data type, you would use code like this:

```
rec.Fields("urn:schemas-microsoft-com:datatypes#type") _
    = "string"
```

The section "Data Types" lists the various data types. That's all you need to create a property definition, but you can configure the property further for more specific behavior. Table 3.4 lists some of the optional properties you can set.

Table 3.4 Optional properties used to define a new custom property

Property	Data type	Purpose
urn:schemas-microsoft-com: exch-data:isindexed	Boolean	If True, the property is indexed with other store properties for efficient searches. It is also returned with a SELECT * query.
urn:schemas-microsoft-com: exch-data:ismultivalued	Boolean	Property can contain multiple values. Must be enforced by the custom application.
urn:schemas-microsoft-com: exch-data:defaultvalue	String	Indicates what value is placed in the property by default.
urn:schemas-microsoft-com: exch-data:isrequired	Boolean	If True, the property definition must be set to some value. Must be enforced by the custom application.

Listing 3.6 shows how to use ADO to define a custom property in an application schema. The procedure uses a number of parameters to determine the qualities for the new property definition. Only the URL for the application schema folder, the namespace name, and the property name are required. The other parameters are optional. By default, the procedure creates a single-valued string property that doesn't have a default value and is not indexed.

Listing 3.6 Define a custom property.

```
Function DefineProperty( _
    ByVal AppSchemaFld As String, _
    ByVal Namespace As String, _
    ByVal PropertyName As String, _
    Optional DataType As String = "string", _
    Optional IsMultiValued As Boolean = False, _
    Optional Default As String = "", _
    Optional IsIndexed As Boolean = False)
```

```
' This function creates a property definition
' in an application schema folder. The default
' is to create a single-valued, string property
' that has no default value and is not indexed.

' If you are using VBScript, use this With:
' With CreateObject("ADODB.Record")
With New ADODB.Record
    ' Create the new property record
    .Open AppSchemaFld & PropertyName _
        , _
        , adModeReadWrite _
        , adCreateNonCollection
    ' Define the property
    .Fields _
        ("DAV:contentclass") _
        = "urn:content-classes:propertydef"
    .Fields _
        ("urn:schemas-microsoft-com:xml-data#name") _
        = Namespace & PropertyName
    .Fields _
        ("urn:schemas-microsoft-com:datatypes#type") _
        = DataType
    .Fields _
        ("urn:schemas-microsoft-com:exch-data:ismultivalued") _
        = IsMultiValued
    .Fields _
        ("urn:schemas-microsoft-com:exch-data:defaultvalue") _
        = Default
    .Fields _
        ("urn:schemas-microsoft-com:exch-data:isindexed") _
        = IsIndexed
    ' Save the changes
    .Fields.Update
    .Close
End With
End Function
```

NOTE You can also create custom properties by appending them directly to the item or folder. By using ADO, you can append to the Fields collection for that folder or item and define a new property ready to set immediately. This is a quick and easy way to add the custom property. However, the custom property exists only on that resource and not in a schema anywhere. If you want to use it again, you must append it to each record.

DATA TYPES

You can set the urn:schemas-microsoft-com:datatypes#type property to a number of data types. Table 3.5 lists some of the possible values.

Table 3.5 Some of the possible data types for defining custom properties

String value	Description
bin.base64	Binary data (base64 encoded)
boolean	True (1) or false (0) value
dateTime	Date and time value
i2	Two-byte integer
i4	Four-byte integer
i8	Eight-byte integer
float	Double value
string	Two-byte character string (Unicode)
uuid	Universally unique identifier

DEFINING CONTENT CLASSES

You define a custom content class in the application schema folder. To define a
new content class, create a new item in the schema folder and set the
DAV:contentclass property to urn:content-classes:contentclassdef. Then name the
content class. The name you used with the URL to create the new content class
definition item is the name of only the item in the folder, not the actual content
class name. To name the content class, set the urn:schemas-microsoft-com:xml-
data#name property to a qualified name. You can use anything you like as the
name, but you should employ some sort of naming convention to distinguish a
content class from a property. For example, you could name the custom content
class using a format similar to that employed by Exchange but prefixed with the
name of your application instead of urn. The following code sample names a
content class for the Zoo Management application:

```
rec.Fields("urn:schemas-microsoft-com:xml-data#name") _
  = "zoomgt:content-classes:animal"
```

After you have named the new content class, indicate which, if any, existing
content class the new class is extending. This lets the new content class inherit
existing properties. Exchange supports both single and multiple inheritances. For
example, you can set your new content class to inherit the properties of the
existing urn:content-classes:person content class if you want the new content class
to have all the properties normally associated with a contact as well as your own
custom properties. If the new content class also needs messaging properties, you
could have the new content class inherit properties from the urn:content-
classes:message content class and the urn:content-classes:person content class. To
use inheritance, set the urn:schemas-microsoft-com:xml-data#extends property to
an array of values. The following code sample indicates that the new content class
definition inherits properties from the urn:content-classes:item content class:

```
rec.Fields _
("urn:schemas-microsoft-com:xml-data#extends") = _
  Arrary("urn:content-classes:item")
```

The last step is to indicate which custom properties will be added to the content class. To associate custom properties with the new content class, set the urn:schemas-microsoft-com:xml-data#element property to an array that contains the qualified names of all the custom properties. The following code sample sets the urn:schemas-microsoft-com:xml-data#element property to a previously populated array named CustomPropsList:

```
rec.Fields _
("urn:schemas-microsoft-com:xml-data#element") = _
 CustomPropsList
```

Listing 3.7 shows how to use ADO to define a custom content class in an application schema. The procedure uses a number of parameters to determine the qualities for the new content class definition including: the URL to the application schema folder, the content class prefix including the trailing colon (for example, "zoomgt:content-classes:"), the friendly name of the content class, an array that contains the existing content classes to extend, and an array that contains the custom properties to add to the class.

Listing 3.7   Define a custom content class.

```
Function DefineContentClass( _
    AppSchemaFld As String, _
    CCPrefix As String, _
    CCName As String, _
    ExtendsCCList As Variant, _
    CustomPropsList As Variant)

    ' This procedure creates a new custom
    ' content class in the schema folder
    ' you specify. Make sure to name the
    ' content class using some sort of
    ' naming convention such as:
    ' zoomgt:content-classes:animal.
```

```
' If you are using VBScript, use this With:
' With CreateObject("ADODB.Record")
With New ADODB.Record
    ' Create the new property record
    .Open AppSchemaFld & CCName _
        , _
        , adModeReadWrite _
        , adCreateNonCollection

    ' Indicate this is a content class definition
    .Fields("DAV:contentclass") = _
        "urn:content-classes:contentclassdef"

    ' Name the content class
    .Fields("urn:schemas-microsoft-com:xml-data#name") = _
        LCase(CCPrefix) & LCase(CCName)

    ' Indicate which content class the new content class
    ' will inherit properties from
    .Fields("urn:schemas-microsoft-com:xml-data#extends") = _
        ExtendsCCList

    ' Indicate the custom properties added to this content class
    .Fields("urn:schemas-microsoft-com:xml-data#element") = _
        CustomPropsList

    ' Save change
    .Fields.Update
    .Close
End With
End Function
```

CREATING A CUSTOM SCHEMA

The previous section explained how to use ADO to define a custom application schema. This section explains how to apply those procedures and create a custom application schema for the Zoo Management application, including how to define the Zoo Management schema and create an instance of the Animal content class.

NOTE If you have installed the Zoo Management application, the schema is already defined. However, you can run the code here to see how a new schema would be configured without harming the current schema configuration. If you have not installed the Zoo Management application on the Applications Web Storage System, you must do so to execute this code successfully. For information about installing the application, see the introduction to the book.

DEFINING THE ZOO MANAGEMENT SCHEMA

The Zoo Management application uses a custom schema to obtain functionality not readily available in Exchange. For example, the application needs to store information about the animals in the zoo. An entry about a specific animal must store information such as an ID value, species name, and the exhibit where the animal is kept. You can add each of these properties individually whenever a new entry for an animal is made, or you can define a custom content class so that these properties are available every time you create a new instance of the content class. This example defines a new animal content class.

Listing 3.8 is the main force behind creating the Zoo Management schema and defining the custom properties and animal content class. The procedure starts by defining the string literals that will be passed to the other procedures that actually do the configuration. You can adjust any of these accordingly if you have installed the application elsewhere. Then the procedure checks to see if the Zoo Management application exists on the Applications Web Storage System. If not, the procedure alerts you and exits. If it connects to the application, the procedure continues with the core tasks: it creates the application schema folder structure, defines the properties, and defines the animal content class.

Listing 3.8   Create a custom schema for the Zoo Management Web Storage System application.

```
Sub ConfigureZooMgtApplication()
    ' Configure the Zoo Management application
    ' with a custom schema

    Dim strWebStorageSystem As String
    Dim urlWSS As String
    Dim urlWSSApp As String
    Dim urlAppSchema As String
    Dim strNamespace As String
    Dim rec As ADODB.Record
    Dim PropertyList()

    ' This is the name of the Web Storage System
    ' If you set up the folders on the MAPI Web Storage System
    ' Change this to "public folders"
    strWebStorageSystem = "Applications"
    ' URL to the Web Storage System
    urlWSS = GetStorageName & strWebStorageSystem & "/"
    ' URL to the Web Storage System application
    urlWSSApp = urlWSS & "zoo management/"

    ' Enable error trapping for VB and VBS
    On Error Resume Next

    ' Check to see if the zoo application exists
    ' By opening an ADO record using the above URL
    Set rec = New ADODB.Record
    rec.Open urlWSSApp
    If Err.Number <> 0 Then
        ' The application does not exist
        MsgBox "Error accessing the Zoo Management Application. " & _
            "Make sure that the folder exists.", _
            vbCritical, "Zoo Management Sample Application"
        rec.Close
        GoTo ExitHere
    End If
```

```
' Turn error handling back to the system
' You can change this to go to your current error handler
' if you are using VB
On Error GoTo 0

' URL to the application schema folder
urlAppSchema = urlWSSApp & "schema/"
' Namespace to be used with the schema properties
strNamespace = "zoomgt:"

' Configure the Web Storage System application schema folder
DefineSchemaFolder urlWSS, urlAppSchema, True

' Configure the application folders
ConfigureFolders urlWSSApp

' Define the custom properties
DefineProperty _
   urlAppSchema, strNamespace, "animalid", _
   "string", False, , True
DefineProperty _
   urlAppSchema, strNamespace, "species", _
   "string", False, , True
DefineProperty _
   urlAppSchema, strNamespace, "commonname", _
   "string", False, , True
DefineProperty _
   urlAppSchema, strNamespace, "gender", _
   "boolean", False, , False
DefineProperty _
   urlAppSchema, strNamespace, "habitat", _
   "string", False, , False
DefineProperty _
   urlAppSchema, strNamespace, "exhibit", _
   "string", False, , False
DefineProperty _
   urlAppSchema, strNamespace, "specialneeds", _
   "string", False, , False
```

```
' Build an array of the custom properties
ReDim PropertyList(0 To 6)
PropertyList(0) = strNamespace & "animalid"
PropertyList(1) = strNamespace & "species"
PropertyList(2) = strNamespace & "commonname"
PropertyList(3) = strNamespace & "gender"
PropertyList(4) = strNamespace & "habitat"
PropertyList(5) = strNamespace & "exhibit"
PropertyList(6) = strNamespace & "specialneeds"

' Define the content class
DefineContentClass _
    urlAppSchema, _
    "zoomgt:content-classes:", _
    "animal", _
    Array("urn:content-classes:item"), _
    PropertyList

    Debug.Print "Application schema created successfully."

ExitHere:
    Set rec = Nothing
End Sub
```

CREATING THE SCHEMA FOLDER STRUCTURE

To create the schema folder structure, the code must first create the Zoo Management application schema folder. The ConfigureZooMgtApplication procedure calls the DefineSchemaFolder procedure and passes the URL for the Web Storage System on which the Zoo Management application is installed, the URL for the application schema folder to be created, and a True value to overwrite the folder if it already exists. The application schema folder is created.

```
' Configure the WSS application schema folder
DefineSchemaFolder urlWSS, urlAppSchema, True
```

Next the code calls the ConfigureFolders procedure and passes the URL for the Zoo Management application. Each subfolder, such as Animals, points to the new schema folder rather than the global schema on the Web Storage System.

```
' Configure the application folders
ConfigureFolders urlWSSApp
```

Defining the Custom Properties

The ConfigureZooMgtApplication procedure calls the DefineProperty procedure for each property that must be defined. The procedure passes several arguments: the URL for the application schema folder where the property is defined, the "Zoo:mgt:" namespace prefix, the name of the property being created, the data type, a Boolean value that indicates whether the property is multi-valued, a default value, and a Boolean value that indicates whether the property is indexed.

```
' Define the custom properties
DefineProperty _
  urlAppSchema, strNamespace, "animalid", "string", False, , True
DefineProperty _
  urlAppSchema, strNamespace, "species", "string", False, , True
DefineProperty _
  urlAppSchema, strNamespace, "commonname", "string", False, , True
DefineProperty _
  urlAppSchema, strNamespace, "gender", "boolean", False, , False
DefineProperty _
  urlAppSchema, strNamespace, "habitat", "string", False, , False
DefineProperty _
  urlAppSchema, strNamespace, "exhibit", "string", False, , False
DefineProperty _
  urlAppSchema, strNamespace, "specialneeds", "string", False, , False
```

DEFINING THE ANIMAL CONTENT CLASS

After you define the custom properties, you can define the animal content class. Before calling the DefineCustomClass procedure, the code builds an array that contains the qualified names for all the custom properties. After the array is complete, the ConfigureZooMgtApplication procedure calls the DefineCustomClass procedure and passes the URL for the application schema folder, the "zoomgt:content-classes" prefix, the friendly name of the animal class, an array of the content classes from which to inherit properties, and the array of custom properties.

```
' Build an array of the custom properties
ReDim PropertyList(0 To 6)
PropertyList(0) = strNamespace & "animalid"
PropertyList(1) = strNamespace & "species"
PropertyList(2) = strNamespace & "commonname"
PropertyList(3) = strNamespace & "gender"
PropertyList(4) = strNamespace & "habitat"
PropertyList(5) = strNamespace & "exhibit"
PropertyList(6) = strNamespace & "specialneeds"

' Define the content class
DefineContentClass _
  urlAppSchema, _
  "zoomgt:content-classes:", _
  "animal", _
  Array("urn:content-classes:item"), _
  PropertyList
```

CREATING AN INSTANCE OF THE ANIMAL CONTENT CLASS

After you have created the Zoo Management application schema, you can test out the new zoomgt:content-classes:animal content class by creating a new instance of the class. Listing 3.9 shows how to create a new instance of the class in the Animals subfolder of the Zoo Management application. To define a new instance of a custom class, you use the same approach as you do to define a new instance of a predefined content class. After a new item is created in the folder, the procedure sets the DAV:contentclass property to the zoomgt:content-classes:animal content class. The procedure then sets the various custom properties that were also defined in the application schema folder and saves those changes.

Although you can use Outlook Web Access to see the new instance of the animal class created in the Animals folder of the Zoo Management application, you will not be able to see the custom properties. You need to build a form to see those properties or use the Content Class Browser discussed earlier in this chapter to view the new item's properties and their values.

Listing 3.9   Create an instance of a custom content class.

```
Sub CreateAnimalInstance()
    ' Test out the schema defined in
    ' Sub ConfigureZooMgtApplication()
    ' by creating a new instance of the
    ' zoomgt:content-classes:animal
    ' content class.

    Dim strURL As String

    ' Build the URL to the new instance
    strURL = GetStorageName & _
        "/Applications/Zoo Management/Animals/Super rooster.EML"

    ' If you are using VBScript, use this With:
    ' With CreateObject("ADODB.Record")
    With New ADODB.Record
        ' Create the new animal record
        .Open strURL, , , adCreateOverwrite
```

```
' Set the custom properties
    .Fields("DAV:contentclass") = "zoomgt:content-classes:animal"
    .Fields("zoomgt:animalid") = "suproos1"
    .Fields("zoomgt:species") = "Divine Roostrus"
    .Fields("zoomgt:commonname") = "Super Rooster"
    .Fields("zoomgt:gender") = 0 'male
    .Fields("zoomgt:habitat") = "Tropics"
    .Fields("zoomgt:exhibit") = "Habitat 1"
    .Fields("zoomgt:specialneeds") = "Lots of exercise"

    ' Save the changes
    .Fields.Update
    .Close
End With

Debug.Print "Instance created."
End Sub
```

RETURNING APPLICATION SCHEMA INFORMATION

Sometimes it's helpful to know what content classes and what properties are already defined in an application schema. This section explains how you can return information on a custom application schema by querying the schema folder.

Using SQL, you can build SELECT statements that retrieve the property definition and content class definition objects as well as their related properties. Listing 3.10 shows how to return the schema information for an application. When you call the procedure, pass a URL for the application schema folder that you want to explore. For example, to read the schema for the Zoo Management Web Storage System application in the MAPI public folder tree, you would call the procedure like this:

```
ReadSchemaFolder _
    "file://./backofficestorage/domain.com/" & _
    "public folders/zoo management/schema/"
```

The procedure takes that URL and uses it to build two SELECT statements. The first statement queries the folder for the names of all content class definitions. After the information is reported, the second SELECT statement queries the folder for information on all property definitions, including the property name, data type, index information, and default values.

Listing 3.10 Return the schema information in an application schema folder.

```
Sub ReadSchemaFolder(ByVal urlSchemaFld As String)
    ' Returns information on a custom schema
    ' for an application including:
    ' Content classes and their custom properties;
    ' Custom properties and the meta-data
    ' on those properties.

    Dim cnn As ADODB.Connection
    Dim rst As ADODB.Recordset
    Dim strSQL As String
    Dim v As Variant

    ' Select only content class definitions
    strSQL = _
        "SELECT " & _
        AddQuotes("urn:schemas-microsoft-com:xml-data#name") & ", " & _
        AddQuotes("urn:schemas-microsoft-com:xml-data#element")
    strSQL = strSQL & _
        " FROM scope('shallow traversal of " & AddQuotes(urlSchemaFld) _
        & "')"
    strSQL = strSQL & _
        " WHERE " & AddQuotes("DAV:contentclass") & _
        " = 'urn:content-classes:contentclassdef'"

    ' Open the connection
    Set cnn = New ADODB.Connection
    With cnn
        .Provider = "exoledb.datasource"
        .Open urlSchemaFld
    End With

    ' Open Recordset based on the SQL string
    Set rst = New ADODB.Recordset
    rst.Open strSQL, cnn

    Debug.Print "----------------------------------------------------"
    Debug.Print "Application Schema Definition"
    Debug.Print urlSchemaFld
    Debug.Print "----------------------------------------------------"
```

```vb
Debug.Print ""
Debug.Print "Content classes:"

' Return the name of the class
Do Until rst.EOF
    Debug.Print rst.Fields("urn:schemas-microsoft-com:xml-data#name")
    For Each v In _
        rst.Fields("urn:schemas-microsoft-com:xml-data#element").Value
            Debug.Print vbTab, v
    Next
    rst.MoveNext
Loop

' Select only property definitions
strSQL = _
    "SELECT " & _
    AddQuotes("urn:schemas-microsoft-com:xml-data#name") _
    & ", " & _
    AddQuotes("urn:schemas-microsoft-com:datatypes#type") _
    & ", " & _
    AddQuotes("urn:schemas-microsoft-com:exch-data:ismultivalued") _
    & ", " & _
    AddQuotes("urn:schemas-microsoft-com:exch-data:defaultvalue") _
    & ", " & _
    AddQuotes("urn:schemas-microsoft-com:exch-data:isindexed")
strSQL = strSQL & _
    " FROM scope('shallow traversal of " & AddQuotes(urlSchemaFld) _
    & "')"
strSQL = strSQL & _
    " WHERE " & AddQuotes("DAV:contentclass") & _
    " = 'urn:content-classes:propertydef'"

' Open Recordset based on the SQL string
Set rst = New ADODB.Recordset
rst.Open strSQL, cnn

Debug.Print ""
Debug.Print "Properties:"

' Return the property information
Do Until rst.EOF
```

```
    Debug.Print rst.Fields("urn:schemas-microsoft-com:xml-data#name")
    Debug.Print vbTab, "Data type: ", _
        rst.Fields("urn:schemas-microsoft-com:datatypes#type")
    Debug.Print vbTab, "Multivalued: ", _
        rst.Fields("urn:schemas-microsoft-com:exch-data:ismultivalued")
    Debug.Print vbTab, "Default value: ", _
        rst.Fields("urn:schemas-microsoft-com:exch-data:defaultvalue")
    Debug.Print vbTab, "Indexed: ", _
        rst.Fields("urn:schemas-microsoft-com:exch-data:isindexed")
    rst.MoveNext
Loop

' Close the ADO objects
rst.Close
cnn.Close

' Clean up
Set rst = Nothing
Set cnn = Nothing
End Sub
```

Summary

No matter how good you already are at writing ADO or CDO code, you will write better code if you understand the Web Storage System schema. The schema is the underlying data definition of Exchange that consists of a large number of predefined properties. By drawing on these properties, Exchange provides many content classes for creating objects. You can extend this base set of properties and content classes with your own and can even define an entire schema to be used with a particular application. This flexibility and extensibility means that you can build applications to meet your business needs in the way that makes the most sense to you.

In Chapter 4, "ActiveX Data Objects and Exchange," you apply your knowledge of the Web Storage System schema to use ADO to interact with folders and items in the Web Storage System.

4

ActiveX Data Objects and Exchange

Earlier versions of Microsoft Exchange offered developers limited data access. Although you could store almost any type of data in Exchange Server 5.5, you were limited when it came to accessing that data programmatically. With the release of Exchange 2000 Server, this has changed. Exchange is still an excellent choice for mass data storage, and now it includes a powerful and efficient data access story. By using Microsoft ActiveX Data Objects (ADO) 2.5 and the Exchange OLE DB (ExOLEDB) provider, you can interact with data stored in a Microsoft Web Storage System as easily as you interact with data stored in Microsoft Access or Microsoft SQL Server. You can create, edit, and delete resources. You can copy and move resources, and you can execute Structured Query Language (SQL) queries. You can even stream the contents of a folder directly to an Extensible Markup Language (XML) document.

This chapter teaches you how to use ADO to access and explore the Web Storage System. Sections include:

- **Overview of ActiveX Data Objects 2.5 and Exchange**

- **Connecting to a Web Storage System**

- **Using the Record Object**

- **Using the Recordset Object**

- **Querying a Web Storage System by Using SQL SELECT Statements**

- **Doing More Using ADO**

- **Using ADO with Microsoft Internet Publishing Provider**

OVERVIEW OF ACTIVEX DATA OBJECTS 2.5 AND EXCHANGE

ActiveX Data Objects 2.5 is the scriptable interface to OLE DB and is used to access and interact with any data store that has an OLE DB provider. ADO is installed automatically with Microsoft Windows 2000 and supports all languages that support Component Object Model (COM) objects, including Visual Basic, Microsoft Visual Basic Scripting Edition (VBScript), and Microsoft Visual C++. This makes ADO the optimal data access interface. Earlier versions of ADO have been used for years to access data stores such as Access and SQL Server. Today, ADO 2.5 can be used to access Web Storage Systems through the ExOLEDB provider.

This section introduces the ADO 2.5 object model and the ExOLEDB provider and then explains the relationship between Records and Recordsets and how security works in ADO.

ADO 2.5 OBJECT MODEL

The ADO 2.5 object model is simple in design and has only a few objects. Figure 4.1 shows the ADO 2.5 object model. The objects and collections in the object model include:

- **Connection**. The Connection object represents the communication link with the server—in this case, Exchange. You can open a connection explicitly, after you indicate a provider and a connection string, or implicitly, by opening a record (or recordset) directly.

- **Command**. The Command object defines a specific command to execute against the data source, usually a SQL statement. A Command object can also work in conjunction with a collection of Parameter objects to execute parameter queries.

- **Recordset**. A Recordset object is a collection of data consisting of records of data. A recordset can be a collection of items in a folder or a collection of folders. A Recordset does not need to have multiple records; it can contain a single folder or item.

- **Record**. A Record object represents a single resource, such as an e-mail item in an Inbox, a post in a Web Storage System folder, or even a single folder.

- **Errors**. The Errors collection contains individual objects that represent the provider errors generated while connecting or connected to a data source.

- **Stream**. The Stream object represents a stream of binary data or text. By using the Stream object, you can create, manage, and read items and files in streams of bits of data rather than in one large chunk.

- **Parameters**. The Parameters collection contains individual arguments or criteria passed to a Command object that is executing a parameter query.

- **Fields**. The Fields collection is made up of schema properties for a resource. For example, a Record object has a Fields collection that holds all the schema properties used to define that resource.

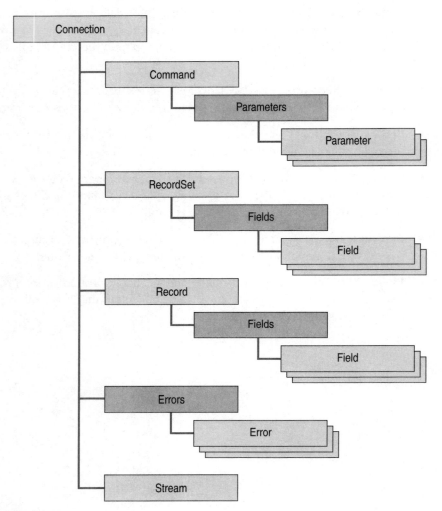

Figure 4.1
The ADO 2.5 object model

EXCHANGE OLE DB PROVIDER

When you write code to access Web Storage System data, you are interacting with the Exchange OLE DB (ExOLEDB) provider. ExOLEDB is the new, high-performance OLE DB provider for accessing Web Storage System resources using ADO 2.5 and Collaboration Data Objects (CDO) for Exchange. ExOLEDB is installed with Exchange 2000 Server and is a server-side-only component, which means that any code that uses ExOLEDB must also reside on the server. Figure 4.2 shows the relationship among ADO, the ExOLEDB provider, and Exchange.

So what can you build with ExOLEDB if it can only reside on the server? Even though your code must reside on the server, you are not severely limited in what you can build. You can build Web applications that use Active Server Pages (ASP) technology. You can wrap functionality into COM components, such as ActiveX DLLs and executable files (.exe files) that are built with Visual Basic or Visual C++. You also use ExOLEDB when building event sinks and workflow event sinks.

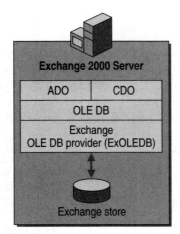

Figure 4.2
The relationship of ADO 2.5 to ExOLEDB

NOTE ADO exposes a variety of properties and methods through the ADO objects. However, it is up to the OLE DB provider to support the properties and methods. Although ExOLEDB supports most of the ADO object model functionality, it does not support certain features, including impersonation via the UserName and Password parameters available on many ADO methods, cursor type selection, record locking options, and nested transactions.

UNDERSTANDING THE RELATIONSHIP BETWEEN RECORDS AND RECORDSETS

You use ADO Record objects and ADO Recordset objects to navigate a Web Storage System and access the data stored there. You can use a Record object to open an item such as a message or contact, and a Recordset object to return a collection of folders or items. Sometimes the Record object and Recordset object are used together to accomplish a task, such as when you access the contents of a folder. This section steps through an example and demonstrates how to use ADO to navigate the contents of an Inbox.

Figure 4.3 shows the relationship between Exchange objects and ADO objects in a hypothetical mailbox. At the top of the figure is an object that represents a mailbox. To use ADO to access the mailbox, you open an ADO Record object and pass the URL for the mailbox. After the Record is open, you can get information about that mailbox. If you want to return the contents, you use a Recordset object. By calling the GetChildren method of the ADO Record object representing the mailbox, you populate a Recordset with the contents of the folder. In this example, calling GetChildren from a mailbox returns a Recordset containing the standard folders generated whenever a mailbox is created, such as Inbox, Contacts, Calendar, and Sent Items. You can enumerate through the collection and read information about each folder.

To navigate to another child folder, such as the Inbox, you again use a combination of the Record object and Recordset object. After you open a Record object on the Inbox, call the GetChildren method, and the contents of the Inbox are returned as a Recordset. The resulting Recordset contains not only the messages in the Inbox but also any subfolders. Recordsets are not homogeneous but instead can contain items of multiple types, such as folders, items, Web files, and Office documents.

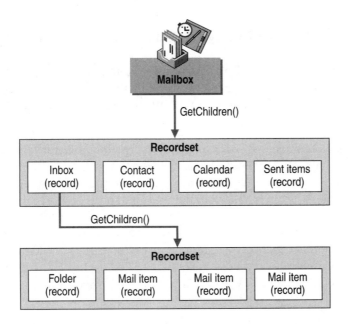

Figure 4.3
ADO Record and Recordset objects represent every piece of data in a Web Storage System.

UNDERSTANDING SECURITY IN ADO

When ADO 2.5 is used with the ExOLEDB provider, all code is run in the ExOLEDB security context, regardless of what user might be running the code. This means that an assistant and an executive could have the same permissions to access and manipulate resources in a Web Storage System. From a security standpoint, this is not the best scenario.

ExOLEDB does not support the IAuthentication interface, so a user cannot impersonate another user in your code and force a different security context. You define a security context with Visual Basic and VBScript by wrapping your ADO 2.5 code into a COM application. You can then use COM+ security roles to allow a group of users to run the code under a particular security context. For more information about COM+ roles, see Chapter 14, "Setting Security and Permissions."

CONNECTING TO A WEB STORAGE SYSTEM

To interact with the data in a Web Storage System, you must first establish a connection by using the ADO Connection object. A single Connection object corresponds to a single connection to ExOLEDB. Once a connection is established, you can access the data in a Web Storage System.

You can establish a connection either explicitly by creating a Connection object or implicitly with the root. When Exchange is installed, it registers ExOLEDB with the OLE DB 2.5 root binder for the File URL namespace on the local server. The root binder is part of the Windows 2000 operating system and is responsible for binding a resource at a URL with an ADO object. The root binder eliminates the need for you to explicitly open a Connection object when accessing resources through OLE DB/ADO. Both approaches, however, require a well-constructed URL to successfully get resources or create new resources. This section explains how to build URLs for ExOLEDB and how to use a Connection object.

BUILDING URLs FOR ExOLEDB

A URL defines the location of a resource in a Web Storage System. Nearly everything in Exchange is accessible with a URL, and nearly everything you do with data is dependent on a URL. You need a URL to create new resources and open existing resources. You also use a URL to copy, move, and delete resources.

Chapter 2, "Exchange and the Web Storage System," explained how to build URLs that use the HTTP/WebDAV protocol to access resources in a Web Storage System. When ExOLEDB is installed with Exchange 2000, Exchange registers the provider for the File:// URL namespace. This registration means that the URLs you build to access a Web Storage System via ExOLEDB also use the File:// namespace. An ExOLEDB URL has the following syntax:

```
File://./backofficestorage/<Domain DNS name>/<path to a resource>
```

In addition to the File:// URL namespace, Exchange also registers for the namespace backofficestorage. The first portion, File://./backofficestorage, of the base ExOLEDB URL is the same for any server on which the code is run. This portion simply identifies the Exchange storage. The <Domain DNS Name> portion identifies the domain in which the code is running. Unlike the HTTP/WebDAV protocol, which uses the name of the Exchange server, the File URL protocol uses the domain name. The following URL shows how to use ExOLEDB to access a Web Storage System on domain.com:

```
file://./backofficestorage/domain.com/
```

The <path to a resource> portion of the URL varies depending on the store in which the resource resides. The complete URL to a resource is stored in the DAV:href schema property of each resource.

The URLs shown in this section and throughout most of this book are absolute URLs. An *absolute URL* is a URL that has all the information necessary to locate a resource in a Web Storage System. With ExOLEDB you can also use relative URLs. A *relative URL* contains only a partial address and uses an absolute URL as a reference point for navigating in a hierarchy.

Note   You can use HTTP with ExOLEDB; however, code that uses HTTP by default uses Microsoft Internet Publishing Provider. To use HTTP URLs with ExOLEDB, you must explicitly set the provider to be ExOLEDB.

ACCESSING PUBLIC WEB STORAGE SYSTEM FOLDERS

To access a public Web Storage System folder, append the name of a Web Storage System folder tree to the base URL and provide the rest of the folder path, separating each level in the folder hierarchy with a forward slash (/). Folder names are not case sensitive, so you can use any combination of uppercase and lowercase without affecting the connection.

To access a folder on the MAPI public folders tree, you use the folder tree name Public Folders and append the folder path. For example, you would use the following URL to access Internet Newsgroups on the MAPI folder tree on domain.com:

```
File://./backofficestorage/
    domain.com/public folders/Internet Newsgroups/
```

To access a non-MAPI folder tree, replace the text "public folders" with the folder tree name of a Web Storage System. For example, you would use the following URL to access the Zoo Management application folder on the Applications folder tree in domain.com:

```
File://./backofficestorage/domain.com/applications/zoo management/
```

The trailing slash is not necessary to access a folder. When used in code, however, it helps you discern between a URL that points to a folder and a URL that points to an item.

ACCESSING MAILBOXES

To access the mailbox of a particular user, you extend the base URL with the suffix /MBX/alias/. MBX is a constant that indicates that you want to access a mailbox, and the alias is the user's Exchange alias. For example, the URL pointing to the mailbox of the user Mindy would look like this:

```
file://./backofficestorage/domain.com/mbx/mindy/
```

To access the standard folders in a mailbox, you use URLs like those that follow, substituting your own Domain Name System (DNS) domain name and e-mail alias:

- `file://./backofficestorage/domain.com/mbx/mindy/Tasks/`
- `file://./backofficestorage/domain.com/mbx/mindy/Notes/`
- `file://./backofficestorage/domain.com/mbx/mindy/Journal/`
- `file://./backofficestorage/domain.com/mbx/mindy/Drafts/`
- `file://./backofficestorage/domain.com/mbx/mindy/Contacts/`
- `file://./backofficestorage/domain.com/mbx/mindy/Calendar/`
- `file://./backofficestorage/domain.com/mbx/mindy/Sent Items/`
- `file://./backofficestorage/domain.com/mbx/mindy/Deleted Items/`
- `file://./backofficestorage/domain.com/mbx/mindy/Outbox/`
- `file://./backofficestorage/domain.com/mbx/mindy/Inbox/`

ExOLEDB URLs are specific to entire domains, not to individual Exchange databases; this means you don't have to concern yourself with the physical location of the data. This is particularly significant when creating URLs for private mailbox stores. No matter where a mailbox physically resides, the URL is always constructed in the same way, even if the mailbox is eventually moved from one server to another.

ACCESSING ITEMS

You can build a URL that points directly to an item in a folder without accessing the folder first. To build a URL pointing to an item, you append the base URL with the appropriate store information (folder tree or mailbox), folder path, and the DAV:displayname schema property value. The following URL accesses the first mailbox item with a DAV:displayname value of "Hello.eml" from the Inbox:

```
file://./backofficestorage/domain.com/mbx/mindy/inbox/hello.eml
```

> **NOTE**   If there is more than one item with the same subject in the folder, any additional instances must be identified by appending a number to the subject to indicate which instance you want to return. For more information, see Chapter 2, "Exchange and the Web Storage System."

To access an item other than a Multipurpose Internet Mail Extensions (MIME) message, such as a Microsoft Word document or Microsoft Excel spreadsheet, use the standard file extension (.doc or .xls). The following URL accesses a Word document stored in a public folder:

```
file://./backofficestorage/domain.com/public folders/mindy/cdo final.doc
```

You can also use an ADO Stream object to get a structured document as bytes of information, as explained in "Streaming Contents," later in this chapter.

USING A CONNECTION OBJECT

Although it's definitely easier to let the URL provide all the information necessary to establish a connection with ExOLEDB, you may want to explicitly open a Connection object. By opening a Connection object, you can:

- Use relative URLs to access resources in a folder hierarchy in relation to the current connection point.

- Use a transaction to conduct a mass of changes to a Web Storage System all at once.

- Use the Errors collection to trap ADO-provider errors as they occur and to recover gracefully without stopping the program.

To use SQL to search or query a Web Storage System, you must open a Connection object. For more about querying a Web Storage System, see "Querying a Web Storage System by Using SQL SELECT Statements" later in this chapter.

OPENING AND CLOSING A CONNECTION

To open a connection, you must provide the name of the OLE DB provider to use and the URL for the point in the Web Storage System to which you are connecting. To connect to a Web Storage System, set the Connection.Provider property to the ExOLEDB provider, ExOLEDB.datasource. Next, call the Connection.Open method and pass the URL for the appropriate store as a string argument. After you finish with the connection, close each connection by calling the Close method of the Connection object.

Listing 4.1 shows how to create an ADO Connection object, set the Provider property, and open the connection. The code then returns some information about the current connection and closes the Connection object before exiting.

> **NOTE** The code listings shown in this chapter are available in the Microsoft Visual Basic project CH_04.vbp on the companion CD. If you want to run the samples as they are written, you must have the Zoo Management sample installed on your Exchange 2000 Server. For information about installing the application, see the introduction to the book. In addition, the code samples repeatedly call a function named GetStorageName. This function returns the name of the domain in which the code is running. For more information about the GetStorageName function, see Chapter 8, "Interacting with Active Directory."

Listing 4.1   Connect to a Web Storage System folder.

```
Sub ConnectToWSSFolder()
    ' By explicitly opening a connection,
    ' you can use relative URLs, use single
    ' transactions, and trap OLE DB errors.

    Dim cnn As ADODB.Connection
    Dim strURL As String
```

```
    ' File URL to the Zoo Management application
    strURL = GetStorageName & _
        "applications/zoo management/"

    Set cnn = New ADODB.Connection
    With cnn
        ' Indicate the EXOLEDB provider
        .Provider = "exoledb.datasource"
        ' Open the connection
        .Open strURL

        ' Return some information about
        ' the connection.
        Debug.Print "-------------------------------------"
        Debug.Print _
            "Current Connection Information"
        Debug.Print _
            "Command Timeout: " & .CommandTimeout
        Debug.Print _
            "Connection Timeout: " & .ConnectionTimeout
        Debug.Print "-------------------------------------"

        ' Close the connection
        .Close
    End With

    ' Clean up
    Set cnn = Nothing
End Sub
```

USING RELATIVE URLs

When you explicitly establish a connection with Exchange, you can use relative
URLs. If you develop Web applications, you are already familiar with relative URLs.
A relative URL locates a resource relative to some starting point defined by an
absolute URL. For example, you could connect to a folder with this absolute URL:

```
File://./backofficestorage/domain.com/applications/zoo management/
```

You can then use a relative URL to access a child folder or item in that folder. To navigate down the tree from this point, you build the relative URL beginning with a dot and a forward slash (./) and append the remainder of the path to the resource. For example, to access the Staff child folder in the Zoo Management application, you use a relative URL like this:

```
./Staff/
```

You can also use relative URLs to move up the folder tree. To build a relative URL for navigating up the tree, begin the URL with two dots and a forward slash (../) and append the remainder of the path to the resource. If you are only moving up the tree one level, you do not need to append the path to the resource. For example, to navigate up one level from the Zoo Management application, you use a relative URL like this:

```
../
```

Listing 4.2 shows how to use relative URLs with ADO. After the procedure connects to the Zoo Management application with an absolute URL, it accesses a child folder and then accesses the parent container.

Listing 4.2   Access the parent and child folders from the connection folder.

```
Sub UseRelativeURLs()
    ' By explicitly opening a connection to
    ' EXOLEDB, you can use relative URLs to
    ' navigate to parent and child folders
    ' from the point of connection.

    Dim cnn As ADODB.Connection
    Dim strURL As String
    Dim rec As ADODB.Record

    ' File URL to the Zoo Management application
    strURL = GetStorageName & _
        "applications/zoo management/"

    Set cnn = New ADODB.Connection
    With cnn
        ' Indicate the EXOLEDB provider
        .Provider = "exoledb.datasource"
```

```
        ' Connect to the Zoo Management
        ' application folder
        .Open strURL
    End With

    Set rec = New ADODB.Record
    With rec
        ' Access the Staff child folder of
        ' the Zoo Management folder.
        .Open "./Staff/", cnn
        Debug.Print .Fields("DAV:href")
        .Close

        ' Now access the parent folder of
        ' the Zoo Management folder.
        .Open "../", cnn
        Debug.Print .Fields("DAV:href")
        .Close
    End With

    ' Clean up
    cnn.Close
    Set rec = Nothing
    Set cnn = Nothing
End Sub
```

USING TRANSACTIONS

When you use ADO to make changes to a resource, the changes are propagated back to the Web Storage System as soon as you save the record. Every time a record is created, changed, or deleted, the change is sent back to the store on a per-record basis. This per-record update is acceptable when only a few records are being updated at a time. However, if you are updating a large number of records at one time, this is not optimal and can be very costly in terms of server resources. In such cases, you can use a transaction to create all updates at one time. A *transaction* is an environment in which database calls are cached and then executed at the same time. Either all the updates are successful, or the entire transaction is canceled.

To manage a transaction, you use the BeginTrans, CommitTrans, and RollbackTrans methods of a Connection object. To begin a transaction, open a Connection object and call the BeginTrans method. Changes that are made after you call this method are no longer immediately committed to the store. To save changes made during the transaction and to end the transaction, call the CommitTrans method. To cancel changes made during the transaction and to end the transaction, call the RollbackTrans method. Listing 4.3 shows the transactions template.

NOTE Exchange 2000 does not support nested transactions. You must complete one transaction before beginning another.

Listing 4.3 Transactions template

```
Sub TransactionsTemplate()

    ' Turn on error handling
    On Error GoTo HandleErrors

    Dim cnn As ADODB.Connection
    Dim strURL As String

    ' File URL to the Zoo Management application
    strURL = GetStorageName & _
        "applications/zoo management/"

    Set cnn = New ADODB.Connection
    With cnn
        .Provider = "exoledb.datasource"
        .Open strURL
    End With

    ' Start caching changes
    cnn.BeginTrans
```

```
    '
    ' Make your record changes here
    '


    ' Save the changes to the store
    cnn.CommitTrans

ExitHere:
    On Error Resume Next
    cnn.Close
    Set cnn = Nothing
    Exit Sub

HandleErrors:

    ' Cancel the changes
    cnn.RollbackTrans


    Resume ExitHere
End Sub
```

HANDLING ERRORS

As with any application, errors can occur during an ADO operation. To complicate matters, a single ADO error can generate multiple provider errors. It's these provider errors—not the actual ADO error—that are stored as Error objects in the Errors collection of the Connection object. By creating a mechanism to trap ADO errors and then looping through the resulting Errors collection, you can use the properties of the Error object to determine the cause of the ADO error and then take the appropriate action to recover. The most frequently used properties are listed in Table 4.1.

Table 4.1 Frequently used Error object properties

Property	Data type	Description
Description	String	A string-based description of the error.
Number	Long	A long integer; the number associated with that error.
Source	Object	The object that triggered the error.

The Errors collection maintains a set of errors until the next successful ADO operation, which clears out the Errors collection. That is, if you perform an ADO action that fills the Errors collection and then you perform an action that succeeds, the original set of errors is lost. To manually flush the Errors collection, call the Clear method. Listing 4.4 shows how to use the Errors collection.

Listing 4.4 Use the Errors collection to trap errors generated during ADO calls.

```
Sub TestErrors()
    ' This procedure forces ADO errors to be
    ' generated and then processes each one
    ' with an error handler.

    ' Turn on error handling
    On Error GoTo HandleErrors

    Dim strURL As String
    Dim cnn As ADODB.Connection

    ' This is a bogus URL
    strURL = GetStorageName() & "mbx/administrator"

    Set cnn = New Connection
    With cnn
        .Provider = "exoledb.datasource"
        ' This line of code will trigger an error
        .Open strURL
    End With
```

```
ExitHere:
    On Error Resume Next
    cnn.Close
    Set cnn = Nothing
    Exit Sub

HandleErrors:
    Dim objErr As ADODB.Error
    Dim strError As String

    ' Loop through all of the errors
    For Each objErr In cnn.Errors
        ' Get the error number, description, and source
        strError = _
        strError & "ADO error #" & _
        objErr.Number & ": " & _
        objErr.Description & vbCrLf & _
        "Triggered by: " & _
        objErr.Source & vbCrLf
    Next

    ' Display the errors in a message box
    MsgBox strError
    Resume ExitHere
End Sub
```

USING THE RECORD OBJECT

The ADO Record object represents a resource in a Web Storage System such as a
folder, an item in a folder, or an actual file. Records fall into two categories:
collection records and non-collection records. A *collection record* is a folder that
can contain child resources. A *non-collection record* is an individual item in a
folder, a structured document, or a text file. Non-collection records do not have
child resources. You use Record objects to create new resources in a Web Storage
System or edit existing resources. This section explains how to use the Open
method, open a resource, enumerate properties, save a record, create a resource,
and append a custom property to a resource.

Using the Open Method

You use the Open method to open a Web Storage System resource as a Record object. You also use the Open method to create new resources such as folders and items. The syntax for the Open method is:

```
record.Open [Source][, ActiveConnection][, Mode][, CreateOptions]
    [, Options][, UserName][, Password]
```

Where:

record

is an ADO Record object.

Source

is the URL for the resource to be opened.

ActiveConnection

is an optional parameter that indicates the connection through which the record is to be opened.

Mode

is an optional enumeration that indicates how the resource should be opened: read-only, read/write, with share access, without share access, and so on. The Mode parameter is discussed in more detail in "Understanding the Mode Parameter" later in this section.

CreateOptions

is an optional enumeration that indicates if a new resource is created. The CreateOptions parameter is discussed in more detail in "Understanding the CreateOptions Parameter" later in this section.

Options

is an optional enumeration that specifies additional options for opening a record: open the entity asynchronously or without an associated stream object. ExOLEDB only supports adOpenAsync.

UserName

> is an optional parameter that specifies a user ID to use to access a Web Storage System. This parameter is disabled for the ExOLEDB provider.

Password

> is an optional parameter that specifies the password associated with the preceding user ID. This parameter is disabled for the ExOLEDB provider.

UNDERSTANDING THE MODE PARAMETER

The Mode parameter uses the ConnectModeEnum enumeration and can be set to any of the constants, or combination of constants, listed in Table 4.2. If no value is specified for the Mode parameter, the default value is adModeRead.

Table 4.2 Mode parameter enumerations

Constant	Value	Description
adModeUnknown	0	Unknown status.
adModeRead	1	Client can read the existing values but cannot write changes to the record.
adModeWrite	2	Client can write changes to the record but cannot read existing values.
adModeReadWrite	3	Client can read all the values and write changes to the record.
adModeShareDenyRead	4	Other users cannot read the record while it is open.
adModeShareDenyWrite	8	Other users cannot write changes to the record while it is open.
adModeShareExclusive	12	Other users cannot access the record while it is open.
adModeShareDenyNone	16	Other users can read and write to the record while it is open.
adModeRecursive	4194304	Client has access to all child records of the current record.

UNDERSTANDING THE CREATEOPTIONS PARAMETER

The CreateOptions parameter determines how ADO opens the record and whether or not it creates a new record. The CreateOptions parameter can be set to one or more of the constants listed in Table 4.3. Combine constants by using the Or operator or a PLUS SIGN (+).

Table 4.3   CreateOptions parameter enumerations

Constant	Value	Used for	Description
adFailIfNotExists	-1	Existing	Open fails if the URL is not valid. This is the default.
adOpenIfExists	33554432	Existing, new	Record is opened only if the resource exists. No error is generated.
adCreateNonCollection	0	New	Creates an item such as an e-mail message or appointment.
adCreateCollection	8192	New	Creates a folder.
adCreateOverwrite	67108864	New	If a resource already exists for the given URL, it is deleted and the new information is saved to that same URL.

Some of the ways to use the CreateOptions parameter are:

- To open an item or folder, leave the CreateOptions parameter empty. If the resource specified by the URL does not exist, the code fails with a trappable error.

- To create a folder, set CreateOptions to adCreateCollection enumeration.

- To create an item, set CreateOptions to adCreateNonCollection or leave the parameter empty.

- To overwrite an existing folder or item with new information, set CreateOptions to adCreateCollection + adCreateOverwrite for a folder andadCreateNonCollection + adCreateOverwrite for an item.

- To open a folder or item if it exists or create it if it doesn't exist, use adCreateCollection + adOpenIfExists for a folder and adCreateNonCollection + adOpenIfExists for an item.

OPENING A RESOURCE

You use the Open method of a Record object to open a single resource such as one folder or one item. To open a resource in read-only mode, you need to pass only the URL for the resource you are opening. If you are planning to make changes to the record, you must open it with read/write privileges. To open a folder or item for editing, pass the constant adModeReadWrite to the Mode argument of the Record.Open method:

```
rec.Open urlResource, , adModeReadWrite
```

Listing 4.5 shows how to open an Exchange item in read-only mode, return some information on the item, and return some information on the ADO Record representing the item.

Listing 4.5 Open a resource in a Web Storage System in read-only mode.

```
Sub OpenItem()
    ' Open an item in a Web Storage System
    ' and return the content class.

    Dim urlResource As String

    ' URL to an item in the Zoo Management application
    urlResource = GetStorageName() & _
    "applications/Zoo Management/Announcements/Welcome.eml"
```

```
        With New ADODB.Record
            ' Open the item read-only
            .Open urlResource

            ' Some info on the Exchange item
            Debug.Print .Fields("DAV:displayname")
            Debug.Print .Fields("DAV:contentclass")
            Debug.Print .Fields("DAV:href")

            ' Some info on the ADO Record
            Debug.Print .RecordType
            Debug.Print .State
            Debug.Print .ParentURL

            ' Close the object
            .Close
        End With
    End Sub
```

ENUMERATING PROPERTIES

After you open a resource by using a Record object, you can read and set all the properties saved with it. You access the schema properties associated with a resource through the ADO Fields collection. You can use the Fields collection to read a property, set a property, and get more details about a resource by enumerating through the entire Fields collection.

The Fields collection consists of individual ADO Field objects. A single Field object represents one schema property. Schema properties can be single-valued or multi-valued. A *single-valued property* is the most common property type and can hold only one value at a time. A *multi-valued property* is less common than a single-valued property and can hold multiple values, called an array of values, at the same time.

To enumerate through all the properties (single-valued and multi-valued) in the Fields collection of a Record, you use a For..Next loop. The For..Next loop references each object in a collection, which means that you can investigate each object individually. In the case of the Fields collection of a Record object, the For..Next loop accesses each property associated with the resource. You then return the name of the schema property with the Name property of a Field object.

For example, the following code sample loops through the Fields collection for a Record and evaluates each property type by using the IsArray function and passing the value of the property. The IsArray function returns True if the property is a multi-valued property. If the property is single-valued, the property name and the literal "[SINGLE-VALUED]" are returned. If the property is multi-valued, the property name and the literal "[MULTI-VALUED]" are returned.

```
For Each fd In rec.Fields
  If Not IsArray(fd.Value) Then
    Debug.Print fd.Name, "[SINGLE-VALUED]"
  Else
    Debug.Print fd.Name, "[MULTI-VALUED]"
  End If
Next fd
```

Because a Web Storage System is not a structured database, each resource may have a different set of properties associated with it. Therefore, the Fields collection for one record may not match the Fields collection of another record.

READING SINGLE-VALUED PROPERTIES

To return and set the value for a schema property, you use the Value property of a Field object. To read and set single-valued properties, you don't have to call the Value property explicitly because the Value property is the default property of the Field object. This means that if you don't specify a property of a Field object, the Value property is returned or set by default. However, when you read multi-valued properties, you must explicitly call the Value property (see "Reading Multi-Valued Properties" later in this section). To ensure consistency between the two property types, it is recommended that you always call the Value Property. For example, the previous code sample has been modified here to return the value of a single-valued property in addition to the property name:

```
For Each fd In rec.Fields
  If Not IsArray(fd.Value) Then
    Debug.Print fd.Name, fd.Value
  Else
    Debug.Print fd.Name, "[MULTI-VALUED]"
  End If
Next fd
```

READING MULTI-VALUED PROPERTIES

You can read single-valued properties by calling the Value property of a Field object. However, you cannot access the values in a multi-valued property in the same direct way. One way to get each value is to use a For Each..Next loop to enumerate each value in the array. For example, the following code sample loops through each value in the urn:schemas-microsoft-com:xml-data#element multi-valued schema property:

```
For Each v In
    rec.Fields("urn:schemas-microsoft-com:xml-data#element").Value
    Debug.Print v
Next v
```

If you add this code to the previous sample that enumerates the properties in a Record, the code looks like this:

```
For Each fd In rec.Fields
  If Not IsArray(fd.Value) Then
    Debug.Print fd.Name, fd.Value
  Else
    Debug.Print fd.Name, "[MULTI-VALUED]"
    For Each v In fd.Value
        Debug.Print vbTab, v
    Next v
  End If
Next fd
```

SAVING A RECORD

If you make changes to an open Record object by using the Fields collection, you must explicitly save those changes. When you open a resource for editing, you are not creating a link directly to that resource. Instead, the property values are copied from a Web Storage System to the instance of the ADO object. Any changes that you make to the object are made only to the local copy. To save those changes back to a Web Storage System, you must call the Fields.Update method for the ADO object that has changed. If you do not call the Fields.Update method, no errors are generated, but the changes are not saved and the properties revert to the values they contained when the Record was opened.

When you create a new resource in a Web Storage System by using a Record object, you do not need to call the Fields.Update method to commit the resource. However, if you make any changes by using the Fields collection, you will need to call the Fields.Update method to save the changes.

NOTE To refresh the ADO object with the latest copy of a Web Storage System resource's properties, you can call the Resync method.

CREATING A RESOURCE

To create a new resource in a Web Storage System, you use the Open method and pass the appropriate CreateOptions argument to indicate whether you are creating a folder or an item and how it should be created. If you are going to make any changes immediately by using the Fields collection of the new resource, you must open a Record with read/write privileges by passing adModeReadWrite as the Mode argument.

Here are some ways to create new resources by using the ADO Record.Open method:

- To create a folder:

```
rec.Open urlResource _
    , _
    , adModeReadWrite _
    , adCreateCollection
```

- To create an item:

```
rec.Open urlResource _
    , _
    , adModeReadWrite _
    , adCreateNonCollection
```

- To overwrite an existing item with the new information:

```
rec.Open urlResource _
    , _
    , adModeReadWrite _
    , adCreateNonCollection + adCreateOverwrite
```

- To open a folder if it exists or create a folder if it doesn't exist:

```
rec.Open urlResource _

    , _
    , adModeReadWrite _
    , adCreateCollection + adOpenIfExists
```

CREATING A FOLDER

When you use ADO to create a new folder in a Web Storage System, by default the folder is a message folder. If you want to create a folder of a specific content class, you must explicitly set the DAV:contentclass schema property to the appropriate content class. For example, Listing 4.6 shows how to create a new folder for storing contact information in the Zoo Management application. If the folder already exists, it is replaced with the new folder information.

Listing 4.6   Create a new contacts folder.

```
Function CreateFolder()
    ' Create a new contacts folder in the
    ' Applications folder tree.

    Dim urlNewFolder As String

    'URL to the new folder
    urlNewFolder = GetStorageName & _
        "applications/zoo management/new contact folder/"

    With New ADODB.Record
        ' Create a new folder resource
        ' You must open the Record with Read/write permissions
        .Open urlNewFolder _

            , _
            , adModeReadWrite _
            , adCreateCollection + adCreateOverwrite
```

```
      ' Specifically create a contacts folder
       ' Otherwise, the folder would be a generic
       ' message folder.
       .Fields("DAV:contentclass") = _
          "urn:content-classes:contactfolder"

       ' Save the resource to the WSS
       .Fields.Update
    End With

    Debug.Print "Folder created."
  End Function
```

CREATING AN ITEM

When you use ADO to create a new item in a Web Storage System, by default the item is a message. If you want to create a different type of item, you must explicitly set the DAV:contentclass schema property to the appropriate content class.

For example, Listing 4.7 shows how to create a new contact in the folder that was created by the CreateFolder procedure shown in the previous code sample. If the contact already exists, it is replaced with the new information.

Listing 4.7   Creates a new post item in a public folder.

```
  Sub CreateItem()
      ' Create a new contact in the folder
      ' created by the CreateFolder procedure.

      Dim urlNewItem As String

      'URL to the new message
      urlNewItem = GetStorageName & _
          "applications/zoo management/new contact folder/Robert Brown.eml"
```

```
With New ADODB.Record
    ' Create a new folder resource
    ' You must open the Record with Read/write permissions
    .Open urlNewItem _
        , _
        , adModeReadWrite _
        , adCreateNonCollection + adCreateOverwrite

    ' If you don't set this, you get a message by default
    .Fields("DAV:contentclass") = "urn:content-classes:person"

    ' Save the contact to the WSS
    .Fields.Update
End With

Debug.Print "Contact created."
End Sub
```

APPENDING A CUSTOM PROPERTY TO A RESOURCE

Items and folders used for specific purposes often require custom properties to define them. By using custom properties, you can store information specific to your application. For example, the items and folder in the Zoo Management application use properties that contain information relevant to a zoo. You can create a custom property by defining the property in a custom schema (see Chapter 3, "Web Storage System Schema") or by creating a new property for each resource as needed.

To create a custom property for one resource, append a new property to the Fields collection of a Record object and, at the same time, set the value with the Fields.Append method. The new property and its corresponding value are then saved with the resource to a Web Storage System. The Append method has the following syntax:

```
Sub Append(Name As String, Type As DataTypeEnum[, DefinedSize As Long]
    [, Attrib As FieldAttributeEnum = adFldUnspecified][, FieldValue])
```

To use the Append method, you must supply the Name for the property, the ADO data type, and a value for the property. The following code appends a string property named Specialty to a Record and sets the value to Amphibians:

```
rec.Fields.Append "Specialty", adBSTR, , , "Amphibians"
```

When you create a new property of a resource, that property is not by default available to append to other resources. You must append the property to each resource that needs it.

Listing 4.8 shows how to create a contact in the contact folder created just like the CreateItem procedure shown in the previous section. However, this time the custom property Specialty is appended to the contact record and set to a value. The property is stored with the resource just as predefined properties are.

Listing 4.8   Create a contact that has a custom property.

```
Sub CreateItemWithCustomProperty()
    ' Create a new contact with a custom property
    ' in the folder created by the CreateFolder procedure.

    Dim urlNewItem As String

    'URL to the new message
    urlNewItem = GetStorageName & _
        "applications/zoo management/new contact folder/Robert Brown.eml"

    With New ADODB.Record
        ' Create a new folder resource
        ' You must open the Record with Read/write permissions
        .Open urlNewItem _

            , _
            , adModeReadWrite _
            , adCreateNonCollection + adCreateOverwrite

        ' If you don't set this property, you get a message by default
        .Fields("DAV:contentclass") = "urn:content-classes:person"

        ' Create a custom property
        .Fields.Append "Specialty", adBSTR, , , "Amphibians"
```

```
        ' Because this property is a string value,
        ' you could use this code instead and get the
        ' same result.
        '.Fields("Specialty") = "Amphibians"

        ' Save the contact to the WSS
        .Fields.Update
    End With

    Debug.Print "Contact created."
End Sub
```

UNDERSTANDING ADO DATA TYPES

When you append a new property to a resource, you must pass one of the
DataTypeEnum enumeration constants as the Type argument. The DataTypeEnum
enumeration specifies the ADO data type of the new field. Table 4.4 lists the data
types that are used most often. For a complete list, see the Microsoft Platform SDK.

Table 4.4   DataTypeEnum values

Constant name	Value	Description
AdArray	0x2000	A flag value, always combined with another data-type constant, that indicates an array of that other data type.
adBigInt	20	An eight-byte integer.
adBinary	128	A binary value.
adBoolean	11	A Boolean value.
adBSTR	8	A null-terminated character string (Unicode).
adChar	129	A string value.
adCurrency	6	A currency value with four digits to the right of the decimal point.

Continued on next page

Table 4.4 continued   DataTypeEnum values

Constant name	Value	Description
adDate	7	A date value stored as a double.
adDecimal	14	An exact numeric value with a fixed precision and scale.
adDouble	5	A double-precision floating-point value.
adEmpty	0	No value.
adError	10	A 32-bit error code.
adInteger	3	A four-byte, signed integer.
adNumeric	131	An exact numeric value with a fixed precision and scale.
adSingle	4	A single-precision floating-point value.
adSmallInt	2	A two-byte signed integer.
adTinyInt	16	A one-byte signed integer.
adUnsignedBigInt	21	An eight-byte unsigned integer.
adUnsignedInt	19	A four-byte unsigned integer.
adUnsignedSmallInt	18	A two-byte unsigned integer.
adTinyInt	16	A one-byte signed integer.
adUnsignedBigInt	21	An eight-byte unsigned integer.
adUnsignedInt	19	A four-byte unsigned integer.
adUnsignedSmallInt	18	A two-byte unsigned integer.
adUnsignedTinyInt	17	A one-byte unsigned integer.
adUserDefined	132	A user-defined variable.
adWChar	130	A null-terminated Unicode character string.

USING THE RECORDSET OBJECT

You use Recordset objects to access a group of resources in a Web Storage System—resources such as the contents of a folder, a filtered list of items, or a combination of folders and items. For example, a Recordset can hold the contents of an Inbox or a list of public folder names. The Recordset itself is made up of both columns and rows. Columns are the various fields that contain the data, and rows are the individual records. A Recordset uses a cursor to handle record navigation in the Recordset. Although the Recordset can contain multiple rows, the cursor can point to only one row at a time. This section explains how to open a Recordset, move through a Recordset, and use a Recordset to get the contents of a folder.

OPENING A RECORDSET

You can open an ADO Recordset from several different ADO objects. For example, you can:

- Open a Recordset from a Record using the GetChildren method of a Record object.

- Open a Recordset with the Open method of a Recordset object.

- Open a Recordset from a Connection object by calling the Execute method of a Connection object.

- Open a Recordset from a Command object by calling the Execute method of a Command object.

When you open a Recordset object by using the ExOLEDB provider, the Recordset uses optimistic locking and a dynamic cursor type. In *optimistic locking,* the data page that contains the record being edited is unavailable to other users only while the record is being saved with the Fields.Update method. However, users can make changes to the record anytime before or after the Fields.Update method is called. You can use the dynamic cursor type to navigate forward or backward among the Recordset rows and to make changes to existing records, add records, and delete records. Changes made by other users are also reflected. Although other providers allow you to specify locking options and cursor types, ExOLEDB does not support these other options.

USING THE GETCHILDREN METHOD

Use the GetChildren method to create a Recordset object populated with the child records of an open Record object. Child records can include items, subfolders, and structured documents. For example, you can use the GetChildren method to get the contents of a folder. To use the GetChildren method, open a Record object for a resource and then call the Record.GetChildren method. References to the child records of the Open record are placed in a new object:

```
Dim rst As ADODB.Recordset
Set rst = rec.GetChildren
```

If the source Record does not contain any child records, this method returns an empty Recordset object.

USING THE OPEN METHOD OF A RECORDSET OBJECT

You can also create a Recordset object by opening the Recordset object explicitly with the Open method. The Open method of a Recordset object has the following syntax:

```
Recordset.Open [Source][, ActiveConnection]
    [, CursorType][, LockType][, Options]
```

To get a group of resources from a Web Storage System by using the Open method, you specify the Source parameter and the ActiveConnection parameter. Source is a variant that indicates the source of the rows of the Recordset such as a SQL string, and Activeconnection is the connection to use when executing the query. For example, the following code sample creates a new Recordset object and opens it:

```
Dim rst As ADODB.Recordset

Set rst = New ADODB.Recordset
rst.Open strSQLStatement, cnn
```

All the parameters of the Recordset.Open method are optional, because these parameters also exist as properties of the Recordset object. If you prefer, you can set the properties and call the Open method without passing any arguments. The following code sample is equivalent to the previous one:

```
Dim rst As ADODB.Recordset

Set rst = New ADODB.Recordset
With rst
   .ActiveConnection = cnn
   .Source = strSQLStatement
   .Open strSQLStatement
End With
```

Although the second example has a few more lines of code, you may find it easier to set and maintain the property values in this manner than to pass the values as arguments of the Recordset.Open method.

MOVING THROUGH A RECORDSET

To navigate through the rows of a Recordset, you can use any of the move methods provided by ADO: MoveFirst, MoveNext, MovePrevious, and MoveLast. The name of each method clearly states what it does. You generally use the Move methods with the BOF and EOF properties of a Recordset object to successfully navigate a Recordset. You use the BOF and EOF properties of a Recordset object to determine when the current record position has moved beyond the first or last record. The BOF property is True when the current record position is before the first record, and EOF is True when the current record position is after the last record. When EOF and BOF are both True, the Recordset is empty. Figure 4.4 shows where BOF and EOF would be set to True on a sample Recordset. If the current record is Record 1, and you move the current record pointer back one record, BOF is True. If the current record is Record 3, and you move the current record pointer forward one record, EOF is True.

BOF
Record 1
Record 2
Record 3
EOF

Figure 4.4
When you navigate a Recordset, you can use the BOF and EOF properties to determine when the record cursor has moved beyond the first or last record in the Recordset.

To move through every row in a Recordset, you can use a Do..Loop construction. The loop should be constructed with an Until clause to move through every row until the EOF property is True. Put this clause on the same line as the Do statement; this avoids generating an error if the current record is already at the last record. Within the loop, you can read properties, set properties, or do whatever you need to do. Before you call the Loop statement, be sure to call the MoveNext method to move to the next row in the Recordset. If you do not call the MoveNext method, the loop continues to execute until you explicitly stop the code. The loop continues forever because the current record would never be anything other than the first record, so EOF would never be True.

The following code sample shows how to successfully navigate through the rows of a Recordset:

```
Do Until rst.EOF
  'Print the display name of each record
Debug.Print rst.Fields("DAV:displayname")
  'Move to the next record
  rst.MoveNext
Loop
```

Using ADO to Get the Contents of a Folder

After you understand the basic techniques of using a Recordset object, you are ready to apply those techniques to read the contents of a folder. One way to read the contents of a folder is to use a combination of a Record object, the Record.GetChildren method, and a Recordset object. After you access the parent folder by using a Record object, you call the GetChildren method of a Record object to populate a Recordset with the contents of the parent folder. You can then loop through the rows of the Recordset, reading any of the applicable schema properties.

Listing 4.9 shows how to open the Zoo Management application folder and read the DAV:href value for each child record.

Listing 4.9   Get the contents of a folder.

```
Sub OpenFolderAndContents()
    ' Reads the contents of a folder,
    ' including subfolders, items, and
    ' any structured documents.

    Dim rec As ADODB.Record
    Dim rst As ADODB.Recordset
    Dim urlFolder As String

    'Build the URL
    urlFolder = GetStorageName() & _
        "Applications/Zoo Management/"

    'Create a Record object
    Set rec = New ADODB.Record

    'Open the Zoo Management application folder
    rec.Open urlFolder

    'Extract the contents of the folder
    Set rst = rec.GetChildren

    ' Read the URL for each child record:
    Do Until rst.EOF
        Debug.Print rst.Fields("DAV:href")
        rst.MoveNext
    Loop

    'Close the objects and release memory
    rst.Close
    rec.Close
    Set rst = Nothing
    Set rec = Nothing
End Sub
```

QUERYING A WEB STORAGE SYSTEM BY USING SQL SELECT STATEMENTS

When you get the contents of a folder by using the GetChildren method of a Record object, you get all the child records, whether they are items or other folders. You also get all the properties for each child record. But what if you want only a subset of resources from that folder, or you need to use only one property of each of the returned resources? One way to solve this dilemma is to build and execute an SQL query. You can use a query to search a public Web Storage System or a mailbox store. Exchange supports several SQL commands, including SELECT, WHERE, ORDER BY, GROUP BY, and CONTAINS. However, Exchange does not support SQL commands typically reserved for structured databases, such as JOIN, MAX, MIN, or SUM.

To query an Exchange store, you must explicitly connect to the Web Storage System. You can execute the query with a Connection object or a Command object. Using these objects to execute queries is generally reserved for executing action queries that add records or delete them. If you need to manipulate the results of the query, you can open a Recordset object explicitly and pass the SQL statement as the source. This section describes how to use the AddQuotes function, build a simple SELECT statement, open a Recordset with the query results, and save a Recordset as XML.

USING THE ADDQUOTES FUNCTION

SQL queries require that string values be passed with quotes surrounding the value. You use quotes around the URL being queried as well as property names and string property values. Adding the quotes explicitly to the string can make for a very confusing SQL statement, and you might have a hard time adding the proper number of quotes.

To simplify programming, you can use a function to add quotes around the string values you want "quoted." All the procedures in this book use a function called AddQuotes (see Listing 4.10) to wrap text strings in quotes. The Addquotes takes one argument, strValue, the text string to which you want to add quotes. If the string contains any embedded quotes, they are doubled as well.

Listing 4.10 Add quotes around any text string passed to the function.

```
Public Function AddQuotes(strValue As String) As String
    ' Given a string, wrap it in quotes, doubling
    ' any quotes within the string.

    Const QUOTE = """"
    AddQuotes = QUOTE & _
        Replace(strValue, QUOTE, QUOTE & QUOTE) & QUOTE
End Function
```

BUILDING A SIMPLE SELECT STATEMENT

To get records from a Web Storage System, you use a SELECT statement, supplying the necessary clauses. Every SELECT statement includes the same basic components or phrases:

```
SELECT properties
FROM SCOPE datasource
[WHERE criteria]
[ORDER BY sort fields]
```

The WHERE and ORDER BY clauses are optional clauses and are not necessary for executing a successful query. However, they do lend specific functionality that you may find useful when querying a Web Storage System: you use the WHERE clause to filter the results and the ORDER BY clause to sort the results.

After you have built the query, to execute it you pass the entire SELECT statement as a string to the Open method of a Recordset object. This section constructs an SQL string in pieces so that you can reuse the code and substitute your own values.

SELECT: CHOOSE THE PROPERTIES TO RETURN

You build a SELECT statement, starting with the command SELECT, and then indicate the fields or columns of information to be returned in the result set.

```
SELECT [column1][As Alias], [column2][As Alias],
```

Column 1 and Column 2 are the names of the schema properties to be returned. The As alias allows you to name the property with a nickname so that you don't need to use the actual schema property name in any further references to the property in the code. The number of properties that you can select to be returned is not limited.

The following code sample begins building the sample SELECT statement used later in this section. The SELECT statement returns only the DAV:displayname, DAV:contentclass, and DAV:href schema properties in the result set. As mentioned earlier, all string values, including property names, must be passed in quotes, so each property name is passed to the AddQuotes function to wrap it in additional quotes:

```
strSQL = "Select " & _
    AddQuotes("DAV:displayname") & ", " & _
    AddQuotes("DAV:contentclass") & ", " & _
    AddQuotes("DAV:href")
```

Although you should avoid returning all schema properties in a query because there are quite a few of them, Exchange supports the use of an asterisk (*) in place of field names to return all properties:

```
SELECT *
```

FROM: INDICATING WHERE TO LOOK FOR RECORDS

The FROM clause of the SQL statement indicates where to start searching for the records.

```
FROM SCOPE('[Shallow | Deep] Traversal Of """ & URL & """')
```

URL is a folder in a Web Storage System that indicates the starting point of the query. Because Exchange is based on a hierarchical folder tree structure, you must also indicate how deep in the folder tree to search. The depth of a query is specified by adding the SCOPE statement to the FROM clause and indicating either Shallow or Deep. A Shallow traversal searches only the contents of the folder indicated in the target URL (nested subfolders are ignored). A Deep traversal searches the contents of the folder indicated in the target URL as well as all the child folders. You can only perform Deep traversals on the non-MAPI Web Storage Systems and mailbox stores. The entire traversal phrase is enclosed in single quotes.

The following code sample builds on the previous SELECT statement and specifies that a Shallow traversal of the Zoo Management application folder be conducted. As with property names, the entire URL must be enclosed in quotes:

```
'Begin the search here
urlQueryFld = _
    GetStorageName() & "applications/Zoo Management/"

' Select the properties to be returned
strSQL = "Select " & _
    AddQuotes("DAV:displayname") & ", " & _
    AddQuotes("DAV:contentclass") & ", " & _
    AddQuotes("DAV:href")
' Indicate shallow or deep traversal
' and what URL to begin looking
strSQL = strSQL & _
    " FROM SCOPE('SHALLOW traversal of " & _
    AddQuotes(urlQueryFld) & "')"
```

The SELECT statement searches the Zoo Management application folder and returns the DAV:displayname, DAV:contentclass, and DAV:href schema properties in the result set.

WHERE: FILTERING THE RESULTS

The WHERE clause is an optional clause of the SELECT statement that restricts the rows returned in the Recordset based on criteria that you provide. If the WHERE clause is not included, all the records from the URL are returned. The syntax for the WHERE clause is:

```
WHERE [Expression] And | Or [Expression]
```

Expression is a combined string containing the property to evaluate, a comparison operator, and a value to search for. The property does not need to be included with the SELECT clause to be used in a WHERE clause. You can combine multiple conditions to make the WHERE clause as complex as you want by separating each clause with AND or OR.

For example, the following code sample builds on the previous SELECT statement and specifies some criteria to filter the results of the query. The WHERE clause in this sample restricts the results to only those resources that have a DAV:isfolder schema property of True. This returns only subfolders and no items. Again, text strings must be enclosed in quotes, so the AddQuotes method is called when needed:

```
'Begin the search here
urlQueryFld = _
   GetStorageName() & "applications/Zoo Management/"

' Select the properties to be returned
strSQL = "Select " & _
   AddQuotes("DAV:displayname") & ", " & _
   AddQuotes("DAV:contentclass") & ", " & _
   AddQuotes("DAV:href")
' Indicate shallow or deep traversal
' and what URL to begin looking
strSQL = strSQL & _
   " FROM SCOPE('SHALLOW traversal of " & _
   AddQuotes(urlQueryFld) & "')"

' Build a filter
' This one restricts the results to folders
strSQL = strSQL & _
   " WHERE (" & _
   AddQuotes("DAV:isfolder") & " = True)"
```

The SELECT statement searches the Zoo Management application folder and returns the DAV:displayname, DAV:contentclass, and DAV:href schema properties for only folder resources.

ORDER BY: SORTING THE RESULTS

The ORDER BY clause is also an optional clause in the SELECT statement. You can use it to sort the result set based on the contents of one or more fields. The syntax for the ORDER BY clause is:

```
Order By [[Fieldname] ASC | DESC], [[Fieldname] ASC | DESC], [...]
```

Fieldname is the property that contains the information on which the sort is based. ASC | DESC indicates ascending or descending order. If no sorting method is specified, the results are sorted in ascending order. To sort in descending order, include the DESC keyword. If you want to sort by more than one property, separate each phrase with a comma. The result set is sorted by the first property, then the second, then the third, and so on. As with the WHERE clause, the fields used in the ORDER BY clause need not be included in the FROM field list. If they do not appear in the field list, they are used only for sorting and do not appear in the result set.

For example, the following code sample builds on the previous SELECT statement and sorts the result set in descending order based on the folders' display names. As always, property names must be enclosed in quotes, so the AddQuotes method is called when needed:

```
'Begin the search here
urlQueryFld = _
   GetStorageName() & "applications/Zoo Management/"

' Select the properties to be returned
strSQL = "Select " & _
   AddQuotes("DAV:displayname") & ", " & _
   AddQuotes("DAV:contentclass") & ", " & _
   AddQuotes("DAV:href")
' Indicate shallow or deep traversal
' and what URL to begin looking
strSQL = strSQL & _
   " FROM SCOPE('SHALLOW traversal of " & _
   AddQuotes(urlQueryFld) & "')"
' Build a filter
' This one restricts the results to folders
strSQL = strSQL & _
   " WHERE (" & _
   AddQuotes("DAV:isfolder") & " = True)"
```

```
' Sort the results by the display name
' of the folder in descending order
strSQL = strSQL & _
    " ORDER BY " & AddQuotes("DAV:displayname") & " DESC"
```

The SELECT statement searches the Zoo Management application folder; returns the DAV:displayname, DAV:contentclass, and DAV:href schema properties for only folder resources; and sorts the results in descending order based on DAV:displayname values.

OPENING A RECORDSET WITH THE QUERY RESULTS

Listing 4.11 shows how to open a Recordset object as the source of the records by using the SELECT statement built in the previous sections. After the procedure opens a Connection object, it constructs the SQL statement and passes it to the Open method of a Recordset object. The procedure then returns information about each folder in the result set.

Listing 4.11   Get the subfolders in the Zoo Management application folder.

```
Sub GetZooMgtSubfolders()
    ' Use a SQL SELECT statement
    ' to get the subfolders in the
    ' Zoo Management application.

    Dim cnn As ADODB.Connection
    Dim rst As ADODB.Recordset
    Dim urlQueryFld As String
    Dim strSQL As String

    ' Build the URL string
    urlQueryFld = _
        GetStorageName() & "applications/Zoo Management/"
```

```
' Connect to the calendar URL
Set cnn = New ADODB.Connection
With cnn
    .Provider = "exoledb.datasource"
    .Open urlQueryFld
End With

' Select the properties to be returned
strSQL = "Select " & _
    AddQuotes("DAV:displayname") & ", " & _
    AddQuotes("DAV:contentclass") & ", " & _
    AddQuotes("DAV:href")
' Indicate shallow or deep traversal
' and what URL to begin looking
strSQL = strSQL & _
    " FROM SCOPE('SHALLOW traversal of " & _
    AddQuotes(urlQueryFld) & "')"
' Build a filter
' This one restricts the results to folders
strSQL = strSQL & _
    " WHERE (" & _
    AddQuotes("DAV:isfolder") & " = True)"
' Sort the results by the display name
' of the folder in descending order
strSQL = strSQL & _
    " ORDER BY " & AddQuotes("DAV:displayname") & " DESC"

' Create a Recordset object
Set rst = New ADODB.Recordset
With rst
    'Open Recordset based on the SQL string
    .Open strSQL, cnn
End With
```

```
'Print the folder names to the debug window
Do Until rst.EOF
   Debug.Print rst.Fields("DAV:displayname")
   Debug.Print vbTab, rst.Fields("DAV:contentclass")
   Debug.Print vbTab, rst.Fields("DAV:href")
   rst.MoveNext
Loop

' Close the ADO object
rst.Close
cnn.Close

' Release memory used by object variables
Set rst = Nothing
Set cnn = Nothing
End Sub
```

SAVING A RECORDSET AS XML

A new feature of ADO 2.5 is the ability to save a Recordset in XML format as an
.xml file or as a Stream object. This also means that ADO Recordset objects can be
transmitted through HTTP as easily as any other parts of standard HTML text. For
example, you can use the query from the previous section, which gets the contents
of the Zoo Management application folder, and with it create an XML document
that can be easily and instantly shared on the Web.

To save a Recordset as XML, you call the Save method of a Recordset object and
specify the destination as a file name or a Stream object and pass the constant
adPersistXML. The following code sample saves a Recordset as an .xml file:

```
rst.Save "C:\MyXML.xml", adPersistXML
```

The result is an .xml file that can be opened and read by using the XML Document
Object Model (XML DOM) object model. For more information about reading an
.xml file, see Chapter 13, "XML and Exchange."

If you add the preceding code statement into Listing 4.11, the result looks something like Figure 4.5.

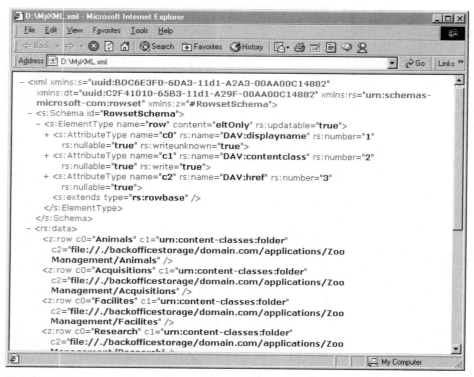

Figure 4.5
You can stream the contents of a Recordset object into an .xml file.

If you prefer to send the XML directly to a Stream object, use code like this:

```
Dim stm As New ADODB.Stream
rst.Save stm, adPersistXML
```

> **NOTE**   Certain data types used by the Web Storage System are not supported by XML, so you cannot use a Recordset that returns all properties.

Doing More Using ADO

In addition to using ADO to open and create resources in a Web Storage System, you can also use ADO in Web Storage System applications to perform record manipulation tasks such as copying, moving, and deleting resources. This section also discusses how to use the Stream object.

Copying a Resource

To copy a resource from one location to another, use the CopyRecord method. The CopyRecord method of a Record object copies a resource from one location and creates a duplicate at another location. The syntax for the CopyRecord method is:

```
Record.CopyRecord ([Source], Destination
    [, UserName][, Password][, Options][, Async])
```

To use the CopyRecord method, open a Record object on the resource to be copied and then pass a destination URL. The destination URL must include the folder path as well as the DAV:displayname for the new resource created by CopyRecord. If a resource already exists at the destination URL, CopyRecord generates an error. You can set the *Options* parameter to the constant adCopyOverwrite (1) to replace the existing resource with the new information.

For example, Listing 4.12 shows how to copy a folder from one location to another by using the CopyRecord method of a Record object. If a folder with the same URL as the destination URL already exists, it is replaced.

Listing 4.12 Copy a resource to another location.

```
Sub CopyResource()
    ' Copies a folder from one
    ' location to another.

    Dim urlCopyFrom As String
    Dim urlCopyTo As String

    ' This is the URL to the resource to be copied
    ' This folder must already exist.
    urlCopyFrom = GetStorageName & _
        "applications/zoo management/surgery/"
```

```
            ' This is the URL to the new resource
            urlCopyTo = GetStorageName & _
               "applications/surgery/"

            With New ADODB.Record
               .Open urlCopyFrom
               .CopyRecord , urlCopyTo, , , adCopyOverWrite
               .Close
            End With
         End Sub
```

MOVING A RESOURCE

To move a resource from one location to another, use the MoveRecord method.
The MoveRecord method of a Record object essentially deletes a resource at one
URL and recreates it at another URL. If the record being moved is a collection, all
the child records move with it. The syntax for the MoveRecord method is:

```
Record.MoveRecord ([Source], Destination [, UserName][, Password][,
Options][, Async])
```

To use the MoveRecord method, open a Record object for the resource to be
moved. You must open the Record with read/write permissions for this method to
work because ExOLEDB must be able to delete the original resource at the source
URL. The Destination URL must include the folder path for where the resource is
being moved as well as the DAV:displayname for the resource being moved. You
can rename the resource by providing a different DAV:displayname from the one in
the source URL. If a resource already exists at the destination URL, MoveRecord
generates an error. To replace the contents of an existing destination record, use
the *Options* parameter constant adMoveOverWrite (1).

For example, Listing 4.13 shows how to move a contact from one folder to another.
If a contact already exists with the same URL as the destination URL, the existing
contact is replaced.

Listing 4.13   Move a contact from one folder to another.

```
Sub MoveResource()
    ' Moves a contact from one folder
    ' to another. You must open the
    ' resource read/write in order to get
    ' this to work.

    Dim urlMoveFrom As String
    Dim urlMoveTo As String

    ' This is the URL to the resource to be moved
    ' This folder and contact must already exist.
    urlMoveFrom = GetStorageName & _
        "applications/zoo management/announcements/Welcome.eml"
    ' This is the URL to the new resource
    urlMoveTo = GetStorageName & _
        "applications/zoo management/research/Welcome.eml"

    With New ADODB.Record
        ' Open a record for the contact to be moved
        ' This must be opened read/write
        .Open urlMoveFrom, , adModeReadWrite
        ' Move the contact to the new destination
        ' If it exists, overwrite with the new info
        .MoveRecord , urlMoveTo
        .Close
    End With
End Sub
```

DELETING A RESOURCE

You can delete a resource in a Web Storage System by using a method of the
Record object or the Recordset object. To delete the resource by using a Record
object, use the DeleteRecord method. To use this method, open a Record on the
resource to be deleted with read/write permissions. Then, call the DeleteRecord
method. The DeleteRecord method does not take any arguments.

If you are deleting a folder with the DeleteRecord method, any items and subfolders in it are also deleted. For example, Listing 4.14 can be used to delete folders as well as items. DeleteAResource takes one argument, which is the URL to the resource to be deleted. If the resource is opened and deleted successfully, DeleteAResource returns a success message.

Listing 4.14 Delete the resource at a URL.

```
Sub DeleteAResource(urlDelete As String)
    ' You can use this procedure to
    ' delete folders or items.

    ' Turn on error trapping for VB
    ' and for VBScript
    On Error Resume Next

    ' Open the resource to be deleted
    With New ADODB.Record
        .Open urlDelete, , adModeReadWrite
        If Err.Number <> 0 Then
            ' Record cannot be found
            Debug.Print "Record does not exist."
        Else
            ' Delete the resource
            .DeleteRecord
            If Err.Number <> 0 Then
                ' Unable to delete the record
                Debug.Print _
                    "Problem deleting. Check permissions."
            Else
                Debug.Print "Record deleted."
            End If
        End If
        ' Close the record
        .Close
    End With
End Sub
```

If you want to delete a resource from an open recordset, move to the item to be deleted and call the Delete method of a Recordset object. This does not delete the Recordset object, only the current item.

STREAMING CONTENTS

You can use the Stream object to access the contents of a resource as a binary stream of bytes. You use Stream objects to open attachments, access parts of an embedded message, and render multimedia data. This section explains how to open and read the default stream for an item and how to save a stream to a file.

OPENING AND READING THE DEFAULT STREAM FOR AN ITEM

Every item in a Web Storage System has a special property for accessing the stream of an item. This property, called the default stream (adDefaultStream), contains a character series of any length and is available only for non-collection records. You access the default stream property in the same way that you access any other multi-valued property. After opening a Record object for the item, call the Fields property and pass the adDefaultStream constant. After the stream is open, you can read the contents by using the Read or ReadText methods. The Read method lets you read from a binary stream and returns the results as a variant. The ReadText method lets you read from a text stream and returns the results as a string.

The following code sample accesses the default stream for an item and returns its contents as a string:

```
rec.Open urlResource
    Set stm = New ADODB.Stream
    Set stm = rec.Fields(adDefaultStream).Value
    Debug.Print stm.ReadText
```

NOTE CDO for Exchange opens the default stream for an object with the GetStream method.

SAVING A STREAM TO A FILE

You can use the SaveToFile method of a Stream object to save the binary contents of a stream to a file at a specified location. For example, you use the SaveToFile method to save attachments in messages to a file. The SaveToFile method has the following syntax:

```
Stream.SaveToFile FileName [, SaveOptions]
```

To use the SaveToFile method, you must provide a fully qualified file name, passed as a string value, for the file to be created. You can also pass one of the *SaveOptions* constants. To create a new file only if the file does not already exist, pass the adSaveCreateNotExist (1) constant to the *SaveOptions* parameter. To replace the file even if it exists, pass the adSaveCreateOverwrite (4) to the SaveOptions parameter.

Listing 4.15 shows how to get the default stream for a Word document in a Web Storage System and save the stream to a file on a local hard disk, replacing any existing file with the same name. To run this procedure as it is currently written, you must have the Word document already created in the Web Storage System folder.

Listing 4.15   Copy a Word document from a Web Storage System folder to the local hard disk.

```
Function GetStreamforWordDocument()
    ' Copies a Word document from a
    ' Web Storage System folder to
    ' the local disk.

    Dim stm As ADODB.Stream
    Dim urlResource As String

    ' URL to the document
    urlResource = GetStorageName() & _
        "applications/Zoo Management/Research/Demo.doc"

    With New ADODB.Record
        .Open urlResource

        ' Get the Stream for the Word document
        Set stm = New ADODB.Stream
        Set stm = .Fields(adDefaultStream).Value
```

```
        ' Save it to a file
        stm.SaveToFile _
            "c:\copy of demo.doc" _
            , adSaveCreateOverWrite
    End With

    ' Clean up
    stm.Close
    Set stm = Nothing
End Function
```

USING **ADO** WITH **MICROSOFT INTERNET** PUBLISHING **PROVIDER**

The rest of this chapter explained how to write ADO code that uses the ExOLEDB provider—code that can only run on the server. However, this limits how you can use the code to server-based applications such as Web applications that use ASP technology or Web Storage System events. If you want to use ADO 2.5 to access a Web Storage System from a client application such as Microsoft Office, you can use Microsoft Internet Publishing Provider on the client machine. Microsoft Internet Publishing Provider (MSDAIPP) is an alternative provider to ExOLEDB and can be used on systems running Microsoft Windows 2000, Microsoft Windows 95 and later, and Microsoft Windows NT 4.0. It is installed with Internet Explorer 5 or later and with Microsoft Office 2000. This means you can build client applications that best suit your needs.

If you are going to build an application that uses Microsoft Internet Publishing Provider, you need to install ADO 2.5 on each client computer as well. ADO 2.5 is installed automatically with Windows 2000. If your client computers are running an earlier version of Windows, you may need to install ADO 2.5. You can download the DLL as part of Microsoft Data Access Components (MDAC) and distribute it throughout your organization. MDAC consists of the latest versions of ADO, OLE DB, and Open Database Connectivity (ODBC), which are released, documented, and supported together. The latest pack is available at http://www.microsoft.com/data/.

Microsoft Internet Publishing Provider registers for the HTTP URL namespace and uses the HTTP/WebDAV protocol, so you need to construct your URLs differently than you do for the ExOLEDB provider. You build a URL for Microsoft Internet Publishing Provider in the same way that you build a URL for use in a Web browser such as Microsoft Internet Explorer. After you build the appropriate URL, you can use ADO to work with items, as you have seen in this chapter. OLE DB automatically uses Microsoft Internet Publishing Provider when you use a URL with HTTP in your code, so you do not need to indicate a provider explicitly. For example, Listing 4.16 shows how to connect to a Web Storage System by using Microsoft Internet Publishing Provider, open a folder in the Zoo Management application, and return information on each of the child folders.

Listing 4.16   Open a folder in a Web Storage System by using Microsoft Internet Publishing Provider.

```
Sub OpenFolderContents_MSDAIPP()
    ' Use the Internet Publishing Provider
    ' to open a folder and return the URLs
    ' to each of the child folders.

    Dim rec As ADODB.Record
    Dim rst As ADODB.Recordset
    Dim urlFolder As String

    ' Build the URL. Modify this for your
    ' own situation.
    urlFolder = _
        "http://cyberserver/zooweb/"

    ' Reference the folder
    Set rec = New ADODB.Record
    rec.Open urlFolder

    ' Get the folder contents
    Set rst = rec.GetChildren
    Do Until rst.EOF
        Debug.Print rst.Fields("DAV:href")
        rst.MoveNext
    Loop
```

```
      ' Clean up
      rst.Close
      rec.Close
      Set rst = Nothing
      Set rec = Nothing
End Sub
```

SUMMARY

By using ADO 2.5 with Exchange 2000 Server, you can manipulate information in a
Web Storage System as easily as you can by using any other database software.
With URLs, you can quickly navigate to a particular item or folder in the store and
then use the Record and Recordset objects to open, edit, create, or delete those
resources. The new Stream object enhances performance by handling standard file
operations as bits of data rather than manipulating resources as one big chunk.
Even SQL SELECT statements can be used against a Web Storage System to access a
subset of information. All in all, the Web Storage System is now fully
programmable.

Chapter 5, "Introduction to CDO for Exchange," explains how you can extend the
record navigation features of ADO by using the collaboration tools of CDO for
Exchange.

5

Introduction to CDO for Exchange

Collaboration Data Objects (CDO) for Exchange is the definitive API for building collaboration applications with Microsoft Exchange 2000 Server. Although Microsoft ActiveX Data Objects (ADO) 2.5 can be used to navigate the Microsoft Web Storage System, ADO lacks even the simplest collaborative capabilities. CDO, in contrast, can be used to build any type of collaboration solution, from an automated messaging application to a scheduling application to an advanced workflow application. CDO even gives you the ability to manage your Exchange objects and interact with the Exchange information stored in the Active Directory directory service of Microsoft Windows 2000. Overall, CDO is the best object model for cracking the powerful collaboration world of Exchange 2000 Server.

This chapter explains the core techniques for building applications with CDO, focusing on how to use CDO to access and manipulate resources in the Web Storage System. This chapter also discusses how to use CDO to manage folders and contacts. Sections include:

- **Overview of CDO**

- **Getting Started with CDO**

- **Understanding and Using the IDataSource Interface**

- **Working with Folders**

- **Working with Contact Information**

OVERVIEW OF CDO

CDO is a technology that you can use to build a wide range of collaboration applications for purposes such as messaging, calendaring, contact management, and workflow, as well as Exchange administrative applications. CDO is designed to enhance ADO by offering methods and properties specific to collaboration operations such as sending e-mail and scheduling appointments. Like ADO, CDO is a server-based API.

Unlike earlier releases of CDO, CDO for Exchange must be installed and used only on a computer running Microsoft Windows 2000 Advanced Server and Exchange 2000 Server, because it requires the Exchange OLE DB (ExOLEDB) provider. CDO is optimized for applications that can run code on the server. These include Exchange server-based applications, such as event sinks and server-management tools, and Web-based applications that use Active Server Pages (ASP) technology. This section explains the three different CDO object models and discusses the uses of each.

NOTE   You can continue to use earlier releases of CDO, such as CDO 1.2 and CDO 1.2.1, in client-side applications to access Exchange 2000 Server.

ADO vs. CDO

Although it is possible to build a Web Storage System solution by using just ADO or just CDO, you are more than likely going to end up incorporating objects from both. ADO and CDO are designed to enhance one another rather than compete, and both use the ExOLEDB. This means you can use the same skills to construct URLs to bind to resources in the Web Storage System for each object model. From there, the object model you use depends on the type of functionality you require.

ADO 2.5 is optimized for navigating, searching, and setting properties within the Web Storage System and specializes in generic, resource-manipulation tasks such as copying and moving records.

You should use CDO when you need to create a collaboration-based application. CDO is the premier object model for creating collaboration applications because it contains objects specifically designed for creating messaging, calendaring, and contact-management systems. You can use CDO to build server-management tools and complex routing systems. You can also use the CDO object model to set object-specific properties easily.

CDO Object Models

CDO is not packaged as a single object model. Instead, it consists of three different object models, each of which serves a unique purpose. You can use these object models individually or together. Table 5.1 lists the three models and the DLL file names associated with them. All three CDO DLLs are installed with Exchange 2000 by default. If they have not been installed, you can rerun Setup and select the **Messaging and Collaboration** option.

Table 5.1   CDO for Exchange DLLs

DLL	File name
CDO for Exchange 2000 Server	Cdo.dll
CDO for Exchange Management Objects	Cdoexm.dll
CDO Workflow for Exchange	Cdowf.dll

UNDERSTANDING THE CDO FOR EXCHANGE 2000 SERVER OBJECT MODEL

CDO for Exchange 2000 Server is the primary CDO object model and the one you will use most often. This object model contains the core objects and interfaces most common to collaboration applications such as messaging applications, contact-management systems, and scheduling applications. In addition, you can use the CDO for Exchange 2000 Server object model to create and configure folders in the Web Storage System. The top-level CDO objects used to build these types of solutions include:

- **Folder**. A container in a mailbox store or public store.

- **Person**. Contact-type information in a Web Storage System folder or a user/contact object in Active Directory.

- **Message**. An e-mail message.

- **Appointment**. A scheduled appointment or meeting.

- **CalendarMessage**. A meeting request.

- **Addressee**. A free-form recipient of e-mail messages or meeting requests.

- **Attendee**. A person involved with an appointment or meeting.

All these top-level objects have two key interfaces in common that provide typical object configuration and file input/output (I/O) functionality. The IConfiguration interface is used to define a behavior model that can be applied to multiple objects. The IDataSource interface is exposed by every CDO object and is used to manage, store, and save data.

In addition to these two key interfaces, some CDO objects also use other interfaces to provide functionality specific to particular tasks. In a messaging application, use the IBodyParts interface to access the parts of a Multipurpose Internet Mail Extensions (MIME) message such as the header or HTML body. Similarly, you can use the ICalendarParts interface to manipulate the calendar portion of a meeting request. Use the IRecurrencePatterns and IExceptions interfaces when scheduling meetings.

If you are using Microsoft Visual Basic to build Component Object Model (COM) components and you want to use early binding, set a reference to the Microsoft CDO for Exchange 2000 library. This object library appears in Object Browser as CDO.

UNDERSTANDING THE CDO FOR EXCHANGE MANAGEMENT OBJECTS OBJECT MODEL

Previously known as Exchange Management Objects, CDO for Exchange Management Objects consists of classes and interfaces for creating and managing Exchange mailboxes and Exchange server components. Although managing the server itself is not a trivial task, you might find yourself more often writing code using these objects to manage your Exchange recipients and mailboxes. For these types of applications, the objects that you use are:

- **IMailRecipient**. Specifies how e-mail is delivered and managed for a user. The object also enables contacts and folders to receive e-mail without a mailbox.

- **IMailboxStore**. Specifies how to create, move, and delete Exchange mailboxes and how to manage the administrative properties of a recipient that has been enabled to use a mailbox.

Although the System Manager Microsoft Management Console (MMC) snap-in will most often be used to manage your Exchange server, you might decide to build your own Exchange Server management tool. For example, perhaps you want to build a Web-based server manager. CDO for Exchange Management Objects also provides objects for managing your server as a whole. The top-level objects used in these scenarios are:

- **ExchangeServer**. Manages your Exchange 2000 Server and returns basic information, such as the server type and version.

- **FolderTree**. Manages folder trees, including any replicas, on the server.

- **StorageGroup**. Manages storage groups that organize the mailbox stores and public stores.

- **MailboxStoreDB**. Manages the mailbox store of a single recipient. You can use the object to mount, move, or dismount a mailbox store and return basic information about the store database.

- **PublicStoreDB**. Creates, manages, and deletes public stores and returns basic information about the store database.

If you are building COM components with Visual Basic and want to use early binding, set a reference to the Microsoft CDO for Exchange Management library. This object library appears in Object Browser as CDOExM.

UNDERSTANDING THE CDO WORKFLOW FOR EXCHANGE OBJECT MODEL

CDO Workflow for Exchange consists of COM classes and interfaces for building and running workflow and routing applications. You can build workflow applications two ways: by using Workflow Designer for Microsoft Exchange 2000 Server or by building the workflow event processes and sinks manually. For most developers, Workflow Designer provides enough functionality and flexibility to fulfill all application-development needs. If you use Workflow Designer, you don't need most of the workflow objects. You need to use these objects only when you write scripts that react to various workflow actions. The objects that you will most likely use in those scripts include:

- **IWorkflowSession**. Provides run-time communication among the workflow engine, your action script, and the workflow item (ProcessInstance) being processed.

- **IWorkflowMessage**. Creates notification messages in the workflow process that can be sent to recipients.

- **AuditTrailEventLog**. Creates entries about workflow event activity in an application log.

If Workflow Designer does not provide what you need to accomplish your design goals, you must build the event sinks manually. Although you gain quite a bit of design flexibility and control over your application this way, you also take on added responsibility. You must build every aspect of the workflow application and use almost all the objects in the workflow object library. In addition to the objects and interfaces listed earlier, you must also become familiar with the following objects:

- **ProcessDefinition**. Defines the logic in a workflow, which includes states and actions.

- **ProcessInstance**. Controls, records, and monitors the status of an individual workflow item moving through a workflow process.

If you are using Visual Basic to build workflow tools and event sinks and you want to use early binding, set a reference to the Microsoft CDO Workflow for Exchange library. This object library appears in Object Browser as CDOWF.

GETTING STARTED WITH CDO

CDO for Exchange uses a paradigm centered on COM classes and interfaces. This section introduces key concepts—concepts that you might find familiar if you are a Visual Basic developer. This section also discusses core programming techniques for writing code with any of the CDO object models.

CREATING OBJECTS FROM CLASSES

CDO consists of a variety of COM classes, which are blueprints for creating new objects. When an object is created, the class determines the standard default functionality that the object has. For example, the CDO Message class is used to define new Message objects. Each Message object has the same standard functionality, which allows the object to be sent and received. You can then customize each object by setting the existing properties or by adding your own properties to the object. The Web Storage System also allows you to define your own custom classes. For more information on custom classes, see Chapter 3, "Web Storage System Schema."

If you are using Visual Basic to create objects from the CDO COM classes, you will want to take advantage of early binding and set a reference to the appropriate object library. In your code, you can then declare your object variables of the appropriate class and use the New keyword to create an instance of the class. The following code sample creates a CDO Message object:

```
Dim msg As CDO.Message
Set msg = New CDO.Message
```

If you are using Microsoft Visual Basic Scripting Edition (VBScript) and ASP, you cannot use the New or As keywords in declarations of variables. Instead, you must declare variables without an object type, and you must use the Server.CreateObject method to create new objects, passing the name of the class being instantiated as a string value. To create a new Message object with VBScript and ASP technology, you use code like this:

```
Dim msg
Set msg = Server.CreateObject("CDO.Message")
```

You can now access the properties and methods of the default interface in addition to any other interfaces exposed by the class.

As with all object-oriented programming, you must clean up your code by releasing memory resources allotted to object variables when you are finished using them. Set the object variable to *Nothing* to release memory resources previously allotted to the variable, as follows:

```
Set msg = Nothing
```

USING INTERFACES

Unlike COM classes, interfaces do not define an object. Instead, interfaces define an encapsulated set of properties and methods. Some interfaces are specific to certain classes, but other interfaces define a common functionality. By encapsulating properties and methods in this way, interfaces can be shared easily among predefined and custom classes.

Classes generally have multiple interfaces associated with them, including one that encapsulates the native functionality of that class—the default interface. A default interface is one that exposes the default functionality for a class. A default interface has the same name as the object it represents but is prefaced with an *I*, indicating that it is an interface as opposed to a class object. For example, the Person class has an IPerson interface that manages all the properties and methods used specifically for defining and managing contact-type information. The default interface is exposed directly from the object, which means you can use it to call the properties and methods directly from the object. You can call the e-mail property of a Person object directly from the object like this:

```
Dim prs As CDO.Person

Set prs = New CDO.Person
prs.Email = "someone@domain.com"
```

In addition to the default interface, most classes use at least one other interface, which is often also used by other classes. For example, the IDataSource interface contains the methods for opening and saving data to and from CDO objects and the Web Storage System. Because every top-level CDO class requires this functionality, objects such as Person and Message implement an IDataSource interface. You can access the properties and methods of these interfaces only after you reference the interfaces. You can easily do this by calling the associated property. The IDataSource interface is accessed through the DataSource property like this:

```
Dim dsrc As IDataSource
Set dsrc = prs.DataSource
```

Some interfaces do not have an associated property for referencing them. For example, the CDOEXM IMailRecipient interface manages the e-mail properties for a person or folder, but the interface cannot be accessed with a matching property name. The way you access the IMailRecipient interface depends on whether you are using Visual Basic or VBScript. If you are using Visual Basic, you can declare the object variable as the proper interface and then reference the interface automatically by pointing the interface object variable at the object exposing the interface. The following code sample references the IMailRecipient interface on a folder:

```
Dim fld As CDO.Folder
Dim rcp As CDOEXM.IMailRecipient

Set rcp = fld
```

If you are using VBScript, you cannot declare variables as data types. Therefore, you must access the interface with the GetInterface method. The GetInterface method is exposed by almost every CDO object for accessing interfaces. The following code sample accesses the IMailRecipient interface using VBScript:

```
Set rcp = fld.GetInterface("IMailRecipient")
```

ACCESSING SCHEMA PROPERTIES

Although ADO requires that you use the Fields collection to change schema properties, CDO offers an easier approach. Many of the more commonly used schema properties are accessible through a CDO property. For example, you can access the urn:schemas:contacts:HomePhone schema property for a Person object with the HomePhone property of the Person object, as follows:

```
prs.HomePhone = "555-555-0101"
```

For schema properties that do not have an equivalent CDO property, you need to use the Fields collection. This is actually the ADO Fields collection; therefore, it has the same properties and methods. To access a specific property in the collection, pass either the fully qualified schema property name or the associated CDO constant equivalent, if it exists. CDO provides named constants for nearly all the predefined schema properties. Prefaced with **cdo**, these constants are included in the CDO object library. You can use them to avoid having to pass the entire property name. To use a CDO constant, pass the constant name without quotations. The following code sample sets the urn:schemas:contacts:FTPSite property:

```
prs.Fields(cdoFtpSite) = "somearchive.edu"
```

TIP To see a complete list of constants, set a reference to the CDO object library in Visual Basic or the Visual Basic Editor of Microsoft Office products and browse with Object Browser.

If the schema property you need to access is not available as a CDO property or constant, you must pass the fully qualified schema property name to the Fields collection. For example, the following code sample also accesses the property but passes the qualified schema name as a string literal:

```
prs.Fields("urn:schemas:contacts:ftpsite") = "somearchive.edu"
```

If you pass the qualified schema name, your code tends to look like an encoded document. More important, because property names are case sensitive, you are more likely to make errors because you must type the schema property name every time you use it. Because of this, you should define your own constants for your application if you use properties for which a CDO property doesn't exist and a schema constant is not created.

USING URLS

Just like ADO, CDO relies on URLs and the ExOLEDB provider to interact with resources in a Web Storage System. The URL must be properly constructed, with both the complete folder path and the display name (DAV:displayname) of the resource being accessed. If you are opening an item such as a contact or an e-mail message and where the item originated is uncertain, append an .eml extension to the URL. Any spaces that appear in the folder path or item display name must also be preserved in the URL. For example, if you have created the Zoo Management application on the Applications tree, you use the following URL to access the Staff folder:

```
File://./backofficestorage/Applications/Zoo Management/Staff/
```

The trailing slash mark (/) is not required when you are opening a folder, but including it is good programming practice. By always including a trailing slash mark on a URL that points to a folder, you can quickly distinguish between a URL for a folder and a URL for an item. To access a contact stored in that folder, you would use a URL like this:

```
File://./backofficestorage/Applications/
    Zoo Management/Staff/Amy Luehmann.EML
```

For more information about the general use of URLs, see Chapter 2, "Exchange and the Web Storage System." For information about using URLs with ExOLEDB, see Chapter 4, "ActiveX Data Objects and Exchange."

NOTE CDO also supports relative URLs.

UNDERSTANDING AND USING THE IDATASOURCE INTERFACE

The IDataSource interface is the key to accessing resources in a Web Storage System using CDO. All CDO objects expose the IDataSource interface through a DataSource property. You use the DataSource property to open resources, detect and save changes, and create resources in a Web Storage System.

This section lists the IDataSource properties and methods; explains how the IDataSource interface works; and shows how to open a resource using CDO, detect and save changes, create a new resource using CDO, open CDO objects from other objects, and check whether an item exists.

IDATASOURCE INTERFACE PROPERTIES AND METHODS

Regardless of what you are trying to do using CDO, you will need to use the IDataSource interface. Table 5.2 lists the properties and methods exposed by the IDataSource interface.

Table 5.2   Properties and methods of the IDataSource interface

Name	Type	Returns	Description
ActiveConnection	Property	Connection	Returns the active Connection object if the resource is bound to an object (read-only).
IsDirty	Property	Boolean	Indicates whether the local copy of the data has changed.
Source	Property	Unknown	Returns the currently bound object (read-only).
SourceClass	Property	String	Returns the name of the interface originally used to open the data source (read-only).
SourceURL	Property	String	Returns the URL of the currently bound object (read-only).

Continued on next page

Table 5.2 continued Properties and methods of the IDataSource interface

Name	Type	Returns	Description
Open	Method	N/A[1]	Opens the data source for an existing resource.
OpenObject	Method	N/A	Opens a CDO object from another object.
Save	Method	N/A	Saves changes to an existing resource.
SaveTo	Method	N/A	Saves a data source to a specific resource URL with a name.
SaveToContainer	Method	N/A	Saves a data source in a container.
SaveToObject	Method	N/A	Saves a data source to another object.

[1]Not available.

HOW THE IDATASOURCE INTERFACE WORKS

When you use CDO to open a resource, you are not dynamically connecting to the Web Storage System. Instead, the data is copied locally from the Web Storage System to the CDO object. Essentially, you have two copies of the data: one in the Web Storage System and another in the CDO object. Any changes that you make to the data by using the CDO object's properties and methods are made to the local copy—not to the Web Storage System copy. The data in the Web Storage System remains unchanged until you explicitly commit the changes from the local copy by using one of the IDataSource save methods. If you do not call one of the save methods, all the changes are lost and the Web Storage System maintains the original copy.

The same is true if you are creating a new resource. The resource will not exist in the Web Storage System until you call one of the save methods. In addition, if you change schema properties through the Fields collection, you must also call the Update method independently of the save methods. Because the Update method commits changes only to the local copy, you must call the Update method before you call one of the IDataSource save methods.

OPENING A RESOURCE BY USING CDO

To open a resource in a Web Storage System, you use the DataSource.Open method of the appropriate CDO object. The DataSource.Open method is based on the ADO Record.Open method. However, not all the parameters are supported in CDO. The Open method syntax that CDO uses is as follows:

```
Sub Open(
    SourceURL As String
    [, ActiveConnection As Object]
    [, Mode As ConnectModeEnum])
```

Where:

SourceURL

is the URL for the resource to be opened, such as a folder or an item in a folder. This is the only required argument.

ActiveConnection

is an optional argument that indicates the connection through which the resource is to be opened. To use the existing connection, leave this blank.

Mode

is an optional enumeration that identifies how the record should be opened. Use one of the following constants: adModeRead, adModeReadWrite, adModeRecursive, adModeShareDenyNone, adModeShareDenyRead, adModeShareDenyWrite, adModeShareExclusive, adModeUnknown, or adModeWrite.

If you do not pass any arguments other than the URL to the Open method, the resource is opened as read-only. To open a resource for editing, you must also pass the Mode argument adModeReadWrite.

NOTE For the code listings shown in this chapter, see the Microsoft Visual
Basic project CH_05.vbp on the companion CD. To run the samples as they
are written, you must have the Zoo Management sample installed on your
Exchange 2000 Server. For information on installing the application, see the
introduction to the book. In addition, the code samples repeatedly call a
function named GetStorageName. This function returns the name of the
domain in which the code is running. For more information about the
GetStorageName function, see Chapter 8, "Interacting with Active Directory."

Listing 5.1 shows how to open a read-only resource with the DataSource.Open
method. The procedure creates a new CDO Folder object and opens the folder by
passing the folder URL to the DataSource.Open method of the Folder object.
Because no other arguments are passed, the folder is opened in read-only mode.
Then the code enumerates the properties of the folder and returns their names and
values if the property is single-valued or just the property name and constant
[MultiValued] if the property is multi-valued.

Listing 5.1. Open a resource in the Web Storage System by using CDO.

```
Sub OpenAResource_CDO()
    ' Return info about a folder

    Dim urlFolder As String
    Dim fd As ADODB.Field

    urlFolder = GetStorageName & "Applications/Zoo Management/"

    ' If you are using VBScript, use this With:
    ' With CreateObject("cdo.folder")
    With New CDO.Folder

        ' Open the folder
        .DataSource.Open urlFolder
```

```
' Enumerate through the properties
For Each fd In .Fields
  If Not IsArray(fd.Value) Then
    ' If the property is single valued,
    ' return the name and the current value
    Debug.Print fd.Name, fd.Value
  Else
    ' If the property is multi-valued,
    ' Identify it as such
    ' For info on enumerating multi-valued properties,
    ' See Chapter 4 for ADO and Chapter 13 for XML
    Debug.Print fd.Name, "[MULTIVALUED]"
  End If
Next
End With

' Clean up
Set fd = Nothing
End Sub
```

DETECTING AND SAVING CHANGES

After a resource is opened and displayed in a client application, the user might make changes to it. If the user makes changes, those changes should be saved back to the Web Storage System by calling the Save method. However, if no changes are made, calling the Save method is unnecessary. By using the DataSource.IsDirty property of the IDataSource interface, you can determine whether changes were made locally to the open data source.

The DataSource.IsDirty property is a Boolean value indicating whether fields in the local copy of the data have changed. After the CDO object opens a resource, two copies of the same data exist: one copy is cached locally in the CDO object, and the other copy is in the Web Storage System. When the information is initially cached, the local copy is considered clean, and the DataSource.IsDirty property returns a value of False. If the client makes changes, the local copy of the data is then considered dirty, and the DataSource.IsDirty property is set to True. The property is reset to False when any of the following situations occur:

- The Save method (see the following text) is called to push changes from the local copy of the data back to the Web Storage System.

- The CDO object variable referencing the local copy of the data is set to Nothing.

- The CDO object variable referencing the local copy of the data is bound to a different resource.

If the client has indeed made changes and those changes should be saved, it is necessary to call the DataSource.Save method for the changed object. The DataSource.Save method does not take arguments. You just call the method after you have finished editing an object to commit those changes to the Web Storage System. If you do not call the DataSource.Save method, the changes are lost. This method is not used on objects that have never been saved (new objects).

The following code sample demonstrates how to use the DataSource.IsDirty property and the DataSource.Save method. You can use this code sample in almost any procedure to test for changes. The DataSource.IsDirty property is evaluated to determine whether the CDO object has been changed locally. If the property returns True, then the code saves the changes with the DataSource.Save method. If the local copy has not been changed, no action occurs.

```
If cdoObject.DataSource.IsDirty Then
    'Save changes to the source.
    cdoObject.DataSource.Save
End If
```

CAUTION   The DataSource.IsDirty property checks only the local copy of the data. It does not determine whether another client application has made changes to the copy in the Web Storage System. For example, if one user's application opens a resource for editing and another application opens the same resource a second later, any changes the second application makes are not reflected in the first local copy. This means that one user can inadvertently overwrite another user's changes. For more control over this type of situation, consider using server events to monitor changes on the server. For more information about using and building Web Storage System events, see Chapter 9, "Using Web Storage System Events."

CREATING A NEW RESOURCE BY USING CDO

You create a new resource in a Web Storage System folder by first defining the object and then saving it to the Web Storage System by calling the DataSource.SaveTo method or the DataSource.SaveToContainer method. As mentioned earlier in this chapter, if you have used the Fields collection to set any property values, you also need to call the Fields.Update method before you call either of the save methods. This section describes how to create a new resource by saving to a URL and by saving to a container.

SAVING TO A URL

One way to create a new resource in a Web Storage System is to build a URL for it and then save the information to that URL. The DataSource.SaveTo method lets you specify the URL of the resource you are creating. In other words, you must build the URL exactly as it would appear if the resource already existed. This includes the folder path as well as the DAV:displayname for the resource.

TIP   If you are creating a folder, append the trailing slash onto the URL. If you are creating an item, append the .eml extension to the URL. This unofficial standard can save you time later by distinguishing between a URL for a folder and a URL for an item.

The DataSource.SaveTo method has parameters similar to what you have used with the DataSource.Open method. The syntax for the DataSource.SaveTo method used by CDO is:

```
Sub SaveTo(
    SourceURL As String
    [, ActiveConnection As Object]
    [, Mode As ConnectModeEnum]
    [, CreateOptions As RecordCreateOptionsEnum])
```

Where:

SourceURL

is the URL for the resource to be saved (created), such as a folder or an item in a folder. This is the only required argument. If you are creating an item, the URL should also include the .eml extension.

ActiveConnection

is an optional argument indicating the connection through which the resource will be opened. Leave this empty if you want to use the existing connection.

Mode

is an optional enumeration that identifies how the record should be opened. Use one of the following constants: adModeRead, adModeReadWrite, adModeRecursive, adModeShareDenyNone, adModeShareDenyRead, adModeShareDenyWrite, adModeShareExclusive, adModeUnknown, or adModeWrite.

CreateOptions

is an optional enumeration that specifies how the resource is created. To overwrite an existing resource at the same URL, set this to the adCreateOverwrite constant. Other constants for this parameter are not supported for this method.

Listing 5.2 shows how to create a new resource in a Web Storage System folder by using the DataSource.SaveTo method. Before anything else, the URL to the new resource is created. In this case, because the code is creating an item, the .eml extension is appended to the URL. Then, the procedure creates a new CDO Person object and sets some of the properties, including one that can be accessed only through the Fields collection. To save those changes, the code calls the Fields.Update method. Finally, the procedure calls the DataSource.SaveTo method and passes the URL for the new contact.

Listing 5.2   Create a new contact in a folder.

```
Sub CreateAResourceAtAURL()
    ' Create a new contact in
    ' a Web Storage System folder
    ' using a specific URL.

    Dim urlStaffMember As String

    urlStaffMember = GetStorageName & _
        "Applications/Zoo Management/Staff/Amy Luehmann.EML"

    ' If you are using VBScript, use this With:
    ' With CreateObject("cdo.person")
    With New CDO.Person
```

```
        ' Set some of the basic contact properties
        .FirstName = "Amy"
        .LastName = "Luehmann"
        .HomeCity = "Redmond"
        .HomeState = "Washington"
        .Email = "amy@domain.com"

        ' You can use one or the other
        ' of the following:
        '.Fields("urn:schemas:contacts:ftpsite") = "somearchive.edu"
        .Fields(cdoFtpSite) = "somearchive.edu"

        'Save the changes made through the Fields collection
        .Fields.Update

        'Save the information to the URL and overwrite any existing contact
        .DataSource.SaveTo urlStaffMember, , , adCreateOverwrite
    End With
End Sub
```

NOTE Because the adCreateOverwrite constant was not passed to the DataSource.SaveTo method in Listing 5.2, the procedure will fail if the contact already exits. To avoid this scenario, you must check first to see if the resource with that same URL already exists before attempting to save to the same URL. For information about how to validate a URL, see "Checking for the Existence of a Folder or Item," later in this chapter.

SAVING TO A CONTAINER

The DataSource.SaveToContainer method provides you with another option for creating resources in the Web Storage System. You can use this method to create a resource in a specified folder without naming the resource in the URL. The DataSource.SaveToContainer method appears to be the same as the DataSource.SaveTo method because it has the same arguments, but it does not use URLs in the same way. The DataSource.SaveToContainer method requires a URL for the folder in which you are creating the item. The URL cannot include the DAV:displayname value for the new item. Instead, the DAV:displayname value is automatically generated by Exchange when the resource is saved.

The DataSource.SaveToContainer method is especially useful when you are creating appointments in calendars because display names are often duplicated in the container. For example, if you use the DataSource.SaveTo method to create an appointment in your calendar with a display name of Dentist Appointment. If you attempt to use the DataSource.SaveTo method to create another Dentist Appointment, an error message is generated. If you use the overwrite option, you will replace the first dentist appointment, even though the second appointment occurs six months later. However, if you use the DataSource.SaveToContainer method, you can be sure that the new appointment is created without replacing an existing one.

For example, Listing 5.3 shows how to create a new appointment in a calendar. After the code creates the appointment and sets some properties, it calls the DataSource.SaveToContainer method and passes a URL that points to the calendar folder instead of to the item. The DAV:displayname property is set by CDO and Exchange.

Listing 5.3   Create a new resource with an automatically generated DAV:displayname.

```
Sub SaveToContainer()
    ' Save the appointment to the container
    ' Exchange will provide the display name

    Dim urlSurgeryFld As String

    urlSurgeryFld = _
    GetStorageName & "Applications/Zoo Management/Surgery/"

    ' If you are using VBScript, use this With:
    ' With CreateObject("cdo.appointment")
    With New CDO.Appointment
        ' Set the Appointment properties
        .StartTime = "9/29/2001 1:30:00 PM"
        .EndTime = "9/29/2001 2:30:00 PM"
        .Subject = "Tooth extraction"
        .Location = "Zoo hospital"
        .TextBody = "Tiger needs an incisor extracted."

        ' Save the appointment to a calendar
        .DataSource.SaveToContainer urlSurgeryFld
    End With
End Sub
```

OPENING CDO OBJECTS FROM OTHER OBJECTS

You use the DataSource.OpenObject method to open a CDO object from another in-memory object. The in-memory object can be either another CDO object or an object from another library, such as ADO 2.5.

The syntax for the OpenObject method is:

```
Sub OpenObject(Source As Unknown, InterfaceName As String)
```

Where:

Source

    is the reference to the object that's already open, such as an ADO record or a previously opened e-mail message. This is generally an object variable.

InterfaceName

    is the string name of the interface exposed by Source. For example, if *Source* is a BodyPart object of an e-mail message, *InterfaceName* is IBodyPart. This is a case-sensitive argument.

The DataSource.OpenObject method works well for opening embedded messages as their own individual message objects or streaming data from an attachment to a file on disk. You can also use the DataSource.OpenObject method to bind CDO objects to ADO objects. Why would you want to do this? Perhaps you are already navigating through the Web Storage System by using a Recordset object, or perhaps you are using the Connection object to run an SQL query that filters a list of items, or maybe you are creating new items in batches. All these tasks require ADO, but you might also need to use CDO to set object-specific properties.

If you make changes to the CDO object after opening it this way, you need to use the DataSource.SaveToObject method to save those changes back to the parent object. Pass the same arguments to the DataSource.SaveToObject method as you did to save the changes to the DataSource.OpenObject method.

The code in Listing 5.4 opens a CDO Folder object from an ADO Record object to make use of the CDO Folder object properties. To open the folder this way, the Record object variable is passed along with the _Record interface name to the DataSource.OpenObject method of the Folder object. The underscore indicates that the name refers to an interface and not an object. After testing the folder description, the code then uses the DataSource.IsDirty property to determine whether changes were made while the object was open. If so, the changes are saved to the open Record object.

Listing 5.4 Open a CDO Folder from an ADO Record.

```
Sub BindingCDOFoldertoADORecord()
  ' Open a CDO Folder object from
  ' an ADO Record object

  Dim rec As ADODB.Record
  Dim rst As ADODB.Recordset

  ' Create a new ADO record object
  Set rec = New ADODB.Record

  ' Open the demo folder with ADO
  rec.Open _
    GetStorageName & "Applications/Zoo Management/" _
    , , adModeReadWrite

  ' If you are using VBScript, use this With:
  ' With CreateObject("cdo.folder")
  With New CDO.Folder
    ' Link the folder datasource to the data in the open ADO record
    ' "_Record" is the interface name.
    ' Note that the interface name is
    ' case-sensitive.
    .DataSource.OpenObject rec, "_Record"
```

```
      ' Create a new description if blank
      If Len(.Description) = 0 Then
        .Description = "This folder contains zoo information."
      End If

      ' If changes have been made...
      If .DataSource.IsDirty Then
        ' Save the changes back to the record
        .DataSource.SaveToObject rec, "_Record"
      End If

      ' Print some of the stats of the folder
      Debug.Print .HasSubFolders
      Debug.Print .ContentClass
      Debug.Print .Description
   End With

   ' Open a recordset on the objects within
   ' the folder including any subfolders
   Set rst = rec.GetChildren
   Do Until rst.EOF
      ' Print the HREF for each resource in the folder
      Debug.Print rst.Fields("DAV:href")
      rst.MoveNext
   Loop

   ' Close the ADO objects and clean up
   rec.Close
   rst.Close
   Set rec = Nothing
   Set rst = Nothing
End Sub
```

CHECKING FOR THE EXISTENCE OF A FOLDER OR ITEM

Developers of collaboration applications often face the issue of duplicate items. CDO does not provide an easy way to check whether a folder or item exists. Using the parameters of the save methods, you can overwrite existing folders or items, but what if you want to create the item only if one doesn't already exist? For example, you might need to create a folder only if it isn't already present. Or, perhaps you want to create a contact for a person only if a contact for that person doesn't exist. The easiest way to test for the presence of an item is to attempt to open an ADO Record with the URL in question. By using the ADO Open method, you can check the validity of a URL before any property changes are made. For more information about using the Open method with an ADO Record, see Chapter 4, "ActiveX Data Objects and Exchange."

The code in Listing 5.5 checks whether a URL already exists. When you call the function, you pass the URL string that you want to test. The code then attempts to open a Record with that URL but fails if the URL does not exist. To enable error handling in both Visual Basic and VBScript, error trapping is turned off, and the code continues to run regardless of whether the ADO Open method generates an error. If an error is generated, the URL does not point to an existing resource in the Web Storage System, and the function returns a value of False. If an error is not generated, the URL already points to a valid resource in the Web Storage System, and the function returns a value of True. You can use the AlreadyExists function to test for the existence of any item.

Listing 5.5.   Check to see if an item exists.

```
Function AlreadyExists(ResourceURL As String) As Boolean
    ' Checks to see if a resource already exists
    ' at the URL passed to the function

Dim rec As ADODB.Record

    ' Allow error trapping in both VB and VBScript
On Error Resume Next
```

```
' Attempt to open an ADO record for the URL
Set rec = New ADODB.Record
rec.Open _
   ResourceURL _
   , _
   , adModeReadWrite _
   , adFailIfNotExists

' Check to see if an error was generated
If Err.Number <> 0 Then
   ' URL does not already exist
   AlreadyExists = False
Else
   ' URL already exists
   AlreadyExists = True
   rec.Close
End If

' Turn error handling back to the system
' Change this to go to your current error handler
' if you are using VB
On Error GoTo 0

' Clean up
Set rec = Nothing
End Function
```

WORKING WITH FOLDERS

The CDO Folder object represents a single folder in the Web Storage System. You can use the Folder object to create a new folder or open an existing folder and set folder-specific properties. You can also use ADO to manipulate folders. Because folders are stored as records in the Web Storage System, ADO can accomplish tasks with folders that CDO cannot. For example, you can use ADO to query for all folders of a specific type, such as contact folders. However, for setting folder properties, you should use CDO.

This section lists the properties of the CDO Folder object and explains how to use CDO to create a folder, enable e-mail in a folder, and count the contents of a folder.

CDO FOLDER OBJECT PROPERTIES

CDO provides a number of properties for Folder objects that you can use to set folder-specific operations and obtain status information. Table 5.3 lists the properties of the CDO Folder object.

Table 5.3 Properties of the CDO Folder object

Property	Data type	Description
Configuration	Configuration	Returns the Configuration object associated with the folder.
ContentClass	String	Sets or returns the content class of the folder.
DataSource	IDataSource	Returns the IDataSource interface (read-only).
Description	String	Sets or returns the text description associated with a folder.
DisplayName	String	Returns the name of the folder without a path (read-only).
EmailAddress	String	Returns the e-mail address assigned to a folder (if any) (read-only).
Fields	Fields	Returns a collection of fields specific to the folder content class (read-only).
HasSubFolders	Boolean	Returns True if the folder has child folders (read-only).
ItemCount	Long	Returns a count of all items in a folder, not including subfolders (read-only).
UnreadItemsCount	Long	Returns a count of all items marked as unread in a folder (read-only).
VisibleCount	Long	Returns a count of all items that are not hidden (read-only).

CREATING A FOLDER BY USING CDO

To create a folder by using CDO, you create a new CDO Folder object and then set its properties to make it operate the way you want. If you configure the folder to hold a specific type of item, set the ContentClass property to one of the predefined folder content classes. If you also want the folder to be usable by MAPI clients, set the http://schemas.microsoft.com/exchange/outlookfolderclass property. After you set all the necessary properties, commit the changes to the store. If you have set properties by using the Fields collection, call the Update method first. Next, call the DataSource.SaveTo method to create the folder.

Listing 5.6 shows how to create a new folder in the Zoo Management Web Storage System application for storing contact information about Vets. After checking to see if a folder with the same name already exists by calling the AlreadyExists function, the procedure creates a new folder object and sets a number of properties describing the folder. The procedure also sets the ContentClass property to optimize the folder for storing contacts. To allow MAPI clients to use all functionality of the folder, the MAPI equivalent property is also set. Finally, the folder is created in the Web Storage System, and any existing folder with the same URL is overwritten with the new information. For more information about content classes, see Chapter 3, "Web Storage System Schema."

Listing 5.6   Create a public folder.

```
Sub CreateFolder_CDO()
  ' Create a new folder in the Zoo Management application

  Dim urlVetsFld As String

  ' Build the URL to the new folder
  urlVetsFld = _
    GetStorageName & "Applications/Zoo Management/Vets/"

  If AlreadyExists(urlVetsFld) Then
    ' Contact already exists
    Debug.Print "This folder already exists: " & urlVetsFld
    Exit Sub
  End If
```

```
' If you are using VBScript, use this With:
' With CreateObject("cdo.folder")
With New CDO.Folder
  ' Set a description about the folder
  .Description = "Information about vets."

  ' Configure the folder to hold contact information
  .ContentClass = "urn:content-classes:contactfolder"

  ' Make the contact folder usable by Outlook
  .Fields("http://schemas.microsoft.com/exchange/outlookfolderclass")
= _
    "IPF.contact"

  ' Save the changes
  .Fields.Update

  ' Create the new folder by saving it to the public store
  .DataSource.SaveTo urlVetsFld
End With
End Sub
```

TIP To delete a folder from the folder hierarchy, use ADO to access the folder record, and then call the DeleteRecord method. For more information, see Chapter 4, "ActiveX Data Objects and Exchange."

ENABLING A FOLDER FOR E-MAIL

When a folder is created, by default it is not enabled to receive e-mail messages through Simple Mail Transfer Protocol (SMTP). You must explicitly enable the folder to receive e-mail. This is done with the MailEnable method of the CDO IMailRecipient interface. When you call this method, Exchange automatically assigns an e-mail address to the folder.

To enable a folder to receive e-mail, the folder must already exist in a folder tree. If you are creating a new folder and want to enable it to receive e-mail at the same time you create the folder, you must first save the folder and then call the MailEnable method. If you are simply enabling a folder that already exists to receive e-mail, it is not necessary to save it again before calling the MailEnable method.

Listing 5.7 shows how to create and enable a folder to receive e-mail. The procedure first calls the AlreadyExists function to determine if the folder already exists. If it does exist, the procedure opens the folder in edit mode. If the folder does not exist, the procedure creates a new folder and saves it to the folder tree. To enable the folder to receive e-mail, the procedure must access the IMailRecipient interface. Because the code is written using Visual Basic and the IMailRecipient interface object variable is declared as CDOEXM.IMailRecipient, the code can point the IMailRecipient interface object variable to the Folder object variable, and the folder will return the proper interface automatically. After the interface is referenced, the procedure calls the MailEnable method. To be sure that the folder e-mail address will appear in the Microsoft Outlook address book, the procedure also sets the HideFromAddressBook property to False.

Listing 5.7 Create a folder that can receive messages via SMTP.

```
Sub MailEnableFolder()
  ' Create a folder that can receive email

    Dim urlNotices As String
    Dim fldr As CDO.Folder
    Dim rcp As CDOEXM.IMailRecipient

    Set fldr = New CDO.Folder

    'Build the URL to the new folder
    urlNotices = GetStorageName & _
      "applications/zoo management/facilities/"

    If AlreadyExists(urlNotices) Then
      ' Open the folder
      fldr.DataSource.Open urlNotices, , adModeReadWrite
    Else
      ' Create a new folder
      fldr.DataSource.SaveTo urlNotices, , adModeReadWrite
    End If
```

```
' Reference the IMailRecipient interface
' If you are using VBScript, access the interface like this
'Set rcp = fldr.GetInterface("IMailRecipient")
Set rcp = fldr

' Mail enable the folder and generate the email addresses
With rcp
   .HideFromAddressBook = False
End With

' Save the folder again
fldr.DataSource.Save

'Clean up
Set fldr = Nothing
Set rcp = Nothing
End Sub
```

NOTE   For more information about configuring e-mail recipients, see Chapter 8, "Interacting with Active Directory."

COUNTING THE CONTENTS OF A FOLDER

Another reason to use the CDO Folder object when you work with folders is to count the folder contents. When using ADO to count resources in a folder, you must navigate to the folder, populate a Recordset object with the folder contents, and then call the RecordCount property. Not only does this property disregard whether the record is an item or another folder, but depending on the type of cursor the Recordset object uses, you might often get ambiguous results that indicate items exist in the folder but that the exact count is unknown. The other alternative with ADO is to enumerate through the contents of the Recordset object and use a variable to count the number of times the loop runs. Because this requires that each resource in the Recordset object be touched, this approach can add unnecessary stress to the server when the Recordset object is very large.

Using CDO, you can avoid both ambiguity in your code and overhead to the server. The Folder object offers three properties for counting the contents of a folder:

- The ItemCount property counts all items in a folder, excluding any subfolders.

- The UnreadItemCount property counts only those items that are not marked as read.

- The VisibleCount property counts only those items that are visible to users with access. The property disregards hidden system items that might be stored in the folder.

The code in Listing 5.8 reads some of the properties for a CDO Folder object. After a folder is opened, the code returns the content class for the folder and the counts of various items.

Listing 5.8 Get item count information for a folder.

```
Sub CountFolderContents()
    ' Return the various item counts on a folder

    Dim urlKeepersFld As String

    ' Build the URL to the folder
    urlKeepersFld = GetStorageName & _
        "Applications/Zoo Management/Staff/"

    ' If you are using VBScript, use this With:
    ' With CreateObject("cdo.folder")
    With New CDO.Folder
        ' Open the folder
        .DataSource.Open urlKeepersFld
```

```
        ' Return some information including the counts
        Debug.Print _
            "DisplayName      = " & .DisplayName
        Debug.Print _
            "ContentClass     = " & .ContentClass
        Debug.Print _
            "EmailAddress     = " & .EmailAddress
        Debug.Print _
            "Description      = " & .Description
        Debug.Print _
            "ItemCount        = " & .ItemCount
        Debug.Print _
            "UnreadItemCount  = " & .UnreadItemCount
        Debug.Print _
            "VisibleCount     = " & .VisibleCount
    End With
End Sub
```

WORKING WITH CONTACT INFORMATION

What is a contact? That's not an easy term to define these days. As business practices become more complex, so do the objects used to represent the practices —especially those used to define information about a person. In Exchange, a contact can represent a resource in a Web Storage System folder and in Active Directory. In a folder, a contact is a compilation of information about a person. In Active Directory, a contact can be both an entry for storing basic information about a person and a user object for logging on to the network. For either kind of resource, you use the CDO Person object to create new contacts and edit existing ones.

The way that you bind the Person object to the target resource depends on where the contact is located. When working with contact information in a Web Storage System folder, you use the typical URL that you create with the ExOLEDB provider. To bind a Person object to information in Active Directory, you need to create a different URL that uses the Lightweight Directory Access Protocol (LDAP) provider. After you have bound the Person object to the appropriate resource, you can then use any of the properties available in the urn:schemas:contacts namespace to store a variety of information about a person, such as name, telephone numbers, e-mail address, and physical address. Using this contact data, you can call people on the telephone, send e-mail messages to them, and schedule meetings with them at their offices. This section lists the Contact properties and explains how to create a contact in the Web Storage System and retrieve vCard information.

NOTE This chapter does not discuss using the Person object with objects in Active Directory. However, in most cases, the same core features of the CDO Person object can be applied to contact and user objects in Active Directory. You also cannot use the Person object to create and manage distribution lists, now known as groups. Groups are maintained in Active Directory and must be accessed by using Active Directory Service Interfaces (ADSI). For information about using the CDO Person object to manage user objects in Active Directory and more information about ADSI and groups, see Chapter 8, "Interacting with Active Directory."

CONTACT PROPERTIES

It takes a quite a bit of information to describe people and their behaviors. Everything from a person's hobbies and gender to more computer-specific information, such as the proxy address for a person's computer, must be saved when a new contact is created in either the Web Storage System or Active Directory. To accommodate all this information, the schema defines a wide range of properties. In fact, with more than 140 properties, the urn:schemas:contacts: namespace is one of the largest compilations of schema properties defined in Exchange. Because only a small percentage of properties are implemented as CDO interface properties, you must know the name of the schema property or constant to access it through the Fields collection of the Person object.

Tables 5.4 through 5.14 list contact properties based on functionality. This should make name discovery easier. In addition to the data type and description, each table lists the following information:

- **urn:schemas:contacts: property name**. This is the name of the property as it is identified in a Web Storage System schema. Schema property names are case sensitive, so use the name exactly as it appears in this column. Because some of these names can be lengthy, some property names wrap into multiple lines. When this happens in the table, it does not mean that you should use a space in the name.

- **CDO constant**. This column contains the CDO constant for the schema property if it exists. You can use this constant in place of the full schema property name. As with the schema property names, some of the constant names can be lengthy and wrap into multiple lines. When this happens in the table, it does not mean that you should use a space in the name.

- **CDO property**. This column contains the CDO Person object property, if it exists, for the schema property. CDO object properties are the easiest to use.

Table 5.4 Name properties

urn:schemas:contacts: property	CDO constant	CDO property	Data type	Description
givenName	cdoFirstName	FirstName	String	Given name (first name).
middlename	cdoMiddle Name	Middle Name	String	Middle name.
sn	cdoSurname	LastName	String	Surname (last name).
namesuffix	cdoNamesuffix	Name Suffix	String	Name suffix (such as Sr., Jr., II, or III).
personaltitle	cdoPersonalTitle	Name Prefix	String	Title prefix (such as Miss, Ms., Mrs., M., or Mr.).

Continued on next page

Table 5.4 continued Name properties

urn:schemas:contacts: property	CDO constant	CDO property	Data type	Description
initials	cdoInitials	Initials	String	Initials (the first letter of a person's first, middle, and last names).
cn	cdoCommon Name	N/A	String	Common name (an alternative to the person's full name).
nickname	cdoNickName	N/A	String	Nickname (friendly name).
fileas	cdoFileAs	FileAs	String	Indicates how the contact name is ordered in views.

Table 5.5 Identification properties

urn:schemas:contacts: property	CDO constant	CDO property	Data type	Description
customerid	cdoCustomerID	N/A	String	User defined.
fileasid	cdoFileAsID	N/A	Long	User defined.
governmentid	cdoGovernment Id	N/A	String	User defined.
internationalisdn number	cdoInternational ISDNNumber	N/A	String	User defined.
employeenumber	cdoEmployee Number	N/A	String	User defined.

Table 5.6 E-mail address and URL fields

urn:schemas:contacts: property	CDO constant	CDO property	Data type	Description
email1	cdoEmail1 Address	Email	String	Primary e-mail address of the contact.
email2	cdoEmail2 Address	Email2	String	Secondary e-mail address of the contact.
email3	cdoEmail3 Address	Email3	String	Third e-mail address of the contact.
proxyaddresses	cdoProxy Addresses	Email Addresses	Variant	String containing one or more client e-mail addresses.
sourceurl	cdoSourceURL	N/A	String	URL of the data source on the server for a contact.
personalHome Page	cdoPersonalURL	N/A	String	URL of the personal home page of a contact.
businesshome page	N/A	N/A	String	URL of the business home page of a contact.
ftpsite	cdoFTPSite	N/A	String	URL of the File Transfer Protocol (FTP) site of a contact.
mapurl	cdoMapURL	N/A	String	Map URL of the contact. Read-only.

Table 5.7 Other computer properties

urn:schemas:contacts: property	CDO constant	CDO property	Data type	Description
authorig	cdoOriginal Author	N/A	String	User name of the person who created the contact.
submission contlength	cdoSubmission ContentLength	N/A	Long	Maximum size, in kilobytes, of a message that can be sent to the contact.
usercertificate	cdoUser Certificate	N/A	Byte	Digital certificate used to validate a contact.
protocolsettings	cdoProtocol Settings	N/A	String	A binary string that indicates Internet communications.
dn	cdo Distinguished Name	N/A	String	Distinguished name of the contact, including domain information (read-only).
contact	N/A	N/A	String	Extensible Markup Language (XML) element used by Microsoft Hotmail to retrieve contact information (read-only).
computernetwork name	cdoComputer NetworkName	N/A	String	Computer network name.

Table 5.8 Telephone number properties

urn:schemas:contacts: property	CDO constant	CDO property	Data type	Description
othertimezone	cdoOtherTimeZone	N/A	String	Work time zone.
telephoneNumber	cdoWorkPhone	Work Phone	String	Work telephone number.
telephonenumber2	cdoWorkPhone2	N/A	String	Alternative work telephone number.
otherTelephone	cdoOtherTelephone	N/A	String	Other alternative work telephone number.
facsimile telephonenumber	cdoWorkFax	WorkFax	String	Work fax number.
otherfax	cdoOtherFax	N/A	String	Alternative work fax number.
telexnumber	cdoTelexNumber	N/A	String	Telex (work) number.
pager	cdoPager	Work Pager	String	Work pager number.
otherpager	cdoOtherPager	N/A	String	Alternative pager number.
mobile	cdoMobile	Mobile Phone	String	Mobile telephone number.
othermobile	cdoOtherMobile	N/A	String	Alternative mobile telephone number.
callbackphone	cdoCallBackPhone	N/A	String	Callback telephone number.

Continued on next page

Table 5.8 continued   Telephone number properties

urn:schemas:contacts: property	CDO constant	CDO property	Data type	Description
hometimezone	cdoHomeTime Zone	N/A	String	Home time zone.
homePhone	cdoHomePhone	Home Phone	String	Home telephone number.
homephone2	cdoHome Phone2	N/A	String	Alternative home telephone number.
homefax	cdoHomeFax	HomeFax	String	Home fax number.
otherfacsimile telephonenumber	cdoOtherFax Number	N/A	String	Alternative home fax number.

Table 5.9   Physical address properties—work

urn:schemas:contacts: property	CDO constant	CDO property	Data type	Description
o	cdoOrganization Name	N/A	String	Name of the company or organization.
department	cdoDepartment	N/A	String	Name of the department.
roomnumber	cdoRoom Number	N/A	String	Office room number.
location	N/A	N/A	String	Location or area.
workaddress	cdoWorkAddress	Work Postal Address	String	Combination field of work street, city, state, and postal delivery zone (read-only).

Continued on next page

Table 5.9 continued Physical address properties—work

urn:schemas:contacts: property	CDO constant	CDO property	Data type	Description
street	cdoWorkStreet	Work Street	String	Work street address.
postofficebox	cdoPostOffice Box	N/A	String	Work post office box.
l	cdoWorkCity	WorkCity	String	Work city.
st	cdoWorkState	WorkState	String	Work state abbreviation.
postalcode	cdoWorkPostal Code	Work Postal Code	String	Work postal code.
c	cdoWork Country Abbreviation	N/A	String	Work country abbreviation.
co	cdoWorkCountry	Work Country	String	Work country common name. If used, you must also use the work country abbreviation.

Table 5.10 Physical address properties—home

urn:schemas:contacts: property	CDO constant	CDO property	Data type	Description
homepostal address	cdoHomePostal Address	Home Postal Address	String	Combination field of home street, city, state, and postal delivery zone (read-only).
homeStreet	cdoHomeStreet	Home Street	String	Home street address.

Continued on next page

Table 5.10 continued Physical address properties—home

urn:schemas:contacts: property	CDO constant	CDO property	Data type	Description
homepostoffice box	cdoHomePost OfficeBox	HomePost Office Box	String	Home post office box.
homeCity	cdoHomeCity	HomeCity	String	Home city.
homeState	cdoHomeState	HomeState	String	Home state abbreviation.
homePostalCode	cdoHomePostal Code	Home Postal Code	String	Home postal delivery zone.
homeCountry	cdoHome Country	Home Country	String	Home country abbreviation.
homelatitude	cdoHome Latitude	N/A	Double	Home latitude.
homelongitude	cdoHome Longitude	N/A	Double	Home longitude.

Table 5.11 Physical address properties—package and mail delivery

urn:schemas:contacts: property	CDO constant	CDO property	Data type	Description
mailingaddressid	cdoMailing AddressID	Mailing Address ID	Cdo Mailing Address Id Values	Indicates whether these package delivery address fields are built from work, home, or other address fields, or whether a new address is used.

Continued on next page

Table 5.11 continued Physical address properties—package and mail delivery

urn:schemas:contacts: property	CDO constant	CDO property	Data type	Description
mailingpostal address	cdoMailingPostal Address	Mailing Address	String	Combination field of package delivery street, city, state, and postal delivery zone (read-only).
mailingstreet	cdoMailingStreet	N/A	String	Package delivery street address (read-only).
mailingpostoffice box	cdoMailingPost OfficeBox	N/A	String	Package delivery post office box (read-only).
mailingcity	cdoMailingCity	N/A	String	Package delivery city (read-only).
mailingstate	cdoMailingState	N/A	String	Package delivery state abbreviation (read-only).
mailingcountry	cdoMailing Country	N/A	String	Package delivery country abbreviation (read-only).

Table 5.12 Physical address properties—second home or alternative address

urn:schemas:contacts: property	CDO constant	CDO property	Data type	Description
otherpostaladdress	cdoOtherPostal Address	N/A	String	Combination field of alternative street, city, state, and postal delivery zone (read-only).

Continued on next page

Table 5.12 continued   Physical address properties—second home or alternative address

urn:schemas:contacts: property	CDO constant	CDO property	Data type	Description
otherstreet	cdoOtherStreet	N/A	String	Alternative street address.
otherpostofficebox	cdoOtherPost OfficeBox	N/A	String	Alternative post office box.
othercity	cdoOtherCity	N/A	String	Alternative city.
otherstate	cdoOtherState	N/A	String	Alternative state abbreviation.
otherpostalcode	cdoOtherPostal Code	N/A	String	Alternative postal delivery zone.
othercountrycode	cdoOther CountryCode	N/A	String	Alternative country abbreviation.
othercountry	cdoOther Country	N/A	String	Alternative country common name.

Table 5.13   Associated people properties

urn:schemas:contacts: property	CDO constant	CDO property	Data type	Description
manager	cdoManager	N/A	String	Full name of the manager of the contact.
managercn	cdoManager CommonName	N/A	String	Friendly name of the manager of the contact.
secretary	cdoSecretary	N/A	String	Full name of the secretary of the contact.

Continued on next page

Table 5.13 continued Associated people properties

urn:schemas:contacts: property	CDO constant	CDO property	Data type	Description
secretarycn	cdoSecretary Common Name	N/A	String	Friendly name of the secretary of the contact.
secretaryurl	cdoSecretaryURL	N/A	String	URL of the secretary of the contact.
spousecn	cdoSpouse CommonName	N/A	String	Friendly name of the spouse of the contact.
childrensnames	cdoChildren Names	N/A	Variant	Multi-valued list of names of children of the contact.

Table 5.14 Miscellaneous fields

urn:schemas:contacts: property	CDO constant	CDO property	Data type	Description
account	cdoAccount	N/A	String	User-defined.
title	cdoTitle	Title	String	Work title of the contact.
profession	cdoProfession	N/A	String	Professional position or role of the contact.
language	cdoLanguage	N/A	String	Spoken language of the contact in IS639 format.
gender	cdoGender	N/A	Integer	String indicating the gender of the contact (male, female, or unknown).

Continued on next page

Table 5.14 continued Miscellaneous fields

urn:schemas:contacts: property	CDO constant	CDO property	Data type	Description
bday	cdoBirthday	N/A	Date	Birth date of the contact.
hobbies	cdoHobbies	N/A	String	Concatenated list of personal hobbies of the contact.
billinginformation	N/A	N/A	String	String indicating billing information, such as an hourly rate.
wedding anniversary	cdoWedding Anniversary	N/A	Date	Wedding anniversary date of the contact.

CREATING A CONTACT IN THE WEB STORAGE SYSTEM

To create a contact in the Web Storage System by using CDO, you create a new Person object, set the properties that describe the contact, and then call the DataSource.SaveTo method. You also have the option of using the DataSource.SaveToContainer method. However, as mentioned earlier in the chapter, the DataSource.SaveToContainer method does not allow you to explicitly set the DAV:displayname property suffix of the URL in the same way that the DataSource.SaveTo method does. Instead, Exchange automatically sets the DAV:displayname property to a globally unique identifier (GUID) that looks something like this: {E180EECE-36A5-498E-BB80-C8A5FE6C33C8}.

This can cause a number of problems. First, although the GUID means something to the Web Storage System, it has no meaning for your customers. So, if you plan to display the DAV:displayname value or even the URL for the item, the GUID might generate some confusion. Second, because this GUID is generated by Exchange, it is always unique. This means that you could inadvertently enter the same information for a contact multiple times and never generate an error. To avoid multiple entries for the same contact, use the DataSource.SaveTo method when creating contacts and test for the existence of a contact with the same credentials before creating it.

RETRIEVING VCARD INFORMATION

Not all messaging clients can interpret MAPI format. To optimize compatibility with other information management programs, contacts can be exposed as MIME-compliant files of contact information known as *vCards*. Using the GetVCardStream method, you can access or create vCard information for a contact. This method returns an ADO Stream object that can be manipulated. For example, you can store the vCard information in a file on the local hard disk, embed the information in an e-mail message, or attach it to another item.

For example, the code in Listing 5.9 uses the GetVCardStream method to extract vCard information from a contact in a Web Storage System folder. The code writes the vCard information to a file on the local drive. After opening the contact, the GetVCardStream method is called to return the contact information as an ADO Stream object. Because the subprocedure writes only to the local drive, the SaveToFile method is called immediately and passed a name for the new file and instructions to overwrite any existing file with the same URL. By calling the SaveToFile method in the same statement as the GetVCardStream method, it is not necessary to create a Stream object. However, you still need to reference ADO 2.5 in the project. If you are planning to further manipulate the contents of the Stream object, you should create a separate Stream object variable, point it to the results of GetVCardStream, and manipulate the information from there.

Listing 5.9   Return contact information as a vCard.

```
Sub GetVCardInformation()
  ' Return a contact as a vCard file

  Dim urlStaffMember As String

  urlStaffMember = GetStorageName & _
    "Applications/Zoo Management/Staff/Amy Luehmann.EML"

  If Not AlreadyExists(urlStaffMember) Then
    ' This URL does not exist
    Debug.Print "Contact does not exist at that URL."
    Exit Sub
  End If

  ' If you are using VBScript, use this With:
  ' With CreateObject("cdo.person")
  With New CDO.Person
    'Open the existing contact
    .DataSource.Open urlStaffMember
    'Save the vCard information to a local file
    .GetVCardStream.SaveToFile "C:\vCard", adSaveCreateOverWrite
  End With
End Sub
```

When the code in Listing 5.9 runs, a file is generated. If you open the file in Microsoft Notepad, the results would look similar to the file in Figure 5.1.

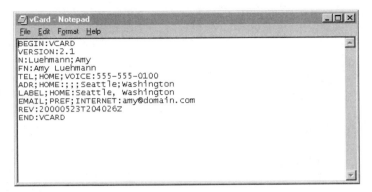

Figure 5.1
When the code in Listing 5.9 runs, it generates a file like this with vCard information for the contact.

SUMMARY

CDO for Exchange provides objects, classes, and interfaces for building powerful collaboration solutions. Although ADO 2.5 is optimal for navigating the Web Storage System, CDO is optimal for manipulating those individual resources when you have collaboration goals in mind. You can use CDO for sending e-mail, scheduling appointments, managing contacts, and maintaining folders. When you use CDO with contact information, it provides you with easy access to the immense selection of contact schema fields through exposed properties. CDO even exposes a method for easy access to vCard information. If folder creation and management is your goal, CDO exposes properties for folder configuration and provides access to folder management objects.

Chapter 6, "CDO Messaging," discusses the core technologies present in any CDO messaging application and explains the techniques you need to build an application—from the simplest application to the most complex solution.

6

CDO Messaging

Remember when the fastest and easiest way to communicate with your coworkers in other offices and with colleagues at other companies was to pick up the telephone and call them? That wasn't very long ago. Now, although the phone is still essential to doing business, e-mail has replaced it as our most important telecommunication link. Today when a phone system goes down, it's a nuisance but not a disaster. (For that matter, many people now have cell phones.) However, when a messaging server goes down, the world seems to stop. Entire businesses come to their knees when e-mail isn't working. People depend on this quick and easy form of communication for everything from handling standard business practices, such as invoice approvals, to providing the necessary link between international offices any time of the day.

More and more applications have messaging integrated into them. To keep up with this increasing demand, Collaboration Data Objects (CDO) for Microsoft Exchange 2000 Server provides a robust set of classes and interfaces to develop rich messaging applications. This chapter explains the core techniques necessary to build the simplest application or the most complex solution. Sections include:

- **Overview of CDO Messaging**
- **Composing and Sending Messages**
- **Composing More Complex Messages**
- **Processing Messages**

OVERVIEW OF CDO MESSAGING

Microsoft Exchange 2000 Server and CDO support the Internet standards that specify how messages should be formatted for transmission across a network. By conforming to these standards, CDO for Microsoft Windows 2000 and CDO for Exchange can be used to build messaging solutions that function across a broad range of protocols, including Simple Mail Transfer Protocol (SMTP) and Network News Transfer Protocol (NNTP). The messages themselves are structured using Multipurpose Internet Mail Extensions (MIME), the currently accepted standard for messaging. This chapter focuses on MIME-formatted messages unless stated otherwise.

MIME enables any client program to decode and display complex message bodies, such as those that contain HTML tags, rich text, and structured attachments. MIME is highly flexible and allows each piece of an electronic mail message to be managed independently of, or in relation to, the other parts without affecting the underlying format of the message.

> **NOTE** Although the Microsoft Web Storage System is optimized for MIME and all messages are stored in MIME format by default, Exchange also supports the RFC 822 format and UUENCODE for attachments. RFC 822 is a simple message format consisting of header fields such as sender, recipient, and subject. This type of message might or might not have a body. If it does, it is separated from the header fields by an empty line. This type of message must consist of US-ASCII characters only.

CDO MESSAGING CLASSES AND INTERFACES

When you use CDO to build message applications, you use the classes and interfaces found in the CDO for Exchange 2000 object library (Cdoex.dll). Messaging applications are not built with a single object and interface but involve a number of classes and interfaces. The more complex the application, the more classes you use to create it. However, some basics always apply.

Predominant among these is the Message class. The Message class is the cornerstone of CDO messaging solutions. It can be either a message or a post, which is a message saved in a folder or posted to a newsgroup, and it is used to create new messages as well as to open and manipulate existing ones. The Message object has an extensive list of properties, but not all possible message fields are exposed as properties. The Message object also provides a Fields collection that you can use to access the schema properties that are not defined as CDO Message properties, including any custom properties. By using the methods of the Message object, you can send or post messages, reply to existing messages, and forward them to other recipients. You can address a message by using the properties of the Message object, but you must use the Addressee object to resolve addresses and eliminate ambiguous names. Figure 6.1 shows the Message object model.

If you work with MIME messages, then you will also use the BodyParts collection. MIME messages are made up of pieces known as BodyPart objects. A BodyPart can, for example, be an attachment, the body text, or the header section. You can create and manage attachments by using the BodyPart object. In addition, you can use the ActiveX Data Objects (ADO) Stream object to save attachments or other BodyPart objects to disk.

If you work with groups of messages, you will undoubtedly use the Configuration object. You use the Configuration object to define how to send or post a message. You can then apply that single configuration to all messages that your application sends, eliminating the need to configure each individual message. And, as with all CDO objects, the IDataSource interface handles the data swapping between the actual resource in the Microsoft Web Storage System and the copy of data in the CDO object.

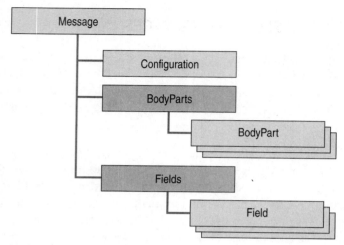

Figure 6.1
The CDO Message object model

DISSECTING A MIME MESSAGE

To successfully build messaging applications by using CDO, you must understand how MIME messages are split into BodyPart objects. BodyPart objects have a media type property (BodyPart.ContentMediaType) that identifies what the BodyPart object contains. This section presents general information about media types. For a more detailed discussion of media types, see "Identifying the Media Type of a BodyPart Object" later in this chapter.

One way to learn how messages are broken into BodyPart objects is to step through a few messaging scenarios. A simple example is a plain-text message that has an attachment. When you create a simple message that uses plain text in the body text, the entire Message object is considered to be a single BodyPart object (see Figure 6.2). The BodyPart contains all the information about the message, including header information and the body text of the message. The BodyPart for the message has a media type of "text/plain."

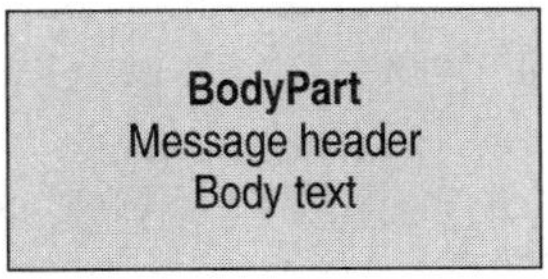

> **BodyPart**
> Message header
> Body text

Figure 6.2
A plain-text message has only one BodyPart object and contains both the message header and the body text.

When you add an attachment, for example, a Microsoft Word document, to that message, the entire structure of the message changes. The message no longer has a single BodyPart object but three BodyPart objects: one for the header information, one for the attachment, and one for the body text. The BodyPart object that represents the header information is considered the parent of the other two BodyPart objects, which constitute a BodyParts collection. The BodyPart object that represents the body text is still plain-text, so it has a media type of "text/plain." The attachment is a Word document, so the media type for that BodyPart object is "application/msword." Because the message BodyPart object contains BodyPart objects with different media types, the message header BodyPart has a media type of "multipart/mixed." Figure 6.3 shows how the message evolves from a single BodyPart object into three BodyPart objects.

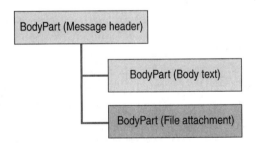

Figure 6.3
A plain-text message with a Word document attachment has three BodyPart objects: one for the message header, one for the body text, and one for the file attachment.

Another example is a message with HTML formatting in the body text. Because not every client is able to process HTML in messages, by default Exchange also generates a plain-text version of the content. In this message, the body text must be rendered in two different BodyPart objects: one BodyPart object that represents the HTML version with a media type of "text/HTML" and one BodyPart object that represents the plain-text version with a media type of "text/plain." Because the message can generate the body text using two different formats, the message header BodyPart object has a media type of "multipart/alternative." Figure 6.4 shows this type of message structure.

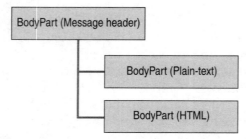

Figure 6.4
A message that uses both plain-text and HTML body text formats consists of three BodyPart objects: one for the message header, one for the plain-text format, and one for the HTML format.

Let's look at one last example: this time, you want to create a message with HTML formatting in the body text and a Word document attachment. Essentially, this example combines the first two examples. When you create a message with two possible formats for the body text, the message has the same structure as that shown in Figure 6.4. When you add the attachment, the message becomes rather complex. The message BodyPart contains a BodyParts collection that consists of another BodyParts collection for the body text formats and a BodyPart object for the file attachment. Because the message contains multiple media types, the message header BodyPart has a media type of "multipart/mixed." The BodyParts collection that represents the body formatting types has a media type of "multipart/alternative" and consists of a BodyPart object for the HTML format with a media type of "text/HTML" and a BodyPart object for the plain-text version with a media type of "text/plain." The BodyPart object that represents the attachment has a media type of "application/msword". Figure 6.5 shows this nested multipart message.

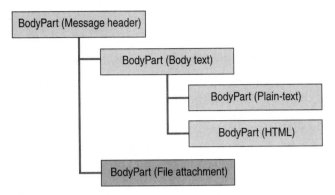

Figure 6.5
A message that uses alternative body text formatting and also includes a file attachment

Although this might seem rather overwhelming, the good news is that CDO provides several properties and methods to make your interaction with BodyPart objects and BodyParts collection as painless as possible. For example, when you add an attachment, you do not have to add a BodyPart object to the message and set the media type. Instead, you can use the AddAttachment method, which does the dirty work for you.

COMPOSING AND SENDING MESSAGES

Whether you're composing a simple message with plain text or a complex message that uses a Web page in the body and a persistent configuration, you need to know the basic techniques involved in composing and sending a message. If you understand the basics behind messaging with CDO, the more advanced tasks don't seem so advanced.

SENDING A SIMPLE MESSAGE

When you send e-mail to someone by using a client application such as Microsoft Outlook Web Access, you create a new message, fill in some information, and then send it. Typically, you address the message to someone, specify the subject matter, and fill in the body with the message. When you send a message with CDO, you do the same thing. To send a simple message by using CDO, create a new Message object and then:

- **Address the e-mail message**. You can use the To, From, and CC properties to indicate who will receive the message. You set each property to a string value consisting of one or more e-mail addresses. If you use multiple e-mail addresses, separate each with a comma.

- **Specify the subject matter**. You set the Subject property to a string value to a short description of the overall content of the message.

- **Fill in the body with some text**. The body can contain plain text, HTML-formatted information, hyperlinks, or even complete Web pages. If you don't need any formatting, you can use the TextBody property or HTMLBody property to fill the body of the e-mail with the message content. The TextBody property uses plain-text formatting in the body, and the HTMLBody property uses HTML formatting.

- **Send the e-mail message**. When you are ready to send the e-mail, you use the Send method of a Message object.

NOTE The code listings in this chapter are available in the project CH_06.vbp on the companion CD. The code samples in this chapter repeatedly call a function named GetStorageName. This function returns the name of the domain in which the code is running. For more information about the GetStorageName function, see Chapter 8, "Interacting with Active Directory."

When you send e-mail using CDO, you must do one additional thing to successfully send the message. You must specify who is sending the e-mail. Client applications such as Outlook Web Access do this for you automatically, but you must set this information explicitly when using CDO. You can set the From property of a Message object to do this. Listing 6.1 shows how to successfully send a very simple e-mail message to two people.

Listing 6.1. Send a simple message.

```
Public Sub CreateandSendMail()
    ' This sends a very simple message

    ' If you are using VBScript, use this With:
    ' With CreateObject("CDO.Message")
    With New CDO.Message
```

```
    ' Indicate who is sending the message
    .From = "mindy@domain.com"

    ' Address the message
    .To = "denise@domain.com, aidan@domain.com"

    ' Set the subject matter
    .Subject = "Siberian Tigers"

    ' Fill in the body text using plain text formatting
    .TextBody = "Did you know there are estimated only " & _
        "about 400 of these magnifcent creatures left in the wild?"

    ' Send the message
    .Send
  End With

  Debug.Print "Message sent."
End Sub
```

ADDRESSING A MESSAGE

When you develop an application by using the Microsoft Outlook 2000 object model or earlier versions of CDO, you address a message by adding to a Recipients collection of the message. CDO does not use a Recipients collection. Instead, when using CDO, you address a message by setting the appropriate CDO properties or schema properties to the appropriate e-mail addresses. The term "recipient" is still used; however, it only defines the receiver of a message. It does not define an object in the CDO object model.

> **NOTE** A CDO Addressee object represents each e-mail address added to the message. You can use the Addressee object to resolve an address, handle ambiguous addresses, and return the free/busy status of a user. However, you do not use the Addressee object to address a message.

Specifying Who Is Sending the Message

As mentioned earlier, you must specify who is sending the e-mail message to successfully send it. You can indicate the sender by setting the From property to the e-mail address of the person who is sending the message. If you set the From property to more than one address, the first address is used as the From address. If you do not indicate a sender, the code fails with a trappable error. For example, this sets the From property for a Message object:

```
msg.From = "mindy@domain.com"
```

If you are sending multiple messages in the same application, you might want to specify a sender with a Configuration object instead of setting the From property on every Message object. By using a persistent Configuration object, you can define a sender with one object and then apply this Configuration to each message. For more information on using a Configuration object to set the sender information, see "Using a Persistent Configuration Object," later in this chapter.

Specifying Who Is Receiving the Message

To indicate who is receiving the message, set one or more of the properties listed in Table 6.1. You can set each property to a string value that consists of one or more e-mail addresses.

Table 6.1 Standard address properties

CDO property	Data type	Description
To	String	Sets or returns the e-mail addresses for the primary recipients of the message.
CC	String	Sets or returns the e-mail addresses for the recipients of a courtesy copy of the message.
BCC	String	Sets or returns the e-mail addresses for the recipients of a courtesy copy of the message as a hidden list.

If you are sending to more than one address, separate each address with a comma. This style of creating multiple recipients is different from that used by some e-mail clients, including Outlook. The following code sample addresses an e-mail message to several recipients:

```
msg.To = "denise@domain.com, aidan@domain.com"
msg.CC = "robert@domain.com"
msg.BCC = "peter@domain.com"
```

CDO supports e-mail addresses in any address format defined by Internet standards. If you are sending a message within your organization, you can use the alias associated with an e-mail address. An alias is a shortcut name for the proper e-mail address and is often the portion of the e-mail address before the @ symbol. For example, an e-mail address of `mindy@domain.com` might have an alias of "mindy."

CONFIGURING FOR REPLIES

In addition to setting the standard address properties for addressing a message, you can also set an alternative address for replies. Normally when you reply to an existing message, the replies go to the address specified in the From property. If you prefer to have replies sent to another address instead, set the ReplyTo property to that e-mail address. Replies then go to the ReplyTo address instead of to the From address.

As with the From property, the ReplyTo property has an equivalent configuration schema property that can be set with a Configuration object instead of setting the ReplyTo property on every Message. By using a persistent Configuration object, you can define the address used for replies with a single Configuration object and then apply this Configuration to each message. For more information about using a Configuration object to set the sender information, see "Using a Persistent Configuration Object," later in this chapter.

ADDING THE BODY TEXT

You can add the body text of a message several different ways. You can add text that uses plain-text formatting, HTML formatting, or MIME Encapsulation of Aggregate HTML Documents (MHTML) formatting. This section discusses how to use these three types of formatting in the body text of a message.

USING PLAIN-TEXT FORMATTING

If you want to add only simple text to the body of a message, set the TextBody property of a Message object to a text string. You can use the TextBody property to add text, but it does not allow you to specify special formatting, such as making some words bold or making bulleted lists. For example, the following code sample adds text to a Message object text body without using any special formatting:

```
msg.TextBody = _
    "This is the main body text without any special formatting."
```

If you want to format the text, you must use HTML to add the formatting features.

USING HTML FORMATTING

If you want to include formatting in the body text, you can use HTML formatting. With HTML, you can specify the font style, add bold or italic, or use bulleted lists. In fact, you can use just about any formatting available in HTML. To use HTML formatting in body text, you set the HTMLBody property to a legitimate HTML string. For example, the following code sample uses HTML formatting to create body text with a header, a rule, italic, and special font styles in the text:

```
msg.HTMLBody = _
    "<H1>Check this out!</H1>" & _
    "<HR><i>Look</i>" & _
    " at this " & _
    "<font color=red size=12>cool</font>" & _
    " HTML message."
```

When you create an HTML body, by default CDO also generates a plain-text version of the body text. The plain-text version of the body uses the same text as the HTML body but without any special HTML formatting. This ensures that clients unable to process HTML-formatted messages can still read the message. If you would rather not automatically generate a plain-text version of the body text, set the AutoGenerateTextBody property to False. Then, if you prefer to create a plain-text body, you can do so by setting the TextBody property to the value you want. For example, Listing 6.2 shows how to create a message with two different formats for the body text.

Listing 6.2   Generate a message with both a text body and an HTML body.

```
Public Sub CreateSeparateTextandHTML()
    ' Use both an HTML and plain text
    ' version for body text formatting.

    ' If you are using VBScript, use this With:
    ' With CreateObject("CDO.Message")
    With New CDO.Message
        .From = "mindy@domain.com"
        .To = "peter@domain.com"

        .Subject = _
            "This message has two different body text versions"

        ' Generate body text for plain text viewers
        .TextBody = _
            "You're missing out by not supporting HTML!"

        ' Generate body text for HTML capable viewers
        .HTMLBody = _
            "<H1>Check this out!</H1>" & _
            "<HR><i>Look</i>" & _
            " at this " & _
            "<font color=red size=12>cool</font>" & _
            " HTML message."

        ' Send the message
        .Send
    End With

    Debug.Print "Message sent."
End Sub
```

Using MHTML Formatting

Many e-mail clients, such as Outlook, can display HTML pages just like a Web browser does. To include all the HTML formatting, graphics, objects, and other elements contained in the Web page in the body of a message, you use MHTML formatting. MHTML is an Internet standard that defines the MIME structure that is used to send HTML content in message bodies along with those elements that are used in the Web page.

To embed a Web page or portions of a Web page as body text, you use the CreateMHTMLBody method of a Message object. The CreateMHTMLBody method has one required parameter: the URL of the Web page must be embedded in the body of a Message object. For example, the following code sample fills the body of a message with the msdn.Microsoft.com/exchange developer center home page:

```
msg.CreateMHTMLBody "http://msdn.microsoft.com/exchange/"
```

If the Web page contains support elements (such as sound files, style sheets, or graphics), they are included with the Web page and attached to the message as file attachments. Although this allows a recipient to view the Web page in its entirety, it also dramatically increases the size of a message in bytes. To avoid this increase in message size, you can use the optional argument Flags to indicate which elements to exclude. To define which elements to exclude, set the Flag parameter to one or more of the numeric constants from Table 6.2.

Table 6.2   Constants for the Flags argument of the CreateMHTMLBody method

CDO constant	Value	Result
cdoSuppressAll	31	Do not include support files.
cdoSuppressBGSounds	2	Do not include sound files.
cdoSuppressFrames	4	Do not include framesets.
cdoSuppressImages	1	Do not include image files.
cdoSuppressNone	0	Include all support files. (Default)
cdoSuppressObjects	8	Do not include object files.
cdoSuppressStyleSheets	16	Do not include style sheets.

The following code sample once again embeds the microsoft.com home page in a message, but this time, suppresses the background sounds and objects:

```
msg.CreateMHTMLBody _
    "http://msdn.microsoft.com/exchange/", _
    cdoSuppressImages + cdoSuppressObjects
```

Listing 6.3 shows how to embed a complete Web page into the body of an e-mail message while suppressing background sounds and objects used in the Web page.

Listing 6.3   Embed a Web page in the body of an e-mail message.

```
Public Sub FillMessageBodywithWebPage()
    ' Creates a mail message with the Microsoft home page
    ' as the body text.

    Dim cnfg As CDO.Configuration

    ' Set the Sender information
    Set cnfg = New CDO.Configuration
    With cnfg
        .Fields(cdoSendEmailAddress) = "peter@domain.com"
        .Fields.Update
    End With

    ' Create the new message
    With New CDO.Message
        Set .Configuration = cnfg
        .To = "mindy@domain.com"
        .Subject = "This is a great web site."

        ' Embed the Microsoft home page into the body
        .CreateMHTMLBody _
            "http://msdn.microsoft.com/exchange/" _
            , cdoSuppressBGSounds + cdoSuppressObjects

        .Send
    End With

    ' Clean up
    Set cnfg = Nothing
End Sub
```

Figure 6.6 shows the result of executing the code in Listing 6.3.

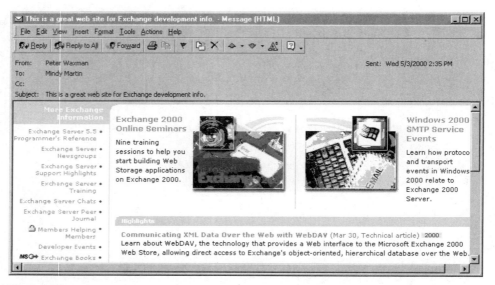

Figure 6.6
The CreateMHTMLBody method of a Message object lets you embed an entire Web page in the body of a message.

ADDING ATTACHMENTS

You often need to send files along with an e-mail message. To add an attachment, use the AddAttachment method of a Message object. The AddAttachment method is a shortcut to manually add a new BodyPart to a message and then set the necessary properties for that BodyPart to be an attachment. In case you need to manipulate the attachment further, the AddAttachment method returns a BodyPart object.

To use the AddAttachment method, pass a string value with the path and file name to be attached. An attachment can be a file on a local or remote computer, a message in an Inbox, or even a Web page. Correct examples of using the AddAttachment method include:

```
msg.AddAttachment _
   "D:\Sales Information\Latest Sales Data.xls"

msg.AddAttachment _
   "http://cyberserver/exchange/mindy/inbox/siberian%20tigers.eml"

msg.AddAttachment _
   "HTTP://www.microsoft.com/index.html"
```

If the attachment doesn't exist, the code fails with a trappable error. Listing 6.4 shows how to attach a file to a message. If the file doesn't exist, an error message is generated.

Listing 6.4   Attach a file to a message.

```
Sub CreateMsgwithAttachment()
    ' Attempts to attach a file
    ' to a message.

    ' Turn on error handling
    On Error GoTo HandleErrors

    ' Create a new message
    With New CDO.Message
        .From = " mindy @domain.com"
        .To = "peter@domain.com"
        .Subject = "Message with attachments"
        .TextBody = "Can you see this?"

        ' Attempt to attach a file
        .AddAttachment "D:\somefile.xls"

        ' Send the message
        .Send
    End With

    Debug.Print "Message sent."
```

```
ExitHere:
    Exit Sub

HandleErrors:
    Dim strError As String
    ' Get the error number, description, and source
    strError = "Error #" & Err.Number & ": " _
        & Err.Description
    ' Display the errors in a message box
    MsgBox strError
    Resume ExitHere
End Sub
```

USEFUL SCHEMA PROPERTIES FOR MESSAGING

When you create a new CDO Message object, you are creating a resource in a Web Storage System with a DAV:contentclass of urn:content-classes:message. The Web Storage System automatically associates a number of properties with the urn:content-classes:message content class, most of which are accessible through a CDO property. However, some of the most useful schema properties cannot be read or set through a CDO property. Table 6.3 lists these schema properties.

Because a CDO object does not explicitly expose these properties, you must use the Fields property of a Message object to set them. You can pass either the schema property name or the CDO constant equivalent. After you set the appropriate properties, save the changes you made with the Fields.Update method. For example, the following code sample sets the importance level of the message to high:

```
Set msg = New CDO.Message
msg.Fields(cdoImportance) = cdoHigh
```

Table 6.3 To retrieve these schema properties for a Message object, you must use the Fields collection.

Schema property	CDO constant	Data type	Read/write?	Description
DAV:parentname	cdoParentName	String	No	URL of the container that owns the message.
DAV:href	cdoHref	String	No	URL of the message that includes the display name.
DAV:ishidden	cdoIsHidden	Boolean	Yes	If True, the message is not visible.
DAV:isreadonly	N/A[1]	Boolean	Yes	If True, the message is read-only.
DAV:creationdate	cdoCreationDate	Date	No	Date the message was created.
DAV:getcontentlength	N/A	Long	No	Size of the message.
DAV:displayname	cdoDisplayName	String	No	Subject of the message with the .eml extension.
DAV:uid	cdoUID	String	No	Unique identifier value assigned by Exchange.
urn:schemas:httpmail:date	cdoDate	Date	Yes	Date the message was sent to the server.
urn:schemas:httpmail:datereceived	cdoDateReceived	Date	No	Date the message was received by the server.

Continued on next page

Table 6.3 continued   To retrieve these schema properties for a Message object, you must use the Fields collection

Schema property	CDO constant	Data type	Read/ write?	Description
urn:schemas:httpmail: hasattachment	cdoHas Attachment	Boolean	No	If True, the message contains attachments.
urn:schemas:httpmail: importance	cdo Importance	Long	Yes	Importance level: cdoLow (0) cdoNormal (1) cdoHigh (2).
urn:schemas:httpmail: read	cdoRead	Boolean	Yes	If True, the message has been read.
urn:schemas:httpmail: submitted	cdo Submitted	Boolean	Yes	If True, the message has been sent to the Outbox for delivery.
urn:schemas:httpmail: thread-topic	cdoThread Topic	String	Yes	The topic in a discussion thread.
urn:schemas:mailheader: message-id	cdoMessage Id	String	Yes	A unique identifier for a message.
urn:schemas:mailheader: received	cdoReceived	String	No	All the received headers for a message in one string.

[1]Not available.

SENDING TO A FOLDER

As mentioned earlier, a Message object can represent an e-mail message as well as a post. A *post* is a message that you save in a folder or post to a newsgroup. A Message object supports two methods for sending a post to the destination folder or newsgroup: Send and Post. The Send method is used to send a Message object to a folder configured for SMTP. These folders are typically public Web Storage System folders used to share information within your organization. Use the Post method to post a Message object to a folder configured for NNTP newsgroups. For more about posting to newsgroups, see "Posting to a Newsgroup," later in this section.

You create a message to send to a Web Storage System folder just like you create a message to send to an e-mail recipient. When you set the To property, use the alias name of the folder. The alias name of a mail folder is generally the same as the display name of the folder but without spaces.

For you to successfully send a Message object to a folder, the folder must already be configured for SMTP. You can configure a folder for SMTP by mail-enabling it with code or by using the Exchange System Manager user interface. If you attempt to send a message to a folder that isn't configured for SMTP, no error is generated. When the message arrives in the folder, the object is rendered in a standard post form rather than a mail message form. For example, Listing 6.5 shows how to send a message to a Web Storage System folder.

Listing 6.5   Post to a Web Storage System folder.

```
Sub SendMailToWSSFolder()
    ' This is the programmatic equivalent to
    ' creating a post in a folder.

    ' If you are using VBScript, use this With:
    ' With CreateObject("CDO.Message")
    With New CDO.Message
        ' Indicate who is sending the message
        .From = "mindy@domain.com"
```

```
      ' Address the message to a folder
      .To = "announcements"

      ' Set the subject matter
      .Subject = "New Siberian Tiger Reserve!"

      ' Fill in the body text using plain text formatting
      .TextBody = "We will be helping establish " & _
         "a new Siberian tiger reserve in Russia."

      ' Send the message
      .Send
   End With

   Debug.Print "Message sent to folder."
End Sub
```

NOTE   When you create a folder by using code, it is not enabled to receive e-mail messages by default. You can enable an existing folder to receive e-mail or you can create a new mail-enabled folder by using CDO. For information about creating a mail-enabled folder by using CDO, see Chapter 5, "Introduction to CDO for Exchange."

POSTING TO A NEWSGROUP

As mentioned earlier, a Message object can be used to post information to an NNTP newsgroup. A *newsgroup* is an Internet discussion group that focuses on a particular category of interest. For example, you could use a newsgroup in the Zoo Management application to allow keepers to share information about wildlife management techniques, or you could set up a newsgroup accessible to the public so that parents and kids could post questions about certain animals and the staff could answer them. In both cases, other people are able to see the original message and replies.

TIP You can set up a new newsgroup by using Newsgroup Wizard in Exchange System Manager. Follow the steps in the wizard, and when you finish, you will have a new newsgroup ready for posting.

To post a message to an Internet newsgroup by using NNTP, create a new Message object and set some properties the way you would to send a message to an e-mail recipient. When you address the post, however, rather than setting the To property, set the Newsgroups property to a string that indicates the name of the newsgroup. This can be a single newsgroup or a list of newsgroups separated by commas. The following code sample sets the Newsgroup property so that a post appears in two newsgroups:

```
msg.Newsgroups = "ZooNews.AnimalTalk, Wolf News"
```

NOTE When you configure a newsgroup with Newsgroup Wizard in Exchange System Manager, you have the option of setting a friendly name for the newsgroup. If you set a friendly name for a newsgroup, you must set the Newsgroup property using the friendly name.

To post the message to the indicated newsgroup or newsgroups, call the Post method. For example, Listing 6.6 shows how to post a message to a newsgroup named ZooNews.AnimalTalk.

Listing 6.6 Post to a newsgroup.

```
Sub PostToNewsgroup()
    ' You must set the From, Subject, and
    ' Newsgroups property or the Post method
    ' will generate an error.

    ' Create a new message for the post
    With New CDO.Message
        ' Indicate who is posting the message
        .From = "mindy@domain.com"

        ' Address the message to a newsgroup name.
        ' If you are using a friendly name for the
        ' newsgroup, use that name instead.
        .Newsgroups = "ZooNews.AnimalTalk"
```

```
        ' Set the subject matter
        .Subject = "Wolves"

        ' Fill in the body text using HTML formatting
        .HTMLBody = _
            "How many species of wolves exist in the wild today?"

        ' Post the message
        .Post
    End With

    Debug.Print "Message posted."
End Sub
```

CAUTION   If you do not set the From, Subject, and Newsgroups properties for a Message object, the Post method generates a trappable error.

If you are using CDO to create several posts in the same application, you might want to specify the sender information by using a Configuration object rather than setting the From property on every Message. By using a persistent Configuration object, you can define a sender with one object and then apply this Configuration to each post. For more information about using a Configuration object to set the sender information, see "Using a Persistent Configuration Object" later in this chapter.

COMPOSING MORE COMPLEX MESSAGES

In the previous section, you learned the basic techniques behind CDO messaging. This section explains how to build on those basic techniques to extend a simple message into a more advanced and intelligent messaging solution.

USING A PERSISTENT CONFIGURATION OBJECT

Some information, such as the sender of a message or post, doesn't usually change in the same application. For example, if your application uses a single account to send all bulk mailings, you will probably set the From property for each message object to the same mailbox address. You can either set this type of information for each individual Message object, or you can use a CDO Configuration object.

You can use a CDO Configuration object to create a persistent configuration that sets general settings such as the sender and then applies those settings to each Message object. Not only is this easier to code, but it's also easier to manage. If the general e-mail address for that sender changes, you need to make the change in only the Configuration object instead of searching your code for all references to the address.

To create a persistent configuration, create a new Configuration object and then set the various schema properties in the CDO configuration namespace (http://schemas.microsoft.com/cdo/configuration/). Table 6.4 lists some of the configuration schema properties that you can use to define an application specific configuration.

Table 6.4 Some of the CDO configuration fields

CDO configuration property	CDO constant	Data type	Description
Languagecode	cdoLanguageCode	String	Sets or returns the language code used for response templates.
SendEmailAddress	cdoSendEmailAddress	String	Sets or returns the e-mail address used to send a message when the From field is not specified. Also used as the organizer of a meeting.
SendUserReply EmailAddress	cdoSendUserReply EmailAddress	String	Sets or returns the address to which message replies are sent.
PostEmailAddress	cdoPostEmailAddress	String	Sets or returns the e-mail address used to post messages when the From field is not specified.
PostUserReply EmailAddress	cdoPostUserReply EmailAddress	String	Sets or returns the address to which post replies are sent.

The Configuration object does not expose the CDO configuration namespace properties explicitly, so you must use the Fields collection to get at them. After you set the appropriate properties, save the changes with the Fields.Update method. For example, the following code sample creates a persistent Configuration object and sets the sender of e-mail messages to a specific e-mail address so that the From property doesn't need to be set with each message:

```
Dim cnfg As CDO.Configuration

Set cnfg = New CDO.Configuration
With cnfg
    .Fields(cdoSendEmailAddress) = "mindy@domain.com"
    .Fields.Update
End With
```

To apply the configuration to a Message object, set the Message.Configuration property to the defined Configuration object. The following code sample sets the configuration for two different Message objects to the same previously defined Configuration object:

```
Set msg1 = New CDO.Message
Set msg2 = New CDO.Message

Set msg1.Configuration = cnfg
Set msg2.Configuration = cnfg
```

After you do this, if you need to change the configuration, you need to make the changes only in the persistent Configuration object rather than in each message.

RESOLVING AN ADDRESS IN YOUR DOMAIN

Before you address a message to a person, you might want to verify that the address belongs to a user in your domain or a contact entry in the Active Directory directory service in Windows 2000. Checking an e-mail address in this way is referred to as *resolving an address*. Resolving an address helps minimize the number of undeliverable alerts that a sender receives.

To resolve an address in your domain, you use a CDO Addressee object. An Addressee object provides the properties and methods for retrieving information about a recipient of a mail message. To get information about a user, you must access Active Directory on your Windows 2000 domain controller. Active Directory manages user information for Exchange 2000 Server as well as for the domain.

For more information about accessing Exchange information in Active Directory, see Chapter 8, "Interacting with Active Directory."

CHECKING FOR USER EXISTENCE

One way to resolve an address in your domain is simply to verify that the address belongs to a user or contact object in Active Directory. You can verify the existence of the object by checking the e-mail address in Active Directory with the CheckName method of an Addressee object. After you create a new Addressee object, set the EmailAddress property of an Addressee object to the e-mail address you are verifying. Then, call the CheckName method of an Addressee object and pass a Lightweight Directory Access Protocol (LDAP) URL to the Active Directory server. This is where the method looks for an Active Directory object that owns that e-mail address. The CheckName method returns True if a user or contact object with that mailbox is found in Active Directory, and it returns a False value if a user or contact object is not found. For more information about using LDAP and Active Directory, see Chapter 8, "Interacting with Active Directory."

Listing 6.7 shows how to check for an object with a particular address in Active Directory. The HasMailboxInDomain function takes one argument, AddressToCheck, which is a string that contains the e-mail address to search for. The HasMailboxInDomain function first dynamically builds the LDAP URL for the Active Directory server in the domain running this function. Then the procedure creates a new Addressee object and checks for the existence of an Active Directory object with the address passed to the AddressToCheck parameter. If the address exists, the function returns True. If it does not exist, the function returns False.

Listing 6.7   Check an address in the current domain's Active Directory.

```
Public Function HasMailboxInDomain( _
    ByVal AddressToCheck As String) _
    As Boolean
```

```
' Return True if the address belongs to an
' Exchange mailbox within the domain.
' Otherwise return False.

Dim rootDSE As ActiveDs.IADs
Dim urlADServer As String

' Use the Root DS Entry to dynamically build
' the LDAP URL string.
Set rootDSE = GetObject("LDAP://RootDSE")
urlADServer = "LDAP://" & rootDSE.Get("dnshostname")

With New CDO.Addressee
    ' Indicate the email address to check
    .EmailAddress = AddressToCheck

    ' If the name exists in the Active
    ' Directory, CheckName returns True.
    If .CheckName(urlADServer) Then
        ' This mailbox exists in the current domain
        HasMailboxInDomain = True
    Else
        ' This mailbox does not exist in the current domain
        HasMailboxInDomain = False
    End If
End With
End Function
```

You can use the HasMailboxInDomain function to dynamically set your To, CC, and BCC properties for a Message object. You can use the function to check an address before you add it to one of these properties. For example, Listing 6.8 shows one way to use the HasMailboxInDomain function. Before the new message is addressed, the procedure calls the HasMailboxInDomain function on each e-mail address in an array. If the address is verified in the domain, the address is added to a string. If the address is not found in Active Directory, the address is not added to the string. After enumerating each address, the message is finally addressed to those recipients in the string and then sent.

Listing 6.8   Apply the HasMailbox function.

```
Sub CallResolve()
    ' Dynamically sets the To property of
    ' a Message after testing each address
    ' in an array with the HasMailboxInDomain
    ' function.

    Dim someArray(0 To 2)
    Dim v As Variant
    Dim strAddress As String

    ' Build an array of addresses
    someArray(0) = "denise@domain.com"
    someArray(1) = "peter@domain.com"
    someArray(2) = "someone@domain.com"

    ' Check each address in the array
    For Each v In someArray
        If HasMailboxInDomain(v) Then
            strAddress = strAddress & v & ","
        End If
    Next

    ' Strip the last comma from the string
    strAddress = Left$(strAddress, Len(strAddress) - 1)

    'Create and send a message
    With New CDO.Message
        .From = "mindy@domain.com"
        .To = strAddress
        .Subject = "Verify existence"
        .HTMLBody = "<H1>These addresses exist in this domain.</H1>"
        .Send
    End With
End Sub
```

HANDLING AMBIGUOUS NAMES

If you are using friendly names or e-mail aliases instead of actual e-mail addresses, you might run into issues with ambiguous addresses. Occasionally, it is possible that a friendly name or address can represent more than one user or contact in Active Directory. In this type of conflict, the name you are checking is considered ambiguous. If you are using friendly names or e-mail aliases to address a message, you should test for ambiguity by getting the ResolvedStatus property of an Addressee object.

The ResolvedStatus property returns a numeric value that indicates the success of the resolution. Table 6.5 lists the possible return values.

Table 6.5   Return values for the ResolvedStatus property

Value	CDO constant	Description
0	cdoUnresolved	Address was not found in Active Directory.
1	cdoResolved	Address was found in Active Directory.
2	cdoAmbiguous	More than one address was found in Active Directory.

If the ResolvedStatus property for an Addressee object returns a value of cdoAmbiguous (2), you can call the AmbiguousNames property of an Addressee object to return a list of Addressee objects that have a potential match with the name or alias in question. You can then look at each Addressee object individually and take the appropriate action. For example, the following code sample handles an ambiguous address:

```
Dim adr As CDO.Addressee

With New CDO.Addressee
   .EmailAddress = "somealias"

   If .ResolvedStatus = cdoAmbiguous Then
   ' The name has more than one possible match
   ' in Active Directory
     For Each adr In .AmbiguousNames
         Debug.Print adr.EmailAddress
     Next adr
   End If
End With
```

PROCESSING MESSAGES

The previous sections discussed various ways to create a message; this section discusses some of the ways you can process an existing message.

NOTE The examples in this section use a test message created by the CreateTestMessage procedure included with the sample code. Run this procedure to create a message in your Inbox before running any of the additional code samples.

FINDING A MESSAGE

You can't reply to a message if you can't find it, so to process a message in any way, you must first find the message. To do anything with a message, you need its URL. If you already know the URL, you can open the message immediately. However, more often than not, you need to discover the URL. You can discover a URL with one of two common approaches:

- Use the Web Storage System OnSyncSave event on a folder to trap a new message that arrives. You can then retrieve the URL of the new item, perform some property evaluation if necessary, and open the message for further action. For more information about using Web Storage System events, see Chapter 9, "Using Web Storage System Events."

- Build a Structured Query Language (SQL) query that looks for a particular message that has specific property values. A SQL query might return more than one e-mail message with the same qualities, so you must loop through the result set. For more information about querying a folder for an item, see Chapter 4, "ActiveX Data Objects and Exchange."

OPENING A MESSAGE

After you have the URL for a message, you can pass the URL string to the DataSource.Open method of a Message object. If the message is opened successfully, you can then read the properties or act on the message accordingly.

For example, Listing 6.9 opens the TestMessage.EML message and enumerates the properties for the message.

Listing 6.9 Open a message and read the properties.

```
Public Sub OpenMsg()
    ' Opens a message and enumerates the properties.
    ' This procedure uses the TestMessage created
    ' by the CreateTestMessage procedure.

    Dim strMBXAlias As String
    Dim urlTestMsg As String
    Dim msg As CDO.Message
    Dim fd As ADODB.Field

    ' Change this to your alias
    strMBXAlias = "mindy"

    ' URL to the TestMessage
    urlTestMsg = GetStorageName & "mbx/" & _
        strMBXAlias & "/inbox/TestMessage.EML"

    ' Open TestMessage
    Set msg = New CDO.Message
    msg.DataSource.Open urlTestMsg

    ' Return all of the properties of the message
    For Each fd In msg.Fields
        If Not IsArray(fd.Value) Then
            Debug.Print fd.Name, fd.Value
        Else
            Debug.Print fd.Name, "[MULTI-VALUED]"
        End If
    Next fd

    ' Clean up
    Set fd = Nothing
    Set msg = Nothing
End Sub
```

DETECTING AND SAVING ATTACHMENTS

Although an attachment to a message is actually a BodyPart object, you do not need to enumerate a message's entire BodyParts collection to detect an attachment BodyPart object. Instead, you read the Attachments property of a Message object. The Attachments property returns all attachments for a message as a BodyParts collection. You can count the number of attachments in this collection, and you can enumerate the contents of the collection and act on each attachment accordingly.

To count the attachments in a message, you can use the Attachments.Count property of a Message object. If a message does not have attachments, this property returns zero (0). For example, the following code sample uses the Count property to determine if a message has attachments:

```
If msg.Attachments.Count > 0 Then
    '
    'Message has attachments
    'Do something
    '
End If
```

If a Message object does have attachments, you can then enumerate the attachments and return information about each one or save each one to a file. To save an attachment to a file, you can use the SaveToFile method of a BodyPart object and pass the path and file name to which the attachment should be saved. For example, the following code sample saves an attachment to a file using the attachment file name:

```
atch.SaveToFile "D:\Downloads\" & atch.FileName
```

Listing 6.10 shows how to enumerate all the attachments in the TestMessage.EML message and save each one to disk, replacing existing files of the same name.

Listing 6.10   Enumerate attachments in TestMessage.

```
Function EnumerateAttachmentsandSaveToFile()
    ' Enumerates each of the attachments in
    ' a message and saves each attachment to disk.
    ' This procedure uses the TestMessage created
    ' by the CreateTestMessage procedure.
```

```
    Dim strMBXAlias As String
    Dim urlTestMsg As String
    Dim msg As CDO.Message
    Dim atch As CDO.IBodyPart

    ' Change this to your alias
    strMBXAlias = "mindy"

    ' URL to the TestMessage
    urlTestMsg = GetStorageName & "mbx/" & _
        strMBXAlias & "/inbox/TestMessage.EML"

    ' Open TestMessage
    Set msg = New CDO.Message
    msg.DataSource.Open urlTestMsg

    ' Check for attachments
    If msg.Attachments.Count > 0 Then
        Debug.Print msg.Subject & " attachments:"
        'Loop through each attachment
        For Each atch In msg.Attachments
            ' Return information about each attachment
            Debug.Print _
                atch.ContentMediaType, atch.FileName
            Debug.Print _
                "-----------------------------------------------"

            ' Save the attachment to disk
            atch.SaveToFile "D:\Downloads\" & atch.FileName
        Next
    End If

    ' Clean up
    Set atch = Nothing
    Set msg = Nothing
End Function
```

NOTE   If you don't care how many attachments the message has and you simply want to determine if attachments exist, you can read the urn:schemas:httpmail:hasattachment schema property. This schema property returns True if the message has attachments and False if the message has no attachments.

READING A MESSAGE AS BODYPART OBJECTS

As discussed earlier, a MIME message is comprised of BodyPart objects. Some BodyPart objects represent the header information, some represent the body text, and some represent attachments. This section shows you how to enumerate through the BodyPart objects of a message.

USING SHORTCUT PROPERTIES

You can gain access to some BodyPart objects by using the special properties of a Message object. For example, use the Attachments property to gain access to attachments in a Message object. As shown in Table 6.6, CDO also provides several properties that you can use to easily read the body of a Message object.

Table 6.6   CDO properties that help you access the text body contents of a Message object

Property	Data type	Description
TextBody	String	Sets or returns only the text of the BodyPart object that contains the plain-text portion of the message.
HTMLBody	String	Sets or returns only the HTML text of the BodyPart object that contains the HTML portion of the message.
TextBodyPart	IBodyPart	Returns a reference to the BodyPart object that contains the plain-text portion of the message. This includes both the header fields and text for the BodyPart object.
HTMLBodyPart	IBodyPart	Returns a reference to the BodyPart object that contains the HTML portion of the message. This includes both the header fields and HTML for the BodyPart object.

IDENTIFYING THE MEDIA TYPE OF A BODYPART OBJECT

A Message object uses BodyPart objects in varying ways. A BodyPart object can be the text portion of a message, an attached Word document, an image file, or a container for additional BodyPart objects. To identify how a BodyPart object is allocated, read the ContentMediaType property of a BodyPart object. You use this property to identify how a BodyPart object is currently being used as well as to indicate the intended purpose of a new BodyPart object. From the server perspective, the purpose of the ContentMediaType property is to supply enough information so that receiving servers can select an appropriate agent for presenting the data.

> **NOTE** The ContentMediaType property maps to the urn:schemas:mailheader:content-type schema property.

The ContentMediaType property sets or returns a string organized into a *"type/subtype"* structure, where *type* is the general concept of the BodyPart object, such as text, image, or multipart, and *subtype* provides more information about the details of the type, such as plain, HTML, JPEG, or an alternative. For example, if a BodyPart object contains unformatted text, the media type is text/plain. If the text contains HTML tags, the media type is still text, but now it has a subtype of HTML, so the media type is text/HTML. The most common media type strings have coordinating CDO constants. Table 6.7 lists these constants and their matching text strings.

Table 6.7   Possible values for the ContentMediaType property

CDO constant	Actual value	Description
cdoGif	image/gif	GIF image file
cdoJpeg	image/jpeg	JPEG image file
cdoMessageExternalBody	message/external-body	External body message
cdoMessagePartial	message/partial	One piece of a fragmented message
cdoMessageRFC822	message/rfc822	Simple message type

Continued on next page

Table 6.7 continued   Possible values for the ContentMediaType property

CDO constant	Actual value	Description
cdoMultipartAlternative	multipart/alternative	Contains additional body parts of different versions of the same type
cdoMultipartDigest	multipart/digest	Different messages, including forwarded messages
cdoMultipartMixed	multipart/mixed	Contains additional body parts of mixed types
cdoMultipartRelated	multipart/related	Contains additional body parts accessed through URLs
cdoTextHTML	text/html	Text with HTML tags
cdoTextPlain	text/plain	Unstructured text

Listing 6.11 shows how to enumerate the BodyPart objects that make up a Message object.

Listing 6.11   Return the media type for each BodyPart object in the TestMessage message.

```
Public Sub ShowBodyPartMediaTypes()
    ' Enumerate BodyPart objects
    ' in the TestMessage.
    ' This procedure uses the TestMessage created
    ' by the CreateTestMessage procedure.

    Dim strMBXAlias As String
    Dim urlTestMsg As String
    Dim bdp As CDO.IBodyPart

    ' Change this to your alias
    strMBXAlias = "mindy"
```

```
          ' URL to the TestMessage
    urlTestMsg = GetStorageName & "mbx/" & _
        strMBXAlias & "/inbox/TestMessage.EML"

    ' Open TestMessage
    With New CDO.Message
        .DataSource.Open urlTestMsg

        ' This is the message type
        Debug.Print .BodyPart.ContentMediaType

        ' Loop through the various BodyPart objects
        For Each bdp In .BodyPart.BodyParts
            Debug.Print vbTab, bdp.ContentMediaType, _
                bdp.BodyParts.Count, _
                bdp.FileName
        Next bdp

        ' No point sending this message.
    End With

    ' Clean up
    Set bdp = Nothing
End Sub
```

STREAMING BODYPART OBJECTS

If you want to access only the body text of a message, you can use a shortcut property. However, if you want to access the header information for the message or another BodyPart object and then do something with that information, you need to use an ADO Stream object. You can return a Stream object by using one of the BodyPart object streaming methods listed in Table 6.8.

Table 6.8 Streaming methods supported by the IBodyPart interface

Streaming method	Description
GetStream	Returns an ADO Stream object that contains header fields and the content of the body part. This method can be used to retrieve attached documents, the entire contents of a message, or the header fields and text.
GetEncodedContentStream	Returns an ADO Stream object that contains the content of the body part in encoded format. Does not retrieve the header fields. When this method is used to view an attached text file, it returns the contents still encoded.
GetDecodedContentStream	Returns an ADO Stream object that contains the content of the body part in decoded format. Does not retrieve the header fields. When this method is used to view an attached text file, it returns the contents in plain text.

The following code sample retrieves the HTML BodyPart object of a message and then calls the GetStream method to retrieve not only the content but also the header fields. The ReadText method returns the contents of the stream in text characters:

```
Set stm = msg.HTMLBodyPart.GetStream
Debug.Print stm.ReadText
```

You can also write the contents of the body part directly to another message. Either way, the result of calling the GetStream method looks something like this:

```
Content-Type: text/html;
    charset="iso-8859-1"
Content-Transfer-Encoding: 7bit

Some text.
```

If you call the GetDecodedContentStream method instead of the GetStream method, you'll receive only the content, not the header information:

```
Some Text.
```

REPLYING TO A MESSAGE

To reply to a message, you can use either the Reply method or the ReplyAll method. Both methods automatically create a new Message object, but they address the new message differently. The Reply method takes the address in the original message's From property and places it in the To property of the new message, ignoring any values in the CC or BCC properties. The ReplyAll method likewise takes the From property value of the original message and places it in the To property of the new message, but the ReplyAll method also takes all the CC recipients of the original message and places them in the CC property of the new message. The BCC recipients are not included.

When either reply method is called, any attachments included with the original message are stripped from the new message. The subject is automatically generated to include the RE: prefix followed by the subject of the original message. By default, the body text from the original message is included in the body of the new message and is formatted something like this:

```
-----Original Message-----
From:     "mindy@domain.com" <mindy@domain.com>
Sent:     Tuesday, November 02, 1999 1:12 PM
To:       "amy@domain.com" <amy@domain.com>
Cc:       "michael@domain.com" <michael@domain.com>
Subject:  Neato!

We've got a new Super Rooster!
```

If you want to place additional text in the body of the reply message, you must use the same body format for the reply message as the original message. For example, if the original message uses HTML to format the body, the new message must use the HTMLBody property. To add more text to the body of the reply message without replacing the text from the original message, you can concatenate the new text string with the current contents of the body text. The following code sample adds a new phrase preceding the reply text already in the body:

```
msgReply.HTMLBody = "This is so cool!" & _
    vbCrLf & msgReply.HTMLBody
```

Now the body of the reply message looks something like this:

```
This is so cool!

-----Original Message-----
From:     "mindy@domain.com" <mindy@domain.com>
Sent:     Tuesday, November 02, 1999 1:12 PM
To:       "amy@domain.com" <amy@domain.com>
Cc:       "michael@domain.com" <michael@domain.com>
Subject: Neato!

We've got a new Super Rooster!
```

Finally, to send the reply message, call the Send method of the new Message object. Listing 6.12 shows how to reply to the sender of the TestMessage message.

Listing 6.12   Reply to the TestMessage message.

```
Public Sub ReplyToMsg()
    ' This procedure uses the TestMessage created
    ' by the CreateTestMessage procedure.

    Dim strMBXAlias As String
    Dim urlTestMsg As String
    Dim msg As CDO.Message
    Dim msgReply As CDO.Message

    ' Change this to your alias
    strMBXAlias = "mindy"

    ' URL to the TestMessage
    urlTestMsg = GetStorageName & "mbx/" & _
        strMBXAlias & "/inbox/TestMessage.EML"

    ' Open TestMessage
    Set msg = New CDO.Message
    msg.DataSource.Open urlTestMsg
```

```
      'Create the reply message with the Reply method
      Set msgReply = msg.Reply
      With msgReply
         'Add a lead in phrase prior to the text of the original message
         .HTMLBody = "This is a reply." & "<hr>" & vbCrLf & .HTMLBody
         'Send the reply
         .Send
      End With

      ' Clean up
      Set msgReply = Nothing
      Set msg = Nothing
   End Sub
```

NOTE   To reply to a post, you use the PostReply method. The PostReply method behaves like the Reply method except that it replies to the newsgroup or folder to which the original message was posted. All other rules still apply.

FORWARDING A MESSAGE

To forward a message to a person who is not already on the list of recipients, use the Forward method of a Message object. When you call the Forward method, you create a new Message object. The From property is automatically set, but you must indicate the person to whom you are forwarding the message.

When you forward a message, it retains any attachments included in the original message and sends them along to the new recipient. The subject is automatically generated to include the FW: prefix followed by the subject of the original message. By default, the body of the new message includes the body text from the original message and formats it like this:

```
   -----Original Message-----
   From: "mindy@domain.com" <mindy@domain.com>
   Sent: Tuesday, November 02, 1999 10:33 AM
   To: "denise@domain.com" <denise@domain.com>
   Subject: Neato!

   We've got a new Super Rooster!
```

If you want to place additional text in the body of the reply message, you must use the same body format in the reply message as in the original message. For example, if the body of the original message uses HTML, the new message must use the HTMLBody property. To add more text to the body of the reply message without replacing the text from the original message, you can concatenate the new text string with the current contents of the body text. The following code sample adds a new phrase preceding the reply text already in the body:

```
msgFwd.HTMLBody = "Look at this stuff you missed:" & _
  "<HR>" &  msgFwd.HTMLBody
```

The body of the new message looks something like this:

```
Look at this stuff you missed:


-----Original Message-----
From: "mindy@domain.com" <mindy@domain.com>
Sent: Tuesday, November 02, 1999 10:33 AM
To: "denise@domain.com" <denise@domain.com>
Subject: Neato!


We've got a new Super Rooster!
```

Finally, to send the forwarded message, call the Send method of the new message. Listing 6.13 shows how to forward the TestMessage message.

Listing 6.13   Forward the TestMessage message.

```
Public Sub ForwardMessage()
    ' This procedure uses the TestMessage created
    ' by the CreateTestMessage procedure.

    Dim strMBXAlias As String
    Dim urlTestMsg As String
    Dim msg As CDO.Message
    Dim msgFwd As CDO.Message

    ' Change this to your alias
    strMBXAlias = "mindy"

    ' URL to the TestMessage
    urlTestMsg = GetStorageName & "mbx/" & _
        strMBXAlias & "/inbox/TestMessage.EML"
```

```
' Open TestMessage
Set msg = New CDO.Message
msg.DataSource.Open urlTestMsg

'Create the forward message with the Forward method
Set msgFwd = msg.Forward
With msgFwd
    'Indicate who is sending the message
    '.From = "mindym@domain.com"
    'Indicate whom the message is being forwarded to
    .To = "mindy@domain.com"
    'Add a lead in phrase prior to the text of the original message
    .HTMLBody = _
        "This is a forwarded message." & "<hr>" & vbCrLf & .HTMLBody
    'Send the forward message
    .Send
End With

' Clean up
Set msgFwd = Nothing
Set msg = Nothing
End Sub
```

SAVING A MESSAGE TO A FILE

You can also save an entire Message object to a file on a disk using the SaveToFile method of an ADO Stream object. To save a Message object to file, open the appropriate message and call the GetStream method of a Message object. This method returns the entire contents of a message—all the header information as well as all the body text—as a stream of text. If the message includes alternate body text, the GetStream method gets both the plain-text version and the HTML version. You can then call the SaveToFile method of the Stream object and pass the path and file name to which to save the message. To replace an existing file, pass the adSaveCreateOverWrite constant as well. Listing 6.14 shows how to save the TestMessage to a file on a disk.

Listing 6.14   Save the TestMessage to a file on a disk.

```
Public Sub SaveMsgtoFile()
    ' Save an entire message
    ' to a file on disk.

    Dim strMBXAlias As String
    Dim urlTestMsg As String

    ' Change this to your alias
    strMBXAlias = "mindy"

    ' URL to the TestMessage
    urlTestMsg = GetStorageName & "mbx/" & _
        strMBXAlias & "/inbox/TestMessage.EML"

    ' Open TestMessage
    With New CDO.Message
        .DataSource.Open urlTestMsg

        ' Save the message to a file and overwrite
        ' if the file exists.
        .GetStream.SaveToFile _
        "D:\msgtext.txt", adSaveCreateOverWrite
    End With
End Sub
```

Figure 6.7 shows an example of the text file that is generated when you open the message in Microsoft Notepad.

Figure 6.7
Message saved as a file

SUMMARY

Messaging continues to be the cornerstone of most collaboration applications. As e-mail gains increasing acceptance as a fundamental form of communication, messaging capabilities appear in more and more applications. CDO meets this demand by providing a diverse selection of objects, interfaces, properties, and methods for building a range of messaging solutions. By using CDO, you can create everything from a simple program that posts information to newsgroups to a complex application that sends a monthly newsletter to a group of recipients. This chapter discusses the core technologies of CDO messaging applications.

Chapter 7, "CDO Calendaring," explains how to use CDO to build calendaring applications.

7

CDO Calendaring

Calendars are part of everyday life. People use calendars to keep track of personal events such as doctor appointments and dinner parties with friends. People rely on calendars to keep track of business engagements such as status meetings and business trips. People even rely on other people's calendars for information about their whereabouts.

CDO (Collaboration Data Objects) for Microsoft Exchange provides the classes and interfaces for creating a variety of calendaring solutions—from those that simply generate appointments to more advanced tools that schedule recurring meetings. This chapter teaches how to use the CDO object models to build calendaring applications. Sections include:

- **Overview of CDO Calendaring**

- **Using the Appointment Object**

- **Scheduling Meetings**

- **Scheduling Recurring Appointments and Meetings**

- **Working with Existing Appointments and Meeting Requests**

- **Setting Reminders**

OVERVIEW OF CDO CALENDARING

You can use CDO to build a variety of calendaring solutions. You can create single appointments in a private mailbox store or schedule meetings with others. You can also use CDO to create recurring appointments and meetings. This section introduces the CDO classes and interfaces used to create these and other calendaring solutions. This section also discusses how Exchange handles dates and times to make your solutions globally accessible.

CDO CALENDARING CLASSES AND INTERFACES

To build any type of calendaring solution with CDO, you use the classes and interfaces found in the CDO for Exchange 2000 object library (Cdoex.dll). Like most solutions, calendaring solutions involve a number of objects and interfaces. If the solution gets more complex, for example, by including recurrence patterns, you need to use more objects and interfaces. One object that you always use, however, is the Appointment object. The Appointment object represents a personal appointment or a meeting. You typically use the Appointment object to create a new appointment or schedule a new meeting, but you can also use the Appointment object to process meeting requests. Figure 7.1 shows the CDO Appointment object model that you use to build all calendaring solutions.

The Appointment class contains five collections that you can use to customize an Appointment object for specific behavior.

- The Attendees collection represents the people who have been invited to attend a meeting. If you are creating a meeting, you add to the Attendees collection to invite people to the meeting.

- The RecurrencePatterns collection contains the recurrence patterns used to define how often a meeting or appointment occurs and when the meetings will cease to occur. For example, you can configure a RecurrencePattern for a meeting so that it occurs every other week.

- The Exceptions collection is used with the RecurrencePatterns collection and contains the exceptions to a recurring meeting or appointment. An exception can be an additional meeting instance or a canceled meeting instance.

- The Attachments collection contains all the attached files for an appointment. You use this collection to attach files and access files already attached to an Appointment object.

- The Fields collection contains those schema properties that are not accessible with a CDO Appointment object property. This includes all the custom properties that you create.

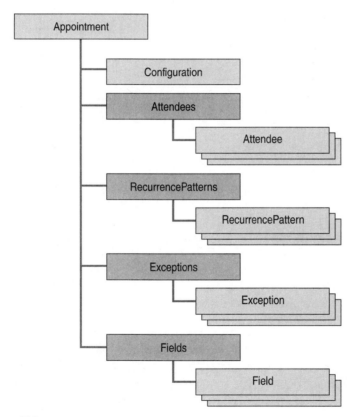

Figure 7.1
The Appointment object model

When you use the Appointment object to schedule meetings, you also work with the CalendarMessage object model (see Figure 7.2). You use the CalendarMessage object to create a meeting request that invites others to a meeting. The CalendarMessage object exposes the Message object and also has a CalendarParts collection. The CalendarParts collection contains the related appointment information and is used to accept, tentatively accept, or decline a meeting request. The Message object in the CalendarMessage object is used for typical messaging actions, such as sending a meeting request.

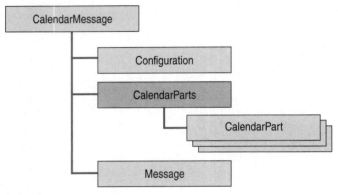

Figure 7.2
The CalendarMessage object model

UNDERSTANDING HOW EXCHANGE STORES AND FORMATS DATES AND TIMES

Probably the most important factor in developing a successful calendaring solution is understanding how Exchange stores and formats dates and times. Exchange stores dates and times based on Coordinated Universal Time (UTC) syntax, so all date/time values are converted into UTC syntax by Exchange when the data is saved to a Microsoft Web Storage System. For example, each time a new appointment is added, Exchange automatically converts the StartTime and EndTime properties of the appointment from the time zone in which the appointment was created to UTC. When a client then sends a request to view the appointment, the date must be converted back to the user's time zone so that the appointment can be viewed properly.

Microsoft Outlook and Outlook Web Access automatically convert the date from UTC to the time zone in the local computer's date and time settings. You can take advantage of this automatic time conversion in custom Web applications by reusing Outlook Web Access components. However, if you use CDO for Exchange to build your own custom client for scheduling, you must explicitly convert the dates and times appropriately, particularly when querying a calendar for a date range.

Exchange also formats the dates and times differently from what you might be accustomed to seeing. Exchange 2000 Server formats dates in International Organization for Standardization (ISO) 8601 format. ISO format is the international format for the representation of dates and times. ISO describes a number of date and time formats, but Exchange uses the complete date plus hours, minutes, and seconds:

```
yyyy-mm-ddThh:mm:ssZ
```

Where:

yyyy

   is a four-digit year.

mm

   is a two-digit month (01=January, etc.).

dd

   is a two-digit day of the month (01 through 31).

t

   is a time designator.

hh

   is two digits of an hour (00 through 23) (A.M. and P.M. are not allowed).

mm

   is two digits of a minute (00 through 59).

ss

   is two digits of a second (00 through 59).

Z

   indicates that the time uses UTC syntax.

For information about how to convert dates and times for querying and for display, see "Converting Dates and Times" later in this chapter.

INDICATING A TIME ZONE

When you create a new appointment, you should save information about the time zone in which the appointment was created. Because Exchange adjusts the time zone to UTC for storage, storing the time zone helps you know how to convert the dates back to the original time zone when displaying the appointment information to the user again. You can set the urn:schemas:calendar:timezoneid schema property (cdoTimeZoneIDURN) when the appointment is created to a constant, which indicates a time zone. When the appointment is opened again, you can then read this property to convert the date back to the original time zone properly. The TimeZoneConverter function that uses these constants to convert a date from one time zone to another is discussed later in this chapter.

NOTE   You can set the time zone on an individual CDO Appointment object or on a CDO Configuration object, which can be applied to multiple Appointment objects.

Table 7.1 lists the possible time zone values for the urn:schemas:calendar:timezoneid schema property (cdoTimeZoneIDURN).

Table 7.1 Constant values for urn:schemas:calendar:timezoneid (cdoTimeZoneIDURN)

CDO constant	Value	Description
cdoEastern	10	Eastern time (UTC - 5:00)
cdoCentral	11	Central time (UTC - 6:00)
cdoMountain	12	Mountain time (UTC - 7:00)
cdoMidAtlantic	30	Mid Atlantic (UTC - 2:00)

Using the Appointment Object

The Appointment object is the key to all calendaring solutions, whether you are creating a simple appointment in a personal calendar or scheduling a meeting for multiple attendees. You handle both scenarios by first creating a new Appointment object and then setting properties that control its behavior. This section introduces the properties of the Appointment object and discusses the core techniques you'll use to create a new appointment and configure appointments.

Creating a Simple Appointment

You can create a simple appointment in either a mailbox store or a public store. Normally, a simple appointment is created for one individual, and nobody else is invited. A dentist appointment is an example of a simple appointment.

To create a simple appointment, create a new Appointment object and set some properties to specify how the appointment occurs. Every new appointment should set a few essential properties: the time zone in which the appointment is created, when the appointment starts, when the appointment ends (or the duration), the subject of the appointment, and where the appointment occurs.

To set the time zone in which the appointment is occurring, set the urn:schemas:calendar:timezoneid schema property (cdoTimeZoneIDURN) to one of the constants listed in Table 7.1. This property is not exposed explicitly, so you must use the Fields collection to set it. To save the changes, you must also call the Fields.Update method. To set the time frame in which the appointment occurs, you set the StartTime property and either the EndTime or Duration property. Both StartTime and EndTime require a string value that is a concatenation of both the date and the time. You can use a space between the date and the time. If you prefer to use the Duration property instead of the EndTime property, set the Duration property of an Appointment object to the number of seconds that the appointment will last. When you are ready to save the appointment, call the DataSource.SaveToContainer method and pass the URL to the parent calendar, not to the appointment itself. The DataSource.SaveToContainer method automatically assigns a GUID as the DAV:displayname to the Appointment object. This is done to ensure that each appointment in a calendar has a unique URL.

NOTE The code listings in this chapter are available in the Microsoft Visual Basic project CH_07.vbp on the companion CD. If you want to run the samples as they are written, you must have the Zoo Management sample installed on your Exchange 2000 Server. For information about installing the application, see the introduction to the book. In addition, the code samples repeatedly call a function named GetStorageName. This function returns the name of the domain in which the code is running. For more information about the GetStorageName function, see Chapter 8, "Interacting with Active Directory."

Listing 7.1, for example, shows how to create a new dentist appointment in a personal calendar. After building the URL to the calendar folder, the procedure creates a new Appointment object and sets the time zone for the appointment to Pacific time. Then, the code sets the StartTime and EndTime properties to string values combining the date and time. Next, the procedure sets the Subject, Location, and TextBody properties to some values to describe the type of appointment and its location. Finally, the code calls the DataSource.SaveToContainer method and saves the appointment to the calendar folder URL.

Listing 7.1   Create an appointment in a private calendar.

```
Sub CreatePersonalAppointment()
    ' Create a simple appoinment in a personal
    ' calendar in the Pacific time zone.

    Dim urlMBXCal As String

    ' Build the URL to the calendar
    urlMBXCal = GetStorageName & "mbx/mindy/calendar/"

    ' If you are using VBScript, use this With:
    ' With CreateObject("CDO.Appointment")
    With New CDO.Appointment
```

```
        ' Add the time zone information
        .Fields(cdoTimeZoneIDURN) = cdoPacific
        .Fields.Update

        .StartTime = "4/17/2001 1:00:00 PM"
        .EndTime = "4/17/2001 2:00:00 PM"
        .Subject = "Dentist appointment"
        .Location = "Examining room 1"
        .TextBody = "Time for a check-up!"

        ' Save the appointment to the calendar
        .DataSource.SaveToContainer urlMBXCal
    End With

    Debug.Print "Appointment created successfully."
End Sub
```

NOTE If an appointment already exists in the same time frame, this code schedules another appointment concurrently. The DataSource.SaveToContainer method ignores the CreateOptions parameter value adCreateOverwrite, so you cannot use this approach to overwrite an appointment that is already scheduled for the same time frame. One possible solution to this dilemma is to check the free/busy status for the person who owns the personal calendar in which you are saving the appointment before you create the appointment. For more information about checking the free/busy status for a person, see the section "Checking Free/Busy Status" later in this chapter.

APPOINTMENT PROPERTIES

In addition to those properties used to create the appointment in the previous section, you can set a number of additional properties on an Appointment object to give the appointment additional functionality or provide more detailed information about the appointment. For example, you can set the Priority property to indicate that the appointment has a high priority with code like this:

```
appt.Priority = cdoPriorityUrgent
```

Table 7.2 lists some of the additional CDO Appointment object properties that you can use to create more detailed appointments.

Table 7.2 Properties of the Appointment object

Name	Data type	Description
AllDayEvent	Boolean	If True, the appointment is scheduled for the entire day.
Contact	String	Sets or returns the name of the person to contact about the appointment.
ContactURL	String	Sets or returns the URL for accessing an alternative format of the contact.
Duration	Long	Sets or returns the length of time the meeting lasts in seconds.
GEOLatitude	Double	Sets or returns the geographic latitude for the appointment location.
GEOLongitude	Double	Sets or returns the geographic longitude for the appointment location.
Keywords	Variant	Sets or returns the keywords used to describe the appointment for indexing and searching.
Location	String	Sets or returns the physical location for the appointment.
LocationURL	String	Sets or returns the URL for accessing the location information.
MeetingStatus	String	Sets or returns the status of the appointment: confirmed, tentative, or canceled.
Priority	Long	Sets or returns the priority level: cdoPriorityNormal (0), cdoPriorityNonUrgent (-1), or cdoPriorityUrgent (1).
Resources	String	Sets or returns a list of resources for the appointment.

Continued on next page

Table 7.2 continued   Properties of the Appointment object

Name	Data type	Description
ResponseRequested	Boolean	If True, a response is requested for the meeting request. If the appointment has been configured with a Meeting Organizer, the default is True.
Sensitivity	Long	Sets or returns the sensitivity description: cdoSensitivityNone (0), cdoPersonal (1), cdoPrivate (2), or cdoCompanyConfidential (3).

USING A PERSISTENT CONFIGURATION OBJECT

Some information, such as the time zone where the appointment is created, usually doesn't change in the same application. For example, if your application is running in eastern time, all the Appointment objects that you create in that application will more than likely be configured for eastern time as well. You can either set the time zone information for each individual Appointment object, or you can use the CDO Configuration object. You can use the CDO Configuration object to create a persistent configuration that sets general settings like the time zone. You can then apply that persistent configuration to each Appointment object.

To create a persistent configuration, create a new Configuration object and then set the various schema properties in the CDO configuration namespace (http://schemas.microsoft.com/cdo/configuration/). The Configuration object does not expose these properties explicitly, so you must use the Fields collection to get at them. After you set the appropriate properties, save the changes with the Fields.Update method. For example, the following code sample creates a persistent Configuration object and sets the time zone to Pacific time:

```
Set cnfg = New CDO.Configuration
With cnfg
  .Fields(cdoTimeZoneIDURN) = cdoPacific
  .Fields.Update
End With
```

To apply the configuration to an appointment, set the Appointment.Configuration property to the defined Configuration object. The following code sample sets the configuration for two different Appointment objects to the same previously defined Configuration object:

```
Set appt1 = New CDO.Appointment
Set appt2 = New CDO.Appointment

Set appt1.Configuration = cnfg
Set appt2.Configuration = cnfg
```

If you need to change the configuration, you only need to make the changes to the persistent Configuration object rather than having to make the changes for each Appointment object. For example, if you need to change the time zone from Pacific time to eastern time, you change the Configuration object instead of each of the Appointment objects that reference the Configuration object.

SCHEDULING MEETINGS

A meeting is a special type of appointment with multiple attendees. Scheduling a meeting with multiple attendees is a bit more complex than creating a simple appointment for one person. In addition to creating the base appointment that represents the meeting information, such as the start time, end time, and location, you also need to send out invitations. This section explains how to schedule a meeting, send out requests, and check the availability of a potential attendee.

SCHEDULING A NEW MEETING

Just as you use the Appointment object to create a simple appointment, you also use the Appointment object to schedule a meeting. You must provide the same basic information essential to every appointment, such as the time zone, the start and end times, the location of the meeting, and the subject matter. In addition to providing the basic appointment information, you must also complete a few additional tasks when scheduling a meeting. These tasks include:

- Setting the meeting organizer

- Adding attendees

- Sending a meeting request

Each of these tasks is discussed in greater detail in the following sections. However, to get a feel for how you use them all together, review Listing 7.2, which schedules a meeting with required and optional attendees. First, the meeting organizer is defined using the Configuration object. Then, the procedure creates a new Appointment object and sets the normal properties to define the appointment, including the StartTime, EndTime, Subject, Location, and BodyText. Next, the procedure adds the required and optional attendees and sends out the meeting request. Finally, the procedure saves the meeting to the meeting organizer's calendar.

Listing 7.2   Schedule a meeting and send the meeting requests.

```
Sub ScheduleMeeting()
  ' Schedules a meeting with
  ' required and optional attendees.

  Dim cnfg As Configuration
  Dim appt As CDO.Appointment
  Dim urlMBXCal As String

  ' URL to the calendar
  urlMBXCal = _
    GetStorageName & "mbx/mindy/calendar/"

  ' Set the configuration information
  Set cnfg = New CDO.Configuration
  With cnfg
    ' Set the meeting organizer
    .Fields(cdoSendEmailAddress) = "mindy@domain.com"
    ' Set the time zone
    .Fields(cdoTimeZoneIDURN) = cdoPacific
    .Fields.Update
  End With

  ' Create an appointment
  Set appt = New CDO.Appointment
  With appt
    ' Associate the configuration with this meeting instance
    .Configuration = cnfg
```

```
    'Set the basic properties
    .StartTime = "1:00 PM 4/18/2001"
    .EndTime = "2:00 PM 4/18/2001"
    .Subject = "Super Rooster security"
    .Location = "Super Rooster Exhibit Hall"
    .TextBody = "We need to discuss the security measures " & _
       "to employ to avoid the theft of our Super Rooster."
  End With

  ' Add the required attendees
  appt.Attendees.Add _
    "peter@domain.com, aidan@domain.com"

  ' Add the optional attendees
  With appt.Attendees.Add
    .Address = "robert@domain.com"
    .Role = cdoOptionalParticipant
  End With

  ' Send out the meeting requests to
  ' everyone who is added to the Attendees
  ' collection in the previous lines of code.
  appt.CreateRequest.Message.Send

  ' Save the meeting to the organizer's calendar
  appt.DataSource.SaveToContainer urlMBXCal

  ' Clean up
  Set cnfg = Nothing
  Set appt = Nothing
End Sub
```

TIP So that others can see the meeting, you can save a meeting to a public calendar instead of to the organizer's calendar. However, if you choose to do this, the meeting is not added to the organizer's calendar nor does the organizer get a meeting request by default. One way to solve this dilemma is to add the organizer to the list of required attendees, so the organizer will receive a meeting request and can then add the meeting to his or her personal calendar.

SETTING THE MEETING ORGANIZER

Every meeting requires an organizer. The meeting organizer is not only the person who generally chairs the meeting, but, more importantly from a programming perspective, the organizer is the sender of the meeting request and the owner of the meeting. Only the meeting organizer can change a meeting.

To indicate the meeting organizer, you use the Configuration object and set the http://schemas.microsoft.com/cdo/configuration/ SendEmailAddress schema property (cdoSendEmailAddress) to the e-mail address for the organizer. The Configuration object does not explicitly expose this property, so you must use the Fields collection to set it. Save the changes with the Fields.Update method. The following code sample sets the meeting organizer to mindy@domain.com:

```
' Define a single configuration
Set cnfg = New CDO.Configuration
With cnfg
   ' These fields are not exposed explicitly
   ' so you must use the Fields collection to
   ' get at them.
   .Fields(cdoSendEmailAddress) = "mindy@domain.com"
   .Fields(cdoTimeZoneIDURN) = cdoPacific
   .Fields.Update
End With
```

NOTE If you do not set a meeting organizer, the code will fail when you attempt to send the meeting request.

ADDING ATTENDEES

The Attendees collection of an Appointment object includes everyone who is invited to the meeting. An Attendee object represents each person in that collection. To invite a person to a meeting, you add to the Attendees collection with the Add method and then specify the e-mail address of the person (or persons) being invited. If you add more than one e-mail address at a time, separate them with commas. The following code sample adds two people to the Attendees collection for an appointment:

```
' Add the required attendees
appt.Attendees.Add _
  "peter@domain.com, aidan@domain.com"
```

You assign every attendee a role in the meeting, either implicitly or explicitly, from the Role property values listed in Table 7.3. The Role property indicates a person's role in the meeting. If you do not specify a role, the attendee is automatically configured to be required for the meeting. This is the case in the previous code sample. However, an attendee can only have one role; the Role property is not bitmapped so you cannot add two of the constant values together to create a new role type.

Table 7.3   Role property values

Constant	Value	Description
cdoRequiredParticipant	0	Attendee is a required participant. This is the Default setting.
cdoOptionalParticipant	1	Attendee is an optional participant.
cdoNonParticipant	2	Attendee is copied only to give him or her the information. This person does not need to respond or attend.
cdoChair	3	Attendee is the meeting chairperson. Attendee is included as a required participant.

The following code sample shows how to add an attendee to an appointment as an optional participant:

```
' Add the optional attendees
With appt.Attendees.Add
  .Address = "robert@domain.com"
  .Role = cdoOptionalParticipant
End With
```

SENDING A MEETING REQUEST

To tell people about a meeting, you need to send a meeting request. A CDO
CalendarMessage object is used to send and process a meeting request. To send a
meeting request to the people in the Attendees collection of an Appointment
object, call the Appointment.CreateRequest method. The method returns a new
CalendarMessage object and automatically addresses the request to everyone in the
Attendees collection for an Appointment object. To actually send the request, call
the Message.Send method exposed by the CalendarMessage object. The following
code sample creates a meeting request for an appointment and sends it:

```
appt.CreateRequest.Message.Send
```

Attendees use the meeting request to accept, tentatively accept, or decline the
invitation to the meeting.

CHECKING FREE/BUSY STATUS

Before adding a person to the list of meeting attendees, you might want to check
to see if that person is available to attend. A person's availability is known as their
free/busy status. To check the free/busy status, you must use the Addressee object
instead of the Attendee object. The Addressee object provides the properties and
methods for retrieving information about an Exchange user, including the user's
free/busy status. However, the Attendee object only has properties for defining the
participation of an Exchange user in reference to an appointment, such as the
person's role in the meeting.

To get information about an Exchange user, including free/busy status, you must
access the Active Directory directory service of Microsoft Windows 2000 on your
Windows 2000 domain controller. Active Directory manages user information for
the Exchange server as well as for the domain. For more information on accessing
Exchange information in Active Directory, see Chapter 8, "Interacting with Active
Directory."

CHECKING THE USER EXISTENCE

To access free/busy information, you must first verify that the user has an Exchange account in the domain. You can verify the existence of the account by checking the e-mail address in Active Directory.

After creating a new Addressee object, set the EmailAddress property to the e-mail address of the person you are checking. Next, call the CheckName method and pass the server name using the Lightweight Directory Access Protocol (LDAP). The method returns a True value if a coordinating user object is found in the Active Directory, and it returns a False value if no user object is found. For more information about using the LDAP protocol and Active Directory, see Chapter 8, "Interacting with Active Directory."

The following code sample checks to see if an e-mail address belongs to a user account in the domain.

```
With New CDO.Addressee
  ' Indicate the email address to check
  .EmailAddress = "mindy@domain.com"
  ' If the name exists in the Active
  ' Directory, CheckName returns True.
  If .CheckName("LDAP://cyberserver") Then
    Debug.Print "This user exists."
  Else
    Debug.Print "This email address does not exist in this domain."
  End If
End With
```

USING THE GETFREEBUSY METHOD

After verifying the existence of the user object in Active Directory, you can then check the free/busy status by using the GetFreeBusy method of an Attendee object. The GetFreeBusy method has three required parameters: StartTime, EndTime, and Interval.

The StartTime and EndTime parameters are the boundaries of the range to check in date/time format. You can specify both the date and the time for each parameter. The Interval parameter indicates the size of each segment in minutes to splice the date range. For example, an interval of 60 generates one segment for every 60 minutes from the StartTime parameter to the EndTime parameter. If the StartTime parameter is 2/14/2000 8:00AM and the EndTime parameter is 2/14/2000 9:00AM, one segment is generated. If the EndTime parameter is 2/14/2000 10:00AM, two segments are generated. Each segment is then assigned one of the values listed in Table 7.4, which indicates the status of the attendee for that particular segment.

Table 7.4 Possible interval segment values indicating free/busy status

Value	Description
0	Free
1	Tentative
2	Busy
3	Out of office (OOF)
4	Data unavailable (The Exchange server may not have the most recent information.)

All these segment values for the time frame are concatenated into a single string and returned by the GetFreeBusy method. The following code sample

```
strResult= adre.GetFreeBusy( _
    "2/14/2000 8:00AM", _
    "2/14/2000 10:00AM", _
    30)
```

might return the string value "2201" for an addressee. The result contains four values, because it requested information about 30-minute segments, over a span of two hours. In this case, the addressee is busy from 8:00 to 9:00 A.M., free from 9:00 to 9:30 A.M., and tentatively busy from 9:30 to 10:00 A.M. If an addressee is busy for half of a segment and free for the other half, a busy value is returned. For example, if you are checking an hour segment and the addressee is marked as Busy for 30 minutes of that hour, a Busy status is returned for the entire hour.

TIP To check the status of an addressee for an entire day, use an interval of 60*24.

Listing 7.3 shows how to check the free/busy status for an addressee. The procedure takes three arguments: the start date and time of the time frame to check, the end date and time of the time frame to check, and the time interval to evaluate. The function looks in Active Directory for a user account with the specified e-mail address. If the e-mail address is valid, the procedure returns the free/busy information for the time frame and interval that you specify and evaluates the return string. If the return string contains values indicating busy or out-of-office status, the function returns False, indicating that the user is not available to meet during the specified time. If the return string contains any other values, the function returns True, indicating that this person is available.

Listing 7.3   Determine if a user is available at the specified meeting time.

```
Function IsAvailable(strEmail As String, _
  dtStart As Date, _
  dtEnd As Date, _
  lngInterval As Long) As Boolean

  ' This function returns True if the
  ' user's time frame is anything
  ' but Busy or OOF.

  Dim strFBStatus As String

  With New CDO.Addressee
    .EmailAddress = strEmail

    If .CheckName("ldap://cyberserver") Then

      ' Get the free/busy string
      strFBStatus = .GetFreeBusy(dtStart, dtEnd, lngInterval)

      'if this string contains a 2 or a 3
      If InStr(1, strFBStatus, "2") = 0 And _
        InStr(1, strFBStatus, "3") = 0 Then
        ' The user is not already marked as busy or OOF
        ' so go ahead and schedule
        IsAvailable = True
      Else
        ' The user is busy or out of office during that interval
        IsAvailable = False
```

```
        End If
    Else
        ' User was not found in Active Directory
        IsAvailable = False
    End If
  End With
End Function
```

NOTE   The Outlook 2000 object model has a similar method named FreeBusy that also returns free/busy information. They are not the same methods. You can use the CDO GetFreeBusy method to specify the exact time frame to return information about, including hours and minutes. However, the Outlook method allows you only to set the start date, and it ignores the time if it is included. The time frame evaluated is always an entire 24-hour period, so you are responsible for parsing through the return string to pull out the exact values that you need.

PUBLISHING A MEETING

For some meetings, you do not need to know whether a person is attending or not attending for the event to occur. In these scenarios, you do want people to know about the event, but sending a meeting request is not necessary. One solution is to *publish* a meeting instead of scheduling it. When a meeting is published, a meeting request is sent out, but no one is required to respond. If you open the meeting itself, you will also notice that it does not have any attendees. To create a published meeting, you must still indicate a meeting organizer, but you do not add to the Attendees collection. When it comes time to create the meeting request, use the Publish method as opposed to the CreateRequest method, add recipients to the message, and then send it.

Listing 7.4 shows how to publish a meeting. The code defines the Configuration object just like a typical meeting request. Next, the procedure creates a new Appointment object and sets the appropriate properties. Instead of inviting people to the meeting, the code jumps ahead and creates a new message request with the Publish method. The Publish method does not add attendees automatically to the meeting request, so the code sets the To property of the Message object part of the meeting request to some e-mail addresses and then sends the request. To preserve the list of invitees with the meeting, the procedure populates the body of the appointment with the recipients list and then saves the appointment to a public calendar.

Listing 7.4 Publish a meeting and send alert notices.

```
Sub CreatePublishedEvent()
    ' Publish an event in a public folder
    ' and tell people about it with
    ' a meeting invitation.

    Dim cnfg As CDO.Configuration
    Dim urlEventsFld As String

    ' URL to the calendar
    urlEventsFld = _
        GetStorageName & "applications/zoo management/events/"

    ' Define a single configuration
    Set cnfg = New CDO.Configuration
    With cnfg
        ' These fields are not exposed explicitly
        ' so you must use the Fields collection to
        ' get at them.
        .Fields(cdoSendEmailAddress) = "mindy@domain.com"
        .Fields(cdoTimeZoneIDURN) = cdoPacific
        .Fields.Update
    End With

    ' If you are using VBScript, use this With:
    ' With CreateObject("CDO.Appointment")
    With New CDO.Appointment
        ' Add the meeting organizer and time zone
        ' information to this meeting.
        Set .Configuration = cnfg

        'Set the basic properties
        .Subject = "Opening of the Super Rooster Exhibit"
        .StartTime = "8:00 PM 5/1/2001"
        .EndTime = "11:00 PM 5/1/2001"
        .Location = "Super Rooster Exhibit Hall"
        .TextBody = "This is going to be great!"
```

```
' Create the meeting request
With .Publish
  .Message.To = "peter@domain.com, robert@domain.com," & _
    "aidan@domain.com, denise@domain.com, amy@domain.com"
  .Message.Send
End With

' Save the meeting to the events calendar
.DataSource.SaveToContainer urlEventsFld
End With

' Clean up
Set cnfg = Nothing
End Sub
```

KEEPING TRACK OF ATTENDEES OF A PUBLISHED EVENT

By default, a published event does not have any attendees. Although you send information about the event to individuals, they are not considered attendees of the meeting. Only the event organizer is listed as an attendee. What happens, then, if the event time changes or the event gets deleted? By default, nothing happens. Nobody is notified of the change because the subscription list is no longer available with the original appointment.

One possible solution to this dilemma is to use a combination of custom properties and Web Storage System events. When you address the calendar message, write each recipient into a custom property in the Appointment object. If you do this, you can keep track of who is invited to the event. In the previous example, the list is simply saved to the body text of the appointment; however, custom properties give you much more control over the list and prevent users from inadvertently making changes to the list. But because you are programmatically maintaining this list, you need to remember that when others are invited.

When you have a list of attendees stored, you can use the Web Storage System events, OnSave and OnDelete, for the calendar folder to trap for changes. These are asynchronous events, so they fire after the actual action occurs. In the event sink, you can check the item that has triggered the event sink to see if the item is a published event item. If so, you can read the custom property that stores the e-mail addresses with the item and send a new CalendarMessage to those addresses. For more information on how to use event sinks, see Chapter 9, "Using Web Storage System Events."

SCHEDULING RECURRING APPOINTMENTS AND MEETINGS

Some appointments and meetings happen at regular intervals. For example, company update meetings might occur every quarter, and project update meetings might occur every other Thursday. These types of appointments and meetings are known as *recurring appointments* and *recurring meetings*.

A recurring appointment or meeting can consist of up to three components—a master Appointment object, a RecurrencePattern object (belonging to the RecurrencePatterns collection), and an Exception object (belonging to the Exceptions collection):

- The master Appointment object defines the main properties of the appointment, such as the StartTime, EndTime or Duration, Subject, and Attendees collection (if used). These properties are then applied to every occurrence of the appointment, known as instances of the master Appointment object. The first instance is defined by the master Appointment object.

- The RecurrencePattern object defines the pattern used to create all instances after the original one. The pattern is defined by values such as the frequency of the occurrence, the time frame between occurrences, and when the occurrences will cease to occur.

- The Exception object is an optional component. It is used to alter the original pattern by deleting single instances, modifying single instances, or defining additional instances. An Exception object can be applied to a single instance or to an entire range of instances.

This section describes how to create and work with recurring appointments and meetings.

CONFIGURING THE MASTER APPOINTMENT

You create a recurring appointment or meeting by creating a master Appointment object and defining the RecurrencePattern object and any Exception objects. However, this can be overwhelming if you try to learn it all at once. This section and the following sections step through how to change a basic meeting into a recurring meeting with an exception.

Let's say that you are scheduling a public feeding of the super rooster in the zoo. You want people to witness the super rooster's strong yet playful behavior during feeding to promote public acceptance of this animal. Because you are unsure of the general reception of this event, you want the public feeding to occur only every other day for 10 instances. To make sure that everyone knows about this trial feeding event, you want to add the meeting to the Events calendar in the Zoo Management application. However, you do need to invite the animal keeper who works with the super rooster so that person knows when to show up.

Listing 7.5 shows how to set up the master appointment for the public feeding of the super rooster. After you set the meeting organizer and time zone information with the Configuration object, create a new Appointment object and set the basic information that describes the appointment, such as where the feeding will take place. Then, set the time frame for the feeding. The date portion of the StartTime property defines the first date that the feeding will occur as well as the time frame. Finally, you need to invite the super rooster keeper and then save the master Appointment object to the Events folder.

Listing 7.5   Create the master Appointment for a recurring meeting.

```
Sub CreateRecurringMeeting_1()
  ' This is the first part of three parts
  ' demonstrating how to create a
  ' recurring meeting or appointment.
  ' Part 1 creates the base appointment.

  Dim cnfg As CDO.Configuration
  Dim urlFeedingFld As String

  ' URL to the Events folder in the
  ' Zoo Management application
  urlFeedingFld = _
  GetStorageName & "applications/zoo management/events/"

  ' Set the configuration information
  Set cnfg = New CDO.Configuration
  With cnfg
    ' Set the meeting organizer
    .Fields(cdoSendEmailAddress) = "mindy@domain.com"
```

```
            ' Set the time zone to Pacific time
            .Fields(cdoTimeZoneIDURN) = cdoPacific
            .Fields.Update
        End With


        ' If you are using VBScript, use this With:
        ' With CreateObject("CDO.Appointment")
        With New CDO.Appointment
            ' Associate the meeting organizer and time zone
            ' info with the Appointment
            Set .Configuration = cnfg

            ' Set some general info
            .Subject = "Public Feeding of the Super Rooster"
            .Location = "Super Rooster Exhibit"
            .TextBody = "We are testing the receptiveness to " & _
              "the public feeding of the super rooster."

            ' Set the date and time frame for the
            ' first meeting in the recurrence
            .StartTime = "6/1/2001 3:00 PM"
            .EndTime = "6/1/2001 3:30 PM"

            ' Invite the super rooster keeper
            .Attendees.Add ("peter@domain.com")

            ' Send the meeting request
            .CreateRequest.Message.Send

            'Save to the Events calendar
            .DataSource.SaveToContainer urlFeedingFld
        End With

        ' Clean up
        Set cnfg = Nothing
    End Sub
```

If you run this code, the feeding of the super rooster is scheduled for 3:00 to 3:30 P.M. at the super rooster exhibit on June 1, 2001 only. The next section explains how to add a recurrence pattern to the master Appointment object so that the public feeding is scheduled for more than one day.

DEFINING A RECURRENCE PATTERN

The master appointment has already defined the date that the first public feeding will occur in the StartTime property. The time portion of the StartTime property and the time portion of the EndTime property define the time frame for the master appointment and all other instances. If the master appointment has a StartTime of 6/1/2001 3:00PM and an EndTime of 6/1/2001 3:30PM, all the additional instances will also be from 3:00 to 3:30 P.M.

To create additional instances of the master appointment, you define a recurrence pattern that the additional Appointment objects follow. To create a recurrence pattern, you call the RecurrencePatterns.Add method of an Appointment object. The RecurrencePatterns.Add method has one parameter, which is a string value indicating the type of pattern that you are adding. The type can be either "Add" or "Delete." You use "Add" when you are creating a new pattern, and you use "Delete" when you are deleting an existing pattern. The following code sample creates a new pattern for an appointment:

```
appt.RecurrencePatterns.Add("Add")
```

You then need to define how the additional instances of the Appointment object will occur by setting the recurrence pattern properties listed in Table 7.5. The Frequency property and the Interval property determine how often the instances will occur, and the PatternEndDate property and the Instances property set when the instances will stop occurring.

Table 7.5   Properties for defining recurrence patterns

Property	Data type	Description
Frequency	cdoFrequency	Type of recurrence used in the pattern, such as daily or weekly.
Interval	Long	Interval between two occurrences.
PatternEndDate	Date	Date that the occurrence ends.
Instances	Long	Number of occurrences in a pattern.

The Frequency property can be set to any of the constants listed in Table 7.6.

Table 7.6 Constants for the cdoFrequency enumeration

Constant	Value	Description
cdoSecondly	1	Appointment occurs every second.
cdoMinutely	2	Appointment occurs every minute.
cdoHourly	3	Appointment occurs every hour.
cdoDaily	4	Appointment occurs every day.
cdoWeekly	5	Appointment occurs every week.
cdoMonthly	6	Appointment occurs every month.
cdoYearly	7	Appointment occurs every year.

You use the Interval property to adjust the frequency of an appointment by specifying the instances between each occurrence. By default, the appointment has an interval occurrence of 1; this means that an appointment with a frequency of cdoDaily occurs once each day. However, if you set the Interval property at 2, the appointment will occur every other day. If you set the Interval property to 3, the appointment will occur every third day.

After you have defined how often the meetings occur, you need to indicate when they end by setting either the Instances property or the PatternEndDate property. To create a recurring appointment that ends after a number of instances, set the Instances property. If you do not know how many times an appointment or meeting needs to occur, you can instead set the PatternEndDate property to end the occurrences after a certain date is reached. An example is scheduling a recurring meeting for an ongoing project; the meetings should continue until the project is over. When the project ends, the meetings should also end. Because projects often have a defined end date, you could set the PatternEndDate property to that same date.

> **TIP** If you want the appointment or meeting to occur indefinitely, do not set either the PatternEndDate property or the Instances property.

So if you want the public feeding of the super rooster to occur every other day, you must add a new RecurrencePattern object passing the "Add" method type argument, and then you set the Frequency property to cdoDaily and the Interval property to 2. If you want the public feeding to end after it occurs 10 times, set the Instances property to 10. Listing 7.6 takes the master Appointment object from the previous section and adds a RecurrencePattern to it. The RecurrencePattern is defined immediately after the basic Appointment properties are set.

Listing 7.6   Create a recurring meeting.

```
Sub CreateRecurringMeeting_2()
    ' This is the second part of three parts
    ' demonstrating how to create a
    ' recurring meeting or appointment.
    ' Part 2 defines the recurrence pattern
    ' so the appointment occurs every other day
    ' until it has occured 10 times.

    Dim cnfg As CDO.Configuration
    Dim urlFeedingFld As String

    ' URL to the Events folder in the
    ' Zoo Management application
    urlFeedingFld = _
    GetStorageName & "applications/zoo management/events/"

    ' Set the configuration information
    Set cnfg = New CDO.Configuration
    With cnfg
        ' Set the meeting organizer
        .Fields(cdoSendEmailAddress) = "mindy@domain.com"
        ' Set the time zone to Pacific time
        .Fields(cdoTimeZoneIDURN) = cdoPacific
        .Fields.Update
    End With

    ' If you are using VBScript, use this With:
    ' With CreateObject("CDO.Appointment")
    With New CDO.Appointment
```

```
        ' Associate the meeting organizer and time zone
        ' info with the Appointment
        Set .Configuration = cnfg

        ' Set some general info
        .Subject = "Public Feeding of the Super Rooster"
        .Location = "Super Rooster Exhibit"
        .TextBody = "We are testing the receptiveness to " & _
          "the public feeding of the super rooster."

        ' Set the date and time frame for the
        ' first meeting in the recurrence
        .StartTime = "6/1/2001 3:00 PM"
        .EndTime = "6/1/2001 3:30 PM"

        ' Make the appointment occur
        ' every other day for 10 instances
        With .RecurrencePatterns.Add("Add")
          .Frequency = cdoDaily
          .Interval = 2
          .Instances = 10
        End With

        ' Invite the super rooster keeper
        .Attendees.Add ("peter@domain.com")

        ' Send the meeting request
        .CreateRequest.Message.Send

        'Save to the Events calendar
        .DataSource.SaveToContainer urlFeedingFld
    End With

    ' Clean up
    Set cnfg = Nothing
End Sub
```

Using the dates specified in the previous listing, the feeding of the super rooster is scheduled from 3:00 to 3:30 P.M. at the super rooster exhibit on the following dates: June 1, 2001; June 3, 2001; June 5, 2001; June 7, 2001; June 9, 2001; June 11, 2001; June 13, 2001; June 15, 2001; June 17, 2001; and June 19, 2001.

USING EXCEPTIONS

An exception is used to modify a recurring appointment or meeting without changing the entire recurrence pattern. You can modify a recurring appointment by adding another Appointment instance that doesn't fit the defined pattern, by deleting an Appointment instance defined by the pattern, or by changing an Appointment instance defined by the pattern. You use the Exception object of an Appointment object to alter a recurring appointment. Here's an example: if you have a recurring meeting scheduled for the 25th of every month, you can use an Exception object to change that rule in December when the meeting will occur on a holiday.

You create an exception to a recurrence pattern by calling the Exceptions.Add method of the master Appointment object. The Exceptions.Add method takes one required parameter, which is the type of exception being added. The method type parameter is a string value and can be set to "Add," "Delete," or "Modify" depending on what you are trying to do.

To add an additional instance to a pattern, you pass the "Add" method type to the Exceptions.Add method. Then, you must set the StartTime and EndTime for the new instance. You do not need to do anything more than this. The new instance inherits the basic information from the master Appointment—information such as the location of the appointment, just like any other instance. The following code sample adds an instance to an appointment on July 1, 2001:

```
With appt.Exceptions.Add("Add")
   .StartTime = "7/01/2001 3:00PM"
   .EndTime = "7/01/2001 3:30PM"
End With
```

To delete an instance from a recurrence pattern, pass the "Delete" string to the Exceptions.Add method. Then, indicate which instance of the recurring appointment will be deleted. Every Appointment instance for a recurring appointment is automatically assigned a RecurrenceID value. When a new instance is created, the RecurrenceID property is automatically set to the StartTime property value of the Appointment instance. You use the RecurrenceID property when deleting Appointment instances to indicate which instance is to be deleted. If an Appointment instance does not exist with the RecurrenceID property you specify, no error is generated. For example, the following code sample deletes an Appointment instance that occurs on June 10, 2001:

```
With appt.Exceptions.Add("Delete")
   .RecurrenceID = "6/10/2001 3:00 PM"
End With
```

When you modify an Appointment instance of a recurrence pattern, you are essentially deleting the existing Appointment instance and creating another Appointment instance at another time. So, to modify an Appointment instance, you combine the techniques for deleting an exception and adding an exception. To modify an Appointment instance of a recurrence pattern, pass the "Modify" string to the Exceptions.Add method. Then, set the RecurrenceID property of the Exception object to the StartTime of the existing Appointment instance to be modified. Next, set the StartTime of the Exception object to reflect the new time. If the RecurrenceID property does not reference an existing Appointment instance, no error is generated and a new Appointment instance is created at the specified StartTime. The following code sample changes the Application instance currently scheduled for June 11, 2001 at 3:00 P.M. to occur instead on June 10, 2001 at 3:00 P.M.:

```
With appt.Exceptions.Add("modify")
   .RecurrenceID = "6/11/2001 3:00 PM"
   .StartTime = "6/10/2001 3:00 PM"
End With
```

Listing 7.7 completes the scheduling of the super rooster's public feedings. After you configure the master appointment with the basic information about the appointment, you add the recurrence pattern so that the feeding will occur every other day for 10 instances. However, one of the instances occurs on Monday, June 11, and you would rather have it occur on Sunday, June 10, when the zoo is much more crowded, so you must add an exception to modify the June 11 instance so that it occurs on June 10. In addition, you no longer want the last scheduled feeding to occur, so you add another exception to delete the June 19 instance.

Listing 7.7 Create a recurring meeting with exceptions.

```
Sub CreateRecurringMeeting_3()
  ' This is the second part of three parts
  ' demonstrating how to create a
  ' recurring meeting or appointment.
  ' Part 3 defines two exceptions to the
  ' pattern by modifying one instance
  ' and deleting another.

  Dim cnfg As CDO.Configuration
  Dim urlFeedingFld As String

  ' URL to the Events folder in the
  ' Zoo Management application
  urlFeedingFld = _
    GetStorageName & "applications/zoo management/events/"

  ' Set the configuration information
  Set cnfg = New CDO.Configuration
  With cnfg
    ' Set the meeting organizer
    .Fields(cdoSendEmailAddress) = "mindy@domain.com"
    ' Set the time zone to Pacific time
    .Fields(cdoTimeZoneIDURN) = cdoPacific
    .Fields.Update
  End With

  ' If you are using VBScript, use this With:
  ' With CreateObject("CDO.Appointment")
  With New CDO.Appointment
    ' Associate the meeting organizer and time zone
    ' info with the Appointment
    Set .Configuration = cnfg

    ' Set some general info
    .Subject = "Public Feeding of the Super Rooster"
    .Location = "Super Rooster Exhibit"
    .TextBody = "We are testing the receptiveness to " & _
      "the public feeding of the super rooster."
```

```
' Set the date and time frame for the
' first meeting in the recurrence
.StartTime = "6/1/2001 3:00 PM"
.EndTime = "6/1/2001 3:30 PM"

' Make the appointment occur
' every other day for 10 instances
With .RecurrencePatterns.Add("Add")
  .Frequency = cdoDaily
  .Interval = 2
  .Instances = 10
End With

' Change the feeding scheduled for
' Monday June 11 to Sunday June 10.
With .Exceptions.Add("modify")
  .RecurrenceID = "6/11/2001 3:00 PM"
  .StartTime = "6/10/2001 3:00 PM"
End With

' Delete the last feeding currently
' scheduled for June 19.
With .Exceptions.Add("delete")
  .RecurrenceID = "6/19/2001 3:00 PM"
End With

' Invite the super rooster keeper
.Attendees.Add ("peter@domain.com")

' Send the meeting request
.CreateRequest.Message.Send
```

```
      'Save to the Events calendar
      .DataSource.SaveToContainer urlFeedingFld
   End With

   ' Clean up
   Set cnfg = Nothing
End Sub
```

If you run this listing as is, the feeding of the super rooster is now scheduled from 3:00 to 3:30 P.M. at the super rooster exhibit on the following dates: June 1, 2001; June 3, 2001; June 5, 2001; June 7, 2001; June 9, 2001; June 10, 2001; June 13, 2001; June 15, 2001; and June 17, 2001. The feeding originally scheduled for June 11 was moved to June 10, and the feeding originally scheduled for June 19 was deleted.

NOTE   You can also create Exception objects for a recurring appointment after the pattern has been defined. However, to do so you still need to access the master appointment. You cannot make changes to the pattern through one of the instances. For more information about retrieving the master appointment from an instance, see "Getting the Recurrence Master."

GETTING THE RECURRENCE MASTER

The way Exchange handles recurring appointments and meetings is unique in the CDO for Exchange calendaring realm. To optimize data storage, Exchange creates only one item in the Web Storage System for the master appointment. However, any time you view a calendar, Exchange evaluates the recurrence pattern and exceptions for the appointment and generates temporary items for those instances. You see only the instances, not the master appointment. The master is more like a template used by Exchange to create the instances, so it is hidden and unavailable for normal user interaction. Any changes made to an individual instance are always stored back to the master appointment.

Figure 7.3 shows how Exchange stores recurring appointments versus how the client calendar views recurring appointments. In this example, Exchange stores two master Appointment objects. Each master appointment defines three instances, so the client calendar shows six appointments, although Exchange is really storing only two Appointment objects.

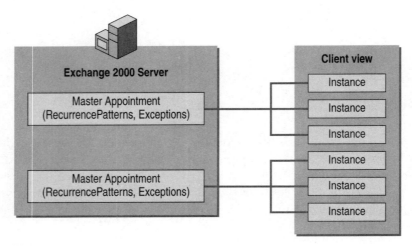

Figure 7.3
Exchange stores only the master Appointment objects, but a client calendar sees all the
instances defined by the master Appointment objects.

To make changes to a recurring appointment, you must access the master
appointment, but you can't access the master directly. You can get the recurrence
master appointment for a recurrence pattern by accessing an instance of the
appointment, and then calling that instance's GetRecurringMaster method. The
GetRecurringMaster method takes one argument, a string indicating where the
calendar containing the master appointment is located.

For example, Listing 7.8 returns a master appointment for an instance and reports
the recurrence pattern information. After the instance appointment is opened, its
InstanceType property is evaluated. If the appointment is anything other than a
single appointment, the procedure retrieves the master appointment and returns
the recurrence pattern information. This function also calls a second function,
GetFrequencyPattern, to convert the Frequency property from a long integer into a
string description.

Listing 7.8   Get the pattern properties for a master recurrence appointment.

```
Function GetMasterPattern(urlAppt As String, urlCalFld As String)
  ' Using a URL to the appointment and
  ' a URL to the owning calendar, this procedure
  ' determines if the appointment is an
  ' instance of a recurrring appointment, and
  ' if so, info on the recurrence pattern of the
  ' master appointment is returned.

  Dim appt As CDO.Appointment
  Dim apptMaster As CDO.Appointment

  'Open the appointment
  Set appt = New CDO.Appointment
  appt.DataSource.Open urlAppt

  ' If the appointment is part of a recurring appointment
  If appt.Fields(cdoInstanceType) > 0 Then
    ' Get the master
    Set apptMaster = appt.GetRecurringMaster(urlCalFld)

    ' Access the recurrence pattern
    With apptMaster.RecurrencePatterns(1)
      Debug.Print _
        "----------------------------------------------------"
      Debug.Print "MASTER APPOINTMENT: " & appt.Subject
      Debug.Print "Start: " & appt.StartTime
      Debug.Print "End: " & appt.EndTime & vbCrLf
      Debug.Print "RECURRENCE PATTERN"
      Debug.Print "Frequency: " & GetFrequencyPattern(.Frequency)
      Debug.Print "Interval: " & .Interval
      Debug.Print "Instances: " & .Instances
      Debug.Print "Pattern End Date: " & .PatternEndDate
      Debug.Print _
        "----------------------------------------------------"
    End With
  End If
```

```
    ' Clean up
    Set appt = Nothing
    Set apptMaster = Nothing
  End Function


  Function GetFrequencyPattern(lngInterval As CdoFrequency) _
    As String

    ' Returns a friendly string describing
    ' the frequency defined for a recurring
    ' appointment.

    Select Case lngInterval
    Case cdoSecondly '1
      GetFrequencyPattern = "Secondly"
    Case cdoMinutely '2
      GetFrequencyPattern = "Minutely"
    Case cdoHourly '3
      GetFrequencyPattern = "Hourly"
    Case cdoDaily '4
      GetFrequencyPattern = "Daily"
    Case cdoWeekly '5
      GetFrequencyPattern = "Weekly"
    Case cdoMonthly '6
      GetFrequencyPattern = "Monthly"
    Case cdoYearly '7
      GetFrequencyPattern = "Yearly"
    End Select
  End Function
```

If you do not know the URL for the master appointment, you can instead use
Structured Query Language (SQL) to build a SELECT query that returns all the
master appointments by adding criteria that evaluate the
urn:schemas:calendar:instancetype schema property. The
urn:schemas:calendar:instancetype schema property contains information about the
appointment type. Queries that use the urn:schemas:calendar:instancetype schema
property are discussed in more detail in "Identifying Appointment Types" later in
this chapter.

WORKING WITH EXISTING APPOINTMENTS AND MEETING REQUESTS

The previous sections taught about how to create various types of Appointment objects. But what if you need to interact with existing Appointment objects in a calendar? This section shows how to query a calendar for information, make changes to appointments, cancel appointments, and send out updates. In addition, this section explains how to process meeting requests.

CONVERTING DATES AND TIMES

To use code to get calendar information from Exchange, you need to structure your request and parse the results properly. The code listings and samples in this chapter use the TimeZoneConverter and the ISOFormat functions to properly convert and format dates and times. The TimeZoneConverter function (see Listing 7.9) takes a date/time string and converts it into the equivalent time in another time zone. Most often, you will use this function to convert date/time strings from your local time zone to UTC so that Exchange can properly process a data request.

The TimeZoneConverter function takes three parameters: *DateToConvert, FromTimeZone,* and *IntoTimeZone. DateToConvert* is a date string to be converted. *FromTimeZone* is a cdoTimeZoneID constant that identifies the current time zone from which the date string will be converted. *IntoTimeZone* is a cdoTimeZoneID constant that identifies the time zone to which you want to convert the date string.

The function uses a temporary Appointment object to set the time and the Configuration object to use Exchange as the engine to make the time zone change to the date value. The TimeZoneConverter function creates a temporary Appointment object, sets the cdoTimeZoneIDURN schema property of the Appointment.Configuration object to be the *FromTimeZone* parameter value, and sets the StartTime property of the Appointment object to the *DateToConvert* parameter. To get the equivalent of *DateToConvert* in the *IntoTimeZone* time zone, the code sets the cdoTimeZoneIDURN schema property of the Appointment.Configuration object to the *IntoTimeZone* parameter value. Through this action, the StartTime of the Appointment object is automatically converted to the equivalent time in the time zone indicated by the *IntoTimeZone* parameter. The function returns this date/time value.

Listing 7.9 Convert a date/time from one time zone to another time zone.

```
Public Function TimeZoneConverter( _
  ByVal DateToConvert As String, _
  FromTimeZone As CdoTimeZoneId, _
  IntoTimeZone As CdoTimeZoneId) As String

  ' Uses the Configuration object and
  ' Exchange to convert a string date
  ' from one time zone into another.

  With New CDO.Appointment
    ' Set the time zone for the Appointment
    ' to the FromTimeZone value.
    With .Configuration
      .Fields(cdoTimeZoneIDURN) = FromTimeZone
      .Fields.Update
    End With

    'Set the starttime to the date to be converted
    .StartTime = DateToConvert

    ' Set the time zone for the Appointment
    ' to the IntoTimeZone value. Exchange will
    ' automatically do the date conversion for you.
    With .Configuration
      .Fields(cdoTimeZoneIDURN) = IntoTimeZone
      .Fields.Update
    End With

    ' Return the new date
    TimeZoneConverter = .StartTime
  End With
End Function
```

To use the function, you pass a date you want to convert, the time zone the date is currently formatted with, and the time zone for the resulting date. If you are converting a date to UTC, this last argument is always set to cdoUTC.

```
TimeZoneConverter("12/16/00 10:00AM", cdoPacific, cdoUTC)
```

The resulting value in UTC is 12/16/2000 6:00:00 PM.

The ISOFormat function (see Listing 7.10) is much less complex. It simply takes a date argument and formats it into ISO format so that Exchange can read it.

Listing 7.10 Format the date in ISO date format.

```
Public Function ISOFormat( _
   ByVal DateToFormat As String) As String

   ' Formats a date as ISO date format
   ' For instance, 12/25/2000 8:00AM
   ' becomes 2000-12-25T08:00:00Z

   ISOFormat = _
     Format(DateToFormat, "yyyy-mm-ddThh:mm:ssZ")
End Function
```

The two functions can be used in conjunction. For instance, the following code sample formats the data after converting it:

```
ISOFormat(TimeZoneConverter("12/16/00 10:00AM", cdoPacific, cdoUTC))
```

The result of the two function calls is 2000-12-16T18:00:00Z. These functions are frequently used when querying a calendar folder. For more information about querying calendars, see the next section, "Querying a Calendar."

QUERYING A CALENDAR

To locate existing appointments, you can query a calendar folder with SQL. Querying a folder allows you to locate appointments to make changes, cancel entire meetings, or retrieve occurrence masters.

You query a calendar by using the same core techniques as when querying any other folder in a Web Storage System. However, calendar folder queries often use a more complex WHERE clause than other queries. To query a calendar efficiently, you should try to specify a date range in which to look for appointments. Otherwise, the query looks at every appointment stored in the calendar, regardless of whether it occurred in the past or will occur in the very distant future. To query for a time frame, you use a WHERE clause using at least two criteria:

- **The start date and time of the date range**. The CDO StartTime property is accessed with SQL using the urn:schemas:calendar:dtstart schema property (cdoDTStart). Test for a cdoDTStart value that is greater than or equal to (>=) some date and time value.

- **The end date and time of the date range**. The CDO EndTime property is accessed with SQL using the urn:schemas:calendar:dtend schema property (cdoDTEnd). Test for a cdoDTEnd value that is less than or equal to (<=) some date and time value.

Because Exchange stores all dates and times in the same format, you must convert the dates and times you specify in the WHERE clause to dates and times Exchange can understand. To correctly build a query that retrieves items from the dates you specify, you must do three things with each date value:

1. **Convert the time zone.** Dates used in queries must be converted to UTC.

2. **Format the string in ISO date format.** You must convert all dates to ISO date format (yyyy-mm-ddThh:mm:ssZ) .

3. **Cast to the DateTime data type.** You need to indicate that the date value being passed is indeed a date data type as opposed to a string.

For example, the following text string shows how the WHERE clause needs to look for Exchange to return the right date range:

```
WHERE ("urn:schemas:calendar:dtstart" _
>= CAST("2000-04-01T16:00:00Z" as 'dateTime')) _
AND ("urn:schemas:calendar:dtend" _
<= CAST("2000-05-02T03:00:00Z" as 'dateTime'))
```

Listing 7.11 shows how to query a calendar for a specific time frame and report information about each appointment. The procedure takes three arguments: the URL for the folder being queried, the start date and time for the data range, and the end date and time for the date range. This SELECT statement calls two custom functions to properly convert the dates and times: TimeZoneConverter and ISOFormat. The TimeZoneConverter function converts a date from some time zone to UTC, and the ISOFormat function formats the UTC in ISO format. In addition, the query calls another function, AddQuotes. AddQuotes surrounds the text string passed to it with additional quotes. For more information on using AddQuotes, see Chapter 4, "ActiveX Data Objects and Exchange."

Listing 7.11   Retrieve appointments for a specific time frame.

```
Sub GetApptsByDate(urlQueryFld As String, _
  ByVal strStartDate As String, _
  ByVal strEndDate As String)

  ' Queries the calendar at the URL
  ' for all appointments that occur
  ' in the specified time frame.

  Dim cnn As ADODB.Connection
  Dim rst As New ADODB.Recordset
  Dim appt As New Appointment
  Dim strSQL As String

  ' Connect to the calendar URL
  Set cnn = New ADODB.Connection
  With cnn
    .Provider = "exoledb.datasource"
    .Open urlQueryFld
  End With

  ' Build the SQL SELECT statement in pieces
  ' Select the properties
  strSQL = "Select " & _
    AddQuotes(cdoDisplayName) & ", " & _
    AddQuotes(cdoHref) & ", " & _
    AddQuotes(cdoSubject) & ", " & _
    AddQuotes(cdoDTStart) & ", " & _
    AddQuotes(cdoDTEnd) & ", " & _
    AddQuotes(cdoInstanceType)
  ' Indicate shallow or deep traversal
  ' and what URL to begin looking
  strSQL = strSQL & _
    " FROM scope('shallow traversal of " & _
    AddQuotes(urlQueryFld) & "')"
```

```
' Build a filter
' This one restricts the results to a date range
strSQL = strSQL & _
  " WHERE (" & _
  AddQuotes(cdoDTStart) & " >= CAST(""" & _
  ISOFormat _
    (TimeZoneConverter(strStartDate, cdoPacific, cdoUTC)) & _
  """ as 'dateTime')) AND (" & _
  AddQuotes(cdoDTEnd) & " <= CAST(""" & _
  ISOFormat _
    (TimeZoneConverter(strEndDate, cdoPacific, cdoUTC)) & _
  """ as 'dateTime'))"
' Sort the results by the start date with the
' latest appointment first
strSQL = strSQL & _
  " ORDER BY " & AddQuotes(cdoDTStart) & " DESC"

' Execute the query and get the results
Set rst = New Recordset
With rst
.Open strSQL, cnn
End With

Debug.Print _
"-----------------------------------------------------"

' Move through the result set
' returning detail information
' about each Appointment object
rst.MoveFirst
Do Until rst.EOF
  Debug.Print "Subject: " & rst.Fields(cdoSubject)
  Debug.Print "Start: " & rst.Fields(cdoDTStart)
  Debug.Print "End: " & rst.Fields(cdoDTEnd)
  Debug.Print "Instance type: " & rst.Fields(cdoInstanceType)
```

```
    Set appt = New CDO.Appointment
    appt.DataSource.Open rst.Fields(cdoHref)
    If appt.Attendees.Count > 1 Then
    Debug.Print "This is a meeting."
    Debug.Print "Attendees count: " & appt.Attendees.Count
    End If
    Debug.Print _
    "----------------------------------------------------"

    rst.MoveNext
  Loop

  ' Close the ADO objects
  rst.Close
  cnn.Close

  ' Clean up
  Set appt = Nothing
  Set rst = Nothing
  Set cnn = Nothing
End Sub
```

NOTE If you are querying a folder that contains recurring appointments or meetings, Exchange automatically expands the recurrence master and creates the instances in the designated time boundaries of the query.

IDENTIFYING APPOINTMENT TYPES

An Appointment object can represent several types of appointments. When you return a result set of Appointment objects, you might want to be able to distinguish between a simple Appointment object and one that is an instance in a recurring meeting. The urn:schemas:calendar:instancetype property (cdoInstanceType) for an appointment identifies the type of appointment with one of the values listed in Table 7.7.

Table 7.7 Possible values for the urn:schemas:calendar:instancetype property

Name	Value	Description
cdoSingle	0	A single appointment.
cdoMaster	1	The master recurring appointment.
cdoInstance	2	A single instance of a recurring appointment.
cdoException	3	An exception to a recurring appointment.

You can use this property to query for specific appointment types. The following SELECT statement retrieves only master recurring appointments in the defined time frame:

```
' Build the SQL SELECT statement in pieces
' Select the properties
strSQL = "SELECT *"
' Indicate shallow or deep traversal
' and what URL to begin looking
strSQL = strSQL & _
   " FROM scope('shallow traversal of " & AddQuotes(urlQueryFld) & "')"
' Build a filter
' This one restricts the results to a date range
strSQL = strSQL & _
   " WHERE (" & _
   AddQuotes("urn:schemas:calendar:dtstart") & " >= CAST(""" & _
   ISOFormat(TimeZoneConverter(strStartDate, cdoPacific, cdoUTC)) & _
   """ as 'dateTime')) AND (" & _
   AddQuotes("urn:schemas:calendar:dtend") & " <= CAST(""" & _
   ISOFormat(TimeZoneConverter(strEndDate, cdoPacific, cdoUTC)) & _
   """ as 'dateTime')) AND (" & _
   AddQuotes("urn:schemas:calendar:instancetype") & " = 1)"
' Sort the results by the start date with the
' latest appointment first
strSQL = strSQL & _
   " ORDER BY " & AddQuotes("urn:schemas:calendar:dtstart") & " DESC"
```

Telling the Difference Between a Meeting and a Simple Appointment

Unfortunately, the urn:schema:calendar:instancetype schema property does not make it possible to distinguish between appointments and meetings. One solution to this dilemma is to open a CDO Appointment object and get the Attendees.Count property value. If the Attendees.Count property is greater than 1, the Appointment object is a meeting. If the Attendees.Count property is not greater than 1, the Appointment object is a simple appointment.

Using Calendar Browser

Included in the CH_07 Visual Basic project on the companion CD is a form titled "Calendar Browser" (frmCalBrowser.frm). You can use Calendar Browser to:

- Browse for Appointment objects in a calendar within some time frame.

- View properties on Appointment objects.

- Distinguish meetings from simple appointments.

- Identify which appointments are instances of a recurring appointment.

- Learn how to build queries that use dates in the WHERE clause of the SQL statement.

NOTE Calendar Browser is also available on the CD as an executable file (Calendar Browser.exe) in the More Helper Tools folder.

To use Calendar Browser, you must be running the CH_07 Visual Basic project or the executable version on your Exchange server computer. Calendar Browser uses the GetStorageName function to connect to the Exchange server on the local domain. It also uses a constant (LOCAL_TZ) to indicate the time zone in which the form is running. By default, LOCAL_TZ is set to Pacific time, so you might have to change it. To run the form, press the F5 key, and Calendar Browser will be visible (see Figure 7.4).

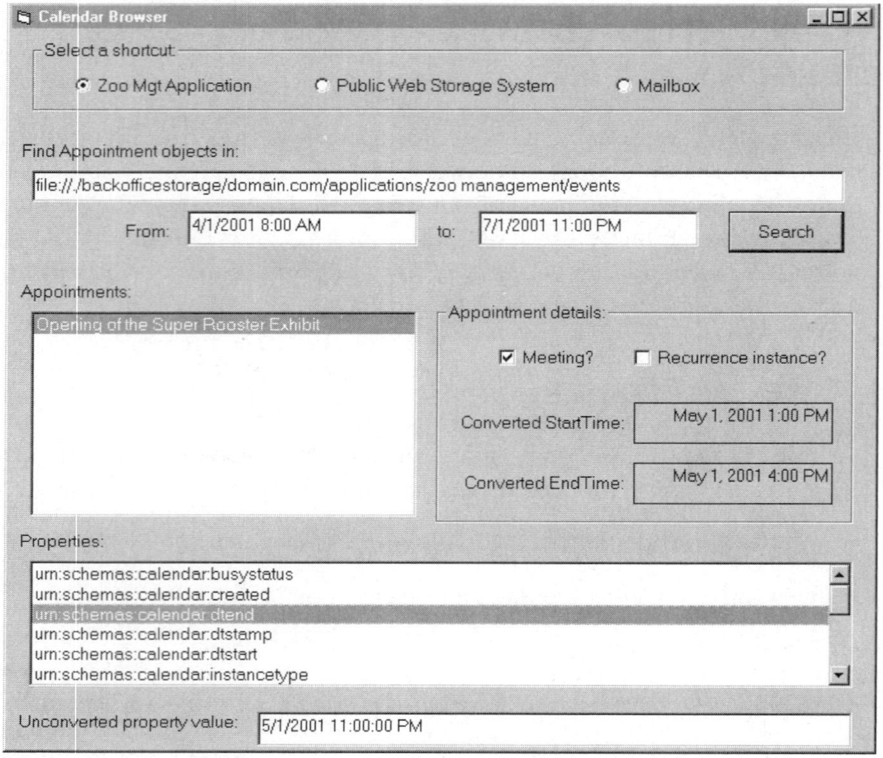

Figure 7.4
You can use Calendar Browser to query calendars for all appointments that occur in a specific time frame and then view the properties on each appointment.

Enter a URL for the calendar you want to search in the URL text box. You can use one of the shortcut option buttons to help build the URL. For example, click **Zoo Mgt Application** to build the URL for the Zoo Management application on the Applications Web Storage System. Next, specify a data and time range. These values determine the time frame in which to search for Appointments. When you click **Search**, the code tries to connect to the Exchange server on the local domain and populate the **Appointments** list with the results of the query. If the query doesn't find any appointments, it populates the **Appointments** list with a text message instead.

If the query returns Appointment objects, click an item in the **Appointments** list to populate the other controls on the form. The **Appointment details** area contains some general information about the selected appointment, including the start and end times converted to the time zone specified by LOCAL_TZ, whether the Appointment object is a meeting, and whether it is an instance of a recurring appointment.

In addition, Calendar Browser populates the **Properties** list with properties specific to an Appointment object when you select an appointment in the **Appointments** list. To see the value for a specific property, click that property in the **Properties** list. The **Unconverted property value** box then displays the current value as it is stored in the Web Storage System. For example, the start date and end date values are in UTC syntax.

SENDING UPDATES

When a meeting changes, you must notify the attendees of the alteration in the original appointment. To send an update about a meeting change, you must first open the Appointment object for the appointment that has changed. Once the Appointment object is open, you can send an update in the same way that you first notified the attendees. After configuring the cdoSendEmailAddress information, you can once again call the CreateRequest method of the Appointment object. If you want to alert people to the change, you can set the TextBody property of the Message portion of the CalendarMessage before sending it. The following code sample shows how to create and send an update to a meeting:

```
Set cmsgUpdate = appt.CreateRequest

cmsgUpdate.Message.TextBody = "This meeting has changed."
cmsgUpdate.Message.Send
```

NOTE   Only the meeting organizer can make changes to a meeting.

CANCELING AND DELETING APPOINTMENTS AND MEETINGS

Personal appointments and meetings are canceled in different ways. This section describes how they are canceled and how the appropriate people are notified of the cancellation.

CANCELING AN APPOINTMENT

To cancel an appointment, you do not need to send out any form of notification to others. Instead, you can simply delete the associated ActiveX Data Objects (ADO) record, but you must first decide how you are going to locate it. You will probably want to construct a query that selects the appointment based on a time range. To verify that the item is indeed an appointment, check the Count property of the Attendees collection to make sure that it is zero. If it is indeed an appointment, you can then call the Delete method of the Recordset to permanently delete the appointment.

Listing 7.12 shows how to delete an appointment from a private calendar. The code first builds an SQL SELECT statement that returns all the appointments for an indicated date range. After the connection is opened, a Recordset is generated from the results of the query. Because more than one appointment may be saved in the date range, the code then loops through the result set. To make sure that the appointment is not a meeting request, the code opens an Appointment object for the record and reads the attendee count. If there are no attendees, the appointment is only an appointment, and the record is deleted.

Listing 7.12   Delete appointments from a private calendar.

```
Sub DeleteAppt(strStartDate As String, strEndDate As String)
    ' Query a folder for a specific time frame
    ' and delete any simple appointment
    ' found there. Meetings are not deleted.

    Dim urlMBXCal As String
    Dim cnn As ADODB.Connection
    Dim rst As New ADODB.Recordset

    ' URL to the personal calendar
    urlMBXCal = GetStorageName & "mbx/mindy/calendar/"

    ' Open the connection
    Set cnn = New ADODB.Connection
    With cnn
      .Provider = "exoledb.datasource"
      .Open urlMBXCal
    End With
```

```
' Build the SQL SELECT statement in pieces
' Select the properties
strSQL = "Select *"
' Indicate shallow or deep traversal
' and what URL to begin looking
strSQL = strSQL & _
  " FROM scope('shallow traversal of" & AddQuotes(urlMBXCal) & "')"
' Build a filter
' This one restricts the results to a date range
strSQL = strSQL & _
  " WHERE (" & _
  AddQuotes("urn:schemas:calendar:dtstart") & " >= CAST(""" & _
  ISOFormat(TimeZoneConverter(strStartDate, cdoPacific, cdoUTC)) & _
  """ as 'dateTime')) AND " & _
  AddQuotes("urn:schemas:calendar:dtend") & " <= CAST(""" & _
  ISOFormat(TimeZoneConverter(strEndDate, cdoPacific, cdoUTC)) & _
  """ as 'dateTime'))"
' Sort the results by the start date with the
' latest appointment first
strSQL = strSQL & _
  " ORDER BY " & _
  AddQuotes("urn:schemas:calendar:dtstart") & " DESC"

' Get the results of the query
Set rst = New Recordset
With rst
  .Open strSQL, cnn
End With

' Go through all of the appointments
' You could list the results in a list box
' and let the user decide which ones get deleted
rst.MoveFirst
Do Until rst.EOF
  With New CDO.Appointment
    .DataSource.Open rst.Fields("DAV:href")
    ' Make certain that there are no attendees
    If .Attendees.Count = 0 Then
      ' Delete the appointment record
      rst.Delete
```

```
    End If

End With
    ' Move to the next appointment
    rst.MoveNext
  Loop

    ' Close the ADO objects
    rst.Close
    cnn.Close

    ' Clean up
    Set rst = Nothing
    Set cnn = Nothing
End Sub
```

CANCELING A MEETING

To cancel an existing meeting, you must send a special update that indicates that the meeting has been canceled. Notifying people of a meeting cancellation is similar to notifying them of a change in the original meeting. However, instead of using the CreateRequest method to create the CalendarMessage object, you use the Cancel method of the Appointment object. By setting the CleanupCalendar parameter to True, you can delete the appointment at the same time.

For example, the following code sample sends out an update indicating that the meeting has been canceled and deletes the meeting from the calendar as well.

```
With appt.Configuration
  .Fields(cdoSendEmailAddress) = "mindy@domain.com"
  .Fields.Update
End With

Set cmsgCancel = appt.Cancel(, True)
cmsgCancel.Message.Send
```

PROCESSING A MEETING REQUEST

To process a meeting request, you need to access a user's Inbox. You can either query the Inbox for a DAV:contentclass value of urn:content-classes:calendarmessage, or you can use a Web Storage System event sink. By using the OnSyncSave event sink on an Inbox, you can trap when a new meeting request arrives and then process it accordingly. For more information about using Web Storage System events, see Chapter 9, "Using Web Storage System Events."

To programmatically handle a meeting request using CDO, you retrieve the Appointment object associated with the meeting request and respond to it appropriately. After you have accessed the CalendarMessage object representing the meeting request, you must retrieve the associated Appointment object to respond to the request. To access the appointment bits, retrieve the CalendarParts collection with the CalendarParts property. Next, call the GetUpdatedItem method to return the Appointment object associated with the meeting request. The method always retrieves the most recent appointment information, whether it's from the calendar message or from the Web Storage System. The GetUpdatedItem method requires one parameter, the URL for a calendar folder. If the meeting request is an update, the calendar folder indicates where to look for the original appointment information. If the meeting request is a new appointment, the URL indicates where to save the appointment information.

Before you can respond to the request, you must first configure the Appointment object just opened for a sender. This is the only way to successfully send out a response. After that is done, you can call one of the three methods for responding to a meeting request: Accept, AcceptTentative, and Decline. These methods return a new CalendarMessage object, which is automatically addressed to the meeting organizer. You can modify the new CalendarMessage object or send it immediately. Once the response is sent, the calendar is automatically updated with the latest information.

After the response has been sent, you still need to process the appointment itself. If you have accepted, you then save the appointment to a calendar folder. Finally, you must explicitly delete the meeting request that you just processed. Unlike e-mail clients such as Outlook 2000, CDO does not automatically delete the meeting request after it has been processed. To delete the request, use ADO to open a Record object and then call the DeleteRecord method.

Listing 7.13 shows how to process a meeting request. The procedure automatically accepts any meeting request that is sent by a particular individual. The procedure takes two arguments: the URL for the CalendarMessage object that triggered the event, and the URL for the calendar that stores the appointment. After the procedure opens the meeting request, it evaluates who the sender is. If the sender is a particular person, the request is automatically accepted and the calendar message is deleted from the Inbox.

Listing 7.13   Automatically accept a meeting request.

```
Sub AcceptMeetingRequest(urlRequest As String, urlCalendar As String)
    ' Automatically accept meeting requests
    ' from a particular sender.

    Dim appt As CDO.Appointment
    Dim cmRequest As CDO.CalendarMessage
    Dim rec As ADODB.Record
    Dim strAlias As String

    ' Open the meeting request
    Set cmRequest = New CDO.CalendarMessage
    cmRequest.DataSource.Open urlRequest, , adModeReadWrite

    ' Indicate the sender that you want to automatically
    ' accept meeting requests from.
    strAlias = "someone"

    ' If the request is from a particular person
    If InStr(1, cmRequest.Message.From, strAlias) <> 0 Then
      ' Get the associated appointment
      Set appt = New CDO.Appointment
      Set appt = _
        cmRequest.CalendarParts(1).GetUpdatedItem(urlCalendar)

      With appt
        ' Reconfigure the sender information
        ' so you can send the response.
        .Configuration.Fields(cdoSendEmailAddress) = _
          cmRequest.Message.From
        .Configuration.Fields.Update
```

```
' Accept the meeting request and send the response
    ' This could also be AcceptTentative or Decline.
    .Accept.Message.Send
  End With

  ' Delete the original message request
  ' from the inbox.
  Set rec = New ADODB.Record
  With rec
    .Open urlRequest, , adModeReadWrite
    .DeleteRecord
    .Close
  End With
End If

  ' Clean up
  Set rec = Nothing
  Set appt = Nothing
  Set cmRequest = Nothing
End Sub
```

TIP   Although you can check the content class for an item within the procedure itself, it is a better idea to use the WHERE clause of the event registration to check for it. The WHERE clause of the event registration prevents unwanted items from triggering the event and reduces the frequency with which the event must be called. For more information on registering events, see Chapter 9, "Using Web Storage System Events."

SETTING REMINDERS

Reminders are a way to alert users to an upcoming appointment or meeting using a sound, a dialog box, or both. When a new appointment is created with CDO, the reminder is turned off. However, when CDO is used to schedule a meeting, the reminder is automatically set to occur 15 minutes before the start time. To change this default behavior, set the urn:schemas:calendar:reminderoffset schema property to the number of seconds before the meeting starts that the reminder should occur. The reminderoffset schema property does not have an associated CDO property with it, so you must use the Fields collection. However, you can use the CDO constant, cdoReminderOffset, instead of the lengthy schema property name.

The following code sample sets the reminder for an appointment to occur 30 minutes before the start of the appointment.

```
With appt
  ' Set the reminder to be 30 minutes before the start time
  .Fields(cdoReminderOffset) = 60 * 30
  .Fields.Update
End With
```

Instead of using the exact seconds count, this example uses a multiplication phrase (60 * [minutes before StartTime]) that can be easily changed depending on the number of minutes desired. Using this multiplication phrase, you can quickly and easily set a reminder for any number of minutes without concern about leaving off a zero during the multiplication.

If you are using a client program such as Outlook, the reminders are automatically processed and rendered. You do not need to do anything more than set the reminder offset property. However, if you are using a custom Web client, you are responsible for detecting and displaying reminders on appointments.

SUMMARY

Keeping track of time commitments is not an easy task. Most personal information management tools have some form of calendaring component; however, they rarely offer everything that you need for full-scale corporate time management. CDO for Exchange exposes the classes and interfaces for building a custom solution tailored to meet your demanding corporate needs. This chapter examined the fundamentals for building a wide range of calendaring applications.

Chapter 8, "Interacting with Active Directory," explains how to interact programmatically with Active Directory to access Exchange server information and manage Exchange directory objects such as mailboxes.

8

Interacting with Active Directory

Managing the users in your organization is as important as managing the data itself and often even more so. Microsoft Exchange 2000 Server takes advantage of the richness of Microsoft Windows 2000 and gives the user and mailbox management responsibilities to the Active Directory directory service in Windows 2000. Active Directory manages the users in a domain, along with other network objects and services, so it makes sense that the directory should also manage the mailboxes that belong to those same users.

Everything in Active Directory—whether a user's Exchange mailbox, a distribution group, or the server itself—is accessible by using Active Directory Service Interfaces (ADSI), Collaboration Data Objects (CDO) for Exchange, and ActiveX Data Objects (ADO). This chapter shows how to use these tools with the Lightweight Directory Access Protocol (LDAP) wire protocol to create User objects and Group objects, delete existing User objects and Group objects, manage computers, and query Active Directory to create your own Exchange management tools. Sections in this chapter include:

- **Connecting to Active Directory**

- **ADSI for the Exchange Developer**

- **Understanding Active Directory Contacts, Users, and Mailboxes**

- **Working with Groups**

- **Querying Active Directory**

- **Using ADSI to Return Information About Your Domain**

CONNECTING TO ACTIVE DIRECTORY

To build an effective directory services solution, you must understand how an application communicates with Active Directory. This section discusses the different APIs and protocols used to connect to Active Directory, how client applications access the data stored there, and how to choose between ADSI and CDO. In addition, this section explains how to build the LDAP string used to bind to any object in Active Directory.

LDAP

Lightweight Directory Access Protocol (LDAP) is the standard Internet protocol used for directory access. It is the wire protocol used to conduct conversations between a client application and an Active Directory across the network. In fact, an LDAP application can access *any* directory service that exposes LDAP. The LDAP client library (WLDAP32.dll) is installed with all versions of Windows 2000. Figure 8.1 shows how LDAP works with Active Directory access.

Although you can write code directly to LDAP to access Active Directory, most developers use one of the implemented interfaces, such as ADSI or CDO. These interfaces use the LDAP wire protocol as the communication layer through an LDAP provider.

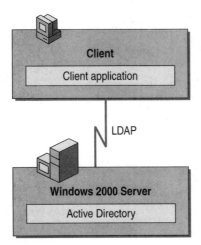

Figure 8.1
LDAP is the wire protocol used by a directory-access application to interchange information with a directory service.

ADSI

Active Directory Service Interfaces (ADSI) are Component Object Model (COM) interfaces that provide an abstraction layer for manipulating resources stored in a directory service. Because many directory services, including Active Directory, use LDAP as the primary means of access, the ADSI LDAP provider is the most widely used. You can use ADSI to create users and groups, manage shared resources (such as printers and faxes), and locate resources in the organization. Because ADSI is implemented as a set of COM interfaces, any application that supports COM, including the Microsoft Visual Basic development system, Microsoft Visual C++, and Active Server Pages (ASP) technology can use it.

Active Directory itself runs on the Windows 2000 operating system, but ADSI client applications can run on Microsoft Windows 95 and later, Microsoft Windows NT Server version 4.0, and Windows 2000 operating systems. ADSI requires components to reside on both the server and the client. The client-side bits of ADSI version 2.5 are automatically installed with Windows 2000. If your computer is running an earlier version of Windows, you must manually install these components. You can download the ADSI client components from the Microsoft Developer Network (MSDN) Web site.

The ADSI client components consist of:

- ADSI LDAP Provider (Adsldp.dll, Adsldpc.dll, and Adsmsext.dll).

- ADSI Router (Activeds.dll). The router implements the core set of objects of the provider and corresponds to the Active DS Type library (Activeds.tlb).

Figure 8.2 shows how an ADSI application works. A client application uses the ADSI library to write ADSI code. The application sends this code to the ADSI LDAP provider. The provider then maps the request to the appropriate directory service on the server through the LDAP wire protocol, in this case, Active Directory. After the requested information is found, it is returned to the client computer and cached locally for further manipulation.

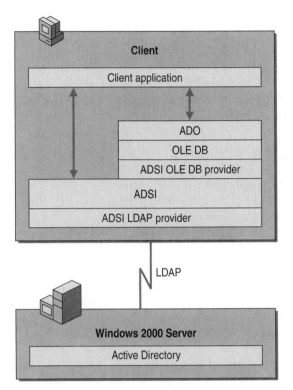

Figure 8.2
The relationship of ADSI and ADO to Active Directory

ADSI delegates some of the responsibility for querying Active Directory to ADO. ADSI supplies an OLE DB provider for ADSI, which enables developers to build applications that use ADO to search Active Directory. Developers can apply their knowledge of ADO to access data in Active Directory in the same way that they access data in other OLE DB providers, such as Microsoft SQL Server and Microsoft Access.

CDO FOR EXCHANGE

ADSI is not the only set of COM interfaces that uses LDAP to access Active Directory. CDO for Exchange also provides a number of objects and interfaces for managing users and mailboxes. Although not as rich as ADSI, CDO makes it easy to manipulate users, mailboxes, and folders. Using CDO to access Active Directory involves two object libraries: CDO for Exchange 2000 (CDO) and CDO for Exchange Management (CDOExM). CDO yields the IPerson interface for manipulating User objects in the directory. If you work with folders that are enabled to receive e-mail messages directly, you will also use the Folder object. CDOExM yields the IMailboxStore and IMailRecipient interfaces for managing Exchange mailboxes and e-mail recipients.

Unlike ADSI, CDO for Exchange cannot be installed on a client. Therefore, any applications that you build with CDO to interact with Active Directory need to run on the Exchange server. Figure 8.3 shows how CDO is also used with LDAP to manipulate Active Directory in a server application.

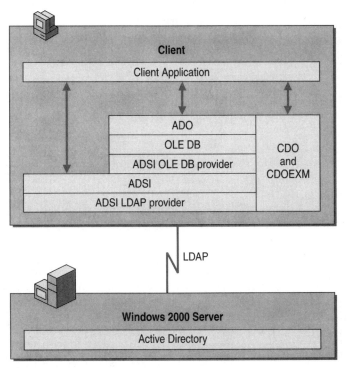

Figure 8.3
CDO can also be used to manipulate the Active Directory store.

CHOOSING BETWEEN CDO AND ADSI

If both CDO and ADSI can access and manipulate the resources stored in Active Directory, how do you choose between them? The best way to approach this question is from a task perspective. What are you trying to do? What type of application houses the code? Are you already familiar with one library but not the other? There is no single answer, and it is likely that you'll find it necessary to use both object libraries. However, there are a few scenarios in which one is better than the other.

Use CDO if:

- You need an application solely to create and manage users and Exchange mailboxes and to move contact information between Active Directory and public folders.

- You want to manage public folders that are enabled to receive e-mail messages directly.

- You are writing a server-based application and are already comfortable with CDO.

Use ADSI if:

- You want to use a single API to do everything with Active Directory. ADSI has the ability to manage everything, including Exchange mailboxes, in the directory store.

- You are building a client application with Visual Basic or Microsoft Office 2000 that must access Active Directory. CDO for Exchange cannot be used on the client.

BUILDING THE LDAP BINDING STRING

Whether you use ADSI or CDO to access Active Directory, you need to build the proper LDAP binding string before you can do anything with the objects found there. As in the Microsoft Web Storage System, everything in Active Directory has an associated path string that represents its exact location in the directory store. When accessing Active Directory, this string is called the "LDAP binding string," and it is used to connect to Active Directory, open user objects, access groups, and navigate containers. Specifically, it is used in the following ways:

- CDO uses the LDAP binding string to open data sources for Person objects and create new entries in Active Directory.

- ADSI uses the LDAP binding string to bind to objects by using the OpenObject function.

> **NOTE** The ADSI ADsPath property can be used to return the current LDAP binding string value for an object in Active Directory.

The LDAP binding string consists of the protocol identifier followed by the server name and the distinguished name (DN) of the object:

```
LDAP://server/DN
```

The provider portion of the string is case sensitive. Attempts to access an object in Active Directory with a string that starts with ldap:// instead of LDAP:// generate an error. *Server* is the name of the server that is the domain controllerfor your domain and that houses the Active Directory. If you stopped right here without providing the DN, your LDAP binding string would look something like this:

```
LDAP://cyberserver
```

Without the DN, this access string uses the domain of the current user and returns a reference to the top level of the Active Directory domain. More often than not, however, you want to navigate straight to an object in Active Directory, and you need the DN to do this. The DN identifies the domain that holds an object as well as the complete path through the container hierarchy that is used to access the object. Table 8.1 lists the attributes that make up the DN.

Table 8.1   Attributes that make up the distinguished name (DN)

Attribute	Description
CN	Common name of the object or container.
OU	Organizational unit. Organizational units behave similarly to containers and are used to manage objects in Active Directory.
DC	Domain controller identifier. Represents one piece. For example, if your domain is microsoft.com, one DC attribute must be used for each piece: DC=Microsoft and DC=com.

A DN can consist of any combination of the above as well as multiples of each type. For example, a DN can have two CN attributes and two DC attributes. However, the order of these attributes is extremely important. Just like a file path, the DN must be provided in a particular order. The CN of the object comes first. This part of the DN is also known as the relative distinguished name (RDN). The RDN to a user object would look like this:

```
CN=Denise Smith
```

This CN is followed by the CN for the direct parent container and then by any additional containers or organizational units in which the object is nested. After this comes the DC information. For example, the following LDAP binding string maps to the user object Denise Smith in the organizational unit Recipients on the domain domain.com:

```
LDAP://cyberserver/CN=Denise Smith,OU=Recipients,DC=domain,DC=com
```

You access a group object in almost the same way. Instead of providing the user common name, you provide the group common name. For example, the following string maps to the group object Keepers in the same location:

```
LDAP://cyberserver/CN=Keepers,OU=Recipients,DC=domain,DC=com
```

To access only the organizational unit, eliminate the CN for the user or group object. The following string binds to the Recipients organizational unit on domain.com:

```
LDAP://cyberserver/OU=Recipients,DC=domain,DC=com
```

ADSI FOR THE EXCHANGE DEVELOPER

Writing ADSI code is very different from writing CDO code. Before you tackle the tasks that are often conducted against Active Directory, you should understand the core concepts of ADSI programming. This section presents the more commonly used ADSI interfaces and explains how to open objects in Active Directory, read and write property values, and conduct standard I/O operations such as creating, moving, copying, and deleting objects.

COMMON SUPPORTED INTERFACES

Active Directory contains many different objects, such as containers, users, and groups. By using the properties and methods of the various ADSI interfaces, you can create and manipulate objects, modify the Active Directory schema, and set security aspects. Table 8.2 lists the interfaces used most frequently by Automation clients, such as Visual Basic, Microsoft Visual Basic for Applications, and Microsoft Visual Basic Scripting Edition (VBScript).

Table 8.2   Common ADSI interfaces

Interface	Description
IADs	Supplies core functions for ADSI objects. Every object supports an IADs interface. You can use this interface to bind to any object in Active Directory.
IADsPropertyList	Retrieves a list of properties for an object, counts properties, and enumerates through properties.
IADsOpenDSObject	Supplies a security context for binding to an object. This provides a means to specify alternative logon credentials for authentication when first binding to an ADSI object.
IADsClass	Manages schema class objects that provide class definitions for any of the object types.
IADsProperty	Creates custom properties and retrieves information about an existing property.
AccessControlEntry	Manages each entry in an Access Control List (ACL).
AccessControlList	Builds and maintains an ACL.
IADsDomain	Represents a network domain. Manages the accounts on that domain.
IADsContainer	Manages containers in the Active Directory store and the objects in them. Provides methods and properties used to filter the contents, count items, and manage the creation, deletion, and enumeration of ADSI objects contained in the object.
IADsOU	Manages an organizational unit in a domain.
IADsUser	Contains properties and methods that are specific to users; some of these properties are also used for contacts and computers.
IADsGroup	Creates and manages group objects, such as distribution lists for sending e-mail. Contains properties for naming the group and adding and removing members.
IADsMembers	Represents all the individuals in a group and can be used to count as well as filter the members.

NOTE   If you are using an automation client such as Visual Basic, you can set a reference to the Active DS Type Library (Activeds.tlb) and use the Object Browser to further explore the object library and the properties and methods.

OPENING AN OBJECT

For code that is running on the server (so it's already using the administrator logon credentials), you can use the GetObject function to open objects in Active Directory. The GetObject function takes one argument: the DN to the object being opened. This section describes how to use the GetObject function to open several different objects with Active Directory. This section also discusses how to specify logon credentials for client applications that must be designed to use a particular user's credentials. Using another person's credentials to accomplish programmatic tasks is *impersonation*.

NOTE   If the user running the client application does not have permission to open objects, you must use the OpenDsObject method instead and provide logon credentials. For more information, see "Opening with Logon Credentials" later in this section.

ACCESSING THE DOMAIN

To access the entire domain, you can use either an IADs interface or an IADsDomain interface. Which one you choose depends on what you want to accomplish. For example, to manage the domain, use the IADsDomain interface. This gives you access to properties and methods specific to domain activity, such as managing access information. To conduct multiple actions on Active Directory itself, such as opening multiple groups and containers in the same procedure, use the IADs interface. The following code sample uses this approach to access a named domain:

```
Dim dom As ActiveDs.IADs
Set dom = GetObject("LDAP://cyberserver/dc=domain,dc=com")
```

NOTE   For information about using ADSI calls to detect the local domain, see "Identifying Your Active Directory Server" later in this chapter.

OPENING A CONTAINER OR ORGANIZATIONAL UNIT

To open a container or organizational unit in Active Directory, use the IADsContainer interface. Pass the container's DN to the GetObject function; include the CN for the container or OU for the organizational unit name. For example, the following code sample binds to the Recipients organizational unit:

```
Dim cntr As ActiveDs.IADsContainer
Set cntr = GetObject _
    ("LDAP://cyberserver/ou=recipients,dc=domain,dc=com")
```

You can also open an organizational unit with the IADsOU interface. However, this interface does not allow you to create or delete objects. IADsOU offers properties for retrieving information about the unit itself. If you need to create or delete objects, you must use the IADsContainer interface.

OPENING GROUP AND USER OBJECTS

You can open a Group or User object by using one of two approaches; which one you use depends on whether a connection with the container is already established. If a connection is established, you can call the GetObject method of the Container object. Although it has the same name and purpose as the GetObject function, the GetObject method requires two parameters: the schema class name, such as group or user, of the object being opened and the RDN of the object being opened.

If no connection is established, you can open the object directly with either the IADsGroup interface or the IADsUser interface. In this case, call the GetObject function directly and pass the DN for the object. The LDAP string must include the object name as well as its parent container. For example, the following code sample opens a group object in the Recipients organizational unit:

```
Dim grp As ActiveDs.IADsGroup
Set grp = GetObject _
    ("LDAP://cyberserver/cn=Keepers,ou=recipients,dc=domain,dc=com")
```

To open a user object instead, take the same approach as in the previous example, but this time use the IADsUser interface and change the name in the DN to that of a legitimate user object:

```
Dim usr As ActiveDs.IADsUser
Set usr = GetObject _
    ("LDAP://cyberserver/cn=Denise Smith,ou=recipients,dc=domain,dc=com")
```

OPENING WITH LOGON CREDENTIALS

To open any object in the Active Directory store, you must have permission to do so and you must be properly authenticated. When a client attempts to access an object in Active Directory, it connects by using a security context. This security context contains the credentials used to authenticate the user to perform particular actions on secured objects. In all the previous examples in this section, the authentication is done implicitly and uses the default credentials. These default credentials are those of the user who is currently logged on and running the program.

Although this is the recommended approach to ADSI programming, you might sometimes need to log on explicitly with alternative credentials. To open an object by specifying credentials, you must use the OpenDSObject method of the IADsOpenDSObject interface. The OpenDSObject uses four parameters:

- *bstrDNName*. The DN of the object to be opened.

- *bstrUserName*. The user account name to be used to access the object.

- *bstrPassword*. The password for the user account.

- ADS_AUTHENTICATION_ENUM. An authentication flag used for binding. For secure binding, set this to ADS_SECURE_AUTHENTICATION.

NOTE The code listings in this chapter are available in the project CH_08.vbp on the companion CD. For more detailed information about Active Directory—what it is, how it works, and what you can do with it—see the Active Directory SDK documentation and the Exchange online documentation.

Listing 8.1 shows how to open a group object by using specific logon credentials. Because the OpenDSObject method belongs to the IADsOpenDSObject interface, you must first access Active Directory by calling the GetObject function and pass the LDAP string. Then you can call the IADsOpenDSObject.OpenDSObject method and pass the name of the object to be opened, the user name, a password, and the ADS_AUTHENTICATION_ENUM value: ADS_SECURE_AUTHENTICATION. This value indicates that Active Directory is to use secure authentication on the specified credentials.

Listing 8.1 Open an object in Active Directory by using the credentials of a specific user account.

```
Sub BindingWithCredentials()
    ' Opens an Active Directory object
    ' Using specific credentials.

    Dim dso As IADsOpenDSObject
    Dim sobj As IADs

    'Bind to the server
    Set dso = GetObject("LDAP:")

    'Open the object using credentials
    Set sobj = dso.OpenDSObject("LDAP://cyberserver/" & _
        "cn=mindy martin,ou=recipients,dc=domain,dc=com" _
        , "administrator" _
        , "somepassword" _
        , ADS_SECURE_AUTHENTICATION)

    Debug.Print sobj.ADsPath

    'Clean up
    Set sobj = Nothing
    Set dso = Nothing
End Sub
```

NOTE For more information about using authentication, see the Platform SDK documentation available at http://msdn.microsoft.com/windows2000/.

UNDERSTANDING THE PROPERTY CACHE

Before you use the syntax necessary to set and read properties, you must understand how Active Directory processes data requests. Because the Active Directory store is on the domain controller for an organization, your code is not likely to be running on that same server but, instead, on a client machine somewhere else in the domain. This means that all client requests for data must be sent across the network. If this were to happen every time a client application needed to access a property, network traffic could increase to a level that would negatively affect other networking tasks, such as printing documents and sending e-mail messages.

To reduce the number of data requests that are made over the network, Active Directory temporarily populates a property cache on a client machine to store information. When a client application requests data about an object, the information is copied from Active Directory to the property cache. Any subsequent requests by the client application for information about that object go to the property cache, not to Active Directory.

You can access and manipulate Active Directory data by using the Get, GetEx, GetInfo, Put, PutEx, and SetInfo methods. Figure 8.4 shows how these methods work with the property cache and Active Directory. The first time the property cache is populated, this is done either implicitly, by accessing a property directly with the Get or GetEx method, or explicitly, by calling the GetInfo method. After the property cache is populated, any further Get or GetEx calls look in the cache rather than on the server. Only the GetInfo method always accesses the server.

You set property values in the property cache by using the Put and PutEx methods. These methods write to the cache even if it has not already been populated with any of the Get methods. Any subsequent Get calls overwrite the work of the Put methods; because of this, you should not set property values before you call one of the Get methods.

To save data to the Active Directory store, use the SetInfo method. This method takes all the data from the property cache and commits it to the directory store. If any changes are not valid, the entire save fails with a trappable error. Because the SetInfo method sends information across the network, avoid calling this method unless necessary.

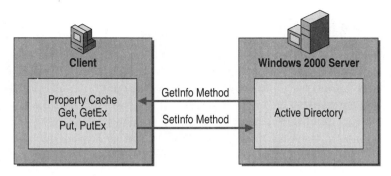

Figure 8.4
When a client application accesses an object in Active Directory, property values are temporarily stored in a property cache on the client. This minimizes network calls to the server.

GETTING PROPERTY VALUES

You read property values by using the Get, GetEx, and GetList methods. This section describes how to use these methods.

USING THE GET METHOD

To retrieve the value for a single-valued property, call the Get method and pass the name of the property you are querying for data. For example, the following code sample retrieves the value for the common name (CN) property of a User object:

```
strCN = usr.Get("cn")
```

Many of the properties have interface properties associated with them as well. This means you can simply use the matching interface property name instead of the Get method. For example, calling the Name property of the object also retrieves the common name property value for a User object. The following code sample does the same thing as the previous sample:

```
strCN = usr.Name
```

USING THE GETEX METHOD

To retrieve values from a multi-valued property, you should use the GetEx method. Multi-valued properties can have more than one value. The GetEx method retrieves all the stored values for a property in an array of variant type. You can loop through the contents of the array to process all the values. The following code sample returns the OtherHomePhone property, which may or may not contain multiple values. A For..Each loop is then used to enumerate each value in the array:

```
varPhNums = usr.GetEx("otherHomePhone")
For Each n In varPhNums
  Debug.Print n
Next
```

The GetEx method works for single-valued properties as well; however, values are still returned as variant type. If you know that the property is single-valued and you know the return data type, use the Get method. If you do not know whether a property is multi-valued, it is best to use the GetEx method.

USING THE GETLIST METHOD

Unlike the Get and GetEx methods, the GetInfo method retrieves every property value for an object instead of just one property. Also unlike the Get and GetEx methods, the GetInfo method retrieves these values directly from the Active Directory store, not from the property cache. The GetInfo method initializes the property cache with property values or refreshes the property cache with the most up-to-date values.

You can call the GetInfo method two ways:

- **Implicitly**. The first time a Get or GetEx method is called, ADSI checks the property cache. If the cache is not initialized, the GetInfo method is called implicitly to fill the cache with all the property values. After this initial GetInfo call, no additional GetInfo calls are made. If any values exist in the cache, the Get or GetEx call returns the value from the property cache, not the Active Directory store, and no GetInfo call is made.

- **Explicitly**. When you call the GetInfo method, it returns all the property values for the object from the Active Directory server. If the property cache already contains values—old or new—they are all replaced. All changes made to the property cache are lost and replaced by the values from the Active Directory store. To save changes made to the property cache, you must explicitly save them to the server by using the SetInfo method, as discussed in "Using the SetInfo Method" in the following section.

The following code sample retrieves all the property values for the User object and stores them in the property cache. If changes are made to the property cache, they are replaced with the stored values from the server.

```
Usr.GetInfo
```

SETTING PROPERTY VALUES

Setting property values is similar to reading property values. The Put and PutEx methods work in much the same way that their Get and GetEx equivalents do. When you set property values, the values are written to the local property cache on the client. To commit the changes to the Active Directory store, you must call the SetInfo method explicitly.

USING THE PUT METHOD

To set the property value for a single-valued property, call the Put method and pass both the name of the attribute to be changed and the new value. For example, to set the e-mail property for a User object to a Simple Mail Transfer Protocol (SMTP) address, use code like this:

```
Usr.Put "mail", "SMTP:mindy@domain.com"
```

This updates the local property cache on the client with the new value and replaces any existing value stored in the cache. However, the change is not committed to the server until you call the SetInfo method.

USING THE PUTEX METHOD

The PutEx method gives you added control when writing to the cache. You can use the PutEx method to append a value to an existing one in a multi-valued property, to make changes to an individual value, to delete all the values, or even to remove a specific value from the set. The PutEx method has the following syntax:

```
Sub PutEx(InControlCode As Long, BstrName As String, vProp)
```

Where:

InControlCode

is one of the ADS_PROPERTY_OPERATION_ENUM values. This indicates the type of modification that will occur, such as adding to the property's existing values or removing a value.

Bstrname

is the name of the property being modified.

vProp

is the value to be added to the property as a variant array. If the property is a single-valued property, this is a single-valued array.

You can use the PutEx method several ways; which you use depends primarily on the InControlCode parameter setting:

- To add to the value list of a property without modifying existing values, use the ADS_PROPERTY_APPEND (3) constant and pass the value to be added. The following code sample adds a value to the value list of a property:

```
usr.PutEx ADS_PROPERTY_APPEND _
        , "OtherHomePhone", Array("555-555-0100")
```

- To change a value in the list of current values, use the ADS_PROPERTY_UPDATE (2) constant and pass a new value for each value to be changed. Each value must correlate with the value in the array to be changed. The following code sample changes the first value in the array:

```
usr.PutEx ADS_PROPERTY_UPDATE _
        , "OtherHomePhone", Array("555-555-0199")
```

- To delete one or more values in the existing list, use the ADS_PROPERTY_
  DELETE (4) constant and pass the values to be removed from the list. You can
  provide the values in any order. If they do not already exist, a trappable error is
  generated. The following code sample removes two values from the
  OtherHomePhone property:

```
x.PutEx ADS_PROPERTY_DELETE _
        , "OtherHomePhone", Array("555-555-0103", "555-555-0199")
```

- To clear the property of all existing values, use the ADS_PROPERTY_CLEAR (1)
  constant and pass the appropriate value. For example, to clear a string property,
  pass a null string. The following code sample clears the OtherHomePhone
  property:

```
x.PutEx ADS_PROPERTY_CLEAR _
        , "OtherHomePhone", vbNullString
```

As with the Put method, the PutEx method writes to the cache. To commit any of
these changes permanently to the Active Directory store, call the SetInfo method.

USING THE SETINFO METHOD

Although the Put and PutEx methods write to only the property cache, the purpose
of the SetInfo method is to commit all those changes to the Active Directory store
on the server. For example, the following code sample changes some properties for
a user object and then commits those changes to the directory store:

```
usr.Put "givenName", "Peter"
usr.Put "sn", "Waxman"
usr.SetInfo
```

Because the SetInfo method sends information across the network, you should
avoid calling this method unless it is necessary. For example, don't call SetInfo
every time you change a property value. Wait until you have finished setting the
properties and then call SetInfo once.

CREATING OBJECTS

To create most objects in Active Directory, including users and groups, you use the same approach. First, you access the container that stores the object, and then you call the Create method of the IADsContainer interface. The Create method takes two parameters:

- The schema class name for the object to be created (such as Group object or User object)

- The RDN for the new object (such as CN=Keepers)

For example, the following code sample creates a new Group object, named Keepers, in the Recipients organizational unit:

```
Dim ctnr As IADsContainer
Dim grp As IADsGroup

Set cntr =
GetObject("LDAP://cyberserver/ou=recipients,dc=domain,dc=com")
Set grp = cntr.Create("group", "cn=Keepers")

'
' Set properties here
'

grp.SetInfo
```

Notice that the code sample calls the SetInfo method at the end. Although the code has created a new object for Active Directory, it does not yet exist permanently in the directory. To save the changes permanently to Active Directory, you must call the SetInfo method. Otherwise, the object is not made persistent, and no error is generated to alert you to the problem.

> **NOTE** If the user running the client application does not have permission to
> create objects, you must use the CreateDsObject method instead and provide
> logon credentials. For more information, see "Opening with Logon
> Credentials" earlier in this chapter.

DELETING OBJECTS

To delete an object permanently from the directory, you must first access the
container or organizational unit that contains the object to be deleted and then call
the Delete method of the container. The Delete method uses two parameters: the
schema-class type of the object to be deleted, and the RDN of the object (as it is
known in Active Directory). For example, the following code sample deletes the
user Aidan Delaney from the Recipients organizational unit:

```
Set cntr = GetObject _
    ("LDAP://cyberserver/ou=recipients,dc=domain,dc=com")
cntr.Delete "user", "cn=Aidan Delaney"
```

The Delete method does not require you to call the SetInfo method to commit the
changes. The deletion is automatically committed to the Active Directory store.

If you want to delete a User object that also has an Exchange mailbox, you need to
delete the mailbox before you delete the User object. CDO does not provide the
means to delete a directory object, so you must use a combination of both CDO
and ADSI. For more information about deleting mailboxes, see "Deleting a
Mailbox" later in this chapter.

> **NOTE** If the user running the client application does not have permission to
> delete objects, you must use the DeleteDsObject method and provide logon
> credentials. For more information, see "Opening with Logon Credentials"
> earlier in this chapter.

UNDERSTANDING ACTIVE DIRECTORY CONTACTS, USERS, AND MAILBOXES

Active Directory supports two objects that you can use to represent people: Contact objects and User objects. You can enable both Contact and User objects to receive messages at a specific e-mail address in the organization, but you can configure only User objects with a security context and an Exchange mailbox.

This section discusses these two objects that you can create in Active Directory to represent people, discusses how to configure these objects to receive messages, and explains how to create, configure, and manage mailboxes.

PERSON, CONTACT, AND USER OBJECTS

The Active Directory objects that represent people are based on the Active Directory schema object class of Person. Two main object classes derive from the Person class: Contact and User. An Active Directory Contact object is an entry in Active Directory for storing basic information about a person, such as name, address, and telephone numbers. A User object is a security principal. A *security principal* is an object that can log on to the network and that can be granted and denied rights to access resources on the network.

A Contact object, however, is not a security principal. This is the primary difference between a User object and a Contact object. By using the security identity of the User object, the person represented by the User object can log on to the network and access any of the shared resources on that network. Because a User object derives from the Active Directory schema object class of Person, it also has properties for storing basic information about a person, such as name, address, and telephone numbers. In addition, it has those properties that are specific to security access. Figure 8.5 shows how the User and Contact objects derive from the Person class.

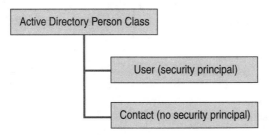

Figure 8.5
The User and Contact objects derive from the Person class.

NOTE   The Computer object class inherits from the User object class. A Computer object represents a computer on the network and, therefore, must also be a security principal.

CDO also defines a Person object. A CDO Person object can be used to access contacts in a Web Storage System folder as well as to access any of the Active Directory Person objects. As do Person objects stored in Web Storage System folders, Person objects in Active Directory have a DAV:contentclass value of urn:content-classes:person.

UNDERSTANDING MAIL-ENABLED VS. MAILBOX-ENABLED

You can configure some Active Directory objects to be either mail-enabled or mailbox-enabled. The difference between the two has to do with whether the object has an Exchange mailbox in the organization:

- A *mail-enabled* object is an object that has an e-mail address on a domain in the organization but has no mailbox that can receive messages. The object appears in the global address list, so other people in the organization can easily locate or send a message to that person, but the administrator doesn't have to manage an unnecessary mailbox. Contacts, users, and even folders can be mail-enabled.

- A *mailbox-enabled* object not only has an e-mail address in the organization, but it also has an Exchange mailbox. Because Exchange uses Windows security and authentication, which require that mailboxes be security principals, only User objects can be mailbox-enabled.

To understand the differences between these types of objects, it helps to consider what different people do with e-mail. Imagine that you are responsible for creating objects in Active Directory. Here are scenarios in which you would create one or the other type of object:

- **Active Directory contact (mail-enabled)**. A consultant works for your company, occasionally from a remote location. Because the work regularly involves other people in the company, your employees need an easy way to send messages to him. If you create a mail-enabled Contact object, people can send messages to the consultant just as easily as to another employee, by using an alias. However, because the consultant does not need to access the network or any shared resources, he does not need to have a security context.

- **User (mail-enabled)**. Another consultant works onsite for your company. This person needs an e-mail address, but she also has a mailbox back at her own company. By mail-enabling the consultant instead of assigning her a mailbox, you can minimize the responsibility of your own administrators and the hardware allowance on the Exchange server hard disk. However, because this consultant works onsite, she does need to access the network and shared resources, such as printers and faxes.

- **User (mailbox-enabled)**. A full-time employee needs to log on to the network and access shared resources. This person needs an Exchange mailbox to receive messages as well as an e-mail address. The mailbox should be managed onsite. A similar type of user would be a consultant at your company who needs to maintain a separate mailbox.

CREATING CONTACT AND USER OBJECTS

This section discusses how to create Contact and User objects in Active Directory. In addition, the section covers the various Active Directory properties that you can set on both objects.

Choosing an Account

It can be hard to determine what type of account you need to create. To help decide which type of object to create, ask yourself two questions:

Does this person need to log on to the network? A person who logs on to a network has access to the shared resources there. They can use the printers and fax machines, have an e-mail address in a domain, and qualify for an Exchange mailbox in which to store messages locally. This type of person must be represented by a User object. If access to the network is not necessary, create a Contact object instead.

Does this person need a mailbox on the system? If a person has a mailbox elsewhere, you only need to mail-enable the person (that is, provide only an e-mail address on a domain in the organization). If the person does not have a mailbox elsewhere, you must create an Exchange mailbox for that person.

CREATING AN ACTIVE DIRECTORY CONTACT OBJECT

An Active Directory Contact object has no security context. Therefore, only basic information, such as name, physical mailing address, and telephone numbers, is normally stored with a Contact object. If you want to use CDO to create the Active Directory contact, you can apply most of the same skills that you use to create a contact in a Web Storage System folder. The main differences are in how you declare the class type of the object and save the object to Active Directory.

Listing 8.2 shows how to create a Contact object in Active Directory. The procedure sets the ObjectClass attribute of the object to "contact" because CDO, by default, attempts to create a User object. To commit the changes to Active Directory, the code calls the SaveTo method and passes the LDAP string to the new object (complete with the RDN to the Contact object).

Listing 8.2   Create a Contact object in Active Directory.

```
Sub CreateADContact(strFirstName As String, strLastName As String)
    ' Create a contact entry in Active Directory

    Dim strLDAP As String

    strLDAP = "LDAP://cyberserver/cn=" & strFirstName & " " & strLastName
    strLDAP = strLDAP & ",ou=recipients,dc=domain,dc=com"

    ' Create a new CDO Person object for Active Directory entry
    With New CDO.Person
        ' Indicate that this is a contact
        .Fields("ObjectClass") = "contact"

        ' Use CDO to set some basic properties
        .FirstName = strFirstName
        .LastName = strLastName

        ' Save the changes made to the property cache
        .Fields.Update

        'Send the content to Active Directory
        .DataSource.SaveTo strLDAP
    End With
End Sub
```

CREATING A USER ACCOUNT

Exchange uses Windows authentication, so a person to whom you want to assign an Exchange mailbox must be able to log on to the network. Because Active Directory Contact objects have no security context, an Exchange mailbox cannot be assigned to a Contact object; therefore, you must create a user account (User object) instead. You can use either CDO or ADSI to do this.

To use CDO, begin just as if you were creating a simple contact. Build the LDAP binding string for the new User object, and then create a CDO Person object. When you use CDO to create a Person object in Active Directory, the Person object is automatically considered a User object in the schema object class of Person, so you do not need to indicate the schema class object type. For more information, see "Understanding Mail-Enabled vs. Mailbox-Enabled" earlier in this chapter.

After setting any general information properties, save the new User object to the Active Directory store by calling DataSource.SaveTo and passing the LDAP binding string. For example, the following code sample creates a User object, sets some basic address book properties, and saves the information:

```
Set prs = New CDO.Person

prs.FirstName = "Peter"
prs.LastName = "Waxman"
prs.WorkPhone = "555-555-0133"

prs.DataSource.SaveTo strLDAP
```

Although this code would generate a new User object in Active Directory, the account, by default, would be disabled. To create an enabled default account type that represents a typical user account, you must explicitly set the UserAccountControl property to ADS_UF_NORMAL_ACCOUNT(512).

The UserAccountControl property does not have a CDO property associated with it, so you must use the Person.Fields property. After you set the account value, save the changes by updating the Fields collection. The following code sample creates a user account that is enabled:

```
prs.Fields("userAccountControl") = ADS_UF_NORMAL_ACCOUNT
prs.Fields.Update
```

When you set the UserAccountControl property to create a normal account, the only option that is set is the option for the user to change the password at the next logon. If you want to explicitly set some of the account options, add one of the options listed in Table 8.3 to the account type.

Table 8.3 UserAccountControl options

Option	Description
ADS_UF_SCRIPT (1)	The logon script will be executed.
ADS_UF_ACCOUNTDISABLE (2)	The user's account is disabled.
ADS_UF_HOMEDIR_REQUIRED (8)	The home directory is required.
ADS_UF_LOCKOUT (16)	The account is currently locked out.
ADS_UF_PASSWD_NOTREQD (32)	No password is required.
ADS_UF_PASSWD_CANT_CHANGE (64)	The user cannot change the password.
ADS_UF_ENCRYPTED_TEXT_PASSWORD _ALLOWED (128)	The user can send an encrypted password.
ADS_UF_DONTEXPIREPASSWD (65536)	Represents the password, which should never expire.
ADS_UF_SMARTCARD_REQUIRED (262144)	When set, forces the user to log on by using smart card.

Listing 8.3 creates a user account in Active Directory. The code creates a normal account for the user by setting the userAccountControl attribute to ADS_UF_NORMAL_ACCOUNT. The changes are then saved to Active Directory.

Listing 8.3 Create a normal User account in Active Directory.

```
Sub CreateUserAccount( _
   strFirstName As String, _
   strLastName As String)

   ' Create a User account that can have an Exchange mailbox

   Dim strLDAP As String

   strLDAP = _
      "LDAP://cyberserver/cn=" & strFirstName & " " & strLastName
   strLDAP = _
      strLDAP & ",ou=recipients,dc=domain,dc=com"
```

```
        'Create the new user account
        With New CDO.Person
            .FirstName = strFirstName
            .LastName = strLastName
            .Fields("userAccountControl") = ADS_UF_NORMAL_ACCOUNT
            .Fields.Update
            .DataSource.SaveTo strLDAP
        End With
    End Sub
```

For a complete list of user account values, see the Active Directory SDK
documentation.

ACTIVE DIRECTORY PROPERTIES FOR ADDRESS BOOK INFORMATION

Active Directory Contact objects and User objects support a variety of properties. If
you use a CDO Person object to create and manage these objects, most of the
Active Directory properties map directly to their CDO counterparts. However, some
Active Directory properties, such as DirectReports, do not map to CDO properties.
If you use CDO, you can access these properties with the Fields collection.
Remember to call the Update method to save changes made this way. If you use
ADSI, you can use the Get, GetEx, Put, and PutEx methods to read and set these
properties. Tables 8.4 through 8.8 summarize commonly used properties, grouped
by category.

Table 8.4   Some of the Active Directory properties used for storing name information

Active Directory property	CDO Person property	Data value	Description
GivenName	FirstName	String	The given name (first name) of the user.
Sn	LastName	String	Last name of the user.
DisplayName	N/A[1]	String	Name displayed in the address book for the user.
Initials	Initials	String	Letters that stand for a user's name (typically, the first letter of each of the user's names).

[1]Not available.

Table 8.5 Some of the Active Directory properties used for business information

Active Directory property	CDO Person property	Data value	Description
Title	Title	String	Job title of the user.
Manager	Fields(cdo Manager)	String	DN of the user who is the user's manager.
DirectReports	N/A	String	List of users that report directly to the user. Multi-valued.
ManagedObjects	N/A	String	List of DNs of objects that are managed by the user. Multi-valued.
Department	Fields(cdo Department)	String	Name of the department in which the user works.
Notes	N/A	String	Comment information.
Description	N/A	String	Description to display for the user. Multi-valued.

Table 8.6 Some of the Active Directory properties used for address information

Active Directory property	CDO Person property	Data value	Description
Street	WorkStreet	String	Business street address.
L	WorkCity	String	Town or city in the address.
St	WorkState	String	State or province in the address.
C	Fields(cdo WorkCountry Abbreviation)	String	Code of country where the user is located.
Co	WorkCountry	String	Common name of the country in the address.
PostalCode	WorkPostal Code	String	Postal code in the postal address.

Continued on next page

Table 8.6 continued   Some of the Active Directory properties used for address information

Active Directory property	CDO Person property	Data value	Description
PostOfficeBox	WorkPost OfficeBox	String	Post office box number.
PostalAddress	WorkPostal Address	String	Complete postal address.
physicalDelivery OfficeName	N/A	String	Office number.

Table 8.7   Some of the Active Directory properties used for telephone numbers

Active Directory property	CDO Person property	Data value	Description
HomePhone	HomePhone	String	Primary home telephone number for the user.
TelephoneNumber	WorkPhone	String	Business telephone number.
Pager	WorkPager	String	Primary pager number.
Mobile	MobilePhone	String	Primary cellular telephone number.
Facsimile Telephone Number	WorkFax	String	Business fax number.
OtherMobile	N/A	String	Alternate cellular telephone numbers. Multi-valued.
OtherPager	N/A	String	Alternate pager numbers Multi-valued.
OtherTelephone	N/A	String	Alternate business telephone numbers. Multi-valued.
otherFacsimile Telephone Number	N/A	String	Alternate fax numbers. Multi-valued.

Continued on next page

Table 8.7 continued   Some of the Active Directory properties used for telephone numbers

Active Directory property	CDO Person property	Data value	Description
IpPhone	N/A	String	Used by telephony.
OtherIpPhone	N/A	String	Other telephone number used by telephony.

Table 8.8   Some of the Active Directory properties used for Web information

Active Directory property	CDO Person property	Data value	Description
WWWHomePage	N/A	String	URL for the user's primary Web page.
url	N/A	String	URLs for the user's alternate Web pages. Multi-valued.

MAIL-ENABLING AN OBJECT

To mail-enable an object, such as a Contact or a Group, you access the CDOEXM IMailRecipient interface of the object and call the MailEnable method. If you are mail-enabling a Contact or User object, pass a string that indicates the e-mail address you want the person to have. The e-mail address can be in any supported e-mail address format, such as SMTP, X.400, cc:Mail, and so on. If you are mail-enabling a group or a folder, you do not need to pass anything. Exchange automatically creates the e-mail address for folders and groups.

Listing 8.4 shows how to create a new Contact object that has an e-mail address in Active Directory. Because the code is written with Visual Basic and the IMailRecipient interface object variable is declared as CDOEXM.IMailRecipient, the procedure points the IMailRecipient interface object variable to the CDO Person object variable and the proper interface is automatically returned. If you use VBScript, you must use the GetInterface method of the folder to retrieve the interface.

Listing 8.4   Create a mail-enabled Contact object.

```
Sub CreateADContact_MailEnabled( _
    strFirstName As String, _
    strLastName As String)

    ' Create a contact entry that has
    ' an email address.

    Dim strLDAP As String
    Dim prs As CDO.Person
    Dim rcp As CDOEXM.IMailRecipient

    ' LDAP URL to the new contact
    strLDAP = "LDAP://cyberserver/cn=" & _
        strFirstName & " " & strLastName & _
        ",ou=recipients,dc=domain,dc=com"

    ' Create a new CDO Person object for Active Directory entry
    Set prs = New CDO.Person
    With prs
    ' Indicate that this is a contact
    .Fields("objectClass") = "contact"

    ' Use CDO to set some basic properties
    .FirstName = strFirstName
    .LastName = strLastName

    ' Reference the IMailRecipient interface
    Set rcp = prs

    ' Enable the contact with an e-mail address
    rcp.MailEnable _
        "SMTP:" & _
        Left$(.FirstName, 5) & _
        Left$(.LastName, 3) & _
        "@domain.com"

    ' Save the changes made to the property cache
    .Fields.Update
```

```
        ' Save the information to Active Directory
        .DataSource.SaveTo strLDAP
        End With

        ' Clean up
        Set rcp = Nothing
        Set prs = Nothing
    End Sub
```

TIP   To disable an account, use the MailDisable method.

WORKING WITH MAILBOXES

An Exchange mailbox is where a user can receive messages and meeting requests, maintain a personal calendar, and store personal contact information. You usually create and manage mailboxes by using standard user interfaces, but you might find it necessary to create your own management tools. This section explains how to create and maintain mailboxes as well as how to move and delete them.

MAILBOX-SPECIFIC PROPERTIES IN ACTIVE DIRECTORY

When you create an Exchange mailbox for a user, you add a number of properties to the Active Directory schema for that User object. Table 8.9 lists some of the properties that are added.

Table 8.9   Some of the properties (attributes) added to the User object when you create an Exchange mailbox

Property (attribute)	CDO property	Data type	Description
altRecipient	MailRecipient. ForwardTo	String	Sets or returns the name of a mailbox to which e-mail should be delivered instead of (or in addition to) this mailbox. Used with DeliverAndRedirect.

Continued on next page

Table 8.9 continued   Some of the properties (attributes) added to the User object when you create an Exchange mailbox

Property (attribute)	CDO property	Data type	Description
publicDelegates	MailboxStore. Delegates	String	Sets or returns a list of other mailboxes that can send on behalf of this mailbox. Multi-valued.
homeMDB	MailboxStore. HomeMDB	String	Returns the DN of the Exchange database for this mailbox. Read-only[1].
authOrig	MailRecipient. RestrictedAddress Lists RestrictedAddresses	String	Sets or returns a list of mailboxes that are exclusively allowed to send e-mail to this recipient. Multi-valued.
displayName	N/A	String	Sets or returns the name of this mailbox as it appears in the global address list.
mail	MailRecipient.SMTP Email	String	Sets or returns the primary SMTP address of this mailbox.
garbageCollPeriod	MailboxStore. DayBefore Garbage Collection	Long	Sets or returns the deleted item retention limit in seconds. The deletedItemFlags must be set as well.
LegacyExchange DN	N/A	String	Returns the Exchange directory DN for this mailbox. Read-only.
proxyAddresses	MailRecipient. ProxyAddresses	String	Sets or returns the Exchange proxy addresses for this mailbox. Multi-valued.
textEncodedOR Address	MailRecipient. x400Email	String	Sets or returns the primary X.400 address of this mailbox.

Continued on next page

Table 8.9 continued Some of the properties (attributes) added to the User object when you create an Exchange mailbox

Property (attribute)	CDO property	Data type	Description
deletedItemFlags	MailboxStore. GarbageCollect OnlyAfterBackup and MailboxStore. OverrideStore GarbageCollection	Integer	Sets or returns how deleted items are handled: use the store default (empty), use the value garbageCollPeriod value (5), do not permanently delete items until the Exchange store has been backed up (3). Used with garbageCollPeriod.
delivContLength	MailRecipient. IntgoingLimit	Long	Sets or returns the maximum message size, in kilobytes, that this mailbox can receive.
DeliverAnd Redirect	MailRecipient. ForwardingStyle	Boolean	If True, e-mail is delivered to both the primary and alternate recipient. Used with altRecipient.
msExchHideFrom AddressLists	MailRecipient.Hide FromAddressBook	Boolean	If True, this mailbox does not appear in address lists.
msExchHome ServerName	N/A	String	Returns the name of this mailbox's server. Read-only.
mailNickname	MailRecipient.Alias	String	Sets or returns the e-mail alias for this recipient.
mDBOverHard QuotaLimit	MailboxStore. HardLimit	Long	Sets or returns the maximum size, in kilobytes, allowed for mailbox after which receiving messages is disabled.
mDBOverQuota Limit	MailboxStore. OverQuotaLimits	Long	Sets or returns the maximum size, in kilobytes, over the store quota after which sending messages is disabled.

Continued on next page

Table 8.9 continued Some of the properties (attributes) added to the User object when you create an Exchange mailbox

Property (attribute)	CDO property	Data type	Description
mDBStorageQuota	MailboxStore. StoreQuota	Long	Sets or returns the size limit, in kilobytes, allowed for this mailbox before regular quota warnings are issued.
mDBUseDefaults	MailboxStore. EnableStore Defaults	Boolean	When set to True, the default storage limit settings are applied to this mailbox.
protocolSettings	N/A	String	Sets or returns the Exchange Internet protocol settings for this mailbox, including the MIME encoding version, RTF version, and whether Outlook Web Access is enabled. Multi-valued.
submissionCont Length	MailRecipient. OutgoingLimit	Long	Sets or returns the maximum message size, in kilobytes, that this mailbox can send.
msExchMailbox Guid	N/A	String	Returns the GUID of this mailbox in the store. Read-only.
msExchMailbox SecurityDescriptor	N/A	String	Returns the security descriptor for this mailbox. Multi-valued and read-only.
msExchRecipLimit	MailboxStore. RecipientLimit	Integer	Sets or returns the maximum number of recipients per message to whom this mailbox can send.
unauthOrig	MailRecipient. RestrictedAddress Lists Restricted Addresses	String	Sets or returns a list of recipients who are not allowed to send e-mail to this mailbox. (Multi-valued)

NOTE An administrator with the correct permissions can write to any attribute. However, as a developer, you should not set certain properties even if you have permissions to do so. Exchange sets some of these properties automatically when a mailbox is created, and changing the property values with code could disrupt normal messaging operations.

CREATING A MAILBOX

To use CDO to create a mailbox, you use a combination of a Person object and the IMailboxStore interface. You use the Person object to access the account to which the mailbox will be added, and you use the CreateMailbox method of the IMailboxStore interface to actually create the mailbox. The CreateMailbox method takes a string argument that indicates where to create the mailbox. This is the HomeMDB URL string for the mailbox (also returned by the CDO HomeMDB property). The following code sample shows the URL of a new mailbox:

```
"LDAP://cyberserver/ CN=Mailbox Store (CYBERSERVER),CN=First Storage
Group," & _
"CN=InformationStore,CN=cyberserver,CN=Servers," & _
"CN=First Administrative Group,CN=Administrative Groups," & _
"CN=First Organization,CN=Microsoft Exchange," & _
"CN=Services,CN=Configuration,DC=domain,DC=com"
```

The HomeMDB URL can seem a bit daunting at first, but that's due more to the number of attributes than to its complexity. Think of building the HomeMDB URL as working your way up through the configuration information stored in Active Directory for the Exchange server.

To step through how the HomeMDB URL is constructed, start with the Active Directory name and follow it with the name of the database that stores the mailbox:

```
LDAP://cyberserver/ CN=Mailbox Store (CYBERSERVER)
```

The next set of information shows the path up from the database, starting with the storage group and proceeding all the way to the top of Exchange:

```
CN=First Storage Group,
CN=InformationStore,
CN=cyberserver,
CN=Servers,
CN=First Administrative Group,
CN=Administrative Groups,
CN=First Organization,
CN=Microsoft Exchange
```

But it doesn't stop there. This configuration information is stored in Active Directory. Therefore, you must also provide the remainder of the path upward. Exchange is considered a service, and services are found under configuration information on the domain.com domain. In this final set of information, notice that the last lines are only DC values:

```
CN=Services,
CN=Configuration,
DC=domain,
DC=com
```

If you look at Active Directory Sites and Services in Microsoft Management Console (MMC) for a server, you will see that the HomeMDB URL maps directly to the location of the Holding Pen database deep in the Services container. Figure 8.6 shows an expanded view of the Services container.

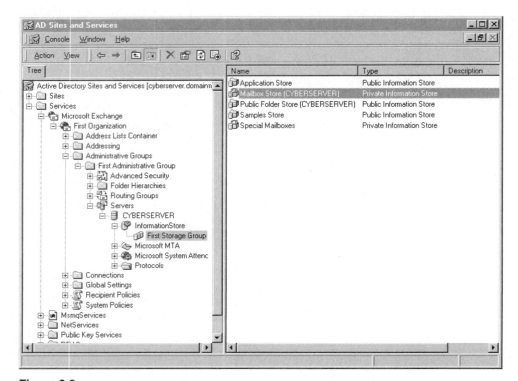

Figure 8.6
Active Directory Sites and Services in MMC can be used as a guide to building the HomeMDB URL of a mailbox store.

Listing 8.5 shows how to create a new User object with an associated mailbox.

Listing 8.5 Create a user and an associated mailbox.

```
Sub CreateUserwithMailbox()
    ' Create a User account and mailbox


    Dim prsmbx As CDO.Person
    Dim mbx As CDOEXM.IMailboxStore
    Dim strFirstName As String
    Dim strLastName As String
    Dim strAlias As String
    Dim strLDAP As String
```

```
    strFirstName = "Aidan"
    strLastName = "Delaney"
    strAlias = strFirstName & Left$(strLastName, 2)

    ' LDAP URL to the new user
    strLDAP = "LDAP://cyberserver/cn=" & strFirstName & " " & strLastName
    strLDAP = strLDAP & ",ou=recipients,dc=domain,dc=com"

    ' Create the new user account
    Set prsmbx = New CDO.Person
    With prsmbx
        .FirstName = strFirstName
        .LastName = strLastName
        .Fields("userAccountControl") = ADS_UF_NORMAL_ACCOUNT
        .Fields.Update
        .DataSource.SaveTo strLDAP
    End With

    ' Create a new mailbox based on the new user information
    Set mbx = prsmbx
    mbx.CreateMailbox _
        "LDAP://cyberserver/CN=Mailbox Store (cyberserver)," & _
        "CN=First Storage Group,CN=InformationStore," & _
        "CN=cyberserver,CN=Servers,CN=First Administrative Group," & _
        "CN=Administrative Groups,CN=First Organization," & _
        "CN=Microsoft Exchange,CN=Services,CN=Configuration," & _
        "DC=domain,DC=com"

    ' Set some additional mail fields
    With prsmbx
        .Email = "SMTP:" & strAlias & "@domain.com"
        .Fields("mailnickname") = strAlias
        .Fields.Update
        .DataSource.Save
    End With

    ' Clean up
    Set mbx = Nothing
    Set prsmbx = Nothing
End Sub
```

Customizing Mailbox Settings

One of the strengths of CDOExM is its ability to manage and maintain mailboxes on a computer running Exchange 2000 Server. By using the properties of the IMailboxStore interface, you can quickly and easily customize a mailbox for cleanup, e-mail limits, and delegated access. Table 8.10 lists the properties of the IMailboxStore used to manage mailboxes.

Table 8.10   Properties of the IMailboxStore interface

Property	Data type	Default	Read/write?	Description
HomeMDB	String	Empty	No	Returns the DN of the mailbox.
EnableStoreDefaults	Boolean	Empty	Yes	If True, only default store values are used for storage limits.
RecipientLimit	Long	-1 (no limit)	Yes	Sets or returns the maximum number of people to which one message can be sent.
StoreQuota	Long	-1 (no limit)	Yes	Sets or returns the maximum size, in kilobytes, allowed for the mailbox before a warning is issued.
OverQuotaLimit	Long	-1 (no limit)	Yes	Sets or returns the maximum size, in kilobytes, over the store quota after which sending messages is disabled.
HardLimit	Long	-1 (no limit)	Yes	Sets or returns the maximum size, in kilobytes, allowed for mailbox, after which receiving messages is disabled.

Continued on next page

Table 8.10 continued   Properties of the IMailboxStore interface

Property	Data type	Default	Read/write?	Description
OverrideStore GarbageCollection	Boolean	Empty	Yes	If True, the store is prevented from permanently deleting messages.
DaysBeforeGarbage Collection	Long	-1 (no limit)	Yes	Sets or returns the number of days deleted messages are kept before being permanently deleted.
GarbageCollectOnly AfterBackup	Boolean	False	Yes	If True, deleted messages are only permanently deleted after the mailbox is backed up.
Delegates	String	Null	Yes	Sets or returns a list of DNs of users who have access to the mailbox.

Listing 8.6 shows how to open an existing mailbox and change some of the default settings.

Listing 8.6   Change the current settings for a mailbox.

```
Sub ChangeMailboxProperties()
    ' You can change mailbox settings
    ' after the mailbox has been created.

    Dim prs As CDO.Person
    Dim mbx As CDOEXM.IMailboxStore
    Dim strmoveto As String
    Dim strLDAP As String

    ' LDAP URL string to the user account
    strLDAP = "LDAP://cyberserver/cn=Aidan Delaney"
    strLDAP = strLDAP & ",ou=recipients,dc=domain,dc=com"
```

```
        Set prs = New CDO.Person
        prs.DataSource.Open strLDAP

        ' Get the mailbox and set some properties
        Set mbx = prs
        With mbx
            .GarbageCollectOnlyAfterBackup = True
            .DaysBeforeGarbageCollection = 7
            .StoreQuota = 10
            .OverQuotaLimit = 2
            .HardLimit = 1
        End With

        ' Save the changes to the User object
        prs.DataSource.Save

        ' Clean up
        Set mbx = Nothing
        Set prs = Nothing
    End Sub
```

MOVING A MAILBOX

You can move a mailbox from one Exchange database to another. This is often done to optimize management of a particular group of mailboxes that have similar requirements or qualities. To move a mailbox programmatically, you must first access the mailbox to be moved. You can then call the MoveMailbox method of the CDOExM IMailboxStore interface and pass an LDAP string to the new location for the mailbox. Because this method changes the HomeMDB property for a User object, you must save your changes to the User object after the move.

Listing 8.7 shows how to move a mailbox from its current location to another database.

Listing 8.7   Move a mailbox to another database.

```
Sub MoveMailbox()
    ' Move a mailbox from one database
    ' to another database.

    Dim prs As CDO.Person
    Dim mbx As CDOEXM.IMailboxStore
    Dim strmoveto As String
    Dim strLDAP As String

    ' LDAP URL to the mailbox
    strLDAP = "LDAP://cyberserver/cn=Aidan Delaney"
    strLDAP = strLDAP & ",ou=recipients,dc=domain,dc=com"

    ' Open the user object
    Set prs = New CDO.Person
    prs.DataSource.Open strLDAP

    ' Reference the mailbox
    Set mbx = prs

    ' Indicate the new mailbox location
    strmoveto = "LDAP://cyberserver/CN=Special mailboxes," & _
        "CN=First Storage Group,CN=InformationStore," & _
        "CN=cyberserver,CN=Servers,CN=First Administrative Group," & _
        "CN=Administrative Groups,CN=First Organization," & _
        "CN=Microsoft Exchange,CN=Services,CN=Configuration," & _
        "DC=domain,DC=com"

    ' Move the mailbox to the new location
    mbx.MoveMailbox strmoveto

    ' Save the changes
    prs.DataSource.Save

    ' Clean up
    Set mbx = Nothing
    Set prs = Nothing
End Sub
```

DELETING A MAILBOX

To delete a mailbox from the Exchange store, you use the DeleteMailbox method of the CDOExM IMailboxStore interface. Before you call the method, though, you must access the mailbox of the User account to be deleted. After you open the User object associated with the mailbox, set a reference to the mailbox store of the user. Then call the DeleteMailbox method to permanently remove the mailbox from the Exchange store.

Because DeleteMailbox generates an error when no mailbox exists, you should test for the existence of the mailbox before you try to delete it. The HomeMDB property returns an empty string when a mailbox does not exist. If HomeMDB returns anything but an empty string, the user has a mailbox and you can safely call the DeleteMailbox method. The following code sample shows how to do this:

```
Dim mbx as As CDOEXM.IMailboxStore
Dim prs As CDO.Person

Set prs = New CDO.Person
prs.DataSource.Open _
    "LDAP://cyberserver/cn=Aidan Delaney,ou=recipients,dc=domain,dc=com"

Set mbx = prs
If mbx.HomeMDB <> "" Then
    mbx.DeleteMailbox
End If
```

Deleting a mailbox does not delete the associated User object. To delete the User object, use ADSI. For more information about deleting the User object, see "Deleting User and Contact Objects" later in this chapter.

MANAGING USER AND CONTACT OBJECTS

This section describes different ways to manage existing User and Contact objects, such as opening, deleting, moving, and enumerating them.

USING CDO TO OPEN USER AND CONTACT OBJECTS

You can take the same approach to open a User or Contact object in Active Directory by using CDO as you do to open a Person object in a Web Storage System folder. The only difference is in how you use the URL string. To access an Active Directory object, you need to use an LDAP string that maps to the object being opened. Listing 8.8 shows how to open a User object in Active Directory by passing the LDAP string to the DataSource.Open method.

Listing 8.8   Use CDO for Exchange to open a User object in Active Directory.

```
Sub OpenUser_CDO()
    ' Use CDO Person object to read
    ' an Active Directory User object.

    Dim strADSPath As String
    Dim prs As CDO.Person

    ' Build the ADsPath
    strADSPath = "LDAP://cyberserver/cn=Peter Waxman"
    strADSPath = strADSPath & ",ou=recipients,dc=domain,dc=com"

    ' Open the account with the CDO Person object
    Set prs = New CDO.Person
    prs.DataSource.Open strADSPath

    ' Do something here

    ' Clean up
    Set prs = Nothing
End Sub
```

For more information about using the CDO Person object, see Chapter 5, "Introduction to CDO for Exchange."

USING ADSI TO OPEN USER AND CONTACT OBJECTS

To use ADSI to open an object in Active Directory, you call the GetObject function and pass the DN to the User object. Listing 8.9 shows how to use ADSI to open a User object in Active Directory:

Listing 8.9   Use ADSI to open a User object in Active Directory.

```
Sub OpenUser_ADSI()
    ' Use ADSI IADsUser interface to read
    ' an Active Directory User object.

    Dim strADSPath As String
    Dim usr As ActiveDs.IADsUser

    ' Build the ADsPath
    strADSPath = "LDAP://cyberserver/cn=Peter Waxman"
    strADSPath = strADSPath & ",ou=recipients,dc=domain,dc=com"

    ' Open the account with the ADSI IADsUser object
    Set usr = GetObject(strADSPath)

    ' Do something here

    ' Clean up
    Set usr = Nothing
End Sub
```

MOVING USER AND CONTACT OBJECTS

You must use ADSI methods to move an object in Active Directory from one location to another. CDO does not provide this capability. To move an object, use the IADsContainer.MoveHere method on the destination container or organizational unit and pass two arguments:

- **SourceName**. This is the DN of the object that you want to move.

- **NewName**. This is the optional, new RDN of the object. If you want the object to maintain its current name, you can pass an empty string (vbNullString) instead.

Listing 8.10 shows how to move a User account from the Recipients organizational unit to the Special Users organizational unit without changing the RDN of the User object.

Listing 8.10 Move an account in Active Directory from one organizational unit to another.

```
Sub MoveUser()
    ' Move the user from one organizational unit
    ' to another organizational unit.

    Dim strMoveThis As String
    Dim ctr As ActiveDs.IADsContainer
    Dim objMoved As ActiveDs.IADsUser

    'Indicate the container where the new object will reside
    Set ctr = GetObject( _
      "LDAP://cyberserver/cn=Users,dc=domain,dc=com")
    'Indicate the object to be moved
    strMoveThis = "LDAP://cyberserver/cn=Peter Waxman," & _
      "ou=recipients,dc=domain,dc=com"

    'Move the object to the new container and keep the RN
    Set objMoved = ctr.MoveHere( _
      strMoveThis, _
      vbNullString)

    'Clean up
    Set ctr = Nothing
    Set objMoved = Nothing
End Sub
```

NOTE Moving a User object in Active Directory does not affect the link between the User object and its Exchange mailbox.

DELETING USER AND CONTACT OBJECTS

Because User and Contact are objects of Active Directory and you need permission to manipulate them, only ADSI can be used for I/O operations such as deleting. To delete an object, you must open the parent container or organizational unit and call the IADsContainer.Delete method and pass two arguments:

- **bstrClassName**. The object class string of the object to be deleted, such as "User" or "Contact."

- **bstrRelativeName**. The RDN of the object to be deleted.

The Delete method commits the deletion directly to Active Directory. You do not need to call the SetInfo method to commit the deletion.

If the user has a mailbox, deleting the User object does not delete the Exchange mailbox. You must do this explicitly before deleting the User object in Active Directory. This ensures there are no orphaned mailboxes—mailboxes that no longer have users. Listing 8.11 shows how to delete a User object from Active Directory. If the user has a mailbox on the Exchange server, the mailbox is deleted first.

Listing 8.11   Use the HomeMDB property of the CDO Person object to check for a mailbox.

```
Sub DeleteUserandMailbox()
    ' Delete both the mailbox and the user

    Dim ctr As IADsContainer
    Dim prs As CDO.Person
    Dim mbx As CDOEXM.IMailboxStore
    Dim strFirstName As String
    Dim strLastName As String
    Dim strRN As String
    Dim strLDAP As String

    strFirstName = "Aidan"
    strLastName = "Delaney"
    strRN = "cn=" & strFirstName & " " & strLastName

    ' LDAP URL to the user
    strLDAP = "LDAP://cyberserver/cn=" & strFirstName & " " & strLastName
    strLDAP = strLDAP & ",ou=recipients,dc=domain,dc=com"
```

```
' Open the user object and the mailbox store
Set prs = New CDO.Person
prs.DataSource.Open strLDAP
Set mbx = prs

' Check to see if a mailbox has been assigned to this user
If mbx.HomeMDB <> "" Then
   mbx.DeleteMailbox
End If
prs.DataSource.Save

' Now delete the user
strLDAP = "LDAP://cyberserver/ou=recipients,dc=domain,dc=com"
Set ctr = GetObject(strLDAP)
ctr.Delete "user", strRN

' Clean up
Set prs = Nothing
Set mbx = Nothing
Set ctr = Nothing
End Sub
```

ENUMERATING USER AND CONTACT OBJECTS

Containers and organizational units often contain items of more than one type. You
should optimize code as thoroughly as possible and request only objects of
interest, because all the information a user requests through ADSI is downloaded to
a local cache. Although you can build a Structured Query Language (SQL) SELECT
statement and use ADO to return only particular objects, it is simpler to filter the
container or organizational unit instead. To filter for specific objects, use the
IADsContainer.Filter property and pass an array of object classes to return:

- To filter for Contact objects, use:

```
cntr.Filter = Array("contact")
```

- To filter for User objects (this includes computers), use:

```
cntr.Filter = Array("user")
```

- To filter for both Contact and User objects, use:

```
cntr.Filter = Array("person")
```

When you apply a filter to the container or organizational unit, only the objects you specify are returned to the local cache. Your code automatically references the local cache whenever possible, so any further action on the container or organizational unit as a whole applies only to those filtered objects. As far as your code is concerned, no other objects exist in that container or organizational unit. Listing 8.12 shows how to filter an organizational unit for User and Contact objects.

Listing 8.12   Filter an organizational unit for User and Contact objects.

```
Sub EnumerateUsers()
    ' Filter a container for users and contacts
    ' This will also return computer objects as well.

    Dim ctr As IADsContainer
    Dim obj As IADs

    'Access the proper container
    Set ctr = _
        GetObject("LDAP://cyberserver/ou=recipients,dc=domain,dc=com")

    'Filter for only group classes
    ctr.Filter = Array("person")

    'Loop through each group
    For Each obj In cntr
        Debug.Print obj.Name, obj.Class
    Next

    Set ctr = Nothing
End Sub
```

> **NOTE** Because a Computer object is derived from the Person object class, this filter also returns Computer objects. To create a result set that contains only User and Contact objects without Computer objects, use an SQL query and the ObjectCategory property.

WORKING WITH GROUPS

A group establishes an association among people. By using groups, you can send a message to several people at one time through a single alias, or you can easily assign access permissions on a shared resource to multiple people at one time. This section describes the types of groups you can create and the scopes in which they can be applied. The section also explains how to create groups, manage the members of a group, and handle basic I/O operations such as copying, moving, and deleting.

NOTE CDO does not have an object that represents an Active Directory group, so you must use ADSI to create and manage distribution and security groups. However, you can use the CDO IMailRecipient interface to mail-enable a distribution group.

USING GROUP TYPE AND GROUP SCOPE

You can create several different groups in Active Directory by setting the group type and group scope attributes. The group type determines how the group can be used. The group scope determines who can be a member of the group, who can use the group, and how the group can be used. You set both group type and group scope programmatically with the groupType attribute.

UNDERSTANDING GROUP TYPE

Active Directory supports two types of groups:

- A *security group* is a security-enabled group type that you use primarily to control access to shared resources by setting permissions. You use a security group to indicate how a resource can be managed. In addition, the group can have an e-mail alias. You can add a security group to Access Control Lists (ACLs) on resources.

- A *distribution group* is not security-enabled, and you use it only for grouping purposes. You use a distribution group most often to send e-mail messages to a collection of recipients. You cannot add distribution groups to ACLs on resources.

Both group types support an e-mail alias, so which one should you use when? If you plan to use the group only for e-mail purposes, create a distribution group. A distribution group improves performance because group members' security tokens do not need to be updated by Windows 2000 during the logon process. However, if you plan to use that same group to assign permissions on resources, such as printers or public folders, create a security group.

UNDERSTANDING GROUP SCOPE

To understand scope, imagine a company that has Active Directory domains configured for Asia, Europe, and North America. This organization contains users and groups from all these domains. When you create a group, you can choose from three different scopes: universal, global, and domain local. The scope you select depends on who needs to belong to the group and who needs to use the group:

- A *universal* group has the broadest reach and allowance in membership. This type of group can contain members from any domain in the organization. You can include users from Asia, Europe, and North America. If you make this group a distribution group (see "Understanding Group Type" in the previous section), the alias for the group appears in the address book of every domain. In addition, a user in any domain can access the details of the distribution list and view the members. If you create a universal scope security group, you can use the group to set security on resources in any native-mode domain. However, a universal group requires more resources when it replicates between domains because the entire group membership needs to replicate. Mail-enabled groups should be universal groups.

- A *global* group also has broad reach but is more specific in membership. A global group can include members from only a single domain—that in which it was created. If you create a global group in the domain North America, the group can include only users and groups from North America. It cannot include users and groups in Asia and Europe. However, users in other domains can still see and use the group. For example, if you create a global scope distribution group in the North America domain, the alias for the group is available in the address books of users in every domain, but only users in the North America domain can access the distribution list details and view the members. The same applies to security groups. If you create a global scope security group, people anywhere can use the group, but it can contain only objects from the domain in which it was created.

- A *domain local* group combines some aspects of both the universal and global scopes. Like a universal group, a domain local group can contain members from any domain in the organization. You can include users from Asia, Europe, and North America. However, the specific ways you use a domain local group scope are more similar to global scope groups. For example, if you create a domain local scope distribution group in the North America domain, the alias for the group is available in the address books of users in every domain, but only users in the North America domain can search the distribution list and view the members. Security groups are completely unique. If you create a domain local scope security group in the North America domain, the group can only be used in that domain. However, it can contain resources from any domain.

NOTE   Universal scope security groups are not supported for a mixed-mode environment, in which domain controllers run a mix of Windows NT 4.0 and Windows 2000; however, universal scope distribution groups are supported.

CREATING A GROUP OBJECT

To create a Group object in Active Directory, you use the ADSI IADsGroup interface. If you want to create a mail-enabled distribution list, you can use the CDOExM IMailRecipient interface. This section discusses how to create mail-enabled distribution groups and security groups.

CREATING A MAIL-ENABLED DISTRIBUTION GROUP

To create a mail-enabled distribution group, you define the group by using ADSI and you mail-enable the group by using CDOExM. To define the group by using ADSI, you create a new Group object, set properties to define the group type and scope, and then set the sAMAccountName property. To mail-enable the group, you reference the IMailRecipient interface and call the MailEnable method. Unlike when you mail-enable contacts and users, you do not need to pass any information to the MailEnable method. Exchange automatically creates the e-mail address for the group.

Listing 8.13 shows how to create a new mail-enabled universal scope distribution
group. After a new Group object is created, the procedure defines the group type
and scope by setting the GroupType property to
ADS_GROUP_TYPE_UNIVERSAL_GROUP. Then the procedure sets the
sAMAccountName property to provide backward compatibility with Windows
NT 4.0 account names. To mail-enable the Group object, the procedure calls the
IMailRecipient.MailEnable method.

Listing 8.13   Create a mail-enabled distribution group.

```
Function CreateMailEnabledGroup(strGroupName As String)
    ' Create a distribution group that has
    ' an e-mail address.

    Dim strGroupCN As String
    Dim ctr As ActiveDs.IADsContainer
    Dim grp As ActiveDs.IADsGroup
    Dim rcp As CDOEXM.IMailRecipient

    ' Build the RDN to the group
    strGroupCN = "cn=" & strGroupName

    'Indicate where to create the group and give it a name
    Set ctr = GetObject _
        ("LDAP://cyberserver/ou=recipients,dc=domain, dc=com")
    Set grp = ctr.Create("group", strGroupCN)

    With grp
        ' Create a global group type
        .Put "grouptype", ADS_GROUP_TYPE_UNIVERSAL_GROUP

        ' Add backward compatibility security name
        .Put "sAMAccountName", strGroupName

        ' Must save the group prior to adding members
        .SetInfo

        'Add a user to the group
        .Add "LDAP://cyberserver/cn=Mindy Martin," & _
            "ou=recipients,dc=domain,dc=com"
```

```
' Reference the IMailRecipient interface
Set rcp = grp
' Enable the group to receive e-mail
rcp.MailEnable

' Save the group with the members list
' and mail information.
.SetInfo
End With

'Clean up
Set rcp = Nothing
Set grp = Nothing
Set ctr = Nothing
End Function
```

INDICATING THE GROUP TYPE

You set both the group type and group scope by using the GroupType property.
You must set the GroupType property to one of the values that indicate the scope
listed in Table 8.11.

Table 8.11   Constants used to indicate the scope of the group

Constant	Value	Description
ADS_GROUP_TYPE_GLOBAL_GROUP	2	Global distribution
ADS_GROUP_TYPE_DOMAIN_LOCAL_GROUP	4	Domain local distribution
ADS_GROUP_TYPE_UNIVERSAL_GROUP	8	Universal distribution

To create a group for use as a distribution list, you need to set this property to only
one of these values. For example, to create a universal scope distribution group,
your code would look like this:

```
grp.Put "grouptype", ADS_GROUP_TYPE_UNIVERSAL_GROUP
```

To create a security group, you need to set the GroupType property to one of the values listed in Table 8.11 and include an additional value, which is the constant for security groups: ADS_GROUP_TYPE_SECURITY_ENABLED. For example, to create a domain local scope security group instead of a domain local scope distribution group, the Put statement would look something like this:

```
grp.Put "grouptype", _
    ADS_GROUP_TYPE_DOMAIN_LOCAL_GROUP _
    + ADS_GROUP_TYPE_SECURITY_ENABLED
```

SETTING THE sAMAccountName

As it must for user accounts, the sAMAccountName property must also be set for groups. This string is the unique name of the object that is used by clients and servers running earlier versions of Windows. The sAMAccountName property cannot contain more than 20 characters. For example, the following code sets the sAMAccountName property to Keepers:

```
grp.Put "sAMAccountName", "keepers"
```

HANDLING GROUP MEMBERSHIP

This section discusses how to add members to a Group object, verify their membership, remove members from the group, and enumerate the existing members.

ADDING MEMBERS

ADSI lets you make any object in Active Directory a member of any group. However, it makes sense to add only certain objects to certain groups. For example, you should add mail-enabled User objects, Contact objects, or other mail-enabled groups to the membership of a mail-enabled distribution group.

To add to the current member list for a group, call the IADsGroup.Add method and pass the DN for the new member. The following code sample adds the user Michael Patten to a group:

```
grp.Add _
    "LDAP://cyberserver/" & _
    "cn= Michael Patten," & _
    "cn=Recipients,dc=domain,dc=com"
```

Before you can add users to a group, that group must already exist. This does not matter when you open an existing group and add a new member, but it's quite important if you create a new group and want to add members at the same time. When you create a new group, call the SetInfo method of a Group object before you attempt to add members. This updates Active Directory with the new group information and allows you to add members to the list. If you do not call the SetInfo method, an error is generated when you attempt to add a member.

CHECKING USER MEMBERSHIP

If a user is already a member of a group, calling the Add method to add the same user generates an error. To avoid this, use the IsMember method of the IADsGroup interface to check whether a member is in a group before you call the Add method. The IsMember method searches the list of group members for the name that was passed. It returns True if the user is already a member. For example, the following code sample checks to see if the user Amy Luehmann is already a member of the group. If IsMember returns False, Amy Luehmann is not yet a member and you can add her to the list.

```
strUser = "LDAP://cyberserver/cn=Amy Luehmann," & _
    "cn=Recipients,dc=domain,dc=com"

If Not grp.IsMember(strUser) Then
    grp.Add strUser
End If
```

> **NOTE**   The IsMember method compares only the name of the user to be added with all existing member names; it does not check whether the user to be added actually exists. Therefore, if the user does not exist in Active Directory, IsMember does not generate errors, but the Add method does.

Removing Members

To remove a member from a group member list, call the Remove method and pass the DN of the user to be removed. The following code sample removes the user Michael Patten from the group list:

```
grp.Remove _
    "LDAP://cyberserver/" & _
    "cn=Michael Patten," & _
    "cn=Recipients,dc=domain,dc=com"
```

As with the Add method, the Remove method generates an error if the user is not a member of the group. Therefore, you should use the IsMember function to check for membership before you attempt to remove a user from the group member list. The following code sample shows how to test for membership:

```
strUser = "LDAP://cyberserver/cn=Michael Patten," & _
    "cn=Recipients,dc=domain,dc=com"

If grp.IsMember(strUser) Then
    grp.Remove strUser
End If
```

Enumerating Members of a Group

The current members of a group are accessible by calling the IADsGroup.Members property. With the Members collection, you can:

- Loop through each member of the collection to return member-specific information.

- Use the IADsGroup.Count property to retrieve a total count of all the individuals in the group.

- Call the IADsGroup.Filter property to return only members that fulfill certain criteria.

When you loop through the members of a group, remember that members can include objects other than users, such as other groups and computers. Therefore, any variable that you apply generically to each object in the Members collection must apply overall and must perform some form of late binding. For example, the following code sample generates an error if the group contains members of any class other than user:

```
Dim mbr As ActiveDs.IADsUser
'
'Bind to the group here
'
For Each mbr In grp.Members
    Debug.Print mbr.DisplayName
Next
```

The variable *m* must bind to a generic interface that every class type in the group would inherit, such as the IADs interface. This eliminates the possibility of a type mismatch error. For example, the following declaration does not generate an error when used to enumerate group members:

```
Dim mbr As ActiveDs.IADs
```

Listing 8.14 shows how to loop through a collection of members of a group and retrieve information about each member. The procedure also returns the total count of members in the group.

Listing 8.14   List the members in a group.

```
Sub EnumerateGroupMembers(strGroupName As String)
    ' Returns information on each member
    ' in a group.

    Dim strGroupCN As String
    Dim grp As ActiveDs.IADsGroup
    Dim mbr As ActiveDs.IADs

    ' Build the RDN to the group
    strGroupCN = "cn=" & strGroupName
```

```
  ' Get the Group object
  Set grp = GetObject _
     ("LDAP://cyberserver/" & strGroupCN & _
     ",ou=recipients,dc=domain, dc=com")

  Debug.Print "Group: " & grp.DisplayName
  Debug.Print "Member Count: " & grp.Members.Count

  ' Loop through each member in the group
  For Each mbr In grp.Members
     Debug.Print vbTab, "------------------------"
     Debug.Print vbTab, "Class: " & mbr.Class
     Debug.Print vbTab, mbr.DisplayName
     Debug.Print vbTab, mbr.Mail
     Debug.Print vbTab, mbr.Parent
  Next

  ' Clean up
  Set mbr = Nothing
  Set grp = Nothing
End Sub
```

MANAGING GROUP OBJECTS

This section describes how to manage existing Group objects by opening, deleting, moving, and enumerating those objects.

OPENING A GROUP OBJECT

To open an existing group in Active Directory, you can bind directly to a Group object if you know the LDAP binding string. The following code sample binds to a Group object in the Recipients organizational unit:

```
Set grp = GetObject( _
  "LDAP://cyberserver/cn=Keepers,cn=Recipients,dc=domain,dc=com")
```

With the binding set, you can retrieve group information, such as the member listing or the group e-mail address, as well as conduct tasks, such as adding and removing members and enumerating the member list for detailed information.

Moving Group Objects

To move an object in Active Directory from one location to another, you must use ADSI methods because CDO does not provide this capability. To move an object, open the container that contains the Group object to be moved and then call the MoveHere method on the destination container. The MoveHere method takes two arguments:

- **SourceName**. This is the DN of the object to be moved.

- **NewName**. This is the optional, new RDN for the object. If you want the object to maintain its current name, you can pass an empty string (vbNullString) instead.

Listing 8.15 shows how to move a Group object from the Recipients organizational unit to the Special Objects organizational unit and retain the original RDN of the group.

Listing 8.15   Move a Group object and retain its RDN.

```
Sub MoveGroup(strGroupName As String)
    ' Move a group object from one
    ' organizational unit to another.

    Dim strGroupCN As String
    Dim strMoveThis As String
    Dim ctr As ActiveDs.IADsContainer
    Dim objMoved As ActiveDs.IADsGroup

    ' Build the RDN to the group
    strGroupCN = "cn=" & strGroupName

    'Indicate the container where the new object will reside
    Set ctr = GetObject _
        ("LDAP://cyberserver/cn=Users,dc=domain,dc=com")

    'Indicate the object to be moved
    strMoveThis = "LDAP://cyberserver/" & strGroupCN & _
    ",ou=recipients,dc=domain,dc=com"
```

```
        'Move the object to the new container and keep the RDN
        Set objMoved = _
            ctr.MoveHere(strMoveThis, vbNullString)

        'Clean up
        Set ctr = Nothing
        Set objMoved = Nothing
    End Sub
```

DELETING A GROUP OBJECT

Deleting a Group object from Active Directory is similar to deleting a User or Contact object. You must first open the Active Directory container that holds the object to be deleted. Then you call the Delete method of the IADsContainer interface and pass the following arguments:

- **bstrClassName**. The object class string of the object to be deleted. In this case, it is "group."

- **bstrRelativeName**. The RDN of the object to be deleted.

Listing 8.16 shows how to delete a Group object from Active Directory.

Listing 8.16   Delete a Group object.

```
    Function DeleteGroup(strGroupName As String)
        ' Delete a Group object.

        Dim ctr As IADsContainer
        Dim strLDAP As String

        ' Build the LDAP string to the container
        strLDAP = _
            "LDAP://cyberserver/ou=users,dc=domain,dc=com"

        ' Open the recipients container
        Set ctr = GetObject(strLDAP)

        'Delete the group
        ctr.Delete "group", "cn=" & strGroupName
```

```
        ' Clean up
        Set ctr = Nothing
    End Function
```

ENUMERATING ONLY GROUP OBJECTS IN A CONTAINER

Containers and organizational units often contain items of more than one type. You should optimize code as thoroughly as possible and request only objects of interest, because all the information a user requests through ADSI is downloaded to a local cache. Although you can build an SQL SELECT statement and use ADO to return only particular objects, it is simpler to filter the container. To filter a container for only specific objects, use the IADsContainer.Filter property and pass an array of object classes to return. For example, to filter for Group objects, first bind to the container holding the object of interest. Then set the Filter property like this:

```
    ctr.Filter = Array("group")
```

When you apply the filter to the container, only Group objects are returned to the local cache. Because your code automatically uses the local cache whenever possible, any further action on the container as a whole applies only to those filtered objects. As far as your code is concerned, no other objects exist in the container. Listing 8.17 shows how to filter a container for Group objects.

Listing 8.17   Filter a container for only Group objects.

```
    Sub EnumerateGroups()
        ' Filter an organizational unit
        ' for group objects

        Dim ctr As IADsContainer
        Dim obj As Object

        ' Access the organizational unit
        Set ctr = GetObject _
            ("LDAP://cyberserver/ou=recipients,dc=domain,dc=com")

        ' Filter for only group classes
        ctr.Filter = Array("group")
```

```
     ' Loop through each group
     For Each obj In ctr
         Debug.Print obj.Name, obj.Class
     Next

     ' Clean up
     Set obj = Nothing
     Set ctr = Nothing
 End Sub
```

QUERYING ACTIVE DIRECTORY

As discussed in earlier sections, you can filter a container or organizational unit to return only specific schema object classes. However, the Filter property cannot specify which properties to return or whether to search multiple locations before returning the result set. Even more complex filters become cumbersome. To overcome these shortcomings in the Filter property, you can use ADO 2.5 to navigate in the Active Directory store and query for particular objects. ADSI also supports the LDAP syntax as documented in RFC 2254 as well as a subset of SQL. This section focuses on how to use the SQL dialect. Some of the searches that you can build by querying Active Directory include:

- Find a user when you do not know where the user is actually located in Active Directory.

- Return only select properties for a user.

- Dynamically locate the nearest resource, such as a printer in a specific building.

- Return the names of all users who have an Exchange mailbox in your organization.

- Find users based on a partial value in a property.

This section discusses the nuances of how to query Active Directory by using ADO 2.5 and the Active Directory SQL dialect. This section also explains how to build everything from a simple SQL SELECT statement that returns all objects of a particular class to a more complex query that returns user objects based on a partial name value.

QUERYING BY USING ADO

Queries that use ADO and ADSI to search Active Directory can be built in a few different ways. However, the following core tasks must always be completed:

1. **Build the SELECT statement**. Determine where in Active Directory you need to search and what results you expect.

2. **Establish the connection to Active Directory**. Use the ADO Connection object to establish a communication link with Active Directory through ADSI. The ADSI OLE DB provider is ADsDSOObject.

3. **Indicate the query settings**. Use the ADO Command object to set options that determine how the data is returned. If you don't want to set any options now, you can skip this step and do it all in the next step.

4. **Return the result set**. You can manually populate the ADO Recordset with the query results or use the Command object to do so.

Listing 8.18 shows how to execute a query that returns a subset of Group objects in the Recipients container of Active Directory that have the word "keepers" in the group name.

Listing 8.18   Return information on all Group objects with a specific name.

```
Sub QueryByGroupName()
    ' Query for groups with 'keepers'
    ' in the group name.

    Dim strLDAP As String
    Dim strSQL As String
    Dim rst As ADODB.Recordset
    Dim cnn As Connection

    ' Indicate where to begin the search
    strLDAP = "LDAP://cyberserver/ou=recipients,dc=domain,dc=com"

    ' Open the connection
    Set cnn = New Connection
    With cnn
        .Provider = "adsDSOobject"
        .Open strLDAP
    End With
```

```
' Build the SQL SELECT statement
strSQL = _
    "SELECT adspath, cn " & _
    "FROM '" & strLDAP & "' " & _
    "WHERE cn='*keepers' and objectcategory='group'"

' Execute the query and return the results
Set rst = New Recordset
rst.Open strSQL, cnn

' Enumerate through the rows
Do Until rst.EOF
    Debug.Print rst.Fields("cn"), rst.Fields("adspath")
    rst.MoveNext
Loop

' Close the ADO objects and clean up
rst.Close
cnn.Close
Set rst = Nothing
Set cnn = Nothing
End Sub
```

BUILDING THE CORE SELECT STATEMENT

The SELECT statement is how you indicate which objects are returned from the Active Directory store. If you don't build the SELECT statement properly, the code fails and generates an error, or it returns the wrong information. To avoid either of these outcomes, you must provide accurate information. The SELECT statement in the Active Directory SQL dialect is similar to the SELECT statement you use with other data sources:

```
SELECT properties
FROM 'ADsPath'
[WHERE criteria]
[ORDER BY sort fields]
```

As with standard SELECT statements, an Active Directory SELECT statement starts with SELECT and then indicates the properties or attributes of information to return in the result set. To return specific properties, separate each property name with a comma. For example, to return the ADsPath property and the CN property, the code would look like this:

```
SELECT ADsPath, cn
```

Notice that property names are not enclosed in quotation marks. Quotation marks are unnecessary in this dialect of SQL. When you want to return all properties, you normally use an asterisk (*) in place of the property names. In this dialect of SQL, however, that approach returns only the ADsPath property. The query simply checks for the existence of the objects.

The FROM portion of the SQL statement indicates where to begin the search for objects. In the case of Active Directory, this is an LDAP binding string just like the one you use to open and create objects in the directory store. This is simply the starting point and does not limit the search to only that container. All subcontainers are searched, too, unless you specify otherwise by using a Command option. You should be as specific as possible when you indicate the starting point for the search. Although you can use an LDAP binding that starts at the top level of the organization and searches the entire Active Directory, this is not recommended.

Because the entire SELECT statement is passed through the OLE DB provider as a string, the ADsPath property name must be enclosed in single quotes. The following code sample returns the same properties as the previous code sample for objects in the Recipients organizational unit:

```
SELECT ADsPath, cn FROM
       'LDAP://cyberserver/ou=recipients,dc=domain,dc=com'
```

At this point, the SELECT statement could be considered complete. It definitely would run; however, without a WHERE clause, it would return all objects. Because this information is cached locally and must be brought across the network, returning all objects would make for an inefficient search and take quite a toll on network traffic. Instead, you can use a filter to limit the result set to only those records that match your requirements. For information about building filter criteria, see "Adding Filter Criteria" later in this section.

The following code sample builds on the previous SELECT statement and returns only objects with a name that ends in "club":

```
SELECT ADsPath, cn FROM
    'LDAP://cyberserver/ou=recipients,dc=domain,dc=com' WHERE cn='*club'
```

The ORDER BY clause is also an optional clause in the SELECT statement. It allows you to sort the result set based on the contents of one or more properties. By default, the results sort in ascending order. To add sorting, indicate the property to sort by, and to optimize efficiency, use only indexed properties. The following code sample adds sorting to the previous SELECT statement:

```
SELECT ADsPath, cn FROM
    'LDAP://cyberserver/ou=recipients,dc=domain,dc=com' WHERE cn='*club'
    ORDER BY cn
```

NOTE The ASC (Ascending) and DSC (Descending) options in the ORDER BY clause are not supported in the Active Directory SQL dialect.

ADDING FILTER CRITERIA

Probably the most complex part of building a SELECT statement is creating the filter criteria for the WHERE clause. The WHERE clause is an optional clause of the SELECT statement that allows you to specify criteria for objects returned in the result set. Here are some basic rules that apply to the WHERE clause:

- String values must be enclosed in single quotes, for example:

  ```
  'Area 51'
  ```

- Criteria consist of one or more expressions. An expression is the combination of a property, a comparison operator (=, <, >, <=, >=, <>), and a value, for example:

  ```
  location = 'Area 51'
  ```

- For criteria that consist of multiple expressions, separate the expressions with concatenation operators such as AND or OR, for example:

  ```
  location = 'Area 51' AND objectCategory = 'Computer'
  ```

- Wildcard characters, such as the asterisk (*), are supported. Use wildcard characters at the beginning of the string whenever possible. A wildcard character used alone tests for only the existence of the property value, for example:

  ```
  cn= '*club' AND mail = '*'
  ```

SEARCHING FOR OBJECT TYPES

All objects in Active Directory belong to a general class category that is defined by the values in the following two properties:

- The ObjectCategory property contains a schema class name that identifies the category to which an object instance belongs. Although the ObjectCategory is often the current class of the object (for example, Group for Group objects), some objects use another class to more easily identify them as being similar. For example, Contact objects and User objects both have an ObjectCategory of Person, which identifies them as representations of people.

- The ObjectClass property contains the schema class of a particular object instance. It is a multi-valued property that contains the specific class for the object and any classes from which it was derived, including the Top class. For example, a User class is derived from the Person class, which is derived from the Top class; therefore, the ObjectClass property for a User object is User, Person, and Top. After you set it, this property never changes.

When you query for an object type, first attempt to build the filter by using only the ObjectCategory property. The ObjectCategory property is an indexed property, but the ObjectClass property is not. Using an indexed property improves the performance of the search. For example, the proper way to filter for Group objects is with a filter like this:

```
ObjectCategory = 'group'
```

Sometimes, however, you might need to use both the ObjectCategory property and the ObjectClass property in a filter. For example, both Contact objects and User objects have an ObjectCategory of Person. To return only User objects, use the following filter:

```
ObjectCategory = 'person' AND objectClass = 'user'
```

To return only User objects, you cannot use only the ObjectClass expression in a filter because computers have an ObjectClass of User as well. Table 8.12 lists the object classes and categories for some of the Active Directory objects as well as the associated filter you need to return them.

Table 8.12 Classes and categories of Active Directory objects and the filters for retrieving them

Active Directory object	ObjectCategory	ObjectClass[1]	Filter
Contact	Person	Top, Person, Contact	ObjectCategory='person' AND ObjectClass='contact'
User	Person	Top, Person, User	ObjectCategory='person' AND ObjectClass='user'
Computer	Computer	Top, Person, User, Computer	ObjectCategory='computer'
Group	Group	Top, Group	ObjectCategory='group'

[1]All these objects also have an object class of Top.

SETTING COMMAND OPTIONS

The ADO Command object issues the actual query statement and sets various optional properties. Before anything can be done, however, you must first create a Command object and then set the ActiveConnection property to indicate which connection to use to communicate with Active Directory. After the connection is established, you can set the CommandText property to the query string to execute against the server. Although this can also be in the LDAP dialect, this section focuses on the SQL dialect. The following code sample demonstrates these tasks:

```
Set cmd = New ADODB.Command
Set cmd.ActiveConnection = conn
cmd.CommandText = strSQL
```

You can also use the Command object to set various properties for more precise control over how the result set is obtained and returned from Active Directory. Table 8.13 lists some of the common properties and their default values. For more information about a property, see the following sections.

Table 8.13   Common command properties and their default values

Command property	Data type	Default value
SearchScope	Enumeration	ADS_SCOPE_SUBTREE
Timeout	Integer	No time-out (0)
Time limit	Integer	No time limit (0)
Page size	Integer	No page size (0)
Cache results	Boolean	True
Chase referrals	Enumeration	ADS_CHASE_REFERRALS_EXTERNAL

The following code sample shows how to customize these properties by setting the SearchScope property for a Command object to indicate one-level searching:

```
cmd.Properties("searchscope") = ADS_SCOPE_ONELEVEL
```

USING THE SEARCHSCOPE PROPERTY

The SearchScope property indicates what objects from the base level are searched. The LDAP binding string used in the SELECT statement determines the base level. From that starting point, you can indicate the search area in which to look for objects that fit the indicated criteria. The possible ADS_SCOPE_SUBTREE enumeration values include:

- **ADS_SCOPE_BASE (0)**. A base search. This search is restricted to only the base object, and it returns only one object. In other words, even if your base is a container, a base search doesn't look at the subobjects in it. It acknowledges only the container object. This type of query is good when you want to determine if an object exists.

- **ADS_SCOPE_ONELEVEL (1)**. A one-level search. This search is restricted to the immediate subobjects of a base object; it excludes the base object. For example, it ignores the container but includes the subobjects.

- **ADS_SCOPE_SUBTREE (2)**. A subtree search. This is the broadest of all searches and includes the base object, all subobjects, and any subnodes. This search is also known as a deep search.

USING THE TIME LIMIT AND TIMEOUT PROPERTIES

The Time Limit property specifies the time, in seconds, that the server can spend processing the search. By default, this property is set to 0, which means that the server can continue processing the search until it is complete. To avoid using too many server resources for a single request and to allow other requests to be processed, you should specify a time limit. When the Time Limit property value is reached, the search is abandoned. Setting a Time Limit property is also a good idea if you have queries that run during peak hours of use. Administrators often set a general time limit value for all request processing. If you specify a search Time Limit property value greater than the administrative time limit, the server ignores your Time Limit property value and uses the administrative time limit instead. The default Active Directory administrative time limit is 2 minutes.

The client sets the TimeOut property. This specifies the time, in seconds, that the server can spend processing the search before returning a result set. By default, the TimeOut value is 0. When the server fails to respond before the specified time-out, the client abandons the search. The TimeOut property is especially useful when a client requests an asynchronous search. In an asynchronous search, the client makes a request and then continues with other tasks rather than waiting on the server. If something were to happen to the server, the client would continue to wait unless a time-out value was specified.

USING THE PAGE SIZE PROPERTY

By default, when you send a query to Active Directory, the server that responds to the query completely calculates the result set before it returns any data. In the case of a large result set, this can consume a large amount of memory on the server and put a heavy burden on the network when the result set is returned. Because the client cannot interrupt this type of search, a user might be unable to conduct other tasks until the server finishes processing the request completely.

By setting the Page Size property, you enable paged searching, or paging. *Paging* allows the server to send the data as it is built in collections of rows called pages. As far as the client is concerned, however, the search comes back as a complete result set. Paging provides benefits to both the server and the client. The server is able to minimize the memory required to process the result set. The client is able to cancel the operation while it is in progress. To turn paging on, set the Page Size property to the number of rows to calculate before a page is sent to the client.

> **NOTE** If the SELECT statement incorporates sorting, the Page Size property is ignored, and the query is completely processed on the server.

USING THE CACHE RESULTS PROPERTY

The Cache Results property determines how long the client keeps a result set in memory. By default, when a result set is retrieved, it is cached in memory on the client. Caching increases performance for the client because it allows the client to revisit the data again and again without sending repeated requests to the server. Caching also provides clients with SQL cursor support. You should set the Cache Results property to True when:

- Your code will probably use the result set more than once.

- The result set requires cursor support.

- The query will return a large or complex result set.

- The connection to the server is slow.

When you set Cache Results to False, the client does not keep the result set in memory. Each row in the Recordset is released from memory after the code has retrieved it. Also, when Cache Results is set to False, cursors are not supported. You should set Cache Results to False when:

- Your code will use the result set only once.

- The result set does not require cursor support.

- The client running the code has limited memory resources.

USING THE CHASE REFERRALS PROPERTY

Often, directory information is spread across multiple servers on the network. When a search uses a one-level or subtree scope, some of the objects required by the search might not reside on the server that you query; they might instead reside on another server. In that case, the object on the server that you query includes a referral to the actual object on the other server. You can determine how the query responds to referrals by setting the Chase Referrals property to one of the following ADS_CHASE_REFERRALS_EXTERNAL enumeration values:

- **ADS_CHASE_REFERRALS_NEVER (0)**. The server does not generate a referral to a client, even if the referral exists.

- **ADS_CHASE_REFERRALS_EXTERNAL (64)**. The server generates a referral to a client only if the request can be resolved on another server of a different directory tree.

- **ADS_CHASE_REFERRALS_SUBORDINATE (32)**. The server generates a referral to a client only if the request can be resolved on a server that has a name that forms a contiguous path from the originating server. In other words, the second server must be used for any subordinate containers or organizational units on the first server. ADS_CHASE_REFERRALS_SUBORDINATE (32) is supported for only subtree searches.

- **ADS_CHASE_REFERRALS_ALWAYS (96)**. The server always generates a referral to a client regardless of the client's type.

USING ADSI TO RETURN INFORMATION ABOUT YOUR DOMAIN

If your collaboration application is installed in multiple organizations and on multiple servers, the last thing you want is to have the server name hard-coded. A hard-coded server name limits the scope of your application and requires special programming to allow the program to run in multiple sites.

This section provides a number of procedures that you can use to dynamically identify the Active Directory server and domain in which your code is running. In addition, this section shows how to return information about the user currently logged on, the names of all the Exchange servers in the current domain, and the Exchange server used by an e-mail address.

IDENTIFYING YOUR ACTIVE DIRECTORY SERVER

The LDAP standard requires that every directory maintain a special entry called Root DS Entry. Root DS Entry contains a set of attributes describing Active Directory and the server on which it runs, and it is accessible through a rootDSE object. You can return the rootDSE object through the IADs interface. For example, the following code sample sets a reference to a rootDSE object:

```
Dim rootDSE As ActiveDs.IADs
Set rootDSE = GetObject("LDAP://rootDSE")
```

Table 8.14 lists the various properties of a rootDSE object. You can use these values to dynamically construct an LDAP string.

Table 8.14   Some of the properties of the rootDSE object

Property	Description
CurrentTime	Current time on the Active Directory server.
SubSchemaSubentry	Distinguished name for the sub-Schema object that contains information about the supported attributes and classes.
DefaultNamingContext	Default distinguished name for the domain to which Active Directory belongs.
SchemaNamingContext	Distinguished name for the schema container.
ConfigurationNamingContext	Distinguished name for the configuration container.
DnsHostName	DNS address for this Active Directory server.
ServerName	Distinguished name for the Server object for this Active Directory server stored in the configuration container.

Listing 8.19 shows how to use the rootDSE object to retrieve some information about Active Directory on the network in which the code is running, including the name of the Active Directory server, the Domain Name System (DNS) host, and a number of DNs. A sample result set follows the listing.

Listing 8.19   Get information about the Active Directory server.

```
Sub GetADInfo()
    ' Use the rootDSE to return information
    ' about Active Directory server

    Dim rootDSE As ActiveDs.IADs

    ' Access the Root DS Entry of the Active Directory
    Set rootDSE = GetObject("LDAP://rootdse")
```

```
Debug.Print "-------------------------------------------------------"
Debug.Print "Server: " & vbCrLf & rootDSE.Get("servername")
Debug.Print "-------------------------------------------------------"
Debug.Print "Time: " & rootDSE.Get("currentTime")
Debug.Print "DNS Host: " & rootDSE.Get("dnshostname")
Debug.Print "Default DN: " & rootDSE.Get("defaultNamingContext")
Debug.Print "Schema DN: " & rootDSE.Get("schemaNamingContext")
Debug.Print "Configuration DN: " & _
    rootDSE.Get("configurationNamingContext")
Debug.Print "Subschema DN: " & rootDSE.Get("subschemaSubentry")


    ' Clean up
    Set rootDSE = Nothing
End Sub
```

The code in Listing 8.19 returns results like these:

```
-----------------------------------------------------------
Server:
CN=CYBERSERVER,CN=Servers,CN=Default-First-Site-
Name,CN=Sites,CN=Configuration,DC=domain,DC=com
-----------------------------------------------------------
Time: 19991124162903.0Z
DNS Host: CYBERSERVER.domain.com
Default DN: DC=domain,DC=com
Schema DN: CN=Schema,CN=Configuration,DC=domain,DC=com
Configuration DN: CN=Configuration,DC=domain,DC=com
Subschema DN: CN=Aggregate,CN=Schema,CN=Configuration,DC=domain,DC=com
```

IDENTIFYING YOUR DOMAIN

You can use Root DS Entry to return information about your Active Directory server and use that information to dynamically build your LDAP string. However, to return information about your domain that you can then use to dynamically build URL strings for the Exchange OLE DB (ExOLEDB) provider, you access the ADSI ADSystemInfo object. The ADSystemInfo object returns information about the system, including the host DNS name.

Throughout this book, code samples and listings refer to a function named GetStorageName. GetStorageName, shown in Listing 8.20, returns the URL string of the domain in which the function is running. The URL string returned is the base for all URL strings that access a Web Storage System by using the ExOLEDB provider. By using this function, you do not need to explicitly state the domain name, and you can run the code on multiple names without having to rewrite it each time.

Listing 8.20   Return an ExOLEDB URL with the current domain DNS name.

```
Public Function GetStorageName() As String
    ' Return the name of the storage for
    ' the current server, using ADSI and the Active Directory.
    ' The return value is in the format:
    ' file://.backofficestorage/<domainname>/

    ' Turn on error trapping for VB and VBS
    On Error Resume Next

    Dim SysInfo As ActiveDs.ADSystemInfo
    Dim strName As String

    ' Reference the ADSystemInfo object in the
    Set SysInfo = New ActiveDs.ADSystemInfo
    ' Get the domain name
    strName = SysInfo.DomainDNSName

    If Len(strName) <> 0 Then
        ' Build the generic part of the EXOLEDB string
        GetStorageName = "file://./backofficestorage/" & strName & "/"
    Else
        ' Problem accessing the AD
        Err.Raise vbObjectError + 1959, "Unable to retrieve domain name."
    End If

    ' Clean up
    Set SysInfo = Nothing
End Function
```

TIP   The procedures throughout this book call the GetStorageName function independently. However, to optimize your application performance, you should call this procedure only when necessary.

IDENTIFYING THE CURRENT USER

If you want to return information about a user, you can use the ADSI WinNTSystemInfo object. The WinNTSystemInfo.UserName property returns the name of the user account that is executing the code. Listing 8.21 shows how to use the WinNTSystemInfo object to return the name of the user who is currently logged on.

Listing 8.21   Return the name of the user currently logged on to the system.

```
Function GetUserInfo() As String
    ' Return the name of the
    ' current user and computer.

    Dim WinNTInfo As New ActiveDs.WinNTSystemInfo

    ' Get the name of the user currently logged on
    GetUserInfo = WinNTInfo.UserName

    ' Clean up
    Set WinNTInfo = Nothing
End Function
```

The user name returned by the UserName property is not always the same as the user currently logged on to the system. For example, if the code is running in a COM+ application (such as an event sink), the UserName property returns the user context under which the COM object is executing. If the code is running in an ASP page and the user has not authenticated for the ASP, the UserName property returns the default user name for Microsoft Internet Information Services (IIS).

RETURNING EXCHANGE MAILBOXES

Because the information about Exchange users and mailboxes is now stored in Active Directory, it can be a little difficult to tell which accounts have mailboxes and which accounts do not. One way to solve this dilemma is to query Active Directory for users with mailboxes. The query begins the search at the root of the Active Directory server and searches all subtrees for objects with an ObjectCategory of Person and an MsExchMailboxGuid value of anything other than an empty string.

Listing 8.22 shows how to query for Exchange mailboxes. Use the Root DataSource Entry to return information about the system running the code.

Listing 8.22   Query Active Directory for users with mailboxes.

```
Sub GetUserswithMailboxes()
    ' Query for all users that have
    ' a mailbox in a domain.

    Dim rootDSE As IADs
    Dim strSearchRoot As String
    Dim strADServer As String
    Dim cnn As ADODB.Connection
    Dim rst As ADODB.Recordset
    Dim cmd As ADODB.Command

    ' Use the Root DS Entry to dynamically build
    ' the LDAP URL string.
    Set rootDSE = GetObject("LDAP://RootDSE")
    strADServer = rootDSE.Get("dnshostname")
    strSearchRoot = "LDAP://" & strADServer

    ' Open the connection
    Set cnn = New ADODB. Connection
    With cnn
        .Provider = "adsDSOobject"
        .Open strSearchRoot
    End With
```

```
' Build the SQL SELECT statement
strSQL = _
    "SELECT adspath, cn " & _
    "FROM '" & strSearchRoot & "' " & _
    "WHERE objectcategory='person' AND MsExchMailboxGuid='*'"

' Pass the querying options to a command object
Set cmd = New ADODB.Command
With cmd
    Set .ActiveConnection = cnn
    .CommandText = strSQL
    .Properties("searchscope") = ADS_SCOPE_SUBTREE
    .Properties("cache results") = False
    .Properties("Chase Referrals") = ADS_CHASE_REFERRALS_ALWAYS
End With

' Return the results in a recordset
Set rst = cmd.Execute

' Enumerate the Exchange servers
Do Until rst.EOF
    Debug.Print rst.Fields("cn"), rst.Fields("adspath")
    rst.MoveNext
Loop

' Close the ADO objects and clean up
rst.Close
cnn.Close
Set rootDSE = Nothing
Set rst = Nothing
Set cnn = Nothing
End Sub
```

RETURNING EXCHANGE SERVERS

You can also use a query to identify the Exchange server or servers in an organization. The query in this case conducts a search of the configuration naming context. The criteria restrict the results to objects with an ObjectCategory of msExchExchangeServer. Listing 8.23 shows how to query for Exchange servers in an organization.

Listing 8.23   Get the names and DN of all Exchange servers in a domain.

```
Sub FindAllExchangeServers()
    ' Returns the names of all Exchange servers
    ' in the current domain.

    Dim rootDSE As IADs
    Dim strSearchRoot As String
    Dim strADServer As String
    Dim strConfigDN As String
    Dim cnn As ADODB.Connection
    Dim rst As ADODB.Recordset
    Dim cmd As ADODB.Command

    ' Use the Root DS Entry to dynamically build
    ' the LDAP URL string.
    Set rootDSE = GetObject("LDAP://RootDSE")
    strADServer = rootDSE.Get("dnshostname")
    strConfigDN = rootDSE.Get("configurationNamingContext")
    strSearchRoot = "LDAP://" & strADServer & "/" & strConfigDN

    ' Open the connection
    Set cnn = New ADODB.Connection
    With cnn
        .Provider = "adsDSOobject"
        .Open strSearchRoot
    End With
```

```
' Build the SQL SELECT statement
    strSQL = _
            "SELECT adspath, cn " & _
            "FROM '" & strSearchRoot & "' " & _
            "WHERE objectcategory='msExchExchangeServer'"

    ' Pass the querying options to a command object
    Set cmd = New ADODB.Command
    With cmd
        Set .ActiveConnection = cnn
        .CommandText = strSQL
        .Properties("searchscope") = ADS_SCOPE_SUBTREE
        .Properties("cache results") = False
        .Properties("Chase Referrals") = ADS_CHASE_REFERRALS_ALWAYS
    End With

    ' Return the results in a recordset
    Set rst = cmd.Execute

    ' Enumerate the Exchange servers
    Do Until rst.EOF
        Debug.Print rst.Fields("cn"), rst.Fields("adspath")
        rst.MoveNext
    Loop

    ' Close the ADO objects and clean up
    rst.Close
    cnn.Close
    Set rootDSE = Nothing
    Set rst = Nothing
    Set cnn = Nothing
End Sub
```

RETURNING AN EXCHANGE SERVER FROM AN E-MAIL ADDRESS

You can return a specific Exchange server by using an e-mail address to query Active Directory for an object with that e-mail address. The query begins the search at the Active Directory server root and searches all subtrees. The criteria restrict the results to objects with an ObjectCategory property value of person and an e-mail property value equal to the e-mail address. If the query successfully locates a User object, you can read the msExchHomeServerName property to return the name of the Exchange server that hosts the mailbox.

Listing 8.24 shows how to query an Active Directory for the name of the Exchange server that hosts the mailbox for a specific e-mail address.

Listing 8.24   Return the Exchange server that hosts the mailbox for an e-mail address.

```
Function GetExchServerViaEmail()
    ' Returns the name of the Exchange server
    ' that hosts the mailbox for an email address.

    Dim rootDSE As IADs
    Dim strSearchRoot As String
    Dim strADServer As String
    Dim cnn As ADODB.Connection
    Dim rst As ADODB.Recordset
    Dim cmd As ADODB.Command

    ' Use the Root DS Entry to dynamically build
    ' the LDAP URL string.
    Set rootDSE = GetObject("LDAP://RootDSE")
    strADServer = rootDSE.Get("dnshostname")
    strSearchRoot = "LDAP://" & strADServer

    ' Open the connection
    Set cnn = New ADODB.Connection
    With cnn
        .Provider = "adsDSOobject"
        .Open strSearchRoot
    End With
```

```
' Build the SQL SELECT statement
strSQL = _
   "SELECT msExchHomeServerName, adspath " & _
   "FROM '" & strSearchRoot & "' " & _
   "WHERE objectcategory='person' AND mail='mindy@domain.com'"

' Pass the querying options to a command object
Set cmd = New ADODB.Command
With cmd
   Set .ActiveConnection = cnn
   .CommandText = strSQL
   .Properties("searchscope") = ADS_SCOPE_SUBTREE
   .Properties("cache results") = False
   .Properties("Chase Referrals") = ADS_CHASE_REFERRALS_ALWAYS
End With

' Return the results in a recordset
Set rst = cmd.Execute

' Return the Exchange server name and DN
Do Until rst.EOF
   Debug.Print _
      rst.Fields("msExchHomeServerName"), _
      rst.Fields("adspath")
   rst.MoveNext
Loop

' Close the ADO objects and clean up
rst.Close
cnn.Close
Set rootDSE = Nothing
Set rst = Nothing
Set cnn = Nothing
End Function
```

SUMMARY

Managing the users of an Exchange organization can be just as complex as managing the data itself. With the release of Windows 2000, Active Directory makes managing that information a little easier. You can access everything in Active Directory, from the user who has an Exchange mailbox to distribution groups to the server itself, by using ADSI, CDO, and ADO. When you use these tools together with the LDAP wire protocol, you can create User objects and Group objects, delete existing User objects and Group objects, manage computers, and query Active Directory to create your own Exchange management tools.

Section III, "Extending Your Application," discusses some ways to extend your Exchange applications with server-side enhancements, including Web Storage System events and workflow logic. In addition, the section discusses how to build solutions for Outlook 2000 clients.

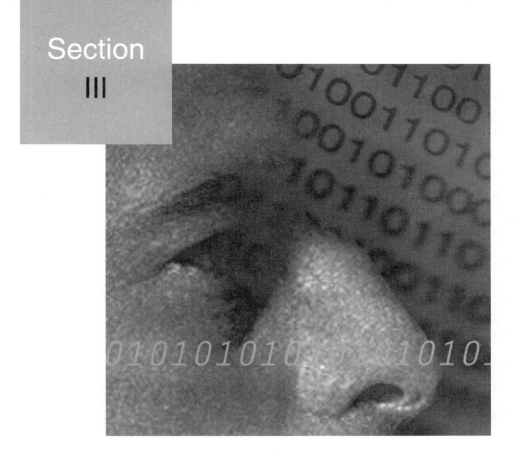

Extending Your Application

Chapter:

9	Using Web Storage System Events	**419**
10	Designing Workflow Applications	**479**
11	Developing with Outlook 2000	**513**

Using Web Storage System Events

Microsoft Exchange 2000 Server uses the new Microsoft Web Storage System event model to provide a way for collaboration applications to trigger code when an event occurs. An *event* is an action that occurs when a client, server, or application does something, such as adding new data. You can write code that reacts to events and runs automatically whenever a particular event occurs. Because the code reacts to events on the server, it doesn't matter what type of client is used to trigger the events. The events occur whether the client is Microsoft Outlook Web Access, Microsoft Outlook 2000, or a custom Web application.

It is possible to build a good application without writing code that responds to events, but you can build an excellent application—one that is interesting and responsive—by incorporating Web Storage System events. This chapter explains what Web Storage System events are and how to use them in applications. Sections include:

- **Overview of Events in Exchange 2000**

- **Building an Event Sink**

- **Creating an Event Registration Item**

- **Using Custom Properties with Events**

- **Investigating Event Errors with the Application Log**

OVERVIEW OF EVENTS IN EXCHANGE 2000

Often the toughest part of building an application is determining when code will run and how it will start. In the case of Exchange applications, code should typically run when a new item is added to a folder, after an existing item is changed, or when an item or folder is deleted. You can account for these scenarios to some degree in a custom client application, but then you assume that all users will make data requests by using only that custom client application. In addition, a client application cannot detect when changes occur by other users. An alternative solution is to monitor data requests on the server-side by using events—actions that occur when a client, server, or application does something.

Events are not completely new to Exchange. In Exchange Server 5.5, you could use Event Agents to respond to events after they had occurred. For example, you could write code in a Delete event agent that responded *after* the delete had taken place. Now, however, with the Web Storage System event model, you can react to events not only after they occur, but you can also react to an event, such as the delete, *before* it finishes executing.

Web Storage System events are happening constantly in Exchange, but they aren't very useful to your application unless you write code to react to them. You can use events to validate data before an item is saved to a folder, and you can use an event to send out notifications when information is changed. You can also use events to execute code at a particular time each day. This section explains some reasons behind why you might want to use events, what types of events are available, how events interact with each other, and the design of the event programming paradigm.

WHY INCORPORATE EVENTS?

Exchange automatically incorporates some events into its day-to-day operations. Content indexing, schema population, workflow, wireless technologies, and unified messaging use events to accomplish their particular tasks. But what can events do for your applications? Events can be used to:

- **Change items from one content class to another**. If you are using a folder with a single custom content class, you can use an event to check for messages with different content classes. If an item is the wrong content class, you can use the code in the event to change it to the correct one, either on a single-instance basis or as a timed occurrence.

- **Create reminders for time-sensitive applications that do not have a built-in reminder system**. You can generate an e-mail message to an administrator when a particular item comes due.

- **Maintain updated files in a Web folder**. When a file is more than a certain number of days old, you can send out notification that the file needs to be updated.

- **Track when changes are made to resources**. You can trap deletion so that other dependent resources are not orphaned. You can use an event to check for these types of resources and make the appropriate changes.

- **Validate or check data before it is saved to Exchange**. You can verify rights to make certain changes or simply check the formatting of the resource being saved.

UNDERSTANDING EVENT TYPES

Before you write code to react to events, you should understand what types of events are available to you. You can't write the same code to react to every event. For example, you can't write code to validate data in an item before it is saved in an event that fires after the save has already taken place. If you understand the different types of events in the beginning, you can avoid lengthy debugging sessions later.

Events are grouped into three category types: synchronous events, asynchronous events, and system events. Synchronous events and asynchronous events react in some way to a data request. A data request can be a new resource request, a change request, a delete request, or a copy or move request. Synchronous events fire before a data request is committed to the Web Storage System, whereas asynchronous events fire after a data request is committed to the Web Storage System. System events do not react to data requests but instead fire when a database starts or stops or at a particular time.

SYNCHRONOUS EVENTS

Synchronous events fire after a client has issued a data request to Exchange but before Exchange processes the data request. You can write code that reacts to synchronous events to validate data before it is saved to a Web Storage System folder, to authorize the deletion of a resource according to detailed criteria, or to change a property value on a resource before it is saved to or deleted from the Web Storage System.

Because synchronous events occur before Exchange processes the data request, your code can either commit the request or abort the request. When you *commit* a data request, you confirm that Exchange can finish processing the initial data request. For example, if a client is attempting to create a new item, Exchange can create the item in the appropriate folder. When you abort a data request, you tell Exchange to ignore the original data request. For example, if the client is attempting to create a new item, the item is not created. The context from when the data request enters Exchange until it is committed or aborted is a single local transaction.

The Web Storage System exposes two synchronous events, OnSyncSave and OnSyncDelete, defined as follows:

- The *OnSyncSave* event fires immediately before an item is saved to the Web Storage System. You can trigger a save when you create a new item, change an existing item and save the changes, copy an item, or move an item to a new location. If you move a folder, the OnSyncSave event fires only once for the parent folder. It does not fire for each child item in the folder.

- The *OnSyncDelete* event fires immediately before an item is removed from its current location in the Web Storage System. You can remove an item by deleting it completely or by moving it from one location to another. The OnSyncDelete event is not fired when an item is moved as a result of moving the folder that contains it or when a mailbox is deleted.

ASYNCHRONOUS EVENTS

Asynchronous events fire after a data request is fully processed by the Web Storage System. For example, if you create a new folder in a Web Storage System, an asynchronous event does not fire until after the folder is created. Because asynchronous events occur after the data request is processed, these events are better for code that sends simple notification e-mail. For example, you can write code that sends a notification message to people when an item in the store is updated with new information.

You can use two asynchronous events, OnSave and OnDelete, defined as follows:

- The *OnSave* event fires after a new resource is saved in a Web Storage System, an existing resource is changed and resaved, or a resource is moved or copied. If you move a folder, an OnSave event fires for only the parent folder. It does not fire for each child item in the folder. If you copy a folder, an OnSave event fires for the parent folder and for each item in the folder.

- The *OnDelete* event fires after a resource is deleted from a Web Storage System and when a resource is moved. A delete can be either soft or hard, as described in the previous section "Using Synchronous Events." If you delete a folder, an OnDelete event fires for the parent folder and once for each child folder. However, an OnDelete event does not fire for any of the items in the folder.

SYSTEM EVENTS

System events do not react to data requests in the same way that synchronous and asynchronous events do. Instead, system events fire at a particular system occurrence, such as when a database starts. However, the events do not fire until after the action happens. Because of this, system events are similar to asynchronous events.

The Web Storage System exposes three system events, OnMDBStartUp, OnMDBShutdown, and OnTimer, defined as follows:

- The *OnMDBStartUp* event fires when an Exchange database starts, and the *OnMDBShutdown* event fires after a database shuts down. You can use these events for application status notification. For example, if an Exchange database that is used for a particular application is taken offline, you can have the system immediately send an e-mail notification that the database is down to the application developer. Then when the database restarts, you can send another automatic notification.

- The *OnTimer* event is called at a specified time period. You use the OnTimer event to execute code at a particular time. For instance, you can use an OnTimer event to run a program that updates a distribution list every Wednesday at midnight. You can also use the OnTimer event for repeated calls during that time period.

UNDERSTANDING THE EVENT PARADIGM

A Web Storage System uses an event paradigm that involves two core constituents: an event sink that contains the code that reacts to an event and an event registration that links the event with the code component. These constituents are described as follows:

- An *event sink* is a Component Object Model (COM) component, such as a Microsoft ActiveX DLL, that contains the code to run when an event occurs. Event sinks organize the actual procedures that react to synchronous, asynchronous, or system events. You can create event sinks by using Microsoft Visual Basic, Microsoft Visual C++, or script. Because the event sink must run on the server, you can use both ActiveX Data Objects (ADO) and Collaboration Data Objects (CDO) for Exchange code in the sink.

- An *event registration* is a hidden item in a Web Storage System that contains the information to associate an event with an event sink. The event registration item must be saved to the folder on which the event is to be enabled. If you create a system event registration item, the item is saved to the folder root. You can create an event registration item by using ADO, Extensible Markup Language (XML), or simple script.

Figure 9.1 shows how the event sink and the event registration work together. When a Web Storage System event occurs, the store checks whether that event is registered to execute code by looking for an event registration item in the folder that triggered the event. If the store finds an event registration item in the folder, the store reads the event registration item to determine what event sink to call and how to call it.

The Web Storage System then calls the event sink named in the event registration item and passes information about the resource that triggered the event as well as any custom information in the registration item. The resource that triggered the event is the *event item*. As shown in Figure 9.1, the event sink is not represented in the Web Storage System. This is because event sinks do not run in process with the Web Storage System. An event sink must run as an out-of-process application.

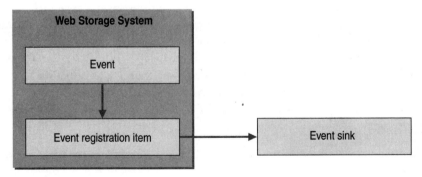

Figure 9.1
Web Storage System event paradigm

SECURITY AND EVENT SINKS

As mentioned earlier, event sinks do not run in process with the Web Storage System; they run as out-of-process COM applications. Because event sinks do not run in process with the Web Storage System, Exchange requires some form of authentication before allowing the event sink to execute any code. For your event sink code to run properly, you must specify a user account to execute the code in the various components. Regardless of who actually authors the event sink, the code always runs with the permissions of this particular account. Anything that account has permission to do, the code has permission to do. Anything the account is denied from doing, the code is denied from doing. The account must, at the very least, have access to the folder in which the event is being triggered. You will specify this user account when you create a COM+ application for the event sink, which is discussed later in this chapter.

BUILDING AN EVENT SINK

Events are always firing in a Web Storage System. However, unless you do something to react to them, they aren't very interesting. To react to an event, you create an event sink that contains the code that should execute whenever the event occurs. You can create event sinks by using Visual Basic, C++, or even a standard scripting language, such as Microsoft Visual Basic Scripting Edition (VBScript). Because Visual Basic is generally easier to use than C++ and using Visual Basic to create an event sink will generally provide better performance than creating an event sink with a scripting language, this section focuses on creating event sinks with Visual Basic.

To create an event sink by using Visual Basic, you create an ActiveX DLL project, write the event procedures in class modules, and then register the event sink as a COM+ application on the server. Use an ActiveX DLL rather than an ActiveX EXE because you can only use an ActiveX DLL as a COM+ component on the server. By using COM components, you can use COM+ security roles to add security to an event sink. For more information about COM+ security roles, see Chapter 14, "Setting Security and Permissions."

> **NOTE** If you need high performance multithreaded event sinks, it is recommended that you build your event sinks with C++.

CREATING THE DYNAMIC-LINK LIBRARY

To create an event sink with Visual Basic, you create a new ActiveX DLL project, set references, implement the appropriate interfaces in a class module, and build the event procedures.

> **TIP** If you create a DLL project from scratch, rename the project and the class modules. These names are also used to generate the COM component names, so if you don't rename the project and class modules, your COM components might have very generic names such as Project1.Class1. A nondescript name like this doesn't help identify the purpose of a component.

SETTING THE REFERENCES

After you create the new DLL, on the **Project** menu, select **References**, and from the list of available references, select **ExOLEDB Type Library (exoledb.dll)**. By setting a reference to the ExOLEDB library, you can create any of the event procedures. Depending on what your event sink is meant to do, you might also want to set references to any or all of the following object libraries:

- **Microsoft ActiveX Data Objects 2.5 Library (adodb.dll)**. Set this reference if you plan to read or set property values for the item that triggered the event.

- **Microsoft CDO for Exchange 2000 Library (cdoex.dll)**. Set this reference to send notification messages and to interact with existing collaboration objects such as contacts, messages, and appointments.

- **Microsoft CDO for Exchange Management Library (cdoexm.dll)**. Set this reference if you need to return information about a user's mailbox.

- **Active DS Type Library (activeds.tlb)**. Set this reference if you want to write code that dynamically identifies the domain, server, and user. You must also set this reference if you want to manage distribution groups.

Figure 9.2 shows the **References** dialog box for a new project with all these references set.

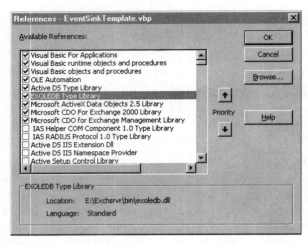

Figure 9.2
After you create a new ActiveX DLL, set references to the object libraries, including the ExOLEDB library, that you want to use.

BUILDING THE EVENT PROCEDURES

After you set references to the appropriate object libraries, you can build the event procedures by implementing the appropriate interface and calling the appropriate event method. Each Web Storage System event type has an Exchange OLE DB (ExOLEDB) interface that contains event methods. For example, the IExStoreSyncEvents interface exposes the OnSyncDelete and OnSyncSave methods that build the event procedures that will react to the OnSyncDelete and OnSyncSave synchronous events.

To use the event methods, you must first implement the event interface in a class module. In the declarations section of a class module, indicate which event interface is being implemented with the Implements statement. For example, the following code sample implements the synchronous events with the IExStoreSyncEvents interface:

```
Implements Exoledb.IExStoreSyncEvents
```

To implement the asynchronous events with the IExStoreAsyncEvents interface, use code like this:

```
Implements Exoledb.IExStoreAsyncEvents
```

To implement the system events with the IExStoreSystemEvents interface, use code like this:

```
Implements Exoledb.IExStoreSystemEvents
```

When you implement an interface, the **Object** combo box at the top of the class module is populated with the name of the implemented interface, and the **Procedure** combo box is populated with the names of the event methods of the implemented interface. Figure 9.3 shows these combo boxes in a class module.

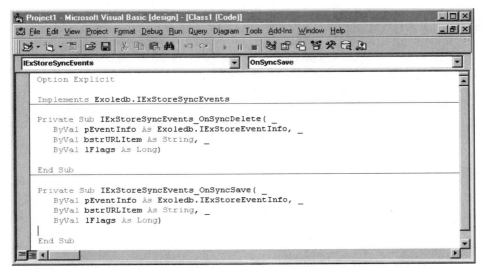

Figure 9.3
When you implement an interface in a class module, the Objects combo box is populated with the interface names, and the Procedure combo box is populated with the method names of the implemented interface.

To build an event procedure for an event, click the interface name in the **Object** combo box and then click the event method in the **Procedure** combo box. The coordinating event procedure is created in the class module. For example, to create the event procedure for the OnSyncSave event in the IExStoreSyncEvents interface, click **IExStoreSyncEvents** in the **Object** combo box, and then click **OnSyncSave** in the **Procedure** combo box. The IExStoreSyncEvents_OnSyncSave event procedure is then automatically generated in the class module.

For Visual Basic to successfully make the DLL file, you must create an event procedure for each method on the implemented interface. Otherwise, the DLL will not compile correctly. You do not, however, need to add any code in the procedure.

NOTE All event procedures must be created in a class module. You can use standard modules for any shared procedures, but the actual event procedures must reside in a class module.

Using CDO to Send Notifications

When you incorporate collaboration capabilities into an Exchange 2000 Server-based application, you use CDO for Exchange. Event sinks are no different. For example, if you want to send notification messages to people from an event sink, you can use a CDO Message object. You can use a notification message to alert people when a new item is added to a folder or when an item is deleted. You can even use notification message to alert developers when a database shuts down. Listing 9.1 shows how to send a notification message from an asynchronous save event procedure by using CDO. You can use the lFlags parameter in your code to test to see if the event is being triggered during replication. The lFlags parameter contains information about the event and the item that triggered the event. The lFlags parameter is discussed in more detail later in the chapter.

NOTE The code listings shown in this chapter are available in the Microsoft Visual Basic project CH_09.vbp on the companion CD. If you want to run the samples as they are written, you must have the Zoo Management sample installed on your Exchange 2000 Server. For information about installing the application, see the introduction to the book. In addition, the code samples repeatedly call a function named GetStorageName. This function returns the name of the domain in which the code is running. For more information about the GetStorageName function, see Chapter 8, "Interacting with Active Directory."

Listing 9.1   Send a notification message from an asynchronous save event procedure.

```
Private Sub IExStoreAsyncEvents_OnSave( _
   ByVal pEventInfo As Exoledb.IExStoreEventInfo, _
   ByVal bstrURLItem As String, _
   ByVal lFlags As Long)

   ' Make sure that this event sink is not
   ' being triggered by replication.
   If Not lFlags And EVT_REPLICATED_ITEM Then

      ' Send a notification message
      With New CDO.Message
         .From = "mindy@domain.com"
         .To = "mindy@domain.com"
         .Subject = "New Information"
         .HTMLBody = "This record has just been added: " _
            & vbCrLf & bstrURLItem
         .Send
      End With
   End If
End Sub
```

USING THE EVENTSINKTEMPLATE PROJECT

To make writing event sinks a little easier, you can use the EventSinkTemplate DLL project (EventSinkTemplate.vbp) included on the companion CD. The EventSinkTemplate project contains three class modules for each event type. The modules are already configured with the coordinating event procedures. The synchronous event procedures even contain the conditional statements for testing for the calling phase. In addition, the project already has references set to the following object libraries:

- ExOLEDB Type Library

- Microsoft ActiveX Data Objects 2.5 Library

- Microsoft CDO for Exchange 2000 Library

- Microsoft CDO for Exchange Management Library

- Active DS Type Library

You can write directly in the template and add your own custom code to each procedure, or you can import the class modules to new projects. If you write code directly in the template, rename the project from RenameMe to something appropriate for your application. Figure 9.4 shows the class module before any additional code is added.

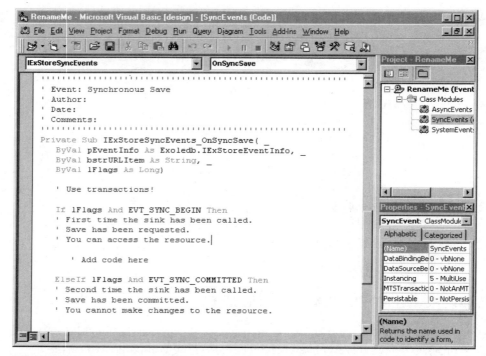

Figure 9.4   You can use the EventSinkTemplate project to get a jump start on writing your event code.

REACTING TO SYNCHRONOUS EVENTS

As mentioned earlier, synchronous events are triggered after a client makes a data request but before Exchange processes the data request. This means that you can use a synchronous event sink to intercept a data request before it completes. For example, you can write code in a synchronous event sink that validates properties of an item before it is saved to a folder. You can then either allow or disallow the save.

Synchronous events occur in the transaction of the data request and result in the synchronous event firing twice for the same data request: once when the transaction begins with the initial data request and once when the transaction completes with a commit or abort of the request. Because a synchronous event fires twice for every data request, a synchronous event sink is called twice as well.

Figure 9.5 shows how this occurs. When a client makes a data request to a Web Storage System, a transaction begins and a synchronous event fires. During this initial phase of the transaction, the event item that triggered the event is passed to the synchronous event sink. The event sink can read or set properties of the event item during this first phase of the transaction. The event sink then either commits the data request by allowing the transaction to complete normally, or the event sink explicitly aborts the transaction by calling the AbortChange method. After the transaction is either committed or aborted, the transaction completes and the synchronous event sink is called the second time—this time to deal with any potential implications that result from the commit or abort, such as to undo changes that were made to other items.

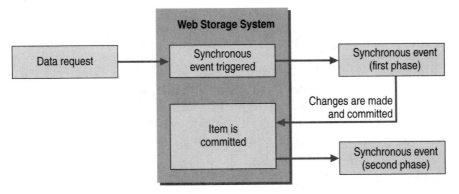

Figure 9.5
Synchronous event sinks are called twice: once when the data request is made and once when the data request is committed or aborted.

While a synchronous event process executes, the event sink has exclusive control over the data request that triggered the event. No other process or request can access the item until the event finishes executing.

USING THE ONSYNCDELETE EVENT PROCEDURE

The OnSyncDelete event fires when a delete is requested. A delete can be requested as a result of a request to destroy a resource completely or a request to move a resource from one folder to another. The syntax for the OnSyncDelete event procedure is:

```
Private Sub IExStoreSyncEvents_OnSyncDelete( _
  ByVal pEventInfo As Exoledb.IExStoreEventInfo, _
  ByVal bstrURLItem As String, _
  ByVal lFlags As Long)

  'Code goes here

End Sub
```

Where:

pEventInfo

is a pointer to the IExStoreEventInfo interface. The IExStoreEventInfo interface is not accessible to OLE Automation compatible languages such as Visual Basic. Instead, you use the OLE Automation compatible version, IExStoreDispEventInfo. The IExStoreDispEventInfo interface is also exposed by the pEventInfo reference. In synchronous events, you use this to get a reference to the item to be deleted, the event registration item, or the session. You can also use it to access the AbortChange method of the IExStoreDispEventInfo interface to cancel the delete.

bstrURLItem

is the URL of the event item that triggered the OnSyncDelete event.

lFlags

is a long integer that contains the status information about the event action. You can use it to determine the type of delete occurring as well as the phase of the transaction. Table 9.1 lists the possible values of lFlags in an OnSyncDelete event procedure. You can also use a combination of these values.

Table 9.1   OnSyncDelete IFlags values

IFlags constant	Value	This flag means...
EVT_IS_COLLECTION	2	The item being deleted is a collection.
EVT_SOFTDELETE	16	The item has been moved to a temporary holding such as the Delete Items folder (soft delete).
EVT_HARDDELETE	32	The item has been permanently deleted from the store (hard delete).
EVT_INITNEW	64	This is the first firing of the event. It is set only once during the lifetime of a created event sink.
EVT_MOVE	256	The item was moved, which resulted in an implicit delete.
EVT_SYNC_BEGIN	16777216	The event sink is being called for the first phase of the transaction.
EVT_SYNC_COMMITTED	33554432	The event sink is being called for the second phase of the transaction and the save has been committed.
EVT_SYNC_ABORTED	67108864	The event sink is being called for the second phase of the transaction and the save has been aborted.
EVT_INVALID_URL	1073741824	The URL passed to the sink is not valid.
EVT_ERROR	2147483648	An error occurred in the event.

USING THE ONSYNCSAVE EVENT PROCEDURE

The OnSyncSave event fires when a new resource is saved to a Web Storage System, when an existing resource is changed and resaved, or when a new item is saved as a result of a copy or move action. The syntax for the OnSyncSave event procedure is:

```
Private Sub IExStoreSyncEvents_OnSyncSave( _
ByVal pEventInfo As Exoledb.IExStoreEventInfo, _
ByVal bstrURLItem As String, _
ByVal lFlags As Long)

'Code goes here

End Sub
```

Where:

pEventInfo

is a pointer to the IExStoreEventInfo interface. The IExStoreEventInfo interface is not accessible to OLE Automation compatible languages such as Visual Basic. Instead, you use the OLE Automation compatible version, IExStoreDispEventInfo. The IExStoreDispEventInfo interface is also exposed by the pEventInfo reference. In an OnSyncSave event, you use this to get an interface to the new or changed item being saved, the event registration item, or the session. If an item is being changed, the pointer returns the unchanged version of the item. You can also use this to access the AbortChange method of the IExStoreDispEventInfo interface to abort the save.

bstrURLItem

is the URL of the event item that triggered the event. If the event item is a new item, this URL is not valid during the first phase of the transaction because the item does not yet exist. If the transaction is committed, the URL of the new item is available during the second phase of the transaction. If an item is being changed, the URL returns the changed version of the item.

lFlags

is a long integer that contains the status information about the OnSyncSave event. It is used to determine the type of save occurring as well as the phase of the transaction. Table 9.2 lists the possible values of lFlags in an OnSyncSave event procedure. You can also use a combination of these values.

Table 9.2   OnSyncSave IFlags values

IFlags constant	Value	This flag means...
EVT_NEW_ITEM	1	The item being saved is new.
EVT_IS_COLLECTION	2	The item being saved is a collection.
EVT_REPLICATED_ITEM	4	The item is saved as a result of replication.
EVT_IS_DELIVERED	8	The item is saved as the result of message delivery.
EVT_INITNEW	64	This is the first firing of the event. It is set only once during the lifetime of a created event sink.
EVT_MOVE	256	The item being saved as a result of a move.
EVT_COPY	512	The item being saved as a result of a copy.
EVT_DRAFT_CREATE	1024	The item being saved is a newly created draft.
EVT_DRAFT_SAVE	2048	The item being saved is a draft.
EVT_DRAFT_CHECKIN	4096	The item being saved is a draft check-in.
EVT_SYNC_BEGIN	16777216	The event sink is being called for the first phase of the transaction.
EVT_SYNC_COMMITTED	33554432	The event sink is being called for the second phase of the transaction and the save is committed.

Continued on next page

Table 9.2 continued OnSyncSave IFlags values

IFlags constant	Value	This flag means...
EVT_SYNC_ABORTED	67108864	The event sink is being called for the second phase of the transaction and the save is aborted.
EVT_INVALID_SOURCE_URL	536870912	The Source URL could not be obtained during a move operation.
EVT_INVALID_URL	1073741824	The URL passed to the sink is not valid.
EVT_ERROR	2147483648	An error occurred in the event.

TIP Replicated items trigger save events in the same way that any other item does. To avoid executing code on a replicated item, test for an IFlags value of EVT_REPLICATED_ITEM.

CHECKING FOR THE PHASE OF A TRANSACTION

Because synchronous events fire twice, the code in a synchronous event sink also executes twice. It is very important to remember that unless you include a conditional structure such as If..End If, the same code will execute for both the first phase of the transaction and the second phase of the transaction.

Running the same code for the first phase and the second phase can trigger unnecessary errors because certain tasks are allowed during only the first phase. For example, you can write code to modify an event item during the first phase, but not to modify the event item during the second phase. If you attempt to modify an item during the second phase, your code will generate an OLE DB error.

To check for the phase of a transaction, use the lFlags parameter and check the current value and the flag type. If the transaction is in its first phase, IFlags returns EVT_SYNC_BEGIN. If the transaction is in the second phase, IFlags returns EVT_SYNC_COMMITTED if the transaction is committed or EVT_SYNC_ABORTED if the transaction is aborted. To test for the value of IFlags, you must check for the existence of a flag as well as the value. For example, you can use the following conditional structure in your code to check for the phase of the transaction:

```
If lFlags And EVT_SYNC_BEGIN Then
    'This is the first phase
    'The item can be modified
ElseIf lFlags And EVT_SYNC_COMMITTED Then
    'This is the second phase
    'The transaction has been committed
    'You cannot make changes to the event item
ElseIf lFlags And EVT_SYNC_ABORTED Then
    'This is the second phase
    'The transaction has been aborted
    'You cannot make changes to the event item
End If
```

DISTINGUISHING BETWEEN A NEW ITEM AND A CHANGED ITEM

If you use the OnSyncSave event, your event sink is triggered when a new resource is saved to a Web Storage System folder as well as when an existing resource is modified and resaved. If you want to distinguish between a new resource and an existing resource, you can check the IFlags parameter for an EVT_NEW_ITEM flag value. If IFlags returns EVT_NEW_ITEM, the event item is a new resource that is saved to a folder.

Knowing whether the event item is a new item or an existing item that is changed can help you determine how to access the event item in your event sink code. If the item is new, the bstrURLItem parameter will return a null value and you cannot use the URL in your code. If the event item already exists, the bstrURLItem parameter will return the URL of the item's current location and you can use it in your code.

For example, the following code sample checks IFlags to determine if the event item is a new item or not:

```
If lFlags And EVT_NEW_ITEM Then
    'This is a new item
    'The URL string will be null
End If
```

MODIFYING THE EVENT ITEM IN A SYNCHRONOUS EVENT SINK

During the first phase of the transaction, you can write code in the synchronous event sink to access and modify the properties of the item that triggered the event. You can access an event item in two ways: the IExStoreDispEventInfo.GetRecord method or the bstrURLItem parameter with the ADO Open method of a Record object.

You use the GetRecord method to access the event item when:

- The event item is a new item.

- The event item is a changed item, and you want to access the version of the item before the change occurred.

- The event item is being deleted.

You use the bstrURLItem parameter to access the event item when the event item is a changed item, and you want to access the version of the item after the change occurred.

To use the GetRecord method to access an event item, declare an object variable for the IExStoreDispEventInfo interface that exposes the GetRecord method and another object variable for an ADO Record object. The following code shows how this looks:

```
Dim iEventInfo As Exoledb.IExStoreDispEventInfo
Dim rec As ADODB.Record
```

Next, set a reference to the IExStoreDispEventInfo interface of the event item by using the pEventInfo parameter passed to the event procedure. The IExStoreDispEventInfo interface is the OLE Automation compatible version of the IExStoreEventInfo interface and is also exposed by the event parameter, pEventInfo. The following code sets the reference:

```
Set iEventInfo = pEventInfo
```

You can then call the GetRecord method and return a reference to the event item:

```
Set rec = iEventInfo.EventRecord
```

After you access the event item by using a Record object, you can read and write to any of the properties and save your changes back to the source. The following code sample shows how to put it all together:

```
Dim iEventInfo As Exoledb.IExStoreDispEventInfo
Dim rec As ADODB.Record

Set iEventInfo = pEventInfo
Set rec = iEventInfo.EventRecord
```

To use the bstrURLItem parameter to access the event item, you can pass the bstrURLItem parameter value directly to the Open method of an ADO Record object. For example, the following code sample shows how to access the changed version of an existing item:

```
Dim rec As ADODB.Record

Set rec = New ADODB.Record
rec.Open bstrURLItem, , adModeReadWrite
```

ABORTING A SYNCHRONOUS EVENT

During the initial phase of the event transaction, you have the option to commit or abort the transaction. *Aborting* a transaction prevents an action from being committed and can be used to:

- Prevent a resource from being created

- Prevent changes to an existing resource from being saved

- Prevent a resource from being moved to a new location

- Prevent a copy of a resource from being made

- Prevent a resource from being deleted

To abort a transaction, you call the IExStoreDispEventInfo.AbortChange method. The AbortChange method takes one argument, which is the error code (long data type) to return to the event that indicates the reason that the synchronous event is to be aborted. To use the AbortChange method, you return a reference to the IExStoreDispEventInfo interface just as you did when accessing a new event item. After you determine that the transaction should be aborted, call the AbortChange method and pass an error code. For example, the following code sample evaluates the subject for an appointment item. If it contains the text "Appointment" or "Cancel," the transaction is aborted.

```
' This is an arbitrary value
Const conInvalidHeader As Long = 1946

Dim iEventInfo As Exoledb.IExStoreDispEventInfo
Set iEventInfo = pEventInfo

' Code here does some processing

If (InStr(1, strSubject, "Appointment", vbTextCompare) = 0) And _
 (InStr(1, strSubject, "Cancel", vbTextCompare) = 0) Then

    ' Abort the event
    iEventInfo.AbortChange conInvalidHeader

End If
```

If the transaction aborts successfully, the event returns an EVT_SYNC_ABORTED flag, which can be evaluated in the final phase of the transaction.

REACTING TO ASYNCHRONOUS EVENTS

Asynchronous events occur after a data request is fully processed by a Web Storage System. This means that you can use an asynchronous event sink only to react to a data request, not to intercept a request as with a synchronous event sink. Asynchronous event sinks are perfect for simple notification programs and any programs in which it's not necessary to evaluate or modify the event item.

Unlike synchronous events, asynchronous event sinks do not have exclusive rights to the event item, so they do not block the Web Storage System from further actions. In turn, the Web Storage System does not wait for the asynchronous event sink to finish executing but continues processing. Because the Web Storage System does not wait for the event sink to complete, asynchronous events are not guaranteed to execute in any particular order. However, the Web Storage System does guarantee that the event sink will eventually be called, even if the event must fire after the Web Storage System stops and restarts.

Figure 9.6 shows how an asynchronous event sink is called. When a client makes a data request of some sort, such as creating a new item or deleting an item, the Web Storage System fully processes the request before the asynchronous event is triggered. The event then reacts to the data change and calls an asynchronous event sink.

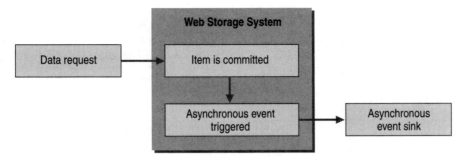

Figure 9.6
Asynchronous events are triggered only after an item is fully processed by the Web Storage System.

USING THE ONDELETE EVENT PROCEDURE

The OnDelete event fires when a delete has occurred. A delete can result when a resource is completely destroyed or when a resource is moved from one folder to another. A move involves deleting a resource from its current folder and recreating it in another folder. The syntax for the OnDelete event procedure is:

```
Private Sub IExStoreAsyncEvents_OnDelete( _
 ByVal pEventInfo As Exoledb.IExStoreEventInfo, _
 ByVal bstrURLItem As String, _
 ByVal lFlags As Long)

 'Enter code here

 End Sub
```

Where:

pEventInfo

> is a pointer to the IExStoreEventInfo interface. In an OnDelete event, this provides a reference to the registration item that called the event sink. You cannot use this parameter to access the event item.

bstrURLItem

> is the URL of the event item that triggered the event. It is used in an asynchronous event sink to access the event item.

lFlags

> is a long integer that contains the status information about the OnDelete event, and it can be used to determine the type of save occurring. Table 9.3 lists the possible values of lFlags in an OnDelete event procedure. You can also use a combination of these values.

Table 9.3   OnDelete lFlags values

lFlags constant	Value	This flag means...
EVT_IS_COLLECTION	2	The deleted item was a collection.
EVT_SOFTDELETE	16	The item is moved to a temporary holding such as the Delete Items folder (soft delete).
EVT_HARDDELETE	32	The item is permanently deleted from the store (hard delete).
EVT_INITNEW	64	This is the first firing of the event. It is set only once during the lifetime of a created event sink.
EVT_MOVE	256	The item was moved, which resulted in an implicit delete.

USING THE ONSAVE EVENT PROCEDURE

The OnSave event is triggered after a resource is saved. A save can occur when a new resource is created, when an existing resource is changed and resaved, or when a resource is copied or moved to a new location. The syntax for the OnSave event method is:

```
Private Sub IExStoreAsyncEvents_OnSave( _
ByVal pEventInfo As Exoledb.IExStoreEventInfo, _
ByVal bstrURLItem As String, _
ByVal lFlags As Long)

'Enter code here

End Sub
```

Where:

pEventInfo

is a pointer to the IExStoreEventInfo interface. In an OnSave event, it provides a reference to the registration item that called the event sink. You cannot use this parameter to access the event item.

bstrURLItem

is the URL of the event item that triggered the event. Use it in an asynchronous event sink to access the event item.

lFlags

is a long integer that contains the status information about the OnSave event and can be used to determine the type of save occurring. Table 9.4 lists the possible values of lFlags in an OnSave event procedure. You can also use a combination of these values.

Table 9.4   OnSave lFlags values

lFlags constant	Value	This flag means...
EVT_NEW_ITEM	1	The saved item is new.
EVT_IS_COLLECTION	2	The saved item is a collection.
EVT_REPLICATED_ITEM	4	The item was saved as a result of replication.
EVT_IS_DELIVERED	8	The item was saved as the result of message delivery.
EVT_INITNEW	64	This is the first firing of the event. It is set only once during the lifetime of a created event sink.
EVT_MOVE	256	The item was saved as the result of a move.
EVT_COPY	512	The item was saved as the result of a copy.

TIP Replicated items trigger save events in the same way that any other item does. To avoid executing code on a replicated item, test for an lFlags value of EVT_REPLICATED_ITEM.

ACCESSING THE EVENT ITEM IN AN ASYNCHRONOUS EVENT SINK

Because asynchronous events fire after an event occurs, you can use the bstrURLItem parameter value to access the event item with an ADO Record object. For example, the following code sample shows how to open an event item in an asynchronous event sink and read the DAV:contentclass value:

```
Dim rec As ADODB.Record
Dim strContentClass As String

Set rec = New ADODB.Record
rec.Open bstrURLItem, , adModeRead

strContentClass = rec.Fields("DAV:contentclass")
```

REACTING TO SYSTEM EVENTS

System events do not react to data requests. Instead, system events fire upon a particular system occurrence, such as the starting of a database. System events behave similarly to asynchronous events; they do not fire until after the Web Storage System completes the action that triggers the event. For example, the OnMDBShutDown event is triggered only after a database shuts down.

Figure 9.7 shows the behavior of system events. When a system action occurs and completes, a system event is triggered. If an event registration item is found for the system event, the appropriate out-of-process event sink is called.

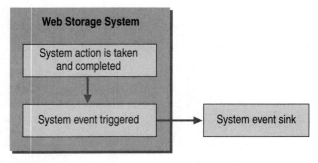

Figure 9.7
System events behave like asynchronous events—they are not called until the Web Storage System process finishes executing.

USING THE ONMDBSTARTUP EVENT PROCEDURE

The syntax for the OnMDBStartUp event method is:

```
Private Sub IExStoreSystemEvents_OnMDBStartUp( _
 ByVal bstrMDBGuid As String, _
 ByVal bstrMDBName As String, _
 ByVal lFlags As Long)

 'Enter code here

 End Sub
```

The bstrMDBGuid parameter is a string globally unique identifier (GUID) that identifies the database that starts, and bstrMDBName is a string that indicates the actual name of the database. The lFlags parameter is not used in an OnMDBStartup event.

USING THE ONMDBSHUTDOWN EVENT PROCEDURE

The syntax for the OnMDBShutDown event procedure is:

```
Private Sub IExStoreSystemEvents_OnMDBShutDown( _
 ByVal bstrMDBGuid As String, _
 ByVal lFlags As Long)

 'Enter code here

 End Sub
```

The bstrMDBGuid parameter is a string GUID that identifies which database shuts down. The lFlags parameter is not used in an OnMDBShutDown event.

USING THE ONTIMER EVENT PROCEDURE

The syntax for the OnTimer event procedure is:

```
Private Sub IExStoreSystemEvents_OnTimer( _
 ByVal pEventRegistrationUrl As Exoledb.IExStoreEventRegistrationURL, _
 ByVal lFlags As Long)
```

```
    'Enter code here

End Sub
```

The pEventRegistrationUrl parameter is the URL of the event registration item. The lFlags parameter is not used in an OnTimer event.

INSTALLING THE EVENT SINK AS A COM+ APPLICATION

After you build the event sink procedures, you are ready to install the event sink as a COM+ application on the server. Installing an event sink involves three steps: making the .dll file, registering the .dll file on the server, and creating the COM components for the DLL interfaces and methods.

MAKING THE .DLL FILE

So that the event sink is accessible to the Web Storage System, you must make a .dll file and register it on the Exchange server computer. To make the .dll file, open the event sink project in Visual Basic. On the **File** menu, click **Make [yourproject].dll**. The **Make Project** dialog box appears, and you must choose the file path and name for the .dll file. You can create the file in just about any folder, but it must physically reside on the server machine.

REGISTERING THE .DLL FILE

After you make the .dll file, you can register it on the server. You can use the Regsvr32 tool (Regsvr32.exe) to register and unregister the .dll file. Regsvr32.exe is included with Microsoft Internet Explorer 3 and later and is installed in the System32 folder on the server running Microsoft Windows 2000. RegSvr32.exe has the following command-line options:

```
Regsvr32 [/u] [/n] [/i[:cmdline]] dllname

    /u - Unregister server
    /i - Call DllInstall passing it an optional [cmdline];
         when used with /u calls dll uninstall
    /n - do not call DllRegisterServer; this option must
         be used with /i
```

To use Regsvr32.exe, open a command window, or click the **Start** button and then click **Run**. To register a .dll file, type the following code:

```
regsvr32 "[full dll path]"
```

where "[full dll path]" is a string that contains the folder path and name of the .dll file. The following code sample registers the ZooMgtEventSink.dll file:

```
regsvr32 "D:\Zoo Management\Event Sinks\ZooMgtEventSink.dll"
```

To unregister the .dll file, pass the /u option along with the full .dll path. The following code sample unregisters the ZooMgtEventSink.dll file:

```
regsvr32 /u "D:\Zoo Management\Event Sinks\ZooMgtEventSink.dll"
```

If the registration is successful, a success message appears. If the attempt is unsuccessful, Regsvr32.exe returns an error message, which might include a Win32 error code. For a list of Win32 error codes and more information about the details of using Regsvr32.exe, see the Microsoft Developer Network (MSDN) Web site.

CREATING THE COM+ COMPONENTS

The final step to register an event sink is to create COM+ components for the DLL interfaces and methods. Exchange does not allow event sinks to run in process with a Web Storage System process. Because a DLL runs in process by default, you must create out-of-process COM+ components for the DLL components so that the event sink is called successfully. If this is the first time that you are creating an event sink, you must create a COM+ application to hold the event sink components before you add the components. If you have already created a COM+ application for the event sink, you can simply add the COM+ components.

CREATING A NEW COM+ APPLICATION FOR EVENT SINK COMPONENTS

To create a COM+ application for the event sink, you use the Component Services console in Microsoft Management Console (MMC). To create the application, follow these steps:

1. Click the **Start** button, and then point to **Programs**. Point to **Administrative Tools**, and then click **Component Services**.

2. Expand **Component Services**, and then double-click the **COM+ Applications** folder. This folder contains all existing COM+ applications. Component Services in MMC should look something like Figure 9.8.

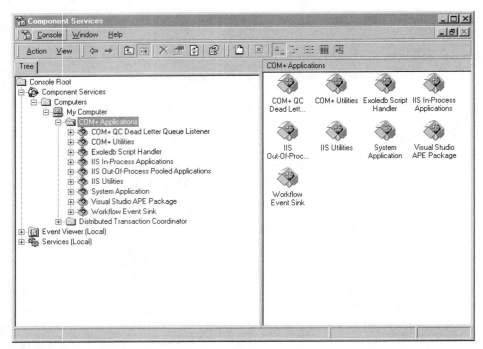

Figure 9.8
Component Services in MMC in Windows 2000

3. Right-click the **Components** folder and click **New**. On the shortcut menu, click **Application**, and then on the **Welcome to the COM Application Install Wizard** page, click **Next** (see Figure 9.9).

Figure 9.9
The Welcome page of the COM Application Install Wizard

4. On the **Install or Create a New Application** page, click **Create an empty application** to create a new application (see Figure 9.10).

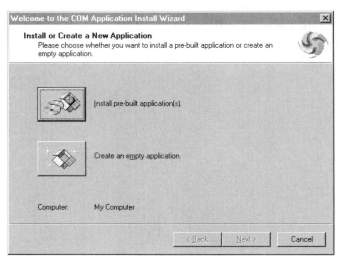

Figure 9.10
Create a new COM+ application.

5. On the **Create Empty Application** page, type a name for the application in the **Enter a name for the new application** text box. Select **Server application** as the Activation type (see Figure 9.11), and then click **Next**.

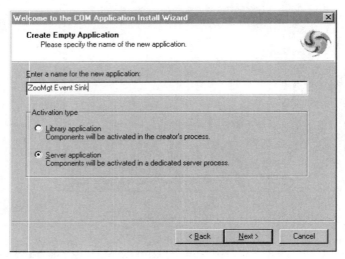

Figure 9.11
Name the new server application.

6. On the **Set Application Identity** page, select **This user** and browse for the appropriate account for running event sinks (see Figure 9.12). Enter a password if necessary, and then click **Next**.

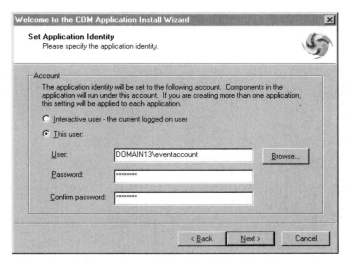

Figure 9.12
Select the user account for executing the event sink code.

7. On the **Thank you** page, click **Finish** to close the wizard.

ADDING COMPONENTS TO A COM+ APPLICATION

After you create a new COM+ application, you can add components to the application. The components encapsulate each of the class modules in the event sink DLL. To add COM+ components to the event sink COM+ application, follow these steps:

1. Click the **Start** button, and then point to **Programs**. Point to **Administrative Tools**, and then click **Component Services**.

2. Expand **Component Services**, and then double-click the COM+ application you have created for the event sink components.

3. Click the **Components** folder to open it. This folder contains all existing components for the application.

4. To add a new component, right-click the **Components** folder and click **New**. On the shortcut menu, click **Component**, and then on the **COM Component Install Wizard Welcome** page, click **Next**.

5. On the **Import or Install a Component** page, click the **Install new component(s)** button to create new COM+ components for a DLL (see Figure 9.13).

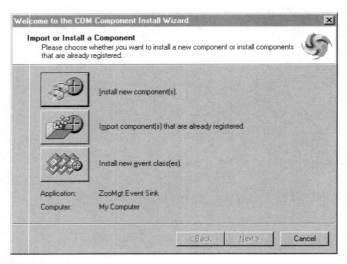

Figure 9.13
To create COM+ components for the event sink components, click the Install new component(s) button.

6. On the **Install new components** page, click your ActiveX DLL to load the class modules (see Figure 9.14). Click **Add**, and then locate the .dll file that you already registered. After adding the DLL, the wizard checks the details and creates a component for each class module in your project. When it is finished, click **Next**.

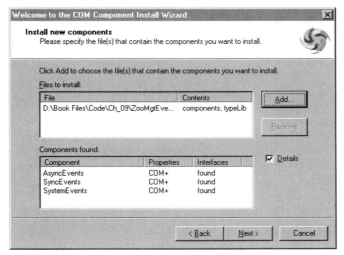

Figure 9.14
When you add your .dll file, the wizard automatically creates a component for each class module in the project.

7. On the **Thank you** page, click **Finish** to close the wizard.

Components Services should now show at least one new component in the Components folder of your COM+ application event sink. A new component is created for each class module in your project. Each component, in turn, contains methods for each exposed Exchange interface. Figure 9.15 shows the new COM+ application.

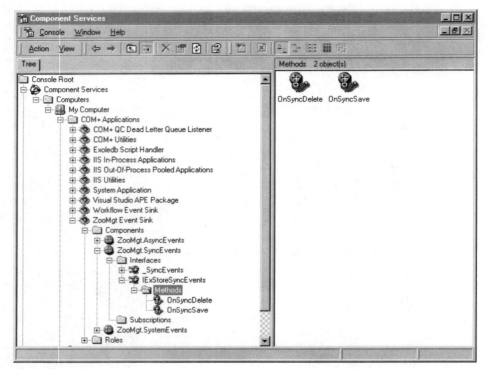

Figure 9.15
Each method on the implemented Exchange interfaces is added as a component of the COM application.

CHANGING AN EVENT SINK

If you make changes to the code in the event sink Visual Basic project, you need to remake the .dll file and register it again to replace the old .dll file with the new .dll file. You do not, however, need to recreate the COM application components.

If you add another class module to the .dll file though, you will need to create a new COM component for the new class module. To add a new component, follow these steps:

1. Click the **Start** button, and then point to **Programs**. Point to **Administrative Tools**, and then click **Component Services**.

2. Expand **Component Services** until you see the event sink COM+ Application you already created, and then double-click the **Components** folder to open it.

3. Right-click the **Components** folder, and then click **New**. On the shortcut menu, click **Component**, and then on the COM Component Install Wizard Welcome page, click **Next**.

4. On the **Import or Install a Component** page, click the **Import Components that are already registered** button.

5. On the **Choose Components to Import** page, select the name of the new class module from the list of registered components, and then click **Next**. The name of the class module will be prefixed with the name of the project.

6. On the **Thank you** page, click **Finish** to close the wizard.

You can also make changes to the COM+ application that manages the event sink. For example, you can change the user account the event sink is running as, enable role-based security, add a description to the event, and indicate how debugging is handled. To make changes to the COM+ application, right-click **COM+ application** in the **Component Services** dialog box, and then click **Properties**.

CREATING AN EVENT REGISTRATION ITEM

For an event sink to fire for a particular event, you must create an event registration item. An *event registration item* is a hidden item that contains the ProgID of the event sink, information about what Web Storage System events will trigger the event sink, and options such as restricting when the event sink is called. You create the event registration item in the same folder that is being monitored. This section explains how to create an event registration item with either ADO or a special script tool, known as RegEvent, which can be used in batch files. This section also describes how to manage event registration items.

> **NOTE**   To create an event registration item, you must be an owner of the parent folder that will contain the event registration item.

CREATING AN EVENT REGISTRATION ITEM BY USING ADO

To create a new event registration item, you create a new item in the folder triggering the event. For example, if you want to trap when new items are added to a Web Storage System folder called Surgery, you create the event registration item in the Surgery folder. If you want the event sink to fire for a parent folder and the child folders, you only need to create the event registration item in the parent folder.

To create a new event registration item by using ADO, you create the appropriate item type, set some required event properties, and possibly set some optional event properties:

1. To create the event item type, create a new ADO Record object and set the DAV:contentclass schema property to urn:content-class:storeeventreg. If you set this content class, the new item will have the schema properties for registering for events associated with it.

2. Next, you must set two required properties to identify the event or events to associate with an event sink and the name of the event sink being called.

3. You can also set some optional event properties to get specific behavior from the event registration, such as adding a filter to restrict the event items.

4. After you have set the properties, save the item. The event and event sink are now linked to each other.

Listing 9.2 shows two procedures: CreateEventReg, which shows how to use ADO to associate an event with an event sink, and AddQuotes, which is called by CreateEventReg to wrap text strings in additional quotes. The CreateEventReg procedure registers for the OnSave asynchronous event in the Zoo Management application Surgery folder to call the ZooMgt.AsyncEvents event sink. Along with the required properties, the procedure sets some optional properties including one that indicates only items visible in a client application will call the event sink. The procedure also configures the event registration item so that an item added to a child folder will also trigger the event sink.

Listing 9.2 Create a new event registration item in the Zoo Management Surgery folder.

```
Sub CreateEventReg()
    ' To create an event registration,
    ' you create the item, set some the
    ' required properties, set any optional
    ' properties, and save the item.

    Dim urlEventFolder As String
    Dim urlEventRegItem As String

    ' Use constants for the events properties
    Const PROP_EVENTMETHOD As String _
        = "http://schemas.microsoft.com/exchange/events/EventMethod"
    Const PROP_SINKCLASS As String _
        = "http://schemas.microsoft.com/exchange/events/SinkClass"
    Const PROP_PRIORITY As String _
        = "http://schemas.microsoft.com/exchange/events/priority"
    Const PROP_MATCHSCOPE As String _
        = "http://schemas.microsoft.com/exchange/events/matchScope"
    Const PROP_CRITERIA As String _
        = "http://schemas.microsoft.com/exchange/events/criteria"

    ' Build URLs to the folder and the new item
    urlEventFolder = _
        GetStorageName & "/applications/zoo management/animals/"
    'urlEventFolder = _
        GetStorageName & "/applications/zoo management/surgery/"
    urlEventRegItem = urlEventFolder & "zooeventreg.eml"

    With New ADODB.Record
        ' Create a new event registration in the taget folder
        .Open urlEventRegItem _
            , _
            , adModeReadWrite _
            , adCreateNonCollection + adCreateOverwrite
        .Fields("DAV:contentclass") _
            = "urn:content-class:storeeventreg"
```

```
    ' Set the required event properties
    .Fields(PROP_EVENTMETHOD) = "OnSave"
    .Fields(PROP_SINKCLASS) = "ZooMgt.AsyncEvents"

    ' Set some optional event properties
    .Fields(PROP_MATCHSCOPE) = "deep"
    .Fields(PROP_PRIORITY) = "0x3f"
    .Fields(PROP_CRITERIA) = _
        "WHERE " & AddQuotes("DAV:ishidden") & " = FALSE"

    ' Save the changes
    .Fields.Update
  End With

  Debug.Print "Event registration item created successfully."
End Sub


Public Function AddQuotes(strValue As String) As String
    ' Given a string, wrap it in quotes, doubling
    ' any quotes within the string.

    Const QUOTE = """"
    AddQuotes = QUOTE & _
        Replace(strValue, QUOTE, QUOTE & QUOTE) & QUOTE
End Function
```

TIP   Both required and optional properties reside in the
http://schemas.microsoft.com/exchange/event namespace. Unfortunately,
these properties do not have any CDO constant equivalents. If you want to
avoid always using the full schema property name, you can define your own
custom constants in the registering application.

If your application uses only one event type, such as the OnSyncSave event, you
need to create only one event registration item. If your application uses more than
one event type, such as the OnSyncSave event and the OnTimer event, you might
need to create multiple event registration items because different event sources use
different registration properties. You can still call class modules from the same DLL.

TIP You can use the Event Registration tool included on the companion CD to create event registration items and return information about existing event registration items.

SETTING THE REQUIRED EVENT PROPERTIES

For an event to successfully trigger an event sink, you must set these two event properties on the event registration item:

- http://schemas.microsoft.com/exchange/events/EventMethod. This identifies the source events that trigger the event sink.

- http://schemas.microsoft.com/exchange/events/SinkClass. This identifies the event sink called by the events.

TIP CDO does not provide constants for these properties, so you must create your own constants.

IDENTIFYING THE SOURCE EVENTS

To identify which events will call the event sink, you set the http://schemas.microsoft.com/exchange/events/EventMethod schema property to a string value that contains the names of the source events. For example, to register for the OnSyncSave event, your code would look like this:

```
rec.Fields _
    ("http://schemas.microsoft.com/exchange/events/EventMethod") _
    = "onsyncsave"
```

You can use a single event registration item to register for more than one event. To register for multiple events, pass the list of event names, separating the values with semicolons. For example, the following code sample shows how to properly register for both the OnSave event and the OnDelete event:

```
rec.Fields _
    ("http://schemas.microsoft.com/exchange/events/EventMethod") _
    = "onsave;ondelete"
```

You can register for multiple events by using the same event registration item only when the events have access to register the same optional properties. For example, you can create a single event registration for OnSyncDelete, OnSyncSave, OnDelete, and OnSave. You can also create a single event registration for OnMDBStartUp and OnMDBShutDown. However, you cannot mix the two categories in a single event registration item. The OnTimer event must always have its own registration item.

IDENTIFYING THE EVENT SINK

To identify the event sink that is called by the events listed in the http://schemas.microsoft.com/exchange/events/EventMethods property, you set the http://schemas.microsoft.com/exchange/events/SinkClass schema property to a string value that contains the name of a registered event sink. This is the sink that contains the code to execute whenever the specified event fires. If you have properly registered your event sink DLL as a COM+ component, the name of the sink is a combination of the project name, followed by a dot (.), and the class module name.

For example, the following code sample indicates that the ZooMgt.AsyncEvents event sink component should be called whenever the events specified in the http://schemas.microsoft.com/exchange/events/EventMethods property fire:

```
rec.Fields _
    ("http://schemas.microsoft.com/exchange/events/SinkClass") _
    = "ZooMgt.AsyncEvents"
```

SETTING OPTIONAL EVENT PROPERTIES

If you want more control over how and when an event calls an event sink, you can set a few additional event properties for an event registration item. By using optional event properties, you can restrict an event sink from being triggered by child folders, set the event firing priority among multiple synchronous event sinks, and restrict which items will actually trigger an event. Table 9.5 describes each of the optional properties.

Table 9.5   Optional properties for an event registration item

http://schemas.microsoft.com/ exchange/events/ property	Description
matchScope	Identifies the range of folders and items affected by the event registration.
criteria	Restricts the event sink from executing unless certain conditions are met.
priority	Establishes a firing order among multiple event registrations of the same type in the same folder.
TimerStartTime	Indicates the number of minutes after the event registration item is created that Exchange begins firing the OnTimer event.
TimerExpiryTime	Indicates the number of minutes past the TimerStartTime that Exchange ceases to fire the OnTimer event.
TimerInterval	Indicates the number of minutes between firings of the OnTimer event.
enabled	If True, the associated event sink executes. The default value is True.

DEFINING THE RANGE OF AN EVENT REGISTRATION ITEM

By default, an event registration triggers an event sink when any resource in a parent folder is created or changed in any way. If you want the event registration to also cover actions in child folders, you need to set the http://schemas.microsoft.com/exchange/event/matchScope schema property. To identify the range affected by an event registration item, set the http://schemas.microsoft.com/exchange/event/matchScope schema property to one of the values in Table 9.6.

Table 9.6 Possible string values for setting the scope of an event

matchScope value	Applies to	Description
Exact	Asynchronous	Fires only for items in that folder.
Deep	Asynchronous, Synchronous	Fires for items in that folder as well as items in child folders.
Shallow	Synchronous	Fires only for items in that folder.
Any	Synchronous	Fires in the scope of the database.

When an event sink is registered for a parent folder and is also triggered by its subfolders, it is called a recursive event. *Recursive events* can be registered at only the top-level folder of a folder tree. Once registered, any new child folders that are added to the top-level folder will inherit the ability to trigger the event.

For example, the following code sample defines a registration item that will apply to the parent folder in which it is created as well as for any child folders.

```
Rec.Fields _
    ("http://schemas.microsoft.com/exchange/events/matchScope") _
    = "deep"
```

NOTES Recursive events are new in Exchange 2000. In Exchange 5.5, if you wanted to register an event agent on more than one folder, you added the agent explicitly to the parent folder as well as every subfolder.

Because system events are not associated with a particular folder in the Web Storage System, they cannot have a scope. Therefore, if you create an event registration for events that will use a scope, you cannot initialize a system event in the same registration.

RESTRICTING EVENT ITEMS

Often, you don't need an event sink to run for every item that can potentially trigger the event. For instance, maybe you want the event sink to run for only Appointment items, or maybe you need the event sink to execute only when a Microsoft Office document is added to a folder. If you want to restrict the event sink to fire only when items fit certain criteria, you can set the http://schemas.microsoft.com/exchange/event/criteria schema property to a Structured Query Language (SQL) WHERE clause. In the clause, you can use the standard comparison operators such as AND, OR, NOT, and EXISTS.

For example, the following code sample restricts the event sink to firing for only those items that are visible in a user interface, restricting the event from firing when new event registrations are added, modified, or deleted:

```
rec.Fields _
    ("http://schemas.microsoft.com/exchange/events/criteria") _
    = "WHERE " & AddQuotes("DAV:ishidden") & " = FALSE"
```

As with all SQL queries of a Web Storage System, you must enclose property names to be evaluated in double quotes. The AddQuotes function takes a string value and puts quotes around it. For more information about using the AddQuotes function and building SQL queries, see Chapter 4, "ActiveX Data Objects and Exchange."

The firing criteria are limited to information that pertains to the item. It is not possible to specify conditions on data outside of this item for the firing criteria. If you use custom properties, they must be explicitly cast to the proper type, like in this code sample:

```
"WHERE cast($MyNumber$ as 'i4')<>11"
```

Although you could perform any of this filtering in the event sink by using If..End If or a Select Case structure, filtering at the registration item is highly recommended. This is because the event registration item conducts the filtering directly in the Web Storage System, meaning that it occurs in process with the Web Storage System thread. The event sink is called only if an item qualifies. Because event sinks are out of process, each call to the event sink is costly in terms of resources. If filtering were done in the sink, the sink would have to fire before the filter could be applied. This would result in poor application performance.

Prioritizing Multiple Event Registrations

You can create more than one registration event item for the same folder. This means that you can call more than one event sink for the same event. Although asynchronous events (including system events) fire in random order, multiple synchronous event registrations can be initialized to fire in a particular order. For example, if you have three different event registrations on the same folder for the OnSyncSave event, each one uses a filter to determine which item will trigger which event sink. However, one event sink is more likely to fire than the other two, and the second is more likely to fire than the third. In this case, you should set the event registration most likely to catch the item to fire first, followed by the second most likely event registration item, and finally the least likely event registration item.

To order synchronous event registrations in this manner, you set the http://schemas.microsoft.com/exchange/event/priority schema property to a long value. The highest priority value fires first. Figure 9.16 shows the direct correlation between the priority value and the firing order. The higher the priority value, the higher the firing order. The value 0x00000000 has the highest priority and will fire before all others. The value 0xffffffff has the lowest priority and will fire only after all other synchronous event registrations have fired. The default value 0x0000ffff is right in the middle.

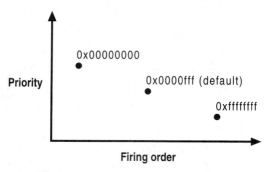

Figure 9.16
The order in which a synchronous event sink fires correlates directly to its priority value.

Consider the three event registration items discussed at the beginning of this section. If EventReg1 has a priority of 0x0000ffff, EventReg2 has a priority of 0xffffffff, and EventReg3 has a priority of 0x00000000, the actual firing order is: EventReg3, EventReg1, and EventReg2. The following code sample shows how the priority is actually set:

```
Rec.Fields _
    ("http://schemas.microsoft.com/exchange/event/priority") _
    = "0x00000000"
```

NOTE Recursive synchronous event sinks fire before any normal sink registered on a subfolder. If there are multiple recursive sinks, the sink priorities are used to decide which recursive sink is run first.

REGISTERING FOR AN ONTIMER EVENT

If you create an event sink for the system event, OnTimer, you need to set some event schema properties specific to timing for the event to fire correctly. The properties used for registering an OnTimer event are:

- **TimerStartTime**. The number of minutes after the event registration item is created that Exchange begins firing the OnTimer event.

- **TimerExpiryTime**. The number of minutes past the TimerStartTime that Exchange ceases to fire the OnTimer event.

- **TimerInterval**. The number of minutes between firings of the OnTimer event. If not set, the event fires only once.

CREATING AN EVENT REGISTRATION BY USING THE REGEVENT SCRIPT

An alternative to using ADO to register for an event is to use the RegEvent.vbs script installed with Exchange 2000 Server.

The RegEvent script can be called directly from a command window, or it can be implemented in a command file. Essentially, this approach to event registration is for developers who prefer to create batch files and who are accustomed to creating command scripts. To create a registration event item with RegEvent.vbs, use the following syntax:

```
cscript RegEvent.vbs Add
                        EventName
                        SinkClass
                        Scope
                        [-p Priority]
                        [-m MatchScope]
                        [-f CriteriaFilter]
```

Where:

EventName

is the name of the event that is being initialized: OnSave, OnDelete, OnSyncSave, OnSyncDelete, OnMDBStartup, OnMDBShutDown, or OnTimer. Separate multiple events with semicolons.

SinkClass

is the name of the event sink as it is registered on the server.

Scope

is the fully qualified URL name of the event registration item to be created in the Web Storage System.

Priority

is an optional parameter that indicates the order to be run.

MatchScope

is an optional parameter that indicates whether child items and folders will fire the event as well. It can be one of the following values: DEEP, SHALLOW, EXACT, ANY. Bindings with no defined scope default to EXACT.

CriteriaFilter

is an optional parameter. It is a SQL WHERE clause that defines additional conditions that a triggering item must meet for the sink to be notified of the event.

NOTE The parameters used by RegEvent script command do not have the same names as their schema property equivalents.

To create an event registration item so that the OnSyncSave event triggers the appoinment.handler sink on all the subfolders and child items in the Web Storage System folder Surgery you would write script like this:

```
cscript eventadmin.vbs Add OnSyncSave appointments.handler
file://./backofficestorage/domain.com/applications/Zoo
Management/Surgery -m Deep
```

MANAGING EVENT REGISTRATION ITEMS

After you successfully create an event registration item in a folder, you will probably need to revisit it at least once. This section discusses some of the ways to manage event registrations.

RETURNING EVENT REGISTRATION INFORMATION

If you want to know if a folder has an event sink already registered, you can search the folder for all event registration items by building an SQL query that restricts the results to items with a DAV:contentclass value of urn:content-class:storeeventreg.

For example, Listing 9.3 shows how to return event registration information for every event registration item in a folder. The procedure takes one parameter, urlQueryFld, which is the URL of the folder to query. In this example, the procedure uses constants for the schema property names.

Listing 9.3   Return information on the event registration items in a particular folder.

```
Sub ReturnEventRegItems(urlQueryFld As String)
    ' Returns all event registration items
    ' at the folder URL passed to the procedure.

    Dim cnn As ADODB.Connection
    Dim rst As ADODB.Recordset
    Dim strSQL As String
    Dim v As Variant

    ' Use constants for the events properties
    Const PROP_EVENTMETHOD As String _
        = "http://schemas.microsoft.com/exchange/events/EventMethod"
    Const PROP_SINKCLASS As String _
        = "http://schemas.microsoft.com/exchange/events/SinkClass"
    Const PROP_PRIORITY As String _
        = "http://schemas.microsoft.com/exchange/events/priority"
    Const PROP_MATCHSCOPE As String _
        = "http://schemas.microsoft.com/exchange/events/matchScope"
    Const PROP_CRITERIA As String _
        = "http://schemas.microsoft.com/exchange/events/criteria"
```

```
' Connect to the folder
Set cnn = New ADODB.Connection
With cnn
    .Provider = "exoledb.datasource"
    .Open urlQueryFld
End With

' Select the properties to be returned
strSQL = "Select " & _
    AddQuotes("DAV:displayname") & ", " & _
    AddQuotes("DAV:href") & ", " & _
    AddQuotes(PROP_EVENTMETHOD) & ", " & _
    AddQuotes(PROP_SINKCLASS) & ", " & _
    AddQuotes(PROP_PRIORITY) & ", " & _
    AddQuotes(PROP_MATCHSCOPE) & ", " & _
    AddQuotes(PROP_CRITERIA)
' Indicate shallow or deep traversal
' and what URL to begin looking
strSQL = strSQL & _
    " FROM SCOPE('SHALLOW traversal of " & _
    AddQuotes(urlQueryFld) & "')"
' Build a filter
strSQL = strSQL & _
    " WHERE (" & _
    AddQuotes("DAV:contentclass") & _
    " = 'urn:content-class:storeeventreg')"
' Sort the results by the display name
strSQL = strSQL & _
    " ORDER BY " & AddQuotes("DAV:displayname") & " DESC"

' Get the results of the query
Set rst = New ADODB.Recordset
rst.Open strSQL, cnn

Debug.Print "-------------------------------------------------"
Debug.Print "Folder registration report for: "
Debug.Print urlQueryFld
Debug.Print "-------------------------------------------------"
```

```
      ' Check to see if any items were returned.
   If rst.EOF And rst.BOF Then
      Debug.Print "No event registration items found."
   Else
      ' Return information about the event registration item
      Do Until rst.EOF
         Debug.Print rst.Fields("DAV:displayname")
         Debug.Print "Events: " & rst.Fields(PROP_EVENTMETHOD)
         Debug.Print "Sink class: " & rst.Fields(PROP_SINKCLASS)
         Debug.Print "Priority level: " & rst.Fields(PROP_PRIORITY)
         Debug.Print "Match scope: " & rst.Fields(PROP_MATCHSCOPE)
         Debug.Print "Criteria: " & rst.Fields(PROP_CRITERIA)
         rst.MoveNext
      Loop
   End If

   ' Close objects and clean up
   rst.Close
   cnn.Close
   Set rst = Nothing
   Set cnn = Nothing
End Sub
```

TIP You can use the Event Registration tool included on the companion CD to create event registration items and return information about existing event registration items.

DISABLING AN EVENT REGISTRATION

To disable an event registration item and prevent it from calling an event sink, set the http://schemas.microsoft.com/exchange/event/enabled property to False. Disabling an event registration item does not remove it from the Web Storage System, but stops it from triggering any code. You can always enable the event registration item again by setting the http://schemas.microsoft.com/exchange/event/enabled property to True. Listing 9.4 shows how to disable an event registration item to stop an event sink from firing.

Listing 9.4 Disable an event registration item.

```
Sub DisableEventRegItem()
    ' By disabling an event registration
    ' item, you can prevent an event sink from
    ' being called.

    Dim urlEventRegItem As String

    ' URL to the event registration item
    ' to be disabled.
    urlEventRegItem = GetStorageName & _
        "applications/zoo management/surgery/eventreg.eml"

    With New ADODB.Record
        ' Open the event registration item
        .Open urlEventRegItem, , adModeReadWrite
        ' Disable the event registration
        .Fields(propEnabled) = False
        .Fields.Update
    End With
End Sub
```

DELETING AN EVENT REGISTRATION

Because an event registration item is just another item in a Web Storage System folder, you can delete it like any other item. To delete an event registration item and remove it completely from the folder, use the DeleteRecord method of a Record object. Listing 9.5 shows how to delete an event registration on a public folder.

Listing 9.5 Delete an event registration item.

```
Sub DeleteEventRegItem()
    ' You can delete an event registration
    ' item just like any other item.

    Dim urlEventRegItem As String

    ' URL to the event registration item
    ' to be deleted.
    urlEventRegItem = GetStorageName & _
        "applications/zoo management/surgery/eventreg.eml"

    ' Open the item to be deleted
    With New ADODB.Record
        .Open urlEventRegItem, , adModeReadWrite
        .DeleteRecord
    End With

    Debug.Print urlEventRegItem & " has been deleted."
End Sub
```

USING CUSTOM PROPERTIES WITH EVENTS

With synchronous, asynchronous, and system events, you can pass custom information from an event registration item to an event sink, create custom properties for client applications, and create custom properties for server applications. For example, you can use a custom property on an event registration to identify the type of application that is calling the event sink. In this way, you can use the same event sink for multiple applications and use custom fields to identify exactly which application triggered the sink.

To use custom properties with events, you must use custom code on both the event registration item and the event sink. You add code to an event registration item to define custom properties and assign a value to each property. You use code in an event sink to read the value of a custom property.

DEFINING CUSTOM PROPERTIES IN THE EVENT REGISTRATION ITEM

You create custom properties for events by appending them to an event
registration item. To use ADO to append a custom property to an item, create or
open the event registration item with an ADO Record object and call the
Fields.Append method. Although the Append method has several optional
parameters, only a name for the property, the data type, and the value are
required. After appending the custom field, call the Update method to save the
changes. For example, the following code sample creates the
zoomgt:events:appName custom property on an event registration item:

```
With New ADODB.Record
    ' Create a new item
    .Open urlEventRegItem _

        , _
        , adModeReadWrite _
        , adCreateNonCollection + adCreateOverwrite

    ' Set the required properties
    ' Set the optional properties

    ' Append a new string property
    ' and set the value
    .Fields.Append _
        "zoomgt:events:appName" _
        , adChar _

        , _

        , _
        , "SurgeryMgt"

    ' Save the changes
    .Fields.Update
End With
```

For more information about using the Fields.Append method of a Record object, see Chapter 4, "ActiveX Data Objects and Exchange."

READING THE CUSTOM FIELDS IN THE EVENT SINK

Custom properties on an event registration item are passed along to an event sink with the item that triggered the event. To access a custom property in the event sink, you must open an ADO Record object for the event information item by using the EventRecord method. Once the record is open, you can access the custom property from the event registration by using the Fields property of the ADO Record object. For example, the following code sample reads the zoomgt:events:appName custom property:

```
Dim iEventInfo As IExStoreDispEventInfo
Dim rec As New ADODB.Record

' Open an ADO record with the event information
Set iEventInfo = pEventInfo
Set rec = iEventInfo.EventRecord

If rec.Fields(propname) _
   = "zoomgt:events:appName" Then
   ' The event registration calling the sink
   ' is the zoo management application

   ' Do something here

End If
```

NOTE Like all schema property names, custom property names are case sensitive.

INVESTIGATING EVENT ERRORS WITH THE APPLICATION LOG

Like other applications, ExOLEDB logs information in the Windows 2000 Application event log when an error occurs in a Web Storage System event. Using Event Viewer, you might be able to determine what went wrong with your application. If you are an administrator of the server running Exchange 2000, you can use Event Viewer to browse the Application log for errors. The Application log contains information about what went wrong when the event attempted to execute the event sink. Table 9.7 lists some of the potential reports made by Exchange.

Table 9.7   Possible log entries reported by the ExOLEDB provider in the Windows 2000 Application event log

Entry	Description
EVENTS_BINDING_DISABLED	ExOLEDB has disabled the event binding due to problems in the event sink.
EVENTS_INVALID_BINDING	ExOLEDB was unable to load event binding.
EVENTS_INVALID_CRITERIA_FILTER	ExOLEDB was unable to process the event criteria filter specified.
EVENTS_INVALID_PROPERTY_VALUE	ExOLEDB was unable to initialize event binding.
EVENTS_INVALID_SINK_CLASS	ExOLEDB was unable to create an event sink object or get necessary interface(s) from the sink class.
EVENTS_MISSING_PROPERTY	ExOLEDB was unable to initialize event binding.
EVENTS_UNABLE_TO_INITIALIZE_SOURCE	ExOLEDB was unable to initialize event binding for the Web Storage System.

Continued on next page

Table 9.7 continued   Possible log entries reported by the ExOLEDB provider in the Windows 2000 Application event log

Entry	Description
EVENTS_UNABLE_TO_REGISTER_BINDING	ExOLEDB was unable to register an event binding.
EXOLEDB_FAILED_TO_REGISTER_OBJECTS	ExOLEDB was unable to successfully register COM objects.

SUMMARY

You don't need to use Web Storage System events to build a useful collaboration application with Exchange 2000. However, events can turn an application that merely does the job into one that truly makes a difference in the workplace. You can use any of the Web Storage System events to make your applications responsive. You can use synchronous events to react after a client has issued a data request but before the Web Storage System processes that request, asynchronous events to react after Exchange has processed some data request, and system events to react to some system action.

Chapter 10, "Designing Workflow Applications," explains how you can build workflow applications by using Workflow Designer for Exchange and the CDO Workflow for Exchange 2000 object model.

10

Designing Workflow Applications

Workflow is server-side logic that you can use to route items in a folder from one user to another as well as to enforce and track an item throughout its lifetime. A folder has traditionally been nothing more than a container. It can hold just about anything—items such as messages and contacts, other folders, or structured documents such as Microsoft Word documents and Active Server Pages (ASP pages)—but it can't automatically do anything other than store these items. After an item is created in a folder, that's basically the end of it. However, by using the workflow functionality provided by Microsoft Exchange 2000 Server, you can have more control over the behavior of an item in a folder. For example, you can use workflow logic to alert a particular person when something needs to be done to an item in a folder, track where an item has been and where it needs to go, and alter the item as it progresses through the workflow process.

This chapter explains how to build workflow applications by using Workflow Designer for Exchange and the Collaboration Data Objects (CDO) Workflow for Exchange 2000 object model. Sections include:

- **Overview of Workflow**

- **Before You Begin**

- **Using Workflow Designer for Exchange**

- **Scripting the Workflow Item**

- **Debugging Workflow Script**

OVERVIEW OF WORKFLOW

This section provides background information about workflow, explains the workflow process and workflow actions, and discusses how to set security and build workflow applications.

WORKFLOW BACKGROUND

The term *workflow* means a variety of things to people. Ask seven people to define workflow, and you'll probably get seven very different responses. In Exchange, workflow is server-side logic that routes items that enforce specific behaviors and tracks the progress of those items. You can create ad hoc, unstructured workflow applications, such as routing slips in Microsoft Office or the voting button in Microsoft Outlook. However, team-processing applications are much more common. Team-processing applications are self-contained applications that typically track an item's status through a series of steps or stages. Bug tracking, help desk requests, document approval and life cycle, and vacation requests are examples.

Like most applications, workflow applications use both client-side components and server-side components. The client bits are generally custom forms that are used for the application. Because just about any client application triggers the workflow with a save or a post to a folder, you can build the client forms in an application such as Office, Outlook, Microsoft FrontPage, Microsoft Visual Basic, or any other client-side forms package. The server-side components are more important, because they define the business rules that apply to the items. The server-side components are the focus of this chapter.

UNDERSTANDING THE WORKFLOW PROCESS

The workflow process is the core component of every workflow application. This is essentially the definition, or business rule, that is applied to each item in the workflow folder. The workflow process determines the routing of the object, how others are notified about the progress of the item, and also when the item can be removed from the folder or marked as completed.

A workflow process is defined by using two key components—states and actions— which automate and enforce the order in which tasks must be completed from start to finish:

- The *state* of an item indicates the status of the workflow item in process. As an item moves through a workflow process, it assumes different states. For example, when an item is first added to the workflow folder, the workflow process might set the state of the item to Active. After another person has evaluated the item, the workflow process might change the state to Tentative. If the item is approved, the workflow process changes the state to Approved. If the item is rejected, the workflow process changes the state to Rejected. You use an item's state to track its progress through a workflow process.

- The *action* of an item does something to the workflow item. An action is an event that occurs in a workflow process. An action can either trigger code or cause a transition from one state to another. Each state can have multiple actions associated with it. For example, you can use a Timer action to execute code after a certain time frame has elapsed. You can also use a Delete action to cause a workflow item to change from its current state to a Deleted state.

Figure 10.1 shows a sample workflow process. State 1 and State 2 indicate the possible states of a workflow item. Two different actions can be used on the states: one action simply triggers code without causing a state change, whereas the other action causes a transition in the workflow item from State 1 to State 2.

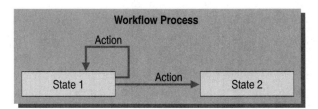

Figure 10.1
In a workflow process, states indicate the status of an item as it progresses through the process, and actions either change the item from one state to another or trigger code that results in no state change.

In addition to using states and actions, you usually also define script in a workflow process by using a scripting language such as Microsoft Visual Basic Scripting Edition (VBScript). You do not need to include script, but your workflow process won't be able to do much without it. You can use script in a workflow process to determine whether an action is triggered. If the action does occur, you can also include script that executes as a result of that action. If an error occurs during execution of the action script, you can also write a compensating action script to "undo" certain actions or to log errors.

UNDERSTANDING ACTIONS

When you create a workflow item, you can define as few or as many states as you need in your workflow process. You do not need to follow any guidelines; you simply create a state to indicate the status of a workflow item and give the state a name. When you add an action to a workflow process, you select from the predefined actions and follow some guidelines to apply the action to an existing state.

You can choose from seven predefined actions to control workflow activities and trigger script. These actions define which events fire for a given state. Table 10.1 lists the actions.

Table 10.1   Workflow actions you can add to a state

Action	Description
Create	Triggered when a new item is created in the folder.
Delete	Triggered when an item is deleted.
Change	Triggered when an item is changed. The Change action can be used to create a state transition.
Enter	Triggered when an item is transitioning into a given state. The Enter action also starts the clock ticking for the Expiry action. The time between the Enter action and the Expiry action is designated in days, hours, or minutes. Fifteen minutes is the minimum duration.
Exit	Triggered when an item is transitioning out of a given state.
Receive	Triggered when an e-mail item, which is an update to an existing item participating in the workflow process, is received in the folder. The Receive action can be used to create a state transition.
Expiry	Triggered when the time defined for the Enter action has elapsed. Expiry is a time-based action. For example, if an item remains at a certain state for more than a specified length of time, an action can be triggered to mark that item as overdue. The Expiry action can be used to create a state transition when an item has been in one state for too long.

When using Workflow Designer, you can add only one Enter, Exit, Create, and Delete action for a single state. For example, you cannot have two Enter events for the Active state. You can, however, assign multiple Change, Expiry, and Receive actions to the same state. For example, you could use two Expiry actions on a state to fire at two different times and trigger two different sets of script. The workflow engine does not impose these sorts of restrictions.

SETTING SECURITY IN WORKFLOW

Because the workflow components run on the server, there is potential to damage the server by interfering with other server tasks. To avoid damage to the server, you can set workflow script to execute in one of two security modes: restricted or privileged.

RUNNING SCRIPT IN RESTRICTED MODE

By default, a workflow process runs in restricted mode. In restricted mode, you can write code to access only the workflow item that is undergoing transition in the workflow process. You can write code that reads the item, makes changes to any of the properties, and even deletes it. However, you cannot create objects by using CreateObject. If you try to use CreateObject, your code will fail with an error. You can still create notification messages, but you need to use the GetNewWorkflowMessage method of a ProcessInstance to create the message.

When code is restricted like this, it is known as *sandboxing*. Just as a sandbox frame keeps the sand in its confines, restricted mode keeps the code confined in the workflow process. This reduces the risk that the code might harm the server, such as by deleting files, adding viruses or worms, or interfering with other services. Sandboxing code also lends server administrators some peace of mind when you must convince them to allow your code to run on their server! Figure 10.2 depicts sandboxing.

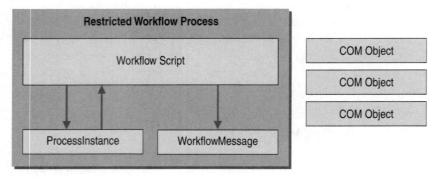

Figure 10.2
When workflow script runs in restricted mode, the script is sandboxed and you cannot create an instance of COM objects.

RUNNING SCRIPT IN PRIVILEGED MODE

You can also run script in privileged mode, although it might be harder to convince a server administrator to allow this. When a script runs in privileged mode, no restrictions are imposed on the actions the script takes. The workflow engine allows any code in privileged mode to execute with full administrative permissions to most Exchange 2000 Server resources. You can use CreateObject to create instances of Component Object Model (COM) objects as well as use the standard script calls allowed in restricted mode. This gives you free rein to do almost anything, including accessing external data sources and interacting with the Active Directory directory service in Microsoft Windows 2000. Figure 10.3 graphically depicts this relationship.

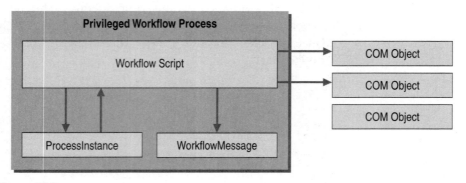

Figure 10.3
When workflow runs in privileged mode, you can do almost anything on the server, including creating instances of COM objects.

You must be a member of the Privileged Workflow Authors role to author privileged scripts. You can add yourself or someone else to the Privileged Workflow Authors role by using Component Services in Microsoft Management Console (MMC). Even if you are just editing privileged scripts, you must still be a member of the Privileged Workflow Authors role, because when the script is executed the workflow engine checks to see who was the last user to touch the script. If the script was edited by anyone other than a privileged author, the script will fail.

BUILDING WORKFLOW APPLICATIONS

You can build workflow applications in several ways: by using Workflow Designer for Exchange, by building the workflow event processes and sinks from scratch, or by automating the workflow engine object from an existing application. Workflow Designer has enough functionality and flexibility to fulfill most developers' application needs. Workflow Designer is a graphical tool that you can use to easily and quickly build workflow processes on folders; if you use it, you don't need to understand the subtle nuances of programming the workflow engine.

If Workflow Designer does not accomplish your design goals, you can build a workflow event sink from scratch. Although you gain quite a bit of flexibility in design and control over your application by doing this, you also take on added responsibility. You need to build every aspect of the workflow and use nearly all the objects in the Workflow object library.

You can also combine the use of the two. You can use Workflow Designer to create a workflow process and then programmatically register the event sink. You can also use Workflow Designer to edit existing processes.

Both approaches to workflow application development use the CDO Workflow for Exchange (cdowf.dll) object model. However, Workflow Designer is designed to use the majority of the objects automatically. In Workflow Designer, you only use the CDO Workflow objects and interfaces when you write script to react to actions. The objects that you will most likely use in those scripts include:

- **IWorkflowSession**. Provides run-time communication between the workflow engine, your action script, and the workflow item (ProcessInstance) being processed.

- **IWorkflowMessage**. Allows you to create notification messages in the workflow process that can be sent to recipients.

- **AuditTrailEventLog**. Used to create entries about workflow event activity in an application log.

This chapter focuses on how to build workflow applications by using Workflow Designer for Exchange. For detailed information about how to build workflow applications from scratch by using the complete CDO Workflow Objects for Microsoft Exchange object model, see the Exchange SDK documentation included on the companion CD.

> **NOTE** Exchange Server 5.5 offered developers the Routing Objects library for building workflow and routing applications. Although similar in purpose to CDO workflow objects for Exchange 2000, routing objects were designed for building only MAPI-based routing applications. Exchange 2000 continues to support MAPI applications developed with routing objects. However, if you want to take advantage of the Microsoft Web Storage System features, you need to use the CDO Workflow Objects for Exchange 2000 library instead.

BEFORE YOU BEGIN

Before you can build a workflow application, you need to properly configure some security settings in your Exchange organization. Although Exchange automatically installs the workflow components for you, you must manually configure a few things to successfully use them. This section discusses the two things that you need to do: define the workflow system account and register workflow authors.

> **NOTE** You can also accomplish these tasks programmatically by using COM+ COMAdmin objects. The Exchange SDK tools contain utility scripts to do just this. For more information, see the Microsoft Exchange developer site at http://msdn.microsoft.com/exchange/.

DEFINING THE WORKFLOW SYSTEM ACCOUNT

For your workflow script to run properly, you must define a user account that will be used to execute the code in the various workflow components. Regardless of who actually authors a workflow process, the workflow script will always run with the permissions of this particular user account. Anything this user account has permission to do, the code has permission to do in privileged mode. Anything the account is denied from doing, the workflow script is denied from doing in privileged mode.

To create the workflow account, open Active Directory Users and Computers on the server configured for workflow. Then follow these steps:

1. Create a new user account in the Users container. You can use any name and password you want for the account, but make sure that you set the account for **Password Never Expires**. In addition, this account must have an Exchange mailbox to send and deliver e-mail, so, when prompted, create an Exchange mailbox. If possible, you should create this mailbox on the same computer where the workflow executes.

2. After the user account is created, open it and make the account a member of the Exchange Domain Servers group. This is a security group created automatically by Exchange during installation and granted access to all Exchange resources. By making the workflow account a member of Exchange Domain Servers group, the workflow script will execute with proper privileges.

After you create the workflow account, you must configure the workflow components to use this account. By default, all workflow application components are set to run under the user account currently logged on to the system. For the workflow scripts to execute properly, you must change this default setting so that the components run under the workflow account you created. On a server running Windows 2000 Server or on a client computer that is configured as an Exchange administrator, open Component Services in MMC, and follow these steps:

1. Expand **Component Services**, then **Computers**, then **My Computer**, and then **COM+ Applications**. Figure 10.4 shows an example of this.

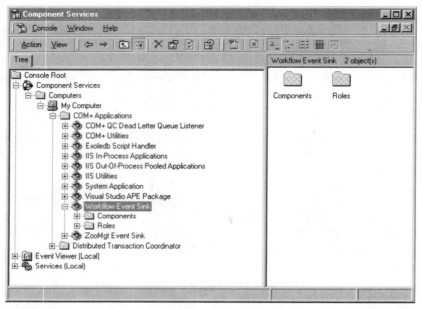

Figure 10.4
Use Component Services in MMC to configure all workflow applications to run under the new workflow account.

2. Right-click Workflow Event Sink, and click Properties.

3. On the **Workflow Event Sink Properties** property sheet, click the **Identity** tab to display account information, as shown in Figure 10.5.

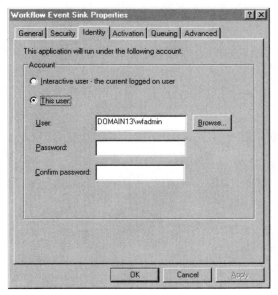

Figure 10.5
Use the Identity tab to indicate which account to use when executing workflow script.

4. Click **This User**, and then browse to select the Workflow user account. Click **OK** to apply the changes.

> **NOTE**   If you have problems assigning the account, right-click **My Computer** and stop the MS DTC.

REGISTERING WORKFLOW AUTHORS

To create and register workflow applications, a workflow author must be an owner of the Web Storage System folder that hosts the workflow process. In addition, a workflow author must be registered as a workflow author on the server. To assign a user the right to author workflow applications, open Component Services on the server where workflow is registered, and follow these steps:

1. Expand Component Services, then Computers, then My Computers, and then COM+ Applications.

2. Double-click Workflow Event Sink, and then expand the Roles folder. Expand the Can Register Workflow role (see Figure 10.6). The users listed in the Users folder under the Can Register Workflow role are allowed to author workflow applications.

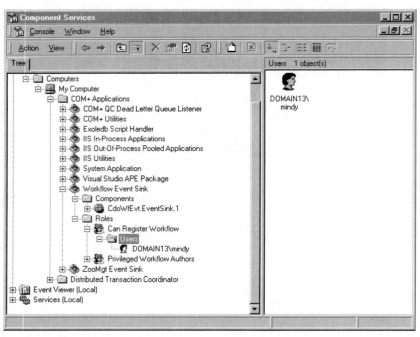

Figure 10.6
To author workflow applications, the author must be assigned rights to do so.

3. Right-click the **Users** folder and select **Add** to add another user account.

4. In the **Select Users or Groups** dialog box, select a user account, and then click **OK**. The selected user now has permission to register workflow applications.

USING WORKFLOW DESIGNER FOR EXCHANGE

When building workflow applications, most people will use Workflow Designer for Exchange. Workflow Designer is a graphical tool that makes constructing workflow processes in a folder quicker and easier than starting from scratch. The best part about the Workflow Designer is that you can install it on any client computer that will be used to author workflow. You do not need to run it directly on the Exchange server.

NOTE Workflow Designer for Exchange is available as part of the Microsoft Office 2000 Developer Version 1.5. Office 2000 Developer 1.5 is an updated release of Office 2000 Developer that includes professional tools for building workflow solutions using Microsoft Exchange 2000 Server. For more information, see the Microsoft Office 2000 Developer Web site at http://msdn.microsoft.com/Officedev/.

INTRODUCING WORKFLOW DESIGNER

Workflow Designer is divided into two panes: a Process List pane and a properties pane that presents your options on one or more tabs. The Process List pane lists the name of the folder you have accessed as well as any processes currently available. The other pane displays the options for the item selected in the Process List. If you select a folder, only the **General** tab is available. The **General** tab offers general options that apply to the folder as a whole.

Figure 10.7 shows Workflow Designer before any processes have been added to a folder.

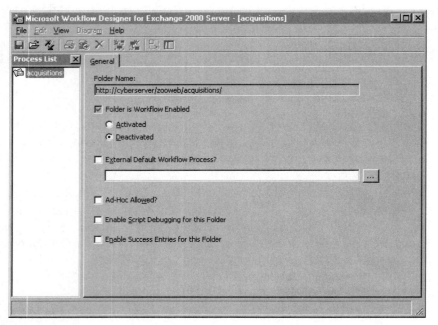

Figure 10.7
Workflow Designer

If a process exists on the folder and you select it in the process list, three tabs become visible:

- **General**. You use this tab to set options for the process, such as whether it is the default process.

- **Design**. This tab contains the graphical depiction of the process, and you use it to add and remove states and actions as well as to add script conditions and procedure calls.

- **Shared Script**. This tab contains a list of procedures that can be called at any point during the process.

USING WORKFLOW DESIGNER: A SIMPLE EXAMPLE

The best way to understand how to use Workflow Designer is to actually build something. This section presents an example of how to use Workflow Designer to create an Animal Request workflow process in the Acquisitions folder of the Zoo Management application on the Applications Web Storage System. In this example, you design the process to track when zoo staff members submit a request to acquire a new animal for the zoo. When a staff member submits a request, a zoologist must evaluate whether the research is complete. For example, there's no point in handling a request for an extinct species. If a request is valid, an expedition team tries to acquire the animal. If the expedition is successful, the animal request is marked "acquired." However, if the initial request is not valid, the person who submitted the request is notified and the expedition team is not alerted.

NOTE   For more detailed information about using Workflow Designer, see the Workflow Designer for Exchange Help documentation installed with the tool.

CONNECTING TO A WORKFLOW FOLDER WITH WORKFLOW DESIGNER

The first step in creating a workflow process is to connect to the workflow folder by using Workflow Designer. To open the designer, click the **Start** menu, point to **Program Files**, point to **Workflow Designer for Exchange**, and then click **Exchange Workflow Designer**. Before Workflow Designer opens, you must provide some essential information, including the name of the Exchange server to host the workflow and the URL of the folder that will contain the workflow elements (see Figure 10.8).

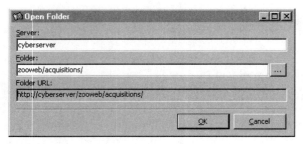

Figure 10.8
Before you can use Workflow Designer, you must indicate the name of the Exchange server and the folder that will contain the workflow.

You can type the folder URL in the **Folder** text box, or you can browse for the folder in the list of public folders on the named server. If you type the URL and it includes spaces, you may need to represent those spaces with the character combination %20. Also, the URL of the folder uses HTTP, so you must use the appropriate virtual directory name. For example, if you created the virtual directory name zooweb to connect to the Zoo Management application, use the following URL to connect to the Acquisitions folder: zooweb/Acquisitions/. After you enter the URL, **Folder URL** displays the complete URL with the server name. Click **OK** to allow Workflow Designer to connect to the folder. If a connection is established successfully, Workflow Designer opens. Only the folder name is visible in the Process list before you add a workflow process to the Acquisitions folder. If you already added workflow processes, the list displays each process name.

CREATING A NEW PROCESS

The next step is to create a new workflow process in the Acquisitions folder. To create a new workflow process, on the **File** menu, click **New Workflow Process**, or on the toolbar, click **New Workflow Process** . You are then prompted to provide a unique name for your workflow process. For this example, enter **Animal Request** and click **OK**.

Workflow Designer generates some information and then requests a name for the first state in the process. Enter the state name **Active**. When you create a new workflow process, Workflow Designer automatically generates a very simple workflow that consists of a Create action, a single state that you name, and a Delete action. Starting and ending blocks indicate the start and end of the process. Figure 10.9 shows how the workflow process should look in Workflow Designer.

TIP   Before you proceed, delete the Delete action. This makes it easier to manipulate the states and actions in the upcoming sections.

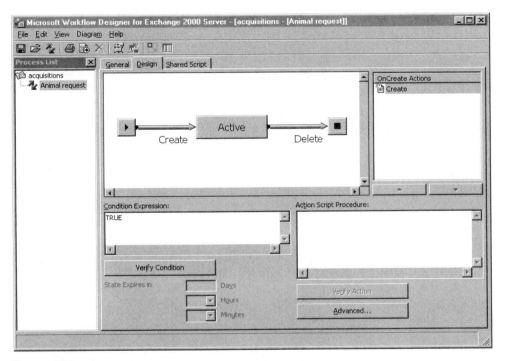

Figure 10.9
Workflow Designer generates a simple, linear workflow process that you can then modify as necessary.

ADDING STATES

You would be hard-pressed to develop a really useful workflow that has only one state. Workflow processes generally consist of multiple states. A state describes the status of a workflow item. Therefore, when the status of the workflow item changes, the state should also change. Although you can insert actions before you insert states, it is much easier to develop a workflow process if you first insert the workflow states because actions often indicate a transition between states. You can create states before knowing all their associated actions.

To insert some more states in the Animal Request workflow process, right-click the background of the Design pane in Workflow Designer, and then click **Insert State**. At the prompt, enter a new name for the state. Enter the state name **Approved**, and then click **OK**. You can repeat this to add the following states: Tentative, Cancelled, and Acquired. After you add the states, you will need to rearrange the Workflow Designer to appear as shown in Figure 10.10.

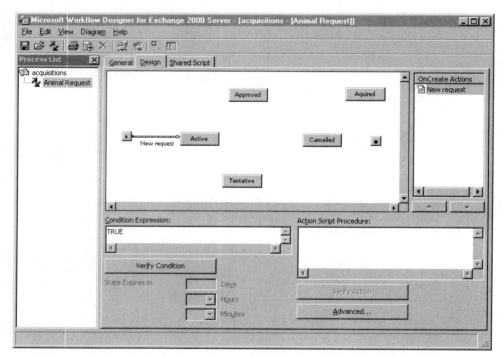

Figure 10.10
A typical workflow process has multiple states.

ADDING ACTIONS

After you add the states, you can add actions to those states. Actions can trigger code for the state or cause a transition from one state to another. Each state can have multiple actions associated with it. For example, the Active state will have at least two actions: one that can change the state to Approved and another that can change the state to Tentative. To add an action to a state, right-click an existing state and select **Insert Action**. The **Insert Action** dialog box appears as shown in Figure 10.11.

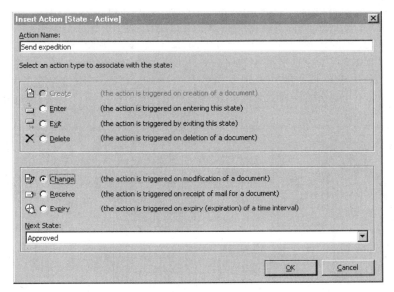

Figure 10.11
Use the Insert Action dialog box to add actions to your workflow process.

The first thing to do is to name your action. An action name should describe what happens to the state, and it can be more than one word. The top list of actions in Figure 10.11 consists of those actions that do not cause a transition in state. You can add only one of each of these actions to a single state. For example, you cannot have two Enter actions for the Active state. The bottom list consists of those actions that cause a state change. You can have multiple instances of these actions. For example, the Active state can have two Change actions. If you select one of these actions, you must indicate the state to which the item is transitioning. Be sure to create the state before you create the action, because you must select the state name from the drop-down list box.

To make the Animal Request process usable, you must add a number of different actions. For example, to add two new actions to the Active state, right-click the **Active** state and click **Insert Action**. Enter **Send Expedition** as the action name. Select the **Change** action, and in **Next State**, click **Approved**.

Figure 10.12 shows what the Animal Request workflow process looks like after you add a few more actions. The diagram displays only those actions used to create state changes. Any actions that do not cause a state change, such as the Expiry action, do not appear in the workflow diagram. You can view all the existing actions for a state by clicking on the state and looking in the action list on the right.

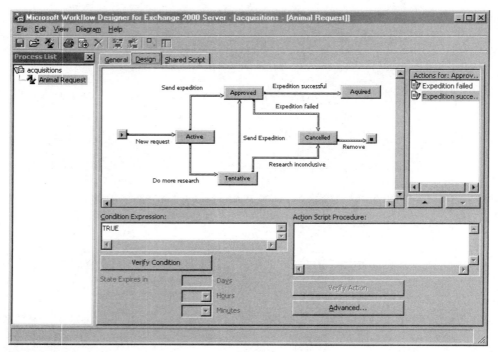

Figure 10.12
Workflow Designer shows a process, complete with states and actions.

ADDING SCRIPT

To make the actions actually do something, you must incorporate scripting into your workflow process. For example, the Active state has two actions: Send expedition and Do more research. Both actions cause a change in state. If the animal request is evaluated as complete, the Send expedition action occurs. If the animal request is evaluated as incomplete, the Do more research action is triggered.

But how do you determine the way in which the animal request is evaluated and, thereby determine which action is triggered? You must provide some way for the user to indicate one of these scenarios. One solution is to use custom properties on the request form. For example, you could add a custom property ResearchComplete to the form. A user looks at the animal request and evaluates it, and then sets this property to True if an expedition should be sent or False if more research is needed. You could add an evaluation script that looks at the property. If ResearchComplete is True, call the Send expedition action and send a message to the expedition team leader. If ResearchComplete is False, call the Do more research action and send a message to the original requester.

CREATING CONDITION SCRIPT STATEMENTS

When you add a new action to a state, Workflow Designer automatically sets the condition expression to True for that action so that the action always fires. In the case of the Active state, this means that both Change actions always fire when the workflow item is changed. However, because a single animal request can't be both Approved and Tentative at the same time, you must add condition script to evaluate the ResearchComplete property. Click the **Send expedition** action, and enter the following information in **Condition Expression**:

```
workflowsession.Fields("ResearchComplete") = True
```

If ResearchComplete is True, the Send expedition action is triggered. To add a condition script for the Do more research action, click **Do more research**, and enter the following information in **Condition Expression**:

```
workflowsession.Fields("ResearchComplete") = False
```

If ResearchComplete is False, the Do more research action is triggered.

You can use expressions in **Condition Expression**, and you can call procedures in **Shared Script**. However, remember that any script you write here runs under the same restrictions as other workflow script.

CREATING ACTION SCRIPT

When a condition evaluates to True, an action fires. However, if you do not add an action script, the action doesn't do much except trigger a state change, if that is its purpose. To make an action do something, you must add action script.

You can add action script in the **Action Script Procedure** text box or on the **Shared Script** tab. The **Action Script Procedure** text box is useful only for simple statements. For example, to add log entries to test for the firing of actions, you can add that script here. To create lengthier procedures, or if you want to call the same type of procedure from more than one action, use the **Shared Script** tab and call the procedure from the **Action Script Procedure** text box. For example, sending notification messages is a common action in workflow script. Rather than building this code for every action that needs to use it, you could create a shared procedure that uses a parameter indicating the subject value and call this procedure from every action that wants to use it. For more information on creating notification messages, see "Sending a Notification Message" later in this chapter.

CREATING COMPENSATING ACTIONS

You can add compensating action script to a workflow process to do something if an action fails to execute properly. For example, you could write code that generates a log to indicate why the action failed. To create compensating script, on the **Design** tab of the Workflow Process pane, click **Advanced**.

USING EXTERNAL SCRIPT FILES

Instead of housing your script in the workflow process, you can create an external script file that can be shared among multiple folders and processes. If you use an external script file, you can also maintain your script in a single location, reducing management efforts. The drawback is that you cannot use procedures on the **Shared Script** tab and in an external script tab. To create an external script file, create a text file with a .vbs or .txt file extension. After you add your code, save the file to an Exchange folder. It doesn't matter which folder, as long as it exists on the same server and you can construct a URL that points to the file.

To use an external script file in a process, follow these steps:

1. In the workflow process, click the **General** tab, and then click **Advanced**.

2. Select the **External Script** check box to enable an external shared script file.

3. In **Script URL**, browse to select the folder and the file name of the shared script file.

4. Click **OK**.

USING MULTIPLE ACTIONS ON A SINGLE STATE

You typically create more than one action for a single state. For example, the Active state uses the Send expedition and Do more research actions. Although the condition expression evaluates which action fires, it does not determine which action is evaluated first. By default, the Workflow engine attempts to fire the first action that was added to the state, followed by the second. So if the Send expedition action was added before the Do more research action, the Send expedition action is evaluated first. If the condition expression for the Send expedition action evaluates to False (if ResearchComplete = False), then the Do more research action is evaluated next. Once an action evaluates to True, no further actions are evaluated.

You can change the way in which actions fire by rearranging them in the **Actions** list on the **Design** tab in Workflow Designer. The action at the top of the list is evaluated first, followed by the actions below it in the order in which they appear. Use the UP ARROW and DOWN ARROW keys to adjust the priority among the actions.

ADDING FINAL TOUCHES TO YOUR WORKFLOW PROCESS

Before you can use the workflow process, you need to add some final touches to both the workflow process and the workflow folder itself. Because the Animal Request is the first process in the folder, it must be set as the default workflow process. Workflow Designer does not do this automatically. To set a workflow process as the default process, click the **General** tab for the process and select the default workflow process for this folder option. The process icon changes from blue to green and has a check mark to indicate that this is the default workflow process. Save the process to commit the changes.

The next step before you can use the workflow process is to activate the folder for workflow activity. By default, workflow is disabled on a folder. To enable workflow, in the list in Workflow Designer, click the folder, and then click the **General** tab. Click **Enabled**, and then save the folder changes.

The last option that you might want to set on the folder is **Enable Success Entries for this Folder**. With this selected, Workflow Designer can log success information about the workflow in the Event log. If you plan to write script that writes directly to the log file, you must check this option. Figure 10.13 shows these options.

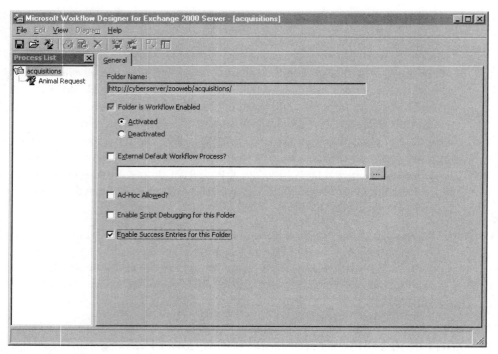

Figure 10.13
To use workflow on a folder, you must activate the folder.

IMPORTING AND EXPORTING PROCESSES

You can import workflow processes to and export workflow processes from Workflow Designer. This lets you create backups of your workflow, apply the same workflow process to multiple folders, and even send the workflow process as an e-mail attachment so that it can be used in different Exchange organizations. Workflow Designer uses Extensible Markup Language (XML) as the default file type. Figure 10.14 shows what the Animal Request process looks like after it is saved as XML.

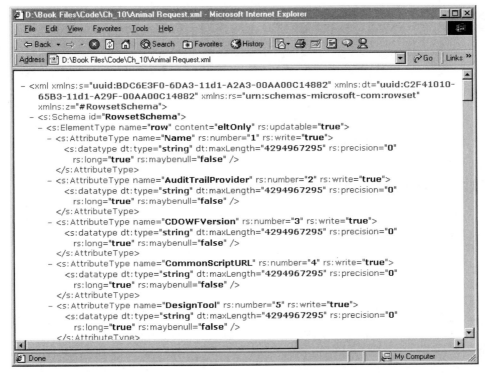

Figure 10.14
Workflow processes can be imported to and exported from Workflow Designer as .xml files.

To export a saved process to an .xml file:

1. In **Active Directory**, click the process to be exported.

2. On the **File** menu, click **Export Workflow Process to XML**.

3. Enter a name for the file, and then click **Save**.

To import a saved process from an .xml file:

1. Open Workflow Designer on the folder to host the imported process.

2. On the **File** menu, click **Import Workflow Process from XML**.

3. Locate the .xml file, and then click **Open**.

SCRIPTING THE WORKFLOW ITEM

As an item moves through a workflow process, advancing from one state to another, you might want to access the workflow item by using code to read properties, set properties, or take action on the item. You can access a workflow item by using a WorkflowSession object. A WorkflowSession object is an intrinsic object passed by the workflow engine to the script environment, and it contains information about the workflow item that is undergoing transition.

WORKFLOWSESSION PROPERTIES AND METHODS

A WorkflowSession object exposes both properties for returning information about a workflow item and methods for taking action on the workflow item. Table 10.2 lists the properties of a WorkflowSession object.

Table 10.2　Properties of a WorkflowSession object

Name	Returns	Description
ActiveConnection	ADODB.Connection	Returns the Session object of the user that initiated the event. This is available only in privileged mode workflows.
Domain	String	Returns the server's domain name.
ErrorDescription	String	Sets and returns the details of an error to be reported back to the audit trail.
ErrorNumber	Long	Sets and returns the error number to be reported back to the calling client and logged to the audit trail.
Fields	Fields	Returns a collection of properties for the ProcessInstance object.

Continued on next page

Table 10.2 continued   Properties of a WorkflowSession object

Name	Returns	Description
ItemAuthors	IMembers	Returns a collection of users allowed to modify an item, in addition to the default collection.
ItemReaders	IMembers	Returns a collection of users allowed exclusive read access to an item.
ReceivedMessage	IWorkflowMessage	Returns a reference to the message that initiated the state transition.
Sender	String	Returns the SMTP address of the user that initiated the state transition.
Server	String	Returns the name of the server.
StateFrom	String	Returns the state of the process instance before the current transition.
StateTo	String	Returns the state of the process instance after the current transition.
TrackingTable	Recordset	Returns a reference to the Recordset object containing data related to the process instance that initiated the state transition.

To access any of these properties in your workflow script, access a WorkflowSession object and call one of the properties. For example, the following code sample returns the name of the domain in which the workflow is running:

```
strDomain = WorkflowSession.Domain
```

A WorkflowSession object also exposes several methods for acting on the workflow item. Table 10.3 lists the methods of a WorkflowSession object.

Table 10.3   Methods of a WorkflowSession object

Name	Description
AddAuditEntry	Adds a log entry to the Windows Applications log file or to a custom AuditTrail provider COM+ object.
DeleteReceivedMessage	Deletes the message correlated with the workflow item.
DeleteWorkflowItem	Deletes the workflow item.
GetNewWorkflowMessage	Returns a new WorkflowMessage object for sending notification messages.
GetUserProperty	Returns the value of an Active Directory attribute property.
IsUserInRole	Returns True if a user is in a folder role.

To call a method in your workflow script, access a WorkflowSession object and call the appropriate method. For example, the following code sample returns True if the user submitting a workflow item is in a specific role:

```
blnIsOk = WorkflowSession.IsUserInRole( _
    WorkflowSession.Sender, "Role13")
```

ADDING AN AUDIT ENTRY

One of the most common scripting tasks is to create custom log entries in the Application Log file. By using log entries, you can track or audit your application for errors and successful transitions. To generate log entries by using the AddAuditEntry method, you must first enable the folder to generate the entries by clicking **Enable Success Entries for this Folder** in Workflow Designer. After you enable log entries, you can call the AddAuditEntry method of a WorkflowSession object in a workflow script and pass a text string message to be added to the log entry. For example, the following code sample adds some text to a log entry:

```
workflowsession.AddAuditEntry "Item created successfully."
```

To view the actual event log entry, you must have access to the server running
Exchange 2000 and Event Viewer. The entry will be added to the Application log.
For example, Figure 10.15 shows what the custom entry created by the previous
code would look like.

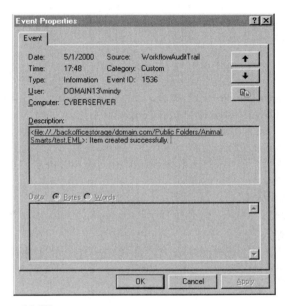

Figure 10.15
A custom Application event log entry showing a successful workflow action

IDENTIFYING THE SENDER

You can use the Sender property to determine who has posted a new workflow
item in a workflow folder or who has triggered a state change in a workflow item.
The Sender property returns the Simple Mail Transfer Protocol (SMTP) address for
the user as a string value. You can use the Sender property to send notification
messages to thank the original poster for their submission or to alert another user
when an item changes state. You could also use the Sender property to log
information that tracks who is posting messages in the folder. For example, you
could use the following action script to log an entry whenever a new item is
created in the workflow folder:

```
WorkflowSession.AddAuditEntry _
    "Posting made by: " & WorkflowSession.Sender
```

SENDING A NOTIFICATION MESSAGE

One of the most common workflow tasks is to send notification messages about the status of an item in the folder. You can use notification messages to alert users when action needs to be taken on a workflow item, when the status of an item has changed, or when an item has been marked as completed.

If your workflow script is running in restricted mode, you will not be able to use the CreateObject function to create an instance of a new CDO Message object. Instead, you must use the GetNewWorkflowMessage method of a WorkflowSession object. The GetNewWorkflowMessage method returns a new WorkflowMessage object, which is the only object that you can create in a restricted workflow script. The WorkflowMessage object is based on the CDO Message object and supports most of the Message object properties and methods. Unlike when you create messages using the CDO message object, you do not need to explicitly set the From property on the WorkflowMessage object. The workflow engine automatically sets the From property to the mailbox of the account under which workflow is executing. This is why the account must have a mailbox. To send the message, you call the SendWorkflowMessage method of a WorkflowMessage object and pass one of the cdoWfSendFlags enumeration values listed in Table 10.4 to indicate whether you want to use tracking.

Table 10.4   Possible values for the CdoWfSendFlags enumeration

Name	Data value	Description
cdowfNoTracking	0	Turns off response tracking.
cdowfAdd	1	Indicates that responses from anyone can be added to the TrackingTable. Allows tracking responses from a distribution list or delegate.
cdowfStrict	2	Indicates that responses from only the original recipient can be added to the TrackingTable. Does not allow tracking of responses from a distribution list or delegate.

NOTE   The code listings shown in this chapter are available in the Microsoft Visual Basic project CH_10.vbp on the companion CD. If you want to run the samples as they are written, you must have the Zoo Management sample installed on your Exchange 2000 Server. For information about installing the application, see the introduction to the book. In addition, the code samples repeatedly call a function named GetStorageName. This function returns the name of the domain in which the code is running. For more information about the GetStorageName function, see Chapter 8, "Interacting with Active Directory."

For example, Listing 10.1 shows how to create a notification message in a restricted workflow script without tracking.

Listing 10.1   Send a notification message a folder monitor about a new art request.

```
Sub SendNotificationMail()
    ' You use the workflow security account
    ' to send a notification message.

    Dim WFMsg

    ' Create a new notification message
    Set WFMsg = WorkflowSession.GetNewWorkflowMessage
    With WFMsg
        ' Set the basic Message properties
        .To = "aidan@domain.com"

        .Subject = "New Art Request"
        .TextBody = _
           "A new animal request has been posted: " & _
           WorkflowSession.Fields("DAV:displayname")
        ' Send the request
        .SendWorkflowMessage cdowfNoTracking
    End With

    ' Clean up
    Set WFMsg = Nothing
End Sub
```

READING THE STATE INFORMATION

Because you can share procedures among multiple actions, you might find it beneficial to identify exactly what action is calling the procedure. One way to do this is to use the StateFrom and StateTo properties of a WorkflowMessage object. The StateFrom property contains the name of the state of the item before the transition occurs. If the item is new, this value will be empty. The StateTo property contains the name of the state the item will be in after the transition occurs. If the item is deleted permanently, this might be an empty string. If the action is not triggering a state change, these values are the same. Listing 10.2 uses the StateTo and StateFrom properties to track the progress of an item through a workflow process.

Listing 10.2   Track state transitions.

```
Sub TrackStateChange()
   workflowsession.AddAuditEntry _
    "Item moving from " & workflowsession.StateFrom & _
    " to " & workflowsession.StateTo
End Sub
```

DELETING THE WORKFLOW ITEM

If you need to delete the workflow item during the workflow process, use the DeleteWorkflowItem method of a WorkflowSession object. The delete is not a synchronous action; therefore, synchronous delete events are not triggered when you delete an item with the DeleteWorkflowItem method. If you need to evaluate a condition to support the delete, you must do that before calling the DeleteWorkflowItem method. For example, the following code sample evaluates a custom property named "somecustomproperty". If the property evaluates to True, the workflow item is deleted and a notification message is sent to alert the folder manager.

```
If workflowsession.Fields("somecustomproperty") = False Then
    workflowsession.DeleteWorkflowItem
    SendNotificationMail "Animal request deleted"
End If
```

DEBUGGING WORKFLOW SCRIPT

Debugging script is more difficult than debugging standard Visual Basic code. Debugging server-side script is even more difficult. Because workflow does not have a user interface associated with the code itself, you cannot use the MsgBox function to track down logical errors. The route you take depends on your access rights to the server running the scripts. This section describes the steps you take to debug workflow script: checking script syntax, using Event Viewer, and using Microsoft Script Debugger.

CHECKING SCRIPT SYNTAX

Before you attempt any of the more time-consuming debugging approaches, you should make sure that your script's syntax is correct. Workflow Designer has several buttons that begin with *Verify* located throughout the tool where script is used. When you click a **Verify** button, a very simple syntax check is conducted on the appropriate code. Then you see either a message stating that no script errors were found or one that indicates the problem. This tool can be used to check for illegal characters or text, such as the use of the As keyword in a variable declaration statement, or missing characters, such as a closing quote on a string. However, the syntax checker does not check the validity of your script, such as whether a property is actually provided by an object.

TIP   If you want your script to have the properly cased text of Visual Basic, write the script in a Visual Basic code module and then paste it in Workflow Designer. Set a reference to the CDO Workflow objects for Microsoft Exchange object library. The script is automatically changed from the typical lowercase text of VBScript to the proper case text of Visual Basic.

USING EVENT VIEWER

When workflow script fails at run time, it rarely generates an error message. More often than not, the process simply does not respond to the client request in the way that you would expect. For example, if a notification message is never sent to the intended recipient, the client application might not display an error message. When these types of errors occur, you should check Event Viewer for information about the error. As long as you are an administrator of the server running Exchange 2000, you can use Event Viewer to browse the Application log for errors. The Application log contains information about what went wrong when the workflow attempted to execute the client request.

USING SCRIPT DEBUGGER

After you have determined that something is wrong and you are unable to quickly identify a problem with your script, you need to turn to a more advanced debugging tool. If you are an administrator and have physical access to the server, you can make use of Script Debugger. Script Debugger must be enabled on every workflow folder in which you want to use it. In Workflow Designer, click the **General** tab for the folder, and click **Enable Script Debugging for this Folder**.

SUMMARY

Workflow adds server-side logic to your applications and transforms folders from simple containers into intelligent monitors. If you add workflow, you can control the behavior of an item throughout its lifetime. By using Workflow Designer, you can quickly and easily add workflow to an Exchange folder. You can write code to alert a user that something needs to be done, track where an item has been and where it needs to go, and even alter the item as it progresses through the workflow process.

Chapter 11, "Developing with Outlook 2000," explains how to extend your Exchange 2000 applications further by incorporating the premier MAPI client to Exchange, Microsoft Outlook 2000.

11

Developing with Outlook 2000

Microsoft Outlook 2000 is a powerful personal information management tool that has increased potential when used in conjunction with Microsoft Exchange 2000 Server. However, Outlook 2000 is a MAPI client and Exchange is no longer configured solely for MAPI clients. This means that you must consider certain design issues when you develop for and in the Outlook environment, but it doesn't mean that you must forgo all the benefits of the Microsoft Web Storage System. For example, server events and workflow logic are client-independent and will work with HTTP and MAPI clients. In addition, you can still access both predefined and custom schema properties from an Outlook form, and you can use ActiveX Data Objects (ADO) 2.5 to access data in any Web Storage System.

This chapter explains how you can create Outlook applications that make the most of the Web Storage System features. Sections include:

- **Introducing the MAPI Folder Tree**

- **Developing for the Outlook Environment**

- **Developing in the Outlook Environment**

INTRODUCING THE **MAPI** FOLDER TREE

By using Exchange 2000 you can create multiple Web Storage Systems and dedicate them to specific applications. However, these additional Web Storage Systems are not accessible to MAPI clients such as Outlook 2000. If you develop an Exchange application that uses Outlook 2000, you must use the Public Folders Web Storage System to store data. The Public Folders store is a folder tree dedicated to MAPI clients such as Outlook, and it is the same Public Folders tree that was available in Microsoft Exchange 5.5. You can still create folders, add data, and create custom Outlook 2000 forms to render and enter data into the Public Folders store. You can also continue to use your existing Outlook forms to access data in the public folder tree in Exchange 2000.

NOTE Because you can't create additional MAPI folder trees, the Public Folders store is often referred to as "the" MAPI store in Exchange 2000.

Other clients, such as Microsoft Outlook Web Access and custom Web clients, can also access the data in Public Folders. If you are developing for a multiple client environment that includes MAPI clients, you must use the Public Folders store to ensure that everyone can access the data. You access the Public Folders tree by using HTTP through the Public virtual directory. For example, the following URL accesses a MAPI folder, Global Calendar, on cyberserver:

```
http://cyberserver/public/Global Calendar/
```

If you are using the Exchange OLE DB (ExOLEDB) provider and ADO or Collaboration Data Objects (CDO) for Exchange, you access the Public Folders tree by using its name. For example, the following URL accesses the same Global Calendar folder:

```
file://./backofficestorage/public folders/Global Calendar/
```

NOTE   The Public Folders store does not support deep traversals in Structured Query Language (SQL), so you cannot query every folder in the Public Folder tree. Only non-MAPI stores and mailbox stores support deep traversals.

DEVELOPING FOR THE OUTLOOK ENVIRONMENT

As discussed in the previous section, Outlook 2000 can interact directly with data in only the MAPI folder tree. When you use Outlook to interact with that data, you needn't do anything special to create a folder or item that displays properly. For example, when you use Outlook to create a new calendar folder, the folder comes with all the proper calendar views and appointment forms.

However, you might also be running code elsewhere that must create resources in the MAPI folder tree. For example, you might execute code that adds resources to the MAPI folder tree in an event sink, in a workflow process, or in a custom Web client. You must set some additional Outlook-specific properties so that Outlook can display this information correctly with the appropriate views and forms. This section explains how to create folders and items that will display correctly in Outlook.

CREATING FOLDERS IN THE MAPI FOLDER TREE

When you create a folder in any folder tree using ADO 2.5 or CDO, you set the DAV:contentclass property to associate the appropriate schema properties with the appropriate folder class. However, if you create the folder in the MAPI folder tree, the DAV:contentclass property doesn't set the MAPI folder class. The MAPI folder class associates an Outlook view type, form, or icon with a folder. To make the association and have the folder display properly in Outlook, you must set the folder class by setting the http://schemas.microsoft.com/exchange/outlookfolderclass schema property.

Table 11.1 lists the content class values and their associated folder class values. If you do not set the http://schemas.microsoft.com/exchange/outlookfolderclass property, Outlook sets the folder class to be an e-mail folder.

Table 11.1 Folder type values for content class and folder class

Content class	Folder class[1]	Description
urn:content-classes:mailfolder	IPF.Note	Folder for e-mail items
urn:content-classes:contactfolder	IPF.Contact	Folder for contact items
urn:content-classes:calendarfolder	IPF.Appointment	Folder for appointments, meetings, and requests
urn:content-classes:taskfolder	IPF.Task	Folder for tasks
urn:content-classes:journalfolder	IPF.Journal	Folder for journal items
urn:content-classes:notefolder	IPF.Stickynote	Folder for notes

[1]These values are not case sensitive.

NOTE The code listings in this chapter are available in the Visual Basic project CH_11.VBP on the companion CD. Unlike the other projects, this project uses folders from the Public Folders store.

Listing 11.1 shows how to create a contact folder that both custom Web clients and Outlook clients can use. The procedure sets the DAV:contentclass property to "urn:content-classes:contactfolder" to associate the appropriate contact schema properties with the new folder resource. The procedure then sets the http://schemas.microsoft.com/exchange/outlookfolderclass schema property to "IPF.Contact" so that the contact folder is displayed in Outlook with the appropriate contact views and forms.

Listing 11.1 Create a contact folder that both a Web client and a MAPI client can use.

```
Function CreateFolderforOutlook()
    ' For a folder to display properly in Outlook,
    ' you must set the
    ' http://schemas.microsoft.com/exchange/outlookfolderclass
    ' schema property.

    Dim urlOutlookFolder As String
```

```
' URL of the new folder
urlOutlookFolder = GetStorageName & _
   "public folders/Zoo Contacts/"

With New ADODB.Record
   ' Create the new folder record
   .Open urlOutlookFolder _
   , _
   , adModeReadWrite _
   , adCreateCollection + adCreateOverwrite

   ' This doesn't associate a front-end display at all
   ' It only associates calendar folder schema properties
   .Fields("DAV:contentclass") _
      = "urn:content-classes:contactfolder"

   ' Make the folder visible to Outlook clients
   ' including OWA, as a calendar folder.
   .Fields _
      ("http://schemas.microsoft.com/exchange/outlookfolderclass") _
         = "ipf.appointment"

   ' Save the changes
   .Fields.Update
   End With
End Function
```

NOTE You must also set the http://schemas.microsoft.com/exchange/ outlookfolderclass schema property to display a folder with the proper views and forms in Outlook Web Access.

CREATING ITEMS IN THE MAPI FOLDER TREE

When you use Outlook 2000 to create and save an item, Outlook sets a message class property on that item that identifies the form used to create it. For example, if you create a new standard contact in Outlook 2000, the new contact has a message class value of IPM.Contact. When you open an item, Outlook looks at the message class value to determine what form to use to display the item.

If you create items in the MAPI folder tree by using Outlook 2000 or Outlook Web Access, the client application automatically sets the message class. If you use CDO for Exchange to create items, it also sets the message class automatically based on the type of item that is being created. For example, if you create a new CDO Person object, set some properties, and save it to a MAPI folder, the message class is set to IPM.Contact. You do not need to do anything more for the item to display properly in Outlook.

However, if you use ADO 2.5 to create items in the MAPI folder tree, you must set both the DAV:contentclass schema property and the http://schemas.microsoft.com/exchange/outlookmessageclass schema property. The DAV:contentclass property associates the appropriate schema properties with the item and the http://schemas.microsoft.com/exchange/outlookmessageclass schema property sets the Outlook message class property. You can set the http://schemas.microsoft.com/exchange/outlookmessageclass schema property to any of the message class values listed in Table 11.2. If you do not set this property when you use ADO to create a new item in a MAPI folder, Outlook displays the new item as a post.

Table 11.2   Item type values for content class and for message class

Content class	Message class	Description
urn:content-classes:message	IPM.Note	Message item
urn:content-classes:appointment	IPM.Appointment	Appointment item
urn:content-classes:person	IPM.Contact	Contact item
urn:content-classes:task	IPM.Task	Task item
urn:content-classes:message	IPM.Post	Post item
urn:content-classes:note	IPM.StickyNote	Note item
urn:content-classes:activity	IPM.Activity	Journal item

NOTE   For a complete list of all the possible pairings of content class and message class, see the Exchange SDK documentation on the companion CD.

Listing 11.2 shows how to create a contact in the Zoo contacts folder that both custom Web clients and Outlook clients can use. The procedure sets the DAV:contentclass property to "urn:content-classes:person" to associate the appropriate contact schema properties with the new contact. The procedure then sets the http://schemas.microsoft.com/exchange/outlookmessageclass schema property to "IPM.Contact" so that the contact will be displayed in Outlook using the appropriate contact form.

Listing 11.2   Create a contact in a MAPI folder.

```
Sub CreateItemForOutlook()
    ' If you create an item in the MAPI folder tree
    ' using ADO, you must set the
    ' http://schemas.microsoft.com/exchange/outlookmessageclass
    ' schema property for the item to
    ' display properly in Outlook.

    Dim urlOutlookItem As String

    ' URL of the new folder
    urlOutlookItem = GetStorageName & _
        "public folders/Zoo Contacts/Michael Patten.eml"

    With New ADODB.Record
        ' Create the new folder record
        .Open urlOutlookItem _
        , _
        , adModeReadWrite _
        , adCreateNonCollection + adCreateOverwrite

        ' This doesn't associate a front-end display at all
        ' It only associates contact item schema properties
        .Fields("DAV:contentclass") _
            = "urn:content-classes:person"

        ' Set some person schema properties
        .Fields("urn:schemas:contacts:givenName") = "Michael"
        .Fields("urn:schemas:contacts:sn") = "Patten"
```

```
         ' Set the message class for the contact item
           ' so that the item is displayed with a contact form.
           .Fields _
             ("http://schemas.microsoft.com/exchange/outlookmessageclass") _
               = "ipm.contact"

           ' Save the changes
           .Fields.Update
      End With

      Debug.Print "Outlook compatible item created."
   End Sub
```

NOTE You must also set the http://schemas.microsoft.com/exchange/outlookmessageclass to display an item with the proper form in Outlook Web Access.

If your Outlook client application uses a custom Outlook form that has been registered, you can also set the http://schemas.microsoft.com/exchange/outlookmessageclass property to the message class name of the custom Outlook form. For example, Listing 11.3 shows how to create a new custom Animal class in a MAPI folder and how to set the message class to use a custom Outlook form.

Listing 11.3 Create a custom item in a MAPI folder and use a custom Outlook message class.

```
   Sub CreateOutlookCompatibleAnimal()
      ' You can automatically apply
      ' a custom Outlook form to an item.

      Dim strURL As String

      ' Build the URL to the new instance
      strURL = GetStorageName & _
      "/public folders/Zoo Management/Animals/Gray Wolf.EML"
```

```
' If you are using VBScript, use this With:
' With CreateObject("ADODB.Record")
With New ADODB.Record
    ' Create the new animal record
    .Open strURL, , , adCreateOverwrite

    ' Set the custom properties
    .Fields("DAV:contentclass") _
        = "zoomgt:content-classes:animal"

    .Fields("zoomgt:animalid") = "Canlup13"
    .Fields("zoomgt:species") = "Canis lupus"
    .Fields("zoomgt:commonname") = "Gray wolf"
    .Fields("zoomgt:gender") = 1 'female
    .Fields("zoomgt:habitat") = "Woodlands"
    .Fields("zoomgt:exhibit") = "Forest preserve 2"
    .Fields("zoomgt:specialneeds") _
        = "Maintain a pack of at least 3 members."

    .Fields("zoomgt:keeper") = "Mindy Martin"

    ' Create a copy of the href value to use
    ' in Outlook forms.
    .Fields("zoomgt:href") = .Fields("DAV:href").Value

    .Fields _
    ("http://schemas.microsoft.com/exchange/outlookmessageclass") _
        = "ipm.contact.animal"

    ' Save the changes
    .Fields.Update
    .Close
End With

Debug.Print "Animal instance created."
End Sub
```

Developing in the Outlook Environment

Just because you want to use a MAPI client such as Outlook doesn't mean that you have to sacrifice all the benefits of a Web Storage System. For example, a common thing to do when developing with any tool is to define custom properties. In a Web Storage System, you can define your own custom schema with property definitions and class definitions. If you use Outlook 2000 as your Exchange client, you can still take advantage of custom schema properties. In addition, you can use ADO 2.5 and Microsoft Internet Publishing Provider to access data in any of the Web Storage Systems. This section explains how to deal with some issues that arise when developing for Exchange 2000 in the Outlook environment.

Adding Collaboration Features

This book consistently describes CDO as the optimal tool to incorporate collaboration capabilities, such as sending e-mail or scheduling meetings, into your applications. Unfortunately, you cannot use CDO in Outlook because CDO uses ExOLEDB, which is a server-side only provider. You do, however, have some options.

The Outlook object model provides nearly everything you need to accomplish standard tasks such as sending e-mail, scheduling meetings, reading attachments, and returning the free/busy status of a recipient. If you need functionality that the Outlook object model does not offer, you can continue to use CDO 1.21 in your applications. CDO 1.21 is a MAPI-based version of CDO, and Exchange 2000 supports it.

Accessing Web Storage System Schema Properties in Outlook Forms

Because Outlook is a MAPI client, it creates and reads MAPI properties. The Web Storage System is not MAPI based and stores properties in native format. When Outlook 2000 accesses properties, it uses MAPI. Fortunately, you can access most of the Web Storage System schema properties by using MAPI properties. For example, you can access the "urn:schemas:contacts:firstname" schema property with the FirstName Outlook property. If you need to access custom schema properties from Outlook, you must create a MAPI property to access the custom schema property. You can create a MAPI property for a custom schema property by using Field Chooser in an Outlook Forms Designer. After you create a MAPI version of your schema property, you can use form controls or the Outlook object model to read and set the custom schema property value.

NOTE   For more information about creating custom Outlook forms, see Appendix B, "Designing Forms with Outlook 2000." For more extensive information, see the Microsoft Press books *Building Applications with Outlook 2000 Technical Reference* (1999) and *Programming Outlook and Exchange* (1999).

Using Field Chooser to Access Schema Properties

To access a custom schema property in an Outlook form with a form control or with the Outlook object model, you must first create a MAPI property for it by using Field Chooser. When you use Outlook Forms Designer to design an Outlook form, you add properties to the form as form controls by using Field Chooser. You drag a property name from the Field Chooser list to a form page, and a new control is created to display and enter data in the field. You can also use Field Chooser to create new properties on a form. If you use custom schema properties on the items that a form displays, you can use Field Chooser to create MAPI properties that access the custom schema properties. Figure 11.1 shows how Field Chooser displays the custom MAPI properties that have been created for an Outlook form.

Figure 11.1
You can use Field Chooser to access custom schema properties.

To create a MAPI property for a Web Storage System schema property by using Field Chooser, follow these steps:

1. In Outlook Forms Designer, click **Field Chooser** on the **Form** menu.

2. Click **New**.

3. Type the name of the custom schema property as the name of the Outlook form property. You don't need to worry about using the proper case of the property name, but the name cannot exceed 32 characters in length, but it is not case sensitive. If necessary, select the **Type** as well.

4. Click **OK** to add the new property to Field Chooser.

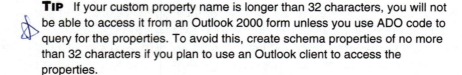

TIP If your custom property name is longer than 32 characters, you will not be able to access it from an Outlook 2000 form unless you use ADO code to query for the properties. To avoid this, create schema properties of no more than 32 characters if you plan to use an Outlook client to access the properties.

After you complete these steps, drag the form field to the form if you want to display the schema property value in a control on the form. When you finish modifying the form, publish the form to one of the forms libraries. For more information about publishing Outlook forms, see Appendix B, "Designing Forms with Outlook 2000."

Figure 11.2 shows a custom Outlook form that was created to display the associated custom schema properties of the custom content class Animal. All the properties shown on the form are custom schema properties. Outlook clients can use this form to create new Animal objects or to edit existing Animal objects.

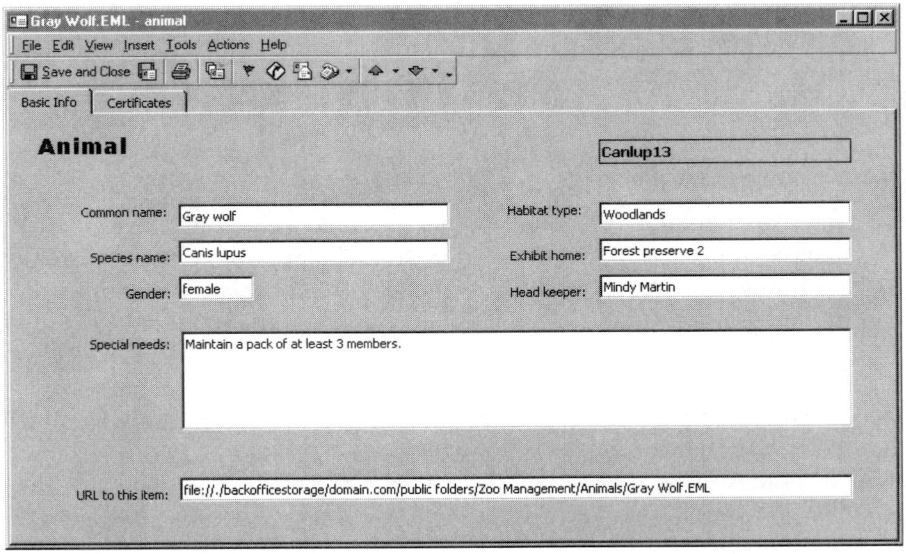

Figure 11.2
You can easily build Outlook forms that display custom schema properties.

TIP If you create custom Outlook form properties for your schema properties and publish the form, you can easily create a custom folder view to display those properties as well. To add a custom schema property to an Outlook folder view, either modify the existing view or create a new one. Then, in the **Show Fields** dialog box, click the custom property on the list of fields associated with the custom Outlook form.

USING THE OUTLOOK OBJECT MODEL TO ACCESS SCHEMA PROPERTIES

You can also use the Outlook object model to access schema properties in an Outlook form. You can access a custom schema property through the UserProperties property of an Outlook item. This property returns a collection of all custom MAPI properties that you created for an Outlook form. To use the collection to retrieve schema properties, you must have already created a new property on the form by using Field Chooser. For example, the following code sample returns the current value of the zoomgt:species custom schema property:

```
strSpeciesName = Item.UserProperties ("zoomgt:species")
```

QUERYING OTHER WEB STORAGE SYSTEMS FROM OUTLOOK FORMS

If you don't have all the information you need for your application saved in the MAPI folder tree, you can query your Outlook form for it. For example, perhaps you have peripheral information stored in another Web Storage System that is used by multiple applications, including your Outlook application. Rather than copy the information to the MAPI folder tree, you can instead query for the information from your Outlook form. You can use ADO and Microsoft Internet Publishing Provider to execute queries from Outlook forms.

Listing 11.4 shows a function in an Outlook form that is called when the form opens to populate a combo box with information. The procedure queries the Staff folder in the Applications Web Storage System for all staff members who have the position of Keeper. The results from the query are then added to a combo box on the Outlook form.

Listing 11.4   Query a non-MAPI folder tree from an Outlook form.

```
Function GetKeeperNames()
    ' Return the names of the keepers
    ' from a folder in a non-MAPI
    ' folder tree.

    Dim cnn              'As ADODB.Connection
    Dim rst              'As ADODB.Recordset
    Dim urlQueryFld      'As String
    Dim strSQL           'As String

    ' Build the URL string
    urlQueryFld = _
        "http://cyberserver/zooweb/Staff/"

    ' Connect to the URL
    Set cnn = CreateObject("ADODB.Connection")
    With cnn
        .Provider = "msdaipp.dso" \
        .Open urlQueryFld
    End With

    ' Select the properties to be returned
    strSQL = "Select " & _
        AddQuotes("urn:schemas:contacts:givenName") & ", " & _
        AddQuotes("urn:schemas:contacts:sn")
    ' Indicate shallow or deep traversal
    ' and the URL to begin the search
    strSQL = strSQL & _
        " FROM SCOPE('DEEP traversal of " & _
        AddQuotes(urlQueryFld) & "')"
    ' Build a filter
    strSQL = strSQL & _
        " WHERE (" & _
        AddQuotes("zoomgt:position") & " = 'keeper')"
    ' Sort the results by the last name
    strSQL = strSQL & _
        " ORDER BY " & _
        AddQuotes("urn:schemas:contacts:sn") & " DESC"
```

```
    'Create a Recordset object
    Set rst = CreateObject("ADODB.Recordset")
    With rst
        'Open Recordset based on the SQL string
        .Open strSQL, cnn
    End With

    ' Return the name in the form of [lastname], [firstname]
    ' and put the results in a combo box
    Do Until rst.EOF
        cboKeepers.AddItem rst.Fields("urn:schemas:contacts:sn") & _
            ", " & rst.Fields("urn:schemas:contacts:givenName")
        rst.MoveNext
    Loop

    ' Close the ADO objects
    rst.Close
    cnn.Close

    ' Release memory used by object variables
    Set rst = Nothing
    Set cnn = Nothing
End Function
```

SUMMARY

Outlook 2000 is the premier MAPI client for Exchange 2000. However, just because Outlook is a MAPI client does not mean you can't benefit by using a Web Storage System. You can incorporate workflow technology into MAPI folders. In addition, MAPI resources, just like any other resources, trigger Web Storage System events. If you build custom Outlook forms for your application, you can even access custom schema properties as form controls.

Section IV, "Building for the Web," explains how to build applications for Exchange that take advantage of the richness of the Web.

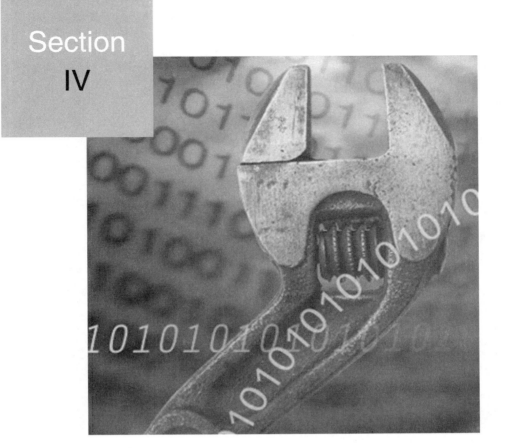

Building for the Web

Chapter:

12 Building Web Applications for Exchange   **531**

13 XML and Exchange   **585**

12

Building Web Applications for Exchange

Microsoft Exchange 2000 Server has many Web features built into it—so many, in fact, that you can develop rich solutions for Exchange with your existing knowledge of Web development. With HTTP access, native Extensible Markup Language (XML) support, and the new Microsoft Web Storage System forms technology for associating Web pages with content classes, the Web is an excellent choice for developing Exchange applications.

Sections in this chapter include:

- **Overview of Web Applications**

- **Using Forms Registry and Forms Registrations**

- **Setting Up a Web Development Environment**

- **Creating and Registering Web Storage System Forms**

OVERVIEW OF WEB APPLICATIONS

This section introduces ways to approach Web development with Exchange and introduces the new Web Storage System forms. The section also discusses a new way of designing Web applications.

APPROACHES TO WEB DEVELOPMENT

To build Web applications for Exchange 2000, you can take advantage of the same skills you use to build Web applications for other data sources, such as Microsoft SQL Server. You can:

- Build simple HTML pages that display static information about a folder.

- Build Active Server Pages (ASP) that use server-side code to return the latest data whenever the Web page is accessed.

- Use ActiveX Data Objects (ADO) and Collaboration Data Objects (CDO) for Exchange to incorporate collaboration features, such as messaging and calendaring, as server-side code to interact with data in a Web Storage System.

- Use custom Component Object Model (COM) components to encapsulate common server-side code functionality and create middle-tier components that you can easily manage and reuse in multiple applications.

- Use the new Web Storage System forms technology to associate Web pages with specific content classes and replace the default Outlook Web Access displays.

THINKING IN TERMS OF DATA, NOT FORMS

The power of the Exchange 2000 Server Web paradigm is its approach to Web development. The standard Web development paradigm is form-focused, which involves a group of Web pages that call other pages by using hyperlinks or code. If a form is used to access data, the form pulls the information from the data source or pushes the data back to the data source. Regardless, the base of the paradigm is the form, not the data.

Exchange, however, deviates from the form-focused approach. In Exchange's data-focused approach, you build hyperlinks to the data, not to the pages. When a client browser requests the data, Exchange sends the data in the appropriate Web page to the client. You don't have to worry about maintaining hyperlinks to the proper form name. In addition, a data-driven approach means that you can build language-neutral solutions. The browser's settings determine what language a form is returned in, and you do not need to build forms in a variety of languages.

UNDERSTANDING HOW WEB STORAGE SYSTEM FORMS WORK

Are the Web Storage System forms just another forms package? Well, not really. Web Storage System forms is more of a catch phrase for Web pages that are registered in a Web Storage System by using a forms registry. A *forms registry* is a collection of form registration items and is part of the standard Exchange installation. A *form registration item* associates a specific content class with a Web page, so that whenever you request an item with that content class, the custom Web page is returned instead of Outlook Web Access.

For example, without the ZooWeb application installed, when you open an Animal item folder in the Animals folder, Outlook Web Access displays the Animal item in a standard post form like that shown in Figure 12.1. Outlook Web Access has no way to know that it should be displaying custom properties.

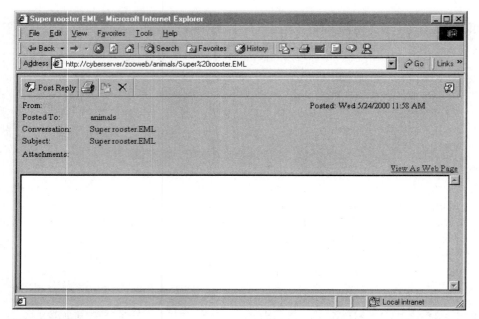

Figure 12.1
By default, Outlook Web Access displays an Animal item using a post form.

When you install the ZooWeb application, a custom Web page is associated with the urn:content-classes:animal content class using a form registration. Now when you request an Animal item using a Web browser, Exchange sends the data in a custom Web page like the one shown in Figure 12.2. This Web page is able to display the custom properties, making the form much more useful than the post form shown previously.

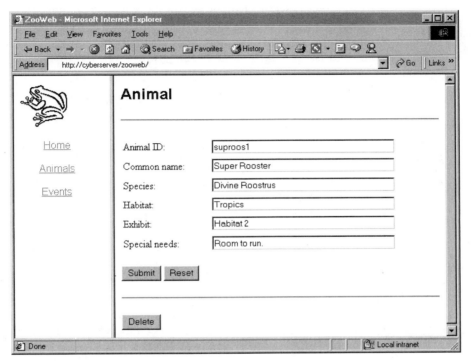

Figure 12.2
You can use a custom Web page to display an item in a Web Storage System folder using the Web Storage System forms.

The forms registry depends on the schema path of the Web Storage System application. The schema path is determined by the urn:schemas-microsoft-com:exch-data:schema-collection-ref property setting on the folders in the application. When a client browser sends Exchange a request for some data resource, Exchange searches the schema path of the Web Storage System application folders for a form registration item with a content class that matches the content class of the requested resource. If a form registration item is found, Exchange searches the information in the form registration and returns the appropriate Web page.

You can create form registration items that return ASP pages as well as HTML pages. If you use an ASP page, all you need to do is create a form registration and save the Web page in a Web Storage System folder in the schema path. To use an HTML page, you must create a form registration and use Forms Renderer to process the HTML properly. Forms Renderer is an ISAPI DLL extension with the name of exwforms.dll. The exwforms.dll file is not part of the standard Exchange installation but is available on the Exchange developer Web site at http://msdn.Microsoft.com/exchange/.

NOTE   You can also download special Microsoft FrontPage 2000 tools to build HTML forms that display and enter Web Storage System data. For more information about these tools, see the Exchange developer Web site (http://msdn.microsoft.com/exchange/).

USING FORMS REGISTRY AND FORMS REGISTRATIONS

The forms registry is the focal point of your Web application. A forms registry enables you to associate Web pages with a content class and a particular set of calling circumstances. As mentioned earlier, almost any Web Storage System folder can be a forms registry. A forms registry consists of registration items that define the set of circumstances under which a Web page is called. This section explains how to create a form registration item by using code and how to set the registration parameters in the resulting Web page. In addition, this section teaches how to install the Forms Registry Explorer, which is a Web-based tool that makes it easy to create and manage form registration items.

CONFIGURING A FORMS REGISTRY

This section explains how to configure a forms registry folder to store form registration items as well as how to optimize form registration items by using custom content classes for folders and items in your application. The section also discusses the Folder Composition tool, which is included on the companion CD to help you configure an application to use a forms registry.

CONFIGURING A FORMS REGISTRY FOLDER

To configure a forms registry folder, you create a schema folder and define the schema path for the application. The schema path is how Exchange searches for the form registration items when a resource with a particular content class is requested.

You can use just about any folder in your application as a forms registry, as long as the folder occurs in the schema path of your application. If you already have a folder designated as the custom schema folder in your application, you can create your form registrations items in that folder. If you do not already have a schema folder, you must create a new application schema folder. Chapter 2, "Exchange and the Web Storage System," explains how to create a custom application schema.

NOTE   When you create a schema folder, you should set the DAV:ishidden property to True to prevent the application schema folder from being displayed in the folder tree. However, hiding a folder from displaying in the tree does not prevent a user who knows the URL of the folder from accessing it. A user who has permission to view the folder can see all the registration items and can potentially disrupt the schema by accidentally or intentionally deleting registrations. To avoid this scenario, explicitly deny access rights to the folder to everyone except the people who manage the schema.

After you create the schema folder, you configure the schema path for an application by setting the urn:schemas-microsoft-com:exch-data:schema-collection-ref property on each folder in the application to point to the application schema folder. If you already have a schema folder, make sure that each child folder is pointing to that schema folder. In addition, if you plan to use a custom Web page for the application parent folder, you must set the urn:schemas-microsoft-com:exch-data:schema-collection-ref property on that folder to point to the custom schema folder as well.

TAKING ADVANTAGE OF CUSTOM CONTENT CLASSES

Because the forms registry associates content classes with Web pages, you must decide ahead of time which content classes will use which custom Web pages. For example, you might want to store information about the staff members at the zoo as items with a content class of urn:content-classes:person. Because you want to use a custom Web page to display the staff members, you create a form registration to display a custom form whenever an item with the urn:content-classes:person is accessed from a Web browser. The custom form contains properties specific to staff members.

However, staff members are not the only objects that use the urn:content-classes:person content class in the Zoo Management application. Perhaps you also store information about people who regularly donate money to the zoo. Because these items also use the urn:content-classes:person content class, the custom form that displays information about staff members also returns information about donators. You must find a way to display one custom form when a staff member item is requested and another custom form when a donator item is requested.

One way to solve this dilemma is to use a custom content class for each folder and item that uses a custom Web page and then create a form registration for each scenario. For example, you can assign staff member items a content class of zoomgt:content-classes:staffmember and assign donator items a content class of zoomgt:content-classes:donator. You create two form registration items for each content class and indicate the appropriate form. This prevents Exchange from sending the donator item data in the staff member Web page.

You do not need to create a content class definition before you assign a custom content class to a folder or item. You can just set the DAV:contentclass schema property of a resource to the custom content class when you create the resource. If the resource already exists, change the DAV:contentclass value to the custom one. See "Using the Folder Composition Tool" for an easy way to do this.

USING THE FOLDER COMPOSITION TOOL

The companion CD includes a tool (Folder Composition.exe) for managing the composition of folders. You can use the Folder Composition tool to:

- Define the schema path of an application by setting the urn:schemas-microsoft-com:exch-data:schema-collection-ref schema properties on a folder.

- Specify custom content classes for folders by setting the DAV:contentclass property to a custom content class name.

Figure 12.3 shows the Folder Composition tool.

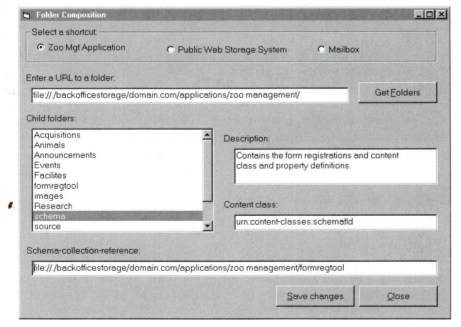

Figure 12.3
Use the Folder Composition tool to adjust schema details.

To use the Folder Composition tool, run the Folder Composition tool application on the companion CD. When the form appears, in **Enter a URL to a folder**, type the URL of the folder you want to open, or use a shortcut button to build the URL. For example, click **Zoo Mgt Application** to build the URL for the Zoo Management application on the Applications Web Storage System. Then click **Get Folders**, and the tool attempts to connect to the Exchange server on the local domain and retrieve the contents of the specified folder.

Child folders lists the child folders in the specified folder. In the list, click a child folder, and **Description** displays the DAV:comment value, **Content Class** displays the content class currently assigned to the folder, and **Schema-collection-reference** displays the urn:schemas-microsoft-com:exch-data:schema-collection-ref schema property. To change any of these values, type a new value in the appropriate text box, and click **Save Changes.**

NOTE To change the content class for an item instead of a folder, set the DAV:contentclass property to the custom content class when you create a new item. If you want to change an existing item from one content class to another, you can modify the source code in the Folder Composition tool to alter the DAV:contentclass schema property on items as well as folders, or you can write a simple query that does the same thing.

USING FORM REGISTRATIONS

This section explains how to create form registration items in a forms registry folder and how to access form registration parameters from the target Web page. The section also discusses the Form Registry tool, which is included on the companion CD to help you create and manage form registration items in a forms registry.

CREATING A FORM REGISTRATION

To define a new form registration, you create a new item in a schema folder and set the DAV:contentclass schema property of the new item to urn:schemas-microsoft-com:office:forms#registration. After you create the item, set some special properties to define the circumstances under which the Web page is called. Table 12.1 describes the more common properties used to define a form registration item. All these properties are string values.

Table 12.1   Core properties for defining a form registration

urn:schemas-microsoft-com: office:forms# property	Description
contentclass	Specifies the DAV:contentclass that triggers the form specified in the registration.
executeurl	Indicates the URL of the engine used to render the form. If you register an ASP page, this is the URL of that page. If you use HTML forms, you must always set this to the exwforms.dll ISAPI filter.
request	Specifies the type of request. Can be either GET or POST. Use GET when you retrieve information. Use POST when you change the data in a Web Storage System or send information in the request.
binding	Indicates where the form executes. Can be "server," "client," or "auto." In the case of ASP forms, this is always "server."
platform	Indicates the platform of the server. WINNT for Microsoft Windows 2000 Server.

The following code sample creates a new form registration that executes the default.asp page whenever a browser opens the Zoo Management application folder.

```
With New ADODB.Record
    .Open "default.reg" _
        , , adModeReadWrite, adCreateNonCollection

    .Fields("DAV:contentclass") _
        = "urn:schemas-microsoft-com:office:forms#registration"

    ' This is the content class that will trigger the form
    .Fields _
        ("urn:schemas-microsoft-com:office:forms#contentclass") _
        = "zoomgt:content-classes:zoowebhome"

    ' This is the executing engine; for an ASP,
    ' this is the name of the ASP page
    .Fields _
        ("urn:schemas-microsoft-com:office:forms#executeurl") _
        = "default.asp"

    ' Get if the form is retrieving data;
    ' Post if the form is putting data onto the server
    .Fields _
        ("urn:schemas-microsoft-com:office:forms#request") _
        = "GET"

    ' Indicates where the form will execute
    .Fields _
        ("urn:schemas-microsoft-com:office:forms#binding") _
        = "server"

    ' Platform of the browser
    .Fields _
        ("urn:schemas-microsoft-com:office:forms#platform") _
        = "WINNT"
End With
```

To be more specific about how a Web page is associated with a content class and when Exchange sends the Web page to the requesting browser, you can set some or all the optional properties listed in Table 12.2. Like the properties in Table 12.1, these properties are all string values.

Table 12.2 Optional properties for a form registration

urn:schemas-microsoft-com: office:forms# property	Description
formurl	Specifies the URL of the form being registered. Can be absolute or relative. If you use ASP pages, you do not need to set this, but you can use it as a base reference.
cmd	Denotes the action or behavior that is calling the Web page. You can use a predefined command or a custom command.
executeparameters	Indicates parameters to pass to the form-rendering engine specified by the executeurl property. You can access these parameters from an ASP page with the QueryString collection.
messagestate	Indicates the state of the item, such as normal, submitted, or important, that triggers the Web page.
contentstate	Performs form matching.
language	Specifies the language of the form. Corresponds to the ISO language country value in the request header.
browser	Indicates the browser type.
version	Indicates the browser version.
majorver	Major version of the browser.
minorver	Minor version of the browser.

If you are not using any of the optional properties, you might still want to set each optional property to the asterisk (*) wildcard character value. When you have multiple form registrations in a folder for the same content class, a form registration with wildcard character values in properties takes precedence over a form registration with properties that are not set.

For more information about form registrations in context with the forms that they call, see "Creating and Registering Web Storage System Forms" later in this chapter.

ACCESSING THE FORM REGISTRATION PARAMETERS FROM A WEB PAGE

The form registration passes two parameters to the Web page assigned to the content class: dataurl and formurl. The dataurl parameter is the URL of the requested resource. When the user clicks a folder hyperlink, the form registration passes that URL to the Web page assigned to the content class of the folder as the dataurl parameter. For example, say you have a Web page with hyperlinks to the various folders of the Zoo Management application. If the user clicks the hyperlink to the Animals folder, the dataurl argument passed to the form contains the string URL:

```
"HTTP://cyberserver/zooweb/animals/"
```

You can use this parameter in your Web pages to determine which resource in the Web Storage System to act on with the code. For example, if the user attempts to delete an item, the dataURL can open the appropriate ADO record to delete the record. You can access the dataurl parameter from an ASP page by using the QueryString collection. The following code sample stores the dataurl value in a script-level variable:

```
<%urlResource = Request.QueryString("dataurl")%>
```

TIP If you want to use multiple procedures in the Web page that all need to access the dataurl, save the parameter value to a script-level variable. A script-level variable is declared near the top of the Web page, not in a procedure. You can use a script-level variable in code anywhere in the page.

The other parameter passed by the form registration is the formurl parameter. The formurl parameter contains the URL of the Web page specified in the form registration optional schema property, urn:schemas-microsoft-com:office:forms#formurl. The formurl parameter lets you establish a point of reference for all other URLs in a Web page. For example, when you access a form named default.asp in the Zoo Management application schema folder, the formurl passes the following string:

```
"HTTP://cyberserver/zooweb/schema/default.asp"
```

You can access the formurl parameter from an ASP page by using the QueryString collection. You can then use this value in a <base> tag as the href attribute value. For example, the following code sample establishes a base reference to a formurl value:

```
<base href=<%=request.querystring("formurl")%>>
```

Avoid using absolute URLs in your Web application to make the application as portable as possible. This way, your application doesn't fail just because you've renamed the application folder. This is one reason to set the urn:schemas-microsoft-com:office:forms#formurl schema property on the form registration item even though it's not required for an ASP page. If all your forms are stored in the schema folder and you do not move the schema folder, you can rely on the formurl as a point of reference for all the other items in your application.

USING THE FORMS REGISTRY EXPLORER

Creating form registration items can be a tedious task if you modify code each time you create a new registration. Make this task easier by using the Forms Registry Explorer included on the companion CD. The Forms Registry Explorer is a Web-based tool that uses ASP pages; you can use it to create form registration items in a schema folder, modify existing registration items, and delete registration items. The tool is actually a set of ASP pages that are also registered in an Exchange schema folder.

To use the Forms Registry Explorer, follow these steps:

1. Run **InstallFormRegExplorer.** You must provide a path to a Web Storage System folder in which to install the tool. Select the parent folder of the application schema folder that you are using. For example, to use the tool for the Zoo Management application schema, install the tool in the Zoo Management folder. The script creates a FormsRegExplorer folder and the necessary form registrations in the folder.

2. Verify that the parent folder in which you have installed the tool has a virtual directory, and enable **Execute scripts** for the directory.

3. Check the permissions for the parent folder. Make sure that everyone who must use the tool has the proper read/write permissions to the parent folder as well as to the FormsRegExplorer folder.

4. Copy the ASP pages from the Forms Registry Explorer folder on the companion CD to the FormsRegExplorer folder on the Web Storage System. These pages are used to list the registrations, display a registration, save information, and delete registrations.

5. Use the Folder Composition application discussed earlier in the chapter to change the DAV:contentclass schema property of your application folder to *urn:content-classes:schemafld*. This is the content class that triggers the Form Registry tool. You must also change the schema-collection-reference property to point to the new FormsRegExplorer folder.

After you complete these steps, if you use Microsoft Internet Explorer to access your application schema folder, you should see a page similar to Figure 12.4. If you haven't added any form registrations to the schema folder yet, the list is empty.

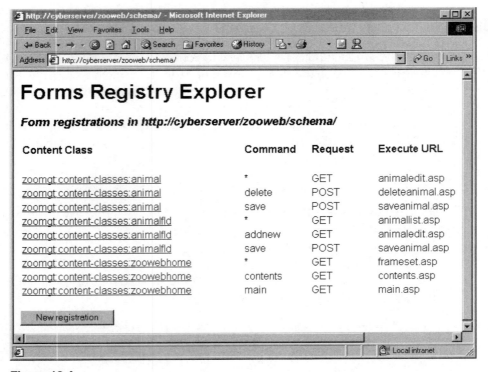

Figure 12.4
You can use the Forms Registry Explorer to easily create, modify, and delete form registrations in any schema folder.

To create a new form registration, click **New registration**. A blank form appears. Fill in the necessary information, and click **Save registration**. You are redirected back to the main page, and the new registration should appear in the list. To view an existing registration, click the content class name. Figure 12.5 shows a form registration.

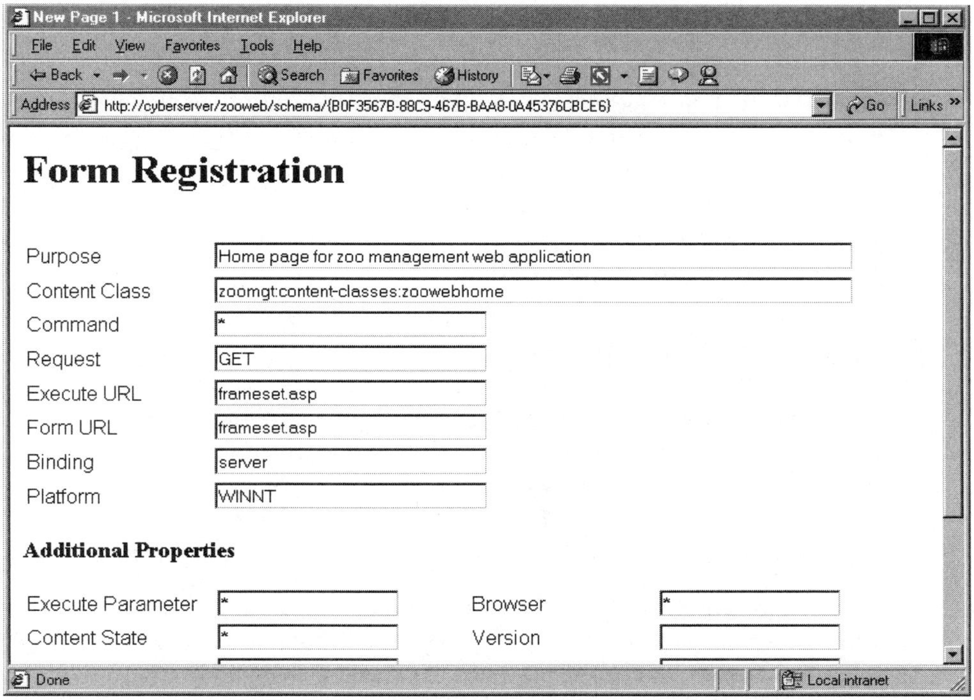

Figure 12.5
An existing form registration

SETTING UP A WEB DEVELOPMENT ENVIRONMENT

To set up a Web environment for an application, you must configure the folders in the application and then open the application by using a Web development tool. This section explains how to configure the Web Storage System folders in a Web application so that Web pages display properly and how to set up the Web development environment by using FrontPage.

NOTE This chapter assumes that you have already created the Applications Web Storage System, installed the Zoo Management folders, and installed the ZooWeb application. If you have not done this, see the introduction of the book for more information about setting up the application.

SETTING EXECUTE PERMISSIONS AND ACCESS RIGHTS

By default, Web Storage System folders are configured as containers for Web information. However, to effectively execute Web pages by using the Web Storage System forms registry, you must set the proper execute permissions and access rights. This section covers how to set execute permissions on a folder so that Web pages execute properly, as well as how to configure anonymous access so that everyone can use your application.

SETTING EXECUTE PERMISSIONS

By default, an Exchange virtual directory is configured without any execute permissions. If you attempt to access a Web page that uses script, such as an ASP page, in the virtual directory folders, Exchange returns an error instead of the Web page. To access an ASP page from the Web Storage System, you must set the execute permissions on the virtual directory to allow scripts to run.

To configure the folder, open Exchange System Manager and access the properties of the virtual directory. Click the **Access** tab. If your Web application uses ASP pages, in **Execute Permissions**, select **Scripts**. If your Web application uses the exwforms.dll, in **Execute Permissions**, select **Scripts and Executables**. Figure 12.6 shows the proper setting for executing ASP pages.

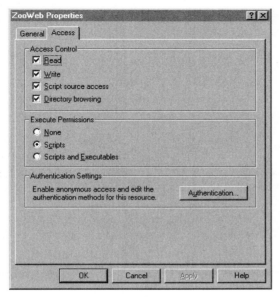

Figure 12.6
For Web pages to execute properly in a Web Storage System folder, you must set the execute permissions on the virtual directory.

USING ANONYMOUS ACCESS

If you need specific control over how people access your Web application, click **Authentication** to display the dialog box shown in Figure 12.7. By default, **Anonymous access** is disabled. When **Anonymous access** is disabled, Windows must be able to authenticate each Web application user in Active Directory. If you prefer to run everything under a single account that allows everyone access, select **Anonymous access**, and select a specific user account that the code in the Web site executes as. If you take this approach, be sure to select a user who has the standard access rights, such as read/write access, to the application folders.

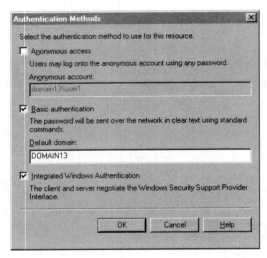

Figure 12.7
With Anonymous access disabled, only users with user accounts in your domain can access your Web site.

If you prefer to have more specific control over how the code executes, you can use COM+ components and security roles for a greater level of security.

> **NOTE** For users to access the contents of a Web Storage System folder by using a Web Storage System form, you must also grant access rights to the users of your application. For example, for a user to open an item for editing, you must grant the user permissions to read and set properties as well as to read and write attributes. For more information about using COM+ security roles and setting permissions, see Chapter 14, "Setting Security and Permissions."

USING A WEB DEVELOPMENT TOOL

You can use FrontPage and Microsoft Visual InterDev to develop an Exchange Web application. You can also use Microsoft Notepad. However, because the Web Storage System form tools are available in FrontPage, this section focuses on FrontPage as the development environment. This section also explains how to use ADO and CDO constants.

USING FRONTPAGE 2000 TO CREATE A WEB DEVELOPMENT ENVIRONMENT

By using FrontPage, you can open a Web application on either a client machine or on the server. To open a Web project for an existing Web Storage System application, follow these steps:

1. In FrontPage, click **File**, and then click **Open Web**. Exchange configured the Web site when you created the virtual directory, so you are not creating a new Web application. The **Open Web** dialog box appears.

2. In the **Open Web** dialog box, enter a URL that uses HTTP and points to the Web Storage System application that you want to open. Be sure that the URL points to the virtual directory you created for the application. Click **Open**. It might take a few seconds, but then FrontPage displays the folders and files of your Web application.

3. If this is the first time that you are opening the Web Storage System folder, FrontPage prompts you for permission to add a few new folders and files. Allow FrontPage to do this. You need those files to develop Web pages that function properly. Figure 12.8 shows what FrontPage looks like when you open the ZooWeb application.

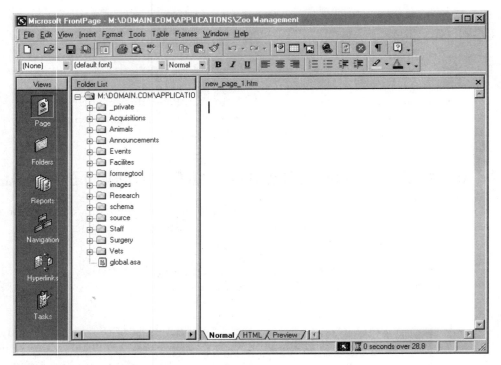

Figure 12.8
You can use FrontPage to build and manage your Exchange Web application.

You can now create any Web pages that you need for your application. Be sure to save all Web pages in the schema folder for the Web Storage System application. If you save forms elsewhere, the forms registry can't find them.

NOTE The global.asa file is one exception to this rule. If you build an ASP application and use a global.asa file, you must save this file in the root application folder.

USING ADO AND CDO CONSTANTS IN WEB PAGES

When you write ADO and CDO code in Web applications, you must use the numerical equivalents of the constants by default. To avoid using the numerical equivalents of constants, Web developers often build a special #include file that contains the constants and then reference this file in every Web page that needs to access the constants. These files can be large and must be included with every page that uses them.

Microsoft Internet Information Services (IIS) 5.0 now offers a more efficient way to reference type libraries. By using METADATA tags in the global.asa, you can reference a type library once and use it on every ASP page. The following code sample references the CDO for Exchange type library:

```
<!--METADATA TYPE="typelib" UUID="CD000000-8B95-11D1-82DB-00C04FB1625D"
    NAME="CDO for Exchange 2000 Type Library" -->
```

NOTE   The code listings in this chapter are available in the Microsoft Visual Basic project CH_12.vbp on the companion CD. If you want to run the samples as they are written, you must have the Zoo Management sample installed on your Exchange 2000 server. For information about installing the application, see the introduction to the book. In addition, the code samples repeatedly call a function named GetStorageName. This function returns the name of the domain in which the code is running. For more information about the GetStorageName function, see Chapter 8, "Interacting with Active Directory."

To use a global.asa file in your Web application, save the file at the virtual directory root folder. For example, if you have created the ZooWeb virtual directory, you save this page in the Zoo Management folder. If you save the file anywhere else in the application, such as in the schema folder, the file will not fire. You know you have stored it in the wrong place if your code fails when you attempt to use one of the constants. Listing 12.1 shows a sample global.asa file that references the ADO 2.5 type library and all three CDO for Exchange type libraries.

Listing 12.1   Reference type libraries in a global.asa page.

```
<SCRIPT LANGUAGE=VBScript RUNAT=Server>

<!--METADATA TYPE="typelib" UUID="CD000000-8B95-11D1-82DB-00C04FB1625D"
    NAME="CDO for Exchange 2000 Type Library" -->
<!--METADATA TYPE="typelib" UUID="CD001000-8B95-11D1-82DB-00C04FB1625D"
    NAME="Microsoft CDO Workflow Objects for Microsoft Exchange"-->
<!--METADATA TYPE="typelib" UUID="25150F00-5734-11D2-A593-00C04F990D8A"
    NAME="Microsoft CDO for Exchange Management Library"-->
<!--METADATA TYPE="typelib" UUID="00000205-0000-0010-8000-00AA006D2EA4"
    NAME="ADODB Type Library" -->

</script>
```

CREATING AND REGISTERING WEB STORAGE SYSTEM FORMS

This section describes how to build Web Storage System forms and create registration items to associate the Web pages with a particular set of request circumstances. The examples shown in this section are from the ZooWeb sample application; this section explains how this application was built.

NOTE This chapter assumes that you have a basic understanding of Web development, including how to use ASP pages. If you are new to Web development, visit the Microsoft Developer Network (MSDN) Web site (http://msdn.microsoft.com) for information about the basics of ASP pages and for information about the new features available with IIS 5.0.

CHOOSING A FOLDER FOR WEB PAGE STORAGE

You can create Web Storage System forms with whatever Web development tool you prefer. You can also save these Web pages in any Web Storage System folder. However, as with the schema folder, you should plan where to save these forms to minimize maintenance later. Regardless of where you save these forms, you must reflect the proper folder path when you create an associated form registration item and set the formurl and executeurl form registration properties. For example, if you save a default.asp page to the same folder as the form registration, you then set the executeurl property to:

```
default.asp
```

If you save the Web page to a folder on the same level in the folder hierarchy as the schema folder, you set the executeurl property to something like this:

```
../WebPages/default.asp
```

The point is to make sure that the form registration executeurl and formurl properties reflect the relative URL properly. The ZooWeb application stores the Web pages in the Schema application folder.

CREATING A SIMPLE HOME PAGE

When you enter the URL to the ZooWeb virtual directory in a Web browser without a form registration, the browser displays the standard Outlook Web Access folder view of the Zoo Management folder. To display a custom Web page whenever a Web browser requests the application folder, create a form registration for the content class of the application folder and indicate the Web page you want Exchange to send back to the client. For example, you could create a form registration with the property settings listed in Table 12.3 to have Exchange send default.asp whenever a Web browser requests a resource with the zoomgt:content-classes:zoowebhome content class. Because you are requesting only data, you set the request property to GET.

Table 12.3   Form registration properties for the ZooWeb simple home page

Form registration property	Value
contentclass	zoomgt:content-classes:zoowebhome
cmd	*
request	GET
executeurl	default.asp
formurl	default.asp
binding	server
platform	winnt

The default.asp page can be an existing Web page or one that you will create. The default.asp in the ZooWeb application is a simple Web page that displays some text and an image. Figure 12.9 shows the simple default.asp Web page that is registered for the ZooWeb application folder. If you request the application folder with a Web browser after creating this form registration, Exchange sends the default.asp Web page.

Figure 12.9
A simple home page for ZooWeb

The simple home page for ZooWeb contains an image that is also stored in the Zoo Management application in an Images folder. Although you can create an absolute URL that points to the image, it is better to use the formurl parameter and a relative URL of the image. For example, the following code uses the formurl parameter and <base> tag to establish a point of reference for URLs used in the Web page:

```
<base href=<%=request.querystring("formurl")%>>
```

The image can then be referenced in the <img> tag by using a URL that is always relative to where the form is stored:

```
<img border="0" src="../images/frog.gif" width="259" height="247">
```

CREATING A FRAMESET HOME PAGE

Another option for a home page is to create a frameset. The ZooWeb application uses a two-page frameset for the home page: one page for the contents pane to provide a way to move through the Web site and one page for the main pane that displays the contents of a folder or the details of an item. The actual frameset page is a third Web page in this solution. This means that Exchange must send three pages to the client when it requests the Zoo Management application folder, so the ZooWeb application uses three different form registrations. This section discusses how each of the three registrations works and what the associated Web pages do. Figure 12.10 shows what the ZooWeb home page looks like when it uses a frameset.

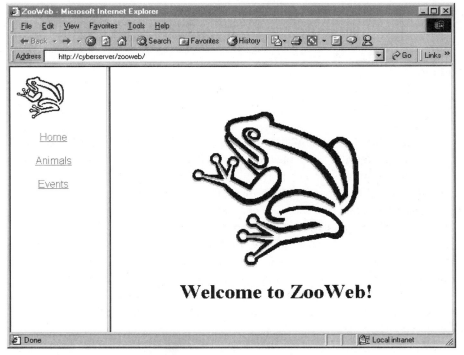

Figure 12.10
ZooWeb home page that uses a frameset

Understanding the Frameset Page

The frameset page manages the display of the other two pages. So that Exchange returns this page whenever a Web browser requests the Zoo Management folder, the ZooWeb application uses a form registration with the property settings listed in Table 12.4.

Table 12.4   Form registration properties for the frameset.asp Web page

Form registration property	Value
contentclass	zoomgt:content-classes:zoowebhome
cmd	*
request	GET
executeurl	frameset.asp
formurl	frameset.asp
binding	server
platform	winnt

You can create a page similar to the frameset.asp page by using FrontPage 2000 and then configure it to display the appropriate pages. The easiest way to configure the frameset to display the other Web pages is to click the **Frames Page HTML** tab and modify the HTML directly. In each <frame> tag, you must set the *src* attribute to indicate the data that each frame displays by default. Unlike in traditional Web application development, however, you are not indicating a Web page to display, you are supplying the URL of a resource. Because the frameset applies the ZooWeb application folder, the URL should still point to the application folder. However, you must provide a parameter value when opening the URL to distinguish the frame page from the frameset itself. For example, the following code sample opens the ZooWeb application folder again but passes a cmd parameter value as well:

```
<frame name="contents" target="main" src="./?cmd=contents"
    scrolling="auto">
```

Listing 12.2 shows the complete source code for the ZooWeb frameset Web page.

Listing 12.2   ZooWeb frameset Web page

```html
<html>
<head>
<title>ZooWeb</title>
<meta name="GENERATOR" content="Microsoft FrontPage 4.0">
<meta name="ProgId" content="FrontPage.Editor.Document">
<link rel="stylesheet" type="text/css" href="zoostyles.css">
</head>

<frameset cols="150,*">
  <frame name="contents" target="main" src="./?cmd=contents"
    scrolling="auto">
  <frame name="main" scrolling="auto" src="./?cmd=main">
  <noframes>
  <body>

  <p>This page uses frames, but your browser doesn't support them.</p>

  </body>
  </noframes>
</frameset>
</html>
```

UNDERSTANDING THE CONTENTS PAGE

The contents page is the navigation bar for the ZooWeb application. The frameset page opens the contents page using a URL like this:

```
"./?cmd=contents"
```

This relative URL points to the ZooWeb application folder but passes a cmd parameter value of *contents* to distinguish this page from the frameset page. The contents page form registration must reflect this scenario as well. For example, the ZooWeb application uses a form registration with the property settings listed in Table 12.5 to return the contents.asp Web page.

Table 12.5 Form registration properties for the contents.asp Web page

Form registration property	Value
contentclass	zoomgt:content-classes:zoowebhome
cmd	contents
request	GET
executeurl	contents.asp
formurl	contents.asp
binding	server
platform	winnt

Listing 12.3 shows the source code for the contents.asp Web page that is called by the previous form registration.

Listing 12.3 Contents Web page

```
<html>
<head>
<meta http-equiv="Content-Language" content="en-us">
<meta http-equiv="Content-Type" content="text/html;
charset=windows-1252">
<meta name="GENERATOR" content="Microsoft FrontPage 4.0">
<meta name="ProgId" content="FrontPage.Editor.Document">
<title>Welcome to the ZooWeb</title>
<base href=<%=request.querystring("formurl")%> target="main">
<link rel="stylesheet" type="text/css" href="zoostyles.css">
</head>
```

```
<body>
<p><img border="0" src="../images/frog.gif" width="73" height="67"></p>
<p align="center"><a href="../?cmd=main">Home</a></p>
<p align="center"><a href="../Animals/">Animals</a></p>
<p align="center">
<a href="../Events/?cmd=contents&view=monthly">Events</a>
</p>
<p> </p>
<p> </p>
</body>
</html>
```

The form registration passes the formurl parameter to the Web page, which can be used to provide a reference point for all URLs used in the contents.asp page. To use this URL, add a <base> tag in the <head> tag of the Web page and set the *href* attribute to the formurl parameter. You also want to set the *target* attribute to Main, which is the ID of the main frame. When a user clicks a link on the contents page, the data is opened relative to the base tag URL, and the results appear in the main target page. The following code sample shows the base tag used in the contents.asp Web page:

```
<base href=<%=request.querystring("formurl")%> target="main">
```

When you create hyperlinks in a Web page that uses a <base> with the formurl attribute, you use the folder that contains the form that owns the hyperlinks as the point of reference for all other URLs. For example, to create a link to the Animals folder in the ZooWeb, you must build a URL that goes up one level in the folder hierarchy from the schema folder to the parent folder and then back down to the Animals folder. The anchor tag and href look something like this:

```
<a href="../Animals/">Animals</a>
```

To access the main page, you need to move up only one level to the parent folder, so you use an anchor tag like this:

```
<a href="../?cmd=main">
```

Understanding the Main Page

The main page is the basic welcome page from the very first example. The frameset page automatically fills the main frame with the main.asp page whenever the frameset is initially displayed. This is done by using a URL like this:

```
"./?cmd=main"
```

This relative URL points to the ZooWeb application folder but passes a cmd parameter value of *main* to distinguish this page from the frameset page and the contents page. To return the main.asp Web page instead of either of the other two pages, the ZooWeb application uses a form registration with the property settings shown in Table 12.6.

Table 12.6 Form registration properties for the main.asp Web page

Form registration property	Value
contentclass	zoomgt:content-classes:zoowebhome
cmd	main
request	GET
executeurl	main.asp
formurl	main.asp
binding	server
platform	winnt

Listing 12.4 shows the source code for the main.asp Web page. As with the Contents.asp page, the main.asp Web page also uses a <base> tag and the formurl parameter to provide a point of reference for the image in the page.

Listing 12.4 ZooWeb main page

```
<% @enablesessionState=false %>
<html>
<head>
<meta http-equiv="Content-Language" content="en-us">
<meta http-equiv="Content-Type" content="text/html;
charset=windows-1252">
<meta name="GENERATOR" content="Microsoft FrontPage 4.0">
```

```
<meta name="ProgId" content="FrontPage.Editor.Document">
<title>Main</title>
<link rel="stylesheet" type="text/css" href="zoostyles.css">
<base href=<%=request.querystring("formurl")%>>
</head>

<body>
<h1 align="center"> </h1>
<h1 align="center">
<img border="0" src="../images/frog.gif" width="259" height="247">
</h1>
<h1 align="center">Welcome to ZooWeb!</h1>
</body>
</html>
```

Getting Folder Contents

One way to access the contents of a folder is to use ADO in a Web Storage System form and then use HTML to display the results in a Web page. The ZooWeb application uses the animalist.asp Web page to display the contents of the Animals folder, which has a DAV:contentclass of zoomgt:content-classes:animalfld. To return this page whenever a user requests the Animal folder, the ZooWeb application uses a form registration item with the property settings listed in Table 12.7.

Table 12.7   Form registration properties for the animalist.asp Web page

Form registration property	Value
contentclass	zoomgt:content-classes:animalfld
cmd	*
request	GET
executeurl	animalist.asp
formurl	animalist.asp
binding	server
platform	winnt

The animalist.asp Web page uses server-side ADO code to access the contents of the folder and HTML to display the results. The ADO code executes a query on the Animals folder and uses the dataurl parameter as the URL of the folder. Because the URL returned by the dataurl parameter uses HTTP, you must explicitly indicate that you use the Exchange OLE DB (ExOLEDB) provider in the connection by setting the Provider property of a Connection object to "EXOLEDB.datasource." The results are then placed in a table.

Listing 12.5 shows the complete source code for the animalist.asp Web page.

Listing 12.5   List the contents of the Animals folder.

```
<%Option Explicit%>
<html>
<head>
<meta http-equiv="Content-Type" content="text/html;
charset=windows-1252">
<meta name="GENERATOR" content="Microsoft FrontPage 4.0">
<meta name="ProgId" content="FrontPage.Editor.Document">
<title>Animals</title>
<base href=<%=request.querystring("formurl")%>>
<link rel="stylesheet" type="text/css" href="zoostyles.css">
</head>

<body>
<table border="0" width="100%" cellpadding="0" height="53">
 <tr>
<td width="50%" height="51">
<h1>Zoo Animals </h1>
</td>
<td width="50%" valign="bottom" height="51">
<h3 align="right"><i>Click on an animal for details</i></h3>
</td>
</tr>
</table>
<hr>

<%
Function AddQuotes(strValue)
```

```
' Given a string, wrap it in quotes, doubling
' any quotes within the string.

  Const QUOTE = """"
  AddQuotes = _
     QUOTE _
     & Replace(strValue, QUOTE, QUOTE & QUOTE) _
     & QUOTE
End Function

' Get a list of animals in the Animals folder
' using ADO.

Dim cnn 'As ADODB.Connection
Dim rst 'As ADODB.Recordset
Dim urlQueryFld 'As String
Dim strSQL 'As String

' Get the URL to the animals folder
urlQueryFld = request.querystring("dataurl")


' Connect to the URL
Set cnn = CreateObject("ADODB.Connection")
With cnn
   .Provider = "exoledb.datasource"
   .Open urlQueryFld
End With


' Build the SQL query
strSQL = "Select " & _
   AddQuotes("DAV:displayname") & ", " & _
   AddQuotes("DAV:contentclass") & ", " & _
   AddQuotes("zoomgt:commonname") & ", " & _
   AddQuotes("zoomgt:species") & ", " & _
   AddQuotes("DAV:href")
strSQL = strSQL & _
   " FROM SCOPE('SHALLOW traversal of " & _
   AddQuotes(urlQueryFld) & "')"
strSQL = strSQL & _
   " WHERE " & AddQuotes("DAV:contentclass") & _
   " = 'zoomgt:content-classes:animal'"
```

```
strSQL = strSQL & _
   " ORDER BY " & AddQuotes("DAV:displayname")

' Get the results of the query
Set rst = CreateObject("ADODB.Recordset")
With rst
   .Open strSQL, cnn
End With

response.Write "<table>"
Do Until rst.EOF
   response.Write "<tr><td width=200>"
%>

<a href="../animals/<%=rst.Fields("DAV:displayname")%>">
<h2><%=rst.Fields("zoomgt:commonname")%></h2>
</a>

<%
   response.Write "</td></tr>"
   rst.MoveNext
Loop

response.Write "</table>"

' Close the ADO object
rst.Close
cnn.Close

' Release memory used by object variables
Set rst = Nothing
Set cnn = Nothing
%>
<p/>
<form method="GET" action="../animals/">
<p/><input type="submit" value="Add new animal" name="B1">
<input type="hidden" name="cmd" value="addnew">
</form>

</body>
</html>
```

TIP   When you intersperse script and HTML, try to avoid switching between the two. Switches between the scripting engine and HTML reduce your Web application's performance. Instead of making numerous inline calls, you can write a bunch of HTML tags at once by using one call to the Response.Write statement. You can also increase performance by turning on response buffering. In IIS 5.0, response buffering is on by default.

If you click the Animals hyperlink on the content pane in a Web browser, Exchange sends the animalist.asp page, and the Web browser displays something like Figure 12.11.

Figure 12.11
You can use a Web page to display the contents of a folder.

To provide a way to access details about an item in a folder the animalist.asp page uses an anchor tag around one of the property values and set the *href* attribute to the URL of the item. The following code sample displays the zoomgt:commonname property value to the user, but adds a hyperlink to the text by using a combination of the relative URL for the Animals folder and the DAV:displayname for the animal:

```
<a href="../animals/<%=rst.Fields("DAV:displayname")%>">
   <h2><%=rst.Fields("zoomgt:commonname")%></h2>
</a>
```

DISPLAYING AN ITEM

You can display the properties of an item in a Web page by using ADO to read the item properties and form controls to display the values. The ZooWeb application uses the animaledit.asp Web page to display the properties of an Animal item, which has a DAV:contentclass of zoomgt:content-classes:animal. To send the animaledit.asp whenever a user requests an Animal item, the ZooWeb application uses a form registration with the property settings listed in Table 12.8.

Table 12.8   Form registration properties for the animaledit.asp Web page

Form registration property	Value
contentclass	zoomgt:content-classes:animal
cmd	*
request	GET
executeurl	animaledit.asp
formurl	animaledit.asp
binding	server
platform	winnt

The animaledit.asp Web page uses the dataurl parameter to identify which animal item triggered the form. The ADO Connection object uses this URL to connect to the item, and the ADO Record object uses the URL to access the properties of the item. An HTML form displays the property values. The form includes a submit button and a reset button. Use the submit button to save changes that are made to the item or to save a new item. The Web page also includes a second form with a delete button. Use this button to delete an existing animal item. All these tasks are discussed in more detail later in this chapter.

Listing 12.6 shows the source code for the animaledit.asp Web page.

Listing 12.6   Display the properties of an animal item.

```
<%Option Explicit%>
<html>
<head>
<meta http-equiv="Content-Type" content="text/html; charset=windows-
1252">
<meta name="GENERATOR" content="Microsoft FrontPage 4.0">
<meta name="ProgId" content="FrontPage.Editor.Document">
<title>New Page 1</title>
<base href=<%=request.querystring("formurl")%>>
</head>

<%
Dim rec
Dim cnn
Dim strDataUrl

strDataUrl = request.querystring("dataurl")

' Open a connection
Set cnn = CreateObject("adodb.connection")
With cnn
   .Provider = "exoledb.datasource"
   .Open strDataUrl
End With
```

```
' Open a Record on the item that triggered
' the form.
Set rec = server.CreateObject("adodb.record")
rec.Open strDataUrl, cnn, adModeReadWrite
%>

<body>
<h2><font face="Arial">Animal</font></h2>

<hr align="Left">
<form method="POST" Action="<%=strDataUrl%>?cmd=save"
    name="FrontPage_Form1">
<table border="0" width="465" height="187">
<tr>
<td width="131" height="25">Animal ID:</td>
<td width="318" height="25">
<input type="text" name="txtAnimalID"
    Value="<%=rec.fields("zoomgt:animalid")%>" size="43">
</td>
</tr>
<tr>
<td width="131" height="25">Common name:</td>
<td width="318" height="25" >
<input type="text" name="txtCommonname"
    Value="<%=rec.fields("zoomgt:commonname")%>" size="43">
</td>
</tr>
<tr>
<td width="131" height="25">Species:</td>
<td width="318" height="25" >
<input type="text" name="txtSpecies"
    Value="<%=rec.fields("zoomgt:species")%>" size="43">
</td>
</tr>
<tr>
<td width="131" height="25">Habitat:</td>
<td width="318" height="25">
<input type="text" name="txtHabitat"
    Value="<%=rec.fields("zoomgt:habitat")%>" size="43">
</td>
</tr>
```

```
<tr>
<td width="131" height="25">Exhibit:</td>
<td width="318" height="25">
<input type="text" name="txtExhibit"
    Value="<%=rec.fields("zoomgt:exhibit")%>" size="43">
</td>
</tr>
<tr>
<td width="131" height="25">Special needs:</td>
<td width="318" height="25">
<input type="text" name="txtSpecialNeeds"
    Value="<%=rec.fields("zoomgt:specialneeds")%>" size="43">
</td>
</tr>
</table>

<p>
<input type="submit" value="Submit" name="B1">
<input type="reset" value="Reset" name="B2">
</p>
</form>

<hr align="Left">
<form method="post" action="<%=strDataUrl%>?cmd=delete">
<input type="submit" value="Delete">
</form>

<%
' Clean up
rec.Close
cnn.Close
Set rec = Nothing
Set cnn = Nothing
%>
</body>
</html>
```

To provide users with a means to open this Web page, the animalist.asp Web page uses a hyperlink on the common name of the animal in the animal list. The anchor tag looks something like this:

```
<a href="../animals/<%=rst.Fields("DAV:displayname")%>">
   <%=rst.Fields("zoomgt:commonname")%>
</a>
```

The *href* attribute is dynamically built for each animal and consists of a relative URL for the Animals folder and the DAV:displayname for that particular Animal item. This URL maps to an existing Animal item. When you click the hyperlink in a Web browser, Exchange sends the animaledit.asp Web page along with the properties for the animal. Figure 12.12 shows a Web browser displaying the animaledit.asp page for an existing Animal item.

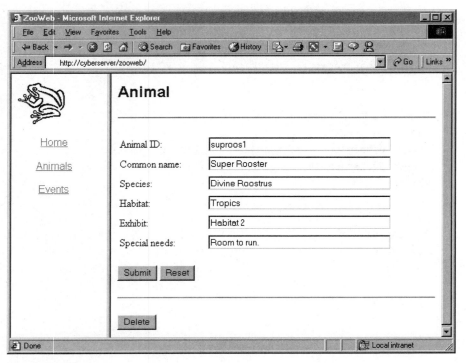

Figure 12.12
Animaledit.asp displays the properties of an Animal item.

CREATING AN ITEM

When you create a new item, you can use the same Web page to set and to read the properties. Rather than displaying the Web page with the existing data, you open the page and leave the form fields blank. The ZooWeb application uses the same form, animaledit.asp, to create a new animal and to edit an existing one. The form doesn't have any functionality specific to one purpose or the other. To specify when the form fields display data and when they are empty, the application uses two form registration items that call the same Web page in different ways. To create a new animal item in the Animals folder, the ZooWeb application uses a form registration with the property settings shown in Table 12.9.

Table 12.9 Form registration properties for creating a new animal item

Form registration property	Value
contentclass	zoomgt:content-classes:animalfld
cmd	addnew
request	GET
executeurl	animaledit.asp
formurl	animaledit.asp
binding	server
platform	winnt

The animalist.asp has a form button at the bottom of the page that you can use to create a new animal item. When you click the button, the form submits a request to the Animals folder with a cmd parameter value of addnew. The following code sample shows the form used to submit the request:

```
<form method="GET" action="../animals/">
  <p><input type="submit" value="Add new animal" name="B1">
  <input type="hidden" name="cmd" value="addnew">
</form>
```

A hidden form control passes the command value to the form registration. You must pass the cmd value as a hidden form field because the request is a GET, not a POST. If the request were a POST, you could pass the cmd value as a parameter of the action string.

As mentioned earlier, editanimal.asp won't behave differently when it is called from this registration item than when it is called from the edit animal registration. However, the difference lies in the dataurl value that is passed to the form. When you create a new Animal item with this approach, the dataurl points to the Animals folder. When the page is displayed, the form fields are empty.

SAVING AN ITEM

If you have a Web page that displays the same information in two different scenarios, such as when an item is edited and when an item is created, you must also create a Web page that can save the data in two different ways.

When you use the editanimal.asp to edit an existing Animal item, the code must save the changes back to the same data source. When you use editanimal.asp to create a new Animal item, the code must create that item in the folder as well as save the property settings. The ZooWeb application uses the same Web page to handle both of these tasks, but it requires two different form registrations to tell the difference between an edit and a new item.

One way to tell the difference between an edit and a new animal is to create form registrations that use different execute parameters to uniquely identify themselves to the Web page. For example, you could use a mode execute parameter on both form registration items and set one to "edit" and one to "addnew." The mode parameter is then passed to the Web page in the QueryString collection along with the dataurl and the formurl parameters. The ZooWeb application uses a form registration with the property settings listed in Table 12.10 to save changes to an animal item being edited.

Table 12.10 Form registration properties for saving an existing animal item

Form registration property	Value
contentclass	zoomgt:content-classes:animal
cmd	save
request	POST
executeurl	saveanimal.asp
formurl	saveanimal.asp
binding	server
platform	winnt
execute parameter	mode=edit

To display an empty form in animaledit.asp when you create a new Animal item, the ZooWeb application uses a form registration with the property settings listed in Table 12.11 to associate the animaledit.asp Web page with the zoomgt:content-classes:animalfld content class and a different execute parameter.

Table 12.11 Form registration properties to create a new animal item

Form registration property	Value
contentclass	zoomgt:content-classes:animalfld
cmd	save
request	POST
executeurl	saveanimal.asp
formurl	saveanimal.asp
binding	server
platform	winnt
execute parameter	mode=addnew

For both registrations, set the cmd parameter to *save* to distinguish among the multiple registration items for each content class. To indicate the cmd parameter, pass the parameter along with the dataurl in the <form> tag *action* attribute. For example, the following code sample is the <form> tag used in the animaledit.asp Web page form:

```
<form method="POST" Action="<%=strDataUrl%>?cmd=save"
    name="FrontPage_Form1">
```

The <form> tag uses a method of POST because you send form data along with the request to the server.

Listing 12.7 shows the actual source code of the saveanimal.asp used to conduct the save. The Web page has no graphic display and consists primarily of ADO and CDO code. After the formurl establishes a base reference point, an ADO Connection item is opened to the dataurl.

Next the Web page tests the value of the mode parameter to determine if a new Animal item is being created or if this an existing Animal is being edited. If mode returns "edit," then the user is editing an existing animal item and the dataurl maps to an existing Animal item. The code opens an ADO Record item for the Animal item, set the various properties, and save the changes back to the Web Storage System.

If mode returns "addnew," then the user is creating a new animal item and the dataurl maps to the Animals folder. You can use several different programmatic approaches to create the new item. This Web page uses CDO for Exchange to create a generic item with a CDO Item object. A CDO Item object is a generic item without any special properties. To associate the appropriate properties and properly identify the item as an Animal item, the Web page sets the DAV:contentclass schema property to zoomgt:content-classes:animal and sets the same properties as when editing an Animal item. Finally, the Web page calls the Fields.Update method to save the changes. To let CDO automatically assign a display name for the new Animal item, this Web page uses the DataSource.SaveToContainer method and passes the URL of the Animals folder (dataurl).

After the Web page finishes saving, it uses a Response.Redirect to make the browser request a different Web Storage System resource. In this case, the saveanimal.asp redirects to the animallist.asp.

Listing 12.7   Save a changed item or a new item.

```
<%option explicit%>
<html>
<head>
<meta http-equiv="Content-Type" content="text/html; charset=windows-
1252">
<meta name="GENERATOR" content="Microsoft FrontPage 4.0">
<meta name="ProgId" content="FrontPage.Editor.Document">
<base href=<%=request.querystring("formurl")%>>
</head>
<body>

<%
Dim rec
Dim cnn
Dim strDataURL
Dim itm

strDataURL = Request.querystring("dataurl")

Set cnn = CreateObject("adodb.connection")
With cnn
   .Provider = "exoledb.datasource"
   .Open strDataURL
End With

If Request.querystring("mode") = "edit" Then
   ' Open the animal record being edited using ADO
   Set rec = server.CreateObject("adodb.record")
   rec.Open strDataURL, cnn, adModeReadWrite
   ' Make the changes
   With rec
      .Fields("zoomgt:animalid") = CStr(Request.Form("txtAnimalID"))
      .Fields("zoomgt:commonname") = CStr(Request.Form("txtCommonname"))
      .Fields("zoomgt:species") = CStr(Request.Form("txtSpecies"))
      .Fields("zoomgt:habitat") = CStr(Request.Form("txtHabitat"))
      .Fields("zoomgt:exhibit") = CStr(Request.Form("txtExhibit"))
      .Fields("zoomgt:specialneeds") = _
          CStr(Request.Form("txtSpecialNeeds"))
      .Fields.Update
```

```
            .Close
        End With
    ElseIf Request.querystring("mode") = "addnew" Then
        ' Create a new animal using CDO Item object
        Set itm = server.CreateObject("cdo.item")
        With itm
            .ContentClass = "zoomgt:content-classes:animal"
            .Fields("zoomgt:animalid") = CStr(Request.Form("txtAnimalID"))
            .Fields("zoomgt:commonname") = CStr(Request.Form("txtCommonname"))
            .Fields("zoomgt:species") = CStr(Request.Form("txtSpecies"))
            .Fields("zoomgt:habitat") = CStr(Request.Form("txtHabitat"))
            .Fields("zoomgt:exhibit") = CStr(Request.Form("txtExhibit"))
            .Fields("zoomgt:specialneeds") = _
                  CStr(Request.Form("txtSpecialNeeds"))
            .Fields.Update

            ' Let CDO assign a displayname
            .DataSource.SaveToContainer strDataURL, cnn
        End With
    End If

    ' Clean up
    cnn.Close
    Set rec = Nothing
    Set cnn = Nothing

    response.redirect "../animals/"
%>
</body>
</html>
```

NOTE IIS 5.0 has introduced a function called Server.Transfer that you can use instead of Response.Redirect. Unlike Response.Redirect, Server.Transfer does not require an extra roundtrip from the browser to the Web server to retrieve a different ASP page, and it results in better performance and response time. However, you cannot use Server.Transfer to transfer requests to another relative URL to a data source other than an ASP page. However, you can use relative data URLs with Response.Redirect to redirect to different Web Storage System resources.

DELETING AN ITEM

One way to delete an item is to create an ASP page that does nothing but execute delete code. Whenever an item must be deleted, a form registration calls this ASP page to do the actual delete. To trigger the deletion of an Animal item, the ZooWeb application uses the deleteanimal.asp Web page and a form registration for the zoomgt:content-classes:animalfld content class with a cmd parameter of "delete." Because this registration sends a data request to the Web Storage System instead of just requesting data, you use a POST request in the form registration. Table 12.12 lists the form registration properties to call the deleteanimal.asp to delete an animal.

Table 12.12   Form registration properties for the deleteanimal.asp Web page

Form registration property	Value
contentclass	zoomgt:content-classes:animal
cmd	delete
request	POST
executeurl	deleteanimal.asp
formurl	deleteanimal.asp
binding	server
platform	winnt

To initiate the delete. the ZooWeb application uses a **Delete** form button on the animaledit.asp Web page. In this approach, the user must view the details of an item before it can be deleted. When the user clicks the delete button, a delete request and the cmd parameter value are sent to the server. The following code sample shows how to call the delete.asp page from the animaledit.asp page:

```
<form method="post" action="<%=strDataUrl%>?cmd=delete">
<input type="submit" value="Delete">
</form>
```

Listing 12.8 shows the actual source code of the deleteanimal.asp used to conduct the delete. The Web page has no graphic display and consists primarily of ADO code. After the formurl establishes a base reference point, an ADO Connection object is opened to the dataurl. The dataurl is the record to be deleted. The Web page opens an ADO Record object for the Animal item and calls the DeleteRecord method to delete the Animal item. After the delete is complete, the Web page uses a Response.Redirect to request a different Web Storage System resource through the browser. In this case, the deleteanimal.asp redirects to the animallist.asp.

Listing 12.8   Delete an animal.

```
<html>
<head>
<meta http-equiv="Content-Type" content="text/html; charset=windows-
1252">
<meta name="GENERATOR" content="Microsoft FrontPage 4.0">
<meta name="ProgId" content="FrontPage.Editor.Document">
<base href=<%=request.querystring("formurl")%>>
</head>
<body>
<%
Dim rec
Dim cnn
Dim urlAnimal

urlAnimal = request.querystring("dataurl")

' Open a connection
Set cnn = CreateObject("adodb.connection")
With cnn
   .Provider = "exoledb.datasource"
   .Open urlAnimal
End With

' Open a record for the animal to be deleted
Set rec = server.CreateObject("adodb.record")
rec.Open urlAnimal, cnn, adModeReadWrite

' Attempt to delete the record
On Error Resume Next
rec.DeleteRecord
```

```
' Clean up
rec.Close
cnn.Close
Set rec = Nothing
Set cnn = Nothing

' Check for an error
If Err.Number <> 0 Then
    response.Write "Unable to delete."
Else
    response.redirect "../animals/"
End If
%>
</body>
</html>
```

REUSING OUTLOOK WEB ACCESS

In some cases, you do not need to build a custom Web page to achieve the
functionality you want. You can simply reuse Outlook Web Access to display your
data. For example, Outlook Web Access does a great job of rendering calendar
folders. Rather than build a calendar display yourself, you can reuse the calendar
display of Outlook Web Access in your custom application. The Events folder in
ZooWeb reuses Outlook Web Access to display the data in the folder with the
calendar view.

To reuse Outlook Web Access with a folder or an item, you simply build a
hyperlink to the resource and do not register the content class with a form
registration. For example, the following anchor tag uses a relative URL to open the
events folder in ZooWeb:

```
<a href="../Events/">Events</a>
```

When a user clicks the hyperlink, the main page displays the calendar by using
Outlook Web Access, complete with the Outlook Web Access navigation bar—just
as if you entered the URL directly in the browser. To display the folder contents
without the navigation bar, pass a cmd parameter value of *contents*:

```
<a href="../Events/?cmd=contents ">Events</a>
```

This is a predefined parameter that suppresses the Outlook Web Access navigation bar and returns only the contents pane. You can use the Outlook Web Access predefined parameters to control the behavior of Outlook Web Access. Table 12.13 lists the predefined Outlook Web Access parameters.

Table 12.13   Outlook Web Access parameters

Parameter name	Description
cmd=x	Issues command x. See Table 12.14 for the various commands that you can call.
page=x	Displays page x.
view=x	Displays Outlook view named x. These are the views already created in Outlook.
sort=x	Sorts by column x. Use the column display names.
date=x	Displays date x in calendar.

To use multiple parameters, concatenate the parameters with an ampersand (&) character, but do not use any spaces between the parameters. For example, the following anchor tag uses a relative URL to return the contents of the events folder in ZooWeb in monthly view:

```
<a href="../Events/?cmd=contents&view=monthly">Events</a>
```

When a user clicks this hyperlink, only the contents pane is returned for the calendar, and it appears in monthly view. Figure 12.13 shows the results.

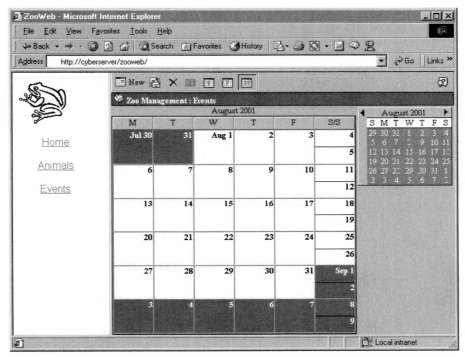

Figure 12.13
Rather than creating a calendar folder view from scratch, the ZooWeb application reuses
Outlook Web Access to render a calendar view of a calendar folder.

Besides applying the cmd parameter to render only the contents of a folder by
using Outlook Web Access, you can also set the cmd parameter to any of the
values listed in Table 12.14 for additional behaviors from Outlook Web Access. For
example, the following URL returns the Options page for a user:

```
http://cyberserver/exchange/mindy/?cmd=options
```

Table 12.14   Defined Outlook Web Access command values

Parameter name	Description
Post	Indicates that data is being sent to a folder.
Get	Indicates that data is being requested from a folder.
New	Creates a new resource in a folder.
Reply	Creates a reply message to an existing message.
Forward	Creates a forward message to an existing message.
Save	Saves a resource to a folder.
Send	Sends a message to a recipient.
Navbar	Displays the Outlook Web Access navigation bar.
Contents	Displays only the contents of a folder without the navigation bar.
Options	Displays the options settings for a user. Pass this command after the alias name.

SUMMARY

Exchange 2000 Server offers a wide range of Web development options. You can use your existing Web development knowledge to quickly and easily develop Web solutions for Exchange. By taking advantage of the new forms registry technology, you can build a client interface that is data driven rather than forms driven. Users can spend more time interacting with the data and less time learning how to use the forms.

Chapter 13, "XML and Exchange," explains how to use XML and XSL in your Web pages for even more control over data retrieval and display flexibility.

13

XML and Exchange

XML (Extensible Markup Language) is a markup language that provides a way for developers to label pieces of data, separating the data layer from the presentation layer. By separating data from presentation, you can easily rearrange pieces of data in a Web page display, filter or sort a specific piece of data, or query for a value. XML itself doesn't do anything but instead works with a number of other components and technologies—HTTP, Extensible Stylesheet Language (XSL), Hypertext Markup Language (HTML), and the XML Document Object Model (XML DOM)—to deliver a full Web development experience and be the future of data interchange on the Web.

This chapter introduces how these protocols, technologies, and components are used and how you can make the most of their abilities with Exchange 2000 Server. Sections include:

- **Overview of XML and Exchange**

- **Understanding the Basics of XML**

- **Making HTTP Requests from a Client**

- **Using XMLHTTP**

- **Rendering XML with XSL**

- **Response Codes**

NOTE This chapter is an overview of XML from an Exchange developer perspective. For more specific information about XML, see the Microsoft Developer Network (MSDN) Web site at http://msdn.microsoft.com/xml/ and the World Wide Web Consortium Web site at http://www.w3c.org.

OVERVIEW OF XML AND EXCHANGE

XML is much more than a simple markup language for Web pages. This section explores the benefits of developing solutions by using XML as well as ways to use XML to develop solutions for Exchange.

WHY DEVELOP USING XML?

XML brings a lot of power and flexibility to Web-based applications. There are many compelling reasons to develop with XML and its associated tools:

- **Native data storage in Exchange**. When it comes to building applications with Exchange, XML is a logical choice because Exchange already stores all property definitions in a Microsoft Web Storage System schema as XML. In addition, Exchange stores data natively as XML.

- **Data from a variety of applications**. XML provides a way to represent data in a neutral format that can be accessed by a wide range of tools. Such neutrality makes it possible to develop one application that can share data among many teams and companies. XML can describe data contained in a wide variety of applications—from collections of Web pages to data records. Because XML is fully extensible, you can also use previously defined elements to build your data definitions.

- **Flexible views**. Typically, when you retrieve data in a Web page, the data can be presented in a limited number of ways without sending another request to the server or accessing another page. By using XML, you can "label" your data in a Web page and then sort, filter, and rearrange the data just by rearranging the XML elements.

- **Multiple data source integration**. In the classic development model, you create one front-end for each data source. By using XML, you can retrieve data from multiple locations and present it in a single fashion with XML elements. You can then manipulate these XML elements without regard as to what data source provided the data.

- **Improved performance through granular updates**. XML enables granular updating. Developers do not have to send the entire structured data set each time there is a change. With granular updating, only the changed element must be sent from the server to the client. The changed data can be presented without the need to refresh the entire page or table.

BUILDING APPLICATIONS BY USING XML

After you understand the benefits of using XML to build Web applications for Exchange server, you should understand the basics behind incorporating XML into your collaboration solutions. As mentioned earlier, you don't build solutions exclusively with XML; you use XML in conjunction with several additional tools to communicate with a Web Storage System in Exchange, process the resulting XML, and display the data in a browser. To get at the data in a Web Storage System, you can use a number of different approaches, including the following approaches:

- **Rendering XML on the server**. One way to incorporate XML into your solutions is to use XML in Active Server Pages (ASP) with server-side rendering to encapsulate data as XML. You start with a standard ASP page that uses ActiveX Data Objects (ADO) to retrieve data from the Web Storage System. However, instead of displaying the results in HTML, you wrap each property in an XML element. Because the XML is generated in an ASP page, the server does the processing and sends the results to the client. When you open the ASP page, however, Microsoft Internet Explorer displays only the XML by using the MSXML Component Object Model (COM) component. The MSXML COM component ships with Internet Explorer. It consists of an XML parser and related tools including the XML Document Object Model (DOM). The XML DOM (Msxml.dll) is a scriptable interface to an XML document.

- **Rendering XML from the client**. You can also use XML to communicate with Exchange from the client side by using script and the XML DOM. The XML DOM exposes an XMLHTTP object that provides a scriptable interface to HTTP and the WebDAV extensions. You can write this code in a typical HTML page. In this scenario, the client makes requests to the server only when necessary, which reduces the server's workload and makes the solution more scalable.

In either case, a typical user cannot use the XML returned to the client. You can use XSL to transform the XML into HTML-formatted data that users can understand. XSL renders the XML and formats the data using HTML. The true power behind XML lies in this separation of the data from the display. You can send the XML data to the client once and then allow the client to rearrange the data in multiple views without requerying the server for a new page.

You can also use XML to incorporate collaboration features into your application. For example, you can use XML to create and define contact entries and post messages to folders and newsgroups. However, you might find it easier to use Collaboration Data Objects (CDO) for Exchange for more complicated tasks, such as scheduling meetings.

NOTE You can build XML Web pages with your favorite editor, including Microsoft FrontPage, Microsoft Visual InterDev, and Microsoft Notepad.

Understanding HTTP and WebDAV

If you want to use the XML object model to issue and receive data requests from a client, you should understand how these tools work together. HTTP is the network protocol used to deliver nearly all content on the Web, including files, images, and query results. These pieces of information are known as resources and are identified with a URL. Resources are interchanged between HTTP clients and HTTP servers through TCP/IP sockets as requests for information and responses with that information or an error code.

HTTP uses the client-server model for data transactions where the Web browser is the HTTP client and the Exchange server is the HTTP server. When a user enters a URL in the address field, the browser establishes a connection, creates a request message, and sends it to the server. The server then responds with either the requested information or an error code. Unless configured, the connection is closed after the transaction is complete.

The request from the browser comes in one of two forms: a simple request to retrieve a page (GET) or a request with extra information to be used in creating the response (POST). To handle this interchange of information, request and response messages have two parts: a header and a body. You rarely see the *header,* which consists of the method being enacted and certain header fields. The *body* contains any information being sent to the server or any information being returned by the server.

Web Distributed Authoring and Versioning (WebDAV) is a protocol extension to HTTP. HTTP alone makes the Web a read-only medium. By adding the features of WebDAV to the mix, people can now write as well as read documents over the Web in a standards-based way. WebDAV provides methods for moving resources, copying, locking and unlocking, and creating collections (folders). Simply put, you can use WebDAV to access files across the Web with essentially the same richness found in a traditional client/server network.

WebDAV extends the same basic data model used by HTTP and focuses on three entities: resources, collections, and properties. When you use WebDAV, everything you access is considered a resource and can be located using a URL. This includes e-mail messages, contacts, and meeting requests, as well as structured documents and folders. When a resource contains other resources, such as with a folder, that resource is considered a collection. Collections are not created in the same way as basic resources, so they use a special method. Both resources and collections are made up of many different properties; each property is identified with a namespace. These properties are centered on XML. XML is used to query properties, read the current values, and populate properties with new values.

WebDAV is based completely on XML data encoding. This approach means that users can share and work with Exchange data regardless of how that information was created or on what platform. Microsoft already supports WebDAV in a number of products, including Microsoft Windows 2000, Microsoft Office 2000, Microsoft Internet Explorer 5, Microsoft Internet Information Server (IIS) 5.0, and now Exchange 2000 Server.

UNDERSTANDING THE BASICS OF XML

Extensible Markup Language (XML) is a markup language that provides a neutral format for describing structured data. Data can be easily interchanged between clients regardless of the authoring tool used and the platform on which it was written. Because XML is an open, text-based format, it can be delivered through HTTP in the same way HTML can, as well as through any other means of sending and saving data, including Simple Mail Transfer Protocol (SMTP) and standard file access. This section explains the basics of creating XML documents.

BUILDING AN XML DOCUMENT

You build an XML document using one of two approaches: by creating a stand-alone XML document or by embedding the XML document in an HTML document as a data island. This section covers how to build a stand-alone XML document; data islands are covered later in this section.

Every XML stand-alone file starts with a processing instruction that indicates the file contains XML. The processing instruction looks like this:

```
<?xml version="1.0"?>
```

After the XML is identified in the Web page, you create all the necessary XML tags and save the file with the appropriate file extension. For example, if you are using XML with ASP, save the file with the .asp file extension. If not, save the file with an .xml file extension.

To create a stand-alone XML document by using FrontPage, follow these steps:

1. Open FrontPage and create a new Web or open an existing Web.

2. Create a new page. Click **File**, select **New**, and then click **Page**.

3. In the HTML view of the document, delete all existing HTML and add the XML-processing instruction to indicate that the Web page contains XML.

4. Enter the XML elements and their data to the page.

5. Save the page with an .xml file extension.

NOTE By default, all XML documents are Unicode.

Listing 13.1 shows how a stand-alone XML document might look.

Listing 13.1 A stand-alone XML document

```
<?xml version="1.0"?>

<staff>
<staffmember>
<fileas>Martin, Mindy</fileas>
<jobtitle>Administrator</jobtitle>
```

```
<email>mindy@domain.com</email>
</staffmember>
</staff>
```

NOTE   The code listings in this chapter are available as individual Web pages in the CH_13 folder on the companion CD. If you want to run the samples as they are written, you must have the Zoo Management sample installed on your Exchange 2000 server. For information about installing the application, see the introduction to the book.

If you open an XML document with Internet Explorer 5 or later, the XML structure is displayed in the browser as a collapsible and expandable XML tree. Use plus (+) and minus (-) signs next to the various elements to see how each element is nested in the XML data. At this point, XML is only providing labels for some data in your document. Figure 13.1 displays an example of an XML file.

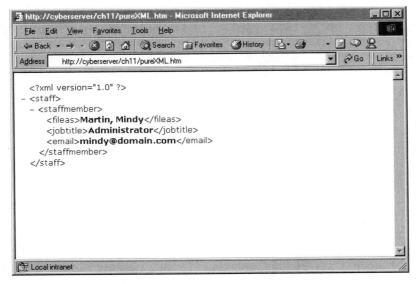

Figure 13.1
A stand-alone XML document

CREATING XML ELEMENTS

XML is a meta-markup language that provides a format for describing structured data using elements. One of the coolest aspects of XML is the flexibility it gives you to design your own XML elements. XML elements are labels for data, and you can create any elements that make sense for your application. For example, you can create an XML element for the species name of an animal and another for the habitat type. This lets you associate similar data in a Web page with that element. If a Web page displays multiple animals and you create elements for the species name and habitat type, you can use these elements to sort the Web page display by an element type, to filter the page, or simply to rearrange the page layout. XML elements might sound similar to table fields, and, indeed, they have essentially the same purpose. However, an XML element is only a label. It doesn't impose any forms of data restriction on the data it represents, unless you configure it that way.

Elements work like containers for data, with a start tag, end tag, and the data value in between. XML tags are similar in structure to HTML tags: all tags must be structured with an open angle bracket (<), followed by the tag name, and a close angle bracket (>). However, the similarities end there. Whereas you use HTML tags to display data in a particular format, such as bold or italic, you use XML tags simply to label a piece of data. The following code sample shows an XML element that is used to label a staff member's full name:

```
<staffmember>Mindy Martin</staffmember>
```

Unlike HTML tags, XML tags are case sensitive. For example, <STAFFMEMBER> is not the same as <staffmember>. When you define your XML elements, plan to use one case style for the tags and stick with it. Otherwise, you might run into problems later.

XML elements can also use attributes. An attribute is metadata about the XML element, and the attribute is set in the opening tag of the element. If you use an attribute with an element, you must enclose the attribute in quotes. The following XML element uses an attribute:

```
<staffmember gender="Female">Mindy Martin</staffmember>
```

Sometimes, XML elements do not contain any data at all. If an element does not contain data, you must still provide a start tag and an end tag. However, you can use a shortcut and denote an empty element tag by ending the start tag with a forward slash (/) before the close angle bracket. The following element does not contain any data but is correctly defined:

```
<staffmember/>
```

When you use XML elements together, they make up an XML document. Every XML document is arranged in a tree format with one element as the root element. That root element generally describes all the data in the XML document. For example, in the previous section, you saw how to build an XML document that used the following elements:

```
<staff>

<staffmember>
<fileas>Martin, Mindy</fileas>
<jobtitle>Administrator</jobtitle>
<email>mindy@domain.com</email>
</staffmember>

</staff>
```

In this example, <staff> is the root element, and it describes all the data in the document. You could not add another XML element after the close tag of the <staff> element. In addition to a singular root element, XML demands that all child elements are strictly nested. Strict nesting means that you cannot overlap the start and close tags of any child elements. For example, in the previous code sample, the close tag of the <staffmember> element is not used until all the child elements are closed.

Some additional tips to writing XML include:

- Certain characters are reserved for use by XML, so they cannot be used directly in your XML text. Instead, you must use certain substitute characters, called *entities*. These are also case sensitive:
  -    <   &lt;
  -    &   &amp;
  -    >   &gt;
  -    "   &quot;
  -    '   &apos;

- Comments are indicated with the <!—and the --> open element tags. Do not include spaces between the hyphens! The following comment is a well-formed comment:
  <!—This is a comment! -->

- To learn to write well-formed XML, start by altering how you write HTML code. Start closing all your HTML tags even if they don't require it, and use quotes around your string attributes even if they are not required.

NOTE When XML is properly structured in a document and uses the techniques described in this section for writing XML, the XML is known as well-formed XML.

INTEGRATING XML NAMESPACES

A Web Storage System schema uses namespaces to identify and distinguish among properties. The fundamentals of namespaces in a Web Storage System schema derive from XML namespaces. A namespace is essentially a way to make properties unique. Because you define your own elements in XML, there is the possibility that you might accidentally use the same tag name to identify two different pieces of information. For example, you could define a title tag to identify an employee's job title, but perhaps you also want to use a title tag to identify a book title. To eliminate any confusion, you can use a namespace with the property name to ensure that elements do not conflict. You can use any kind of namespace name that you want, but it should be unique.

A common technique is to use the name of your domain as the namespace name. Essentially, because you own the domain name, you own that namespace. It would be inappropriate for someone else to define properties in that namespace. If you do use your domain name as your namespace name, it should not be a resolvable URL or something that you can retrieve when you click on it.

When writing XML, you declare namespaces in the root element of the XML document. Any tags used with the XML document have access to that namespace name as well. You set the attribute by using a combination of the xmlns: keyword, followed by a prefix name for the namespace, and ending with the actual namespace name in quotes. The prefix name is usually just a few letters and allows you to reuse the namespace name throughout the XML document with the appropriate element tags. The following code sample declares the DAV namespace in a root element:

```
<staff xmlns:d="DAV:">
```

In order to use properties from multiple namespaces, you must declare each namespace. You can declare as many namespaces as necessary in the root element. To use multiple namespace attributes in the element, separate the attributes with a space. For instance, the following root element declares two namespaces:

```
<staff xmlns:d="DAV:" xmlns:c="urn:schemas:contacts:">
```

Then, when fields from either namespace are used in the child elements, they can be labeled with the prefix. Here's the rest of the XML document:

```
<?xml version="1.0"?>

<c:staff xmlns:c="urn:schemas:contacts:" xmlns:d="DAV:">

  <c:staffmember>
  <c:fileas>Martin, Mindy</c:fileas>
  <d:href>http://cyberserver/ZooWeb/Staff/Mindy Martin.eml</d:href>
  <c:jobtitle>Administrator</c:jobtitle>
  <c:email>mindy@domain.com</c:email>
  <c:workphone>555-555-0106</c:workphone>
  </c:staffmember>

</c:staff>
```

GENERATING XML WITH AN ASP PAGE

You have seen how XML is used to label data, but you might wonder: how does the data get there? One way to use XML is to retrieve the data using ADO in an ASP page and then label the data using XML elements. Using ADO in an ASP page is nothing new. Listing 13.2 shows a traditional ASP page that retrieves the contents of the Keepers folder of the Zoo Management application and renders the results as a Web page that uses HTML.

Listing 13.2   An ASP page that uses ADO and HTML

```
<html>
<head>
<meta http-equiv="Content-Type" content="text/html;
    charset=windows-1252">
<meta name="GENERATOR" content="Microsoft FrontPage 4.0">
```

```
<meta name="ProgId" content="FrontPage.Editor.Document">
<title>Only ADO</title>
</head>
<body>

<%
Function AddQuotes(strValue)
    ' Given a string, wrap it in quotes, doubling
    ' any quotes within the string.

    Const QUOTE = """"
    AddQuotes = _
        QUOTE _
        & Replace(strValue, QUOTE, QUOTE & QUOTE) _
        & QUOTE
End Function

Dim cnn 'As ADODB.Connection
Dim rst 'As ADODB.Recordset
Dim urlFolder 'As String
Dim strSQL 'As String

' URL to the staff folder
urlFolder = _
    "http://cyberserver/ZooWeb/staff/"

' Connect to the folder
Set cnn = CreateObject("ADODB.connection")
With cnn
    .Provider = "exoledb.datasource"
    .Open urlFolder
End With
```

```
' Select the properties to be returned
strSQL = "Select " & _
    AddQuotes("DAV:href") & ", " & _
    AddQuotes("urn:schemas:contacts:telephoneNumber") & ", " & _
    AddQuotes("urn:schemas:contacts:title") & ", " & _
    AddQuotes("urn:schemas:contacts:fileas") & ", " & _
    AddQuotes("urn:schemas:contacts:email1")
strSQL = strSQL & _
    " FROM SCOPE('SHALLOW traversal of """ & _
    urlFolder & """')"
strSQL = strSQL & _
    " WHERE " & _
    AddQuotes("DAV:ishidden") & " = False"
strSQL = strSQL & _
    " ORDER BY " & _
    AddQuotes("urn:schemas:contacts:sn") & " ASC"

' Get the results of the query
Set rst = CreateObject("ADODB.Recordset")
With rst
    .Open strSQL, cnn
End With

Do Until rst.EOF
%>
    <h2><%=rst.Fields("urn:schemas:contacts:fileas")%></h2>
    <%=rst.Fields("DAV:href")%><p/>
    <%=rst.Fields("urn:schemas:contacts:title")%><p/>
    <%=rst.Fields("urn:schemas:contacts:email1")%><p/>
    <%=rst.Fields("urn:schemas:contacts:telephoneNumber")%><p/>
<%
    rst.MoveNext
Loop

' Close the objects and release memory
rst.Close
Set rst = Nothing
%>

</body>
</html>
```

Because the data isn't using XML elements, you cannot easily change the resulting layout. If you want to sort or rearrange the page, you will more than likely need to generate a new Web page, which requires sending a request to the server for the new information.

By incorporating XML elements into an ASP page, you can generate a dynamic result set. You can easily sort, filter, and rearrange the display of the data on the client without sending a new request to the server. To change the previous listing into an XML document, you must add a few things to the Web page. First add the following line of code to indicate to the Web Storage System that you want the results in XML instead of typical HTML:

```
response.contentType = "text/xml"
```

The ADO code remains the same in the new document. However, before returning any of the properties, you indicate that the XML results should be generated with the XML processing command element:

```
<?xml version="1.0"?>
```

You can now wrap each of the <%=> ASP tags in an XML element. As the ADO returns the data, it is immediately encapsulated in the appropriate XML tag. Listing 13.3 shows how the previous listing was changed to return XML elements in addition to the data.

Listing 13.3   An ASP page that uses XML as the response

```
<%
' Indicate the data is to be returned in XML
response.contentType = "text/xml"

Function AddQuotes(strValue)
    ' Given a string, wrap it in quotes, doubling
    ' any quotes within the string.

    Const QUOTE = """"
    AddQuotes = _
        QUOTE _
        & Replace(strValue, QUOTE, QUOTE & QUOTE) _
        & QUOTE
End Function
```

```
Dim cnn 'As ADODB.Connection
Dim rst 'As ADODB.Recordset
Dim urlFolder 'As String
Dim strSQL 'As String

' URL to the staff folder
urlFolder = _
    "http://cyberserver/ZooWeb/staff/"

' Connect to the folder
Set cnn = CreateObject("ADODB.connection")
With cnn
    .Provider = "exoledb.datasource"
    .Open urlFolder
End With

' Select the properties to be returned
strSQL = "Select " & _
    AddQuotes("DAV:href") & ", " & _
    AddQuotes("urn:schemas:contacts:telephoneNumber") & ", " & _
    AddQuotes("urn:schemas:contacts:title") & ", " & _
    AddQuotes("urn:schemas:contacts:fileas") & ", " & _
    AddQuotes("urn:schemas:contacts:email1")
strSQL = strSQL & _
    " FROM SCOPE('SHALLOW traversal of """ & _
    urlFolder & """')"
strSQL = strSQL & _
    " WHERE " & _
    AddQuotes("DAV:ishidden") & " = False"
strSQL = strSQL & _
    " ORDER BY " & _
    AddQuotes("urn:schemas:contacts:sn") & " ASC"

' Get the results of the query
Set rst = CreateObject("ADODB.Recordset")
With rst
    .Open strSQL, cnn
End With
%>
```

```
<?xml version="1.0"?>
<c:staff xmlns:c="urn:schemas:contacts:" xmlns:d="DAV:">
<%Do until rst.eof%>

<c:staffmember>

<c:fileas><%=rst.Fields("urn:schemas:contacts:fileas")%></c:fileas>

<d:href><%=rst.Fields("DAV:href")%></d:href>

<c:jobtitle><%=rst.Fields("urn:schemas:contacts:title")%></c:jobtitle>

<c:email><%=rst.Fields("urn:schemas:contacts:email1")%></c:email>

<c:workphone>

<%=rst.Fields("urn:schemas:contacts:telephoneNumber")%>

</c:workphone>

</c:staffmember>

<%rst.MoveNext%>
<%Loop%>
</c:staff>

<%
' Close the objects and release memory
rst.Close
Set rst = Nothing
%>
```

This listing returns only XML elements and the data. It doesn't provide any way to display the results. By stripping the HTML from this Web page, you are free to dictate how the XML is arranged and displayed in the Web page. The XSL template itself uses HTML tags to actually display the data. Figure 13.2. shows how Internet Explorer would display the results of the Listing 13.3.

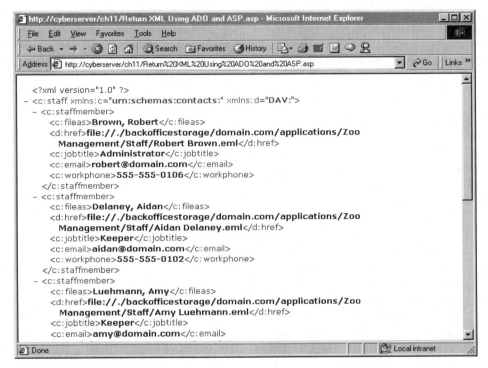

Figure 13.2
XML unparsed in Internet Explorer

USING XML DATA ISLANDS

An XML document does not have to exist as its own page. In fact, it's common to embed chunks of XML in HTML documents. These chunks of data are known as *data islands*. To embed an XML data island in an HTML document, use the <XML> element. You can use the <XML> element to load XML documents into a Web page or to indicate XML elements. To load an external XML document by using the <XML> element, set the SRC attribute to indicate the path of the XML document. This can be a file path, a URL, or a relative URL. In addition, the <XML> element uses an ID attribute to name the XML data island. The ID is used later when parsing through the resulting XML document by using the XML DOM. The following code sample loads an external XML document into a Web page:

```
<XML SRC="xmlFile.xml" ID="somexml"/>
```

If you are adding the XML directly to the document, the <XML> element should be the root element of the XML document. You can use an XML data island in this manner to embed XSL elements in an HTML page. The following code sample shows how to create a data island in a Web page that is also an XML document:

```
<XML ID="stafflisting">
<staff>
<staffmember>
<fileas>Martin, Mindy</fileas>
<jobtitle>Administrator</jobtitle>
<email>mindy@domain.com</email>
</staffmember>
</staff>
</XML>
```

A Web browser does not display a data island. As with a stand-alone .xml file, you must use a tool such as XSL to render the results and display them in the browser by using HTML or Cascading Style Sheets (CSS). However, you must first access the XML elements in the data island as an XML document by using the XML DOM. You can access the island by using the data island id and calling the DocumentElement property. Then, to return the data, you can use the XML property. The following code sample accesses the previously defined data island and sends the results to a DIV tag on the HTML page:

```
<SCRIPT language="vbscript" FOR="window" EVENT="onload">
    divTarget.innerHTML = KeeperInfo.documentElement.xml
</SCRIPT>
```

The data returned is unparsed, and each data piece runs into the next one without any spacing or character to indicate that it is a new property value. For example, the previous code sample returns the data island looking something like this:

```
Martin, Mindy http://cyberserver/ZooWeb/Staff/Mindy Martin.eml
Administrator mindy@domain.com 555-555-0106
```

You can also use the InnerText property in place of the InnerHTML property to return the data with XML tags displayed in the browser, but the results are still not very helpful to the average user. Instead, you can send the results to an XSL template, which can render them as something more readable. For more information on using XSL to render XML, see "Rendering XML with XSL" later in this chapter.

MAKING HTTP REQUESTS FROM A CLIENT

The previous section discussed how to use an ASP page to retrieve data as XML from a Web Storage System. As with any ASP page, the server does all the processing. However, you can instead use XML to build a Web page that initiates the requests from the client. The XML DOM included with Internet Explorer exposes an XMLHTTPRequest object for making HTTP requests from the client. The client can use this object not only to get data in a Web Storage System folder, but also to issue changes to the data. In either case, the client makes the requests through HTTPby using HTTP and WebDAV methods.

XMLHTTPRequest is actually the name of the class in the object library. However, if you use script to create a new instance of the XMLHTTPRequest class, you use the progID of "Microsoft.XMLHTTP". This chapter focuses on script and refers to this object as the XMLHTTP object.

> **NOTE** The samples in this section are written in Microsoft Visual Basic Scripting Edition (VBScript); however, you can use Microsoft JScript if you prefer.

XMLHTTP METHODS AND PROPERTIES

You use the methods of an XMLHTTP object to communicate with the HTTP server, in this case, Exchange. You use the methods to define the HTTP request, send the HTTP request, and maintain the connection. Table 13.1 lists the methods of an XMLHTTP object.

Table 13.1   Methods of the XMLHTTP object

Method	Description
Open	Opens the XMLHTTP object and sets some initial values.
SetRequestHeader	Sets a value for a request header field.
Send	Sends the HTTP request to Exchange.
GetAllResponseHeaders	Retrieves all the header fields from the response message.
Abort	Aborts a connection before it is complete.

The XMLHTTP object also exposes a number of properties that can be used to return information about the connection to Exchange. The ReadyState property returns an integer value that indicates the status of an asynchronous connection. You also use the properties of an XMLHTTP object to return the response body in several formats. For example, you use the ResponseXML property to return the response message as an XML document. Table 13.2 describes each of the properties. All of these are read-only properties, except OnReadyStateChange, which is a write-only property.

Table 13.2 HTTPRequest properties

Property	Data value	Description
OnReadyStateChange	Event Handler reference	Sets a reference to an event handler to be called when the ready state changes. If you use VBScript, you must use the GetRef function to set the function reference. Used only with asynchronous connections.
ReadyState	Integer	Returns the status of an asynchronous operation: uninitialized (0), loading (1), loaded (2), interactive (3), or completed (4).
ResponseBody	Variant array	Returns the body of the response as an array.
ResponseStream	Istream	Returns the body of the response as an ADO Stream object.
ResponseText	String	Returns the body of the response as a string value using UTF-8 encoding.
ResponseXML	XMLDocument	Returns the body of the response as an XML document.
Status	Long	Returns the HTTP status code returned by the server.
StatusText	String	Returns the HTTP response line status code description.

MAKING A SIMPLE HTTP REQUEST

No matter what type of HTTP request you make, you always follow the same basic steps:

1. Create an instance of a new XMLHTTP object by calling the CreateObject function and passing the string value "Microsoft.xmlhttp."

2. Call the Open method of the XMLHTTP object to create the HTTP request.

3. Set any required and optional header fields. For example, to move a resource, you must set the Destination header field.

4. Send the request with the Send method. After the request is processed, you can access the data by using the appropriate properties.

Listing 13.4 shows how to make a simple HTTP request from a client. When you click a command button, the code sends a request to get an item and return the contents as XML.

Listing 13.4   Make a simple HTTP request from a client.

```vbscript
<script language="vbscript">
Dim xmlDoc

Sub cmdGetItem_OnClick()
    Dim strURL, strUser, strPW
    Dim xmlo

    strURL = "http://cyberserver/" & _
      "zooweb/Announcements/Welcome.eml"

    Set xmlo = CreateObject("microsoft.xmlhttp")
    xmlo.Open "PROPFIND", strURL, False, "domain\user1", "password"
    xmlo.setRequestHeader "Content-type:", "text/xml"

    xmlo.send ("")

    Set xmlDoc = xmlo.responseXML
End Sub
</script>
```

USING THE OPEN METHOD

The Open method of an XMLHTTP object has the following syntax:

```
Function XMLHTTP.Open(method, url, async, user, password)
```

Where:

method

> is a string that indicates the verb being enacted, such as GET, PROPFIND, PROPPATCH, or COPY. These values must always be uppercase.

url

> is a string value. This can be a relative or absolute URL of the requested resource.

async

> is a Boolean value that indicates whether the connection is made synchronously (False) or asynchronously (True).

user

> is the name of a user for authentication. This parameter is ignored if the value is missing or NULL.

password

> is the password used for authentication. This parameter is ignored if the value is missing or NULL.

You can set the *method* parameter to one of the HTTP 1.1 methods to send and receive data across the Web. For example, you might be familiar with the normal GET and POST methods used to construct Web applications. WebDAV expands on this list with additional methods that you can use to write data to a Web Storage System. Using the HTTP and WebDAV methods, you can create, copy, and move resources using HTTP as easily as you do across your standard network. All the method names are case sensitive. Table 13.3 lists some of the methods.

Table 13.3 Methods exposed by HTTP 1.1 and the WebDAV extension to HTTP

Method	Description
GET	Returns a resource, such as an item or a folder, with both the header fields and the body.
PUT	Creates a resource in a Web Storage System (basic authoring).
DELETE	Removes a resource from a Web Storage System.
OPTIONS	Discovers server capabilities; used to determine what extensions Exchange supports.
HEAD	Gets metadata about a resource: returns the same thing as GET but without the body information.
POST	Submits an HTML form with data. Can also be used to submit a document to a folder without passing a name for the item.
MOVE	Moves a resource or collection to a new location in a Web Storage System.
COPY	Copies a resource or collection to another location in a Web Storage System.
MKCOL	Makes a collection, such as a folder in a Web Storage System.
PROPFIND	Enumerates properties on a resource.
SEARCH	Queries for resources in a Web Storage System.
PROPPATCH	Sets a property value or removes one.
LOCK	Locks a resource so while it is open other clients cannot edit it.
UNLOCK	Unlocks a resource.

SETTING HEADER FIELDS

For some HTTP requests, you must specify additional information for the server to process the HTTP request properly. This additional information is provided in the header fields of a request. For example, you might set the *Content-Type* header field to indicate the media type used in the body of the response message. In addition, header fields are also returned in the HTTP response generated by the server and can be used to retrieve more detailed information about the response data. Table 13.4 lists some of the header fields and their descriptions.

Table 13.4 Header fields used with HTTP requests and responses

Header field	Used with	Description
Accept	Request	Indicates the content type allowed to be returned.
Content-Type	Both	Indicates the media type contained in the body.
Date	Response	Indicates the date and time the response was generated.
Destination	Request	Indicates the destination URL when a resource is copied or moved.
Depth	Request	Indicates how deep to search for information when accessing a folder or querying for information.
Expires	Response	Indicates the date and time the content is considered obsolete.
If-Modified-Since	Request	Used with the GET request method to return a page only if the page has been modified after the specified date.
Location	Response	Returns the absolute URL of the page.
Refer	Request	Indicates the URL initiating the request.
Translate	Request	Indicates whether the request should go to the underlying source storage or to the application (ASP scripts or OWA).

Continued on next page

Table 13.4 continued   Header fields used with HTTP requests and responses

Header field	Used with	Description
User-Agent	Request	Returns information about the client software initiating the request.
Server	Response	Indicates name and version of server responding to request.
If-None-Match	Request	Used with the GET request method to return a response only if no matching results are found.
Lock-Token	Both	Indicates the lock-token to be used to access a locked resource.

To set a request header for an HTTP request, you set the SetRequestHeader property and pass the name of the header field being set as a string and the value for the header field. The following code sample sets the Content-Type header field to send XML as text/xml:

```
xmlo.setRequestHeader "Content-type:", "text/xml"
```

> **NOTE**   If you don't set the Content-Type header field, the server returns the response as a normal HTML document.

SENDING THE HTTP REQUEST AND GETTING THE RESULTS

To actually send the request to the server and return a response, you call the Send method of an XMLHTTP object. The Send method behaves differently depending on whether the connection is opened synchronously or asynchronously. If the connection is opened synchronously, the Send method does not return anything until the entire response is processed or the connection times out. This can result in poor user experience because the user must always wait for information to be returned. If the connection is established asynchronously, the Send method returns the state of the connection immediately.

The Send method takes one parameter, which is the request body to use. For example, if you want to send an XML DOM object, you create a string of XML elements and send the XML data as the body of the request.

```
strR = "<?xml version='1.0'?>"
strR = strR & "<d:propfind xmlns:d='DAV:'>"
strR = strR & "<d:prop>"
strR = strR & "<d:displayname/>"
strR = strR & "<d:creationdate/>"
strR = strR & "</d:prop>",
strR = strR & "</d:propfind>"

xmlo.send(strR)
```

If you do not want to send a request body, simply call the Send method and pass an empty string:

```
xmlo.send ("")
```

After the request is processed, the server returns some sort of information. If you requested data, the information is returned in the body of the response. For example, if you set the Content-Type header field to *text/XML*, you can access the response by calling the ResponseXML property. This property returns the XML data as an object that can later be parsed and displayed by the XML DOM and rendered by using XSL. The following code sample references the XML in a response message to an HTTP request:

```
Set xmlDoc = xmlo.responseXML
```

In addition to the response information, a request will also return a response code that indicates the success of the request. You can access this response text with the Status and StatusText properties of an XMLHTTP object. The following code sample writes the response code and description to a DIV tag on an HTML page:

```
rsp.innerText = xmlo.Status & " " & xmlo.StatusText
```

If you use an HTTP request that *does* something—such as a delete—as opposed to return something, the server returns only a response code. For detailed information on response codes, see "Response Codes" later in the chapter.

CHECKING THE STATE OF AN ASYNCHRONOUS CONNECTION

Whenever possible, you should open a connection to the HTTP server asynchronously to allow the client to continue processing other operations instead of waiting exclusively for the HTTP server to return some kind of response. If you open a connection asynchronously, you must check the state of the connection to determine when the request is completed. To check the state of an asynchronous connection, you need to do three things:

1. Create a script-level variable to reference the XMLHTTP object variable. This allows all the procedures in the Web page to access the variable and thus the state of a connection.

2. Enable the callback function by setting the OnReadyStateChange header field. Set the field value to a reference to some procedure that processes the state value. If you are using VBScript, you get a reference to a procedure by passing the procedure name to the GetRef function. Whenever the status of the connection changes, this function is called to process the change.

3. Create a callback function that checks the status of the connection. This is the function that you indicated in the OnReadyStateChange header field. A callback routine uses the ReadyState property to determine when the server has completed and returned the entire response. When the ReadyState property returns a value of 4 (Completed), the client has received all the data and the complete results are available in the response body.

Listing 13.5 shows how to check for the status of an asynchronous connection. The script level object variable *xmlo* stores the connection status. When the script opens the connection asynchronously, it also sets the OnReadyStateChange header field to reference the function *HandleStateChange*, which is used to check the status of the connection. Whenever the status of the connection with the HTTP server changes, the code calls this function. If the ReadyState property returns anything other than 4 (Completed), the function returns a still busy message that is sent to the HTML page. When the connection does return 4 (Completed), indicating that the processing is complete, the function returns the response status code and message.

Listing 13.5 Check the state of an asynchronous connection.

```vbscript
<script language=vbscript>
Private xmlo

Sub cmdGetRecords_onclick()
    strUser = "domain\user1"
    strPW = "password"

    strURL = "http://cyberserver/zooweb/staff/"

    Set xmlo = CreateObject("microsoft.xmlhttp")
    xmlo.Open "PROPFIND", strURL, True, strUser, strPW
    xmlo.setRequestHeader "Content-type:", "text/xml"
    xmlo.onreadystatechange = GetRef("HandleStateChange")
    xmlo.send ("")
End Sub

' This is the event handler
Function HandleStateChange()
    If xmlo.readyState = 4 Then
        rsp.innerHTML = xmlo.Status & " " & xmlo.StatusText
    Else
        rsp.innerHTML = "<h4>Working...</h4>"
    End If
End Function

</script>
```

NOTE For simplicity sake, the samples in this chapter do not use asynchronous connections. Before you use these listings in your own applications, make sure to change the code to use asynchronous connections.

USING XMLHTTP

By using an XMLHTTP object, you can generate and process HTTP requests on a client and reduce server responsibility. This section describes how you can create resources, open resources, and query for a subset of resources, as well as move, copy, and delete resources.

RETURNING A RESOURCE WITH ALL PROPERTIES

You can return a resource, such as a folder or an item, using the HTTP PROPFIND method. The PROPFIND method can retrieve all the properties on a resource or a subset of properties.

RETURNING ALL THE PROPERTIES FOR A RESOURCE

To return all the properties on a resource, open the connection passing the PROPFIND method and the URL of the resource to be returned. When you send the request, pass an empty string to the Send method. Listing 13.6 returns all the properties for a welcome message in the Zoo Management application folder when you click a button on a Web page. The results are returned in XML as a multistatus message, which can then be displayed using XSL and XML DOM.

Listing 13.6   Get all the properties for a resource.

```
<script language=vbscript>
Dim xmlDoc

Sub cmdGetAllProps_OnClick()
   Dim strURL

   ' URL to the resource to return
   strURL = "http://cyberserver" & _
       "/zooweb/announcements/welcome.eml"
```

```
With CreateObject("microsoft.xmlhttp")
    .Open "PROPFIND", strURL, _
        True, "domain\user1", "password"
    .setRequestHeader "Content-type:", "text/xml"
    ' Return only the contents of a folder
    .setRequestHeader "Depth", "0"

    'Send the request
    .send ("")

    ' responsehere is a DIV tag on an HTML page
    responsehere.innerText = _
        .Status & " " & .statusText
End With
End Sub
</script>
```

RETURNING AN ITEM WITH SPECIFIC PROPERTIES

Although the previous example works fine to return the properties for an item, returning all the properties is not efficient. To return only specific properties for a resource, you still open the connection passing the PROPFIND method and the URL of the resource to be returned. However, rather than passing an empty string to the Send method, you construct an XML body string that indicates the properties that should be returned. Listing 13.7 returns only the DAV:displayname schema property and the DAV:creationdate schema property for the Welcome message opened in Listing 13.6. Once again, the results are returned as XML.

Listing 13.7   Return specific properties for a resource.

```
<script language=vbscript>
Dim xmlDoc

Sub cmdGetSpecificProperties_OnClick()
    Dim strURL

    ' URL to the resource to return
    strURL = "http://cyberserver" & _
    "/zooweb/announcements/welcome.eml"
```

```
With CreateObject("microsoft.xmlhttp")
    .Open "PROPFIND", strURL, _
        False, "domain\user1", "password"
    .setRequestHeader "Content-type:", "text/xml"
    ' Return only the contents of a folder
    .setRequestHeader "Depth", "0"

    'Send the request
    .send ("")

    ' responsehere is a DIV tag on an HTML page
    responsehere.innerText = _
        .Status & " " & .statusText
    End With
End Sub
</script>
```

RETURNING FOLDER CONTENTS

To return the contents of a folder, you must set the Depth header to indicate which child resources to return. You can set the Depth field to a string value of "0", "1", "1,noroot", or "infinity". To return only the folder, set the Depth header field to "0". To return the folder and the child resources in the folder, set the Depth header field to "1". To return only the child resources in the folder, not the parent folder, set the Depth header field to "1,noroot". To return the folder, the child resources, and the contents of any subfolders, set the Depth header field to "infinity". The default value is "infinity".

Listing 13.8 shows how to return all properties for the contents of a folder without the parent folder.

Listing 13.8   Get the contents of a folder.

```
<script language=vbscript>
Dim xmlDoc

Sub cmdButton_OnClick()
    Dim strURL, strPropReq

    strURL = "http://cyberserver/zooweb/"
```

```
    ' Build the string indicating which
    ' properties to return
    strPropReq = "<?xml version='1.0'?>"
    strPropReq = strPropReq & "<d:propfind xmlns:d='DAV:'>"
    strPropReq = strPropReq & "<d:prop>"
    strPropReq = strPropReq & "<d:displayname/>"
    strPropReq = strPropReq & "<d:creationdate/>"
    strPropReq = strPropReq & "</d:prop>"
    strPropReq = strPropReq & "</d:propfind>"

    With CreateObject("microsoft.xmlhttp")
        .Open "PROPFIND", strURL, _
            True, "domain\user1", "password"
        .setRequestHeader "Content-type:", "text/xml"

        ' Return only the contents of a folder
        .setRequestHeader "Depth", "1,noroot"

        ' Send the XML body string
        .send (strPropReq)

        ' Return the results as XML
        Set xmlDoc = .responseXML
    End With
End Sub
</script>
```

NOTE If you set the Depth header and you are returning anything other than a collection, the HTTP server disregards the Depth header value. However, it is still safer to set the header to zero (0), even if you don't think it is necessary, to avoid the possibility of traversing deep into a collection that you thought was an item.

CREATING A FOLDER

To create a folder, open the connection passing the MKCOL method and the URL of the folder to be created. The URL you provide must include the name of the new folder as well as the path to it. Because the request doesn't have a body and you are returning only a response code, you can pass an empty string to the Send method. If the folder is created successful, the server returns a response code of 201 Created. If the folder already exists, the server returns a response code of 405 Method Not Allowed instead. Listing 13.9 shows how to create a new folder in the Applications Web Storage System by using an HTTP request. The response code and test are returned and displayed on the calling HTML page.

Listing 13.9   Create a folder by using an HTTP request.

```vbscript
<script language="vbscript">
Sub cmdMakeFolder_onclick()
    Dim strURL, strPropReq

    ' URL to the new folder
    strURL = "http://cyberserver/" & _
        "zooweb/Recruiting/"

    With CreateObject("microsoft.xmlhttp")
        .Open "MKCOL", strURL, _
            True, "domain\user1", "password"

        ' Send the request
        .send ("")

        ' responsehere is a DIV tag on an HTML page
        responsehere.innerText = _
            .Status & " " & .statusText
    End With
End Sub
</script>
```

CREATING AN ITEM

To create a new resource other than a folder, you open the connection passing the PROPPATCH method and the URL of the folder to be created. The URL must include the name of the new resource as well as the path to it. In order to set properties on the item with the same request, you pass a body string that actually sets the properties. The string is an XML document that uses a <propertyupdate> element to indicate which properties to set. Listing 13.10 shows how to create a new contact in a contacts folder by using an HTTP request.

Listing 13.10   Create a new item by using an HTTP request.

```vbscript
<script language="vbscript">
Sub cmdCreateItem_OnClick()
    Dim strURL, strPropSet

    ' URL to the new item
    strURL = "http://cyberserver/zooweb/recruiting/" & _
        "Michael Patten.eml"

    ' Set some properties
    strPropSet = "<?xml version='1.0'?>"
    strPropSet = strPropSet & _
        "<d:propertyupdate xmlns:d='DAV:'" & _
        " xmlns:c='urn:schemas:contacts:'>"
    strPropSet = strPropSet & "<d:set>"
    strPropSet = strPropSet & "<d:prop>"
    strPropSet = strPropSet & "<c:fileas>Patten, Michael</c:fileas>"
    strPropSet = strPropSet & "<c:givenName>Michael</c:givenName>"
    strPropSet = strPropSet & "<c:sn>Patten</c:sn>"
    strPropSet = strPropSet & "</d:prop>"
    strPropSet = strPropSet & "</d:set>"
    strPropSet = strPropSet & "</d:propertyupdate>"

    With CreateObject("microsoft.xmlhttp")
        .Open "PROPPATCH", strURL, _
            FalseTrue, "domain\user1", "password"
```

```
    ' Indicate that you are passing XML
    .setRequestHeader "Content-type:", "text/xml"

    ' Send the XML body string
    .send (strPropSet)

    ' Write out the response
    responsehere.innerText = .Status & " " & .statusText
  End With
End Sub
</script>
```

COPYING A RESOURCE

To copy a resource to another location, open the XMLHTTP object and pass the COPY method and the URL of the resource to be copied. You must also build a second URL that indicates the destination of the copy operation, including the name of the resource. You set the Destination header field to this second URL. You do not need to pass a body, so simply call the Send method and pass an empty string. If the copy is successful, the server returns a response code of 201 Created. If either the resource to be copied or the target folder doesn't exist, the server returns a response code of 404 Not Found. Listing 13.11 shows how to send an HTTP request to copy an item from one folder to another. The response code is printed on the HTML page.

Listing 13.11   Copy an item from one folder to another by using an HTTP request.

```
<script language="vbscript">
Sub cmdCopyResource_OnClick()
  Dim strURLtoCopy, strURLTarget

  ' URLs to the item being moved and the target
  strURLtoCopy = "http://cyberserver/zooweb/" & _
    "Recruiting/Michael Patten.eml"
  strURLTarget = "http://cyberserver/zooweb/" & _
    "CopiedItem.eml"

  With CreateObject("microsoft.xmlhttp")
    .Open "COPY", strURLtoCopy, _
      False, "domain\user1", "password"
```

```
        ' Indicate the new URL for the item
        .setRequestHeader "Destination", strURLTarget

        .send ("")

        ' Write out the response
        responsehere.innerText = _


.Status & " " & .statusText
    End With
End Sub
</script>
```

MOVING A RESOURCE

To move a resource from one location to another, open the connection and pass
the MOVE method and the URL of the resource to be moved. You must also build
a second URL that indicates the destination of the move, including the name of the
resource. You set the Destination header field to this second URL. You do not need
to pass a body, so simply call the Send method and pass an empty string. If the
resource is moved successfully, the server returns a response code of 201 Created.
If either the resource to be moved or the target folder doesn't exist, the server
returns a response code of 404 Not Found. Listing 13.12 shows how to send an
HTTP request to move an item from one folder to another. The response code is
printed on the HTML page.

Listing 13.12   Move a resource by using an HTTP request.

```
<script language="vbscript">
Sub cmdButton_MoveResource()
    Dim strURLtoMove, strURLTarget

    ' URLs to the item being moved and the target
    strURLtoMove = "http://cyberserver/zooweb/" & _
        "Recruits/Michael Patten.eml"
    strURLTarget = "http://cyberserver/zooweb/" & _
        "MovedXMLItem.eml"
```

```
With CreateObject("microsoft.xmlhttp")
    .Open "MOVE", strURLtoMove, _
        True, "domain\user1", "password"

    ' Indicate the new URL for the item
    .setRequestHeader "Destination", strURLTarget

    .send ("")

    ' Write out the response
    responsehere.innerText = _
        .Status & " " & .statusText
End With
End Sub
</script>
```

DELETING A RESOURCE

To delete a resource completely from the Web Storage System, use the DELETE HTTP method. If you do not want to remove the resource completely, you should use the MOVE method to move the resource to a deleted items folder. You can fully delete it later or move it back to the original parent folder.

To use the DELETE method, open an XMLHTTP object, and pass the DELETE method. You do not need to pass a body with the Send method, so simply call the Send method and pass an empty string. If the deletion was successful, the server returns a response code of 200 OK. If the item to be deleted doesn't exist, the server returns a response code of 404 Not Found. Listing 13.13 shows how to permanently delete an item and print the response code and description in a named location on the HTML page.

Listing 13.13   Delete a resource by using an HTTP request.

```vbscript
<script language="vbscript">
Sub cmdDeleteResource_OnClick()
    Dim strURL

    ' URLs to the item being deleted
    strURL = "http://cyberserver/zooweb/" & _
        "MovedXMLItem.eml"

    With CreateObject("microsoft.xmlhttp")
        .Open "Delete", strURL, _
            False, "domain\user1", "password"
        .send ("")

        ' Write out the response
        responsehere.innerText = _
            .Status & " " & .statusText
    End With
End Sub
</script>
```

RENDERING XML WITH XSL

An XML document alone does not display any useful information. It simply labels what each piece of data represents. To actually render the data and display in a format that people can read, you must use some sort of markup or a style sheet such as XSL. XSL is very flexible and allows you to use one format with multiple views. With an XSL template, you download the XML data once from the server. Anytime the client wants to sort, filter, or rearrange the data, the XSL template is reapplied on the client, without issuing additional requests to the server.

This section explains how to use XSL-specific elements, build an XSL template as a stand-alone file, identify XML elements to XSL, build a table, and use an XML data island for an XSL template.

How It Works

To display an XML document in a Web browser, you must convert the XML to some sort of HTML presentation. HTML is still ideal for marking up a document for display. XSL is simply a style sheet and does not replace HTML. To actually draw something on the screen, either the server or the browser must convert the XML data to an HTML presentation. One way to convert XML to HTML is to use XSL. XSL can display XML data in a number of ways and provides both semantic and structural independence for the content and presentation. You are free to display XML data in multiple formats without issuing a request to the server each time you display the data in a new format. Figure 13.3 shows how the XML data is processed and rendered in HTML before it is displayed in the browser. Anytime the data needs to be filtered, sorted, or rearranged, the XSL template is reapplied at the client.

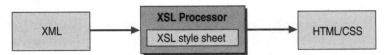

Figure 13.3
XML is rendered by an XSL processor and then displayed in the browser.

Using XSL-Specific Elements

XSL exposes a few predefined elements to indicate how data is arranged in the template and to establish the format and layout. For a complete list of XSL elements, see the Microsoft Platform SDK. The code samples in this chapter use the most common and basic elements:

- <xsl:template> indicates the beginning of an XSL template in an XML data island.

- <xsl:value-of> inserts the current value of a property.

- <xsl:for-each> applies a template (such as a table row) repeatedly to one or more properties.

- <XSL:eval> evaluates a script expression to generate a text string.

The <xsl:value-of> element and the <xsl:for-each> element have a select attribute that identifies the property to be used in the element. For example, the following XSL element applies to the email property:

```
<xsl:value-of select="email"/>
```

The following sections describe how to use the various XSL element tags.

> **NOTE** XSL is essentially an XML document that has XSL specific elements defined. As such, the document has to obey all the guidelines for well-formed XML discussed earlier in this chapter.

BUILDING AN XSL TEMPLATE AS A STAND-ALONE FILE

As with XML documents, you can incorporate an XSL template as either a stand-alone file or as an embedded data island in the Web page. To build a stand-alone XSL template, follow the same basic guidelines as for an XML document, but save the template with an .XSL file extension. In the document, you use a mixture of XSL elements and HTML tags. The XSL elements identify the XML elements that are being formatted, and the HTML tags do the actual rendering. Listing 13.14 shows how a simple XSL template looks.

Listing 13.14   A simple XSL template

```
<?xml version="1.0"?>
<html xmlns:xsl="http://www.w3.org/TR/WD-xsl" >
<head></head>
<body>
<h1>Zoo Staff Members</h1>
<table>
<xsl:for-each select="staff/staffmember">
<tr>
<td>
<div style="background-color:#ffffb0;border-color:#00d0d0;border-style:groove">
<h3><xsl:value-of select="fileas" /></h3>
<h4><xsl:value-of select="jobtitle" /></h4>
<h4><xsl:value-of select="email" /></h4>
```

```
</div>
</td>
</tr>
</xsl:for-each>
</table>
</body>
</html>
```

> **NOTE** Because the HTML tags are in an XML document, the HTML tags must follow the guidelines for well-formed XML. For example, you must close all your tags and properly nest multiple tags, or the code will fail.

To call the XSL template from an XML document, you need to add another XML-processing command to the Web page to tell it where to look for the template and the type of template being used. The following code sample indicates that the XML document should apply an XSL template at a relative URL:

```
<?xml:stylesheet type="text/xsl" href="simplexsltemplate.xsl" ?>
```

Listing 13.15 shows how the whole Web page looks with the XML and the appropriate processing calls.

Listing 13.15   Call an external XSL template from an XML document.

```
<?xml version="1.0"?>
<?xml:stylesheet type="text/xsl" href="simplexsltemplate.xsl" ?>

<staff>
<staffmember>
<fileas>Martin, Mindy</fileas>
<jobtitle>Administrator</jobtitle>
<email>mindy@domain.com</email>
</staffmember>
</staff>
```

Without the XSL template, the XML elements are displayed in Internet Explorer as tree nodes with the data. After an XSL template is applied, the data looks much more like what you want to present to a user. Figure 13.4 shows what the XML looks like when a template is applied.

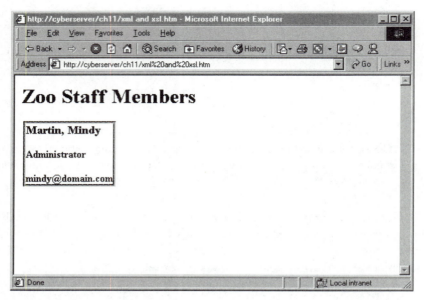

Figure 13.4
XSL applies HTML formatting to an XML document to present it in a Web browser.

IDENTIFYING XML ELEMENTS WITH XSL PATTERNS

XSL Patterns provide a simple way to identify nodes in an XML document. You use these XSL patterns in XSL tags to identify which element node to display. The XSL patterns use an XML Query Language (XQL) format to access the elements that navigate from the root element of the XML document, down through the tree, separating each level it traverses with a forward slash (/). For example, to access the <staffmember> element from the <staff> XML root element, you would use an XSL pattern like this:

```
staff/staffmember
```

XSL patterns can also use special characters for more flexible pattern matching. For example, you can use an asterisk to select any given element in a particular node. The following pattern selects all child nodes of the <staffmember> element:

```
staff/staffmember/*
```

If you do not know the exact location of the node you are looking for in the XML document, you can use square brackets around a node name to indicate that the node might be one or more levels below the child node. For example, the following XSL pattern returns the <givenName> element no matter where in the tree it resides:

```
staff[givenName]
```

You can also use XSL patterns to search for particular values. For example, the following XSL pattern searches for a <givenName> element value of "Mindy":

```
givenName='Mindy'
```

To use an XSL pattern with the XSL elements, you set the select attribute to the XSL pattern. For example, to access each of the instances of the <staffmember> element in the <staff> root element, you could use an <xsl:for-each> element and pass the XML element path to the select attribute. The following code sample would loop over each <staffmember> in the <staff> root element:

```
<xsl:for-each select="staff/staffmember">
</xsl:for-each>
```

If you are using an XMLHTTP object to return XML, the root element is called multistatus. *Multistatus* indicates that more than one chunk of information is returned in the response. To access a chunk of information in an HTTP response, you access the multistatus node and then navigate down to the response node. The following path navigates to the response element in a multistatus response:

```
d:multistatus/d:response
```

If you are reading schema property values in the response, you must traverse through two more elements before you indicate the property name. The first element is the propstat element, and the second is the prop element. You can then provide the exact name of the property you want to access. For instance, the following path accesses the value of the displayname property for a response:

```
d:multistatus/d:response/d:propstat/d:prop/d:displayname
```

For many XSL style sheets, the use of element names and the / operator is powerful enough to transform the XML element into formatted data without using the XML DOM. For more detailed information about using XSL pattern matching and XQL, see the MSDN Web site at http://msdn.Microsoft.com/xml/.

NOTE   This path is applicable only to reading property values. You use a
different path to set property values.

BUILDING A TABLE

HTML is unsurpassed in its table-building capabilities. Because HTML does this so
well, the best way to create a table is to use HTML tags for the table structure and
to insert the XSL elements where you need the data. The example in this section
shows how to build a table using HTML and XSL for each staff member in the Staff
folder.

The first step in building a table in an XSL template is to decide which piece of the
table will be repeated and for which XML element. For example, do you want to
build a table with a different row for each staff member? Or do you want a
different table for each staff member? This example creates a different table for
each staff member, so you use the XSL element <xsl:for-each> before the HTML
table tag:

```
<xsl:for-each>
<table>

<!-- Table details here -->

</table>
</xsl:for-each>
```

In the <xsl:for-each> element, you must use the Select attribute to indicate which
XML element contains the information for each table. If you want to add sorting
capabilities, you can also use the order-by attribute to sort the results. For example,
the following code sample modifies the previous code to build a table for each
node in the response and sorts the results in ascending order by staff title:

```
<xsl:for-each select="d:multistatus/d:response" order-by="c:title">
<table width="330">

<!-- Table details here -->

</table>
<p/>
</xsl:for-each>
```

Within the <table> tags, you add the typical HTML tags to create each detail row. For example, the following code shows how to use HTML tags to create four detail rows for the staff member name, title, e-mail address, and telephone number. The first row contains only one detail. The other three rows contain two details: a label and the actual data:

```
<xsl:for-each select="d:multistatus/d:response" order-by="c:title">
<table width="330">
<tr>
    <td bgcolor="silver" colspan="2">
    <b><xsl:value-of select="d:propstat/d:prop/c:fileas"/></b></td>
</tr>
<tr>
    <td>Job title: </td>
    <td><xsl:value-of select="d:propstat/d:prop/c:title"/></td>
</tr>
<tr>
    <td>Email: </td>
    <td><xsl:value-of select="d:propstat/d:prop/c:email1"/></td>
</tr>
<tr>
    <td>Work phone: </td>
    <td><xsl:value-of
select="d:propstat/d:prop/c:telephoneNumber"/></td>
</tr>
</table>
<p/>
</xsl:for-each>
```

You insert the value of a property into a table cell using the XSL <xsl:value-of> element and set its *select* attribute to the property path. Because you already indicated a path to each response node in the <xsl:for-each> element, you do not need to indicate the entire path again for each detail. XSL automatically applies the <xsl:for-each> *select* value to each detail in the table. For example, the following code sample inserts the value of the fileas schema property in a table cell:

```
<td>
<xsl:value-of select="d:propstat/d:prop/c:fileas"/>
</td>
```

When you put it all together, the complete XSL template looks like this:

```
<xml id="xsltemplate">
<xsl:template    xmlns:xsl="uri:xsl" xmlns:d="DAV:"
xmlns:c="urn:schemas:contacts:">

<xsl:for-each select="d:multistatus/d:response" order-by="c:title">
<table width="330">
<tr>
<td bgcolor="silver" colspan="2">
    <b><xsl:value-of select="d:propstat/d:prop/c:fileas"/></b></td>
</tr>
<tr>
<td>Job title: </td>
<td><xsl:value-of select="d:propstat/d:prop/c:title"/></td>
</tr>
<tr>
<td>Email: </td>
<td><xsl:value-of select="d:propstat/d:prop/c:email1"/></td>
</tr>
<tr>
<td>Work phone: </td>
<td><xsl:value-of select="d:propstat/d:prop/c:telephoneNumber"/></td>
</tr>
</table>
<p/>
</xsl:for-each>
</xsl:template>
</xml>
```

Using an XML Data Island for an XSL Template

In addition to building stand-alone XSL templates, you can also embed an XSL template directly in an HTML document as an XML data island. To create an XSL template as a data island, use the <XML> element and name the island with the ID attribute. You use this ID later to apply the template to the XML data returned by an HTTP response. The next element in the data island should be the <xsl:template> element to indicate that the data island is an XSL template. Because XSL uses the uri:xsl namespace, you must identify the namespace in the <xsl:template> element along with any other namespaces you use. The following code sample defines an XML data island and indicates that the island is an XSL template:

```
<xml id="xsltemplate">
<xsl:template xmlns:xsl="uri:xsl" xmlns:d="DAV:">

<!--template details go here -->

</xsl:template>
</xml>
```

To apply the XSL template to the XML data, you need two things: a place to put the formatted data and the command to push the XML data into the XSL template. The easiest way to mark a location for the results is with the dynamic HTML (DHTML) <DIV> tag. The <DIV> tag works like a bookmark—you place it in the HTML document wherever you want the resulting data to appear. The ID attribute is used like an address by other tags and script. The following <DIV> tag identifies a spot in an HTML page with the ID name of putdatahere:

```
<DIV id=putdatahere />
```

After you identify a place to put the formatted data, you can use the properties and methods of the XML DOM to push the XML data through to the XSL processor and out to the area marked in the HTML document with the <DIV> tag.

You can send the XML document from an HTTP response to the XSL template by calling the TransformNode method of a DOMDocument object and passing the root element of the XML data island. The following code sample applies the XSL template in the data island, myxsltemplate, to the XML document, xmldoc:

```
xmldoc.transformNode(myxsltemplate.documentElement)
```

The TransformNode method returns an HTML blob that can then be sent to the place in the Web page marked with the <DIV> tag. To identify the HTML portion of the area marked with the <DIV> tag, call the InnerHTML property of the tag. The following code sample builds on the previous example and sends XSL template results to a place marked with a <DIV> tag:

```
putdatahere.innerHTML= _
    xmldoc.transformNode(myxsltemplate.documentElement)
```

Listing 13.16 puts it all together and shows the source code of an HTML document that uses an XML data island for an XSL template. When the page loads in Internet Explorer 5, an HTTP request is sent to the Applications Web Storage System and a list of the Zoo staff members is returned.

Listing 13.16   HTML document that uses a data island for an XSL template.

```
<HTML>
<HEAD>
<TITLE>XML Sample</TITLE>
</HEAD>

<xml id="xsltemplate">
<xsl:template    xmlns:xsl="uri:xsl" xmlns:d="DAV:"
xmlns:z="zoomgt:" xmlns:c="urn:schemas:contacts:">

<xsl:for-each select="d:multistatus/d:response" order-by="c:title">
<table width="330">
<tr>
<td bgcolor="silver" colspan="2">
    <b><xsl:value-of select="d:propstat/d:prop/c:fileas"/></b></td>
</tr>
<tr>
<td>Job title: </td>
<td><xsl:value-of select="d:propstat/d:prop/c:title"/></td>
</tr>
<tr>
<td>Email: </td>
<td><xsl:value-of select="d:propstat/d:prop/c:email1"/></td>
</tr>
```

```
<tr>
<td>Work phone: </td>
<td><xsl:value-of select="d:propstat/d:prop/c:telephoneNumber"/></td>
</tr>
</table>
<p/>
</xsl:for-each>
</xsl:template>
</xml>

<SCRIPT language="vbscript" FOR="window" EVENT="onload">
    Dim xmlo
    Dim strURL, strPropReq

    strURL = "http://cyberserver/zooweb/staff/"

    ' Build the string indicating which
    ' properties to return
    strPropReq = "<?xml version='1.0'?>"
    strPropReq = strPropReq & _
    "<d:propfind xmlns:d='DAV:' xmlns:c='urn:schemas:contacts:'>"
    strPropReq = strPropReq & "<d:prop>"
    strPropReq = strPropReq & "<d:href/>"
    strPropReq = strPropReq & "<c:fileas/>"
    strPropReq = strPropReq & "<c:telephoneNumber/>"
    strPropReq = strPropReq & "<c:email1/>"
    strPropReq = strPropReq & "<c:title/>"
    strPropReq = strPropReq & "</d:prop>"
    strPropReq = strPropReq & "</d:propfind>"

    With CreateObject("microsoft.xmlhttp")
        .open "PROPFIND", strURL, _
            False, "domain\user1", "password"
        .setRequestHeader "Content-type:", "text/xml"
        .setRequestHeader "Depth", "1,noroot"
        .send (strPropReq)

        ' Return the results as XML
        Set xmlDoc = .responseXML
```

```
       ' Apply the XSL template
       ListMembersHere.innerHTML = _
           xmlDoc.transformNode(xsltemplate.documentElement)
    End With
</script>

<BODY>
<H1>Zoo Staff</H1>
<hr>
<div id="ListMembersHere"/>
</BODY>
</HTML>
```

Figure 13.5 shows how the Web page looks when this HTML document is opened in Internet Explorer 5.

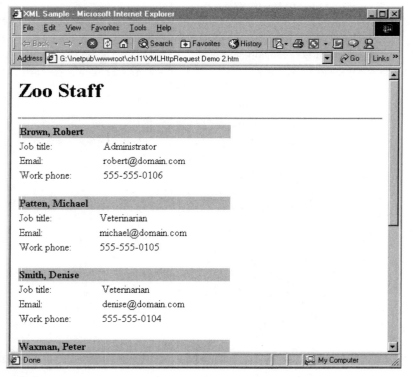

Figure 13.5
Internet Explorer 5 displays the HTML page built from Listing 13.16.

RESPONSE CODES

When you submit a request to your Exchange server via HTTP, a number of things can happen to that request. The request might be processed successfully or the request might be denied for any of several reasons. To help you determine the outcome, Exchange returns a response code about the HTTP request. Each HTTP response code is part of a code level that indicates the general type of response:

- **Level 100 codes**. These are information codes used to deliver basic information about the connection. These codes generally do not give either good or bad news; they simply supply information about the processing that occurs on the HTTP client or the HTTP server.

- **Level 200 codes**. These codes indicate that a successful action has been completed. These codes are returned when you successfully create, move, copy, or delete resources. They can also indicate partial success.

- **Level 300 codes**. These codes indicate that further action must be taken to complete the request. The request is being processed; however, you must take further action before the request can be fully processed by either the client or the server.

- **Level 400 codes**. These codes indicate a failure by the HTTP client. The failure can be anything from a lack of authentication to the proxy server to a request to the server for an unsupported media type.

- **Level 500 codes**. These codes indicate a failure by the HTTP server. The server might not be able to process the request due to an overload or an unrecognized method. These codes can also alert you that there is not enough space on the server to create new resources.

Table 13.5 lists the HTTP response codes and their descriptions.

Table 13.5   HTTP response codes

Response code	Description
100 Continue	The request can be continued.
101 Switching Protocols	The server has switched protocols in an upgrade header.
102 Processing	The server is processing the request.

Continued on next page

Table 13.5 continued HTTP response codes

Response code	Description
200 OK	The server has completed the request successfully. Typical success response for reading a resource.
201 Created	The server has completed the request successfully. Also returned for a successful move.
202 Accepted	The server has accepted the request, but the Resource has not been created or deleted yet.
203 Non-authoritative Information	Meta-information in the header did not come from original server. The returned meta-information in the header is not from the original server.
204 No Content	The server has completed the request successfully, but there is no new information to send back. The server has fulfilled the request but does not need to return an entity-body. Standard success response for a deletion or unlocking. If you are copying or moving something, the action was successful.
205 Reset Content	The server has fulfilled request and client should reset document view. Must not include an entity. The server has completed the request successfully, and the client program should reset the document view that caused the request to be sent.
206 Partial Content	Only some of the resource was returned, with a range header to indicate how much. The server has partially fulfilled the request.
207 MultiStatus	Typical success response when searching or manipulating properties.
300 Multiple Choices	The server doesn't return a response because the requested resource corresponds to multiple representations.
301 Moved Permanently	The requested resource has been assigned to a new permanent URI (Uniform Resource Identifier), and any future references to this resource should be done using one of the returned URIs.

Continued on next page

Table 13.5 continued   HTTP response codes

Response code	Description
302 Redirect	The requested resource resides temporarily under a different URI.
303 Redirect Method	The response to the request can be found under a different URI and should be retrieved using a GET method on that resource.
304 Not Modified	The requested resource has not been modified.
305 Use Proxy	The requested resource must be accessed through the proxy given by the location field.
400 Bad Request	The server could not process the request because the syntax is not valid; this could be an illegal combination of headers, a search scope that's not valid, or bad XML data.
401 Unauthorized	The requested resource requires user authentication.
403 Forbidden	The server understood the request but will not process the request. Authorization will not help.
404 Not Found	The server did not find a resource with the requested Uniform Resource Identifier (URI).
405 Method Not Allowed	The method used was not allowed for the resource named. You might get this response if you attempt to create a folder that already exists.
406 Not Acceptable	No responses acceptable to the client were found.
407 Proxy Authentication Required	This code is similar to 401 Unauthorized, but it indicates that the client must first authenticate itself with the proxy server.
408 Request Timeout	The client did not produce a request in the time that the server is set up to wait.
409 Conflict	The request could not be completed due to a conflict with the current state of the resource. The user should resubmit with more information.

Continued on next page

Table 13.5 continued HTTP response codes

Response code	Description
410 Gone	The requested resource is no longer available at the server, and no forwarding address is known.
411 Length Required	The server cannot accept the request without a defined content length.
412 Precondition Failed	The precondition given in one or more of the request-header fields evaluated to false when it was tested on the server.
413 Request Entity Too Large	The server cannot process the request because the request entity is larger than the server is allowed or able to process.
414 Request URI Too Long	The server cannot service the request because the request URI is longer than the server is allowed to interpret.
415 Unsupported Media Type	The server cannot service the request because the entity of the request is in a format not supported.
422 Unprocessable Entity	The server is unable to process the content type of the request entity. Non-zero depth was specified for a checkout lock, or the Depth header was omitted. If you are searching, the query operator is unsupported.
423 Locked	Cannot set properties on, delete, move, or lock a locked resource without the lock token. The item is already locked. If you are copying something, the destination resource is locked.
424 Method Failure	A property could not be set, so the entire transaction failed.
425 Insufficient Space on Resource	A query produced more results than the server is allowed to transmit. Partial results have been transmitted.
500 Internal Server Error	The server encountered an unexpected condition that prevented it from fulfilling the request.

Continued on next page

Table 13.5 continued   HTTP response codes

Response code	Description
501 Not Implemented	The server does not support the functionality required to fulfill the request, such as using a method not recognized by the server or attempting to save with an unrecognized content type.
502 Bad Gateway	The server, while acting as a gateway or proxy, received an invalid response from the upstream server it accessed in attempting to fulfill the request.
503 Service Unavailable	The server is currently unable to handle the request due to temporary overloading or maintenance of the server. In reference to Exchange, this is often an indication that the MSEXCHANGEIS service is not running.
504 Gateway Timeout	The request timed out while waiting for a gateway.
505 HTTP Version Not Supported	The server does not support the HTTP version that was used in the request message.
507 Insufficient Storage	The resource does not have enough space to set the properties or make the collection.

SUMMARY

Exchange 2000 is the first Microsoft product to natively store XML. Not only are all the properties in a Web Storage System schema stored as XML, but you can also store pure XML documents in a Web Storage System folder. This native support for XML makes developing Web applications by using XML and its associated tools a natural fit. You can use XML to create documents in a neutral format that can be accessed by a wide range of tools. This makes it easy to build applications for sharing data among teams without concern for which tool was used to author it or on which platform it was developed.

Section V, "Preparing for the Enterprise," explains how to set security and grant permissions for an application built with Exchange 2000 as well as how to test and deploy an application.

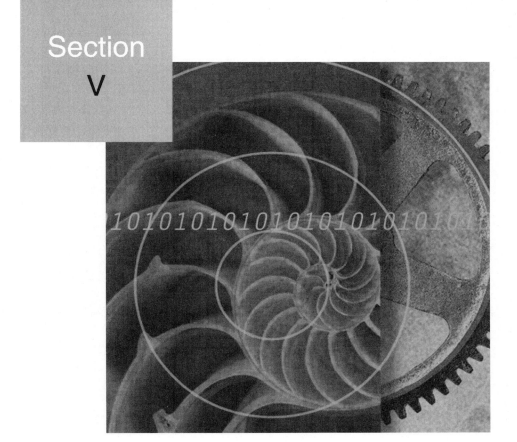

Preparing for the Enterprise

Chapter:

14   Setting Security and Permissions   **643**

15   Testing and Deploying Your Applications   **683**

14

Setting Security and Permissions

Security. No other task in application development requires as much responsibility from a developer, and no other task is as intimidating. A properly secured application keeps data and ideas safe from prying eyes. In a world where sharing data is crucial, you must be careful to keep data secure without making the application too difficult to use. Data should be easily shared among people and teams in an organization, across offices, and sometimes even with curious strangers. Security settings determine exactly what each person can access.

This chapter discusses how to set security and grant permissions for an application built with Microsoft Exchange 2000 Server. It explains how to set permissions on Exchange items and folders as well as how to add security to middle-tier Component Object Model (COM) components. Sections include:

- **Understanding Exchange 2000 Server Security**

- **Managing Client Permissions on Web Storage System Folders**

- **Using the Security Descriptor Property**

- **Enforcing Security on Code with COM+ Components**

UNDERSTANDING EXCHANGE 2000 SERVER SECURITY

Exchange and Microsoft Web Storage System are fully integrated with Microsoft Windows 2000 security infrastructures. The Exchange 2000 Server security model is very different from that of Exchange Server 5.5. With Exchange Server 5.5, you granted permissions to users of your application primarily by setting specific rights on folders. With Exchange 2000 Server, you can still grant permissions on folders, but now you can also grant permissions on specific items and even on individual properties. This section discusses how Exchange 2000 security works and how to plan security for your applications.

HOW EXCHANGE 2000 SERVER SECURITY WORKS

When a user logs on to a Windows 2000 domain, the domain controller attempts to authenticate the user's account name and password. If the user is successfully authenticated, the domain controller generates an access token for that user account. An *access token* is used in all processes that this user executes in the Windows domain and contains the security identifier (SID) of the user and the groups that user account belongs to. An *SID* is a piece of information that identifies the User or Group object to which access permissions are granted or denied.

Most Web Storage System resources have a security descriptor (SD). A *security descriptor* contains information about the security attributes for the Web Storage System resource and includes an access control list (ACL). Derived from the ACL used in the paradigm of the Active Directory directory service of Windows 2000, the ACL of a Web Storage System resource indicates which users and groups have which permissions to the resource. An ACL consists of individual entries known as access control entries (ACE). Each ACE represents a single User or security Group object that has access to the resource, and it contains that User or Group object's SID.

You can modify the security descriptor for a Web Storage System resource with the Exchange System Manager or with the http://schemas.microsoft.com/exchange/security/descriptor schema property. By changing the security descriptor of a resource, you determine who can see a folder and its contents, who can add items to a folder, who can edit and delete which objects, and who can change the permissions on an Exchange object.

When a user tries to open a resource in a Web Storage System, the system attempts to match the SID in the user's access token with an SID in an ACE of the security descriptor for that Web Storage System resource. If a match is made, the user can open the resource. If no match is made, the user cannot open the resource. This type of authorization is performed down to the item level. Therefore, each user might have a different view of the contents of a Web Storage System.

Introducing Exchange Roles

In addition to extending security to items, with Exchange 2000 you can define a new security principal called an Exchange *role*. Similar to a Windows security group stored in Active Directory, an Exchange role is also a named collection of users and groups. However, an Exchange role is stored with the Web Storage System resource and can be created and populated with users and security without a privileged directory service operation. Exchange roles are also different from the roles used to set folder permissions in Exchange 5.5.

You create an Exchange role using Microsoft Visual C++. Once the role is defined, you grant or deny permissions to Exchange roles in much the same way you grant or deny permissions to individual users or security groups. For information about how to create an Exchange role, see the Exchange Developer site at http://msdn.microsoft.com/exchange/.

PLANNING SECURITY IN APPLICATIONS

When you create a new Web Storage System application, it typically has only the default security settings. Before you can deploy this application in your enterprise, you must set certain security features. Some of the questions you should answer before you begin designing your security system are:

- Who will use this application?

- What types of permissions do they need?

- Can users with similar permissions be grouped together in a security group object?

- Will any folder, such as a schema folder, be used exclusively by a certain group?

- Will permissions on folders and items be inherited from parent objects to child objects?

- Should everyone who uses the application be able to execute the same code?

After you know the security features you need, you can proceed to integrating security into your application.

MANAGING CLIENT PERMISSIONS ON WEB STORAGE SYSTEM FOLDERS

You can control how users interact with Web Storage System folders by granting or denying permissions to a folder. Permissions include viewing the items in a folder, creating new items, editing someone else's items, and creating new child folders. In addition, you can set permissions that specify if a user can modify the existing permissions list for an object, create workflow scripts, write event agents, and register event sinks.

This section discusses how to use the user interface tools to set permissions on a folder, inheritance of permissions among Web Storage System resources, and what happens when permissions overlap.

ASSIGNING CLIENT PERMISSIONS BY USING THE USER INTERFACE

This section explains how to assign client permissions to folders in the MAPI folder tree as well as to folders in other Web Storage Systems.

ASSIGNING PERMISSIONS TO MAPI PUBLIC FOLDERS

To view or set permissions to a MAPI folder, follow these steps:

1. Open Exchange System Manager, and expand the folder tree until you see the folder you must set permissions on.

2. Right-click the folder, click **Properties**, and then click the **Permissions** tab. Figure 14.1 shows the **Permissions** tab.

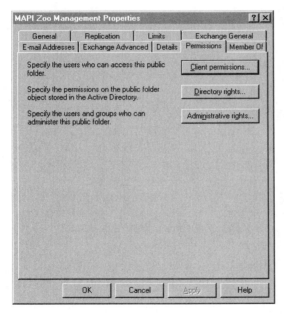

Figure 14.1
Use the Permissions tab to set permissions for a folder.

3. Click **Client permissions**. When you set permissions on a MAPI folder, the **Client Permissions** dialog box appears (see Figure 14.2). The list displays all the users currently assigned permissions on this folder.

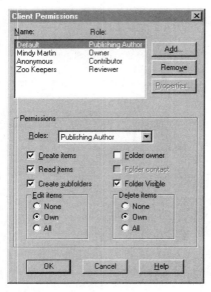

Figure 14.2
Permissions determine what users can do with a folder.

TIP You can also access the **Client Permissions** dialog box from Microsoft Outlook 2000. Locate the folder in the Outlook folder tree, right-click the folder, click **Properties**, and click the **Permissions** tab.

You assign client permissions to MAPI folders by using roles. A role is nothing more than a compilation of permissions that define a particular behavior. For example, the Publishing Editor role has permissions for editorial behavior on a folder. The system evaluates a role when a user opens a folder or item to determine which permissions that user has.

NOTE These roles are not the same as roles defined in Exchange 2000 or COM+ roles.

Table 14.1 lists and describes the defined roles. You assign roles to a user either implicitly or explicitly. If a user accesses the folder anonymously, that person is automatically assigned the role of the Anonymous account. To define roles explicitly, change the currently assigned role for a user by clicking the name and then selecting a role. In addition to the defined roles in Table 14.1, you can select or clear any of the specific options in a role and create a Custom role.

Table 14.1   Defined security roles

Role	Description
Owner	User has high-level permissions. They can create and read items as well as edit and delete any items. They can also create subfolders.
Publishing Editor	User has the same basic permissions as Owner but is not a folder owner; therefore, they do not have administrative rights.
Editor	User has the same permissions as Publishing Editor but cannot create additional subfolders.
Publishing Author	User can create and read items but can only edit and delete their own items. They can create subfolders.
Author	User has same permissions as Publishing Author but cannot create additional subfolders.
Nonediting Author	User can create and read items and can delete their own items. They cannot make changes to any items or create subfolders.
Reviewer	User can only read items in the folder.
Contributor	User can only create new items in the folder.
None	User or group cannot access or use the folder.

To add a new user or distribution group to this list, click the **Add** button. A dialog box with a list of all mail-enabled users appears, and you can select objects to add. You can add only objects with an Exchange mailbox on the system. When a new user is added to the list, he or she is automatically granted the role indicated in the Default account listed for the folder. You can change that role at any time.

When you set client permissions on a folder, the changes do not propagate to existing subfolders. However, new subfolders inherit the client permissions from the parent folder.

ASSIGNING PERMISSIONS TO NON-MAPI FOLDERS

When you assign permissions to a non-MAPI folder in a Web Storage System, you have much more control over what a user can and cannot do. To manage Client permissions on a non-MAPI folder, follow these steps:

1. Open Exchange System Manager, and expand the folder tree until you see the folder you are setting permissions on.

2. Right-click the folder, click **Properties**, and then click the **Permissions** tab.

3. Click **Client Permissions**. The **Client Permissions** dialog box for the folder appears. For example, Figure 14.3 shows the **Permissions** dialog box for the Zoo Management folder.

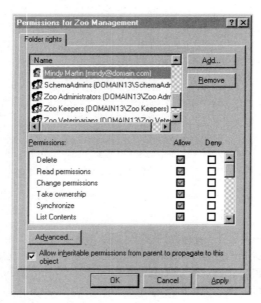

Figure 14.3
Client permissions for a non-MAPI folder

You'll see that the options have changed from the MAPI folder **Client Permissions** dialog box. The **Name** list displays the User and Group objects that are currently assigned rights to the folder, but these objects are actually objects defined in Active Directory. In addition, you don't see any roles assigned to these User and Group objects. Instead, you assign one or more of the detailed permissions in the **Permissions** list. Not only is this list much more extensive and robust than its MAPI counterpart, but you can explicitly deny permissions, rather than not granting or simply not setting them. A denied permission takes precedence over all other settings.

Table 14.2 lists the permissions that you can grant or deny. The first five permissions listed in the table correspond to the standard access rights and are defined by the Windows security system. The remaining permissions are a compilation of permissions that can apply to the folder, to items in the folder, and to any child folders.

Table 14.2   Available permissions

Permission	If granted, the user can...
Delete	Delete this resource.
Read Permissions	Read the ACL and owner information for this resource.
Change Permissions	Change the ACL on the resource.
Take ownership	Change the owner to herself or himself without explicit rights to the resource via the ACL.
Synchronize	Synchronize access and allow a process to wait for a resource to enter the signaled state. Not relevant to most developers.
List Contents	Enumerate the contents (subfolders and items) of a folder.
Create Item	Add an item to a folder. This permission is generally set along with the Write Body permission.
Create Container	Create a subfolder.
Read Property	Read extended attributes associated with that resource. This permission is generally set along with the Read Body permission.

Continued on next page

Table 14.2 continued   Available permissions

Permission	If granted, the user can...
Write Property	Write extended attributes associated with that resource. This permission is generally set along with the Write Body permission.
Execute	Execute a program file. On folders, this specifies the right to traverse the directory.
Delete Child	Delete an item or subfolder.
Read Attributes	Read attributes associated with that resource. This permission is generally set along with the Read Body permission.
Write Attributes	Write attributes associated with that resource. This permission is generally set along with the Write Body permission.
View Item	View an item in the folder.
Owner	The security principal is the owner of the folder. This permission corresponds to the fRightsOwner permission in previous versions of Exchange and is provided for backward compatibility.
Contact	Not used for security. Identifies the user as the contact for the folder. This permission corresponds to the fRightsContact permission in previous versions of Exchange and is provided for backward compatibility.

To change permissions for a user, in the **Name** list, click a user or security group. The current permissions for that object are listed and are organized in Allow and Deny groupings. To grant a permission, select the check box; to deny a permission, clear it.

To add a new User or Security Group object to the list of users granted permission to the folder, click **Add**. A list of Active Directory contents appears, and you can use it to add objects to the users list. Unlike the **Client Permissions** dialog box, in the **Permission**s dialog box you can add any User or Group object already registered in the Active Directory. Select a user or group, and click **OK**. You can now grant or deny permissions to the user or group. Click **Apply** to apply your changes to the folder permissions settings.

UNDERSTANDING PERMISSIONS INHERITANCE

When you create a new folder tree, specific permissions are automatically granted to a number of User and Group objects. When you create a new folder in this folder tree, by default, that new folder inherits the permissions of the parent folder. For example, if you grant permissions to the Applications folder tree to the Zoo Administrators security group, the group automatically has the same permissions to any new folder that you create in that folder tree.

In some applications, you do not want all users and groups to have the same permissions for every child folder in the application. For example, Zoo Administrators should be able to do anything they want in a folder containing administrative information, but they should not be able to change items in the surgery schedule folder (a task of the Zoo Veterinarians). Because the permissions are inherited by default when you create a new folder, you need to find a solution to this problem.

One solution to this dilemma is to modify the inherited User or Group object permissions on each folder so that new folders continue to inherit permissions from the parent folder and also have a customized permissions list. When you modify an inherited group on a folder by granting or denying additional properties, you do not affect how the group behaves in the parent folder. The modifications affect only that folder and any additional child folders you select.

When you make a change to an inherited group, the permissions list for that group appears as a combination of shaded, unavailable check marks and black check marks. The black check marks indicate permissions that apply only to this folder and not to parent folders. For a detailed list of which properties are specific to a folder and which are inherited, in the **Client Permissions** dialog box, click **Advanced**. The **Access Control Settings** dialog box appears (see Figure 14.4).

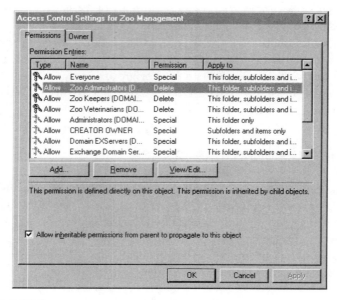

Figure 14.4
The Access Control Settings dialog box is used to view all permissions for each user and security group.

The **Access Control Settings** dialog box lists all the deny and grant entries on the folder. If you have modified the permissions for an inherited object, that object appears in the list twice. The bold entries at the top of the list are specific to that folder. The shaded entries indicate inherited permissions.

For more detail on an entry, select the entry from the list, and click **View/Edit**. A **Permission Entry** dialog box appears (see Figure 14.5).

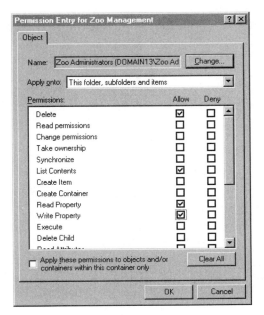

Figure 14.5
Use the Permission Entry dialog box for greater control over how permissions are propagated to child resources.

You can use this dialog box to edit the permissions, or you can change the **Apply onto** option to indicate how the current permissions are propagated to the items in the folder and the child folders. Table 14.3 lists the optional settings for the **Apply onto** option.

Table 14.3 Apply onto option settings

Option	Description
This folder only	Permissions do not propagate to items or child folders.
This folder and subfolders	Permissions apply to the folder and propagate to child folders but not to items in the folder.
This folder and items	Permissions apply to the folder and propagate to items but not child folders.
Subfolders only	Permissions propagate to child folders but not to items.
Items only	Permissions propagate to items but not to child folders.
This folder, subfolders and items	Permissions apply to the folder and propagate to items or child folders. This is the default.
Subfolders and items only	Permissions propagate to items or child folders but are not applied to this folder.

Inheritance among folders is enabled by default. However, you can disable inheritance and prevent permissions from being propagated from a parent folder to a child folder. To disable inheritance, right-click the folder, click **Properties**, and then click the **Permissions** tab. On the **Permissions** tab, clear the **Allow inheritable permissions from parent to propagate to this object** check box. When you clear this check box, a warning message appears (see Figure 14.6).

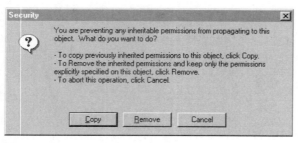

Figure 14.6
Disable user permissions inheritance.

You have three options:

- **Copy**. If you click **Copy**, all the objects and their permissions currently available on the folder remain available. For example, if the folder has inherited a group named Zoo Keepers, when you click **Copy**, the group and its current permissions are copied to the folder as if you created it there in the first place.

- **Remove**. If you click **Remove**, all the inherited User and Group objects currently available on the folder are removed from the permissions list. If you have not added new objects or modified objects for specific behavior on this folder, the **Permissions** list will be empty and you can populate it from scratch.

- **Cancel**. If you click **Cancel**, you leave inheritance in place.

OVERLAPPING PERMISSIONS

You can explicitly grant permissions to a user, or you can implicitly grant permissions by granting permissions to a group to which the user belongs. In some situations, you might want to explicitly grant or deny permissions to a User object that has already been granted permissions implicitly. For example, by default every user in your domain belongs to an Everyone group. The Everyone group is automatically added to the permissions list of a folder tree. Any time you change the permissions of this group, it affects how every user interacts with the folder. If you want to grant or deny permissions for a specific user, you can add the user to the list and modify that entry. In this case, the user now has multiple permission entries.

Here are some permissions scenarios:

- A user is granted explicit permission to view the folder contents. The user can view the folder contents.

- A user is not explicitly granted permission to view the folder contents but belongs to a group that is granted permission to view the folder contents. The user can view the folder contents.

- A user is not explicitly granted permission to view the folder contents and belongs to a group that is not explicitly granted permission to view the folder contents. The user cannot view the folder contents.

- A user is not explicitly granted permission to view the folder contents and belongs to a group that is denied permission to view the folder contents. The user cannot view the folder contents.

- A user is explicitly denied permission to view the folder contents but belongs to a group that is granted permission to view the folder contents. The user cannot view the folder contents.

- A user is explicitly granted permission to view the folder contents but belongs to a group that is denied permission to view the folder contents. The user cannot view the folder contents.

NOTE A denied permission takes precedence over all other settings.

USING THE SECURITY DESCRIPTOR PROPERTY

This section describes how to use code to access and set the security descriptor for a folder or an item.

UNDERSTANDING THE SECURITY DESCRIPTOR PROPERTY

You can read and configure the security descriptor for a particular folder or item with the http://schemas.microsoft.com/exchange/security/descriptor schema property. This book refers to this property as the security descriptor property.

You can access the security descriptor for a resource in a Web Storage System just like any other schema property. However, the security descriptor property returns the value as an Extensible Markup Language (XML) string. When you request this property, the XML string is generated dynamically by the system from the same property that http://schemas.microsoft.com/exchange/ntsecuritydescriptor comes from. The returned XML string takes the following format:

```
<security_descriptor>
<revision/>
<owner/>
<group/>
<dacl/>
<sacl/>
</security_descriptor>
```

Where:

\<revision\>

is information about the revision made.

\<owner\>

is the SID of the owner of this particular object.

\<group\>

is the primary group of the owner of the object.

\<dacl\>

is a discretionary ACL specifying the access permissions for the object.

\<sacl\>

is a security ACL specifying system level security.

NOTE   These security descriptor XML elements are part of the "http://schemas.microsoft.com/security/" namespace.

Listing 14.1 shows how to read the security descriptor for any resource and read the XML.

Listing 14.1   Get a security descriptor on an item.

```
Sub GetEntireSD(urlResource As String)
    ' Return the entire XML string for
    ' the security descriptor on a resource.

    With New ADODB.Record
        ' Open the resource
        .Open urlResource

        ' Get the security descriptor as XML
        Debug.Print .Fields( _
        "http://schemas.microsoft.com/exchange/security/descriptor")
    End With
End Sub
```

NOTE The code listings in this chapter are available in the Microsoft Visual Basic project CH_14.vbp on the companion CD. If you want to run the samples as they are written, you must have the Zoo Management sample installed on your Exchange 2000 server. For information about installing the application, see the introduction to the book.

When you run the code in Listing 14.1, you get results something like this:

```
<S:security_descriptor xmlns:S="http://schemas.microsoft.com/security/"
xmlns:D="urn:uuid:c2f41010-65b3-11d1-a29f-00aa00c14882/"
:dt="microsoft.security_descriptor">
 <S:revision>1</S:revision>
 <S:owner S:defaulted="0">
  <S:sid>
   <S:string_sid>S-1-5-32-544</S:string_sid>
   <S:type>alias</S:type>
   <S:nt4_compatible_name>BUILTIN\Administrators</S:nt4_compatible_name>
   <S:ad_object_guid>{ac6614a5-3dd6-457b-a5ef-
fc76eb2c95d}</S:ad_object_guid>
  </S:sid>
 </S:owner>
 <S:primary_group S:defaulted="0">
  <S:sid>
   <S:string_sid>S-1-5-21-1343757750-1744411205-18798897-
513</S:string_sid>
   <S:type>group</S:type>
   <S:nt4_compatible_name>DOMAIN13\Domain Users</S:nt4_compatible_name>
   <S:ad_object_guid>{bcf52d2f-e5f7-4169-8dab-
4c4926ead2e}</S:ad_object_guid>
  </S:sid>
 </S:primary_group>
 <S:dacl S:defaulted="0" S:protected="1" S:autoinherited="1">
  <S:revision>4</S:revision>
  <S:effective_aces>
   <S:access_allowed_ace S:inherited="0">
    <S:access_mask>1fcfff</S:access_mask>
    <S:sid>
     <S:string_sid>S-1-5-21-1343757750-1744411205-18798897-
1105</S:string_sid>
     <S:type>user</S:type>
     <S:nt4_compatible_name>DOMAIN13\mindy</S:nt4_compatible_name>
```

```
    <S:ad_object_guid>{2f80e4fb-dfb2-4fbe-b410-
2548e62ba5d}</S:ad_object_guid>
      <S:display_name>Mindy Martin</S:display_name>
     </S:sid>
    </S:access_allowed_ace>
    <S:access_allowed_ace S:inherited="0">
     <S:access_mask>10400</S:access_mask>
     <S:sid>
      <S:string_sid>S-1-5-21-1343757750-1744411205-18798897-
1150</S:string_sid>
      <S:type>group</S:type>
      <S:nt4_compatible_name>DOMAIN13\Zoo Keepers</S:nt4_compatible_name>
      <S:ad_object_guid>{e7de6ec7-85d6-472e-84cb-
4b4758a808dc}</S:ad_object_guid>
      <S:display_name>Zoo Keepers</S:display_name>
     </S:sid>
    </S:access_allowed_ace>
   </S:effective_aces>
   <S:subcontainer_inheritable_aces>
    <S:access_allowed_ace S:inherited="0" S:no_propagate_inherit="0">
     <S:access_mask>1fcfff</S:access_mask>
     <S:sid>
      <S:string_sid>S-1-5-21-1343757750-1744411205-18798897-
1105</S:string_sid>
      <S:type>user</S:type>
      <S:nt4_compatible_name>DOMAIN13\mindy</S:nt4_compatible_name>
      <S:ad_object_guid>{2f80e4fb-dfb2-4fbe-b410-
62548e62ba5d}</S:ad_object_guid>
      <S:display_name>Mindy Martin</S:display_name>
     </S:sid>
    </S:access_allowed_ace>
    <S:access_allowed_ace S:inherited="0" S:no_propagate_inherit="0">
     <S:access_mask>10400</S:access_mask>
     <S:sid>
      <S:string_sid>S-1-5-21-1343757750-1744411205-18798897-
1150</S:string_sid>
      <S:type>group</S:type>
      <S:nt4_compatible_name>DOMAIN13\Zoo Keepers</S:nt4_compatible_name>
      <S:ad_object_guid>{e7de6ec7-85d6-472e-84cb-
4b4758a808dc}</S:ad_object_guid>
      <S:display_name>Zoo Keepers</S:display_name>
     </S:sid>
```

```
  </S:access_allowed_ace>
 </S:subcontainer_inheritable_aces>
 <S:subitem_inheritable_aces>
  <S:access_allowed_ace S:inherited="0" S:no_propagate_inherit="0">
   <S:access_mask>1fcfff</S:access_mask>
   <S:sid>
    <S:string_sid>S-1-5-21-1343757750-1744411205-18798897-
1105</S:string_sid>
    <S:type>user</S:type>
    <S:nt4_compatible_name>DOMAIN13\mindy</S:nt4_compatible_name>
    <S:ad_object_guid>{2f80e4fb-dfb2-4fbe-b410-
62548e62ba5d}</S:ad_object_guid>
    <S:display_name>Mindy Martin</S:display_name>
   </S:sid>
  </S:access_allowed_ace>
  <S:access_allowed_ace S:inherited="0" S:no_propagate_inherit="0">
   <S:access_mask>10400</S:access_mask>
   <S:sid>
    <S:string_sid>S-1-5-21-1343757750-1744411205-18798897-
1150</S:string_sid>
    <S:type>group</S:type>
    <S:nt4_compatible_name>DOMAIN13\Zoo Keepers</S:nt4_compatible_name>
    <S:ad_object_guid>{e7de6ec7-85d6-472e-84cb-
4b4758a808dc}</S:ad_object_guid>
    <S:display_name>Zoo Keepers</S:display_name>
   </S:sid>
  </S:access_allowed_ace>
 </S:subitem_inheritable_aces>
 </S:dacl>
</S:security_descriptor>
```

NOTE The Ch 14 Visual Basic Project (Ch_14.vbp) includes a form that you can use to test this code. When you enter a URL of a resource into a text box, the form displays the existing security descriptor of the resource in another text box.

INTERPRETING A DACL

The discretionary access control list (DACL) specifies the users and groups that can access a resource and the permissions granted to those users and groups. A DACL consists of a set of ACEs that either grant or deny a user or group certain permissions to an Exchange object. Only the users and groups with an associated ACE can interact with the Web Storage System resource.

The DACL takes the following format:

```
<dacl>
<revision/>
    ACE
</dacl>
```

An ACE can be an:

- Access allowed ACE. This is used to grant permissions to a user or group. <access_allowed_ace>

- Access denied ACE. This is used to deny permissions to a user or group. <access_denied_ace>

An individual ACE has the following syntax:

```
<access_allowed_ace>
access_mask
SID
</access_allowed_ace>
```

Where:

access_mask

is a hexadecimal value that identifies the permissions controlled by the ACE.

SID

identifies the security principal that the ACE refers to, such as a User or Group object.

Using Access Masks

The access mask contains a set of permissions that are being granted or denied with a particular ACE. An *access mask* is a 32-bit number in which the upper 16 bits define standard and generic access permissions and the lower 16 bits define access permissions that are specific to the folder or item.

You can build the access mask by using a combination of values from Table 14.4 and either Table 14.5 or Table 14.6 (depending on whether you secure a folder or an item). Table 14.4 defines the standard access permissions specified by Windows and available to every resource in a Web Storage System.

Table 14.4   Standard access permissions

Permission	Hexadecimal
Delete	0x00010000
Read Permissions	0x00020000
Change Permissions	0x00040000
Take ownership	0x00080000
Synchronize	0x00100000

Table 14.5 defines the access permissions specific to folder objects.

Table 14.5   Folder access permissions

Permission	Hexadecimal
List Contents	0x00000001
Create Item	0x00000002
Create Container	0x00000004
Read Property	0x00000008
Write Property	0x00000010
Read Attributes	0x00000080
Write Attributes	0x00000100

Continued on next page

Table 14.5 continued   Folder access permissions

Permission	Hexadecimal
Write Own Property	0x00000200
Delete Own Item	0x00000400
View Item	0x00000800
Owner	0x00004000
Contact	0x00008000

Table 14.6 defines the access permissions specific to items such as messages and appointments.

Table 14.6   Item access permissions

Permission	Hexadecimal
Read Body	0x00000001
Write Body	0x00000002
Append Message	0x00000004
Read Property	0x00000008
Write Property	0x00000010
Execute	0x00000020
Read Attributes	0x00000080
Write Attributes	0x00000100
Write Own Property	0x00000200
Delete Own Item	0x00000400
View Item	0x00000800

To grant or deny multiple permissions, you add the associated hexadecimal values together. Numbers in hexadecimal notation are represented by either a digit between 0 and 9 or a letter between a and f inclusive. When the hexadecimal number exceeds the value of 9, you represent each succeeding number with a letter, starting with "a". For example, 10 is represented by "a"; 11 is represented by "b"; and so on. You do not carry a value from one column to the next as you would in standard addition.

For example, to grant a user the following permissions, you would use an access mask value of 1f019b:

- 0x00000001   Read Body

- 0x00000002   Write Body

- 0x00000008   Read Property

- 0x00000010   Write Property

- 0x00000080   Read Attributes

- 0x00000100   Write Attributes

- 0x00010000   Delete standard permission

- 0x00020000   Read Permissions

- 0x00040000   Change Permissions

- 0x00080000   Take ownership

- 0x00100000   Synchronize

You can drop off the leading zeros and the "x" when you set the access mask.

NOTE To read and edit other people's items in a folder, you must grant read and write permission to both properties and attributes.

READING AND BUILDING AN SID

As discussed earlier, an SID is a piece of code that identifies the User or Group object being granted or denied access permissions. An SID has the following syntax:

```
<sid>
<string_sid/>
<nt4_compatible_sid/>
<type/>
<ad_object_guid/>
<display_name/>
</sid>
```

Where:

string_sid

> is string identifier for the User or Group object.

nt4_compatible_sid

> is the pre-Windows 2000 logon name of the User or Group object in the format of [domain]\[logonname].

type

> is the type of object, such as User or Group, being granted or denied permissions.

ad_object_guid

> is a string representation of the globally unique identifier (GUID) for the User or Group object.

display_name

> is the friendly name of the User or Group object and comes from the display name of the address book entry.

When you read an SID for an ACE, you get all the previous information that is available for the User or Group object. When you build an SID for an ACE that will be appended to a security descriptor property for a resource, you need to provide only one of the values. To avoid conflicting display names, set the *nt4_compatible_sid* parameter instead of the *display_name* parameter when you create a new ACE. The system fills in the remaining values for you if it is able to locate the user or group in Active Directory.

You can also grant or deny permissions to an Exchange role by using a role SID. A role SID has the following syntax:

```
<S:role_sid>
<S:scope/>
<S:property_name/>
</S:role_sid>
```

Where:

scope

is where to read the role information, on the item or the folder.

property_name

is the name of role property that contains the list of SIDs.

READING THE DETAILS OF A SECURITY DESCRIPTOR

If you want to use ActiveX Data Objects (ADO) to read the security descriptor, you can only do so much with the property value before you must incorporate another object model. For example, if you want to read the details of the security descriptor, such as the User and Group objects that have been granted permissions to a resource, you can use the XML Document Object Model (XML DOM) to parse through the XML.

Listing 14.2 shows how to use the XML DOM to read a security descriptor on any given resource. The procedure starts with basic ADO code to access the security descriptor value on the resource. Then the code uses the XML DOM to load the property value in an XML document object. Once the value is associated with an XML document, the XML DOM can easily traverse through the document nodes, searching for specific ones. For example, this procedure uses the SelectNodes method to return a collection of all XML nodes representing the access allowed ACEs. The code then loops through this collection and uses the SelectSingleNode method to return both the NT4 compatible name and the access mask. The code repeats this process for the access denied ACEs.

Listing 14.2   Get allow and deny ACE entries.

```
Sub GetACEs(urlResource As String)
    ' Return the names of users and groups
    ' granted or denied permissions on a resource.

    Dim rec As New ADODB.Record
    Dim fld As ADODB.Field
```

```
Dim strURL As String
Dim xmlDoc As MSXML.DOMDocument
Dim nodelist As MSXML.IXMLDOMNodeList
Dim n As MSXML.IXMLDOMNode

' Open the resource
rec.Open urlResource

' Get the security descriptor as XML
Set fld = rec.Fields _
("http://schemas.microsoft.com/exchange/security/descriptor")

Debug.Print "Security Descriptor for "
Debug.Print strURL

Set xmlDoc = New DOMDocument
xmlDoc.validateOnParse = False

' Load the SID
xmlDoc.loadXML fld.Value

Debug.Print "-------------------------------------"
Debug.Print "Users and groups granted permissions:"
Debug.Print "-------------------------------------"

' Get the access_allowed_ace node instances
Set nodelist = xmlDoc.documentElement.selectNodes( _
   "//S:access_allowed_ace")

' Return the name of each user granted permissions
For Each n In nodelist
   Debug.Print n.selectSingleNode _
      ("S:sid/S:nt4_compatible_name").Text
   Debug.Print n.selectSingleNode _
      ("S:access_mask").Text
Next

Debug.Print "-------------------------------------"
Debug.Print "Users and groups denied permissions:"
Debug.Print "-------------------------------------"
```

```
' Get the access_denied_ace node instances
Set nodelist = xmlDoc.documentElement.selectNodes( _
   "//S:access_denied_ace")

' Return the name of each user denied permissions
For Each n In nodelist
   Debug.Print n.selectSingleNode _
      ("S:sid/S:nt4_compatible_name").Text
   Debug.Print n.selectSingleNode _
      ("S:access_mask").Text
Next

' Clean up
rec.Close
Set rec = Nothing
Set fld = Nothing
Set xmlDoc = Nothing
Set nodelist = Nothing
Set n = Nothing
End Sub
```

BUILDING A SECURITY DESCRIPTOR

One way to create a new security descriptor is to build an XML string and then save it to the security descriptor property on a Web Storage System resource. When you create the XML string, you must assign a data type to the XML document of "Microsoft.security_descriptor" with the dt property. The dt property belongs to the following namespace:

```
urn:uuid:c2f41010-65b3-11d1-a29f-00aa00c14882/
```

You set the dt property in the security_descriptor root element of the XML document like this:

```
<S:security_descriptor
xmlns:S="http://schemas.microsoft.com/security/"
xmlns:D="urn:uuid:c2f41010-65b3-11d1-a29f-00aa00c14882/"
D:dt="microsoft.security_descriptor">
```

The security_descriptor element is constant from resource to resource when you set the security descriptor property. Listing 14.3 shows how to build a security descriptor for a folder that contains a single access allowed ACE in a DACL.

Listing 14.3 Create a security descriptor.

```
Sub BuildNewSD()
    ' This creates and assigns a new SD
    ' The procedure will overwrite any
    ' existing SD on the resource.

    Dim strURL As String
    Dim strXML As String

    ' Security descriptor property
    Const strSD As String = _
    "http://schemas.microsoft.com/exchange/security/descriptor"

    ' URL to the resource
    strURL = GetStorageName & "applications/developers/"

    ' Build the XML
    strXML = "<S:security_descriptor"
    strXML = strXML & _
        " xmlns:S=""http://schemas.microsoft.com/security/"""
    strXML = strXML & _
        " xmlns:D=""urn:uuid:c2f41010-65b3-11d1-a29f-00aa00c14882/"""
    strXML = strXML & " D:dt=""microsoft.security_descriptor"">"
    strXML = strXML & "<S:dacl>"
    strXML = strXML & "<S:effective_aces>"
    strXML = strXML & "<S:access_allowed_ace>"
    strXML = strXML & "<S:access_mask>1fcfff</S:access_mask>"
    strXML = strXML & "<S:sid>"
    strXML = strXML & _
        "<S:nt4_compatible_name>domain13\mindy</S:nt4_compatible_name>"
    strXML = strXML & "</S:sid>"
    strXML = strXML & "</S:access_allowed_ace>"
    strXML = strXML & "</S:effective_aces>"
    strXML = strXML & "</S:dacl>"
    strXML = strXML & "</S:security_descriptor>"
```

```
With New ADODB.Record
    ' Open the resource
    .Open strURL, , adModeReadWrite
    ' Assign the SD to the resource
    .Fields(strSD) = strXML
    .Fields.Update
    .Close
End With
End Sub
```

ENFORCING SECURITY ON CODE WITH COM+ COMPONENTS

This section focuses on setting security on application code rather than on Web Storage System resources. One way to set security on your code is to write your ADO and CDO code in ActiveX DLLs and then wrap the DLL in COM+ components. COM+ components not only provide an easy way to share and manage code used by multiple applications, but they also let you make use of COM+ role-based security. *COM+ role-based security* is a type of security that assigns access permissions on COM+ components to a user or group of users. You can grant a role access to every component in a COM+ application or just to specific components, such as an interface or a method. This level of control often eliminates the need to incorporate security-based code in the application itself.

This section describes why you might want to use COM+ role-based security, how to configure COM+ role-based security, and how to disable anonymous access to effectively use COM+ roles.

WHY USE COM+ ROLE-BASED SECURITY?

Both ADO and Collaboration Data Objects (CDO) for Exchange use the Exchange OLE DB (ExOLEDB) provider to communicate with a Web Storage System. One shortcoming of the ExOLEDB provider is that it does not allow you to open a resource with specific credentials. ExOLEDB instead uses a predefined security context. Every application that uses ADO and CDO code on the server runs with the same permissions no matter what the code is attempting to do. Because the ADO and CDO code run on the server under the same security context, this also means that by default, the code will attempt to execute regardless of who is the currently logged on user.

To understand this better, consider the ZooWeb application. This application uses several Web pages that contain both ADO and CDO code. To begin with, no security is set. As long as you have access permissions to the application folders, you can execute the code in the Web pages. Animal handlers can add and delete veterinarians, veterinarians can add new animals, and zoo administrators can schedule surgeries. Obviously, this is not an optimal solution. Data is very insecure and vulnerable to both malicious and accidental alterations.

To avoid this vulnerable situation, you must add one or more types of security. Although you can specify client permissions on the Web Storage System folders to control who can access and edit the data, you do not prevent the code from running in the first place. By moving the code out of the Web pages and into an ActiveX DLL, you can create COM+ components and add COM+ role-based security to the components to restrict execute access to only those users who should be able to run the code. For example, you can build a COM+ security role for each group: handlers, vets, and administrators. You can then indicate which roles can run which code component. For example, only veterinarians should be able to schedule surgery. If only the veterinarian role is enabled on the surgery component, other users can no longer access those code bits.

CONFIGURING COM+ ROLE-BASED SECURITY

To configure a Web Storage System application to use COM+ role-based security, you must complete several tasks. After the components have been registered with Component Services, you must:

1. Enable COM+ role-based security for the application group type.

2. Define COM+ roles that group users together by some common trait.

3. Add Active Directory users or groups to their respective COM+ roles.

4. Assign the COM+ roles to the appropriate components, interfaces, and methods.

ENABLING SECURITY FOR THE COM+ APPLICATION

To use COM+ roles on your COM+ components, you must first enable role-based security for the entire COM+ application type. By default, an application is not configured to use COM+ roles and performs access checks only at the process level by using a user's SID and the process security descriptor. Role checking is turned off at the component, method, and interface levels and is performed only at the application level.

COM+ role-based security, however, relies on more detailed role checking. Role checking occurs at both the process and the component levels. At the process level and component level, both process security descriptor checks and role-based security checks are made. The security call context information is also made available, so you can write code in the component to access security information about the user attempting to connect to the Web site. This is the required option for COM+ applications. You must still specifically enable access checks at the component level, as discussed in later sections.

To enable COM+ roles on an application group, follow these steps:

1. In the **Component Services** console, expand the tree until you see the **COM+ Applications** folder, and click the folder to open it.

2. Locate the COM+ application that will use role-based security. Right-click the application, click **Properties**, and then click the **Security** tab. If you are building DLL components, the application is probably **IIS Out-of-Process Pooled Applications**.

3. Select **Enforce access checks for this application**.

4. Select the second **Security level** option for access checks at both the process and component levels. Figure 14.7 shows how the **Security** tab should look.

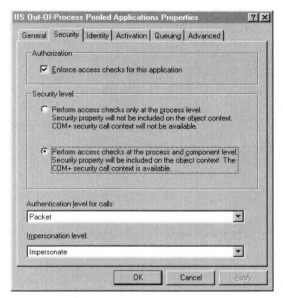

Figure 14.7
To use COM+ roles, you must enforce access checks for the application type and perform these checks at the process and component levels.

5. Restart the application. Only users assigned to roles that have been assigned to the application can access the application.

After you enable COM+ role-based security on the application type, the change applies to all applications and all components registered in the application type. For example, if you enable security for the IIS Out-of-process Pooled Applications group type, the change affects all the applications and components registered there. However, you can manually turn off specific applications.

DEFINING COM+ ROLES

Once you enable COM+ role-based security for the COM+ application type, you must define the COM+ roles to be used in your application. The COM+ roles determine who can access and execute each component, interface, or method.

You can define or create roles that make sense in your application. You can create roles that indicate a level of authority, such as Managers and Administrators. You can use such roles to allow certain individuals to conduct basic maintenance tasks applicable throughout an application. For example, the Administrator role should be able to read information about everything that happens at the zoo, such as surgery schedule, accounting information, and the current animal roster. You can also create roles that describe job functionality, such as Veterinarians or Zoo Keepers. You can use these roles to assign permissions to access components specific to their work. For instance, the Veterinarian role should be able to create and maintain the surgery schedule but doesn't need to access the accounting information for the zoo as Administrators do.

To define a COM+ role, follow these steps:

1. Locate the COM+ application, and expand the tree until you see a Roles folder.

2. Right-click the Roles folder, and click **New**. Then, on the shortcut menu, click **Role**. A **Role** dialog box appears (see Figure 14.8).

Figure 14.8
Use the Role dialog box to create a new role.

3. Enter a name for the role, such as *Zoo Administrators* or *Vets*, and click **OK**. The role now appears in the Roles folder.

TIP You can add a description to a role after the role is created. Right-click the role icon in the Roles folder, and click **Properties**. A **Description** text box appears along with other role information.

ADDING USERS TO COM+ ROLES

After you define the COM+ roles, you add individuals to the role to grant permissions to execute each component. Users can be individual User objects or security Group objects registered in the Active Directory. To assign a user to a COM+ role, follow these steps:

1. Locate the COM+ application, and expand the tree until you see a Roles folder.

2. Expand the Roles folder tree to locate the role you want. Expand it to show a Users folder.

3. Click the Users folder.

4. Right-click the Users folder, and click **New**. Then, on the menu, click **User**. A **Select Users or Groups** dialog box appears (see Figure 14.9).

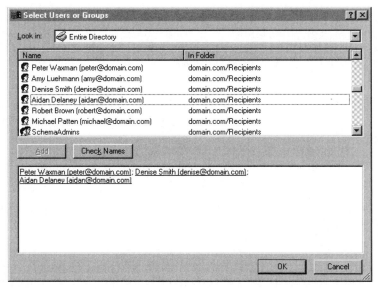

Figure 14.9
Both users and groups in the Active Directory can be added as users of a COM+ role.

5. Select a user or group from the list, and click **Add**.

6. Add users to the list, and then click **OK** to apply the changes and close the dialog box.

Assigning COM+ Roles to Components

The final step to configuring COM+ role-based security is to assign the COM+ roles to the components. You can grant a role access to every component in a COM+ application or just to a specific component, such as an interface or a method. This can eliminate the need to incorporate security-based code in the application itself.

When you assign a role to a component, only users in that role can access the component. No other users or groups can access the COM+ component. For example, if you define roles for Zoo Administrators and Vets, and you assign the Vets role to a surgery component, Administrators are not allowed to access the component or any child components.

In addition, when you assign a role to a component, the users in that role also have access to all methods and interfaces in that COM+ component. If you need to secure only one method instead of the entire component, you should assign the role at the method level rather than force component checking for every method.

To assign COM+ roles to a component, follow these steps:

1. In the **Component Services** console, expand the tree until you see the COM+ Applications folder, and then click the folder to open it.

2. Locate the COM+ application that will use role-based security, expand the tree until you see a Components folder, and then click the Components folder to open it.

3. Locate the component that will use the assigning roles. Expand the component to show the interfaces and methods.

4. Right-click the component, interface, or method. Click **Properties**, and then click the **Security** tab.

5. Select **Enforce component level access checks**.

6. In the **Roles explicitly set for selected item(s)** list, select the roles that are allowed to use this component. Figure 14.10 shows what your dialog box might look like.

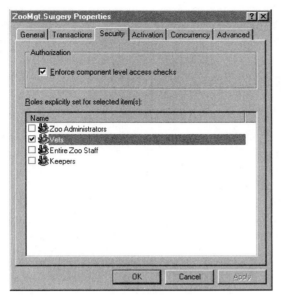

Figure 14.10
Only members of the selected roles have access to a component.

7. Restart the COM services to make the changes take effect.

NOTE   If you do not assign a COM+ role to a component and you have enabled access checks, all attempts by the client application to access the COM+ component fail.

DISABLING ANONYMOUS ACCESS TO EFFECTIVELY USE COM+ ROLES

Anonymous access allows users outside of your network to access a Web Storage System folder by using an anonymous account. When the server running Windows 2000 is installed, this anonymous account is created with a name of IUSR_*computername*, where *computername* is the name of the server. The account is also added to the Guests security group in Active Directory, which has security restrictions on the level of access and content availability to public users. You can specify any account to be used to authenticate anonymous access.

If anonymous access is enabled, Microsoft Internet Information Services (IIS) attempts to authenticate by using the anonymous account first, even if other security methods are in place. When a user attempts to access your Web Storage System application, IIS impersonates the IUSR_*computername* account before accessing any files or executing any code. If the IUSR_*computername* account has permissions, the file is returned and the code is executed. Otherwise, an error is returned.

This scenario changes when COM+ role-based security is enabled for a folder that has anonymous access enabled. IIS continues to impersonate the user as IUSR_*computername*, even if another valid user account is being used to connect to the Web site. This means that the IUSR_*computername* account must be added to a defined role so the file can be returned successfully, or the anonymous access must be disabled. Because adding this generic account to every role defeats the purpose of role-based security, you should leave anonymous access disabled.

To verify that anonymous access to the application has been disabled, follow these steps:

1. In Exchange System Manager, expand the Server group, and navigate to the Protocols group. Expand the HTTP protocol and Exchange Virtual Server until you see your virtual directory.

2. Right-click the virtual directory for your application, and click **Properties**.

3. In the **Properties** dialog box, click the **Access** tab, and then click **Authentication**. The **Authentication Methods** dialog box (Figure 14.11) appears.

4. Make sure the **Anonymous access** check box is clear.

Figure 14.11
To effectively use COM+ Roles in Web applications, disable Anonymous access for your virtual directory.

After anonymous access is disabled, all users must be explicitly defined in COM+ roles to access the application if code is being executed.

SUMMARY

As Web sites become more complex, developers must take precautions to make certain that the applications are secure. As more and more data becomes available on networks and across the Internet, the threat of malicious attacks increases. Developers are now faced with the challenge of providing broad data access throughout a corporation while excluding unwanted guests. Exchange and the Web Storage System offer several methods for keeping unwanted guests out of your Web site, including role-based security, item level security, and folder permissions.

Chapter 15, "Testing and Deploying Your Applications," explains how to test and deploy your applications successfully.

15

Testing and Deploying Your Applications

After you successfully build an application using Microsoft Exchange 2000 Server, you must thoroughly test it in an environment that closely matches your target environment. If you have been developing on your corporate Exchange server, move the application to another computer before you put the application through extensive testing. If you do this, one small bug won't accidentally disable the entire server (and nobody will yell at you because their e-mail is down). After you successfully test your application, you can deploy it. Building your own Exchange environment from scratch minimizes problems you might encounter when deploying an application.

This chapter explains how to test and deploy an application successfully. Sections include:

- **Setting Up Exchange in a Single Server Domain**

- **Setting Up the Development Environment**

- **Deploying Application-Specific Tools**

- **Using Windows Script Files to Automate Installations**

SETTING UP EXCHANGE IN A SINGLE SERVER DOMAIN

The first step to successful deployment of an Exchange application is to understand what goes into an Exchange installation. The best way to understand this is to set up a server computer from scratch and then use this computer as your test environment. Although Exchange is easy to install and use, it is a complex tool, and any developer who wants to write code against the server should have a firm understanding of what goes into building an Exchange environment. If you understand what components need to be installed from which application, it is easier to identify potential solutions to problems that might arise during the actual application deployment.

In the recommended setup of Microsoft Windows 2000 and Exchange, one computer is configured with Microsoft Windows 2000 Advanced Server and the Active Directory directory service of Windows 2000 as the primary Windows domain controller. The other computer is configured with Windows 2000 member server and Exchange 2000 as the collaboration server for the organization. However, for a single computer test environment, you must configure a computer to be both the domain controller and the collaboration server. This means that Windows 2000 Server, Active Directory, and Exchange 2000 must all be installed on the same computer.

INSTALLING WINDOWS 2000 SERVER

Because you configure a single-server network topology, you must install Windows 2000 Server to configure Active Directory. Exchange relies on Active Directory as its directory service, and you can configure Active Directory only on a computer running Windows 2000 Server.

If you suspect that you might need to reinstall Windows 2000 and Exchange from scratch more than once on the same computer, install Microsoft Windows NT version 4.0 or Windows 2000 Professional on one partition of your system and Windows 2000 Advanced Server on another. If you install Windows NT 4.0, upgrade to Service Pack 5 (SP5) so that Windows NT 4.0 can access the Windows 2000 NTFS partitions. You should have about 500 megabytes (MB) of hard disk space for the first partition and at least 2 gigabytes (GB) of hard disk space for the Windows 2000 Server partition. Although this approach is not necessary, it can save you time by making it easier to install Windows Server and Exchange the second time.

To install Windows 2000 Server, start the currently installed version of Windows (Windows NT 4.0 with SP5 or Windows 2000 Professional) and follow these steps:

1. Start Windows 2000 Advanced Server Setup. If you are installing from a Windows 2000 Professional partition, a message appears indicating that you cannot upgrade your Windows edition. Click **OK**. You want to install the server on another partition.

2. On the **Windows 2000 Setup** page, click **Install a new copy of Windows 2000 (Clean install)**, and then click **Next**.

3. Read the agreement, click **Accept**, and then click **Next**. You must accept the agreement to continue.

4. On the **Select Special Options** page, click **Advanced Options**.

5. Select **I want to choose the installation partition during Setup**, click **OK**, and then click **Next**.

6. On the **Upgrading to the Windows 2000 NTFS File System** page, select **Yes, upgrade my drive**, and then click **Next**.

7. On the **Directory of Applications for Windows 2000** page, you can choose to get more information about applications compatible with Windows, and then click **Next** to continue installation.

8. Windows copies the necessary files. This part can take awhile. After copying the files, Windows automatically restarts.

9. When Setup resumes, you are prompted for some general information about the Windows installation, including your name, the name of your organization, and date and time settings. When you are prompted, provide a name for your computer; the name you provide should be the name of your Exchange server. You use the server name in code whenever you use the Microsoft Internet Publishing Provider (msdaipp.dso) to access a Microsoft Web Storage System.

10. On the **Windows 2000 Components** page, you are prompted to add or remove components. In the **Components** list, select **Internet Information Services (IIS)**, and then click **Details**.

11. On the list of subcomponents of the **Internet Information Services (IIS)** list, select **NNTP Service**, click **OK**, and then click **Next**. You can install this component later.

12. On the **Networking Settings** page, you can select **Typical settings**, and then click **Next**.

13. On the **Workgroup or Computer Domain** page, select **No, this computer is not on a network, or is on a network without a domain**, and then click **Next**. You'll configure the domain after Windows has finished installing.

14. After the computer restarts, log on as an administrator. When the **Windows 2000 Configure Your Server** dialog box appears, select **I will configure this server later**, and then click **Next** or close the dialog box.

Microsoft Internet Information Services 5.0, ActiveX Data Objects (ADO) 2.5, MSXML 2.5, Microsoft Internet Explorer 5, Microsoft Visual Basic Scripting Edition (VBScript) 5.1, and Microsoft JScript 5.1 are now installed and available for use.

Configuring Your Domain Controller

Exchange 2000 can be installed only on a computer in a Windows 2000 domain. Because you are using a single server setup, you must configure your test computer to be the domain controller by using Active Directory Installation Wizard. This section takes you through the process step by step.

1. Click the **Start** button, and click **Run**. In the text box, type **dcpromo**, and then click **OK**.

2. On the **Active Directory Installation Wizard** welcome page, click **Next**.

3. On the **Domain Controller Type** page, select **Domain Controller** for a new domain, and then click **Next**. This server is the first domain controller in the domain.

4. On the **Child Tree or Child Domain** page, select **Create a new domain tree**, and then click **Next**.

5. On the **Create or Join Forest** page, select **Create a new forest of domain trees**, and then click **Next**.

6. On the **New Domain Name** page, enter a name for your domain. Enter the same name that you use in URLs using Exchange OLE DB (ExOLEDB) to access a Web Storage System. If you are registered for a domain name, you can use that name. However, if you are just creating a simple test computer that doesn't need to mimic your actual organization names, you can use your own unique domain name. For example, Figure 15.1 shows the creation of domain.com. After you enter a name for your domain, click **Next**.

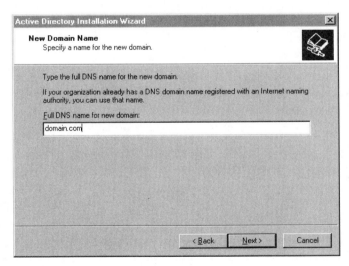

Figure 15.1
Name your domain.

7. On the **NetBIOS Domain Name** page, enter the same name for the domain as you indicated in step 5, and then click **Next**. If you are connected to your network and a conflicting domain name is discovered, the wizard suggests a different NetBIOS name for your computer. You can use the suggested name. You need to use the NetBIOS name only when you provide user credentials.

8. On the **Database and Log Locations** page, accept the default values, and then click **Next**.

9. On the **Shared System Volumes** page, accept the default values, and then click **Next**. At this point, a message might alert you that the wizard cannot contact the DNS server for the DNS name. That's okay. You don't need to install your own DNS server.

10. On the **Configure DNS** page, select **Yes, install and configure DNS on this computer**, and then click **Next**.

11. On the **Permissions** page, select the option that matches the environment you are developing for, and then click **Next**. If possible, select **Permissions compatible only with Windows 2000 servers** to avoid weakening security.

12. On the **Directory Services Restore Mode Administrator Password** page, enter a password for restore mode, and then click **Next**.

13. On the **Summary** page, verify your installation, and then click **Next**. The wizard configures your Active Directory. This step might take awhile, but if you interrupt the wizard, you have to start over.

14. When prompted, click **Finish**, and then restart the computer as prompted.

After the computer restarts, log on as an administrator. The **Configure Your Server** dialog box appears again for informational purposes only. You have successfully configured your server as the primary domain controller.

INSTALLING EXCHANGE 2000 SERVER

To configure Exchange for an actual organization, you would use a configuration topology that includes one computer as the primary domain controller and another computer as your Exchange server. However, for this test environment, you are using a single computer, so you install Exchange on the domain controller.

To install a new copy of Exchange, create a new Exchange organization and select the components that you need for development. If you want an Exchange server that has only the core components, you can use the default settings. Figure 15.2 shows a setup screen that depicts the default settings.

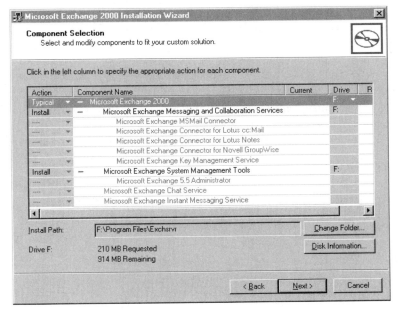

Figure 15.2
Default components settings for a new Exchange installation

You must provide a name for your first organization. This is the name that is used in Exchange System Manager to organize Web Storage Systems. You need to use this name when writing code to create new mailboxes or manage existing mailboxes. You can leave the default name, First Organization, if you like.

The complete setup of an Exchange server can take an hour or more, so plan to do something else during that time. After setup is complete, you do not need to restart Windows. To verify a successful installation, open Windows Explorer and look for drive M named Exchange. This is the location of your Exchange stores. If you have already mapped something to drive M, Exchange attempts to use drive N. If that is taken as well, Exchange attempts to map the stores to drive O, and so on, until it finds an available drive.

CREATING A NEW ADMINISTRATOR ACCOUNT

You are now logged on as the default administrator on your server. You must create a new account for yourself that has the same permissions as the administrator account. To create a new user account, use Active Directory Users and Computers in Microsoft Management Console (MMC) as outlined in these steps:

1. Click the **Start** button, point to **Programs**, point to **Administrative Tools**, and then click **Active Directory Users and Computers**. You can create a User object for yourself in the Users container or create a new organizational unit to organize the users and contacts that you create. During testing, you might find it helpful to have a separate organizational unit for the User objects that you create.

2. To create a new container, right-click the domain name, select **New**, and then select **Organizational Unit**. Enter a name for the organizational unit, and then click **OK**.

3. To create a new User object for yourself in the new organizational unit, right-click the **Organizational Unit** folder, select **New**, and then click **User**. Enter the appropriate information, including a password. Be sure to create an Exchange mailbox as well.

4. Double-click the new User object to display the **Properties** dialog box. Click the **Member of** tab, and then click **Add**. This is a list of the groups your User object belongs to, and to complete necessary tacks on your new network configuration, you should be a member of the following groups:

   - Administrators

   - Domain Admins

   - Enterprise Admins

   - Group Policy Creator Owners

   - Schema Admins

5. Log off as Administrator, and then log back in as the new user you just created.

After you log in as yourself, you can open Internet Explorer and connect to your mailbox by using Microsoft Outlook Web Access. After configuring Internet Explorer (you can even ignore all the connection settings if you like), enter the URL of your mailbox by using this template:

```
HTTP://[computername]/exchange/[youralias]
```

It might take a few seconds the first time you access the mailbox, but you should soon see the contents of your mailbox in Outlook Web Access.

SETTING UP THE DEVELOPMENT ENVIRONMENT

After you have configured Windows 2000 Advanced Server, Active Directory, and Exchange 2000 Server, you can create your development environment. This section explains how to install Microsoft Office 2000 and Microsoft FrontPage 2000 Server Extensions, install development environments and tools, create an Exchange development console in MMC, and add additional users.

INSTALLING OFFICE 2000 AND FRONTPAGE SERVER EXTENSIONS

To easily create and manage a Web application built with Exchange, you must install FrontPage 2000 and FrontPage 2000 Server Extensions. You can use FrontPage Server Extensions to publish Web sites; manage your FrontPage Web content remotely; and keep track of hyperlinks, virtual directories, and other content. As a FrontPage administrator, you can remotely configure permissions and manage users on your FrontPage Web sites.

You can install FrontPage Server Extensions by installing Office 2000 Premium edition or Office 2000 Developer. When the extensions are installed, three new security groups are automatically created on your computer:

- <SERVER> Admins

- <SERVER> Authors

- <SERVER> Browsers

If anyone else needs to create Web applications by using FrontPage, you must add them to these groups to allow them to publish successfully. After you install FrontPage Server Extensions, you can create Web-based solutions for Exchange.

INSTALLING DEVELOPMENT ENVIRONMENTS AND TOOLS

You must install your development tools on the computer you're using for development, whether it's the server or a client. Just make sure to share the Exchange folders that you or other developers need to access. The development environments and tools include:

- **Microsoft Visual Studio**. To create event sinks and Component Object Model (COM) objects, you should install Visual Studio 6.0, including Microsoft Visual Basic and/or Microsoft Visual C++ and Microsoft Visual InterDev.

- **Exchange SDK**. The Help files for development are not installed with Exchange 2000 Server and must be installed manually. You can get the Exchange SDK from the companion CD to this book or from the Microsoft Developer Network (MSDN) Web site at http://msdn.Microsoft.com/exchange/.

- **Sample files from the companion CD**. If you want to reuse the code in this book, copy the sample files from the companion CD to your computer. Create the Applications Web Storage System and add the Zoo Management application folders to run the code as it is written.

CREATING AN EXCHANGE DEVELOPMENT MMC CONSOLE

When you develop an Exchange application, you spend quite a bit of time using various Windows administrator tools, such as Component Services and Active Directory Users and Computers. Rather than opening these as individual tools in separate dialog boxes, you can define a custom console in MMC that includes all the tools you access most often during the development process. To create an Exchange development console in MMC, follow these steps:

1. Click the **Start** button, and then click **Run**. In the text box, type **MMC**, and then click **OK**. An empty console appears (see Figure 15.3).

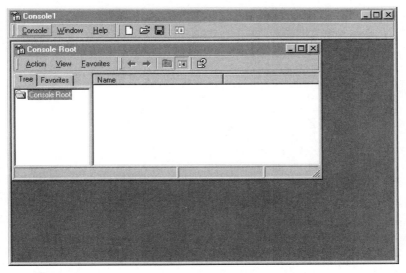

Figure 15.3
An empty console in MMC

2. On the **Console** menu, select **Add/Remove Snap-in**. The **Add/Remove Snap-in** dialog box displays the snap-ins currently linked to the console. Because this is a new console, the list is empty. You can use this list to remove snap-ins from the console as well.

3. Click **Add** to display the **Add Standalone Snap-in** dialog box (see Figure 15.4).

Figure 15.4
Choose the snap-ins you use most often during development.

4. To add a snap-in, select it from the list, and then click **Add**. Some of the snap-ins, such as Event Viewer, can be used to manage multiple computers. When you select one of these snap-ins, a message asks if the snap-in is for managing the local computer. For a single server testing topology, you can select the default value. Snap-ins in the same console that you might find useful include:

- Active Directory Users and Computers

- Component Services

- Event Viewer

- Exchange System

5. After you add the snap-ins, click **Close**, and then on the next dialog box, click **OK**.

6. Select the **Console** menu, and then click **Save As** to save the dialog box. Enter a name, such as **Exchange Development**, for the console, and then click **Save**. By default, the console is saved to the **Administrative Tools** folder. Figure 15.5 shows what the console looks like.

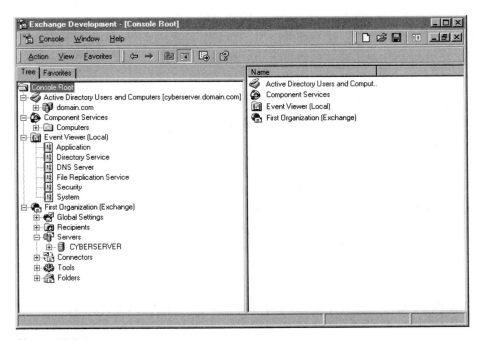

Figure 15.5
The Exchange Development console

To access the Exchange Development console, click **Start**, point to **Programs**, point to **Administrative Tools**, and then click **Exchange Development**. By associating several snap-ins together, you can use your Exchange Development console to:

- Create new user objects in Active Directory.

- Create mailboxes, manage mailboxes, and delete mailboxes.

- Build security and distribution groups.

- Debug workflow and event scripts by using Event Viewer.

- Create new Web Storage Systems, stores, and folders.

- Configure virtual directories.

- Set security and permissions.

- Create COM+ components for event sinks and DLLs for use in Web applications.

- Enable workflow.

ADDING ADDITIONAL USERS

When developing for an environment that includes many clients, you should create additional users in your test domain. This allows you to send e-mail to one or more recipients, schedule meetings, and use specific logon credentials to access objects in Active Directory or in a Web Storage System by using the Microsoft Internet Publishing Provider with ADO. If you test security scenarios, it is particularly important to create multiple accounts. Don't mess with your own security settings if you can help it. It's much easier to create another user, change the permissions on that object, and recreate the User object, if necessary, rather than messing with your own settings, breaking something, and then trying to set them back. In addition, you might find that inherited permissions allow you to do almost anything as an administrator.

DEPLOYING APPLICATION-SPECIFIC TOOLS

When it comes to actually deploying an application, missing a single step can easily trip you up. The following lists are meant to help you remember the details of deploying specific technologies. You can find information on each of these technologies in the specified chapter.

Deploying a custom schema (Chapter 3):

- In the Web Storage System, use code to create the application schema folder as a hidden folder.

- Configure the schema folder with a base schema and a schema content class.

- Set the Schema collection reference for each application folder, including the parent folder, to point to the application schema.

- Create the content class and property definitions in the schema folder by using code.

Deploying events (Chapter 9):

- In Active Directory, create the event account for executing code. You can also use an existing account that has the permissions you need.

- In Component Services, set the event sink application to run under that account.

- Using a command prompt, register the .dll file on the Exchange server computer by using regsvr32.exe.

- In Component Services, create the COM components for the DLL. If you want, you can also add COM+ security roles to the event sink.

- Create the event registrations items in the appropriate folders.

Deploying workflow (Chapter 10):

- In Active Directory, create the workflow account for executing code.

- In Component Services, set the workflow application to run under that account.

- In Component Services, register all workflow authors.

- By using Workflow Designer for Exchange, create the workflow process or import an existing workflow process .xml file.

Deploying a Web solution that uses the Web Storage System forms registry (Chapter 12):

- Make sure that FrontPage Server Extensions are installed on the server.

- Copy the Web pages used by the application to a folder acting as a forms registry. Make sure that the folder is in the schema path of the application.

- Create your form registrations in a schema folder by using code.

- By using Exchange System Manager, set Execute Permissions to **Scripts** if you are running Active Server Pages (ASP) or set it to **Scripts and executables** if you are using the exwforms.dll engine.

- If your Web application uses middle-tier components, register the DLL and create the COM+ components.

Above all, remember to set security and grant permissions on your folders and on COM+ components.

USING WINDOWS SCRIPT FILES TO AUTOMATE INSTALLATIONS

One way to automate the installation of certain components of your Exchange application is to use script files and Windows Scripting Host. Windows Scripting Host is a scripting utility you can use to run scripts in the base operating system. It is supported by all 32-bit operating systems and comes with all the Windows 2000 operating systems. You can use Windows Scripting Host to automate tasks, such as creating folder structures; create definition items, including content class definitions, property definitions, event registrations, and form registrations; define users and roles; and configure security.

Windows Scripting Host comes with VBScript and JScript ActiveX scripting engines, so you can write script files by using either of these engines without any further configuration. To create a script file, you can use Microsoft Notepad (or any text editor) to write your code and then save the file with the appropriate file extension. VBScript files typically have a .vbs file extension, and JScript files typically have a .js file extension. All the same limitations of writing script in any other application apply to script files.

When you write script in the file, you do not need to include procedures if you don't need them. The entire file is considered a single procedure and executes similarly to traditional MS-DOS programs with a start and an end point. If you want to include procedures in the script file, you must explicitly call them. The scripting engine won't automatically execute a procedure. For example, Figure 15.6 shows a sample .vbs file. When you execute this file, you are prompted to install the application. If you click **Yes**, the procedure calls the InstallTool procedure. If you click **No**, the procedure is never called.

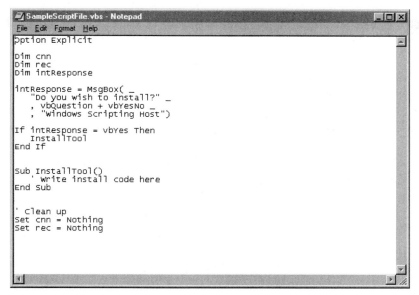

Figure 15.6
Sample VBS script file

Windows Scripting Host provides two applications for executing a script file:
WScript.exe and CScript.exe. WScript runs scripts from the Windows desktop, and
CScript runs scripts from the command prompt (CScript.exe). To run a script from
the desktop, double-click a script file. To run a script from the command prompt,
run the Cscript.exe application from a command prompt, and pass the complete
path to the script file. For more information about using the Windows Scripting
Host, see the Microsoft Platform SDK.

> **NOTE**   You can also use Visual Basic executables to automate some of the
> installation process instead of using script files.

SUMMARY

To successfully deploy an Exchange application, you should be aware of the potential pitfalls that can occur during the deployment process. If you understand how Exchange works and you install and configure it from scratch, it is much easier to diagnose and fix problems. Before you attempt to install an application in your organization or in someone else's organization, first install it on your own system and conduct your tests. Although this can seem a time-consuming process, it will save you more time and energy later—time you would otherwise spend tracking down a simple bug that could have been avoided.

Web Storage System Schema Properties

Tables A.1 through A.18 list the Microsoft Web Storage System schema properties.

NOTE N/A in these tables means *not available at this time*.

DAV

This namespace defines properties for the Web Distributed Authoring and Versioning (WebDAV) protocol. Nearly all predefined content classes have properties from this namespace. Table A.1 lists the DAV: namespace schema properties.

Table A.1 DAV: namespace schema properties

Schema property	CDO constant	Microsoft Visual Basic data type	Description
abstract	cdoAbstract	String	Sets or returns a summary of a resource's content. This property is used by Microsoft Outlook to display previews.
autoversion	N/A	Boolean	If True, the resource is versioned automatically. Read-only.

Continued on next page

Table A.1 continued   DAV: namespace schema properties

Schema property	CDO constant	Microsoft Visual Basic data type	Description
checkintime	N/A	Date	Returns a time stamp set by the server indicating when a report resource was checked in.
child autoversioning	N/A	String	Sets or returns a version for child items if childversioning is True.
childcount	cdoChildCount	Long	Returns the total number of resources, including subfolders in a folder.
childversioning	N/A	Boolean	If True, versioning is set on a folder's items and subfolders. Read-only.
comment	cdoDAV Comment	String	Sets or returns a comment string for a resource.
contentclass	cdoContentClass	String	Sets or returns the content class of a resource.
creationdate	cdoCreationDate	Date	Returns the date a resource is created.
defaultdocument	cdoDefault Document	String	Sets or returns a resource that automatically displays when the folder is accessed by an application.
displayname	cdoDisplayName	String	Returns a calculated property containing the subject of a message, the urn:schemas:contact:fileas value for a contact, or an XML language attribute.

Continued on next page

Table A.1 continued   DAV: namespace schema properties

Schema property	CDO constant	Microsoft Visual Basic data type	Description
getcontent language	cdoGetContent Language	String	Returns the language header intended for use in an object such as a MIME-formatted message body part or a Web document.
getcontentlength	cdoGetContent Length	Long	Returns the size of a resource in bytes.
getcontenttype	cdoGetContent Type	String	Returns the content type of a resource.
getetag	cdoGetETag	String	Returns the entity tag associated with a cached entry.
getlastmodified	cdoGetLast Modified	Date	Returns the time a resource was last modified.
haschildren	cdoHasChildren	Boolean	If True, the folder or structured document resource has child objects. Read-only.
hassubs	cdoHasSubs	Boolean	If True, the folder resource has subfolders. Read-only.
href	cdoHref	String	Returns the absolute URL of a resource.
id	cdoID	String	Returns the unique identifier for a resource.
iscollection	cdoIsCollection	Boolean	If True, the resource is a collection. Read-only.
isfolder	cdoIsFolder	Boolean	If True, the resource is a folder. Read-only.

Continued on next page

Table A.1 continued   DAV: namespace schema properties

Schema property	CDO constant	Microsoft Visual Basic data type	Description
ishidden	cdoIsHidden	Boolean	If True, the resource is hidden from displaying in a client application. Can only be set when a resource is created. After that, the property is read-only.
isreadonly	N/A	Boolean	If True, the resource cannot be modified or deleted.
isroot	cdoIsroot	Boolean	If True, the resource is a root folder.
isstructured document	cdoIsstructured document	Boolean	If True, the resource is a structured document. Read-only.
isversioned	N/A	Boolean	If True, the resource is currently being versioned. Read-only.
lastaccessed	CdoNSDAV.cdo Lastaccessed	Date	Returns the date and time the resource was last accessed.
lockdiscovery	cdoLock discovery	String	Returns a list of current locks on a resource.
mergedfrom	N/A	String	Sets or returns text that indicates a revision based on previous revisions.
nosubs	cdoNosubs	Boolean	If True, subfolders cannot be created in this folder. Read-only.

Continued on next page

Table A.1 continued   DAV: namespace schema properties

Schema property	CDO constant	Microsoft Visual Basic data type	Description
objectcount	cdoObjectcount	Long	Returns the number of items in a folder that are not folders.
parentname	cdoParentname	String	Sets or returns the name of the folder that contains the child folder.
resourcetype	cdoResourcetype	String	Returns the resource type.
revisioncomment	N/A	String	Sets or returns a comment for a particular version of a resource.
revisionid	N/A	String	Returns the unique identifier of the resource version.
revisionlabel	N/A	String	Sets or returns a label for a particular version of a resource.
revisionuri	N/A	String	Reserved for future use.
searchrequest	N/A	String	Returns the original query used to build the search folder.
searchtype	N/A	String	Returns either "static" or "dynamic" to indicate whether the search folder will change.
supportedlock	cdoSupported lock	String	Returns an .xml file of nodes describing lock conditions for the resource. This property can be accessed by using HTTP 1.1 extensions and WebDAV.

Continued on next page

Table A.1 continued   DAV: namespace schema properties

Schema property	CDO constant	Microsoft Visual Basic data type	Description
uid	cdoUid	String	Returns a unique identifier for the resource.
visiblecount	cdoVisiblecount	Long	Returns the number of visible items in a folder that are not folders.
vresourceid	N/A	String	Returns the unique identifier for a resource that is being versioned.

CDO CONFIGURATION

This namespace defines properties used with the Collaboration Data Objects (CDO) Configuration object to determine configurations for several CDO objects, such as CDO Message and CDO Appointment. Table A.2 lists the http://schemas.microsoft.com/cdo/configuration/ namespace schema properties.

Table A.2   http://schemas.microsoft.com/cdo/configuration/ namespace schema properties

Schema property	CDO constant	Microsoft Visual Basic data type	Description
activeconnection	cdoActive Connection	ADO Connection	Sets or returns an ADO Connection object to use when sending messages through Microsoft Exchange 2000 Server.
autopromote bodyparts	CdoAutoPromote BodyParts	Boolean	If True, multipart body parts that contain a single child body part are replaced with the child when the MIME stream is constructed.

Continued on next page

Table A.2 continued   http://schemas.microsoft.com/cdo/configuration/ namespace schema properties

Schema property	CDO constant	Microsoft Visual Basic data type	Description
flushbufferson write	cdoFlushBuffers OnWrite	Boolean	If True, file system buffers are to be flushed when messages are written to the SMTP and NNTP pickup directories.
httpcookies	cdoHTTP Cookies	String	Sets or returns cookies sent along with HTTP requests for HTML pages through the CreateMHTMLBody and AddAttachment methods of a CDO Message.
languagecode	cdoLanguage Code	String	Sets or returns the language code used to localize message response text inserted when replying or forwarding messages.
mailboxurl	cdoMailboxURL	String	Sets or returns a URL to a user's mailbox folder.
nntpaccount name	cdoNNTP AccountName	String	Returns a Microsoft Outlook Express NNTP account name available for information purposes only.
nntpauthenticate	cdoNNTP Authenticate	Long	Sets or returns the authentication mechanism to use when authenticating to an NNTP service across the network.

Continued on next page

Table A.2 continued   http://schemas.microsoft.com/cdo/configuration/ namespace schema
properties

Schema property	CDO constant	Microsoft Visual Basic data type	Description
nntpconnection timeout	cdoNNTP Connection Timeout	Long	Sets or returns the number of seconds that can elapse without a response from the NNTP service before the connection attempt is aborted.
nntpserver	cdoNNTPServer	String	Sets or returns the DNS or NetBIOS name of the host to which to post messages by using NNTP.
nntpserverpickup directory	cdoNNTPServer PickupDirectory	String	Sets or returns the full path to the NNTP service pickup directory.
nntpserverport	cdoNNTPServer Port	Long	Sets or returns the port on which the NNTP service is listening for connections.
nntpusessl	cdoNNTPUseSSL	Boolean	If True, the Secure Sockets Layer (SSL) should be used when posting messages over the network by using NNTP.
postemailaddress	cdoPostEmail Address	String	Sets or returns the e-mail address used when posting messages.
postpassword	cdoPost Password	String	Sets the password used in conjunction with postusername when authenticating over the network.

Continued on next page

Table A.2 continued   http://schemas.microsoft.com/cdo/configuration/ namespace schema properties

Schema property	CDO constant	Microsoft Visual Basic data type	Description
postusername	cdoPostUser Name	String	Sets or returns the username used in conjunction with postpassword when authenticating with an NNTP service over the network.
postuserreply emailaddress	cdoPostUser ReplyEmail Address	String	Sets or returns the reply e-mail address for the message.
postusing	cdoPostUsing Method	Long	Sets or returns the mechanism to use to post messages.
savesentitems	cdoSaveSent Items	Boolean	If True, messages are to be saved in a user's Sent Items folder when sent through Exchange 2000 Server by using the Microsoft Web Storage System OLE DB provider or the HTTP/WebDAV protocol.
sendemail address	cdoSendEmail Address	String	Sets or returns the e-mail address used when sending a message.
sendpassword	cdoSend Password	String	Sets the password used in conjunction with the sendusername property when authenticating to an SMTP or Exchange HTTP/WebDAV service over the network.

Continued on next page

Table A.2 continued http://schemas.microsoft.com/cdo/configuration/ namespace schema properties

Schema property	CDO constant	Microsoft Visual Basic data type	Description
sendusername	cdoSendUser Name	String	Sets or returns the username used in conjunction with the sendpassword property when authenticating to an SMTP or Exchange HTTP service over the network.
senduserreply emailaddress	cdoSendUser ReplyEmail Address	String	Sets or returns the e-mail address used for replying when sending messages using an SMTP service.
sendusing	cdoSendUsing Method	Long	Sets or returns the mechanism to use to send messages.
smtpaccount name	cdoSMTP AccountName	String	Sets or returns the Outlook Express SMTP account name available for informational purposes only.
smtpauthenticate	cdoSMTP Authenticate	Long	Sets or returns the authentication mechanism to use when authenticating to an SMTP service over the network.
smtpconnection timeout	cdoSMTP Connection Timeout	Long	Sets or returns the number of seconds that can elapse without a response from the SMTP service before the connection attempt is aborted.

Continued on next page

Table A.2 continued   http://schemas.microsoft.com/cdo/configuration/ namespace schema properties

Schema property	CDO constant	Microsoft Visual Basic data type	Description
smtpserver	cdoSMTPServer	String	Sets or returns the DNS or NetBIOS name of the host to which to post messages by using SMTP.
smtpserver pickupdirectory	cdoSMTPServer PickupDirectory	String	Sets or returns the full path to the local SMTP service pickup directory.
smtpserverport	cdoSMTPServer Port	Long	Sets or returns the port on which the SMTP service is listening.
smtpusessl	cdoSMTPUseSSL	Boolean	If True, the Secure Sockets Layer (SSL) should be used when posting messages over the network by using SMTP.
urlgetlatest version	cdoURLGetLatest Version	Boolean	If True, any locally cached Web pages should be bypassed and the latest version of a resource retrieved over HTTP.
urlproxybypass	cdoURLProxy Bypass	String	If set to "<local>", indicates that the proxy server set in the http:// schemas.microsoft.com/ cdo/configuration/ urlproxyserver is to be bypassed for local addresses.

Continued on next page

Table A.2 continued http://schemas.microsoft.com/cdo/configuration/ namespace schema
properties

Schema property	CDO constant	Microsoft Visual Basic data type	Description
urlproxyserver	cdoURLProxy Server	String	Sets or returns the DNS or NetBIOS name and port number of the proxy service to use when retrieving resources over the network.
urlsource	cdoURLSource	Long	Sets or returns the location of the mailbox to use when sending or posting messages. Default is 0 (cdoExchangeServerURL).
usemessage responsetext	cdoUseMessage ResponseText	Boolean	If True, response text is inserted when replying to or forwarding messages.

CDO NNTP ENVELOPE

This namespace defines properties that are accessible in the IMessage.EnvelopeFields property of a CDO Message object when it is passed to a transport event sink handling one of the NNTP transport events. These properties are only available in a transport event sink. Table A.3 lists the http://schemas.microsoft.com/cdo/nntpenvelope/ namespace schema properties.

Table A.3   http://schemas.microsoft.com/cdo/nntpenvelope/ namespace schema properties

Schema property	CDO constant	Microsoft Visual Basic data type	Description
newsgrouplist	N/A	String	Returns the newsgroups to which the message is to be posted.
nntpprocessing	N/A	Integer	Sets or returns a bit-mask specifying which NNTP processing should occur for a message.

CDO SMTP ENVELOPE

This namespace defines properties for message transport envelope fields. These properties are only available in a transport event sink. Table A.4 lists the http://schemas.microsoft.com/cdo/smtpenvelope/ namespace schema properties.

Table A.4   http://schemas.microsoft.com/cdo/smtpenvelope/ namespace schema properties

Schema property	CDO constant	Microsoft Visual Basic data type	Description
arrivaltime	N/A	Date	Returns the date and time the message arrived.
clientipaddress	N/A	String	Returns the IP address of the client that submitted the message to the SMTP service.
messagestatus	CdoMessage Stat enumeration	Long	Sets or returns the transport status of the message.
pickupfilename	N/A	String	Returns the file name that housed the submitted message in the SMTP service pickup directory.
recipientlist	N/A	String	Sets or returns the list of recipients for the message.
senderemail address	N/A	String	Returns the e-mail address of the message submitter.

CDO WORKFLOW

This namespace defines properties for building workflow logic into folders by using Collaboration Data Objects Workflow (CDOWF) functionality. Most of these properties are accessible through CDOWF object properties. Table A.5 lists the http://schemas.microsoft.com/cdo/workflow/ namespace schema properties.

Table A.5   http://schemas.microsoft.com/cdo/workflow/ namespace schema properties

Schema property	CDO constant	Microsoft Visual Basic data type	Description
actiontable	cdowfAction TableXML	String	Sets or returns the XML-encoded record set containing the state transition rules for a workflow process.
adhocflows	cdowfAdhoc Flows	Integer	Sets or returns a flag indicating how ad hoc activity is processed in the workflow folder or application.
audittrail	CdoWfAuditTrail	String	Sets or returns a string of comma-separated values listing the states and actions through which a process instance has transitioned.
audittrailprovider	cdowfAuditTrail Provider	String	Sets or returns a COM class identifier (CLSID) of the object used by a workflow to build the audit trail.

Continued on next page

Table A.5 continued   http://schemas.microsoft.com/cdo/workflow/ namespace schema
properties

Schema property	CDO constant	Microsoft Visual Basic data type	Description
commonscripturl	cdowfCommon ScriptURL	String	Sets or returns a URL to the common script, for a process definition. If the process definition resource contains the common script, this property is empty or contains the string file://self.
currentstate	cdowfDefault Process DefinitionURL	String	Returns the current state of a workflow, expressed as a string containing any character. Read-only to all except the workflow engine and enforced by per-property access control list (ACL).
designtool	cdowfDesign Tool	String	Sets or returns a string identifying the tool, if any, used to create the workflow process.
disablesuccess entries	cdowfDisable SuccessEntries	Boolean	If True, success entries for the workflow process are not logged in a log file.
enabledebug	cdowfEnable Debug	Boolean	If True, allows you to debug a workflow process.
expirytime	cdowfExpiry Time	Date	Sets or returns a date and time that a ProcessInstance will expire.
mode	cdowfSecurity Mode	Long	Sets or returns the security mode under which a workflow process definition should be run.

Continued on next page

Table A.5 continued http://schemas.microsoft.com/cdo/workflow/ namespace schema properties

Schema property	CDO constant	Microsoft Visual Basic data type	Description
parentproc instance	cdowfParent ProcessInstance	String	Returns a URL to the parent workflow process. Included on WorkflowMessage replies; used to correlate incoming message to process instance. Created in outgoing WorkflowMessage.
processdefinition	cdowfProcess DefinitionURL	String	Returns a URL that points to the ProcessDefinition resource used by the current ProcessInstance.
response	cdowfResponse	String	Sets or returns a string that contains a voting response of a user.
trackingtablexml	cdowfTracking TableXML	String	Sets or returns the TrackingTable property as XML.
workflow messageid	cdowfMessageID	String	Created as part of an outgoing WorkflowMessage.

EXCHANGE

This namespace defines properties specific to Microsoft Exchange. Table A.6 lists the http://schemas.microsoft.com/exchange/ namespace schema properties.

Table A.6   http://schemas.microsoft.com/exchange/ namespace schema properties

Schema property	CDO constant	Microsoft Visual Basic data type	Description
addressbook displayname	N/A	String	Sets or returns the name for a mail-enabled Microsoft Web Storage System folder in the Active Directory directory service of Microsoft Windows 2000.
adminfolder description	N/A	String	Sets or returns the description of a public folder normally provided by the Microsoft Exchange 2000 Server administrator.
alias	N/A	String	Sets or returns an e-mail alias for a person.
altrecipient	CDOAltRecipient	String	Sets or returns an alternative e-mail address for receiving e-mail.
archive	N/A	Boolean	If True, the resource has changed and needs to be archived. An archive application sets this property to False upon completion.

Continued on next page

Table A.6 continued   http://schemas.microsoft.com/exchange/ namespace schema
properties

Schema property	CDO constant	Microsoft Visual Basic data type	Description
companies	cdoCompanies	String	A multi-valued property used by Microsoft Outlook to list one or more companies associated with Web Storage System content.
contentexpiryage limit	N/A	Long	Sets or returns the expiry age limit in days for resources in public folders.
contentstate	N/A	String	Sets or returns text that describes the state, or status, of a resource.
defaultrevision	N/A	String	Returns a default revision identifier.
deleteditemflags	N/A	Long	Returns the number of items in the deleted items folder.
deleteditemsage limit	N/A	Long	Sets or returns the number of days, on a per-folder basis, to retain deleted items.
delivcontlength	N/A	Integer	Sets or returns the amount of data, in kilobytes (KB), that a mailbox is allowed to receive.
deliverand redirect	N/A	Boolean	If True, messages are forwarded to another recipient.

Continued on next page

Table A.6 continued http://schemas.microsoft.com/exchange/ namespace schema
properties

Schema property	CDO constant	Microsoft Visual Basic data type	Description
disableperuser read	N/A	Boolean	If True, per-user read processing is disabled.
extension attribute1	N/A	String	Sets or returns an attribute for any text without having to extend Active Directory.
extension attribute10	N/A	String	Sets or returns an attribute for any text without having to extend the Active Directory.
extension attribute2	N/A	String	Sets or returns an attribute for any text without having to extend Active Directory.
extension attribute3	N/A	String	Sets or returns an attribute for any text without having to extend Active Directory.
extension attribute4	N/A	String	Sets or returns an attribute for any text without having to extend Active Directory.
extension attribute5	N/A	String	Sets or returns an attribute for any text without having to extend Active Directory.
extension attribute6	N/A	String	Sets or returns an attribute for any text without having to extend Active Directory.
extension attribute7	N/A	String	Sets or returns an attribute for any text without having to extend Active Directory.
extension attribute8	N/A	String	Sets or returns an attribute for any text without having to extend Active Directory.

Continued on next page

Table A.6 continued   http://schemas.microsoft.com/exchange/ namespace schema properties

Schema property	CDO constant	Microsoft Visual Basic data type	Description
extension attribute9	N/A	String	Sets or returns an attribute for any text without having to extend Active Directory.
foldersize	N/A	Long	Returns the total size, in bytes, of all the items in a folder.
freebusypublish amount	N/A	Integer	Sets or returns the number of months to publish free/busy status information for a user. The default is three months.
hardlinklist	N/A	Array (Strings)	Sets or returns a list of folder URLs in which to post a message.
homemdb	N/A	String	Sets or returns the URL to the recipient's store.
longdateformat	N/A	String	Sets or returns the format for long dates in Microsoft Outlook Web Access.
mdboverhard quotalimit	N/A	Long	Sets or returns the maximum mailbox size, in KB, before sending and receiving e-mail is disabled.
mdboverquota limit	N/A	Long	Sets or returns the mailbox quota overdraft limit in KB.
mdbstoragequota	N/A	Integer	Sets or returns the Exchange database quota in KB.

Continued on next page

Table A.6 continued http://schemas.microsoft.com/exchange/ namespace schema properties

Schema property	CDO constant	Microsoft Visual Basic data type	Description
mdbusedefaults	N/A	Boolean	If True, the store uses the default quota, rather than the per-mailbox quota.
mid	N/A	Long	Reserved for Future Use.
mileage	N/A	String	Used for Outlook interoperability.
noaging	N/A	Boolean	Used for Outlook interoperability.
ntsecurity descriptor	N/A	N/A	Sets or returns the security descriptor for the resource. The security descriptor contains the resource's primary owner and group and a discretionary access control list granting and denying various rights to particular users and groups.
originaldate	N/A	Date	Indicates the original date a message was sent when returned in a report. Used for Web client reports.
originaldisplay bcc	N/A	String	Sets or returns the original BCC list of a message referred to in a report.
originaldisplaycc	N/A	String	Indicates CC list of a message. Used in reports for Outlook Web Access.

Continued on next page

Table A.6 continued   http://schemas.microsoft.com/exchange/ namespace schema properties

Schema property	CDO constant	Microsoft Visual Basic data type	Description
originaldisplayto	N/A	String	Indicates the display names for the original BCC list on a report. Used in reports for Outlook Web Access.
originalsender name	N/A	String	Indicates the original name of the sender of a report. Used in reports for Outlook Web Access.
originalsubject	N/A	String	Indicates the original subject of a report. Used for reports in Outlook Web Access.
outlookfolder class	N/A	String	Provides access to the MAPI PR_CONTAINER_CLASS.
outlookmessage class	N/A	String	Provides access to the MAPI PR_MESSAGE_CLASS.
patternend	N/A	Date	Returns the absolute maximum time when an instance of a recurring appointment ends. If there are no exceptions, this is the end time of the last instance.
patternstart	N/A	Date	Returns the absolute minimum time when an instance of a recurring appointment starts. If there are no exceptions, this is the start time of the first instance.

Continued on next page

Table A.6 continued   http://schemas.microsoft.com/exchange/ namespace schema properties

Schema property	CDO constant	Microsoft Visual Basic data type	Description
permanenturl	N/A	String	Indicates the permanent URL that can always be used to access a resource, even if the URL of the resource is renamed or moved.
publicdelegates	N/A	String	Sets or returns the list of URLs of all users that have access to the mailbox.
publicfolderemail address	N/A	String	Sets or returns the e-mail address of a public folder.
publishinaddress book	N/A	Boolean	If True, an address book displays a mail-enabled public folder.
receipttime	N/A	Date	Used by Outlook Web Access to show received time for a message as reported in a delivery report.
recipientlimit	N/A	Long	Sets or returns the maximum number of people to whom the recipient can send e-mail.
replication messagepriority	N/A	Long	Indicates the replication message priorities configured in Exchange System Manager. Can be Normal, Not Urgent, or on a per-folder basis.
replication schedule	N/A	N/A	Indicates the replication schedule on a per-folder basis.

Continued on next page

Table A.6 continued   http://schemas.microsoft.com/exchange/ namespace schema
properties

Schema property	CDO constant	Microsoft Visual Basic data type	Description
replicationstyle	N/A	Integer	Sets or returns the replication styles available for public folders on a per-folder basis.
sensitivity	N/A	Long	Sets or returns the message and appointment sensitivity: None (0); Personal (1); Private (2); Company Confidential (3).
shortdateformat	N/A	String	Indicates the short date format to use for a user. Used by Outlook Web Access.
storagequota issuewarning limit	N/A	Integer	Sets or returns the storage size in KB of a public folder after a storage quota warning is issued for the folder.
targetaddress	N/A	String	Sets or returns the address where e-mail is redirected when the intended recipient is unavailable.
textencodedor address	N/A	String	Sets or returns the primary X.400 address used for the recipient.
timeformat	N/A	String	Indicates the time format of the user. Used by Outlook Web Access.
timezone	N/A	String	Indicates the time zone used for calendaring. Used by Outlook Web Access.

Continued on next page

Table A.6 continued   http://schemas.microsoft.com/exchange/ namespace schema properties

Schema property	CDO constant	Microsoft Visual Basic data type	Description
weekstartday	N/A	Long	Indicates a user's preference that indicates the first day of the week. Used by Outlook Web Access.
workdayendtime	N/A	Long	Sets or returns the time used as the end of the workday.
workdays	N/A	Long	Indicates the workdays for a user. Used by Outlook Web Access.
workdaystarttime	N/A	Long	Indicates the time of day that work starts for a user. Used by a Web client.
yomifirstname	N/A	String	Used in Japan for the searchable or phonetic spelling for a Japanese first name.
yomilastname	N/A	String	Used in Japan for the searchable or phonetic spelling for a Japanese last name.
yomiorganization	N/A	String	Used in a Japanese organization.

EVENT REGISTRATIONS

This namespace defines properties used to create and manage event registration items for Microsoft Web Storage System events. Table A.7 lists the http://schemas.microsoft.com/exchange/events/ namespace schema properties.

Table A.7   http://schemas.microsoft.com/exchange/events/ namespace schema properties

Schema property	CDO constant	Microsoft Visual Basic data type	Description
Criteria	N/A	String	Sets or returns a SQL WHERE condition that restricts the criteria for when an event fires.
Enabled	N/A	Boolean	If True, an event registration will trigger an event sink.
EventMethod	N/A	Array (Strings)	Sets or returns a list of events that will trigger an event sink.
MatchScope	N/A	String	Sets or returns where the event will fire relative to where it is saved as well as if the event is for items, folders, or both.
Priority	N/A	Long	Sets or returns the priority of the event registration with respect to other event registrations for the same events.
ScriptUrl	N/A	String	When using the scripting host, this property specifies the URL of the file that contains the script code to execute.

Continued on next page

Table A.7 continued   http://schemas.microsoft.com/exchange/events/ namespace schema
properties

Schema property	CDO constant	Microsoft Visual Basic data type	Description
SinkClass	N/A	String	Sets or returns the COM class identifier (CLSID) in registry format or the programmatic identifier (ProgID) of the event sink COM class.
TimerExpiryTime	N/A	Date	Sets or returns the absolute time at which Microsoft Exchange no longer notifies event sinks of the OnTimer event.
TimerInterval	N/A	Integer	Sets or returns the period (time interval) in minutes between OnTimer event notifications.
TimerStartTime	N/A	Date	Sets or returns the absolute time at which Exchange begins notifying event sinks of the OnTimer event.

EXCHANGE SECURITY

This namespace defines properties that contain information about security settings on Microsoft Web Storage System folders and items. These properties contain XML strings that describe Microsoft Windows 2000 security descriptors (SDs) and security identifiers (SIDs). Table A.8 lists the http://schemas.microsoft.com/exchange/security/namespace schema properties.

Table A.8   http://schemas.microsoft.com/exchange/security/ namespace schema properties

Schema property	CDO constant	Microsoft Visual Basic data type	Description
admindescriptor	N/A	String	Sets or returns the XML representation of the admin security descriptor for a Web Storage System folder or collection. An admin security descriptor identifies the object's owner and primary group.
creator	N/A	String	Sets or returns the XML representation of a security identifier of the creator of the Web Storage System resource.
descriptor	N/A	String	Sets or returns the XML representation of the security descriptor for a Web Storage System resource.
lastmodifier	N/A	String	This property is the XML representation of a security identifier of the last modifier of the Web Storage System resource.

Continued on next page

Table A.8 continued   http://schemas.microsoft.com/exchange/security/ namespace schema properties

Schema property	CDO constant	Microsoft Visual Basic data type	Description
originalauthor	N/A	String	Sets or returns the XML representation of a security identifier of the original author of the Web Storage System resource.
originalsender	N/A	String	Sets or returns the XML representation of a security identifier of the original sender of the Web Storage System resource.
originalsent representing	N/A	String	Reserved for future use.
originator	N/A	String	Sets or returns the XML representation of a security identifier of the originator of the Web Storage System resource.
readreceiptfrom	N/A	String	Sets or returns the XML representation of a security identifier of the reader of the Web Storage System resource.
receivedby	N/A	String	Sets or returns the XML representation of a security identifier of the recipient of a Web Storage System resource.
received representing	N/A	String	Reserved for future use.

Continued on next page

Table A.8 continued http://schemas.microsoft.com/exchange/security/ namespace schema properties

Schema property	CDO constant	Microsoft Visual Basic data type	Description
reportdestination	N/A	String	Reserved for future use.
reportfrom	N/A	String	Reserved for future use.
sender	N/A	String	Sets or returns the XML representation of a security identifier of the sender of a Web Storage System resource.
sentrepresenting	N/A	String	Reserved for future use.

FULL TEXT QUERYING

This namespace defines properties used with full text querying. Table A.9 lists the urn:schemas.microsoft.com:fulltextqueryinfo: namespace schema properties.

Table A.9   urn:schemas.microsoft.com:fulltextqueryinfo: namespace schema properties

Schema property	CDO constant	Microsoft Visual Basic data type	Description
all	N/A	String	Reserved for future use.
catalogname	N/A	String	Sets or returns the name of the search catalog the result came from.
crawlmodified time	N/A	Date	Reserved for future use.
docsignature	N/A	String	Sets or returns the MD5 digest of a document.
filename	N/A	String	Sets or returns the long file name.
filepath	N/A	String	Sets or returns the path to the file.
hitcount	N/A	Long	Returns the number of search results that matched a query.
htmlcomment	N/A	String	Sets or returns the comments in HTML documents.
nlprank	N/A	Long	Reserved for future use.
rank	N/A	Long	Returns the relevance rank of search results.

Continued on next page

Table A.9 continued   urn:schemas.microsoft.com:fulltextqueryinfo: namespace schema properties

Schema property	CDO constant	Microsoft Visual Basic data type	Description
rankvector	N/A	Long	Sets or returns the ranks of individual components of a vector query.
shortfilename	N/A	String	Sets or returns the short file name.
sitename	N/A	String	Sets or returns the Web site name.
unfiltered	N/A	Boolean	If True, the collection is unfiltered.
usn	N/A	Long	Reserved for future use.
workid	N/A	Long	Reserved for future use.

CALENDAR

This namespace defines properties used to create calendaring solutions with Collaboration Data Objects (CDO) objects, including the Appointment object and the CalendarMessage object. Most of these properties can be accessed by using CDO object properties. Table A.10 lists the urn:schemas:calendar: namespace schema properties.

Table A.10 urn:schemas:calendar: namespace schema properties

Schema property	CDO constant	Microsoft Visual Basic data type	Description
alldayevent	cdoAllDayEvent	String	Sets or returns whether an appointment is for an entire day. Setting this property does not affect the start time or end time of an appointment or meeting.
attendeerole	cdoAttendeeRole	Long	Sets or returns the role of an attendee for an appointment: chair, required, optional, or not attending but copied for reference.
attendeestatus	cdoAttendee Status	Long	Sets or returns the status of an attendee for an appointment: accepted, declined, tentative, or has not responded.
busystatus	cdoBusyStatus	String	Indicates how an appointment displays a free/busy status view.
contact	cdoContact	String	Sets or returns the name of a person as a contact for an appointment.

Continued on next page

Table A.10 continued   urn:schemas:calendar: namespace schema properties

Schema property	CDO constant	Microsoft Visual Basic data type	Description
contacturl	cdoContactURL	String	Sets or returns a URL for accessing contact information in HTML format.
created	cdoCreated	Date	Indicates the date and time an appointment was created in the originator's calendar. This value is the same in the organizer's copy of the appointment and each attendee's copy.
descriptionurl	cdoDescription URL	String	Sets or returns a URL of a resource that contains a description of the appointment or meeting.
dtend	cdoDTEnd	Date	Indicates an appointment's ending date and time.
dtstamp	cdoDTStamp	Date	Indicates the date and time the appointment was created. This value is updated by CDO when the CreateRequest or Invite method of an Appointment object is called.
dtstart	cdoDTStart	Date	Sets or returns the starting date and time of an appointment.
duration	cdoDuration	Long	Sets or returns the duration of the appointment in seconds.

Continued on next page

Table A.10 continued   urn:schemas:calendar: namespace schema properties

Schema property	CDO constant	Microsoft Visual Basic data type	Description
exdate	cdoExDate	Array (Strings)	Sets or returns a list of recurring appointment instances that are deleted.
exrule	cdoExRule	String	Sets or returns the complete recurrence/ exception rule string.
fburl	cdoFburl	String	Sets or returns the URL of the free/busy public folder.
geolatitude	cdoGEOLatitude	Double	Sets or returns the geographical latitude of an appointment's location. Positive values from 0 to 90 are degrees north latitude. Negative values from 0 to -90 are degrees south latitude.
geolongitude	cdoGEO Longitude	Double	Sets or returns the geographical longitude of an appointment's location. Positive values from 0 to 180 are degrees east longitude. Negative values from 0 to -180 are degrees west longitude.

Continued on next page

Table A.10 continued   urn:schemas:calendar: namespace schema properties

Schema property	CDO constant	Microsoft Visual Basic data type	Description
instancetype	cdoInstanceType	Long	Indicates the type of appointment: single appointment, master recurring appointment, instance of a recurring appointment, or exception to a recurring appointment. These values are described by the CdoInstanceType enumeration.
isorganizer	cdoIsOrganizer	Boolean	If True, an attendee is the organizer of an appointment.
lastmodified	cdoLastModified	Date	Sets or returns the last modified value stored in an appointment stream and is separate from the DAV:getlastmodified. This is not mapped to the MAPI PR_LAST_MODIFICATION_TIME.
lastmodifiedtime	cdoCalendarLast ModifiedTime	Date	Returns the last time an appointment was saved. This property is stored in the organizer's copy and in each attendee's copy of the appointment. The value can be different in each copy. This value is updated when any method saves an appointment.
location	cdoLocation	String	Sets or returns the meeting location of an appointment.

Continued on next page

Table A.10 continued urn:schemas:calendar: namespace schema properties

Schema property	CDO constant	Microsoft Visual Basic data type	Description
locationurl	cdoLocationURL	String	Sets or returns a URL for accessing meeting location information in HTML format.
meetingstatus	cdoMeeting Status	String	Sets or returns the status of an appointment: Tentative, Confirmed, or Cancelled.
method	cdoMethod	String	Specifies the method associated with an appointment object.
organizer	N/A	String	Sets or returns the SMTP e-mail name of the organizer of a meeting. This value corresponds to the meeting attendee when the isorganizer property is set to True.
prodid	cdoProdId	String	Sets or returns the identifier of the product that created the appointment type stream.
rdate	cdoRDate	Array (Strings)	Contains an array of appointment instances that are additions to a recurring appointment. The instances are stored as the dates and times of the appointment.

Continued on next page

Table A.10 continued   urn:schemas:calendar: namespace schema properties

Schema property	CDO constant	Microsoft Visual Basic data type	Description
recurrenceid	cdoRecurrenceId	String	Returns the recurrence identifier of a specific instance of a recurring appointment. The value of the recurrence identifier is the starting date and time of the specific instance.
recurrenceid range	cdoRecurrence IdRange	String	Indicates how an exception is handled by a recurring meeting. Can be one of the following values: ThisAndFuture, ThisAndPrior, or None.
reminderoffset	cdoReminder Offset	Long	Sets or returns the number of seconds before an appointment start that a reminder is to be displayed.
replytime	cdoReplyTime	Date	Sets or returns the time a recipient replied to a meeting request. This value is updated by CDO when a meeting request is accepted or rejected and can be used to determine which response is the most recent when an attendee sends more than one response to a meeting request.

Continued on next page

Table A.10 continued urn:schemas:calendar: namespace schema properties

Schema property	CDO constant	Microsoft Visual Basic data type	Description
resources	cdoResources	String	Sets or returns a list of supportive resources for an appointment. The resources are represented as e-mail to Uniform Resource Identifiers (URIs) and are separated by commas.
response requested	cdoResponse Requested	Boolean	Indicates if the originator of the meeting requested a response.
rrule	cdoRRule	String	Indicates the rule for the pattern that defines a recurring appointment. The dtstart property specifies the first instance of the appointment; the rule is based on the date and time of the first instance.
rsvp	cdoRSVP	Boolean	If True, a response is expected to a meeting request. This value is synchronized to the responserequested property.

Continued on next page

Table A.10 continued   urn:schemas:calendar: namespace schema properties

Schema property	CDO constant	Microsoft Visual Basic data type	Description
sequence	cdoSequence	Long	Sets or returns the sequence number of this appointment. The sequence number is incremented by CDO when one or more of the following fields is changed: dtstart, dtend, duration, rdate, rrule, exdate, or exrule.
timezone	cdoTimeZone URN	String	Sets or returns the time zone value of an appointment. This property enables you to define time zones that are not defined by the CdoTimeZoneId enumeration. If this property is specified, the timezoneid property is ignored.
timezoneid	cdoTimeZoneID URN	Long	Sets or returns the local time zone identifier.
transparent	cdoTransparency	String	Indicates if the appointment is opaque or transparent to busy time searches.
uid	cdoCalendarUID	String	Sets or returns the unique identifier for an appointment.

Continued on next page

Table A.10 continued urn:schemas:calendar: namespace schema properties

Schema property	CDO constant	Microsoft Visual Basic data type	Description
version	cdoVersion	String	Sets or returns the iCalendar specification version required to correctly interpret an iCalendar object.

CONTACTS

This namespace defines properties used to create contact solutions with the Collaboration Data Objects (CDO) Person object. Some of these properties are accessible with CDO object properties. For information about which schema properties can be accessed by using CDO object properties, see Chapter 5, "Introduction to CDO for Exchange." Table A.11 lists the urn:schemas:contacts: namespace schema properties.

Table A.11 urn:schemas:contacts: namespace schema properties

Schema property	CDO constant	Microsoft Visual Basic data type	Description
account	cdoAccount	String	Sets or returns the account, typically the account number, for a contact.
authorig	cdoOriginal Author	String	Sets or returns the identity of the person who wrote the original message or body part.
bday	cdoBirthday	Date	Sets or returns the birthday of the contact.
billing information	N/A	String	Sets or returns the billing information for the contact.

Continued on next page

Table A.11 continued   urn:schemas:contacts: namespace schema properties

Schema property	CDO constant	Microsoft Visual Basic data type	Description
businesshome page	N/A	String	Sets or returns the URL of the home page of a business's Web site.
c	cdoWorkCountry Abbreviation	String	Sets or returns the work country code for a contact.
callbackphone	cdoCallback Phone	String	Sets or returns the callback telephone number, in international dialing format, of a contact.
childrensnames	cdoChildrens Names	Array (Strings)	Sets or returns the contact's children, with their names separated by semicolons if there is more than one entry in a property.
cn	cdoCommon Name	String	Sets or returns the friendly name of the contact. This property has a maximum length of 20 characters and should not be the same as a user's name in Microsoft Exchange 2000 Server.
co	cdoWorkCountry	String	Sets or returns the work country for the contact.
computer networkname	cdoComputer NetworkName	String	Sets or returns the computer network name for the contact.
customerid	cdoCustomerId	String	Sets or returns the customer ID of the contact.
department	cdoDepartment	String	Sets or returns the department for the contact.

Continued on next page

Table A.11 continued   urn:schemas:contacts: namespace schema properties

Schema property	CDO constant	Microsoft Visual Basic data type	Description
dn	cdo Distinguished Name	String	Sets or returns the distinguished X.500 name of the contact.
email1	cdoEmail1 Address	String	Sets or returns the primary e-mail address of the contact.
email2	cdoEmail2 Address	String	Sets or returns the secondary e-mail address of the contact.
email3	cdoEmail3 Address	String	Sets or returns the tertiary e-mail address of the contact.
employeenumber	cdoEmployee Number	String	Sets or returns the employee number of the contact.
facsimile telephone number	cdoWorkFax	String	Sets or returns the business fax number.
fileas	cdoFileAs	String	Sets or returns the format of how the contact information is displayed in a folder view. For example, "lastname, firstname."
fileasid	cdoFileAsId	Integer	Specifies how the contact information is displayed.
ftpsite	cdoFtpSite	String	Sets or returns the URL of the FTP site for the contact.
gender	cdoGender	Integer	Sets or returns the gender of the contact.

Continued on next page

Table A.11 continued   urn:schemas:contacts: namespace schema properties

Schema property	CDO constant	Microsoft Visual Basic data type	Description
givenName	cdoFirstName	String	Sets or returns the first name of the contact.
governmentid	cdoGovernment Id	String	Sets or returns the government identifier, typically the social security number in the United States, of the contact.
hobbies	cdoHobbies	String	Sets or returns the hobbies of the contact.
homeCity	cdoHomeCity	String	Sets or returns the home city of the contact.
homeCountry	cdoHome Country	String	Sets or returns the home country of the contact.
homefax	cdoHomeFax	Double	Sets or returns the home fax number of the contact.
homelatitude	cdoHome Latitude	Double	Sets or returns the home latitude of the contact.
homelongitude	cdoHome Longitude	Double	Sets or returns the home longitude of the contact.
homePhone	cdoHomePhone	String	Sets or returns the home telephone number, in international dialing format, of the contact.
homephone2	cdoHome Phone2	String	Sets or returns the alternative home telephone number, in international dialing format, of the contact.

Continued on next page

Table A.11 continued   urn:schemas:contacts: namespace schema properties

Schema property	CDO constant	Microsoft Visual Basic data type	Description
homepostal address	cdoHomePostal Address	String	Sets or returns the home postal address of the contact.
homepostalcode	cdoHomePostal Code	String	Sets or returns the postal code, typically the ZIP code in the United States, of the contact.
homepostoffice box	cdoHomePost OfficeBox	String	Sets or returns the post office box number of the contact.
homestate	cdoHomeState	String	Sets or returns the home state of the contact.
homestreet	cdoHomeStreet	String	Sets or returns the home street of the contact.
hometimezone	cdoHomeTime Zone	String	Sets or returns the home time zone of the contact.
initials	cdoInitials	String	Sets or returns the initials of the contact.
internationalisdn number	cdoInternational ISDNNumber	String	Sets or returns the ISDN number, in international dialing format, of the contact.
l	cdoWorkCity	String	Sets or returns the work city of the contact.
language	cdoLanguage	String	Sets or returns the language, in ISO639 format, of the contact.
location	N/A	String	Sets or returns the location of the contact.

Continued on next page

Table A.11 continued   urn:schemas:contacts: namespace schema properties

Schema property	CDO constant	Microsoft Visual Basic data type	Description
mailingaddressid	cdoMailing AddressId	Integer	Sets or returns the address entries from which the mailing address entries of the contact are constructed.
mailingcity	cdoMailingCity	String	Sets or returns the city portion of the mailing address of the contact.
mailingcountry	cdoMailing Country	String	Sets or returns the country portion of the mailing address of the contact.
mailingpostal address	cdoMailingPostal Address	String	Sets or returns the postal address portion of the mailing address of the contact.
mailingpostal code	cdoMailingPostal Code	String	Sets or returns the postal code portion of the mailing address of the contact.
mailingpostoffice box	cdoMailingPost OfficeBox	String	Sets or returns the post office box portion of the mailing address of the contact.
mailingstate	cdoMailingState	String	Sets or returns the state portion of the mailing address of the contact.
mailingstreet	cdoMailingStreet	String	Sets or returns the street portion of the mailing address of the contact.
manager	cdoManager	String	Sets or returns the distinguished name (DN) of the contact's manager.

Continued on next page

Table A.11 continued   urn:schemas:contacts: namespace schema properties

Schema property	CDO constant	Microsoft Visual Basic data type	Description
mapurl	cdoMapURL	String	Sets or returns the map URL of the contact.
members	cdoMembers	String	Sets or returns the members of a group contact.
middlename	cdoMiddleName	String	Sets or returns the middle name of the contact.
mobile	cdoWorkMobile Phone	String	Sets or returns the mobile telephone number, in international dialing format, of the contact.
namesuffix	cdoNameSuffix	String	Sets or returns the generation qualifier of the contact.
nickname	cdoNickname	String	Sets or returns the nickname of the contact.
o	cdoOrganization Name	String	Sets or returns the name of the organization or company of the contact.
office2telephone number	N/A	String	Sets or returns the secondary office phone number of the contact.
officetelephone number	N/A	String	Sets or returns the primary office phone number of the contact.
organizationmain phone	N/A	String	Sets or returns the main telephone number of a company.

Continued on next page

Table A.11 continued   urn:schemas:contacts: namespace schema properties

Schema property	CDO constant	Microsoft Visual Basic data type	Description
othercity	cdoOtherCity	String	Sets or returns the alternative city of the contact.
othercountry	cdoOther Country	String	Sets or returns the alternative country of the contact.
othercountry code	cdoOthercountry Code	String	Sets or returns the alternative two-letter country code of the contact.
otherfax	OtherFax	String	Sets or returns the alternative work fax number, in international dialing format, of the contact.
othermobile	cdoOtherMobile	String	Sets or returns the alternative mobile telephone number, in international dialing format, of the contact.
otherpager	cdoWorkPager	String	Sets or returns the alternative pager telephone number, in international dialing format, of the contact.
otherpostal address	cdoOtherPostal Address	String	Sets or returns the alternative postal address of the contact.

Continued on next page

Table A.11 continued urn:schemas:contacts: namespace schema properties

Schema property	CDO constant	Microsoft Visual Basic data type	Description
otherpostalcode	cdoOtherPostal Code	String	Sets or returns the alternative postal code, typically a ZIP code in the United States, of the contact.
otherpostoffice box	cdoOtherPost OfficeBox	String	Sets or returns the alternative post office box of the contact.
otherstate	cdoOtherState	String	Sets or returns the alternative state, province, or parish, of the contact.
otherstreet	cdoOtherStreet	String	Sets or returns the alternative work street address of the contact.
othertelephone	cdoOtherWork Phone	String	Sets or returns the alternative work telephone, in international dialing format, of the contact.
othertimezone	cdoOtherTime Zone	String	Sets or returns the alternative work time zone of the contact.
pager	cdoPager	String	Sets or returns the work pager telephone number, in international dialing format, of the contact.
personalhome page	cdoPersonalURL	String	Sets or returns the URL of the home page of the contact.
personaltitle	cdoNamePrefix	String	Sets or returns the prefix title for the contact.

Continued on next page

Table A.11 continued   urn:schemas:contacts: namespace schema properties

Schema property	CDO constant	Microsoft Visual Basic data type	Description
postalcode	cdoWorkPostal Code	String	Sets or returns the work postal code, typically the ZIP code in the United States, of the contact.
postofficebox	cdoWorkPost OfficeBox	String	Sets or returns the work post office box number of the contact.
profession	cdoProfession	String	Sets or returns the profession of the contact.
proxyaddresses	cdoProxy Addresses	String	Sets or returns a list containing one or more client e-mail addresses.
referredby	N/A	String	Sets or returns the full name of the person who referred the contact.
roomnumber	N/A	String	Sets or returns the room number of the contact.
secretary	N/A	String	Sets or returns the full name of the secretary of the contact.
secretarycn	cdoSecretary CommonName	String	Sets or returns the common (or friendly) name of the secretary of the contact.
secretaryphone	N/A	String	Sets or returns the phone number of the contact's secretary.
secretaryurl	cdoSecretaryURL	String	Sets or returns the URL of the secretary for the contact.

Continued on next page

Table A.11 continued   urn:schemas:contacts: namespace schema properties

Schema property	CDO constant	Microsoft Visual Basic data type	Description
sn	cdoLastName	String	Sets or returns the surname of the contact.
sourceurl	cdoSourceURL	String	Sets or returns the URL of the source of the contact.
spousecn	cdoSpouse CommonName	String	Sets or returns the friendly name of the spouse of the contact.
st	cdoWorkState	String	Sets or returns the work state of the contact.
street	cdoWorkStreet	String	Sets or returns the work address of the contact.
submissioncont length	cdoSubmission ContLength	String	Sets or returns the maximum length, in kilobytes (KB), of a message that can be sent to the contact.
telephone number	cdoWorkPhone	String	Sets or returns the work telephone number, in international dialing format, of the contact.
telephone number2	cdoWorkPhone2	String	The alternative work telephone number, in international dialing format, of the contact.
telexnumber	cdoTelex Number	String	Sets or returns the work telex number, in international dialing format, of the contact.
title	cdoTitle	String	Sets or returns the work title or job position of the contact.

Continued on next page

Table A.11 continued   urn:schemas:contacts: namespace schema properties

Schema property	CDO constant	Microsoft Visual Basic data type	Description
ttytddphone	N/A	String	Sets or returns the ttytdd phone number.
unauthorig	N/A	String	Sets or returns the e-mail addresses that cannot send messages to this e-mail address.
usercertificate	cdoUser Certificate	N/A	Sets or returns the certificate used to authenticate the contact.
wedding anniversary	cdoWedding Anniversary	Date	Sets or returns the wedding anniversary of the contact.
workaddress	cdoWorkAddress	String	Sets or returns the work address of the contact.

HTTP MAIL

This namespace defines the core properties that you use to create messages. All string properties encoded with Multipurpose Internet Mail Extensions (MIME) standards are returned decoded as Unicode characters. Table A.12 lists the urn:schemas:httpmail: namespace schema properties.

Table A.12   urn:schemas:httpmail: namespace schema properties

Schema property	CDO constant	Microsoft Visual Basic data type	Description
attachment filename	cdoAttachment Filename	String	Sets or returns the name of the attached file.
bcc	cdoBcc	String	Sets or returns the BCC recipients of the message.
calendar	cdoHTTPMail Calendar	String	Returns the URL to a user's calendar folder.
cc	cdoCc	String	Sets or returns the CC recipients of the message.
contacts	cdoHTTPMail Contacts	String	Returns the URL of the user's contacts folder.
content-disposition-type	cdoContent DispositionType	String	Sets or returns the type portion of the Content-Disposition MIME header for a body part. Can be: unspecified, other, attachment, and inline.
content-media-type	cdoContent MediaType	String	Indicates the content media type for the body part.
date	cdoDate	Date	Indicates the date and time at which the message was sent.

Continued on next page

Table A.12 continued   urn:schemas:httpmail: namespace schema properties

Schema property	CDO constant	Microsoft Visual Basic data type	Description
datereceived	cdoDate Received	Date	Indicates the date and time that the message was received by the server.
deleteditems	cdoHTTPMail DeletedItems	String	Returns the URL of a user's Deleted Items folder.
displaybcc	N/A	String	Returns the display names of the BCC recipients of the message.
displaycc	N/A	String	Returns the display names of the CC recipients of a message.
displayto	N/A	String	Returns the display names of the primary (To) recipients of the message.
drafts	N/A	String	Returns the URL of a user's Drafts folder.
expiry-date	N/A	Date	A resource's expiration date.
flagcompleted	N/A	Date	Indicates the date and time a message resource was flagged as completed.
from	cdoFrom	String	Sets or returns the addressee from whom the message was sent.
fromemail	N/A	String	Returns the e-mail address from which the message was sent.

Continued on next page

Table A.12 continued   urn:schemas:httpmail: namespace schema properties

Schema property	CDO constant	Microsoft Visual Basic data type	Description
fromname	N/A	String	Returns the display name of the user or entity from which the message was sent.
hasattachment	cdoHas Attachment	Boolean	If True, the message has attachments. Read-only.
htmldescription	cdoHTML Description	String	Sets or returns the HTML content of the message.
importance	cdoImportance	Long	Sets or returns the message's importance.
inbox	cdoInbox	String	Returns the URL of a user's Inbox folder.
journal	cdoJournal	String	Returns the URL of a user's Journal folder.
messageflag	N/A	String	Sets or returns the message flag value for the message.
msgfolderroot	cdoMsgFolder Root	String	Returns the URL of a user's mailbox folder root.
normalized subject	cdoNormalized Subject	String	Returns the subject text string with all prefixes such as "Re:" and "Fwd:" removed.
notes	cdoNotes	String	Returns the URL of a user's Notes folder.
outbox	cdoOutbox	String	Returns the URL of a user's Outbox folder.
priority	cdoPriority	Long	Sets or returns the message's priority.

Continued on next page

Table A.12 continued   urn:schemas:httpmail: namespace schema properties

Schema property	CDO constant	Microsoft Visual Basic data type	Description
read	N/A	Boolean	If True, the message has been read.
reply-by	N/A	Date	Indicates when there should be a reply to the message.
reply-to	cdoReplyTo	String	Sets or returns the recipients to whom replies should be sent.
savedestination	N/A	String	Sets or returns where the resource should be saved after it is transmitted by using the Microsoft Exchange 2000 Server e-mail transmission Uniform Resource Identifier (URI).
saveinsent	N/A	Boolean	If True, the resource should be saved in the Sent Items folder after it is transmitted by using the Exchange e-mail transmission URI, through either the Microsoft Web Storage System OLE DB provider or the HTTP/WebDAV protocol.
sender	cdoSender	String	Indicates the actual message sender, if different than the From: property.
senderemail	N/A	String	Sets or returns the e-mail address of the message sender.

Continued on next page

Table A.12 continued   urn:schemas:httpmail: namespace schema properties

Schema property	CDO constant	Microsoft Visual Basic data type	Description
sendername	N/A	String	Sets or returns the display name of the message sender.
sendmsg	cdoSendMsg	String	Returns the e-mail submission URI to which outgoing e-mail should be submitted.
sentitems	cdoSentItems	String	Returns the URL of a user's Sent Items folder.
subject	cdoSubject	String	Sets or returns the subject of the message.
submitted	cdoSubmitted	Boolean	If True, a message has been submitted to the Outbox.
tasks	N/A	String	Returns the URL of a user's Tasks folder.
textdescription	cdoText Description	String	Sets or returns the plain-text content of the message.
thread-topic	cdoThreadTopic	String	Indicates the topic for conversation threading and is used when correlating the conversation threads.
to	cdoTo	String	Sets or returns the primary (To) message addressees.

Continued on next page

Table A.12 continued   urn:schemas:httpmail: namespace schema properties

Schema property	CDO constant	Microsoft Visual Basic data type	Description
unreadcount	cdoUnreadCount	Long	Indicates the number of unread messages in a folder.

Mail Header

This namespace defines the properties used to create messages. This namespace contains properties similar to those in the urn:schemas:httpmail: namespace. However, properties in the urn:schemas:mailheader: namespace define fields that contain Internet standard message header values. Each property value (with a few exceptions) is stored as US-ASCII characters and is identical to the ASCII string found in the message stream. Non-US-ASCII characters are encoded according to Multipurpose Internet Mail Extensions (MIME) standards, and no conversion is performed when the property value is set or updated. Table A.13 lists the urn:schemas:mailheader: namespace schema properties.

Table A.13   urn:schemas:mailheader: namespace schema properties

Schema property	CDO constant	Microsoft Visual Basic data type	Description
approved	cdoApproved	String	Sets or returns the address of the moderator who approved and posted a message.
bcc	N/A	String	Sets or returns the BCC addressees of the message.
cc	N/A	String	Sets or returns the CC addressees of the message.
comment	cdoComment	String	Sets or returns a comment for the message.

Continued on next page

Table A.13 continued   urn:schemas:mailheader: namespace schema properties

Schema property	CDO constant	Microsoft Visual Basic data type	Description
content-base	cdoContentBase	String	Indicates a base for relative Uniform Resource Identifiers (URIs) occurring in other header fields and in HTML documents that do not have any BASE element in HTML.
content-description	cdoContent Description	String	Sets or returns an optional description of a body part.
content-disposition	cdoContent Disposition	String	Sets or returns an intended disposition of the body part.
content-id	cdoContentId	String	Indicates the unique identifier for the body part.
content-language	cdoContent Language	String	Indicates the language identifier for the body part text content.
content-location	cdoContent Location	String	Indicates the URI that corresponds to the content of the body part.
content-transfer-encoding	cdoContent Transfer Encoding	String	Indicates the encoding mechanism used to encode the body part content.
content-type	cdoContentType	String	Indicates the body part content type.
control	cdoControl	String	Contains a Usenet control command.
date	N/A	Date	The date on which the message was sent.

Continued on next page

Table A.13 continued   urn:schemas:mailheader: namespace schema properties

Schema property	CDO constant	Microsoft Visual Basic data type	Description
disposition	cdoDisposition	String	Contains a Mail Delivery Notifications (MDN) status indicator for the message.
disposition-notification-to	cdoDisposition NotificationTo	String	Indicates where disposition notifications should be sent.
distribution	cdoDistribution	String	Sets or returns a comma-separated list similar to the Newsgroups header property, intended to restrict the distribution of a message.
expires	cdoExpires	String	Indicates the date on which the message expires.
expiry-date	N/A	String	Indicates expiry date of a message in an e-mail header. Outlook uses this in Internet mode for setting the expiration date of a message.
followup-to	cdoFollowupTo	String	Sets or returns the newsgroups to which follow-up messages are to be posted.
from	N/A	String	Sets or returns the addressees from whom the message was sent.
importance	CdoImportance Values.cdoLow	String	Sets or returns the level of importance for a message as low, normal, or high.

Continued on next page

Table A.13 continued   urn:schemas:mailheader: namespace schema properties

Schema property	CDO constant	Microsoft Visual Basic data type	Description
in-reply-to	cdoInReplyTo	String	Returns the message identifier of the message to which this is a reply.
keywords	N/A	String	Sets or returns the keywords for the message.
lines	cdoLines	String	Contains a count of the number of lines in the body of the (newsgroup) message.
message-id	cdoMessageId	String	Sets or returns a unique identifier of the message.
mime-version	cdoMIMEVersion	String	Sets or returns the version of MIME used to format the message.
newsgroups	cdoNewsgroups	String	Sets or returns the newsgroup addressees of the message.
organization	cdoOrganization	String	Sets or returns the organization of the sender.
original-recipient	cdoOriginal Recipient	String	Sets or returns the e-mail address of an original recipient of the message.
path	cdoPath	String	Returns a list of NNTP hosts through which this message was relayed before arriving at the current host.
posting-version	cdoPosting Version	String	Indicates the software used to post the message.

Continued on next page

Table A.13 continued   urn:schemas:mailheader: namespace schema properties

Schema property	CDO constant	Microsoft Visual Basic data type	Description
priority	cdoPriority	String	Sets or returns the priority of a message or appointment: normal, urgent, or nonurgent.
received	cdoReceived	String	Returns the SMTP host Received headers for a message.
references	cdoReferences	String	Indicates the Usenet header used to correlate replies with their original messages.
relay-version	cdoRelayVersion	String	Indicates the version of the program responsible for transmitting this article over the immediate link.
reply-by	N/A	String	Indicates when there should be a reply to a message.
reply-to	N/A	String	Sets or returns the address to which replies should be sent.
return-path	cdoReturnPath	String	Sets or returns the address of the message originator.
return-receipt-to	cdoReturn ReceiptTo	String	Sets or returns the address to which return receipts should be sent.
sender	N/A	String	Sets or returns the sender of the message.

Continued on next page

Table A.13 continued   urn:schemas:mailheader: namespace schema properties

Schema property	CDO constant	Microsoft Visual Basic data type	Description
sensitivity	cdoSensitivity	String	Sets or returns the sensitivity of the message or appointment. Can be: None, Personal, Private, or Company Confidential.
subject	N/A	String	Sets or returns the subject of the message.
summary	cdoSummary	String	Sets or returns the summary of the message.
thread-index	cdoThreadIndex	String	Indicates a particular conversation thread; computed from message references.
thread-topic	N/A	String	Sets or returns the topic of a discussion thread.
to	N/A	String	Sets or returns the primary (To) message addressees.
x-mailer	cdoXMailer	String	Indicates the software used to send the message.
x-message-completed	N/A	String	Contains a Microsoft Outlook header for message flag completion.
x-message-flag	N/A	String	Contains a message flag used by Outlook.
xref	cdoXref	String	Contains the name of the host (with domains omitted) and a white–space-separated list of colon-separated pairs of newsgroup names and message numbers.

Continued on next page

Table A.13 continued   urn:schemas:mailheader: namespace schema properties

Schema property	CDO constant	Microsoft Visual Basic data type	Description
x-unsent	cdoXUnsent	String	Indicates whether a message has been completed during authoring.

DATA TYPES

This namespace contains a property used to define data types for property definitions in a Microsoft Web Storage System. Table A.14 lists the urn:schemas-microsoft-com:datatypes# namespace schema properties.

Table A.14   urn:schemas-microsoft-com:datatypes# namespace schema properties

Schema property	CDO constant	Microsoft Visual Basic data type	Description
type	N/A	String	Sets or returns the data type for a property definition.

EXCHANGE DATA

This namespace defines data types specific to Microsoft Exchange for Microsoft Web Storage System properties. Table A.15 lists the urn:schemas-microsoft-com:exch-data: namespace schema properties.

Table A.15   urn:schemas-microsoft-com:exch-data: namespace schema properties

Schema property	CDO constant	Microsoft Visual Basic data type	Description
baseschema	N/A	Array (Strings)	Sets or returns an array of URLs identifying other folders in the same store that contain schema definition items.
closedexpected contentclasses	N/A	Boolean	Reserved for future use.
codebase	N/A	String	Sets or returns a URL where clients can download Microsoft ActiveX components to render or handle items of this content class.
comclassid	N/A	String	Sets or returns a COM class to handle items of this content class.
comprogid	N/A	String	Sets or returns a COM class that is expected to handle items of this content class.
default	N/A	String	Sets or returns a default value for a custom property definition.
dictionary	N/A	String	Reserved for future use.
expected-content-class	N/A	Array (Strings)	Sets or returns an array of resource content classes that are expected to appear in a folder.
iscontentindexed	N/A	Boolean	Reserved for future use.
isindexed	N/A	Boolean	If True, the property is indexed.

Continued on next page

Table A.15 continued   urn:schemas-microsoft-com:exch-data: namespace schema
properties

Schema property	CDO constant	Microsoft Visual Basic data type	Description
ismultivalued	N/A	Boolean	If True, the property can contain multiple values of the type defined with the urn:schemas-microsoft-com:datatypes#type property.
isreadonly	N/A	Boolean	If True, the property should be read-only. If this is a custom property, your application must enforce this setting.
isrequired	N/A	Boolean	If True, the property is required to be set. If this is a custom property, your application must enforce this setting.
isvisible	N/A	Boolean	If True, the property is visible to clients.
propertydef	N/A	String	Sets or returns the name of the property overridden by a property override.
schema-collection-ref	N/A	String	Sets or returns a URL identifying the first folder in which to look for schema definition items.
synchronize	N/A	Boolean	If True, the resource's stream should be updated when this property is set on the row.

Continued on next page

Table A.15 continued urn:schemas-microsoft-com:exch-data: namespace schema properties

Schema property	CDO constant	Microsoft Visual Basic data type	Description
version	N/A	Long	Sets or returns an optional version value for schema definition items. This property has no effect on the schema definitions or their operation in the store.

FORM REGISTRATIONS

This namespace defines properties used to create and manage form registration items for Microsoft Web Storage System forms. Table A.16 lists the urn:schemas-microsoft-com:office:forms# namespace schema properties.

Table A.16 urn:schemas-microsoft-com:office:forms# namespace schema properties

Schema property	CDO constant	Microsoft Visual Basic data type	Description[1]
binding	N/A	String	Sets or returns the binding type, such as "server" or "client."
browser	N/A	String	Sets or returns the type of browser.
cmd	N/A	String	Sets or returns the action or behavior being performed on an object.
contentclass	N/A	String	Sets or returns the content class for which a Web page is registered.

Continued on next page

Table A.16 continued   urn:schemas-microsoft-com:office:forms# namespace schema properties

Schema property	CDO constant	Microsoft Visual Basic data type	Description
contentstate	N/A	String	Sets or returns the value to match forms against the value of the http://schemas.microsoft.com/exchange/contentstate property.
execute parameters	N/A	String	Sets or returns the parameters to pass to the form-rendering engine specified by the executeurl property.
executeurl	N/A	String	Sets or returns the URL of the engine used to render a form. This can be an ASP form or an ISAPI filter.
formurl	N/A	String	Sets or returns the URL of the form or template. The form URL being registered; this can be a relative or absolute URL.
language	N/A	String	Sets or returns the language of the Web form. Provided as part of the HTTP request headers.
majorver	N/A	String	Sets or returns the major version of the browser.
messagestate	N/A	String	Sets or returns the state of the resource. Values include normal, submitted, read, unread, and importance.

Continued on next page

Table A.16 continued   urn:schemas-microsoft-com:office:forms# namespace schema properties

Schema property	CDO constant	Microsoft Visual Basic data type	Description
minorver	N/A	String	Sets or returns the minor version of the browser.
platform	N/A	String	Sets or returns the platform of the browser.
request	N/A	String	Specifies whether the form uses a GET or POST request.
version	N/A	String	Sets or returns the browser version.

[1]An asterisk (*) can be used as a wildcard character for these properties. Properties explicitly set with a wildcard character take precedence over properties that are not set. Content class and executeurl should be actual values.

Microsoft Office

This namespace defines properties used with Microsoft Office documents and applications. Table A.17 lists the urn:schemas-microsoft-com:office:office# namespace schema properties.

Table A.17   urn:schemas-microsoft-com:office:office# namespace schema properties

Schema property	CDO constant	Microsoft Visual Basic data type	Description
Author	N/A	String	Sets or returns the name of the document author.
Bytes	N/A	Long	Sets or returns the size of the document in bytes.

Continued on next page

Table A.17 continued   urn:schemas-microsoft-com:office:office# namespace schema properties

Schema property	CDO constant	Microsoft Visual Basic data type	Description
Category	N/A	String	Sets or returns a comma-delimited list of categories that apply to the document.
Characters	N/A	Long	Sets or returns the number of characters in the document.
Checked_x0020_ by	N/A	Long	Sets or returns a status property used by Microsoft Office applications.
Client	N/A	String	Sets or returns a status property used by Office applications.
Comments	N/A	String	Sets or returns the comments for the document.
Company	N/A	String	Sets or returns the author's company.
Created	N/A	Date	Sets or returns the date and time that an Office document was created.
Date_x0020_ completed	N/A	String	Sets or returns a status property used by Office applications.
Department	N/A	String	Sets or returns the author's department.
Destination	N/A	String	Sets or returns a status property used by Office applications.

Continued on next page

Table A.17 continued   urn:schemas-microsoft-com:office:office# namespace schema properties

Schema property	CDO constant	Microsoft Visual Basic data type	Description
Disposition	N/A	String	Sets or returns a status property used by Office applications.
Division	N/A	String	Sets or returns a status property used by Office applications.
Document_ x0020_number	N/A	String	Sets or returns a status property used by Office applications.
Editor	N/A	String	Sets or returns a status property used by Office applications.
Forward_x0020_ to	N/A	String	Sets or returns a status property used by Office applications.
Group	N/A	String	Sets or returns a status property used by Office applications.
HeadingPairs	N/A	String	Sets or returns a status property used by Office applications.
HiddenSlides	N/A	Long	Sets or returns a status property used by Office applications.
Keywords	N/A	String	Sets or returns a list of keywords for a document.
Language	N/A	String	Sets or returns the language in which the document was written.

Continued on next page

Table A.17 continued   urn:schemas-microsoft-com:office:office# namespace schema properties

Schema property	CDO constant	Microsoft Visual Basic data type	Description
LastAuthor	N/A	String	Sets or returns a status property used by Office applications.
LastPrinted	N/A	Date	Sets or returns a status property used by Office applications.
LastSaved	N/A	Date	Sets or returns a status property used by Office applications.
Lines	N/A	Long	Sets or returns a status property used by Office applications.
LinksUpToDate	N/A	Boolean	Sets or returns a status property used by Office applications.
MailStop	N/A	String	Sets or returns a status property used by Office applications.
Manager	N/A	String	Sets or returns a status property used by Office applications.
Matter	N/A	String	Sets or returns a status property used by Office applications.
MultimediaClips	N/A	Long	Sets or returns a status property used by Office applications.
NameOf Application	N/A	String	Sets or returns a status property used by Office applications.

Continued on next page

Table A.17 continued urn:schemas-microsoft-com:office:office# namespace schema properties

Schema property	CDO constant	Microsoft Visual Basic data type	Description
Notes	N/A	Long	Sets or returns a status property used by Office applications.
Office	N/A	String	Sets or returns a status property used by Office applications.
Owner	N/A	String	Sets or returns a status property used by Office applications.
Pages	N/A	Long	Sets or returns a status property used by Office applications.
Paragraphs	N/A	Long	Sets or returns a status property used by Office applications.
PartTitles	N/A	String	Sets or returns a status property used by Office applications.
Presentation Format	N/A	String	Sets or returns a status property used by Office applications.
Project	N/A	String	Sets or returns a status property used by Office applications.
Publisher	N/A	String	Sets or returns a status property used by Office applications.
Purpose	N/A	String	Sets or returns a status property used by Office applications.

Continued on next page

Table A.17 continued   urn:schemas-microsoft-com:office:office# namespace schema properties

Schema property	CDO constant	Microsoft Visual Basic data type	Description
Received	N/A	String	Sets or returns a status property used by Office applications.
Recorded	N/A	String	Sets or returns a status property used by Office applications.
Recorded_ x0020_date	N/A	String	Sets or returns a status property used by Office applications.
Reference	N/A	String	A status property used by Office applications.
Revision	N/A	String	A status property used by Office applications.
ScaleCrop	N/A	Boolean	A status property used by Office applications.
Security	N/A	Long	A status property used by Office applications.
Slides	N/A	Long	A status property used by Office applications.
Source	N/A	String	A status property used by Office applications.
Status	N/A	String	A status property used by Office applications.
Subject	N/A	String	A status property used by Office applications.
Telephone_ x0020_number	N/A	String	A status property used by Office applications.

Continued on next page

Table A.17 continued   urn:schemas-microsoft-com:office:office# namespace schema properties

Schema property	CDO constant	Microsoft Visual Basic data type	Description
Template	N/A	String	A status property used by Office applications.
ThumbNail	N/A	N/A	A status property used by Office applications.
Title	N/A	String	A status property used by Office applications.
TotalTime	N/A	Date	A status property used by Office applications.
Typist	N/A	String	A status property used by Office applications.
Version	N/A	Long	A status property used by Office applications.
Words	N/A	Long	A status property used by Office applications.

XML DATA

This namespace defines properties used to create and manage Microsoft Web Storage System content class definitions and property definitions. Table A.18 lists the urn:schemas-microsoft-com:xml-data# namespace schema properties.

Table A.18   urn:schemas-microsoft-com:xml-data# namespace schema properties

Schema property	CDO constant	Microsoft Visual Basic data type	Description
element	N/A	Array (Strings)	Sets or returns the property definitions associated with a custom content class.
extends	N/A	Array (Strings)	Sets or returns the content classes a custom content class extends.
name	N/A	String	Sets or returns the name of a custom content class definition or custom property definition.

Designing Forms with Outlook 2000

Microsoft Outlook 2000 is a powerful and easy-to-use personal information management tool. When you pair it with Microsoft Exchange 2000 server, you have instant groupware capabilities in shared calendars, assigned tasks, and workflow applications. When you build custom solutions for Outlook, you focus your programming efforts primarily on folders and forms. Exchange public folders allow Outlook users to quickly and easily share information among individuals and teams. By creating a custom Outlook form, you increase the potential of an Outlook application. Use a custom Outlook form to display and enter custom properties that are specific to your solution, include functionality with form events to control how the form behaves, and add complex validation to form fields. When it comes to distributing and managing an Outlook form, it's easy to deploy any version of an Outlook form with the forms registration libraries.

Sections in this appendix include:

- **Introduction to Outlook Forms Designer**. Learn how to use Outlook Forms Designer, the tool you use when customizing any Outlook form.

- **Using Outlook Form Events**. Learn how to incorporate Event objects into your Outlook forms to make them more reactive to users.

- **Using Script to Access Parts of an Outlook Form**. Learn how to use code to access an Outlook form.

- **Using Custom Command Bars**. Learn how easy it is to create and use custom command bars.

- **Distributing Outlook Forms**. Learn about the three different ways to save a form to make it available to other users.

- **Managing and Maintaining Outlook Forms**. Learn how to use Exchange and Outlook together to make managing and maintaining Outlook forms easier than managing many other types of forms.

INTRODUCTION TO OUTLOOK FORMS DESIGNER

To customize an Outlook form, you use Outlook Forms Designer. Outlook Forms Designer exists behind every Outlook form and is the environment in which a form is designed for additional functionality. To use Outlook Forms Designer to design a new form, in Outlook, click the **Tools** menu, select **Forms**, and then select **Design a Form**. Double-click the form type you want to customize. Outlook Forms Designer opens for the select form type. A form open in Outlook Forms Designer is also referred to as being in design mode. Figure B.1 shows a contact form open in design mode.

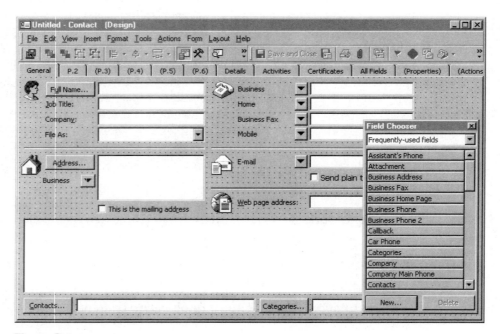

Figure B.1
Outlook Forms Designer exists behind every Outlook form and is used to add custom controls, write code, and make other customizations.

Outlook Forms Designer provides several tools for designing custom Outlook forms:

- **Field Chooser**. Adds fields to an Outlook form as form controls. When you drag a field from Field Chooser to a form page, you create a new control to display and enter data in the field. You can also use Field Chooser to create new fields. If you use custom schema properties, you can use Field Chooser to create fields for accessing custom schema properties. By default, Field Chooser is open whenever Outlook Forms Designer is open.

- **Toolbox**. Adds a selection of ActiveX controls to the Outlook form. You can also add additional controls to the toolbox and create custom toolbox pages for organizing controls. You can even create custom control groups by dragging control from a form to the toolbox.

- **Properties**. Sets ActiveX control properties in Outlook forms. You can use the Properties tool to set display properties, add data validation, and set data formatting options.

- **Advanced Properties**. Like the Properties tool, this tool sets ActiveX control properties in Outlook forms. The Advanced Properties tool is similar to the Properties sheet used in other development environments, such as Microsoft Visual Basic or Microsoft Access. You can use the Properties tool to set more advanced properties, such as configuring a multiple column list box. You can also use the Advanced Properties tool to change properties for more than one control on the form at a time.

- **Script Editor**. Manages all the Microsoft Visual Basic Scripting Edition (VBScript) code in an Outlook form. The Script Editor provides only basic editing functionality. You can display the Script Editor in design mode: On the **Form** menu, click **View Code**, or click the **View Code** toolbar button.

TIP If you prefer to write code in a richer development environment, you can write the code in Visual Basic and then copy the code to Script Editor. This approach lets you use the powerful Microsoft IntelliSense features of the Visual Basic Editor—features such as coloring of code text and proper casing the code commands. However, you may have to change some named constants you have used to their numerical equivalents because VBScript does not support all named constants. You must also change all uses of the New keyword for creating objects to the supported CreateObject function.

USING OUTLOOK FORM EVENTS

You can use events in Outlook forms to trigger code to run at a particular time. Events are actions that occur, such as sending e-mail or opening a contact form. Events are associated with most of the common form behaviors, such as opening and closing a form, saving a form, and even reading attachments. In some cases, these events can even be canceled. This means that you can write code in the event that evaluates whether the event should fully execute. If your code determines that the event should not finish executing, you can cancel the event.

For example, you can write code in the Open event of a form that prompts the user for a password. If the user provides the correct password, the Open event continues and the form opens. If the user does not provide the correct password, the event is canceled and the form does not open. Table B.1 describes the Outlook form events and indicates if the event can be canceled.

Table B.1   Outlook form events

Event	Description	Able to be canceled?
AttachmentAdd	Occurs after an attachment has been added to an item.	No
AttachmentRead	Occurs after an attachment has been opened.	No
BeforeAttachmentSave	Occurs just before an attachment is saved.	Yes
BeforeCheckNames	Occurs once before the recipient names are resolved.	Yes
Open	Occurs when the item is opened in an Inspector object.	Yes
Read	Occurs when the item is read for inline editing but before any changes are saved. Also occurs when the item is opened in an Inspector object.	Yes
Write	Occurs after changes have been saved to the underlying fields, but before the entire item is saved.	Yes

Continued on next page

Table B.1 continued   Outlook form events

Event	Description	Able to be canceled?
Close	Occurs when the Inspector object associated with an item is closed.	Yes
Send	Occurs before an item is sent.	Yes
Reply	Occurs when the user selects the Reply action but before the reply is sent.	Yes
ReplyAll	Occurs when the user selects the ReplyAll action but before the reply is sent.	Yes
Forward	Occurs when the user selects the Forward action but before the item is sent.	Yes
PropertyChange	Occurs after a standard property of an item has been changed.	No
CustomPropertyChange	Occurs after a custom property of an item has been changed.	No
CustomAction	Occurs immediately before a custom action is executed.	Yes

CREATING AN EVENT PROCEDURE

You create an event procedure in the script editor of an Outlook form by using Event Handler. Click the **Script** menu, and select **Event Handler**. The **Insert Event Handler** dialog box appears (see Figure B.2).

Figure B.2
Use the Insert Event Handler dialog box to add event procedures.

From the list of event procedures, select one, and click **Add**. Depending on the particular event chosen, either the sub procedure statements or the function statements are added. If function statements are added, the user can cancel the event. The next section discusses canceling event procedures.

Some event procedures also include parameters in the procedure statements. These parameters contain information about the triggered event. For example, the Reply event includes the parameter *Response,* which represents the response item created in reply to the current item. You can then use this variable to reference the new item and discern between the two open items. You can use this variable to add subject matter to the item, include additional recipients, or add an attachment. Because the information is passed by value, you can't change the original information in the variable and inadvertently interfere with the execution of the item. Table B.2 lists the events that use parameters with an explanation of the variables.

Table B.2 Some events also provide parameters that you can manipulate to control the behavior of the event and any resulting objects.

Event	Parameter	Reference
AttachmentAdd	*NewAttachment*	Attachment object that was added.
AttachmentRead	*ReadAttachment*	Attachment object that was opened for editing.
BeforeAttachmentSave	*SaveAttachment*	Attachment object to be saved.

Continued on next page

Table B.2 continued Some events also provide parameters that you can manipulate to control the behavior of the event and any resulting objects.

Event	Parameter	Reference
PropertyChange	*Name*	String name of the built-in property that was changed.
CustomPropertyChange	*Name*	String name of the custom property (field) that was changed.
CustomAction	*Action*	String name of the custom action that triggered the event.
	NewItem	Object variable pointing to the new item that was created by the action.

CANCELING AN EVENT

As mentioned earlier in this section, when you create some event procedures with Event Handler, they are created as functions rather than as sub procedures. Events that are added as functions are cancelable. Canceling events allows you to prevent the remainder of the action from occurring. For example, you can cancel the Open event to stop a form from opening or cancel the Send event to suppress an item from being sent. By using this option, you can include advanced functionality in your Outlook form to verify users before the form is opened, include advanced field validation that compares fields with each other, and even prompt users for additional information before following through on an action. If an event procedure is not added as a function, you cannot cancel it. Simply changing an event sub procedure to a function does not allow the event to be canceled!

To cancel an event, set the event procedure name to False. For example, the following line of code stops the Open action from completing:

```
Item_Open = False
```

Although this code stops the action from completing, it does not suppress the remainder of the procedure from running. To avoid running unnecessary code after an event has been canceled, exit the function with the Exit Function procedure.

> **NOTE** The code listings in this appendix are available in the Microsoft Visual Basic project CH_03.VBP on the companion CD. If you want to run the samples as they are written, you must have the Zoo Management sample installed on your Exchange 2000 server. For information about installing the application, see the introduction to the book. In addition, the code samples repeatedly call a function named GetStorageName. This function returns the name of the domain in which the code is running. For more information about the GetStorageName function, see Chapter 8, "Interacting with Active Directory."

Listing B.1 shows how to add password access to a form by using the Open event. If the user does not type the correct password (for example, "password1"), the Open event is canceled, the form never opens, and a message stating that the form will terminate appears.

Listing B.1   Open an Outlook form only when the right password is entered.

```
Function Item_Open()
    Dim strPassword
    Dim i

    'Set a counter variable to count attempts.
    i = 0

    Do
        'If the user has already made three attempts,
        'cancel the opening.
        If i = 3 Then
            MsgBox "Form will now terminate.", vbCritical, _
                "Illegal Form Access"
            'Cancel the event
            Item_Open = False
            'To prevent any further code from running,
            'exit the function.
            Exit Function
        End If
        'Display an input box.
        strPassword = InputBox("Password to open:", "Validate")
```

```
        'Increment the counter.
         i = i + 1
     Loop Until strPassword = "password1"
End Function
```

USING CONTROL EVENTS

In addition to the form events, you can also use one control event. Every control that you add to an Outlook form exposes a Click event. You must create a Click event manually by typing the procedure statements into a script editor. To create a Click event procedure for a control, name the event procedure with a combination of the *controlname*, followed by an underscore, and finished with the word Click. For example, the following code sample runs when you click a command button named cmdShowMessage:

```
Sub cmdShowMessage_Click()
    MsgBox "Hello!"
End Sub
```

A common mistake to make when creating control event procedures is to use the wrong name for the control in the procedure. If you find that the code you wrote is not firing properly, check that the control name is the same name used in the event procedure name.

ORDER OF EVENT FIRING

To write code in more than one event, you must understand the order in which these events fire in relation to one another. This helps you write code that fires in the order you need it to fire.

OPENING

```
Opening a new item: Open [PropertyChange] / [CustomPropertyChange]
Opening an existing item: Read -> Open [PropertyChange] /
[CustomPropertyChange]
```

When you create a new item, the Open event is the only event that fires. The Read event doesn't fire because there is no existing data to read. When you open an existing item, the Read event fires, followed by the Open event. If you have any code in the Open event that places data in a built-in field or custom field, the program flow is interrupted and rerouted to the PropertyChange event or to the CustomPropertyChange event. When those procedures finish executing, program control returns to the Open event and it finishes loading the form. This is also true if the code that fills in the fields exists in the Read event.

So if the events fire close together, where do you put the code? You should write code in an Open event when:

- You want the code to run when a new item is created.

- You want the code to run when a new item is created as well as when an existing item is opened.

- If your code that renders any graphical components, such as controls or pages, write the code in the Open event. At the time of the Read event, the form itself has not yet been rendered and controls do not yet exist. Any code that refers to graphical components causes a trappable error.

You should write code in a Read event procedure when:

- You need the code to run only for an existing item, not for a new item.

- When a user might use inline editing to access the item. Inline editing occurs when the user changes a property value for an item in Outlook Explorer without first opening the item. For example, you can edit a task item in an Outlook Explorer without opening it.

SAVING AND CLOSING

```
Closing without saving changes: Close

Closing and saving changes: Close -> Write [SaveAttachment]
```

When you **Close** an item, the Close event fires. If you made any changes, a message prompts you to save changes, but only after the Close event has finished executing completely. If you do not save changes, the form closes. If you do save changes, the Write event is then triggered. Both events are able to access fields and controls. If you have added an attachment to the item or have changed a currently attached item, the SaveAttachment event fires afterward.

SENDING

```
BeforeCheckNames -> Send -> Write -> [SaveAttachment] -> Close
```

When you **Send** an item to someone, the BeforeCheckNames event fires when Exchange attempts to resolve the recipients of the message. Resolving a recipient means Exchange attempts to match the name against an entry in the global address book and at least verifies that the recipient address is in a supported format. If Exchange is unable to resolve a recipient, the Check Names dialog box appears to prompt the user to manually check the recipient name that cannot be resolved. If Exchange is able to resolve all recipient names, the Send event fires as the item is sent to the server. The Write event fires next when the item is saved to the **Sent items** folder or whatever folder is selected for saving sent items. If the message has an attachment, the SaveAttachment event fires next. Finally, the Close event fires when the item is completely unloaded from memory.

REPLYING

```
Select either the Reply or Reply to All: Reply or ReplyAll -> [Close]
(of the original message)
Send the reply: Write (of the original message)
```

When you **Reply** or **Reply All** to a message, the corresponding event fires and the reply form opens. If you set the option to close an item on response or forward, the Close event for the original message fires. Otherwise, the Close event of the original message does not fire until the Inspector displaying the form is explicitly closed. If the reply is actually sent, the Write event of the original message occurs as the reply information is written to the original message.

NOTE If you use a custom reply form that also has code in it, those events fire as well.

FORWARDING

```
Selecting to Forward:
Forward -> Open (of the new item) -> [Close] (of the original message)
Send the forward:
BeforeCheckNames -> Send (of new item) -> Write (of new item) -> Write
(of the original message) -> Close (of the new item)
```

When you **Forward** an item, the Forward event fires and the new form is opened. The Open event of the new item is then triggered. If you set the option to close an item on response or forward, the Close event for the original message fires. Otherwise, the Close event of the original message does not fire until the Inspector displaying the form is explicitly closed.

When the forwarded message is sent, the Send event of the new item fires, followed by the Write event of the new item as it is saved to the **Sent Items** folder or whatever folder is selected for saving sent items. The Write event of the original message fires as the forwarding information is written to the original message. Finally, the Close event of the new item fires as it is completely erased from memory.

USING SCRIPT TO ACCESS PARTS OF AN OUTLOOK FORM

Unlike other form models, Outlook forms do not explicitly employ a forms object model. To use code to navigate in the form , you must understand how forms and the associated item are related. Some key points to remember include:

- The item is the actual data stored in Exchange and is graphically rendered by the Inspector and its team of Pages and Controls.

- When you open an item by using a form, you are actually opening an Inspector object.

- An Inspector object contains a collection of pages exposed as the tabs on a form. Each page owns its own set of controls.

- The term "form" is more of a friendly name for the entire Inspector/Pages/Controls structure.

RETURNING THE CURRENT ITEM

Depending on what you are attempting to accomplish in the form, you write code to navigate either through the Inspector object or through the item itself. If you need to get to the data itself, including the built-in properties and custom fields, you do not need to navigate the Inspector object. Instead, you can use a reference to the item using the keyword Item. When used in VBScript for Outlook forms, the keyword Item refers to the current item displayed by the active Inspector. For example, if you use the following code sample in a Contact form, it returns the full name for the contact currently open:

```
MsgBox Item.FullName
```

GETTING THE INSPECTOR

To access controls on a form, you use an Inspector object of the current item. To return the active inspector for an item, call the GetInspector property of the current item. For example, the following code returns the active inspector:

```
Set ispActive = Item.GetInspector
```

You can use an Inspector object to:

- Determine whether the window is maximized, minimized, or floating.

- Access pages and their controls.

- Reference the body of the item by using an HTML editor or Microsoft Word as the editor.

- Control command bars for the current item.

CONTROLLING PAGES

You access the pages in an Inspector by using the ModifedFormPages property of an Inspector object. This property returns a collection of pages that were manipulated in design view. To return a specific page, pass the name of the page. For example, the following code sets a reference to a page titled Order Information:

```
Set pgOrderInfo = Item.GetInspector.ModifiedFormPages("Order
Information")
```

To access the default page of an e-mail message form or a post form by using the ModifedFormPages property, you must touch the page first. *Touching* involves accessing the form definition of the page in some way. The easiest way to do this is to display the Properties dialog box for any control on that page. As you might have guessed, because you have to touch the default page in order to return it with the ModifedFormPages property, you cannot access the default page from any other item. To manipulate the default page of any of these other items, you need to use the built-in properties to change the data itself instead.

ACTIVATING A PAGE

By default, the standard or default page of a form is displayed when the form is opened. If you would prefer to see a custom page instead, you can use the SetCurrentFormPage method and pass the name of the page to be displayed. As with most Outlook objects, you must be case specific when identifying page names with VBScript behind Outlook forms. The following code displays the custom page "Sales Info" whenever the form is opened:

```
Function Item_Open()
    Item.GetInspector.SetCurrentFormPage _
        "Sales Info"
End Function
```

> **NOTE** Use the SetCurrentFormPage method to display hidden pages as well as visible pages. If you activate a hidden page, the corresponding tab is not displayed.

HIDING AND SHOWING PAGES

You can also hide and show pages by using code. This allows you to display pages for specific users and hide those same pages from other users. To show a form page that is currently hidden, call the ShowFormPage method and pass the name of the page to be shown. The page tab is then displayed, but the page is not activated.

```
Item.GetInspector.ShowFormPage "Administration"
```

To hide a page, use the HideFormPage method and pass the name of the page. The tab is then hidden from view and inaccessible. For example, the following code sample hides a page:

```
Item.GetInspector.HideFormPage "Administration"
```

ACCESSING CONTROLS ON A PAGE

To access the controls in an Outlook form, you use the Controls collection of a Page object. In order to access the controls in a form, you must first navigate to the appropriate page. Next call the Controls property of a Page object to return a collection on controls on a page. To return a specific control, pass the name of the control to the Controls property. As with page names, control names are case sensitive in VBScript behind Outlook forms.

Listing B.2 shows how to use the Open event procedure to reference a collection of controls on a Sales Info page. Because you must often access controls from more than one procedure in the script, you should use object variables declared at the script level. After you declare the variables, you use the Open event of the form to reference the controls. The code then drills into each control individually and sets individual references.

Listing B.2   Access controls on an Outlook form.

```
'Declare the variable at script level for use.
'by all procedures.
Private lstSelected
Private txtSubTotal
Private txtTotal

Function Item_Open()
    'Reference the Sales Info page.
    Set pgSales = Item.GetInspector _
        .ModifiedFormPages("Sales")
    'Reference all of the controls on that page.
    Set ctlsSales = pgSales.Controls

    'Reference each individual control.
    Set lstSelected = ctlsSales("lstSelected")
    Set txtSubTotal = ctlsSales("txtSubTotal")
    Set txtTotal = ctlsSales("txtTotal")
End Function
```

TIP   To imitate as many of the standards of Microsoft Visual Basic for Applications (VBA) development as possible, you can use an object variable of the same name as the control itself. Then throughout the rest of the code, you can simply refer to the control by name just as you would in VBA.

A common question about accessing controls and fields is, "Why should you access the control instead of accessing the field directly?" You should use a reference to a control rather than a field in the following circumstances:

- You need to affect the appearance of the control.

- The control is not bound to any fields.

- You don't want to change the underlying data, but only the data displayed by the control.

- You don't want to trigger the CustomPropertyChange event.

DELVING INTO CUSTOM FIELDS

An alternative to accessing the controls themselves is to go directly to the underlying MAPI field. In Outlook forms, a custom (or user-defined) field is also known as a custom property of that form. If you make changes to the custom field associated with a control, you can update the associated control with the new information as well.

To get into a custom field, you must access the UserProperties collection of the item, not the Inspector object. As mentioned earlier, data belongs to the item. The UserProperties collection contains all custom fields that have been added to a form. To return a reference to a specific field, pass the name of the field as string. Remember, field names are case sensitive in VBScript behind Outlook forms. The following code changes the value of the custom field, strLastName, to a new value:

```
Item.userProperties("strLastName") = "Martin"
```

You use the UserProperties collection instead of the Controls collection in these circumstances:

- You want to simultaneously change the underlying data and what the control is displaying.

- You want to trigger the CustomPropertyChange event. The program pauses execution of the code at this point and runs the Change event code before continuing with the rest of the code.

- You want to trigger any validation associated with the field underlying the control.

CONTROLLING CONTROLS

You can do quite a bit to configure controls during the design period of the form. However, it is inevitable that some tasks cannot be accomplished until the form is actually running and certain scenarios occur. For example, perhaps you need to read values in text boxes to export them to a Word report. Or maybe you want to dynamically populate a list control with data from a database. Or maybe you want to format the text that a user enters in the body of a message that uses Word as the editor. All these situations require you to take control of your controls at run time by using code.

CONTROLLING TEXT BOXES

Text boxes are perhaps the easiest control to manipulate. To fill a text box with data, set the Text or Value property of the control equal to the desired value. Unlike with other forms packages, you cannot simply set the control name equal to the value. Although doing so does not generate an error, you won't get the intended result. As always, be sure that the reference to the control is valid. To read a text box, call one of the same properties. The following code sample fills a text box with data and then displays the current value in a message box:

```
Set txtFirstName = ctlsInfo("txtFirstName")
'Fill the text box with text.
txtFirstName.Text = "Mindy"
'Read the text box.
MsgBox txtFirstName.Text
```

CONTROLLING LIST CONTROLS

You can fill a list control with data in design mode or when code opens the form. If the list control uses multiple columns, you must populate the control by using code.

Populating a List Control Array

One way to populate a single column list control is to use the AddItem method of a list control. The AddItem method lets you add one item at a time to a list control, and it takes two parameters: text and index. *Text* is the text value that is added to the list, and *index* is an optional argument that indicates the positioning of the text in the list. If you omit index, the item is added to the end of the list. The following code sample adds an item to a list box named lstFolders:

```
lstFolders.AddItem "Inbox"
```

To select an item from a list control, use the ListIndex property. Because it's a zero-based array, a value of 0 selects the first control in the list. For example, the following code selects the first item in a list box named lstFolders:

```
lstFolders.ListIndex = 0
```

An alternative to the AddItem method is to first populate an array with the data and then push the array contents into the list control. This approach is preferred when you fill a list control that uses multiple columns of information. The first step is to populate the array. When you declare the array, keep in mind that arrays in VBScript must be zero-based. If you use a multiple dimension array, the first dimension of the array determines the number of rows in the list. The second dimension configures the number of columns. For example, the following code sample creates an array with two dimensions:

```
ReDim aFolders(fdsCurrent.Count - 1, 1)
```

TIP If you work with dynamic arrays that fluctuate in size, you might want to resize the array and employ the Preserve keyword to maintain data integrity. However, be aware that the Preserve keyword generates an error in VBScript when used with arrays with multiple dimensions.

After the array is populated with the data you need, you are ready to fill the list control. If you want to avoid adding duplicate values to a list control, you should start by calling the Clear method of the list control to empty it first. The following line of code clears the contents of the lstFolders list box:

```
lstFolders.Clear
```

Then set the List property of the list control equal to the array. This pushes all the data into the list control at one time, as opposed to one row at a time. Listing B.3 puts all these tools together to populate a list box with two columns of information. The first column contains folder names and the other holds item type constants.

Listing B.3   Use an array to populate a multiple column list control with data.

```
Sub FillFolderListBox()
    Dim fdsCurrent
    Dim fd
    Dim i

    'Reference the folder level currently displayed
    'in the Explorer window.
    Set fdsCurrent = Application.ActiveExplorer _
        .CurrentFolder.Parent.Folders

    'Declare an array.
    ReDim aFolders(fdsCurrent.Count - 1, 1)

    i = 0
    'Loop through all of the folders and
    ' add the names to the array.
    For Each fd In fdsCurrent
        aFolders(i, 0) = fd.Name
        aFolders(i, 1) = fd.DefaultItemType
        i = i + 1
    Next

    'Fill the list box and set a default value.
    With lstFolders
        .Clear
        .List = aFolders
        .ListIndex = 1
    End With
End Sub
```

RETURNING A VALUE FROM A LIST CONTROL

To read the contents of a list control that is using only one column, you can call either the Text property or the Value property. Both of these return a string value that represents the currently selected item. If you prefer to return an index number that indicates the selection, use the ListIndex property. All three of the following lines of code return the currently selected item in the cboFolders combo box:

```
cboFolders.Text
cboFolders.Value
cboFolders.ListIndex
```

Multiple column list controls work differently. More often than not, you want to return a particular column of information, not the entire row. To get to a particular column in the selected item, pass the ListIndex property as well as the column index number to the List property of the control. For example, the following code returns a string for the value in the first column of the currently selected item in a list box named lstFolders:

```
StrResult = lstFolders.List(lstFolders.ListIndex, 0)
```

DETECTING WHEN DATA CHANGES

To detect when data in an item changes, you must write code in one of two events designed to trap such occurrences: the PropertyChange event and the CustomPropertyChange event. To trap when data in a built-in field changes, use the PropertyChange event. This event is triggered when fields such as Subject and StartTime change. If you want to trap when a custom field that you created changes, write code in the CustomPropertyChange event.

Both of these events are triggered when any field changes. In other words, if you have three user-defined fields in a form, any code in the CustomPropertyChange event is triggered when any of these three fields change. Although this is a nice touch, it's not so nice if you have 30 custom fields and want to know only when 2 or 3 specific fields change. To filter out fields, both of these events are passed a *Name* argument indicating the field that triggered the event. You can then use this argument to filter out unwanted fields. For example, the following CustomPropertyChange event procedure is triggered when any custom field on the current form changes, but only the field strLastName actually allows the code to run:

```
Sub Item_CustomPropertyChange(ByVal Name)
    'Test for the custom field name
    ' that triggered the event.
    If Name = "strFolderName" Then
        'Display the current value.
        MsgBox Item.UserProperties(Name)
    End If
End Sub
```

MOVING FOCUS TO A CONTROL AND SELECTING TEXT

Although you can set the tabbing order for the controls on an Outlook form using **Tab Order** on the **Layout** menu, situations might often require you to interrupt that pattern and move the cursor to a particular control. You can use the SetFocus method to force the cursor to go to a control nearly any time. Cursor control is helpful when you need to urge the user to address an issue of a control at a particular time. For example, consider a form that uses the Close event for validation of multiple controls. If one of those controls contains data that violates a validation rule, you want to alert the user to the error and also place the cursor in the control that contains the illegal information. The SetFocus method of a control allows you to do this, which saves the user time searching for the correct field.

To move the cursor to a particular control, call the SetFocus method of the control in which to place the focus. For example, the following code places the cursor in a control named TxtDescription:

```
TxtDescription.SetFocus
```

Once a control has the focus, you can also take charge of the highlighting inside of the control if it is a text box or a combo box. This highlighting not only "pulls" the eye to the problem area, but also saves the user time by selecting the data for quick deletion. A number of properties work together to control the highlighted text:

- **SelStart**. Sets or returns the starting point of the selected text or the cursor position.

- **SelLength**. Sets or returns the number of characters selected.

- **SelText**. Returns a string that represents the currently selected text. If no text is selected, this property returns a Null value.

In the following code sample, a text box is tested to see if it contains any alphabetical characters. Because the ID field should be all numeric, the user is alerted to the problem and then the SetFocus method is used to send the cursor to that control. Next the SelStart property sets the start of the highlighting to right before the first character. The SelLength property makes sure that the highlighting covers all contents of the text box.

```
Sub ValidateContents()
    'Test for alpha characters in the text box.
    If Not IsNumeric(txtEmpID.Text) Then
        MsgBox "ID must contain only numbers.", vbInformation
        With txtEmpID
            'Move the focus to the control.
            .SetFocus
            'Set the start and length of the highlighting.
            .selstart = 0
            .sellength = Len(txtEmpID.Text)
        End With
    End If
End Sub
```

CONTROLLING THE BODY OF ITEMS

In previous versions of Outlook, the only way to fill the body of an item was through the Body property. For example, the following line of code places text and a hyperlink in the body of an item:

```
Item.Body = "Check out this Web site for information on Outlook
development: " _
& vbCrLf & "<http://www.microsoft.com/outlookdev>"
```

Although this was fine for simply entering and reading information, you were unable to do much in the way of formatting the text. This was also the reason why many users didn't use the standard editors in Outlook. Many users switched to special editors with extra features, such as Word or HTML editors, to edit the body of the item. Although this was great for users, developers had no way to take advantage of those same features. Until Outlook 2000, that is. Now you have the ability to format the body when different editors are used. You can control Word or the Microsoft Internet Explorer Document object through special objects in the Outlook object model.

NOTE   You can only format the body for e-mail messages and posts.

USING WORD AS THE EDITOR

Microsoft Word is by far the more popular editor because of its extensive formatting capabilities. To determine if Word is used as the editor in a message, you use the IsWordMail property of an Inspector object. The IsWordMail property returns True if Word is used as the editor. If Word is used, you can then access a Word editor through the WordEditor property of an Inspector object. This property returns a reference to the Word document being used in the body of the message.

```
If Not inspCurrent.IsWordMail Then
    Exit Sub
End If


Set wdeDoc = Item.GetInspector.WordEditor
```

Before going any farther, you should be aware of the odd behavior of Outlook and the Word editor. If you attempt to access the Word document when the cursor has not been placed in the body of the message, an error message states that you are not in the control. If the user has already clicked inside the body, this message won't appear, but you can't always rely on users to do what you want them to do! To avoid this scenario completely, place the focus of the cursor in the body with the SetFocus method. To navigate to that page, you must have changed it in some way. Simply accessing the Properties page for any control on that page accomplishes this. Now you can go ahead and access the Word object model. These following few lines of code add text as well as some formatting to the item.

```
Set rng = wdeDoc.Range(0, 0)
With rng
    .Text = "This is the Word editor."
    .Font.Size = 16
    .InsertParagraphAfter
    .InsertAfter "How about that?"
End With
```

Listing B.4 shows how to interact with the body of a message that uses Word as the editor.

Listing B.4   Access the body of a message when Word is the editor.

```
Sub FillWordEditor()
    'Reference the current irspector.
    Set inspCurrent = Item.GetInspector
    'Reference the Message page. Page must have been
    ' altered in some way for this code to work.
    Set pgGeneral = inspCurrent.ModifiedFormPages("Message")
    'Reference the body control and set the focus in it.
    Set ctlBody = pgGeneral.Controls("Message")
    ctlBody.SetFocus

    'Test to see if Word is really being used as the editor.
    ' If not, exit the sub.
    If Not inspCurrent.IsWordMail Then
        Exit Sub
    End If

    'Return a Word document object reference.
    Set wdeDoc = Item.GetInspector.WordEditor

    'Return a Word document range object.
    Set rng = wdeDoc.Range(0, 0)
    'Insert some text and format it.
    With rng
        .Text = "This is the Word editor."
        .Font.Size = 16
        .InsertParagraphAfter
        .InsertAfter "How about that?"
    End With

    'Clean up.
    Set rng = Nothing
    Set wdeDoc = Nothing
End Sub
```

USING HTML AS THE EDITOR

When you use an HTML body as the message body, you can choose one of two ways to manipulate the body text of an e-mail message or post: the HTMLBody property of the item and the HTMLEditor property of the Inspector object. If you only want to fill the body with text, the HTMLBody property of the item is easier. Even if the item is not already configured to use HTML, this sets the body to use HTML, at least temporarily. Pass a string that uses HTML tags to the property. For example, the following lines of code fill the body of an item with text formatted in various ways:

```
Item.HTMLBody = _
    "<h1>hello there</h1><font color=red>How are you doing
today?</font>"
```

If you want to delve further into the HTML Document Object Model, you must use the other route and return a reference to the HTML Document object library. The HTMLEditor property of the Inspector objects returns a reference to the Explorer object, but only if HTML is the default editor. To check for the editor type, use the EditorType property of the Inspector object. Table B.3 lists the possible return values for this property.

Table B.3   EditorType values

Constant	Value	Description
OlEditorText	1	Basic text
OlEditorHTML	2	HTML
OlEditorRTF	3	Rich text formatting
OlEditorWord	4	Microsoft Word

Listing B.5 shows how to put all these techniques together to reference the HTML Explorer object behind an Outlook item.

Listing B.5 Control the body of a message when HTML is the editor.

```
Sub FillHTMLBody()
    'Reference the Inspector for the current item.
    Set inspCurrent = Item.GetInspector
    'If the editor type is set at anything other than HTML,
    ' exit the procedure.
    If inspCurrent.EditorType <> 2 Then
        Exit Sub
    End If

    'Return a reference to the HTML Explorer object.
    Set htmeExp = inspCurrent.HTMLEditor
    'Fill in the body of the item.
    htmeExp.Body.innerhtml = "<h1>Hello there again!</h1>"

    'Clean up
    Set htmeExp = Nothing
End Sub
```

USING CUSTOM COMMAND BARS

Outlook forms support custom command bars in the same way that other forms do. In previous versions of Outlook, creating custom command bars for forms was rather difficult. In Outlook 2000, however, you can create custom command bars with much less effort.

CREATING THE COMMAND BAR WITH THE OPEN EVENT

Because you want the command bar to be available as soon as the form is open, write the code that creates the command bar in the Open event of the form. To create a custom command bar for a form, add to the CommandBars collection of an Inspector object by using the Add method. Pass the name for the command bar as well as any positioning information. To display the command bar, you must also set the Visible property of a CommandBar object to True.

To create a control on the new command bar, add to the Controls collection of a CommandBar object and set the appropriate control properties. You should at least provide a caption or ID. To trigger code to run when the button is clicked, set the OnAction property to a string value with the procedure name.

Listing B.6 shows how to create a custom command bar for an Outlook form.

Listing B.6   Create a custom command bar on a form.

```
Function Item_Open()
    Set isp = Item.GetInspector
    Set nsMAPI = Application.GetNamespace("MAPI")

    'Create the command bar.
    Set cbr = isp.CommandBars.Add("NewCommandBar", msoBarTop)
    'Add a control.
    Set cbt = cbr.Controls.Add
    With cbt
        'Give the button a caption.
        .Caption = "Display Current User Name"
        'Attach a procedure to run when the button is clicked.
        .OnAction = "DisplayUserName"
    End With

    'Display the command bar.
    cbr.Visible = True
End Function


Sub DisplayUserName()
    'Display the name of the user currently logged.
    MsgBox nsMAPI.CurrentUser
End Sub
```

MAKING COMMAND BARS TEMPORARY

The temp argument flushes the cache after a user exits Outlook but not after the user closes each item. Therefore, if your custom form uses a custom command bar that is built with the Open event, a new command bar is created each time an item that uses the form is opened. Let's say a custom contact form is used with a public folder for contacts. A user regularly investigates 50+ other users a day. That means 50+ instances of that custom command bar are currently stored in memory on that user's machine!

An alternative is to detect the custom toolbar before recreating it. Once detected, options are to delete and then recreate it to assure it is the most up-to-date version (users do modify things they shouldn't) or to create the toolbar only if it isn't detected.

As you might expect, VBScript requires you to access command bars in a slightly different manner than you would by using VBA. To access an individual command bar with the CommandBars collection, you must first point to the CommandBars collection and then proceed to loop through the contents. To determine if you have located the proper command bar, call the Name property of each command bar and test it against the name of your custom command bar. If you locate it, you can then take whatever action you desire. For example, the following code sample loops through the command bars for an Inspector object and deletes a custom command bar named Test if it is found in the collection.

```
For Each cbr In isp.CommandBars
    If cbr.Name = "Test" Then
        cbr.Delete
        Exit For
    End If
Next
```

DISTRIBUTING OUTLOOK FORMS

After you finish customizing your Outlook form, you need to make the form available to other users. You can save a form in one of three ways:

- Save the current instance of the form, including the currently entered data.

- Save the form as a template file.

- Save the form to a forms library to make it readily available to other users in addition to yourself.

For all these scenarios, you should consider protecting the form design with a password.

PROTECTING YOUR FORM DESIGN

Even if not intentionally malicious, a misguided user can inadvertently wreak havoc in a custom form if they have access to it. To protect your form design from curious users, you can add password protection. To add password protection, click on the Properties page when the form is open in design mode. Select Protect form design and set a password, preferably one that uses a combination of letters, numbers, and characters. This password doesn't prevent people from opening the form, but it does prevent the form from being opened in design mode. Once a password is in place, whenever someone attempts to open the form in design mode, a **Password** dialog box appears (see Figure B.3).

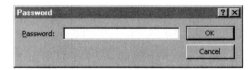

Figure B.3
The Password dialog box

SAVING THE CURRENT INSTANCE OF A FORM

One way to save a form is to create a one-off form. A one-off form is a custom form saved with data in it and it is not reused. While testing your form, you have probably come across a dialog box that prompts you to save your work in this manner. You create a one-off by saving an item after you have modified the underlying form. You can save the item either through the **Save** command on the **File** menu or with the **Save** dialog box.

CREATING A FORM TEMPLATE

Probably the smartest thing you can do when developing a custom form is to save your form as a template file and save it often. An Outlook form template is a file with an .oft extension that can be stored on a local or remote machine like any other file. You can use a form template as a backup in case the actual form is lost during development. Because the template exists as an actual file, you can attach a template to e-mail messages and distribute it in this manner. To save a form as a template, on the **File** menu, click **Save As**. The standard **Save As** dialog box appears and allows you to select a folder and a name for your template file.

PUBLISHING TO A FORMS LIBRARY

To make an Outlook form available throughout your organization, publish the form to a forms library. A forms library is a storage location for form definitions. You can select from a number of forms libraries, depending on the intended outcome:

- **Personal Forms Library**. This library is maintained in your inbox. Forms stored here are available only to you and from any folder. To access a form stored in the Personal Forms library, on the **File** menu, click **New**, and then click **Choose Form**. on **Look In** list, select **Personal Forms Library**.

- **Folder Forms Library**. A form library is available for every personal and public folder. Forms published to a specific folder library are available from only that folder. If a form is published to a personal folder, the form is accessible to anyone with access to the personal folder. If a form is published to a public folder, the form is accessible to anyone with access to the public folder. These forms can be created from the **Actions** menu by configuring the folder to use the form as the default message class.

- **Organizational Forms Library**. This library is maintained on the computer running Exchange Server. Forms published here are available to anyone from any folder. You must have appropriate permissions to publish forms to the Organization forms library. To access a form stored in the Personal Forms Library, on the **File** menu, click **New**, and then click **Choose Form**. On the **Look In** list, select **Organizational Forms** from.

To publish a form to a forms library, on the **Tools** menu, point to **Personal Forms**, and click **Publish Form As**. The **Publish Form As** dialog box appears (see Figure B.4).

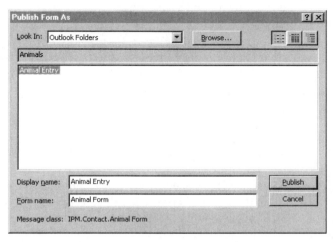

Figure B.4
The Publish Form As dialog box lets you set the form name and the library in which the form is
published.

To successfully publish the form:

1. Enter a display name. The display name can be different from the form name
    and is generally a bit friendlier. It is used to identify a form in a library, provide
    the menu command name on the Actions menu if the form is published to a
    folder library, and determine the caption on the Inspector window.

2. Enter a name for the form. This value determines the message class name for
    the form, which is used by Outlook to identify the form used to create an item.

3. On the **Look In** list, select a form library. If you want to publish to a folder
    library, select **Outlook Folders**, and then click **Browse** to select the folder.

4. Click **Publish** to save the form definition to the library.

UNDERSTANDING HOW PUBLISHED FORMS WORK

Once a form is published to a forms library, you can create items by using the new
custom form. But how exactly does this work? The answer lies in understanding
message classes and the forms cache.

When a form is published, the message class name and its associated form definition are stored in the appropriate library, not with each individual item. Instead, the message class name is stored in the MessageClass property of the custom form. When an item is created and saved for the first time, a dialog box titled **Installing the Form on Your Machine** appears with a status bar. Meanwhile, in the background two things happen: the message class information is saved to this property, and the form definition is copied from the form library to a local forms store known as the forms cache.

The forms cache is a folder on each user computer (C:\\windows\..\application Data\Forms) for locally storing information about Outlook forms. The purpose of the forms cache is to improve performance times by loading the form from a local file rather than downloading it from the server each time a user opens an item with the same form definition. When a new item is created with a custom form, a subfolder with nearly the same name is created, and the form definition file is added to the new folder. All these folders and their contents are managed by a forms table (frmcache.dat) located in the **Forms** folder as well.

The real benefit of the forms cache is apparent when you look at what happens when a user opens an existing item. When a user opens an existing item, Outlook checks the MessageClass property to determine which form definition to use. Outlook then finds the associated form definition file. The search order utilized by Outlook is:

1. Standard forms in the Application forms library. Because the majority of forms use the standard form definitions, Outlook checks this library first.

2. Forms already stored in the forms cache. If the message class isn't found in the Application forms library, Outlook checks the local forms cache in case the definition is stored locally.

3. Form library for the current folder. Fewer forms are be stored in folder libraries than elsewhere, so Outlook can quickly check the folder library. If the form definition is found, Outlook copies it to the forms cache.

4. Personal forms library. Because this is a local library, Outlook checks it before the Organization library. If the form definition is found, Outlook copies it to the forms cache.

5. Organization forms library. This is done last to minimize network traffic. If the form definition is found, it is copied to the forms cache.

Once Outlook locates the form, it abandons any further searching, and the item is opened with the appropriate form definition. To really appreciate the benefit of the forms cache, imagine accessing forms stored in the Organizational Forms Library. If the forms cache didn't exist, Outlook would need to refer to the server each time an item that uses the form is opened.

PUBLISHING WITH THE FORM DEFINITION

If you attempt to publish a custom message form, Outlook prompts you to save the form definition along with the item (see Figure B.5).

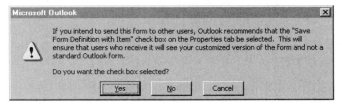

Figure B.5
When you publish a message form, Outlook prompts you to set a property to save the form definition along with every item created by using the form.

Whenever you create and save an item that uses a custom form, the message class name is stored in the MessageClass field of the item. When you open the item, Outlook locates the form definition identified by the message class name and uses it to render the graphical form interface. When you save an item with the form definition, the actual form definition file is stored along with the item. This assures that recipients of the e-mail message can access the custom form used to create the item. As you would imagine, this greatly increases the size of the item.

> **NOTE**   If the form is published to Organizational Forms Library, this is not necessary because everyone in the organization has access to the form definition.

After you publish a form and attempt to close it, the **Save** dialog box usually appears. Don't worry; the form was successfully published. Outlook just checks that you also want to save the form with the current data in it to a default folder store. Regardless of what you decide to do, the form is now registered in the form library.

USING A CUSTOM FORM AS THE DEFAULT FORM IN A FOLDER

If the custom form you created is to be used with a specific folder, you want to be sure that the user can create a new item based on that form in more than one way. When a form is published to a folder, a menu command is added to the Actions menu for the folder explorer window. However, if the user double-clicks in an empty area of the explorer window or clicks **New** on the **File** menu to create a new item of that type, or clicks **New**, a new item is opened based on the default form type, not the custom form. This can be quite confusing and frustrating to people who use your solution. Rather than forcing the users to conform to one method of creating items, you can change the behavior of the folder by setting a folder property to use your custom form as opposed to the default form.

To change the property, on the folder list, right-click the folder of interest. On the shortcut list, select **Properties**. On the default page, set the **When Posting to This Folder Use** option to the custom form.

MANAGING AND MAINTAINING OUTLOOK FORMS

Your work is not over after you have distributed an Outlook form. Form maintenance is a nearly constant task. Fortunately, you can manage an Outlook form much easier than you can manage another form type. Exchange and Outlook work together to make sure that clients always use the latest version of all custom forms.

DISTRIBUTING A NEW VERSION OF A FORM

When you update a form in other form packages, you must redistribute the form to every client computer. Not so with Outlook. In Outlook, you need to republish the revised form to only the appropriate library. The new form information is then replicated down into the forms cache. As long as the message class name has not been changed, any item that used the old version of the form automatically uses the new version of the form.

UPDATING THE MESSAGECLASS PROPERTY

As mentioned earlier, each item has a MessageClass property that indicates which Outlook form is used to display the item. When you publish a new version of a form, all items that currently use that form automatically use the new version. However, if you want items that currently use one message class to use another message class, you must change the property with code.

One way to change the MessageClass property on existing items is to use code that loops through the contents of the folder and sets the MessageClass property for each item to the appropriate form name. For example, Listing B.7 shows code written in an Outlook form that updates the MessageClass property for all items that do not use a specified form.

Listing B.7 Change the MessageClass property to change the form associated with an item.

```
Sub cmdReplaceForm_Click()
    Dim fdChange
    Dim i

    'Reference the actively displayed folder.
    Set fdChange = Application.ActiveExplorer.CurrentFolder

    For Each itm In fdChange.Items
        'If the form is using anything other than the custom form,
        ' change the MessageClass property and save the item.
        If itm.MessageClass <> txtformname.Text Then
            itm.MessageClass = txtformname.Text
            itm.Save
            i = i + 1
        End If
    Next

    MsgBox "Form change completed. " & i & " items changed."
End Sub
```

Glossary

absolute URL

A URL that has the full address necessary for locating a resource in a Web Storage System. For example, HTTP://cyberserver/zoo management/.

access control entry (ACE)

An individual item in an access control list (ACL). Every user or group object that has rights to access a Web Storage System resource is listed in the resource's ACL as an individual ACE.

access control list (ACL)

A listing for a Web Storage System resource that indicates which users and groups have access permissions. Individual entries in the list are known as access control entries (ACE).

access mask

A 32-bit number in which the upper 16 bits define standard and generic access rights and the lower 16 bits define access rights that are specific to the folder or item.

access token

Information that the domain controller generates for a user account when the user is successfully authenticated. The token consists of the security identifier (SID) of the user and of the groups that the user account belongs to. The token is used in all processes that this user executes in the Windows domain.

action

Workflow task detailing how an item moves from state to state or executes script without causing a change in state. An action table is used to automate and enforce the order in which various tasks must be completed from start to finish.

action table

A set of rules that define how workflow items can change state. Each row in the table represents a possible state transition in the workflow.

Active Directory

The directory service for Windows 2000 Server. It stores information about objects on the network and makes this information available for authorized administrators and users. Active Directory gives network users access to permitted resources anywhere on the network using a single logon process. It provides administrators with an intuitive hierarchical view of the network and a single point of administration for all network objects.

Active Directory Service Interface (ADSI)

A dual-interfaced model that allows programmatic access to underlying directory services through a common command set. ADSI is dual-interfaced in that it extends the IDispatch interface and provides access to defined methods through the v-table and through the seven methods defined by the IDispatch interface.

Active Server Pages (ASP)

The server-side scripting environment of Microsoft Internet Information Server (IIS) that can be used to build interactive high-performance Web-based applications. The phrase *ASP page* refers to the Web page that actually appears in the browser, and *.asp file* refers to the file that generates the Web page.

ActiveX Data Objects (ADO)

A collection of data access objects in a hierarchical object library. ADO enables you to write a client application to access and manipulate data in a database server through a provider (database interface) such as Microsoft Internet Information Server 4.0.

addressee

A recipient of e-mail or meeting requests. An addressee is identified using a complete e-mail address or newsgroup name. Represented by the CDO Addressee object.

asynchronous events

A type of event that fires after a change has been fully committed to the Web Storage System. Asynchronous events do not block the Web Storage System thread but instead fire after the action has been committed. They are best used for simple notification tasks.

attendee

A person invited to attend a meeting or appointment. An attendee can accept, decline, or ignore a meeting request. Represented by the CDO Attendee object.

bind

To associate two pieces of information with one another. *Bind* is most often used with reference to associating a symbol (such as the name of a variable) with some descriptive information (such as a memory address, a data type, or an actual value). Binding is also sometimes referred to as *linking*.

child node

In a tree structure, the relationship of a node to its immediate predecessor.

class

In object-oriented programming, a generalized category that describes a group of more specific items, called *objects*, which can exist within it. A class is a descriptive tool used in a program to define a set of attributes or a set of services that characterize any member (object) of the class.

Collaboration Data Objects (CDO)

An application programming interface that allows users and applications high-level access to data objects in Exchange. CDO defines the concept of different object classes, including messages, posts, appointments, and tasks.

collection record

A folder resource that contains a collection of child resources. A child resource can be an item, a structured document, or a folder. Compare this to *non-collection records*, which can be individual items in a folder, structured documents, or text files that do not have child resources.

COM+ role-based security

A type of security that assigns permissions known as roles to a group of users. A role can then be assigned to the entire application or to specific parts, such as an interface or a method, to restrict only the necessary parts of an application. This level of control often eliminates the need to incorporate security-based code in the application itself.

common name (CN)

The first part of a relative distinguished name. There are two types of CNs: the name of an object or container and its direct parent container.

contact

A resource in either a Web Storage System folder or in Active Directory. In a folder, a contact is a compilation of information about an individual. In Active Directory, a contact can be an entry for storing basic information about a person. For either kind of resource, you use the CDO Person object to create new contacts and edit existing ones.

content class

A name identifying the intent or purpose of an item. Content class determines which Web Storage System schema properties are associated with a resource when it is created.

coordinated universal time (UTC)

For all practical purposes, the same as Greenwich Mean Time. Appointments are stored in the Web Storage System in UTC and converted by the client program to the appropriate time zone. Also known as *Universal Time Coordinate* (UTC).

data island

XML data that is embedded in a well-formatted HTML document.

distinguished name (DN)

An identifier for an object that is unique across the entire Active Directory. For example, /O=Internet/DC=COM/DC=Domain/CN=Users/CN=Peter Waxman refers to the "Peter Waxman" user object in the Domain.com domain. The name identifies the domain that holds an object as well as the complete path through the container hierarchy used to access the object.

distribution group

A type of Group object used to group user objects together. Distribution groups are not security enabled. Distribution groups are used most predominantly to send e-mail messages to a collection of recipients.

dynamic-link library (DLL)

An operating system feature that allows executable routines (generally serving a specific function or set of functions) to be stored separately as files with .dll extensions. These routines are loaded only when needed by the program that calls them.

event

The occurrence of some particular action or the occurrence of a change of state that can be handled by an event sink. For example, the arrival of a message to the SMTP service is an event that can be handled by a number of event sinks.

event registration

An item residing in a folder that uses an event sink. The item provides the information store with information that includes what events will trigger the sink, the name of the sink, and options such as restrictions for when the event will fire. The event registration item can be created with either ADO or with a special script tool that can be used in batch files known as RegEvent.

event sink

Code that gets activated through a defined trigger, such as the receipt of a new message. The code is normally written in any COM-compatible programming language, such as Microsoft Visual Basic, Microsoft Visual Basic Scripting Edition (VBScript), Netscape JavaScript, and C/C++. Microsoft Exchange 2000 supports transport, protocol, and store event sinks. Event sinks on the store can be synchronous (code executes as the event is triggered) or asynchronous (code executes sometime after the event).

Exception

A specific appointment that is added, modified, or deleted from the pattern of a recurring appointment or meeting.

Exchange Message Link (EML)

The file format returned by Exchange items. It has the .eml file name extension.

Exchange roles

A compilation of permissions that define a particular behavior. Exchange roles are not defined in Active Directory but rather in the Exchange 2000 stores with the item itself. The system evaluates a role at run time when a user accesses a folder or item to determine which permissions that user has and what exactly they are allowed to do.

Extensible Markup Language (XML)

A tag language based on Standard Generalized Markup Language (SGML) that is optimized for delivery over the World Wide Web. XML defines data layout for a document but not display characteristics, which are commonly defined using HTML. It permits data to be manipulated using Hypertext Transfer Protocol (HTTP), Web Distributed Authoring and Versioning (WebDAV), and Extensible Stylesheet Language (XSL) among different applications on different platforms. XML is not required to conform to the HTML specification.

folder tree

A hierarchy of folders in the Web Storage System, very similar in structure to the standard file system. A single folder can contain child folders, which, in turn, can contain other child folders.

free/busy status

The availability of a person. In addition to free and busy, the status can also be out of office (OOF) or tentative.

Hypertext Transfer Protocol (HTTP)

An Internet standard protocol that lets Web browsers like Microsoft Internet Explorer access Web Storage Systems. Web Distributed Authoring and Versioning (WebDAV) is an extension to HTTP that you can use to build applications that are writeable instead of just read-only.

impersonation

Using another user object's credentials to accomplish programmatic tasks.

information store

Storage technology used by Exchange to store users' mailboxes and folders. There are two kinds of stores: mailbox stores and public stores. An information store consists of a rich-text database (.edb), plus a "streaming" native Internet content database (.stm). Each information store is a single Web Storage System.

Installable File System (IFS)

A technology in Exchange 2000 Server that makes mailboxes and public folders available as traditional folders and files through shared network drives. You can use IFS to treat Exchange as a file repository for any application.

interface

An encapsulated set of properties and methods, some of which are specific to certain classes, but others define a common functionality. By encapsulating properties and methods in this way, interfaces can be easily shared among predefined and custom classes.

Internet Mail Access Protocol version 4 (IMAP4)

An Internet messaging protocol that enables a client to access e-mail on a server rather than downloading it to the user's computer. IMAP4 is designed for an environment where users log on to the server from a variety of different workstations.

interrupt

A request for attention from the processor. When the processor receives an interrupt, it suspends its current operations, saves the status of its work, and transfers control to a special routine known as an interrupt handler, which contains the instructions for dealing with the particular situation that caused the interrupt. Also known as *trap*.

LDAP binding string

A path string associated with an item in Active Directory that represents its exact location in the directory store. This string is known as the LDAP binding string (or the *ADsPath string*), and it is used to connect to Active Directory, open user objects, access groups, and navigate containers.

Lightweight Directory Access Protocol (LDAP)

The standard Internet protocol used for directory access. It is the wire protocol used to conduct conversations between a client application and Active Directory across the network. An LDAP application can access any directory service that exposes an LDAP protocol. The LDAP client library (WLDAP32.dll) is installed with all versions of Microsoft Windows 2000.

mailbox store

A database for storing mailboxes in Exchange 2000 Server. Mailbox stores store data that is private to an individual and contain the mailbox folders generated when a new mailbox is created for an individual.

mailbox-enabled object

A type of object that not only has an e-mail address in the organization but also has an Exchange mailbox to go with it. Because Exchange uses Microsoft Windows security and authentication and thus requires that mailboxes have a security principal, only User objects can be mailbox-enabled.

mail-enabled object

A type of object that has an e-mail address on a domain in the organization, but the object does not have a mailbox in the domain at which to receive messages. The object appears in the global address list, which allows other people in the organization to easily locate or send a message to that person, but the administrator has no need of managing an unnecessary mailbox. Contacts, users, and even folders can be mail-enabled.

Messaging Application Programming Interface (MAPI)

A messaging architecture enabling multiple applications to interact with different messaging systems across a variety of hardware platforms. MAPI is built on the COM foundation.

metadata

Detailed information about a piece of data. For example, the title, subject, author, and size of a file constitute metadata about the file.

Microsoft Data Access Components (MDAC)

The latest versions of ActiveX Data Objects (ADO), OLE DB, and Open Database Connectivity (ODBC), which are released, documented, and supported together.

Microsoft Internet Publishing Provider (MSDAIPP)

An alternative provider to ExOLEDB. MSDAIPP is a provider that is used on the client machine so that you can use ADO 2.5 to access a Web Storage System. It can be used on systems running Microsoft Windows 2000, Microsoft Windows 95 and later, and Microsoft Windows NT 4.0. It is installed with Internet Explorer 5.0 and later and with Microsoft Office 2000.

Microsoft Management Console (MMC)

A management display framework that hosts administration tools and applications. Using MMC, you can create, save, and open collections of tools and applications. Saved collections of tools and applications are called consoles.

MIME Encapsulation of Aggregate HTML Documents (MHTML)

An Internet standard that defines the MIME structure used to send HTML content in message bodies along with those elements used in a Web page.

multistatus indicator

The top-level object in an XML response. The multistatus indicator indicates that more than one chunk of information has been returned in the response.

multi-valued property

A property that can hold multiple values, called an array of values. A multi-valued property is a less common than a single-valued property.

namespace

A logical collection of properties in Web Storage System schema. A namespace serves to group related properties together for easy property discovery and, more importantly, to keep the property names unique.

Network News Transfer Protocol (NNTP)

An Internet standard protocol used across Transmission Control Protocol/Internet Protocol (TCP/IP) networks for accessing newsgroups through an NNTP-compatible client such as Microsoft Outlook Express. You can use NNTP to build online discussions and set up newsgroup applications.

newsgroup

An Internet discussion group that focuses on a particular category of interest.

non-collection records

Individual items in a folder, structured documents, or text files. Compare this to collection records, which are folders that may contain child resources.

persistence

A property of a programming language where created objects and variables continue to exist and retain their values between runs of the program.

Post Office Protocol version 3 (POP3)

An Internet standard protocol that allows a user to download e-mail from his or her Inbox on a server to the client computer where messages are managed. This protocol works well for computers that are unable to maintain a continuous connection to a server.

public store

A database for storing public folders in Exchange 2000 Server. A public store can be accessible to everyone in an organization or can be restricted to a subset of individuals such as a department or team.

recurring meeting

A meeting that occurs multiple times following a specific pattern that indicates how often the individual instances will occur.

recursive event

An event that can be registered for a parent folder as well as for any child folders.

relative distinguished name

The first part of a distinguished name. The RDN is the common name of the Active Directory object. For example, CN=Peter Waxman.

relative URL

A URL that contains only a partial address and uses an absolute URL as a reference point for navigating in a hierarchy.

reminder

A way to alert users about an upcoming appointment or meeting using a sound and/or a dialog box.

remote procedure call (RPC)

A protocol standard used to write routines that send information in packet format over the network.

replica

A copy of a public folder store that contains all of the folder's contents, permissions, and design elements, such as forms behavior and views. Replicas are useful for distributing user load on servers, distributing public folders geographically, and for backing up public folder data.

resolve (an address)

To check that an e-mail address belongs to a user in a specific domain or to a contact entry in Microsoft Active Directory. Resolving an address helps minimize the number of undeliverable alerts that a sender receives.

resource

Anything placed in the Web Storage System. A resource can be an e-mail message, an appointment, another folder, a Web page, or any structured document such as an Excel spreadsheet.

sandbox

A feature, such as restricted mode, that prevents code from tampering with the system.

security descriptor

Contains information about the security attributes for a Web Storage System resource including a list of users and groups that have access permissions to the resource.

security group

A type of Group object used to group user objects together. Security groups are security enabled. They are used primarily to control access to shared resources by setting permissions. They can also be used to indicate how a resource can be managed. In addition, the group can also have an e-mail alias. These groups can be added to Access Control Lists (ACLs) on resources.

security identifier (SID)

A value that identifies the user or group object being granted or denied access rights. The user or group object's SID identifies the specific access control entry (ACE).

security principal

An object that can be granted and denied rights to access resources on the network.

semantics

The logic that serves as the underpinning of programming syntax. A program that is syntactically correct can be semantically incorrect.

Simple Mail Transfer Protocol (SMTP)

An industry standard for Internet e-mail delivery. This is the native protocol that Microsoft Exchange uses to transfer messages.

single-valued property

A property that can hold only one value at a time. This is the most common property type.

snap-in

A Microsoft Management Console (MMC) extension. A snap-in is used to manage services for a component or product.

state

The status of an item in a workflow process. As an item moves through a workflow process, it assumes different states. You use an item's state to track its progress through a workflow process. Also, see *action*.

storage group

Storage groups are created with Exchange System Manager and are used to organize multiple Web Storage Systems into more manageable units in Exchange. Used primarily for building or returning and setting mailbox settings stored in Active Directory. The name of a storage group is not needed to access the contents of a mailbox or of a public Web Storage System.

synchronous events

Events that fire immediately before an item is committed to the Web Storage System. These events block the Web Storage System thread until the event thread has finished executing. While executing, a synchronous event has exclusive control over the item that triggered the event. No other process or request can access the item until the event sink is finished executing.

system events

Events that are not tied to any particular item or folder in the Web Storage System. Instead, they are associated with general actions such as the starting of a database or the system clock reaching a certain time. Within their context, they behave as asynchronous events and do not fire until after the Web Storage System has completed the action triggering the event.

transaction

A kind of database processing in which calls are cached and executed at the same time.

trap

See *interrupt*.

virtual directory

A name used to access the contents of any Web Storage System using a Web browser. The virtual directory name is used to open a mailbox as well as browse the folders of a public store. This name is also used in URLs using the Microsoft Internet Publishing Provider (MSDAIPP), which includes both hyperlinks in Web pages as well as ADO client-side code.

Web Storage System

A storage platform that provides a single repository for managing multiple types of unstructured information in one infrastructure. The Web Storage System combines the features and functionality of the file system, the Web, and a collaboration server (such as Exchange 2000 Server) through a single, URL addressable location for storing, accessing, and managing information, as well as building and running applications. The Web Storage System is based on the technology that drives Exchange Server Information Store.

Web Storage System schema

The data definition of a single Web Storage System—used to define all of the resources, such as folders, items, and Web files, found in the store. The schema consists of a large number of predefined schema properties, which determine the qualities, such as the creation date or the display name, for a resource.

WebDAV protocol

A protocol that can be used to access items in a Web Storage System. It provides a means to access not only an item's contents but also an extensible set of associated properties. Also known as the *HTTP/WebDAV protocol.*

workflow

Server-side logic that you can use to route items in a folder from one user to another and enforce and track an item throughout its lifetime.

Workflow Designer

A graphical tool that can be used to easily and quickly build workflow processes on folders.

workflow engine

An in-process server (CDOWF.DLL) that implements the IProcessInstance Advance method.

wrapper

Code that is combined with another piece of code, the wrapped code, to determine how that code is executed. The wrapper acts as an interface between its caller and the wrapped code. This may be done for compatibility—that is, if the wrapped code is in a different programming language or uses different calling conventions, or for security—that is, to prevent the calling program from executing certain functions. The implication is that the wrapped code can only be accessed via the wrapper.

Index

A

AbortChange method 441
aborting transactions 441–442
access control entries (ACE)
   access masks 664–666
   discretionary access control list
     (DACL) 663–668
   getting allow and deny entries 668–670
   overview 644
   security identifier (SID) 667
access control list (ACL) 644
access masks 664–666
access rights 548–550
access tokens 644
accessing controls vs. fields 794
accounts
   creating new administrator 690–691
   user See User objects
ACE (access control entries)
   access masks 664–666
   discretionary access control list
     (DACL) 663–668
   getting allow and deny entries 668–670
   overview 644
   security identifier (SID) 667
ACL (access control list) 644
actions, workflow 480–483, 496–501
Active Directory
   accessing domains 338
   adding members to groups 386
   ADO Command objects See Command
     objects
   ADSI See Active Directory Service
     Interfaces
   ADsPath property 397
   CDO for Exchange See CDO
     (Collaboration Data Objects) for
     Exchange
   Command objects See Command objects
   connecting to 328–336
   Contact objects See Contact objects
   creating mailboxes 366–369
   creating objects 348
   creating user accounts 354–357
   customizing mailbox settings 370–372
   deleting mailboxes 374
   deleting objects 349
   distribution groups 5
   distribution lists 5
   GetObject function 338–341
   Group objects See Group objects

Active Directory *(continued)*
   groups See groups
   identifying current users 408
   identifying domains 406–407
   LDAP See Lightweight Directory Access
     Protocol
   mailbox-enabled objects 351
   mailbox-specific properties 362–365
   mail-enabled objects 351
   moving mailboxes 372–373
   ObjectCategory property 399
   ObjectClass property 399
   objects, list of 400
   opening containers 339
   opening objects 338–341
   opening organizational units 339
   overview 5–6, 10, 327
   Person class 350
   Person objects 351
   properties 362–365
   properties for address book
     information 357–360
   property cache 342
   property values 343–347
   querying See querying Active Directory
   Root DS Entry 404, 406–407
   security principals 350
   servers 404–406
   summary 415
   Top class 399
   user accounts 354–357
   User objects See User objects
Active Directory Service Interfaces (ADSI)
   accessing domains in Active
     Directory 338
   adding members to groups 386
   ADSystemInfo objects 406–407
   compared to CDO for Exchange 333
   connecting to Active Directory 329–331
   creating objects in Active Directory 348
   deleting Contact objects 378–379
   deleting objects in Active Directory 349
   deleting User objects 378–379
   domains 404
   enumerating Contact objects 379–380
   enumerating User objects 379–380
   GetObject function 338–341
   IADsGroup interface 383
   identifying Active Directory servers 404–
     406
   identifying current users 408
   identifying domains 406–407

Active Directory Service Interfaces (ADSI)
  (*continued*)
   interfaces, common supported 336–337
   LDAP provider 330
   mail-enabled distribution groups 383–385
   moving Contact objects 376–377
   moving Group objects 391–392
   moving User objects 376–377
   opening Contact objects in Active
      Directory 376
   opening containers in Active
      Directory 339
   opening objects in Active
      Directory 338–341
   opening organizational units in Active
      Directory 339
   opening User objects in Active
      Directory 376
   overview 16–18
   property cache 342
   property values 343–347
   querying for mailboxes 409–410
   querying for servers 411–414
   Router (Activeds.dll) 330
   WinNTSystemInfo objects 408
Active DS Type Library (Activeds.tlb) 330,
   338, 427
Active Server Pages (ASP) 595–601
ActiveConnection property 400–404
Activeds.dll 330
Activeds.tlb (Active DS Type Library) 330,
   338, 427
ActiveX Data Objects (ADO) 2.5
   Active Directory querying 395–396
   ASP 595–601
   Command objects 400–404
   Connection objects *See* Connection
      objects
   constants used in Web pages 552–553
   copying resources 165–166
   creating event registration items 458–467
   creating items in MAPI folder trees 518
   data types 148–149
   deep traversal 11–13
   deleting resources 167–168
   error handling 133–135
   event registration items 458–467
   folder contents, reading 153–154
   Microsoft Internet Publishing Provider
      (MSDAIPP) 171–173
   moving resources 166–167
   object model 118–120
   overview 11–13, 117–118
   querying Active Directory 395–396
   Record objects *See* Record objects
   Recordset objects *See* Recordset objects
   relative URLs 130–131

ActiveX Data Objects (ADO) 2.5
   (*continued*)
   security 123
   security descriptor (SD) 668–670
   setting optional event properties 462–467
   setting required event properties 461–462
   streaming contents 169–171
   summary 173
ActiveX Data Objects 2.5 Library
   (Adodb.dll) 427
Add method 804–805
AddAttachment method 240–242
AddAuditEntry method 506
AddItem method 796
AddQuotes function 155, 312–315, 458
address book properties 357–360
address properties 234
Addressee objects
   AmbiguousNames property 254
   free/busy status 287
   ResolvedStatus property 254
   resolving addresses in domains 251
addresses
   ambiguous names 254
   querying Active Directory for servers
      using 413–414
   resolving in domains 250–254
addressing messages 233–235
ADO *See* ActiveX Data Objects 2.5
Adodb.dll (ActiveX Data Objects 2.5
   Library) 427
ADSI *See* Active Directory Service Interfaces
ADSI LDAP provider 330
ADSI Router 330
Adsldp.dll 330
Adsldpc.dll 330
Adsmsext.dll 330
ADsPath property 397
ADSystemInfo objects 406–407
Advanced Properties tool 781
Advanced Server 685
AmbiguousNames property 254
anonymous access 549, 679–681
Append method 146
appending custom properties to
   resources 146–149
Application forms library 810
Application log
   event errors 476–477
   workflow 506
application schema folders
   configuring 96–98
   creating 93–95, 109–110

application schema folders *(continued)*
    custom properties 99–101
    defining content classes 103–105
applications, custom schema *See* custom
  application schema
Applications Web Storage System
    creating application schema folders 93
    defining custom application schema 106
Appointment class 272
Appointment object model 273
Appointment objects
    Attendees collection 285–286
    canceling simple appointments 320–322
    converting dates and times 309–311
    identifying appointment types 315–316
    master 294–296
    modifying existing 309
    overview 272, 277
    persistent Configuration objects 281–282
    processing meeting requests 323–325
    properties 279–281
    reminders 325–326
    sending updates 319
    simple appointments 277–279
ASCII characters 759–765
ASP (Active Server Pages) 595–601
asynchronous connections 611–612
asynchronous events
    accessing event items 446
    OnDelete events 423, 443–444
    OnSave events 423, 444–445
    overview 30, 423
    reacting to 442–446
Attachments collection 273
Attachments property 257
attachments to messages, detecting and
  saving 257–258
Attendee objects 288–291
Attendees collection 272, 285–286
AuditTrailEventLog objects 180, 486
authentication for Web applications 549
AutoGenerateTextBody property 236
automatic time conversion 275

B

BeforeCheckNames events 789
BeginTrans method 132–133
benefits
    events 420
    Exchange 2000 4–9
    public folder trees 47

benefits *(continued)*
    Web Storage Systems 38–40
    XML 586
Body property 800
BodyPart objects
    ContentMediaType property 260–262
    detecting and saving attachments 257
    identifying media types 260–262
    MIME messages 228–231
    overview 227
    reading messages as 259–264
    SaveToFile method 257
    streaming 262–264
BodyParts collection 227
BOF property 152

C

Cache Results property 403
caching properties in Active Directory 342
Calendar Browser xl, 317–319
calendar folder querying
    Calendar Browser 317–319
    distinguishing between meetings and
      simple appointments 317
    identifying appointment types 315–316
    overview 311–315
Calendar namespace 734–742
calendaring *See* CDO calendaring
CalendarMessage object model 274
CalendarMessage objects 274, 323–325
CalendarParts collection 323–325
Cascading Style Sheets (CSS) 602
CD, companion xxxvi–xli, 431
CDO (Collaboration Data Objects)
  Configuration namespace 706–712
CDO (Collaboration Data Objects)
  Configuration objects 706–712
CDO (Collaboration Data Objects) Folder
  objects 207
CDO (Collaboration Data Objects) for
  Exchange
    calendaring *See* CDO calendaring
    COM classes 181
    compared to ADSI 333
    connecting to Active Directory 332
    constants used in Web pages 552–553
    contacts *See* contacts
    counting folder contents 206–208
    creating contacts in Web Storage
      Systems 221
    creating folders using CDO 203–204
    creating items in MAPI folder trees 518
    creating new resources using 192–195
    creating objects from classes 181–182

CDO (Collaboration Data Objects) for
Exchange *(continued)*
   creating user accounts 354–357
   e-mail, enabling folders for 204–206
   Folder objects 201–208
   getting started 181–185
   HomeMDB property 366–369
   IDataSource interface *See* IDataSource
     interface
   interfaces 182–183
   messaging *See* CDO messaging
   notification messages 430–431
   object library (Cdoex.dll) 227, 332
   object models 177–181
   opening Contact objects 375
   opening objects from other objects 196–
     198
   opening User objects 375
   overview 14–16, 175–181, 224
   Person objects 351
   retrieving vCard information 222–224
   schema properties 184–185
   software requirements 176
   URLs 185
   vCards 222–224
CDO (Collaboration Data Objects) Message
  objects 713
CDO (Collaboration Data Objects) NNTP
  Envelope namespace 713
CDO (Collaboration Data Objects) SMTP
  Envelope namespace 714
CDO (Collaboration Data Objects)
  Workflow namespace 715–717
CDO calendaring
   Appointment object model 273
   Appointment objects *See* Appointment
     objects
   Attachments collection 273
   Attendees collection 272
   CalendarMessage object model 274
   CalendarMessage objects 274
   canceling appointments 320–322
   canceling meetings 322
   classes 272–274
   converting dates and times 309–311
   DataSource.SaveToContainer
     method 277–279
   date storage and formatting 274–276
   Duration property 277–279
   EndTime property 277–279
   Exceptions collection 273
   Fields collection 273
   Fields.Update method 277–279
   interfaces 272–274
   meeting organizers 285, 319

CDO calendaring *(continued)*
   meetings, updating 319
   modifying existing Appointment
     objects 309
   modifying existing meeting requests 309
   overview 271–272
   persistent Configuration objects 281–282
   processing meeting requests 323–325
   querying calendars *See* querying
     calendars
   RecurrencePatterns collection 272
   reminders 325–326
   scheduling meetings *See* scheduling
     meetings
   scheduling recurring appointments and
     meetings *See* recurring appointments
     and meetings
   simple appointments 277–279
   StartTime property 277–279
   summary 326
   time storage and formatting 274–276
   time zones 276–277
CDO for Exchange Management (CDOExM)
   customizing mailbox settings 370–372
   IMailboxStore interface *See*
     IMailboxStore interface
   IMailRecipient interface 183, 360–362
   mail-enabled distribution groups 383–
     385
   object library 332
CDO for Exchange Management Library
  (Cdoexm.dll) 427
CDO for Exchange object library
  (Cdoex.dll) 427
CDO Message object model 228
CDO messaging
   classes 227
   composing messages *See* composing
     messages
   detecting attachments 257–258
   finding messages 255
   forwarding messages 266–268
   interfaces 227
   MIME messages 228–231
   opening messages 255
   overview 225–231
   persistent Configuration objects 248–250
   posting messages to newsgroups 246–
     248
   processing messages 255
   reading messages as BodyPart
     objects 259–264
   replying to messages 264–266
   resolving addresses in domains 250–254
   saving attachments 257–258
   saving messages to files 268–270
   schema properties 242–244
   sending messages *See* sending messages
   summary 270

CDO Workflow for Exchange (Cdowf.dll)
  object model 485
cdoDTEnd 312
cdoDTStart 312
Cdoex.dll (CDO for Exchange object
  library) 227, 272, 332, 427
CDOExM *See* CDO for Exchange
  Management
Cdoexm.dll (CDO for Exchange
  Management Library) 427
cdoInstanceType 315
cdoReminderOffset 325
cdoTimeZoneIDURN 276, 309
CDOWF (Collaboration Data Objects
  Workflow) object properties 715–717
Cdowf.dll (CDO Workflow for Exchange)
  object model 485
Chase Referrals property 403
classes
  Appointment 272
  CDO calendaring 272–274
  CDO messaging 227
  content *See* content classes
  folder 515
  Message 227
  Person 350
  Top 399
  XMLHTTPRequest 603
Clear method 796
Click events 787
client permissions
  assigning to MAPI public folders 647–
    649
  assigning to non-MAPI folders 650–653
  roles 648–649
  Web Storage System folders 646–658
Close events 788–789
Collaboration Data Objects for Exchange
  See CDO (Collaboration Data Objects) for
  Exchange
Collaboration Data Objects Workflow
  (CDOWF) object properties 715–717
collection records 135
collections
  Attachments 273
  Attendees 272, 285–286
  BodyParts 227
  CalendarParts 323–325
  CommandBars 804–806
  Controls 793, 804
  Errors 133–135
  Exceptions 273, 294
  Fields 140–142, 146, 184, 273
  Members 388–390
  QueryString 544

collections *(continued)*
  RecurrencePatterns 272, 294
  UserProperties 794–795
COM classes, creating objects from 181
COM Component Install Wizard 454
COM+ applications 448–457, 674–675
COM+ role-based security
  adding users to COM+ roles 677
  assigning COM+ roles to
    components 678–679
  configuring 673–679
  defining COM+ roles 675–676
  disabling anonymous access 679–681
  enabling security for COM+
    applications 674–675
  overview 672–673
command bars 804–806
Command objects
  ActiveConnection property 400–404
  ADO 400–404
  Cache Results property 403
  Chase Referrals property 403
  Page Size property 402
  properties 400–401
  SearchScope property 401
  Time Limit property 402
  TimeOut property 402
CommandBar objects 804–805
CommandBars collection 804–806
CommitTrans method 132–133
companion CD xxxvi–xli, 431
Component Services Microsoft Management
  Console (MMC) 449–456, 485
composing messages
  adding attachments 240–242
  adding body text 235–240
  addressing messages 233–235
  formatting 236–240
  HTML formatting 236–237
  MHTML formatting 238–240
  plain-text formatting 236
  schema properties 242–244
Configuration objects
  CDO messaging 227
  persistent 248–250, 281–282
configuring domain controllers 686–688
connecting to Web Storage Systems
  accessing public Web Storage System
    folders 125–126
  building URLs for ExOLEDB 124–127
  Connection objects 127
  handling errors 133–135
  overview 124

connecting to Web Storage Systems
    (continued)
    relative URLs 129–131
    transactions 131–133
Connection objects
    BeginTrans method 132–133
    closing 128–129
    CommitTrans method 132–133
    Error objects 133–135
    handling errors 133–135
    opening 128–129
    overview 124, 127
    Provider property 128–129
    relative URLs 129–131
    RollbackTrans method 132–133
    transactions 131–133
connections, asynchronous 611–612
ConnectModeEnum enumeration 137
Contact objects
    compared to User objects 352
    creating 352–360
    deleting 378–379
    enumerating 379–380
    mail-enabling 360–362
    managing 374–380
    moving 376–377
    opening 375–376
    overview 350
contacts
    computer properties 213
    creating in Web Storage Systems 221
    e-mail address and URL field
        properties 212
    identification properties 211
    miscellaneous properties 220–221
    name properties 210–211
    overview 208
    people properties 219–220
    physical address properties-home 216–
        217
    physical address properties-package and
        e-mail delivery 217–218
    physical address properties-second
        home or alternative address 218–219
    physical address properties-work 215–
        216
    properties 209–221
    telephone number properties 214–215
Contacts namespace 742–753
Container objects 339
containers
    enumerating Group Objects in 393–394
    filtering 393–394
    opening in Active Directory 339
    saving new resources to 194–195
Content Class Browser xl, 84

content classes
    Content Class Browser 84
    creating new instances of 112–113
    custom 538
    DAV:contentclass schema property 75,
        79–82
    defining 103–105, 111
    folders 76–79
    form registration items 541
    forms registry 538
    inheritance 103–105
    items 79–82
    overview 75–76
    searching for specific 82–84
ContentMediaType property 260–262
contents page of frameset pages 559–561
control events 787
controls
    controlling 795–800
    detecting data changes 798
    focus 799–800
    list controls 795–798
    selecting text 799–800
    text boxes 795
Controls collection 793, 804
Controls property 793
conventions xlii–xlvi
coordinated universal time format 274
COPY method 619–620
copying resources 165–166
CopyRecord method 165–166
Count property 257, 388–390
counting folder contents 206–208
Create method 348
CreateEventReg procedure 458
CreateMailbox method 366–369
CreateMHTMLBody method 238–240
CreateObject function 605
CreateOptions parameter 138–139
creating event sinks
    asynchronous events 442–446
    building procedures 428–430
    changing event sinks 456–457
    creating COM+ components 449–456
    creating DLLs 448
    creating dynamic-link libraries 427–432
    EventSinkTemplate DLL project 431–432
    ExOLEDB Type Library
        (Exoledb.dll) 427
    installing event sinks as COM+
        applications 448–457
    overview 426
    procedures 428–430
    reacting to asynchronous events 442–
        446
    reacting to synchronous events 432–442

creating event sinks *(continued)*
    reacting to system events 446–448
    registering DLLs 448–449
    sending notification messages 430–431
    setting references 427–428
    synchronous events 432–442
    system events 446–448
creating new administrator accounts 690–691
CScript.exe 699
CSS (Cascading Style Sheets) 602
custom application schema
    benefits 90–91
    configuring application schema
        folders 96–98
    creating 106
    creating application schema folders 93–95
    creating new instances of content
        classes 112–113
    creating schema folder structures 109–
        110
    data types 102
    defining 93–98, 106–111
    defining content classes 103–105, 111
    defining properties 99–102, 110
    how custom schema works 91–92
    inheritance 103–105
    overview 89
    returning information 113–116
custom clients, accessing resources 65
custom command bars 804–806
custom content classes 538
custom fields 794–795
custom properties
    appending to resources 146–149
    data types 102
    defining 99–102, 110
    Outlook forms 794–795
CustomPropertyChange events 788, 794–
    795, 798

D

DACL (discretionary access control
    list) 663–668
data display options 22–29
data islands 601–602, 631–634
data storage
    accessing data using URLs 56–57
    accessing individual items using
        URLs 61–62
    accessing mailboxes using URLs 59–60
    accessing public stores using URLs 58–59
    accessing resources using custom
        clients 65
    accessing resources using Windows
        Explorer 62–64
    Exchange 2000 architecture 42–43
    Exchange 2000 vs. SQL Server 40–41

data storage *(continued)*
    highly structured data 40
    overview 37
    querying Web Storage Systems 65
    replicating Web Storage System folder
        trees 66
    semistructured storage model 41
    using Exchange 2000 for 38–40
    Web Storage Systems vs. Exchange 2000
        databases 44–45
data types 102, 148–149
Data Types namespace 765
DataSource property 183
DataSource.IsDirty property 190–191
DataSource.Open method 188–190
DataSource.OpenObject method 196–198
DataSource.Save method 191
DataSource.SaveTo method 192–194
DataSource.SaveToContainer method 194–
    195, 277–279
DataSource.SaveToObject method 196–198
DataTypeEnum enumeration 148–149
dataurl parameter 544–545, 564, 569
dates
    converting 309–311
    ISO 8601 format 275
    retrieving appointments for
        specific 312–315
    storing and formatting 274–276
DAV: namespace schema properties 701–
    706
DAV:contentclass 75, 79–82, 515–521
debugging workflow script 511–512
deep traversal 11–13
default stream property 169
Delete method
    containers 349, 378–379, 392
    HTTP 621–622
    Recordset objects 168
DeleteMailbox method 374
DeleteRecord method 167–168, 323, 472–
    473
DeleteWorkflowItem method 510
deleting mailboxes 374
deleting resources 167–168
deploying applications *See* testing and
    deploying applications
developing with Exchange
    Active Directory 5–6
    ADO 11–13
    ADSI 16–18
    CDO for Exchange 14–16
    data access tools 9–22
    deploying applications 34–35
    displaying data 22–29
    Exchange System Manager 4–5

developing with Exchange *(continued)*
features of Exchange 4–9
HTTP 8
IMAP4 8
LDAP 8
NNTP 8
Outlook 2000 23–24
Outlook Web Access 24–28
overview 3
POP3 8
protocol support 8
security 33
SMTP 8
summary 35
Web Storage System events 30–31
Web Storage System forms 28–29
Web Storage System schema 9
Web Storage Systems 7
WebDAV 8
workflow logic 31–32
XML 19–22
development environments, setting
up 691–696
discretionary access control list
(DACL) 663–668
distinguished name (DN) 335–336
distribution groups
mail-enabled 383–385
overview 5, 381
distribution lists 5
DLLs (dynamic-link libraries) *See* dynamic-
link libraries
DN (distinguished name) 335–336
document conventions xlii–xlvi
DocumentElement property 602
domain controllers 686–688
domain local groups 383
domains
accessing 338
ADSI 404
identifying 406–407
identifying current users 408
querying for mailboxes 409–410
querying for servers 411–414
resolving addresses in 250–254
setting up Exchange in single
server 684–691
DOMDocument objects 631–634
dt property 670–672
Duration property 277–279
dynamic-link libraries (DLLs)
ActiveX Data Objects 2.5 Library
(Adodb.dll) 427
Adsldp.dll 330
Adsldpc.dll 330
Adsmsext.dll 330

dynamic-link libraries (DLLs) *(continued)*
CDO for Exchange (Cdoex.dll) 427
CDO for Exchange Management Library
(Cdoexm.dll) 427
CDO for Exchange object library
(Cdoex.dll) 227, 272, 332
creating 427–432, 448
ExOLEDB Type Library
(exoledb.dll) 427
registering 448–449
Router (ActImeds.dll) 330
WLDAP32.dll 328

E

EditorType property 803–804
elements, XML 592–594
e-mail
enabling folders for 204–206
messages *See* messages
EML (Exchange Message Link) 61–62
EndTime property 277–279
entities 593
enumerating Contact objects 379–380
enumerating Group objects in
containers 393–394
enumerating members of groups 388–390
enumerating User objects 379–380
enumeration, ConnectModeEnum 137
EOF property 152
error handling, ADO 133–135
Error objects 133–135
errors, event 476–477
Errors collection 133–135
Event Agents 420
Event Handler 783–785
event items 425
event registration items
creating using ADO 458–467
creating using RegEvent script 467–468
defining custom properties 474
defining ranges 463–464
deleting 472–473
disabling 471–472
http://schemas.microsoft.com/exchange/
events/EventMethod 461–462
http://schemas.microsoft.com/exchange/
events/SinkClass 461–462
identifying event sinks 462
identifying source events 461
managing 469–473
overview 425, 457
prioritizing multiple event
registrations 466–467
registering for OnTimer events 467

event registration items *(continued)*
    restricting event items 465
    returning information 469–471
    setting optional event properties 462–467
    setting required event properties 461–462
Event Registration tool xl, 461, 471
Event Registrations namespace 727–728
event sinks
    associating with events 425
    changing 456–457
    creating *See* creating event sinks
    identifying 462
    installing as COM+ applications 448–457
    overview 31, 424
    reading custom fields 475
    security 426
    transport 714
Event Viewer, debugging workflow script 512
EventRecord method 475
events
    asynchronous *See* asynchronous events
    BeforeCheckNames 789
    benefits 420
    canceling 785–787
    Click 787
    Close 788–789
    control 787
    creating procedures 783–785
    custom properties 473–475
    CustomPropertyChange 788, 794–795, 798
    errors 476–477
    event items 425
    event registration items *See* event registration items
    event sinks *See* event sinks
    features 420
    Forward 790
    IExStoreAsyncEvents interface 428
    IExStoreSyncEvents interface 428
    IExStoreSystemEvents interface 429
    OnDelete 293, 423, 443–444
    OnMDBShutDown 424, 447
    OnMDBStartUp 424, 447
    OnSave 293, 423, 444–445
    OnSyncDelete 422, 434–435
    OnSyncSave 255, 422, 435–438
    OnTimer 424, 447, 467
    Open 788, 804–805
    order of firing 787–790
    Outlook forms 782–790
    overview 419–420
    paradigm 424
    PropertyChange 788, 798

events *(continued)*
    Read 788
    recursive 464
    Reply 789
    ReplyAll 789
    SaveAttachment 788–789
    schema properties 727–728
    Send 789
    summary 477
    synchronous *See* synchronous events
    system *See* system events
    types 421–424
    Web Storage System 30–31
    Write 788–789
EventSinkTemplate DLL project 431–432
Exception objects 294
exceptions 301–305
Exceptions collection 273, 294
Exchange 2000
    accessing data using URLs 56–57
    data access paradigm 10
    data storage architecture 42
    data storage compared to SQL Server 40–41
    databases compared to Web Storage Systems 44–45
    developing with *See* developing with Exchange
    features 4–9
    Web Storage Systems *See* Web Storage Systems
Exchange 2000 SDK Help files xxxvi
Exchange Data namespace 765–768
Exchange databases compared to Web Storage Systems 44–45
Exchange development MMC console 692–696
Exchange Installable File System (IFS) 62
Exchange Message Link (EML) 61–62
Exchange Management Objects *See* CDO (Collaboration Data Objects) for Exchange
Exchange namespace 718–726
Exchange OLE DB (ExOLEDB) provider *See* ExOLEDB provider
Exchange SDK 692
Exchange Security namespace 729–731
Exchange System Manager
    assigning permissions to MAPI public folders 647–649
    assigning permissions to non-MAPI folders 650–653
    execute permissions 548
    installing Exchange 2000 servers 689
    overview 4–5
execute permissions 548–550

executeurl property 554
ExOLEDB provider
    accessing mailboxes 126
    building URLs for 124–127
    interacting with resources 185
    overview 117, 121, 176
    security 123
ExOLEDB Type Library (Exoledb.dll) 427
Explorer objects 803–804
exporting workflow processes 502
Extensible Markup Language (XML) *See* XML
Extensible Stylesheet Language (XSL) *See* XSL
exwforms.dll 536, 548

F

features
    events 420
    Exchange 2000 4–9
    public folder trees 47
    Web Storage Systems 38–40
    XML 586
Field Chooser 523–525, 781
Field objects 140–142
fields, custom 794–795
Fields collection
    Append method 146
    CDO calendaring 273
    enumerating properties 140–142
    schema properties 184
Fields.Update method 277–279
files
    .oft 808
    .xml *See* XML (Extensible Markup Language)
    Activeds.dll 330
    Activeds.tlb (Active DS Type Library) 330, 338, 427
    Adodb.dll (ActiveX Data Objects 2.5 Library) 427
    Adsldp.dll 330
    Adsldpc.dll 330
    Adsmsext.dll 330
    Cdoex.dll (CDO for Exchange object library) 227, 272, 332, 427
    Cdoexm.dll (CDO for Exchange Management Library) 427
    Cdowf.dll (CDO Workflow for Exchange) object model 485
    CScript.exe 699
    EventSinkTemplate.vdp 431–432
    Exchange 2000 SDK Help xxxvi
    Exchange Message Link (EML) 61–62
    Exoledb.dll (ExOLEDB Type Library) 427

files *(continued)*
    exwforms.dll 536, 548
    Folder Composition.exe 539
    global.asa 553
    Msxml.dll *See* XML Document Object Model (XML DOM)
    Regsvr32.exe 448–449
    WLDAP32.dll 328
    WScript.exe 699
Filter property 379–380, 393–394
filtering containers 393–394
finding messages 255
folder class 515
Folder Composition tool xli, 539–540
Folder Forms Library 808
Folder objects 201–208
folder trees
    MAPI 125, 514
    overview 43, 48
    public *See* public folder trees
    Public Folders stores 514
    replicating 66
folders
    access permissions 664–665
    accessing contents 563–568
    accessing public Web Storage System 125–126
    activating for workflow activity 501
    application schema *See* application schema folders
    assigning permissions to non-MAPI 650–653
    calendar *See* calendar folder querying; CDO calendaring
    checking for existence 199–201
    client permissions on Web Storage System 646–658
    collection records 135
    content classes 76–79
    creating 144–145, 617
    creating in MAPI folder trees 515–517
    custom forms used as default forms 812
    enabling success entries 501
    execute permissions 548
    Folder Composition tool 539–540
    forms registry 537
    Helper Tools xl
    reading contents 153–154
    returning contents 615–616
    sample application xxxviii–xl
    schema 537
    sending messages to 245–246
    Web page storage 554

folders *(continued)*
  workflow 493
  workflow logic 31–32
form registration item properties
  accessing folder contents 563
  contents page of frameset pages 560
  core properties 541
  creating items 573
  displaying items 568
  frameset pages 558
  main page of frameset pages 562
  optional properties 543
  saving items 575
  simple home pages 555
form registration items
  accessing folder contents 563–568
  accessing parameters from Web
    pages 544–545
  creating 541–543, 554, 573–574
  deleting 579–581
  displaying 568–572
  folders for Web page storage 554
  frameset home page creation 557–563
  Outlook Web Access 581–584
  overview 533
  properties *See* form registration item
    properties
  saving 574–578
  simple home page creation 555–556
Form Registrations namespace 768–770
forms
  Outlook 2000 *See* Outlook forms
  Web Storage System *See* Web Storage
    System forms
forms registry
  configuring 537–540
  content classes 538
  folders 537
  Forms Registry Explorer tool xli, 545–547
  overview 533
Forms Registry Explorer tool xli, 545–547
Forms Renderer 536
formurl parameter 544–545
formurl property 554
Forward events 790
Forward method 266–268
forwarding messages 266–268
frameset home page creation 557–563
free/busy status 287–291
Frequency property 297–298
From property 234
FrontPage 2000 551–552, 691
FrontPage 2000 Server Extensions 691

Full Text Querying namespace 732–733
functions
  AddQuotes 155, 312–315, 458
  CreateObject 605
  GetObject 338–341
  GetStorageName 407
  HandleStateChange 611–612
  HasMailboxInDomain 251–253
  ISOFormat 311–315
  Response.Redirect 576, 578
  Server.Transfer 578
  TimeZoneConverter 309–315

G

Get method 342–343
GetChildren method 151
GetDecodedContentStream method 264
GetEx method 342, 344
GetFreeBusy method 288–291
GetInfo method 342, 344
GetInspector property 791
GetInterface method 183
GetList method 344
GetNewWorkflowMessage method 508–509
GetObject function 338–341
GetObject method 339
GetRecord method 440–441
GetRecurringMaster method 306
GetStorageName function 407
GetStream method 263, 268
GetUpdatedItem method 323–325
GetVCardStream method 222–224
global groups 382
global schema 91–92
global.asa 553
Group objects
  See also groups
  creating 383–386
  deleting 392
  enumerating in containers 393–394
  group membership 386–390
  mail-enabling 360–362
  managing 390–394
  moving 391–392
  opening 339, 390
group scope 382, 385
group types 381, 385
groups
  See also Group objects
  adding members 386
  checking user membership 387
  distribution groups 381

groups *(continued)*
  domain local groups 383
  enumerating members 388–390
  global groups 382
  group scope 382, 385
  group types 381, 385
  membership 386–390
  overview 381
  removing members 388
  sAMAccountName property 386
  security groups 381
  universal groups 382
GroupType property 384–386

H

HandleStateChange function 611–612
handling errors, ADO 133–135
hard-coded server names 404
hardware requirements xxxvi
HasMailboxInDomain function 251–253
header fields 608–609
Help files xxxvi
Helper Tools folder xl
HideFormPage method 792
HideFromAddressBook property 205–206
highly structured data 40
home page creation 555–563
HomeMDB property 366–369
HomeMDB URL 366–369
HTML
  ASP 595–598
  building tables 628–630
  Document Object Model 803–804
  message formatting 236–237
  Outlook forms 803–804
HTML Document object library 803–804
HTML Document Object Model 803–804
HTMLBody property 264, 267, 803–804
HTMLEditor property 803–804
HTTP
  asynchronous connections 611–612
  methods 606–607
  overview 8
  request header fields 608–609
  requests from clients 603–612
  response codes 635–639
  sending requests 609–610
  Web Storage System schema 87
  XML 588–589
HTTP Mail namespace 754–759

http://schemas.microsoft.com/cdo/configuration
  / namespace schema properties 706–712
http://schemas.microsoft.com/cdo/nntpenve
  lope/ namespace schema properties 713
http://schemas.microsoft.com/cdo/smtpenv
  elope/ namespace schema properties 714
http://schemas.microsoft.com/cdo/workflow
  /namespace schema properties 715–717
http://schemas.microsoft.com/exchange/
  namespace schema properties 718–726
http://schemas.microsoft.com/exchange/
  outlookfolderclass schema property 515
http://schemas.microsoft.com/exchange/event/
  criteria schema property 465
http://schemas.microsoft.com/exchange/event/
  enabled schema property 471–472
http://schemas.microsoft.com/exchange/event/
  matchScope schema property 463–464
http://schemas.microsoft.com/exchange/event/
  priority schema property 466–467
http://schemas.microsoft.com/exchange/events/
  namespace schema properties 727–728
http://schemas.microsoft.com/exchange/
  events/property 463
http://schemas.microsoft.com/exchange/events/
  EventMethod schema property 461–462
http://schemas.microsoft.com/exchange/events/
  SinkClass schema property 461–462
http://schemas.microsoft.com/exchange/
  outlookmessageclass schema property 521
http://schemas.microsoft.com/exchange/
  security/namespace schema properties
  729–731
http://schemas.microsoft.com/exchange/
  security/descriptor schema
  property 644, 658–662
Hypertext Transfer Protocol *See* HTTP

I

IADs interface 338, 404
IADsContainer interface 339, 348, 392
IADsContainer.Filter property 379–380,
  393–394
IADsContainer.MoveHere method 376–377
IADsDomain interface 338
IADsGroup interface 339, 383, 387
IADsOpenDSObject interface 340–341
IADsOU interface 339
IADsUser interface 339
IConfiguration interface 178
IDataSource interface
  CDO for Exchange 2000 Server object
    model 178
  CDO messaging 227
  creating new resources using CDO 192–195

IDataSource interface *(continued)*
  DataSource.IsDirty property 190–191
  DataSource.Open method 188–190
  DataSource.Save method 191
  detecting changes 190–191
  folders, checking for existence 199–201
  methods 186–187
  opening CDO objects from other
    objects 196–198
  opening resources using 188–190
  operation 187
  overview 183, 186
  properties 186–187
  saving changes 190–191
IExStoreAsyncEvents interface 428
IExStoreDispEventInfo interface 440–442
IExStoreSyncEvents interface 428
IExStoreSystemEvents interface 429
IFS (Installable File System) 62
IIS (Internet Information Services) 553, 680
IMailboxStore interface
  CreateMailbox method 366–369
  creating mailboxes 366–369
  deleting mailboxes 374
  moving mailboxes 372–373
  overview 332
  properties 370–371
IMailboxStore objects 179
IMailRecipient interface
  accessing 183
  MailEnable method 204–206
  mail-enabled distribution groups 383–385
  mail-enabling objects 360–362
  overview 332
IMailRecipient objects 179
IMAP4 (Internet Mail Access Protocol
  version 4) 8
IMessage.EnvelopeFields property 713
impersonation 338
importing workflow processes 502
information stores 42
inheritance
  content classes 103–105
  permissions 653–657
InnerHTML property 602, 632–634
InnerText property 602
Inspector objects
  accessing controls on pages 793–794
  activating pages 792
  Add method 804–805
  CommandBars collection 804–805
  controlling pages 791–794
  GetInspector property 791

Inspector objects *(continued)*
  hiding pages 792
  HTMLEditor property 803–804
  IsWordMail property 801–802
  ModifedFormPages property 791
  overview 790
  returning current items 791
  showing pages 792
  touching pages 792
  WordEditor property 801–802
Installable File System (IFS) 62
installing chapter sample code files xxxvii
installing Exchange 2000 servers 688–689
installing Exchange in single server
  domains 684–691
installing FrontPage 2000 691
installing FrontPage 2000 Server
  Extensions 691
installing Office 2000 691
installing Windows 2000 Server 684–686
Instances property 298
integrating XML namespaces 594–595
IntelliSense 781
interfaces
  ADSI 336–337
  CDO calendaring 272–274
  CDO messaging 227
  IADs 338
  IADsContainer 339, 348, 392
  IADsDomain 338
  IADsGroup 339, 383, 387
  IADsOpenDSObject 340–341
  IADsOU 339
  IADsUser 339
  IConfiguration 178
  IDataSource *See* IDataSource interface
  IExStoreAsyncEvents 428
  IExStoreDispEventInfo 440–442
  IExStoreSyncEvents 428
  IExStoreSystemEvents 429
  IMailboxStore 332
  IMailRecipient *See* IMailRecipient
    interface
  IPerson 332
  overview 182–183
International Organization for
  Standardization (ISO) 8601 format 275
Internet Information Services (IIS) 553, 680
Internet Mail Access Protocol version 4
  (IMAP4) 8
Internet Publishing Provider 49, 171–173,
  522
Interval property 298
introduction xxix–xxxv
IPerson interface 332
islands, data 601–602, 631–634

IsMember method 387
ISO (International Organization for
　Standardization) 8601 format 275
ISOFormat function 311, 312–315
IsWordMail property 801–802
ItemCount property 207–208
IWorkflowMessage objects 180, 486
IWorkflowSession objects 180, 485

L

Lightweight Directory Access Protocol
　(LDAP)
　　binding strings 334–336
　　client library 328
　　connecting to Active Directory 328
　　distinguished name (DN) 335–336
　　identifying Active Directory servers 404–
　　　406
　　overview 8
　　rootDSE objects 404–406
list controls 795–798
List property 797–798
ListIndex property 796, 798
locking, optimistic 150

M

Mail Header namespace 759–765
mailbox stores 42
mailbox-enabled objects 351
mailboxes
　accessing using ADO 126
　accessing using URLs 59–60
　creating 366–369
　customizing settings 370–372
　deleting 374
　HomeMDB URL 366–369
　moving 372–373
　overview 362
　properties 362–365
　querying Active Directory 409–410
MailDisable method 362
MailEnable method 204–206, 360–362, 383–
　385
mail-enabled distribution groups 383–385
mail-enabled objects
　compared to mailbox-enabled
　　objects 351
　mail-enabling 360–362
　overview 351
main page of frameset pages 562–563
MAPI folder class 515
MAPI folder trees
　accessing folders 125
　creating folders in 515–517

MAPI folder trees (continued)
　creating items in 517–521
　overview 514
MAPI properties 523–526
MAPI public folders 647–649
MAPI stores 514
master Appointment objects 294–296
meeting organizers 285, 319
meeting requests 287
meetings
　canceling 322
　converting dates and times 309–311
　distinguishing from simple
　　appointments 317
　modifying existing requests 309
　organizers 285, 319
　processing requests 323–325
　publishing 291–293
　recurring See recurring appointments
　　and meetings
　reminders 325–326
　requests 287
　scheduling See scheduling meetings
　updating 319
Members collection 388–390
Members property 388–390
membership of groups 386–390
memory, releasing resources 182
Message class 227
message class property 517
Message object model 228
Message objects
　AddAttachment method 240–242
　Count property 257
　CreateMHTMLBody method 238–240
　From property 234
　properties 259
　TextBody property 236
message transport envelope field
　properties 714
MessageClass property 810–811, 813
messages
　addressing 233–235
　attachments 240–242, 257–258
　composing See composing messages
　finding 255
　forwarding 266–268
　HTML formatting 236–237
　MHTML formatting 238–240
　MIME 228–231
　notification 430–431, 508–509
　opening 255
　plain-text formatting 236
　post 227
　posting to newsgroups 246–248

messages *(continued)*
  processing 255
  reading as BodyPart objects 259–264
  replying 264–266
  saving to files 268–270
  schema properties 242–244
  sending *See* sending messages
  sending to folders 245–246
  simple 231–233
messaging *See* CDO messaging
meta-markup languages 592
methods
  AbortChange 441
  Add 804–805
  AddAttachment 240–242
  AddAuditEntry 506
  AddItem 796
  Append 146
  BeginTrans 132–133
  Clear 796
  CommitTrans 132–133
  COPY 619–620
  CopyRecord 165–166
  Create 348
  CreateMailbox 366–369
  CreateMHTMLBody 238–240
  DataSource.Open 188–190
  DataSource.OpenObject 196–198
  DataSource.Save 191
  DataSource.SaveTo 192–194
  DataSource.SaveToContainer 194–195,
    277–279
  DataSource.SaveToObject 196–198
  Delete *See* Delete method
  DeleteMailbox 374
  DeleteRecord 167–168, 323, 472–473
  DeleteWorkflowItem 510
  EventRecord 475
  Fields.Update 277–279
  Forward 266–268
  Get 342–343
  GetChildren 151
  GetDecodedContentStream 264
  GetEx 342, 344
  GetFreeBusy 288–291
  GetInfo 342, 344
  GetInterface 183
  GetList 344
  GetNewWorkflowMessage 508–509
  GetObject 339
  GetRecord 440–441
  GetRecurringMaster 306
  GetStream 263, 268

methods *(continued)*
  GetUpdateItem 323–325
  GetVCardStream 222–224
  HideFormPage 792
  HTTP 1.1 606–607
  IsMember 387
  MailDisable 362
  MailEnable 204–206, 360–362, 383–385
  MKCOL 617
  MOVE 620–621
  MoveHere 376–377, 391–392
  MoveMailbox 372
  MoveNext 153
  MoveRecord 166–167
  Open 136–139, 143–144
  OpenDSObject 340–341
  Post 245, 247
  PostReply 266
  PROPFIND 613–616
  PROPPATCH 618–619
  Put 342, 345
  PutEx 342, 346–347
  Read 169
  ReadText 169
  Remove 388
  Reply 264
  ReplyAll 264
  RollbackTrans 132–133
  Save 163–164
  SaveToFile 169–171, 257, 268
  SelectNodes 668–670
  SelectSingleNode 668–670
  Send 245, 267
  SetCurrentFormPage 792
  SetFocus 799, 801
  SetInfo 342, 347
  ShowFormPage 792
  TransformNode 631–634
  WebDAV 606–607
  WorkflowSession objects 504–506
  XMLHTTP objects 603–604
MHTML message formatting 238–240
Microsoft ActiveX Data Objects 2.5 Library
  (Adodb.dll) 427
Microsoft CDO for Exchange Management
  Library (Cdoexm.dll) 427
Microsoft CDO for Exchange object library
  (Cdoex.dll) 427
Microsoft Developer Network (MSDN) 586
Microsoft Exchange 2000 *See* Exchange
  2000
Microsoft Exchange namespace 718–726
Microsoft IntelliSense 781

Microsoft Internet Information Services
(IIS) 553, 680
Microsoft Internet Publishing Provider
(MSDAIPP) 49, 171–173, 522
Microsoft Management Console (MMC)
Component Services 449–456, 485
Exchange development console 692–
696
Microsoft Office namespace 770–776
Microsoft Outlook 2000 *See* Outlook 2000
Microsoft Script Debugger 512
Microsoft SQL Server 40–41
Microsoft Visual Studio 692
Microsoft Web Storage Systems *See* Web
Storage Systems
Microsoft Windows NT 685
Microsoft Word 801–802
MIME
messages 228–231
standards 754–765
MKCOL method 617
MMC (Microsoft Management Console)
Component Services 449–456, 485
Exchange development console 692–
696
Mode parameter 137
ModifedFormPages property 791
MOVE method 620–621
move methods 152–153, 620–621
MoveHere method 376–377, 391–392
MoveMailbox method 372
MoveNext method 153
MoveRecord method 166–167
moving Contact objects 376–377
moving Group objects 391–392
moving mailboxes 372–373
moving resources 166–167
moving User objects 376–377
MSDAIPP (Microsoft Internet Publishing
Provider) 49, 171–173, 522
MSDN (Microsoft Developer Network) 586
Msxml.dll *See* XML Document Object Model
(XML DOM)
multiple public Web Storage Systems 45–48
Multipurpose Internet Mail Extensions
(MIME)
messages 228–231
standards 754–765
multistatus 627
multi-valued properties 140–142

N

Name property 806
namespaces
Calendar 734–742
CDO Configuration 706–712
CDO NNTP Envelope 713
CDO SMTP Envelope 714
CDO Workflow 715–717
Contacts 742–753
Data Types 765
DAV 701
defining properties 99–101
Event Registrations 727–728
Exchange 718–726
Exchange Data 765–768
Exchange Security 729–731
Form Registrations 768–770
Full Text Querying 732–733
HTTP Mail 754–759
list of predefined 73–75
Mail Header 759–765
Microsoft Office 770–776
overview 70
property names 72
resources 71
XML 594–595
XML Data 777
Namespaces in XML W3C (World Wide
Web Consortium) 72
Network News Transfer Protocol (NNTP) 8
Newsgroup Wizard 247
newsgroups 246–248
Newsgroups property 247
NNTP (Network news Transfer Protocol) 8
non-collection records 135
non-US-ASCII characters 759–765
Nothing value 182
notification messages 430–431, 508–509

O

object libraries
Active DS Type Library
(Activeds.tlb) 427
ActiveX Data Objects 2.5 Library
(Adodb.dll) 427
CDO for Exchange 227, 332
CDO for Exchange Management
(CDOExM) 332, 427
CDO for Exchange object library
(Cdoex.dll) 427
HTML Document 803–804

object models
   CalendarMessage 274
   CDO Workflow for Exchange
     (Cdowf.dll) 485
   HTML Document Object Model 803–804
   Message 228
   Microsoft Word 801
   Outlook 526
   XML DOM *See* XML Document Object
     Model (XML DOM)
object properties, Collaboration Data
  Objects Workflow (CDOWF) 715–717
ObjectCategory property 399
ObjectClass property 399
objects
   Active Directory 400
   Addressee 251, 287
   ADSI 338–341
   ADSystemInfo 406–407
   Appointment *See* Appointment objects
   Attendee 288–291
   AuditTrailEventLog 180
   BodyPart *See* BodyPart objects
   CalendarMessage 274, 323–325
   CDO Configuration 706–712
   CDO Folder 207
   CDO Message 713
   Command *See* Command objects
   CommandBar 804–805
   Configuration *See* Configuration objects
   Connection *See* Connection objects
   Contact *See* Contact objects
   Container 339
   creating from COM classes 181
   creating in Active Directory 348
   deleting in Active Directory 349
   DOMDocument 631–634
   Error 133–135
   Exception 294
   Explorer 803–804
   Field 140–142
   Folder 201–208
   Group *See* Group objects
   IMailboxStore 179
   IMailRecipient 179
   Inspector *See* Inspector objects
   IWorkflowMessage 180
   IWorkflowSession 180
   mailbox-enabled 351
   mail-enabled 351, 360–362
   master Appointment 294–296
   opening from other objects 196–198

objects *(continued)*
   opening in Active Directory with logon
     credentials 340–341
   Page 793
   persistent Configuration 281–282
   Person *See* Person objects
   ProcessDefinition 181
   ProcessInstance 181
   Record *See* Record objects
   Recordset *See* Recordset objects
   RecurrencePattern 294
   rootDSE 404–406
   security principals 350
   Stream *See* Stream objects
   User *See* User objects
   WinNTSystemInfo 408
   WorkflowMessage 508–510
   WorkflowSession 504–506, 508–509
   XMLHTTP *See* XMLHTTP objects
   XMLHTTPRequest 603
Office 2000 691
Office namespace 770–776
oft files 808
OLE DB provider for ADSI 331
OnAction property 804
OnDelete events 293, 423, 443–444
one-off forms 807
OnMDBShutDown events 424, 447
OnMDBStartUp events 424, 447
OnSave events 293, 423, 444–445
OnSyncDelete events 422, 434–435
OnSyncSave events 255, 422, 435–438
OnTimer events 424, 447, 467
Open events 788, 804–805
Open method
   Record objects 136–139, 143–144, 440–
     441
   Recordset objects 151–152
   XMLHTTP objects 605–607
OpenDSObject method 340–341
opening messages 255
optimistic locking 150
organization xxxvi–xxxv
Organizational Forms Library 808, 810
organizational units 339
Outlook 2000
   accessing Web Storage System schema
     properties 523–526
   adding collaboration features 522
   creating folders in MAPI folder
     trees 515–517
   creating items in MAPI folder trees 517–
     521
   developing for the environment 515–
     521
   developing in the environment 522–528
   Field Chooser 523–525

Outlook 2000 *(continued)*
  forms *See* Outlook forms
  MAPI folder trees 514
  Outlook Forms Designer 523–524
  overview 23–24, 513
  querying Web Storage Systems 526–528
  summary 528
  Web Storage System schema 89
  ZipOut 2000 xli
Outlook forms
  accessing controls on pages 793–794
  accessing using script 790
  activating pages 792
  Advanced Properties tool 781
  canceling events 785–787
  command bars 804–806
  control events 787
  controlling body of items 800–804
  controlling controls 795–800
  controlling list controls 795–798
  controlling pages 791–794
  controlling text boxes 795
  creating event procedures 783–785
  custom command bars 804–806
  custom fields 794–795
  custom forms used as default forms in
    folders 812
  custom properties 794–795
  design protection 807
  distributing 806–812
  distributing new versions of forms 812
  Event Handler 783–785
  events 782–790
  Field Chooser 781
  Folder Forms Library 808
  hiding pages 792
  HTML 803–804
  Inspector objects *See* Inspector objects
  libraries 808–809
  managing and maintaining 812–813
  Microsoft Word 801–802
  order of event firing 787–790
  Organizational Forms Library 808
  Outlook Forms Designer 780–781
  overview 779
  passwords 807
  Personal Forms Library 808
  Properties tool 781
  protecting designs 807
  published forms 809–811
  publishing to forms libraries 808–809
  publishing with form definitions 811
  returning current items 791

Outlook forms *(continued)*
  saving current instances of 807
  Script Editor 781
  showing pages 792
  templates 808
Outlook Forms Designer 523–524, 780–781
Outlook object model 526
Outlook Web Access
  accessing data using URLs 57
  accessing individual items using
    URLs 62
  accessing mailboxes using URLs 60
  accessing public stores using URLs 58
  command values list 584
  creating items in MAPI folder trees 518
  overview 24–28
  parameters list 582
  Web application creation 581–584
overlapping permissions 657–658
overview xxix–xxxv

P

Page objects 793
Page Size property 402
paging 402
parameters
  CreateOptions 138–139
  dataurl 544–545, 564, 569
  formurl 544–545
  Mode 137
password protection for Outlook forms 807
PatternEndDate property 298
permissions
  See also security
  access masks 664–666
  assigning client 646–653
  assigning to MAPI public folders 647–
    649
  assigning to non-MAPI folders 650–653
  execute 548-550
  folder access 664–665
  inheritance 653–657
  overlapping 657–658
  overview 643
  roles 648–649
  standard access 664
  summary 681
  Web Storage System folders 646–658
persistent Configuration objects 248–250,
  281–282
Person class 350

Person objects
   creating mailboxes 366–369
   overview 351
   schema properties 742–753
Personal Forms Library 808
plain-text message formatting 236
POP3 (Post Office Protocol version 3) 8
post 227, 245
Post method 245, 247
Post Office Protocol version 3 (POP3) 8
posting messages to newsgroups 246–248
PostReply method 266
private mailbox stores 42
privileged security mode 484
Privileged Workflow Authors role 485
procedure, CreateEventReg 458
ProcessDefinition objects 181
ProcessInstance objects 181
properties
   Active Directory 357–360
   ActiveConnection 400–404
   address 234
   ADsPath 397
   AmbiguousNames 254
   appending custom properties to
     resources 146–149
   Attachments 257
   AutoGenerateTextBody 236
   Body 800
   BOF 152
   Cache Results 403
   caching in Active Directory 342
   Chase Referrals 403
   Collaboration Data Objects Workflow
    (CDOWF) objects 715–717
   Command objects 400–401
   contacts 209–221
   ContentMediaType 260–262
   Controls 793
   Count 257, 388–390
   custom 99–102, 146–149, 473–475, 794–
    795
   data types 102
   DataSource 183
   DataSource.IsDirty 190–191
   default stream 169
   defining 99–102, 110
   DocumentElement 602
   dt 670–672
   Duration 277–279
   EditorType 803–804
   EndTime 277–279
   enumerating 140–142
   EOF 152

properties *(continued)*
   events 473–475
   executeurl 554
   Filter 379–380, 393–394
   Folder objects 202
   form registration items *See* form
    registration item properties
   formurl 554
   Frequency 297–298
   From 234
   GetInspector 791
   GroupType 384–386
   HideFromAddressBook 205–206
   HomeMDB 366–369
   HTMLBody 264, 267, 803–804
   HTMLEditor 803–804
   IADsContainer.Filter 379–380, 393–394
   IMailboxStore interface 370–371
   IMessage.EnvelopeFields 713
   InnerHTML 602, 632–634
   InnerText 602
   Instances 298
   Interval 298
   IsWordMail 801–802
   ItemCount 207–208
   List 797–798
   ListIndex 796, 798
   mailboxes 362–365
   MAPI 523–526
   Members 388–390
   message class 517
   Message objects 259
   message transport envelope field 714
   MessageClass 810–811, 813
   ModifedFormPages 791
   multi-valued 140–142
   Name 806
   names 72
   Newsgroups 247
   ObjectCategory 399
   ObjectClass 399
   OnAction 804
   Page Size 402
   PatternEndDate 298
   Provider 128–129
   ReadyState 604, 611–612
   RecordCount 206
   recurrence pattern 297
   ReplyTo 235
   ResolvedStatus 254
   ResponseXML 604, 610
   Role 286
   rootDSE objects 405

properties *(continued)*
    sAMAccountName 383–386
    schema *See* schema properties
    SearchScope 401
    security descriptor (SD) 658–662
    SelLength 799
    SelStart 799
    SelText 799
    Sender 507
    SetRequestHeader 609
    single-valued 140–142
    SMTPEmail 204–206
    StartTime 277–279
    StateFrom 510
    StateTo 510
    Status 610
    StatusText 610
    Text 795, 798
    TextBody 236
    Time Limit 402
    TimeOut 402
    To 245
    UnreadItemCount 207–208
    UserAccountControl 355–357
    UserName 408
    UserProperties 526
    Value 141, 795, 798
    values, getting 343–345
    values, setting 345–347
    Visible 804–805
    VisibleCount 207–208
    WordEditor 801–802
    WorkflowSession objects 504–506
    X400Email 204–206
    XMLHTTP objects 603–604
Properties tool 781
property cache 342
PropertyChange events 788, 798
PROPFIND method 613–616
PROPPATCH method 618–619
protocols, list of supported 8
Provider property 128–129
public folder trees
    accessing folders 125
    creating 50–51
    overview 45–48
public folders
    assigning permissions to MAPI 647–649
    creating using CDO 203–204
Public Folders stores 514
public stores
    accessing using URLs 58–59
    overview 42

public Web Storage Systems 125–126
published events 293
published forms 809–811
publishing meetings 291–293
publishing to forms libraries 808–809
Put method 342, 345
PutEx method 342, 346–347

Q

querying Active Directory
    ADO 395–396
    Cache Results property 403
    Chase Referrals property 403
    Command objects 400–404
    mailboxes 409–410
    overview 394
    Page Size property 402
    SearchScope property 401
    SELECT statement building 396–400
    servers 411–414
    Time Limit property 402
    TimeOut property 402
querying calendars
    Calendar Browser 317–319
    distinguishing between meetings and
        simple appointments 317
    identifying appointment types 315–316
    overview 311–315
querying Web Storage Systems
    AddQuotes function 155
    building SELECT statements 156–161
    opening Recordsets with query
        results 161–163
    Outlook forms 526–528
    overview 65, 155
    saving Recordsets as XML 163–164
QueryString collection 544

R

RDN (relative distinguished name) 335
Read events 788
Read method 169
ReadText method 169
ReadyState property 604, 611–612
Record objects
    appending custom properties to
        resources 146–149
    compared to Recordset objects 122
    CopyRecord method 165–166
    creating folders 144–145
    creating items 145–146
    creating resources 143–146

Record objects *(continued)*
　DeleteRecord method　167–168
　enumerating properties　140–142
　folder contents, reading　153–154
　MoveRecord method　166–167
　Open method　136–139, 440–441
　opening resources　139–140
　overview　135
　saving records　142–143
RecordCount property　206
Recordset objects
　BOF property　152
　compared to Record objects　122
　Delete method　168
　EOF property　152
　folder contents, reading　153–154
　GetChildren method　151
　move methods　152–153
　Open method　151–152
　opening　150–152
　opening with query results　161–163
　optimistic locking　150
　overview　150
　Save method　163–164
　saving as XML　163–164
recurrence master appointments　305–308
recurrence patterns　297–301
RecurrencePattern objects　294
RecurrencePatterns collection　272, 294
recurring appointments and meetings
　configuring master Appointment
　　objects　294–296
　Exception objects　294
　exceptions　301–305
　Exceptions collection　294
　GetRecurringMaster method　306
　master Appointment objects　294–296
　overview　294
　recurrence master appointments　305–
　　308
　recurrence patterns　297–301
　RecurrencePattern objects　294
　RecurrencePatterns collection　294
recursive events　464
RegEvent.vbs script　467–468
registering workflow authors　489–491
registration items *See* form registration
　items
Regsvr32.exe　448–449
relative distinguished name (RDN)　335
relative URLs　129–131
releasing memory resources　182
reminders　325–326
Remove method　388

rendering XML with XSL
　building tables　628–630
　building XSL templates as stand-alone
　　files　624–626
　identifying XML elements with XSL
　　patterns　626–627
　overview　622–623
　XML data islands used for XSL
　　templates　631–634
　XSL-specific elements　623
replicating Web Storage System folder
　trees　66
Reply events　789
Reply method　264
ReplyAll events　789
ReplyAll method　264
replying to messages　264–266
ReplyTo property　235
Request for Comments (RFC)　226, 394
requirements, system　xxxvi
ResolvedStatus property　254
resolving addresses in domains　250–254
resources
　accessing using custom clients　65
　accessing using Windows Explorer　62–
　　64
　appending custom properties to　146–
　　149
　copying　165–166, 619–620
　creating　143–146
　creating new using CDO　192–195
　deleting　167–168, 621–622
　moving　166–167, 620–621
　namespaces　71
　opening using IDataSource
　　interface　188–190
　opening using Record objects　139–140
　overview　43
　returning with all properties　613–616
　returning with specific properties　614–
　　615
　saving to containers　194–195
　saving to URLs　192–194
response codes　635–639
Response.Redirect function　576, 578
ResponseXML property　604, 610
restricted security mode　483
retrieving vCard information　222–224
RFC (Request for Comments)　226, 394
Role property　286
roles
　assigning client permissions　648–649
　COM+ *See* COM+ role-based security
　Privileged Workflow Authors　485
RollbackTrans method　132–133
Root DS Entry
　identifying domains　406–407
　overview　404

root elements 593, 627
rootDSE objects 404–406
Routing Objects library 486

S

sAMAccountName property 383–386
sample application xxxviii–xl
sandboxing 483
Save method 163–164
SaveAttachment events 788–789
SaveToFile method 169–171, 257, 268
saving messages to files 268–270
saving records 142–143
scheduling meetings
    Attendees collection 285–286
    free/busy status 287–291
    meeting organizers 285
    meeting requests 287
    new meetings 282–287
    overview 282
    published events 293
    publishing meetings 291–293
    Role property 286
    user existence, checking 288
schema
    creating folder structures 109–110
    custom application *See* custom
      application schema
    folders 537
    global 91–92
    Web Storage System *See* Web Storage
      System schema
schema properties
    accessing in Outlook forms 523–526
    accessing using Field Chooser 523–525
    CDO for Exchange 184–185
    configuration 249
    DAV 701–706
    DAV:contentclass 75, 79–82, 515–521
    events 727–728
    Field Chooser 523–525
    http://schemas.microsoft.com/cdo/
      configuration/ namespace 706–712
    http://schemas.microsoft.com/cdo/
      nntpenvelope/ namespace 713
    http://schemas.microsoft.com/cdo/
      smtpenvelope/ namespace 714
    http://schemas.microsoft.com/cdo/workf
      low/ namespace 715–717
    http://schemas.microsoft.com/exchange/
      namespace 718–726

schema properties *(continued)*
    http://schemas.microsoft.com/exchange/
      outlookfolderclass 515
    http://schemas.microsoft.com/exchange/
      event/criteria 465
    http://schemas.microsoft.com/exchange/
      event/enabled 471–472
    http://schemas.microsoft.com/exchange/
      event/matchScope 463–464
    http://schemas.microsoft.com/exchange/
      event/priority 466–467
    http://schemas.microsoft.com/exchange/
      events/ namespace 727–728
    http://schemas.microsoft.com/exchange/
      events/ property 463
    http://schemas.microsoft.com/exchange/
      events/EventMethod 461–462
    http://schemas.microsoft.com/exchange/
      events/SinkClass 461–462
    http://schemas.microsoft.com/exchange/
      outlookmessageclass 521
    http://schemas.microsoft.com/exchange/
      security/ namespace 729–731
    http://schemas.microsoft.com/exchange/
      security/descriptor 644, 658–662
    messaging 242–244
    Record objects 140–142
    security 729–731
    security descriptor (SD) 658–662
    TimerExpiryTime 467
    TimerInterval 467
    TimerStartTime 467
    urn:schemas.microsoft.com:fulltextqueryi
      nfo: namespace 732–733
    urn:schemas:calendar: namespace 734–
      742
    urn:schemas:calendar:dtend
      (cdoDTEnd) 312
    urn:schemas:calendar:dtstart
      (cdoDTStart) 312
    urn:schemas:calendar:instancetype
      (cdoInstanceType) 308, 315
    urn:schemas:calendar:reminderoffset
      (cdoReminderOffset) 325
    urn:schemas:calendar:timezoneid
      (cdoTimeZoneIDURN) 276, 309
    urn:schemas:contacts: namespace 742–
      753
    urn:schemas:httpmail: namespace 754–
      759
    urn:schemas:mailheader:
      namespace 759–765
    urn:schemas-microsoft-com:datatypes#
      namespace 765
    urn:schemas-microsoft-
      com:datatypes#type 99–102

schema properties *(continued)*
    urn:schemas-microsoft-com:exch-data:
      namespace 765–768
    urn:schemas-microsoft-com:exch-
      data:baseschema 93
    urn:schemas-microsoft-com:exch-
      data:schema-collection-ref 96–98
    urn:schemas-microsoft-com:office:forms#
      namespace 768–770
    urn:schemas-microsoft-
      com:office:forms#formurl 544
    urn:schemas-microsoft-com:office:office#
      namespace 770–776
    urn:schemas-microsoft-com:xml-data#
      namespace 777
    urn:schemas-microsoft-com:xml-
      data#element 104–105
    urn:schemas-microsoft-com:xml-
      data#extends 103–105
    urn:schemas-microsoft-com:xml-
      data#name 99–101, 103–105
    Web Storage System 524, 701
script
    accessing Outlook forms 790
    running in privileged mode 484
    running in restricted mode 483
Script Debugger 512
Script Editor 781
scripting workflow items 504–510
SD (security descriptor)
    building 670–672
    discretionary access control list
      (DACL) 663–668
    overview 644
    property 658–662
    reading details of 668–670
    schema properties 729–731
    security identifier (SID) 666–668
SDK (software developer's kit) 692
SDK (software developer's kit) Help
    files xxxvi
SearchScope property 401
security
    access control entries (ACE) *See* access
      control entries
    access control list (ACL) 644
    access tokens 644
    ADO 123
    COM+ role-based *See* COM+ role-based
      security
    discretionary access control list
      (DACL) 663–668
    enforcing on code with COM+
      components 672–681

security *(continued)*
    event sinks 426
    overview 33, 643–646
    permissions *See* permissions
    planning in applications 645
    privileged mode 484
    restricted mode 483
    roles 648–649
    running script in privileged mode 484
    running script in restricted mode 483
    sandboxing 483
    schema properties 729–731
    security descriptor (SD) *See* security
      descriptor
    security identifier (SID) 644, 666–668,
      729–731
    summary 681
    workflow 483–485
security descriptor (SD)
    building 670–672
    discretionary access control list
      (DACL) 663–668
    overview 644
    property 658–662
    reading details of 668–670
    schema properties 729–731
    security identifier (SID) 666–668
security groups 381
security identifier (SID) 644, 666–668, 729–
    731
security principals 350
SELECT statements
    AddQuotes function 155
    building 156–161, 396–400
    choosing properties to return 156–157
    filter criteria 398
    filtering results 158–159
    FROM clause 157–158
    opening Recordsets with query
      results 161–163
    ORDER BY clause 159–161
    querying Active Directory 396–400
    querying Web Storage Systems *See*
      querying Web Storage Systems
    retrieving master recurring
      appointments 316
    saving Recordsets as XML 163–164
    searching for object types 399
    SELECT clause 156–157
    sorting results 159–161
    WHERE clause 158–159
    where to look for records 157–158
SelectNodes method 668–670
SelectSingleNode method 668–670
SelLength property 799
SelStart property 799

SelText property 799
semistructured storage model 41
Send events 789
Send method
  forwarding messages 267
  Message objects 245
  XMLHTTP objects 605, 609–610
Sender property 507
sending messages
  addressing messages 233–235
  posting to newsgroups 246–248
  schema properties 242–244
  sending to folders 245–246
  simple messages 231–233
Server.Transfer function 578
servers
  Active Directory 404–406
  hard-coded names 404
  installing 688–689
  querying Active Directory 411–414
Service Pack 5 (SP5) 685
SetCurrentFormPage method 792
SetFocus method 799, 801
SetInfo method 342, 347
SetRequestHeader property 609
setting up development environments 691–696
setting up Exchange in single server domains 684–691
ShowFormPage method 792
SID (security identifier) 644, 666–668, 729–731
simple appointments
  canceling 320–322
  creating 277–279
  distinguishing from meetings 317
Simple Mail Transfer Protocol (SMTP) 8
simple messages, sending 231–233
single instancing 45
single server domains 684–691
single-valued properties 140–142
SMTP (Simple Mail Transfer Protocol) 8
SMTPEmail property 204–206
software developer's kit (SDK) 692
software developer's kit (SDK) Help files xxxvi
software requirements xxxvi, 176
SP5 (Service Pack 5) 685
SQL SELECT statements See SELECT statements
SQL Server 40–41
stand-alone XML documents 590–591
standard access permissions 664
StartTime property 277–279
StateFrom property 510

states, workflow
  adding 495–496
  multiple actions 501
  overview 480
  reading information 510
StateTo property 510
Status property 610
StatusText property 610
storage groups 43, 48
stores 49
Stream objects
  BodyPart objects 262–264
  opening 169
  overview 169
  reading 169
  SaveToFile method 169–171
  saving Recordsets as XML 163
  saving to files 169–171
streaming BodyPart objects 262–264
strict nesting 593
synchronous events
  aborting 441–442
  distinguishing between new and changed items 439
  modifying event items 440–441
  new items vs. changed items 439
  OnSyncDelete events 422, 434–435
  OnSyncSave events 422, 435–438
  overview 30, 422, 432
  reacting to 432–442
  transaction phase 438–439
system events
  OnMDBShutDown events 424, 447
  OnMDBStartUp events 424, 447
  OnTimer events 424, 447, 467
  overview 30, 423
  reacting to 446–448
system requirements xxxvi

T

testing and deploying applications
  additional users, adding 696
  application-specific tools 696–697
  automating installations 698–699
  configuring domain controllers 686–688
  creating new administrator accounts 690–691
  Exchange development MMC console 692–696
  Exchange SDK 692
  installing Exchange 2000 servers 688–689
  installing FrontPage 2000 691

testing and deploying applications
(*continued*)
installing FrontPage 2000 Server
Extensions 691
installing Office 2000 691
installing Windows 2000 Server 684–686
overview 34–35, 683
setting up development
environments 691–696
setting up Exchange in single server
domains 684–691
summary 700
Visual Studio 692
Windows script files 698–699
text boxes 795
Text property 795, 798
TextBody property 236
Time Limit property 402
time zones 276–277
TimeOut property 402
TimerExpiryTime schema property 467
TimerInterval schema property 467
TimerStartTime schema property 467
times
automatic conversion 275
converting 309–311
ISO 8601 format 275
retrieving appointments for
specific 312–315
storing and formatting 274–276
time zones 276–277
TimeZoneConverter function 309–311, 312–315
To property 245
Top class 399
touching pages 792
transactions
aborting 441–442
Connection objects 131–133
synchronous events 438–439
TransformNode method 631–634
transport event sinks 714
tree formats 593

U

Unicode 590, 754–759
Uniform Resource Locators (URLs) *See* URLs
universal groups 382
Universal Time Coordinate (UTC) 274
UnreadItemCount property 207–208
URLs
accessing Exchange 2000 data using 56–57
accessing items 61–62, 127
accessing mailboxes 59–60, 126

URLs (*continued*)
accessing public stores 58–59
accessing public Web Storage System
folders 125–126
building for ExOLEDB 124–127
CDO 185
HomeMDB 366–369
relative 129–131
saving new resources to 192–194
Web Storage System schema 87
urn:schemas.microsoft.com:fulltextqueryinfo
: namespace 732–733
urn:schemas:calendar: namespace 734–742
urn:schemas:calendar:dtend 312
urn:schemas:calendar:dtstart 312
urn:schemas:calendar:instancetype 308, 315
urn:schemas:calendar:reminderoffset 325
urn:schemas:calendar:timezoneid 276, 309
urn:schemas:contacts: namespace 742–753
urn:schemas:httpmail: namespace 754–759
urn:schemas:mailheader: namespace 759–765
urn:schemas-microsoft-com:datatypes#
namespace 765
urn:schemas-microsoft-
com:datatypes#type 99–102
urn:schemas-microsoft-com:exch-data:
namespace 765–768
urn:schemas-microsoft-com:exch-
data:baseschema 93
urn:schemas-microsoft-com:exch-
data:schema-collection-ref 96–98
urn:schemas-microsoft-com:office:forms#
namespace 768–770
urn:schemas-microsoft-
com:office:forms#formurl 544
urn:schemas-microsoft-com:office:office#
namespace 770–776
urn:schemas-microsoft-com:xml-data#
namespace 777
urn:schemas-microsoft-com:xml-
data#element 104–105
urn:schemas-microsoft-com:xml-
data#extends 103–105
urn:schemas-microsoft-com:xml-
data#name 99–101, 103–105
US-ASCII characters 759–765
user accounts *See* User objects
user existence, checking 251–253, 288
User objects
compared to Contact objects 352
creating 352–360
deleting 378–379
deleting mailboxes 374

User objects *(continued)*
   enumerating 379–380
   managing 374–380
   moving 376–377
   moving mailboxes 372–373
   opening 339, 375–376
   overview 350
   properties 362–365
   security principals 350
UserAccountControl property 355–357
UserName property 408
UserProperties collection 794–795
UserProperties property 526
UTC (Coordinated Universal Time) 274

V

Value property 141, 795, 798
vCards 222–224
virtual directories
   creating 54–56
   overview 49
Visible property 804–805
VisibleCount property 207–208
Visual Studio 692

W

W3C (World Wide Web Consortium) 72, 586
Web applications
   access rights 548–550
   accessing folder contents 563–568
   accessing form registration parameters from Web pages 544–545
   ADO constants used in Web pages 552–553
   anonymous access 549
   authentication 549
   CDO constants used in Web pages 552–553
   content classes 538
   contents page of frameset pages 559–561
   creating items 573–574
   creating Web Storage System forms 554
   dataurl parameter 544–545
   deleting items 579–581
   development environment 547
   displaying items 568–572
   Exchange System Manager 548
   execute permissions 548–550
   Folder Composition tool 539–540
   folders for Web page storage 554
   form registration items *See* form registration items
   forms registry *See* forms registry
   Forms Registry Explorer tool 545–547

Web applications *(continued)*
   formurl parameter 544–545
   frameset home page creation 557–563
   FrontPage 2000 551–552
   home page creation 555–563
   main page of frameset pages 562–563
   Outlook Web Access 581–584
   overview 531–536
   registering Web Storage System forms 554
   saving items 574–578
   schema folders 537
   simple home page creation 555–556
   summary 584
   Web development tools 551–553
   Web Storage System forms 533
Web development tools 551–553
Web Distributed Authoring and Versioning (WebDAV)
   methods 606–607
   overview 8
   schema properties 701–706
   XML 588–589
Web Storage System forms
   accessing folder contents 563–568
   creating 554
   overview 28–29, 533
   registering 554
Web Storage System schema
   access scenarios 86–89
   content classes *See* content classes
   custom application schema *See* custom application schema
   global schema 91–92
   namespaces *See* namespaces
   Outlook 2000 89
   overview 9, 69–72
   returning application schema information 113–116
   summary 116
   URLs and HTTP 87
   Web applications using ASP technology 88
   XML namespaces 594–595
Web Storage Systems
   accessing data using URLs 56–57
   accessing individual items using URLs 61–62
   accessing mailboxes using URLs 59–60
   accessing public folders 125–126
   accessing public stores using URLs 58–59
   accessing schema properties in Outlook forms 523–526
   ADO *See* ActiveX Data Objects 2.5
   asynchronous events *See* asynchronous events

Web Storage Systems *(continued)*
  benefits 38–40
  CDO Collaboration Data Objects for
    Exchange
  client permissions 646–658
  compared to Exchange 2000
    databases 44–45
  connecting to *See* connecting to Web
    Storage Systems
  creating contacts in 221
  creating new 49–56
  events *See* events
  execute permissions 548
  ExOLEDB provider *See* ExOLEDB
    provider
  features 38–40
  folder trees 43
  folders 646–658
  forms *See* Web Storage System forms
  mapping to individual stores 42
  Microsoft Internet Publishing Provider
    (MSDAIPP) 171–173
  mounting 51–53
  multiple public 45–48
  namespaces *See* namespaces
  overview 7, 10, 37
  querying *See* querying Web Storage
    Systems
  querying from Outlook forms 526–528
  replicating folder trees 66
  resources 43
  saving new resources to containers 194–
    195
  saving new resources to URLs 192–194
  schema *See* Web Storage System schema
  schema properties 524, 701
  security descriptor (SD) *See* security
    descriptor
  security planning in applications 645
  summary 66
  synchronous events *See* synchronous
    events
  system events *See* system events
WebDAV (Web Distributed Authoring and
  Versioning)
  methods 606–607
  overview 8
  schema properties 701–706
  XML 588–589
well-formed XML 594
Windows 2000 Advanced Server 685
Windows 2000 Component Services
  Microsoft Management Console
  (MMC) 449–456, 485
Windows 2000 Professional 685
Windows 2000 Server, installing 684–686
Windows Explorer, accessing resources 62–64
Windows NT 685
Windows Scripting Host 698–699

WinNTSystemInfo objects 408
wizards
  COM Component Install 454
  Newsgroup 247
WLDAP32.dll 328
Word 801–802
WordEditor property 801–802
workflow
  actions, adding 496–498
  actions, adding script 499
  actions, compensating script 500
  actions, list of 482
  actions, overview 480–483
  actions, using multiple on single
    states 501
  Application log 506
  AuditTrailEventLog objects 486
  building applications 485–491
  creating accounts 487–489
  creating processes 493–502
  custom log entries 506
  debugging script 511–512
  enabling 501
  Event Viewer 512
  folders 493
  identifying senders 507
  IWorkflowMessage objects 486
  IWorkflowSession objects 485
  logging 506
  overview 31–32, 479–486
  registering authors 489–491
  Script Debugger 512
  scripting items 504–510
  security 483–485
  Sender property 507
  sending notification messages 508–509
  states, adding 495–496
  states, overview 480
  states, reading information 510
  states, using multiple actions on 501
  summary 512
  system accounts 487–489
Workflow Designer for Exchange
  action script 499
  activating folders for workflow
    activity 501
  adding actions 496–498
  adding script 498–500
  adding states 495–496
  checking script syntax 511
  compensating actions 500
  condition script statements 499
  connecting to workflow folders 493
  creating new processes 494–495
  enabling success entries for folders 501

Workflow Designer for Exchange
(continued)
  enabling workflow 501
  example process creation 493–502
  exporting processes 502
  external script files 500
  importing processes 502
  overview 32, 180, 485–486, 491–492
  setting default processes 501
  using multiple actions on single
    states 501
WorkflowMessage objects 508–510
WorkflowSession objects 504–506, 508–509
World Wide Web Consortium (W3C) 72,
586
Write events 788–789
WScript.exe 699

X

X400Email property 204–206
XML (Extensible Markup Language)
  attributes 592
  benefits 586
  building applications 587–588
  building documents 590–591
  creating elements 592–594
  data islands 601–602, 631–634
  entities 593
  generating with ASP 595–601
  HTTP overview 588–589
  HTTP requests from clients 603–612
  integrating namespaces 594–595
  overview 19–22, 585–589
  rendering with XSL See rendering XML
    with XSL
  root elements 593, 627
  saving Recordsets as 163–164
  security descriptor (SD) property 658–
    662
  strict nesting 593
  summary 639
  tags 592
  tree formats 593
  Unicode 590
  WebDAV 588–589
XML Data namespace 777
XML Document Object Model (XML DOM)
  data islands 601–602
  rendering XML 587
  saving Recordset objects 163
  security descriptor (SD) 668–670
XML Query Language (XQL) 626
XMLHTTP objects
  copying resources 619–620
  CreateObject function 605
  creating folders 617

XMLHTTP objects (continued)
  creating items 618–619
  deleting resources 621–622
  HTTP requests 605
  methods 603–604
  moving resources 620–621
  Open method 605–607
  overview 603
  properties 603–604
  returning resources with all
    properties 613–616
  Send method 605, 609–610
  Status property 610
  StatusText property 610
XMLHTTPRequest class 603
XMLHTTPRequest objects 603
XQL (XML Query Language) 626
XSL (Extensible Stylesheet Language)
  elements 623
  generating XML with ASP 600
  overview 588
  patterns 626–627
  rendering XML See rendering XML with
    XSL
  templates See XSL templates
  XML data islands 602
XSL templates
  building tables 628–630
  data islands 631–634
  overview 622
  stand-alone files 624–626

Z

ZipOut 2000 xli

Biography

Mindy Martin is an independent developer, trainer, and author specializing in solutions built with Microsoft Exchange. She traces her interest in computers back to a time her father took her to his office when she was 10, and she discovered Zork on the IBM 3090 mainframe. She later received a bachelor's degree in Wildlife Biology, but after one too many wild animal bites and a long stint aging disemboweled deer, she decided she had missed her true calling and became a full-time developer.

Mindy now owns her own consulting business, which specializes in Exchange development with a heavy emphasis on research and writing. She has published many articles in developer magazines and is co-author of the book "Mastering Excel 2000" (Sybex). Mindy is a regular speaker at developer conferences world wide, including Microsoft Tech*Ed, Microsoft Exchange Conference, Informant VBA Developer Conference, and Advisor DevCons. Mindy spends her free time scuba diving, hiking with her Alaskan malamute, and drinking wine—not necessarily at the same time.

Microsoft® Resource Kits—powerhouse resources to minimize costs while maximizing performance

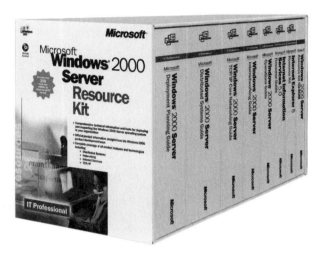

Deploy and support your enterprise business systems using the expertise and tools of those who know the technology best—the Microsoft product groups. Each RESOURCE KIT packs precise technical reference, installation and rollout tactics, planning guides, upgrade strategies, and essential utilities on CD-ROM. They're everything you need to help maximize system performance as you reduce ownership and support costs!

Microsoft® Windows® 2000 Server Resource Kit
ISBN   1-57231-805-8
U.S.A. $299.99
U.K.   £189.99 [V.A.T. included]
Canada $460.99

Microsoft Windows 2000 Professional Resource Kit
ISBN   1-57231-808-2
U.S.A. $69.99
U.K.   £45.99 [V.A.T. included]
Canada $107.99

Microsoft BackOffice® 4.5 Resource Kit
ISBN   0-7356-0583-1
U.S.A. $249.99
U.K.   £161.99 [V.A.T. included]
Canada $374.99

Microsoft Internet Explorer 5 Resource Kit
ISBN   0-7356-0587-4
U.S.A. $59.99
U.K.   £38.99 [V.A.T. included]
Canada $89.99

Microsoft Office 2000 Resource Kit
ISBN   0-7356-0555-6
U.S.A. $59.99
U.K.   £38.99 [V.A.T. included]
Canada $89.99

Microsoft Windows NT® Server 4.0 Resource Kit
ISBN   1-57231-344-7
U.S.A. $149.95
U.K.   £96.99 [V.A.T. included]
Canada $199.95

Microsoft Windows NT Workstation 4.0 Resource Kit
ISBN   1-57231-343-9
U.S.A. $69.95
U.K.   £45.99 [V.A.T. included]
Canada $94.95

Microsoft®

mspress.microsoft.com

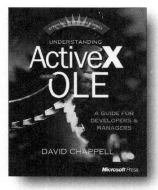
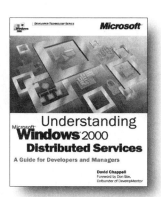

MICROSOFT LICENSE AGREEMENT
Book Companion CD

IMPORTANT—READ CAREFULLY: This Microsoft End-User License Agreement ("EULA") is a legal agreement between you (either an individual or an entity) and Microsoft Corporation for the Microsoft product identified above, which includes computer software and may include associated media, printed materials, and "online" or electronic documentation ("SOFTWARE PRODUCT"). Any component included within the SOFTWARE PRODUCT that is accompanied by a separate End-User License Agreement shall be governed by such agreement and not the terms set forth below. By installing, copying, or otherwise using the SOFTWARE PRODUCT, you agree to be bound by the terms of this EULA. If you do not agree to the terms of this EULA, you are not authorized to install, copy, or otherwise use the SOFTWARE PRODUCT; you may, however, return the SOFTWARE PRODUCT, along with all printed materials and other items that form a part of the Microsoft product that includes the SOFTWARE PRODUCT, to the place you obtained them for a full refund.

SOFTWARE PRODUCT LICENSE

The SOFTWARE PRODUCT is protected by United States copyright laws and international copyright treaties, as well as other intellectual property laws and treaties. The SOFTWARE PRODUCT is licensed, not sold.

1. **GRANT OF LICENSE.** This EULA grants you the following rights:

    a. **Software Product.** You may install and use one copy of the SOFTWARE PRODUCT on a single computer. The primary user of the computer on which the SOFTWARE PRODUCT is installed may make a second copy for his or her exclusive use on a portable computer.

    b. **Storage/Network Use.** You may also store or install a copy of the SOFTWARE PRODUCT on a storage device, such as a network server, used only to install or run the SOFTWARE PRODUCT on your other computers over an internal network; however, you must acquire and dedicate a license for each separate computer on which the SOFTWARE PRODUCT is installed or run from the storage device. A license for the SOFTWARE PRODUCT may not be shared or used concurrently on different computers.

    c. **License Pak.** If you have acquired this EULA in a Microsoft License Pak, you may make the number of additional copies of the computer software portion of the SOFTWARE PRODUCT authorized on the printed copy of this EULA, and you may use each copy in the manner specified above. You are also entitled to make a corresponding number of secondary copies for portable computer use as specified above.

    d. **Sample Code.** Solely with respect to portions, if any, of the SOFTWARE PRODUCT that are identified within the SOFTWARE PRODUCT as sample code (the "SAMPLE CODE"):

    i. **Use and Modification.** Microsoft grants you the right to use and modify the source code version of the SAMPLE CODE, *provided* you comply with subsection (d)(iii) below. You may not distribute the SAMPLE CODE, or any modified version of the SAMPLE CODE, in source code form.

    ii. **Redistributable Files.** Provided you comply with subsection (d)(iii) below, Microsoft grants you a nonexclusive, royalty-free right to reproduce and distribute the object code version of the SAMPLE CODE and of any modified SAMPLE CODE, other than SAMPLE CODE, or any modified version thereof, designated as not redistributable in the Readme file that forms a part of the SOFTWARE PRODUCT (the "Non-Redistributable Sample Code"). All SAMPLE CODE other than the Non-Redistributable Sample Code is collectively referred to as the "REDISTRIBUTABLES."

    iii. **Redistribution Requirements.** If you redistribute the REDISTRIBUTABLES, you agree to: (i) distribute the REDISTRIBUTABLES in object code form only in conjunction with and as a part of your software application product; (ii) not use Microsoft's name, logo, or trademarks to market your software application product; (iii) include a valid copyright notice on your software application product; (iv) indemnify, hold harmless, and defend Microsoft from and against any claims or lawsuits, including attorney's fees, that arise or result from the use or distribution of your software application product; and (v) not permit further distribution of the REDISTRIBUTABLES by your end user. Contact Microsoft for the applicable royalties due and other licensing terms for all other uses and/or distribution of the REDISTRIBUTABLES.

2. **DESCRIPTION OF OTHER RIGHTS AND LIMITATIONS.**

    - **Limitations on Reverse Engineering, Decompilation, and Disassembly.** You may not reverse engineer, decompile, or disassemble the SOFTWARE PRODUCT, except and only to the extent that such activity is expressly permitted by applicable law notwithstanding this limitation.

    - **Separation of Components.** The SOFTWARE PRODUCT is licensed as a single product. Its component parts may not be separated for use on more than one computer.

    - **Rental.** You may not rent, lease, or lend the SOFTWARE PRODUCT.

    - **Support Services.** Microsoft may, but is not obligated to, provide you with support services related to the SOFTWARE PRODUCT ("Support Services"). Use of Support Services is governed by the Microsoft policies and programs described in the user manual, in "online" documentation, and/or in other Microsoft-provided materials. Any supplemental software code provided to you as part of the Support Services shall be considered part of the SOFTWARE PRODUCT and subject to the terms and conditions of this EULA. With respect to technical information you provide to Microsoft as part of the Support Services, Microsoft may use such information for its business purposes, including for product support and development. Microsoft will not utilize such technical information in a form that personally identifies you.

- **Software Transfer.** You may permanently transfer all of your rights under this EULA, provided you retain no copies, you transfer all of the SOFTWARE PRODUCT (including all component parts, the media and printed materials, any upgrades, this EULA, and, if applicable, the Certificate of Authenticity), **and** the recipient agrees to the terms of this EULA.

- **Termination.** Without prejudice to any other rights, Microsoft may terminate this EULA if you fail to comply with the terms and conditions of this EULA. In such event, you must destroy all copies of the SOFTWARE PRODUCT and all of its component parts.

3. **COPYRIGHT.** All title and copyrights in and to the SOFTWARE PRODUCT (including but not limited to any images, photographs, animations, video, audio, music, text, SAMPLE CODE, REDISTRIBUTABLES, and "applets" incorporated into the SOFTWARE PRODUCT) and any copies of the SOFTWARE PRODUCT are owned by Microsoft or its suppliers. The SOFTWARE PRODUCT is protected by copyright laws and international treaty provisions. Therefore, you must treat the SOFTWARE PRODUCT like any other copyrighted material **except** that you may install the SOFTWARE PRODUCT on a single computer provided you keep the original solely for backup or archival purposes. You may not copy the printed materials accompanying the SOFTWARE PRODUCT.

4. **U.S. GOVERNMENT RESTRICTED RIGHTS.** The SOFTWARE PRODUCT and documentation are provided with RESTRICTED RIGHTS. Use, duplication, or disclosure by the Government is subject to restrictions as set forth in subpara-graph (c)(1)(ii) of the Rights in Technical Data and Computer Software clause at DFARS 252.227-7013 or subparagraphs (c)(1) and (2) of the Commercial Computer Software—Restricted Rights at 48 CFR 52.227-19, as applicable. Manufacturer is Microsoft Corporation/One Microsoft Way/Redmond, WA 98052-6399.

5. **EXPORT RESTRICTIONS.** You agree that you will not export or re-export the SOFTWARE PRODUCT, any part thereof, or any process or service that is the direct product of the SOFTWARE PRODUCT (the foregoing collectively referred to as the "Restricted Components"), to any country, person, entity, or end user subject to U.S. export restrictions. You specifically agree not to export or re-export any of the Restricted Components (i) to any country to which the U.S. has embargoed or restricted the export of goods or services, which currently include, but are not necessarily limited to, Cuba, Iran, Iraq, Libya, North Korea, Sudan, and Syria, or to any national of any such country, wherever located, who intends to transmit or transport the Restricted Components back to such country; (ii) to any end user who you know or have reason to know will utilize the Restricted Components in the design, development, or production of nuclear, chemical, or biological weapons; or (iii) to any end user who has been prohibited from participating in U.S. export transactions by any federal agency of the U.S. government. You warrant and represent that neither the BXA nor any other U.S. federal agency has suspended, revoked, or denied your export privileges.

DISCLAIMER OF WARRANTY

NO WARRANTIES OR CONDITIONS. MICROSOFT EXPRESSLY DISCLAIMS ANY WARRANTY OR CONDITION FOR THE SOFTWARE PRODUCT. THE SOFTWARE PRODUCT AND ANY RELATED DOCUMENTATION ARE PROVIDED "AS IS" WITHOUT WARRANTY OR CONDITION OF ANY KIND, EITHER EXPRESS OR IMPLIED, INCLUDING, WITHOUT LIMITATION, THE IMPLIED WARRANTIES OF MERCHANTABILITY, FITNESS FOR A PARTICULAR PURPOSE, OR NONINFRINGEMENT. THE ENTIRE RISK ARISING OUT OF USE OR PERFORMANCE OF THE SOFTWARE PRODUCT REMAINS WITH YOU.

LIMITATION OF LIABILITY. TO THE MAXIMUM EXTENT PERMITTED BY APPLICABLE LAW, IN NO EVENT SHALL MICROSOFT OR ITS SUPPLIERS BE LIABLE FOR ANY SPECIAL, INCIDENTAL, INDIRECT, OR CONSEQUENTIAL DAMAGES WHATSOEVER (INCLUDING, WITHOUT LIMITATION, DAMAGES FOR LOSS OF BUSINESS PROFITS, BUSINESS INTERRUPTION, LOSS OF BUSINESS INFORMATION, OR ANY OTHER PECUNIARY LOSS) ARISING OUT OF THE USE OF OR INABILITY TO USE THE SOFTWARE PRODUCT OR THE PROVISION OF OR FAILURE TO PROVIDE SUPPORT SERVICES, EVEN IF MICROSOFT HAS BEEN ADVISED OF THE POSSIBILITY OF SUCH DAMAGES. IN ANY CASE, MICROSOFT'S ENTIRE LIABILITY UNDER ANY PROVISION OF THIS EULA SHALL BE LIMITED TO THE GREATER OF THE AMOUNT ACTUALLY PAID BY YOU FOR THE SOFTWARE PRODUCT OR US$5.00; PROVIDED, HOWEVER, IF YOU HAVE ENTERED INTO A MICROSOFT SUPPORT SERVICES AGREEMENT, MICROSOFT'S ENTIRE LIABILITY REGARDING SUPPORT SERVICES SHALL BE GOVERNED BY THE TERMS OF THAT AGREEMENT. BECAUSE SOME STATES AND JURISDICTIONS DO NOT ALLOW THE EXCLUSION OR LIMITATION OF LIABILITY, THE ABOVE LIMITATION MAY NOT APPLY TO YOU.

MISCELLANEOUS

This EULA is governed by the laws of the State of Washington USA, except and only to the extent that applicable law mandates governing law of a different jurisdiction.

Should you have any questions concerning this EULA, or if you desire to contact Microsoft for any reason, please contact the Microsoft subsidiary serving your country, or write: Microsoft Sales Information Center/One Microsoft Way/Redmond, WA 98052-6399.

For information about Microsoft Press® products, visit our Web site at

mspress.microsoft.com

Microsoft®